Early Charles County Maryland Settlers

1658-1745

Marlene Strawser Bates
&
F. Edward Wright

HERITAGE BOOKS
2006

HERITAGE BOOKS
AN IMPRINT OF HERITAGE BOOKS, INC.

Books, CDs, and more—Worldwide

For our listing of thousands of titles see our website
at
www.HeritageBooks.com

Published 2006 by
HERITAGE BOOKS, INC.
Publishing Division
65 East Main Street
Westminster, Maryland 21157-5026

Copyright © 1995 Marlene Strawser Bates and F. Edward Wright

All rights reserved. No part of this book may be reproduced or transmitted in any form or by any means, electronic or mechanical, including photocopying, recording or by any information storage and retrieval system without written permission from the author, except for the inclusion of brief quotations in a review.

International Standard Book Number: 978-1-58549-392-9

INTRODUCTION

This project began with Eleanor Lukanich who envisioned an index to many of the records she had found on Charles County. Working with her records we found that an index was not feasible, and decided to abandon her project and confine our attention to selected genealogical data. We have restricted our definition of genealogical data to familial relationships (by birth and marriage), births, ages, and deaths.

Following is a list of the sources we used and a description of pitfalls and limitations.

WILLS

We began with the published series of Baldwin's *Calendar of Wills* (Volumes 1-8) and the subsequent volume published by Family Line Publications (Volume 9). In compiling these data with other sources numerous discrepancies became apparent. In numerous instances we referred to the original records to clear up existing errors and omissions. Errors noted in this project and by others in the genealogical community are covered in Volume 16 of *Maryland Calendar of Wills*. Sometimes the county of the decedent was not recorded in the *Calendar of Wills*, either by omission of the author or omitted in the original Prerogative Court records. We were able to rectify many of these omissions. In this work the liber or book is cited followed by page number. These are based on the following sources:

Jane Baldwin Cotton, *The Maryland Calendar of Wills*:
    Volume   I: 1635 to 1685 (1904. Reprint 1988).
                  Book   1, folio   1-638
                  Book   2, folio   1-201, 346-410
                  Book   4, folio   1-206
                  Book   5, folio   1-350
                  Book   9, folio   1-113
                  Book   10, folio 1- 82
    Volume   II: 1685 to 1702 (1906. Reprint 1988).
                  Book   4, folio 188-319
                  Book   6, folio   1- 59
                  Book   2, folio 202-235
                  Book   6, folio 66- 71
                  Book   2, folio 236-255
                  Book   6, folio   1- 51
                  Book   2, folio 255-336
                  Book   7, folio   1-393
                  Book   6, folio 75-406

                    Book   11, folio   1-278
Volume   III: 1703 to 1713 (1907. Reprint 1988).
                    Book   11, folio 279-422
                    Book   3, folio   1-745
                    Book   12, folio 1-356
                    Book   2—12, folio 1-253
                    Book   13, folio 1-623
Volume   IV: 1713 to 1720 (1914. Reprint 1988).
                    Book   13, folio 625-741
                    Book   14, folio 1-736
                    Book   15, folio 1-356
                    Appendix:
                        From Land Office, Annapolis.
                        From Testamentary Proceedings, Annapolis.
                        From Baltimore City Land Office and Baltimore City
                            Court House.
Volume   V: 1720 to 1726 (1917. Reprint 1988).
                    Book   16, folio 1-525
                    Book   17, folio 1-324
                    Book   18, folio 1-548
                    Appendix:
                        From Land Office, Annapolis.
Volume   VI: 1726 to 1732 (1920. Reprint 1988).
                    Book   19, folio 1-924
                    Book   20, folio 1-573
Volume   VII: 1732 to 1738 (1925. Reprint 1988).
                    Book   20, folio 574-927
                    Book   21, folio 1-924
                    Appendix:
                        From Land Office, Annapolis (except where otherwise
                            noted).
Volume VIII: 1738 to 1743 (1928. Reprint 1988).
                    Book   22, folio 1-533
                    Book   23, folio 1-597

Family Line Publications, *Maryland Calendar of Wills*:
    Volume   9: 1744 — 1749 (1991)
                    Liber   23, folio 600-700
                    Liber   24, folio 1-548
                    Liber   25, folio 1-578

INVENTORIES AND ACCOUNTS SERIES

We examined the works of Vernon Skinner and extracted certain data that suggested relationships and correlated these with the wills if one existed. This source was especially useful in picking up subsequent marriages of the widow. The entry "next of kin" offers additional help in research in naming two other relatives (by blood or marriage). In 1718 the series splits into two series. To date Mr. Skinners has abstracted the Inventories up to 1777, the year the Prerogative Court of Maryland was discontinued.

Vernon L. Skinner, Jr., *Abstract of the Inventories and Accounts of the Prerogative Court of Maryland*:
    1674-1678, 1699-1703 (Libers 1 - 5). (January 1992)
    1679-1686 (Libers 6, 7A, 7B, 7C, 8). (January 1992)
    1685-1701 (Libers 9, 10, 10c, 11A, 11B). (June 1992)
    1688-1698 (Libers 12, 13A, 13B, 14, 15). (August 1992)
    1697-1700 (Libers 16, 17, 18, 19, 19½A, 19½B). (September 1992)
    1699-1704 (Libers 20-24). (1993)
    1699-1708 (Libers 25-28). (1993)
    1703-1711 (Libers 29, 30, 31, 32A, 32B). (1994)
    1711-1713 (Libers 32C, 33A, 33B, 34). (1994)
    1712-1716 (Libers 35A, 35B, 36A, 36B, 36C). (1994)
    1715-1718 (Libers 37A, 37B, 37C, 38A, 38B, 39A, 39B, 39C). (1994)

Vernon L. Skinner, Jr., *Abstracts of the Inventories of the Prerogative Court of Maryland*:
    1718-1720 (Libers 1-4). (May 1991)
    1720-1724 (Libers 5-9). (May 1991)
    1724-1727 (Libers 10-11). (May 1991)
    1726-1729 (Libers 12-14). (May 1991)
    1728-1734 (Libers 15-17). (May 1991)
    1733-1738 (Libers 18-23). (November 1990)
    1738-1744 (Libers 24-28). (August 1990)
    1744-1748 (Libers 29-36). (July 1990)

COURT AND LAND RECORDS

These records cover a wide range of types of information. From them we gleaned ages of persons giving depositions; ages, names and relationships of servants; references to cattle marks of relatives; actual dates of births; references to illegitimate children; criminal cases; and other material. We examined the land records including land commissions and the court records which have been published in the *Archives of Maryland* (court series) covering the Charles County Court, Provincial Court records of Maryland and the Chancery Court Records of Maryland. For specific volumes see below.

A major source were the land records as compiled by Elise Jourdan and those published by T.L.C., cited below. Specific data which gave relationships have been extracted; for complete abstracts of the land records one should examine these sources and eventually the original copies when possible. Much more information is available from the records.

Elise Greenup Jourdan, *Abstracts of Charles County Maryland Court and Land Records 1658-1666*. Volume 1. (Westminster, Maryland: Family Line Publications, 1993).

Elise Greenup Jourdan, *Abstracts of Charles County Maryland Court and Land Records 1665-1695*. Volume 2. (Westminster, Maryland: Family Line Publications, 1993).

Elise Greenup Jourdan, *Abstracts of Charles County Maryland Court and Land Records 1694-1722*. Volume 3. (Westminster, Maryland: Family Line Publications, 1994).

T.L.C. Genealogy, P.O. Box 403369, Miami Beach, Florida 33140-1369.
Charles County, Maryland, Land Records, 1722-1733. 1994. Contents: Liber L#2, Liber M#2.
Charles County, Maryland, Land Records, 1733-1743. 1993. Contents: Liber O#2.
Charles County, Maryland, Land Records, 1743-1752. 1993. Contents: Liber X#2, Z#2.

Persons who made depositions in the records of land commissions were included from the records, Charles County Land Commissions, 1716-1721, Liber M2, pp. 1-149, accession No. 89003-1 (Maryland State Archives).

The Charles County Court records have been used. These are described below:

Archives of Maryland, Vol. 53 (LIII): 1936
Ct. Proc. of Charles Co., 1658-1666 (Court Series 6).
Liber A, folio 1-260   Vol. 53, p. 1-271
Liber B, folio 1-528   p. 272-626

Archives of Maryland, Vol. 60 (LX): 1943
Ct. Proc. of Charles Co., 1666-1674 (Court Series 9).
Liber C, folio 1-275   Vol. 60, p. 1-138
Liber D, folio 1-169   p. 138-262

D supplement 1-80   p. 262-281
Liber E, folio 1-189   p. 281-575
Liber F, folio 1-38   p. 575-618

We have also extracted from the Proceedings of the Provincial Court as published in *Archives of Maryland*, Volumes 4, 10, 41, 49, 57, 65, 66, 67, 68, 69 and 70; and from Volume 51, in which are found the Chancery Court records (1669 - 1679).

CHURCH RECORDS

The county was divided into the following parishes when the Anglican Church became The Church of Maryland in 1692: William and Mary or Pickawaxon; Port Tobacco; Nanjemy or Durham; and Piscataway or St. John's.

Piscataway Parish or St. John's at Broad Creek (also King George's Parish). The bounds of this parish begin at the mouth of the Mattawoman Creek and run up the said creek and branch thereof to the utmost limits of the county and run north to the line of the Province and then west to the Potomac River and then down the river to the mouth of the Mattawoman Creek. This parish became a part of Prince George's County. These records were published as *Prince George's County, Maryland: Indexes of Church Registers 1686-1885* (Westminster, Maryland: Family Line Publications, Reprint 1988. Originally published by Prince George's County Historical Society, 1979). Original page number are cited in this work.

Also included here are extracts of the marriages, births and deaths of Trinity Parish. This parish was created in 1744 and consisted of parts of King and Queen Parish and of All Faith Parish which were in Charles County. The boundaries were Zachiah Swamp, the Wicomico River, the St. Mary's County line, the Patuxent River and the Prince's County line. We have examined both the transcription by Lucy Harrison and the original records themselves (relatively easy to read). These are held by the Maryland State Archives. [See Trinity Parish, Charles County. Micro #372. 1729 — 1803. Vestry Proceedings begin 1749. Original accession no. 12645, Micro M227/258].

The county was divided into seven hundreds: Lower part of William and Mary Parish Hundred; Upper part of William and Mary Parish Hundred; East Side of Portobacco Hundred; West Side of Portobacco Hundred; Lower part of Nanjemy Parish Hundred; Upper part of Nanjemy Parish Hundred; Upper part of King and Queen Parish Hundred (a part of St. Mary's County until 1716).

Those few quaker records which are readily identifiable for persons of Patuxent meeting have also been included. Our source was Henry C. Peden Jr., *Quaker Records of Southern Maryland: Births, Deaths, Marriages and Abstracts from the Minutes, 1658-1800* (Westminster, Maryland: Family Line Publications, 1992). Clifts Monthly Meeting Register, 1662-1782. Peden's page numbers were cited.

LAYOUT OF THIS BOOK

We have arranged these entries generally in alphabetical order but combining the spelling of names which we felt were likely to be the same family. For example, we have grouped together the family names of Marloe, Marlowe and Marler. Morris, Maurice and Maris are combined because of the likelihood that these variations in spelling were sometimes used for the same family, etc. Within each family group we have arranged the entries in chronological order. Not all the information on a family will be found in its family grouping; there may be additional genealogical data in other entries; hence the reader must use the index extensively.

This book is intended to get the genealogical researcher to the more obvious data which has survived. We envision it as an aid leading to the use of other published material cited above (Family Line Publications, T.L.C. and the *Archives of Maryland*) and to primary records. One of the more subtle techniques in linking generations is derived from following the descension of land. We have included the tract names when cited in wills and land records, to facilitate further research. The tract names are shown in italics in the text and in the index.

Since we limited our efforts to only data which revealed relationships, ages, dates of birth, etc. it should be obvious that there these records when examined will reveal many other persons and when analyzed will reveal other genealogy.

ABBREVIATIONS

adj. - adjoining
admr. - administrator (of estate)
afsd. - aforesaid
betw. - between
bro. - brother
Chas. - Charles
child. - children

ck. - creek
co. - county
cous. - cousin
dau. - daughter
dwell. - dwelling
e. - east
eld. - eldest

ex. - executor (of estate)
extx. - executrix (of estate)
n. - north
Nunc. - nuncupative (verbal) will
plan. - plantation
pt. - part

R. - River
s. - south
sd. - said
young. - youngest
w. - west

BIBLIOGRAPHY

Jane Baldwin Cotton, *The Maryland Calendar of Wills*, volumes 1-8. (Westminster, MD: Family Line Publications, 1988 and later.

Helen W. Brown and Louise J. Hienton, *Prince George's County Maryland Indexes of Church Register, 1686 - 1885*. (Westminster, MD: Family Line Publications, 1988. Reprinted by Prince George's County Historical Society, 1979.) 2 volumes.

Elisabeth Hartsook and Gust Skordas, *Land Office and Prerogative Court Records Of Colonial Maryland*. (Baltimore, Maryland: Clearfield Co., Inc. by Genealogical Publishing Co., Inc., Reprint 1989. Originally published 1967 by The Hall of Records Commission.)

Elise Greenup Jourdan, *Abstracts of Charles County Maryland Court and Land Records 1658-1666*. Volume 1. (Westminster, Maryland: Family Line Publications, 1993).

Elise Greenup Jourdan, *Abstracts of Charles County Maryland Court and Land Records 1665-1695*. Volume 2. (Westminster, Maryland: Family Line Publications, 1993).

Elise Greenup Jourdan, *Abstracts of Charles County Maryland Court and Land Records 1694-1722*. Volume 3. (Westminster, Maryland: Family Line Publications, 1994).

Edna A. Kanely, *Directory of Maryland Church Records* (Westminster, MD: Family Line Publications, 1987).

Margaret Brown Klapthor and Paul Dennis Brown, *The History of Charles County, Maryland: Written in its Tercentenary Year of 1958*. (Bowie, Maryland: Heritage Books, Inc., Reprint 1995. Originally published 1958).

Maryland State Archives, *A Guide to Maryland State Archives Holdings of Charles County. Records on Microform*. (Annapolis: Maryland State Archives, 1989.)

Maryland State Archives, *A Guide to Government Records At the Maryland State Archives. A Comprehensive List by Agency and Records Series*. (Annapolis: Maryland State Archives, 1991.)

Harry Wright Newman, *Charles County Gentry*. (Baltimore, Maryland: Clearfield Co., Inc. by Genealogical Publishing Co., Inc., Reprint 1971. Originally published 1940).

Henry C. Peden Jr., *Quaker Records of Southern Maryland: Births, Deaths, Marriages and Abstracts from the Minutes, 1658-1800*. (Westminster, MD: Family Line Publications, 1992).

Percy G. Skirven, *The First Parishes of the Province of Maryland*. (Baltimore, Maryland: Clearfield Co., Inc. by Genealogical Publishing Co., Inc., Reprint 1994. Originally published 1923).

Vernon L. Skinner, Jr., *Abstracts of the Inventories and Accounts of the Prerogative Court of Maryland*. 1674-1718. (Westminster, MD: Family Line Publications, Published 1992-1994).

Vernon L. Skinner, Jr., *Abstracts of the Inventories of the Prerogative Court of Maryland*: 1718-1777. (Westminster, MD: Family Line Publications, Published 1990-1992.)

T.L.C. Genealogy, P.O. Box 403369, Miami Beach, Florida 33140-1369.
Charles County, Maryland, Land Records, 1722-1733. 1994. Contents: Liber L#2, Liber M#2.
Charles County, Maryland, Land Records, 1733-1743. 1993. Contents: Liber O#2.
Charles County, Maryland, Land Records, 1743-1752. 1993. Contents: Liber X#2, Z#2.

F. Edward Wright, *The Maryland Calendar of Wills*, volumes 9-16. (Westminster, MD: Family Line Publications, 1991-1995.)

Map of Charles County showing the original parishes of 1692

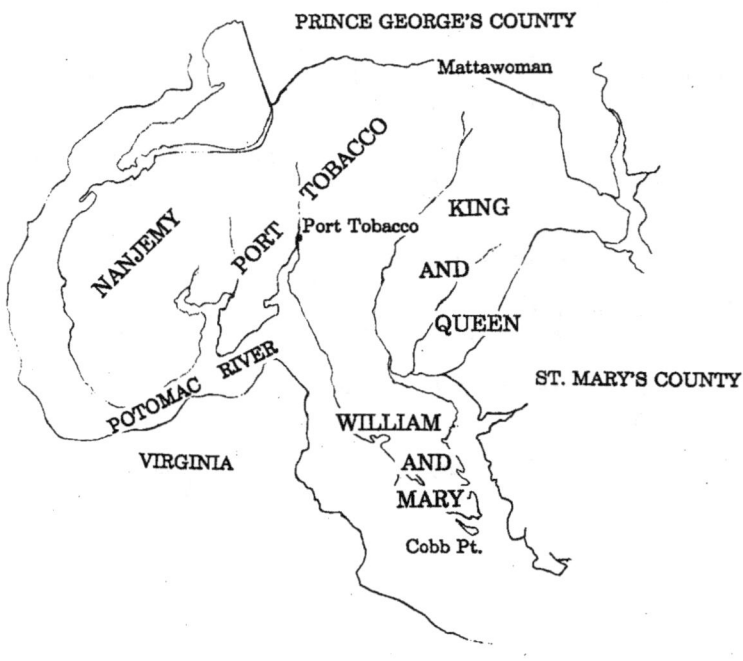

A'GAMBRA. (See GAMBRA.)

ABBOTT, Edward. (Inv.: 9.194; ----; 4 March 1684) Admr./Ex.: Thomas Mitchell. (Acct: 9.461; ----; 19 Jan 1687)

ABBOTT, Thomas. Named in plot of rebellion 5 Aug 1681. (Arch. of Md.: XV:403)

ABERNATHY. (See EBURNATHY.)

ACTON (ACTION), Henry and his wife Anne. Indenture dated 8 Nov 1715; parcel of land called *Abberdeen* on s. side of the main fresh of Mattawoman Ck., cont. 100 acres. (Ct.&Land: F#2.79)

ACTON, Henry Sr. conveyed 4 Oct 1735 and 10 May 1736, to son John Acton, tract *Longnor*, 100 acres and tract *Blueberry*, 125 acres. (Land: O#2.123, 147)

ADAIR, Alexander, Practitioner in Physick, and his wife Christian, conveyed on 15 Nov 1734 a parcel called *Hargrass' Hope*, 200 acres. (Land: O#2.86)

ADAMS (ADDAMES), Henry and wife Marie. Deposition on 1 June 1658 (Ct.&Land: A#1.3)

ADAMS (ADAMES), Henry of Charles County. Married by 9 Jan 1671/2 to Margaret ———, administratrix of Oliver Balse. (Ct.&Land: E#1.53)

ADAMS, Henry, of Portobacco (Roman Cath.). In his will he gives dau. Jane Mathews, 200 acres. Mentions bro. Ignatius Causeene; sons and daus. of Thomas Matthews; Ignatius Williams; and An--. Exs.: Leonard, Robert, and Francis Greene. (Will: 4.204; 13 Oct 1684; 9 July 1686)

ADAMS, Francis. (Inv.: 18.64; 22 Dec 1698; ----) Admr.: Grace Adams. (Acct: 19.47; ----; 7 June 1699)

ADAMS, Mary, wife of Francis Adams. Acquired land from George Godfrey, 5 Oct 1704; part of *Troops Rendezvous*. (Ct.&Land: Z#1.205)

ADAMS (ADDAMS), Charles and wife Elizabeth conveyed on 18 Aug 1718 a tract (patented to Frances Adams, father of Charles) called *Pinner*. Bounded by land of Fran. Adams, cont. 145 acres; also *Pinner Enlargement* bounded by *Pinner* and *Rayly*, cont. 70 acres. (Ct.&Land: H#2.191)

ADDAMS, Charles, age 48. Deposition in 1721 regarding tract called *Wadestones Enlargement* in Durham Parish. (Chas LandComm: M2.127)

ADAMS (ADDAMS), Charles (carpenter). In his will he devises to son George, *Adamses Delight*, to son Charles, *Frogs Nest*. Mentions dau. Sarah, son Lodowick, Anne Skinner and dau. Barbary Allen. Wife Elizabeth extx. (Will: 20.879; 10 Jan 1733/4; 4 Feb 1733/4) Next of kin: Francis Adams, Elisabeth Elgin. Ex.: Charles Adams. (Inv.: 18.491; 27 July 1734; 13 Aug 1734)

ADDAMS, George (planter). To bro. Charles, ex., 110 acres, *Addams' Delight*. To sisters Barbary Alling and Sarah Williams and William Skinner, personalty. (Will: 21.301; 7 Dec 1734; 5 March 1734)

ADAMS, Lodwick, son of Charles Adams, dec'd. and Elizabeth Adams acquired on 25 Feb 1733/4 from his cousin George Thomas, 25 acres, part of a tract called *Mauniss (Mannes) Eleture*; and on 12 March 1733, from his mother, Elizabeth Adams, widow, 75 acres, part of same tract. (Land: O#2.37, 40)

ADAMS, John (planter). To son Richard, 164 acres, *Nailas Range* Prince George's Co. To son Thomas Randolph Greenfield, 100 acres, *Birmingham*, Prince George's Co. Mentions wife Elizabeth, extx., sons John, Luke and George (when age 16 yrs.). (Will: 22.311; 16 Sept 1740; 1 April 1741)

ADAMS, Charles (planter), and his wife Mary, conveyed on 19 June 1742, a tract in Durham Parish called *Addams Delight*, 110 acres. (Land: O#2.592)

ADAMS, Benjamin, and his wife Hester conveyed on 29 June 1742 a tract called *Pork Hall*, 110 acres. (Land: O#2.568)

ADDISON, Jane, servant of John Smith, indicted on 13 March 1710 for having a bastard child. (Ct.&Land: D#2.136)

ADDISON, William (shoemaker), to his son John Addison, on 1 Nov 1731; stock and debts due him. (Land: M#2.266)

AGBOROUGH, Thomas, servant to Alexander Simpson, died 10 Aug 1667. (Ct.&Land: C#1.253; P#1.205; QRev.3)

AILER, Elizabeth, age 20 yrs. and Mary Ailer, age 14 yrs. Servants of Francis Wyne, 9 March 1679. (Ct.&Land: H#1.270)

ALCOCK, Thomas. In his will he left to son Thomas at age 18 yrs., 300 acres, *Manson Folly*, and 75 acres, *Preston*; dau. Mary at age 16 yrs., 209 acres, *St. Davidge*, and 100 acres, *Mounthill*; wife and unborn child, 200 acres, *Hardfrost*. Exs.: Col. Chandler, John Stone. (Will: 4.21; 21 April 1682; 27 Nov 1683) Items in possession of Mathew Dike who married Mary, relict of dec'd. (Inv.: 8.291; 20 April 1684; ----)

ALLCOCK, Thomas. Mentions sister Mary Dike and mother Mary Dike. Father Mathew Dike, ex. (Will: 6.98; 14 Oct 1696; 3 March 1697) (Inv.: 15.359; 5 June 1698; ----) Extx.: Marie Dike. (Inv.: 11B.52; [c1700]; ----)

ALDEN, Mary, age 21 yrs. Servant of John Dent, 12 March 1677. (Ct.&Land: G#1.119)

ALDIS, William, age 10 yrs. Servant of Owen Jones, 8 June 1675. (Ct.&Land: F#1.101)

ALLEN, William. Mentions wife Martha; goddau. Mary dau. of Joseph Harrison; Luke Green of Charles County; John son of John Munn; dau.

Elizabeth (minor). Ex.: Bro. in law John Munn. (Will: 1.413; 3 Jan 1669; 11 Aug 1671)

ALLEN, John and James, eldest sons of John Allen, by Ellinor his wife. Indenture, 16 Nov 1717, to Joseph Harrison, son of Richard Harrison. On 12 March 1666 land was sold to John Lambert and on 13 Aug 1692 it was given to his dau. Ellinor Lambert (now wife of John Allen) by John's wife, Ellen. (Ct.&Land: H#2.135)

ALLEN, Anne, dau. of John and Elinor Allen of Portobacco, born 28 Jan 1694. (Ct.&Land: QRev.25)

ALLEN, Philip. To son Thomas, all land. To daus. Mary and Esther, personalty. Test: Mary Ware, Chas. Baker. (Will: 6.178; 18 May 1698; 24 Aug 1698)

ALLEN, John and Ellinor his wife conveyed on 6 June 1709, 80 acres on w. side of Portobacco Ck. below Plum Tree Point. Deed of gift 10 March 1710, to his children, James, George, and Ann Allen. (Ct.&Land: C#2.138, 233)

ALLEN, James and Virlinda his wife conveyed on 16 Nov 1716, 20 acres at the head of Nanjemy Creek. (Ct.&Land: H#2.52)

ALLEN, John and his wife Katherine (Catherine) conveyed on 18 Feb 1716, to Joseph Harrison, son of Richard Harrison, Gent.; parcel called *Conveniency*; bounded by land in occupation of sd. Allen which he had in marriage to the dau. of John Lambert, dec'd; cont. 36 acres. On 2 Feb 1718 John and Katherine Allen conveyed a parcel of land *Adventure*, located on the easternmost branch of the Avon R., 20 acres. (Ct.&Land: H#2.43, 219)

ALLEN, John, age 56. Deposition, 12 Aug 1719, regarding *Glovers Point*; refers to his father in law John Lambert. (Chas LandComm: M2.48)

ALLEN, James, age 28. Deposition, 20 Aug 1719, regarding tract called *Saint Davids*. (Chas LandComm: M2.50)

ALLIN, John, age 32. Deposition in 1721 regarding tract called *Linsey*. (Chas LandComm: M2.146)

ALLIN, James, age 28. Deposition in 1721 regarding tract called *Wadestones Enlargement* in Durham Parish. (Chas LandComm: M2.50)

ALLEN, Thomas (planter). Lease dated 2 May 1726 of a parcel called *Milford*, 100 acres, and after his decease, to be used by his now wife Mary, and at her death to her son John Kelly. (Land: L#2.285)

ALLIN (ALLEN), George. Next of kin: Thomas Lambert. Admr.: Barbara Allen. (Inv.: 17.251; 29 May 1733; 7 Aug 1733)

ALLIN, James. Mentions wife Jane, extx., son William, bro. George. Son to be in care of wife until age of 20, or in the care of Robert Coward. (Will: 20.665; 21 March 1732/3; 11 May 1733)

ALLEN (ALLIN), James (planter), of Durham Parish. Mentions bros. John and Thomas; nephew Robert (son of Thomas); wife Susanna, extx. Test: Jane Morgan, (living in Virginia at date of probate), William Williams. (Will: 20.667; 9 Nov 1732; 11 May 1733) Ex.: Susanna Allen. (Inv.: 17.347; 16 June 1733; 15 Aug 1733)

ALLEN (ALLIN), Thomas. Next of kin: James Allin, Susan Allin (widow). Admr.: John Allen. (Inv.: 17.247; 2 May 1733; 23 July 1733)

ALLEN, Barbary, widow of Joseph Allen Sr. On 9 April 1734, John Nevit of St. Mary's Co., conveyed to John Allen, part of a tract called *Nevils Desire*, where Joseph Allen Sr., dec'd., did live and his widow, Barbary now lives. (Land: O#2.32)

ALLEN, Joseph Sr. and Barbara his wife. Deed of gift recorded 19 Nov 1729: to his son Joseph Allen Jr., part of two tracts, *Brothwood* and *Nevils Desire*, lying nr. White Oak Swamp, cont. 74 acres. (Land: M#2.184) Next of kin: John Allen, Elisabeth Allen. Admr.: Barbara Allen. (Inv.: 18.486; 31 July 1734; 10 Aug 1734) (Inv.: 19.136; 17 Oct 1734; 22 Oct 1734)

ALLEN (ALLIN), Thomas. To wife Catherine (Katherine), extx. Memo: John Birch, Thomas Smith, Joanna Harben deceased at date of probate. (Will: 21.468; 21 Feb 1729; 31 Oct 1735) Katherine, widow of Thomas Allen, in a deed dated 8 Aug 1741, conveyed to her nephew, John Hearbin (Hearben), tract called *Old Branford Enlarged*, which was devised to her, by her husband; 153 acres. (Land: O#2.518)

ALLEN, Joseph and Susanna Davis, married 2 Nov 1743. (Trinity: 106—rev.)

ALLEN, Pentheceelia, dau. of Joseph and Susanna Allen, born 28 April 1745. (Trinity: 106—rev.)

ALLINSON, Annabella, age 17 yrs. Servant of Philip Lines, 12 June 1676. (Ct.&Land: G#1.37)

ALLANSON, Thomas, age ca. 22. Testified 17 April 1660. (Ct.&Land: A#1.86)

ALLONSON, Thomas, age ca. 24. Testified 4 March 1661. (Ct.&Land: A#1.191)

ALLINSON (ALLERSON), Thomas (gentleman). Next of kin: John Dorsey, Benjamin Posey. Admr./Ex.: William Collyer. (Inv.: 17.349; 13 June 1733; 16 Aug 1733)

ALLENSON, Charles, son of Thomas Allenson, conveyed on 26 Oct 1741 a tract called *Allissons Secret*, 8 acres. (Land: O#2.532)

ALLISON, Charles. In his will he devises to son Thomas, entire estate. Father-in-law Thomas Asten, to be guardian of son Thomas during his minority. In event of death of sd. son estate to pass to the two child. of sister Eliza: and her husband, Edward Ford. (Will: 7.393; 20 Feb 1698; 1 April 1698)

ALLISON, Thomas, deponent on 5 Nov 1719 (age 23) and on 31 May 1721 (age 24), regarding part of tract called *Christian Temple Manor*, on the s. side of Mattawoman. (Chas LandComm: M2.66, 122)

ALLITON, Susannah. Admr.: Humphrey Poley. (Acct: 39C.131; ----; 1 March 1717)

ALLORD, John. Next of kin: Margaret Pase. Admr./Exs.: Tubman Mankin and his wife Jane Mankin, Thomas Hall and his wife Sarah Hall. (Inv.: 27.449; 26 March 1743; 20 June 1743)

ALLWARD, John and Mary of the head of Portobacco Ck. Their children: John, born 18 Dec 1678; Margarett, born 4 March 1680; Mary, born 20 Dec 1676. (Land: P#.206, 207) QRev. 5, 6, 7 shows the parents as John and Anne Allward of Portobacco Creek)

ALLWARD (ALWARD), John. To dau. Margaret Malow, to Dorothy Brown and granddau. Sarah Yopp, personalty. To granddau. Jane Yopp at marriage, *More's Hope, Good Luck,* and *Partnership.* To grandson Charles Yopp, residue of estate. (Will: 14.81; 5 Jan 1715; 19 Jan 1715) Next of kin: John Mallow. (Inv.: 36C.256; 21 Jan 1715; ----) Ex.: Charles Yopp. (Acct: 38B.27; ----; 1 Jan 1716) Legatees: Margaret Marler, wife of John Marler. (Acct: 37B.92; ----; 31 Aug 1717)

ALLWOOD, Susannah, age 59. Deposition, 29 Sept 1719, regarding the tract *Martins Freehold* in which she refers to statments of her brother John Marloe and her husband. (Chas LandComm: M2.59)

ALLWOOD, Susannah, widow of John Allwood. Gift to sons, John and William Allwood, 10 Nov 1719. (Ct.&Land: H#2.312)

ALVEY, Leonard (planter) and Margret Alvey, mother of sd. Leonard, of St. Mary's Co., conveyed on 20 June 1738 part of a tract called *Greens Inheritance,* 200 acres. (Land: O#2.336)

AMBROSS, Richard. Admr./Ex.: Margaret Worrell, relict. (Acct: 6.565; ----; 4 Oct 1679)

AMERY, Samuel (planter), binds himself to Edward Turner, 1 Dec 1730. Said Samuel Amery has married Mary Willson, one of the daus. of John Willson, dec'd., by whom she has right of 1/2 of his lands, part of a tract called *Watsons Choice,* 159 acres, tract called *Partners Purchase,* cont. 25 acres, and one other tract called *Swann Hill,* cont. 100 acres. Deed dated 2 June 1732, to Thomas Dyson Sr., part of a tract called *Nevil's Desire,* cont. 25 acres. and another part of the tract *Swann Hill,* cont. 100 acres. (Land: M#2.245, 286)

AMERY, Samuel and Mary. Their children: Lydia, born 11 Oct 1738; Elinor, born 20 Feb 1740/1; John, born 21 March 1745/6. (Trinity: 105—rev., 111—rev.)

ANCHORAM. (See ANKREM.)

ANCHORAM (ANCCHROM), Richard and his wife Mary, dau. of Anne Foster, and John Ashman (Mary's brother), conveyed on 29 July 1715, a parcel called *Baker's Addition,* cont. 50 acres. On 24 Nov 1726,

Richard and Mary Anchoram conveyed to John Ashman (planter), part of a tract called *St. Edmunds*, lying at the head of Portobacco Ck., 150 acres. (Land: L#2.66, 278, 321)

ANDERSON, John and Mary of Portobacco. Their children: Edward, born 13 Aug 1691; John, born 14 April 1693; George, born 22 March 1694. (Ct.&Land: QRev.20, 22, 25)

ANDERSON, Edward, son of John Anderson. Cattle mark, June-Aug 1694. (Ct.&Land: S#1.329)

ANDERSON, Edward (blacksmith) and Anne his wife conveyed on 22 Sept 1720 part of a parcel called *Bergen-ap-Zome*. (Ct.&Land: H#2.382)

ANDERSON (ANDREWSON), John. (Inv.: 11B.42; 33? April 1700; ----) Admr.: Mary Sims (relict), wife of James Sims. (Acct: 20.262; ----; 9 May 1701)

ANDERSON, John and Elizabeth his wife conveyed on 5 May 1722 a tract *Andersons Chance* in Prince George's Co., on the n. side of Swansons Ck., 81 acres, and on 8 Aug 1722 a tract *Farthings Discovery*, 520 acres. (Land: L#2.16, 67, 170(release))

ANDERSON, Archbald (taylor). Admr.: William Benson. (Inv.: 11.923; 1 April 1727; 23 May 1727)

ANDERSON, John Sr. and his wife Elizabeth. To son in law, Edward Burch (millwright), part of a tract called *New Bradford*, cont. 94 acres. Deed signed 28 Nov 1730. Deed dated 14 July 1733; to son in law, Richard Standforth (planter), part of a tract called *Foxes Race*, cont. 86 acres. (Land: M#2.244; O#2.4)

ANDERSON, John Jr. To bro. Robert, personalty. To bros. and sisters, viz.: Richard, James, Ann and Katherine, residue of personal estate. Ex.: father John Anderson. (Will: 20.745; 15 June 1733; 15 Aug 1733) Next of kin: Robert Anderson, Edward Burch. Ex.: John Anderson Sr. (Inv.: 18.301; 20 Nov 1733; 3 July 1734)

ANDERSON, Edward (nunc.). To wife, real estate. (Will: 20.877; 1 Nov 1733; 28 Jan 1733) Next of kin: Mary Stock, Marmaduke Semmes. Admr.: Ann Anderson. (Inv.: 18.39; 7 Feb 1733; 11 May 1734)

ANDERSON, John (yeoman), and his wife Elizabeth. Deed dated 10 Nov 1735; to his son, Robert Anderson, 100 acres, part of tract called *Fox Race*. (Land: O#2.125)

ANDERSON, Bartholomew (bricklayer). From Edward Neale and his wife Martha, lease, 7 April 1743, of part of a tract called *Aquimsick(?)* for the term of the lives of Bartholomew Anderson, his wife Sarah and his son Daniel Anderson. (Land: X#2.27)

ANDERTON, Jeremiah and his wife Ann. Lease, 23 Feb 1739/40 on a parcel of land in Chinquamuxon being part of a tract called *Wadestones Enlargement*. (Land O#2.346B)

ANDRES, Henry, son of Lawrence Andres and Mary his wife, b. 27 Jan 1717 (recorded 8 Aug 1720) (Ct.&Land: H#2.366)

ANDRES, Elizabeth, dau. of Lawrence Andres and Mary his wife, b. 19 Aug 1716 (recorded 8 Aug 1720). (Ct.&Land: H#2.366)

ANDRASS, Lawrence. Dated 20 Aug 1725, requests births of his two sons be entered: Benjamin born on 2 May 1722, and William born 23 June 1724. (Land: L#2.233)

ANGE, Elizabeth, wife of William Ange, husbandman of the Parish of Hemel Hempstead, County of Hertford. States on 1 Oct 1731, that Francis Wine died ab. 20 Nov 1730; leaving four sons, Henry, aged ab. 10 yrs.; Francis, aged ab. 8 yrs.; William, aged ab. 6 yrs.; and John, aged ab. 3 yrs. That sd. Francis was the only son of Henry Wine of *Pikesley* in county of Northampton (wine cooper) who was the eldest son of the late Francis Wine of Chas. Co. Signed 7 Aug 1732. (Land: M#2.341)

ANGLISH, John, age 16 yrs. Servant of Arthur Turner, 13 March 1676. (Ct.&Land: G#1.16)

ANKREM. (See also ANCHORAM.)

ANKREM, John, of Stafford Co., Virginia, and Mary his wife, conveyed on 9 April 1725 a tract called *Wallingfeild*, 90 acres, called *Woodbridge*. (Land: L#2.224)

ANNES/ANNIS. (See also INNIS.)

ANNIS, Thomas (planter), and Elizabeth his wife, former wife of James Mackey, dec'd, (son of James Mackey by will); [See James Makey's will 14.335 proved 18 May 1717]. Indenture, 13 May 1720, to Thomas Taylor (tailor); a parcel called *Saint John's*, cont. 100 acres. Also other real estate at Maryland Point and Chigamuxon which sd. Thomas Annis and Elizabeth his wife have any right to. (Ct.&Land: H#2.364)

ANNES, Thomas. Next of kin: J. Annis, William Annis. (Inv.: 6.17; 25 March 1720; ----)

ANNIS, Elizabeth, dau. of Thomas Annis (planter). Cattle mark recorded ca. May 1722. (Land: L#2.14)

ANNIS, William. Next of kin: Elisabeth Copper, William Copper. Admr.: Sarah Annes. (Inv.: 20.441; ----; 26 May 1735)

ANSELL, William of Charles Town, (innkeeper). 14 July 1742. James Glasscock, late of Chas. Co., owning lots #60 and 74 in Charles Town, Portobacco Parish, by his will of 1740 bequeathed the same to his son James Glasscock, that he should in the space of 10 years after testator's death, come to enjoy same; in failure thereof, the testator devised same to

William Ansill afsd. and Jane Lucus of Charles Town. Said Jane Lucus died sometime in Aug last past, whereupon William Ansill became entitled, as surviving exr. and legatee of James Glasscock. Said William Ansill on or about last April 22 married Ann Moore, otherwise Church, widow. William Ansell and Ann Ansell to enjoy the property during their lifetimes. (Land: O#2.571)

ANSIL, William. Admr.: Ann Vinton. (Inv.: 29.176; 15 Dec 1742; 8 June 1744)

APPLEYARD, John. Admr.: Susanna Appleyard. (Inv.: 21.407; 12 May 1736; 26 June 1736)

ARCHIBALL, John, age 22 yrs. Servant of Alexander Smith, 9 Feb 1685/6. (Ct.&Land: M#1.89)

ARNLEY, James, age 13 yrs. Servant of Thomas Speeke, St. Mary's Co., 11 March 1678. (Ct.&Land: H#1.129)

ARROWSMITH, Ger(r)ard (merchant). (Inv.: 34.30; 22 July 1713; ----) Admr.: William Thompson. (Acct: 36B.96; ----; 5 Feb 1714)

ASHBROOKE, Thomas. His bro. John Ashbrook and sister Rose Ashbrook, subpoenaed to testify 28 Jan 1661/2. (Ct.&Land: A#1.175)

ASHBROOKE, John, age ca. 39 and Rose Ashbrooke, age ca. 31, both testified in court 29 Jan 1661/2. (Ct.&Land: A#1.186)

ASHBROOKE, Thomas and his wife Lettise. Acknowledge their right to 150 acres in Nangemy Ck., dated 9 Jan 1671/2. (Ct.&Land: E#1.52½)

ASHBROOKE, John, of Nanjemy. To wife (unnamed), extx., plant. during widowhood, and then to son James. To daus., Rose, Eliza: and Anne, personalty. (Will: 10.67; 17 Jan 1677/8; 24 Jan 1678)

ASHBROOKE, John married ——, 1687. (Ct.&Land: P#1.204) (Arch of Md: 60.95)

ASHBROOKE, James and Elizabeth his wife. Indenture, 9 Feb 1705, to Thomas Davis, tailor. Tract called *Hoggs Quarter*, cont. 100 acres. (Ct.&Land: Z#1.230)

ASHBROOKE (ASHBROOK, ASBROOK), James. To son John, personalty. In event of abuse by a father in law, son James to be taken in charge by his godfather, Wm. Perry. Sons afsd. and son Edward to be of age at 20 yrs., dau. Rose at 16 yrs. Extx.: Wife Elizabeth, to be assisted by cousin Brent. (Will: 12.82; ----; -- Jan 1706) (Inv.: 27.3; 24 April 1707; ----) Extx.: Elisabeth Bartlet, wife of Thomas Bartlet. (Acct: 28.99; ----; 28 Jan 1707)

ASHFORD, Rachell, wife of Michael Ashford. Deed of gift 13 Nov 1677, from Thomas Hussey and his wife Johannah. Rachell is the natural dau. of Johannah Hussey; parcel called *Moore's Ditch*, lying on w. side of Zachia Swamp, cont. 500 acres. (Ct.&Land: G#1.72)

ASHFORD, Michaell (carpenter) and Rachell his wife conveyed on 4 Aug 1683 a parcel called *Tatshall*, cont. 40 acres, and on 10 June 1691, a parcel called *Moore's Ditch*, on w. side of Zachia Swamp, cont. 500 acres. (Ct.&Land: K#1.242, R.197)

ASHFORTH, Mary, dau. of Michaell and Rachell Ashforth. Swears Christopher Gregory is the father of the child she now "goes with," 21 Feb 1693. (Ct.&Land: S#1.239)

ASHMAN, Richard and Anne of head of Wicomico R. Their children: Elizabeth, born 29 June 1680; Richard, born 4 Feb 1682; Mary, born 3 Aug 1685; Standidge, born 1 Oct 1687; Allward Hardy, born 12 June 1691. (Ct.&Land: P#1.209; QRev.7, 8, 11, 13, 17)

ASHMAN, Richard. To son Richard, part of tract called *Promise*. To son Standish, residue of *Promise*. To son Allwood Hardy Ashman and hrs., *Ashman Parche*. To son John, half of *Baker's Addition*. To dau. Mary, residue of *Baker's Addition*. Extx.: Wife Ann. (Will: 7.369; 11 May 1698; 20 June 1698) Admr.: Ann Ashman. (Inv.: 17.8; 22 June 1698; ----) Admr.: Ann Hardy (relict), wife of Henry Hardy. (Acct: 20.195; ----; [c1701])

ASHMAN, John and Mary Anchoram, children of Anne Foster. Mary is the wife of Richard Anchoram who binds himself to John Ashman, 22 Feb 1723, to abide by division made of part of a tract called *St. Edmonds*, devised to John Ashman and Mary Anchoram by their mother. Recorded 9 June 1726. (Land: L#2.278)

ASHMAN, John (planter) and Anna his wife. Deed dated 15 March 1722. To Richard Barber (shipwright), tract called *Woodbridge*, cont. 90 acres. John Ashman and his wife conveyed on 1 April 1734 a tract called the *Store Plantation*, 50 acres. (Land: L#2.86; O#2.44)

ASHTON, Burdit of Westmoreland Co., Virginia and his wife Mary. Deed dated 31 July 1722; to Roger Fowke, part of tract *Burdits Rest*, nr. head of Burdits Ck., 229 acres and on 25 April 1726; to Roger Fowke, part of tract *Birds Nest*, nr. head of Birdits Ck., cont. 75 acres. (Land: L#2.43, 315)

ASKIN, George, to his dau. Beththyah Harrison Askin, a Negro girl Charity, &c. Signed 17 April 1731. (Land: M#2.250)

ASPINALL, Henry and his wife Mary acquired on 21 Jan 1667/8, 350 acres of land called *Doags Neck*. (Ct.&Land: D#1.13)

ASPENALL, Henry (gent.) and his wife Elizabeth conveyed on 8 March 1680 a parcel called *Milersie*, cont. 200 acres, and parcels called *Montagues Addition*, cont. 100 acres, and *Aspenalls Chance*, cont. 200 acres. (Ct.&Land: I#1.80)

ASPEANWALL, Henry. (Inv.: 8.105; 11 Oct 1683; ----)

ASPENALL, Henry, Capt. Admr.: Elisabeth Aspenall, wife of Edward Rookwood. (Acct: 9.55; ----; 10 July 1686)

ASTERE, George, age between 14-15 yrs. Servant, presented by Alexander Simpson, 3 Feb 1663/4. (Ct.&Land: B#1.244)

ATCHISON, William. To son John, 100 acres, *Atchison's Hazard*. To son William, 100 acres, dwelling plant., *Atchison's Woodyard*; and personalty. To son James, 86 acres, *Grubb Street*. To son Joseph, 19 acres, *Atchison's Strife*. To child., 2/3 of personal estate; wife Ann, extx. (Will: 21.140; 26 Feb 1733; 17 July 1734) Next of kin: Thomas Cawood, William Cawood. Extx.: Ann Atchison. (Inv.: 20.243; 22 Nov 1734; 15 Jan 1734)

ATHEE, George (planter) and Ann his wife conveyed on 25 May 1683 land called *Hopewell*, cont. 80 acres. (Ct.&Land: K#1.181)

ATHEY (ATHY), George (planter) and Sarah his wife conveyed on 11 March 1689, a parcel called *Yorkshire*, cont. 91 acres in *Zachia Manor*. (Ct.&Land: P#1.198)

ATHEY, John, son of George Athey. Cattle mark recorded 10 Nov 1691. (Ct.&Land: R#1.333)

ATTKINS, William, age 17 yrs. Servant of Robert Henley, 12 Jan 1674. (Ct.&Land: F#1.41)

AUSHISH, William, age 13 yrs. Servant of James Tyre, 13 June 1675. (Ct.&Land: F#1.193)

AUSTIN, Thomas (planter) and Susanna his wife conveyed on 2 Jan 1693 a parcel called *Habnabala Venture*, cont. 250 acres. (Ct.&Land: S#1.205)

AUSTIN, John and Mary his wife. Indenture with Thomas Trueman Greenfield of St. Mary's Co., 13 Sept 1718; for rent, tract in the branches of Zachia called *Wolfs Dam*, lease for 14 years. (Ct.&Land: H#2.202)

AYLMER (AYLMAR), Justinian. (Inv.: 31.143; 27 Feb 1709; ----) Admr.: Isabella Dryden, wife of George Dryden. (Acct: 33A.123; ----; 9 Feb 1711)

AYRES (EYRES), John. To Thomas and Susanna Carvile, Ralph Foster, Robert Charlesworth and William Gile, personalty. Wife Ellinor, extx. and residuary legatee; at her decease estate to pass to John Ayres' brother Joseph of London. (Will: 11.362; 15 Nov 1702; 15 Jan 1702)

AYRES, George. (Inv.: 3.110; 2 Feb 1702; ----) Second account. Exs.: Robert Charlesworth and his wife Elinor Charleworth. (Inv.: 3.112; [c1702]; ----) Extx.: Ellinor Charleworth, wife of Robert Charlesworth. (Acct: 3.210; ----; 3 April 1704)

AYRES (EYRES), George. (Inv.: 34.57; 1 July 1713; ----) Admr.: William Godfrey. (Acct: 35A.149; ----; 9 April 1714)

BABB, Peter (planter) and his wife Elizabeth, conveyed on 12 June 1724; to James Lutwidge, merchant in England, 1 1/2 acres on Potomack R. Deed dated 6 Jan 1724/5; to Joseph Harrison, son of Richard Harrison, two acres of *Wattsons Purchase* which cont. 300 acres, granted to Andrew Wattson. (Land: L#2.143, 191)

BABB, Peter. In his will he mentioned Jean dau. of Ann Muncester, James Burn, Mathew Froner, Robert Aquantance and Jesse Cooper. To William Sisson (ex.), land on n. side of Wharton's Ck. To John Howison (ex.), land on s. side afsd. creek. (Will: 21.522; 22 Dec 1735; 21 Jan 1735) (Inv.: 21.284; 31 Jan 1735; 21 April 1736) (Inv.: 23.28; ----; 15 Feb 1737)

BABTISTA, John. A Moor of Barbary—is a free man, 1 March 1655 (Ct.&Land: A#1.90)

BAGGOTT, Thomas. Next of kin: John Baggot, Samuel Baggot. Admr.: John Parnham. (Inv.: 15.466; 2 April 1720; 27 April 1720)

BAGGOTT, Samuell. Next of kin: John Baggott, Samuell Baggott. Admr.: Alice Baggott. (Inv.: 13.259; ----; 12 Aug 1728)

BAYLY, Nicholas, age 16 yrs. Servant of Ignatius Causine, 2nd Tues in Aug 1673. (Ct.&Land: E#1.135)

BAILY, William, age 14 yrs. Servant of Robert Middletown, 11 April 1676. (Ct.&Land: F#1.173)

BAILEY, Grace, age 20 yrs. Servant of Henry Towne(?) 11 June 1678. (Ct.&Land: G#1.157)

BAYLY, John and Mary, near Pope's Ck. Their children: John, born 20 Jan 1680; James, born 10 Jan 1683. (Ct.&Land: P#1.207; QRev.7, 9)

BAYLY, James, of John Bayly. Cattle mark recorded, 8-9 March 1686. (Ct.&Land: N#1.194)

BALY, John. (Acct: 9.296; 17 March 1687; ----)

BAYLIE (BAYLY), William (merchant). Confirms will made in England, in which he gives to his brother John the greater part of his estate in Md. and Va. Francis Harrison, ex. of sd. estate. (Will: 11.209; 7 Aug 1702; 15 Aug 1702) (Inv.: 22.99; 17 Aug 1702; ----)

BALY (BAYLY), John. Payments include Anne Burford (relict of Thomas Burford). Extx.: Mary Wilson, wife of Joseph Wilson, filed by Hanna Wilson. (Acct: 27.235; ----; 1707)

BAYLEY, James. Next of kin: John Gwinn, Joseph Gwinn. (Inv.: 10.217; 29 April 1724; 4 Nov 1724)

BAITMAN. (See BATEMAN.)

BAKER (See BARKER).

BAKER, Hamlet. Servant, judged to be 14 yrs. old, presented by George Newman, 12 July 1664. (Ct.&Land: B#1.314)

BAKER, Thomas and Martha, of Potomack River. Their children: Martha, born last day in March 1675; Andrew, born 29 March 1679. (Ct.&Land: P#1.205, 206; QRev.5, 6)

BAKER, Martha, dau. of Thomas Baker. Cattle mark recorded ca. June 1678. (Ct.&Land: G#1.156)

BAKER, Thomas. In his will he left to wife Martha, 1/3 of estate; he mentioned children (unnamed). (Will: 4.57; 5 Sept 1684; 18 Nov 1684) (Inv.: 8.238; 18 Nov 1684; ----) (Acct: 9.131; ----; 9 Aug 1686) Payments to: Robert Potts who married widow and executrix of Richard Johns. Extx.: Martha Harrison, wife of John Harrison. (Acct: 9.463; ----; 20 Jan 1687)

BAKER, Andrew, one of the orphan children of Thomas and Martha Baker. Account of estate of William Dent, guardian of Andrew Baker; court held 11 March 1689. (Ct.&Land: Q#1.6)

BAKER, Thomas, and Elizabeth his wife on 14 Sept 1692 conveyed a part of *Hanstone?*, cont. 550 acres, and on 25 Aug 1694, part of a tract called *Harrisson's Gift*, cont. 250 acres, patented by Andrew Baker and his brother, Thomas Baker, father of afsd. Thomas. (Ct.&Land: R#1.466; S.330)

BAKER, Thomas, grandson of Thomas Baker, dec'd., on 12 May 1719, conveyed to Alexander Contee, heir of John Contee, dec'd. John Baker, uncle of Thomas Baker, and Mary his wife, by their deed 13 Nov 1703 sold John Contee land formerly belonging to his father Thomas Baker, known as *Beginning Lott*, cont. 118 acres; this indenture from Thomas Baker, for love of his said uncle, gives warranty to John Contee. (Ct.&Land: H#2.250)

BAKER, Thomas. Quit claim, 14 July 1719, from Thomas Baker, formerly of Richmond County, Virginia, releases rights to land formerly sold by Thomas Baker, father of afsd. to Maj. William Dent (Dant), cont. 118 acres; also a moiety of *Harrisons Guift*, cont. 109 acres. (Ct.&Land: H#2.272)

BAKER, John Jr. Admr.: John Baker. (Inv.: 11.344; 22 Feb 1725; 30 April 1726)

BAKER, Stephen. Admr.: Capt. Charles Somerset Smith. (Inv.: 17.63; ----; 16 March 1732) Admr.: Somersett Smith. (Inv.: 18.505; 22 June 1734; 13 Aug 1734)

BAKER, John. A gift on 19 July 1734, to his grandson, Charles Colvin, cattle. (Land: O#2.46)

BAKER, John. Deed of gift signed 18 July 1738, to his dau. Elizabeth Baker, cattle. (Land: O#2.440)

BAKER, Thomas, and his wife Margaret. Conveyed on 2 Jan 1743/4, Thomas Baker's right to John Olland's estate, dec'd. (Land: X#2.56)

BALL, Thomas, age 17 yrs. Servant of Ignatius Causine, 12 Jan 1668/9. (Ct.&Land: D#1.41)

BALL, John and Winifred his wife of Stafford Co., Virginia, conveyed 9 March 1714 a parcel called *Lanternam*; bounded by Zachia Swamp, cont. 200 acres. (Ct.&Land: F#2.56)

BALTROP, Francis, late of Charles Co., but now of King George Co., Virginia, and his wife Ann. Conveyed on 2 July 1739, 1/2 of tract called *Bowlston*, lying in Kent Co. [Maryland] on n. side of Chester River, 500 acres and 1/2 of tract called *Bowles Purchase*, on Potomack River, 500 acres. (Land: O#2.427)

BALY. (See BAILY.)

BANCKES, Sarah, relict of Richard Banckes, dec'd. (merchant). Deed of gift 26 Aug 1690, to her four children, Mary Banckes, Richard Banckes, Samuel Banckes and Sarah Banckes; cattle, slaves, &c. (Ct.&Land: R#1.facing page 1)

BANISTER (BANESTER), John. In his will he left to son Timothy, at 21 yrs., personalty, including that given him by Humphrey Posey. To rest of children, each 1 shilling at age. Wife Eliza:, extx., to be assisted by Joseph Harrison. (Will: 13.406; 18 March 1711/12; 3 May 1712) Next of kin: Ruld Price. (Inv.: 33B.37; 12 July 1712; ----) Extx.: Elisabeth Hodgson, wife of Richard Hodgson. (Acct: 35A.59; ----; 27 Jan 1713)

BARACLOW, Tobie. Judged to be 18 years old, presented by William Perfect, 8 Nov 1664. (Ct.&Land: B#1.392-393)

BARAN. (See BARRON.)

BARBER, Richard (shipwright). Recorded 30 March 1736. To John Lancaster, in consideration of a marriage to be solemnized between sd. Richard Barber and Mary Leaptrot (spinster); the sd. Richard has given all his estate to John Lancaster. Richard and Mary to stand seized of the estate for their lifetimes. (Land: O#2.122) In his will he left to wife Mary, his entire estate. One of the witnesses to his will was John Lancaster. Note: Charity Garver, only sister of dec'd., refused to be present at probate. (Will: 23.140; 31 March 1743; 14 June 1743)

BAREFOOT, John, son of John Barefoote, dec'd., to serve Richard Boughton to age 21 yrs. 26 April 1694. (Ct.&Land: S#1.284)

BARGESS. (See BURGESS.)

BARKER, William, age 20 yrs. Servant presented by Richard Stone, 8 March 1663/4. (Ct.&Land: B#1.257)

BARKER, Robert, age betw. 21-22 yrs. Servant of Daniell Johnson, 11 Jan 1669/70. (Ct.&Land: D#1.117)

BARKER, John (planter), and Joan his wife conveyed on 13 March 1676, parcel called *Barker's Enlargement*, lying at head of Wicomico River, cont. 50 acres. They conveyed on 10 April 1685 plantation where said Barker dwells called *Barker's Rest*, cont. 150 acres. (Ct.&Land: G#1.19, L.187)

BARKER, John, son of John and ———— Barker of Nanjemy, born 3 April 1691, bapt. 17th day of said month. (Ct.&Land: P#1.211; QRev.17)

BARKER, John. To son John, 100 acres on which Wm. Monkester lives. To dau. Catrine, sons Leonard, Peter, George and William, personalty at majority, and to dau. Eliza:, personalty. To wife Martha, extx., residue of estate. (Will: 12.329; 29 Nov 1708; 20 Jan 1708/9) (Inv.: 30.253; 29 Jan 1709; ————) Legatees: Katherine Barker, John Barker. Extx.: Martha Barker (Acct: 31.280; ————; 11 April 1710)

BARKER, Ann. Deed of gift, 3 Aug 1711, to her son William Barker. (Ct.&Land: C#2.259)

BARKER, William. Next of kin: William Barker, Matha Petters. (Inv.: 31.334; 4 Aug 1710; ————) Admr.: Ann Barker. (Acct: 32C.130; ————; 13 June 1711)

BARKER, Peter (planter). In his will he mentions wife Ann, and son George [at age 18], to whom he left 100 acres lying at the Fish Pond, at Mattawoman. Cousin John. Dau. Elizabeth. Ex.: John Winters. (Will: 21.98; 8 Dec 1733; 25 May 1734) Next of kin: John Barker, Catherine Millstead. (Inv.: 18.513; 17 June 1734; 24 Aug 1734)

BARKER, William. Next of kin: Ann Buttler, Hugh Stone. Admr.: Dorothy Barker. (Inv.: 18.477; 21 May 1734; 7 Aug 1734)

BARLOW, Joel, age 12 yrs. Servant of James Neale Jr., 8 Aug 1671. (Ct.&Land: E#1.43)

BARNES, Henry. To son Matthew Barnes, dau. Christian Barnes, sons Thomas, Francis and John Coster, and to Edmond Barnes, personalty. Wife Sarah, extx. Edward Barnes was a witness. (Will: 5.95; 11 Oct 1675; 5 Oct 1676) (Inv.: 4.430; 10 Sept 1677; ————) Extx.: Sarah Godshall (relict). (Acct: 4.431; ————; 19 Oct 1677)

BARNES, Matthew and Elizabeth, of Portobacco. Their children: Godshall, born 20 Dec 1692; Jane, born 19 Dec 1694. (Ct.&Land: P#1.212; QRev.19, 24)

BARNES, Matthew, son of Matthew Barnes records cattle mark for heifer given him by his uncle Richard Hudson, 18 July 1705. (Ct.&Land: Z#1.208)

BARNES, Elizabeth, dau. of Matthew Barnes. Records cattle mark for heifer given her by her uncle Richard Hudson, 18 July 1705. Formerly the mark of Elizabeth Jones, her mother, the dau. of Owen Jones. (Ct.&Land: Z#1.208)

BARNES, Benjamin. Cattle mark recorded for calf given him by his father Henry Barnes and Barbara his wife, 14 June 1709. (Ct.&Land: (C#2.137)

BARNES, Henry. To son Henry, all real estate. To sons Henry and Thomas, and daus. Barbara and Ann Semms, to neighbor Elizabeth Hudson and to Joanna and Elener Hudson, personalty. Exs.: Son Henry and dau. Barbara. (Will: 22.90; 9 Sept 1738; 18 July 1739) Next of kin: Ann Simms, Thomas Barnes. Exs.: Henry Barnes, Barbara Backer (late Barbara Barnes). (Inv.: 25.394; ----; 21 Feb 1740)

BARNHAM (See PARNHAM).

BARRET, Joseph. Servant, judged to be 19 yrs. old, presented by John Morris, 12 July 1664. (Ct.&Land: B#1.314)

BARRET, Samuel. To Susanna Thomas, personalty. Thomas Polton, ex. (Will: 5.185; 13 Jan 1676; 9 March 1676/7)

BARRETT, John, age 15 yrs. Servant of William Smith, 13 March 1676. (Ct.&Land: G#1.16)

BARRETT, John, age 14 yrs. Servant of Michael Minork, 11 March 1678. (Ct.&Land: H#1.130)

BARRETT, William, age 20 yrs. Servant of Ignatius Causin, 10 Jan 1681. (Ct.&Land: I#1.224)

BARRETT, James and Elizabeth his wife. On 7 Sept 1685 and on 7 Dec 1685, with Henry Moore, portions of tract called *Moore's Fishing Place*, were sold. (Ct.&Land: M#1.31, N.216)

BARROW, John, age 15 yrs. Servant of William Hatch, 10 June 1679. (Ct.&Land: H#1.134)

BARROW, Charles. (Inv.: 1.696; 24 Feb 1702; ----) Ex.: John Booker. (Acct: 24.175; ----; 14 May 1703)

BARON (BARRON, BARROW), Richard, age 15 yrs. Servant of Humphrey Warren Jr., 12 March 1666. Died 27 July 1666. (Ct.&Land: C#1.129, 252; P#1.204; QRev.2)

BARON, Martha, dau. of John and Mary Baron of Portobacco, born 15 Jan 1694. (Ct.&Land: QRev.24)

BARRON, Peter, son of John Barron. Cattle mark recorded on 10 March 1707. (Ct.&Land: Z#1.260)

BARRON, Peter. Cattle mark, 10 June 1707, for calf given him by his sister Martha Barron. (Ct.&Land: Z#1.272)

BARRON, John (planter). In his will he mentions wife Ann, extx.; sons John and Thomas, (at age of 21). Mentions son in law John Watters. (Will: 15.198; 14 Sept 1718; 19 Aug 1719) Next of kin: William Keye, Jobe Key. (Inv.: 3.191; 31 Aug 1719; ----)

BARREN, Thomas. Admr.: John King. (Inv.: 15.75; 25 July 1729; 12 Aug 1729)

BARAN, Richard in St. Mary's Co., and his wife Mary, conveyed, on 23 July 1731, tract called *Cuckholds Delight*, cont. 100 acres. (Land: M#2.263)

BARTLETT, Ralph. Gift of cattle mark, &c. recorded 12 March 1683, to his child.: Ralph and Thomas Bartlett. (Ct.&Land: K#1.335)

BARTLETT, Mary, orphan of Ralph Bartlett, dec'd. Removed from custody of William West to live with Moses Jones, 11 Aug 1691. (Ct.&Land: Q#1.38) [See Q.28—William West charged with bringing up orphan of Ralph Bartlett, in Roman Catholic religion.]

BARTLETT, Thomas. (Inv.: 29.331; 2 June 1709; ---) Admr.: Elisabeth Porfray (relict), now wife of Peter Porfray. (Acct: 31.78; ----; 16 Feb 1709)

BARTON, William Sr., age 52 yrs. 1657. (Arch. of Md.: XLI.9)

BARTON, Grace, dau. of William Barton Jr., born 26 Aug 1659; died last day of "ye s^d. month." (Ct.&Land: A#1.70; P#1.204)

BARTON, Ann, age 20 yrs. On 13 Aug 1661 said that 6-7 yrs. ago her dec'd. husband William Hungerford before she was married, paid Mr. Hatch two hogsheads of tobacco for the use of Mr. Cager in part of payment for a maid servant that William Hungerford had of Mr. Cager which afterwards Vincent Atchison had and married and was to make satisfaction for her to Mr. Cager and "since my husband's death my father hath received two hogsheads of Vincent in the room of the two hogsheads my husband did pay to Mr. Hatch." [She became the wife of William Barton.] (Arch. of Md., v. XLI, p. 455, 469)

BARTON, William, son of William Jr., born 29 June 1662. (Ct.&Land: A#1.240; P.204; QRev.1)

BARTON, William, son of Nathan Barton, born 19 Feb 1667. (Ct.&Land: C#1.252; P#1.204; QRev.3)

BARTON, William, son of William Jr., born 27 Feb 1667. (Ct.&Land: C#1.260)

BARTON, William Jr. had a child born 25 March 1667. (Ct.&Land: C#1.252)

BARTON, William, son of Nathan Barton. Cattle mark recorded, 10 Nov 1668. (Ct.&Land: D#1.6)

BARTON, William, son of Nathan Barton. Deed of gift dated 6 April 1669, from William Barton. (Ct.&Land: D#1.68)

BARTON, Nathan (carpenter) and his wife Martha conveyed on 1 Jan 1670, to William Barton a parcel on w. side of main fresh of Wicomico River, cont. 225 acres. (Ct.&Land: E#1.19½)

BARTON, Nathan. Legacy to Nathan Barton's children, Martha Barton and William Barton in 1684 or 1685; court held 2 March 1690/1. (Ct.&Land: Q.21)

BARTON, Elizabeth, dau. of William Barton Jr., born 27 Feb 1671. (Ct.&Land: E#1.72; P#1.205; QRev.4)

BARTON, George, age 21-22 yrs. Servant of Zachary Wade, 10 March 1673. (Ct.&Land: E#1.153)

BARTON, Robert, age 21 yrs. Servant of William Boareman, 12 June 1682. (Ct.&Land: I#1.293)

BARTON, Nathan. Admr: Francis Hamersley. (Acct: 10.161; ----; 2 Oct 1688) Mentions: three children (unnamed). (Acct: 13B.122; ----; 13 April 1694)

BARTON, Thomas, son of William Barton and Elizabeth Barton of Mattawoman, born 17 July 1689. (Ct.&Land: QRev.14)

BARTON, William, son of William Barton and Elizabeth of Mattawoman, born 11 Nov 1690. (Ct.&Land: QRev.14)

BARTON, William. Petition regarding the estate of his father, Nathan Barton, 10 March 1690. (Ct.&Land: Q#1.27)

BARTON, Elizabeth, wife of William Barton of Mattawoman. Gift dated 22 June 1694, to her god-dau. Elizabeth Parker, dau. of John Parker, a cow calf. (Ct.&Land: S#1.388)

BARTON, David, son of William and Eizabeth Barton of Mattawoman, born 25 June 1695. (Ct.&Land: QRev.26)

BARTON, William of Mattawoman. Mentions Alex Simpson. To wife Eliza:, 500 acres in Stafford Co., Virginia. To son William, ca. 300 acres at Mattawoman, in two tracts, viz., *Wintworth's Woodhouse* and *Cowland*. Mentions "Bartons of Warwickshire, England." Wife and son afsd., exs. (Will: Part 2—12.60; 13 Nov 1708; 10 May 1709)

BARTON, William, son of William Barton, dec'd. Quit claim, 5 Feb 1712, a parcel called *Hedlow*, cont. 500 acres, which by the will of William Barton, was devised to his widow, now wife of James Haddock. (Ct.&Land: D#2.32)

BARTON, William. To son Nathan and dau. Elizabeth, estate. Wife Rachell. Ex.: Francis Bucher. Test: James Boyd, Elizabeth Bucher, James Tinsone. (Will: 14.277; 25 Nov 1716; 18 Feb 1716)

BARTON (BARTTON), Elizabeth. To grandson and granddau., Nathan and Elizabeth Bartton, personalty. Dau. in law Rachel Bartton, extx., to have use of estate during widowhood. (Will: 14.268; 12 Dec 1716; 9 April 1717) (Inv.: 37B.181; 1 May 1717; ----.) Admr.: Rachel Barton, wife of Dave Hopper. (Acct: 39C.134; ----; 31 March 1717)

BARTON, William. Mentions grandsons: Barton Smoot, Barton Warren and William Smoot, granddaus.: Rachell (wife of Mathew Stone), Ann Smoot, Mary Hungerford, Eliza: (wife of Charles Philpott), Eliza (wife of John Neale); three youngest child. of dau. Margaret Miller, and Thomas and Barton (sons of grandson Barton Smoot). Exs.: Dau. Margaret Miller and grandson Barton Smoot. (Will: 14.658; 5 Sept 1717, 22 Sept 1717)

BARTON, William. (Inv.: 37B.182; 1 May 1717; ----) (Inv.: 39C.49; 19 Oct 1717; ----)

BARTON, William. Admr.: Rachell Barton, wife of Dave Hopper. (Acct: 39C.190; ----; 3 March 1717)

BATCHELER, Francis, age ca. 26 yrs. States he found a will of Joseph Lenton among his papers, 4 March 1661. (Ct.&Land: A#1.195)

BATEMAN, Mary, widow of John Bateman. 1663. (Arch. of Md., v. XLIX, p. 162) Mary being the dau of Margaritt Perry of the city of Westminster, county of Mids., widow. John Bateman was once haberdasher of London who signed a bond to said Margaritt Perry on 14 Aug 1649. (Arch. of Md., v. XLI, p. 597)(Arch. of Md., v. XLIX, p. 291, 319) 1665/6. (Arch. of Md., v. LVII, p. 3, 19, 50, 106, 336)

BAITEMAN, Patrick, age 17 yrs. Servant of Wm. Chandler, 11 March 1678. (Ct.&Land: H#1.130)

BATEMAN, George, son of George and Elizabeth Bateman of Pickawaxen, born 7 Dec 1692. (Ct.&Land: P#1.211; QRev.19)

BATEMAN, George Sr. Creditors: Raphael Neale, Thomas Bateman. Next of kin: George Bateman, Thomas Bateman. Admr./Ex.: Mary Bateman. (Inv.: 12.498; 26 Oct 1727; 12 Dec 1727) (Inv.: 13.120; ----; 15 June 1728) Next of kin: Lawrance Bateman, Thomas Bateman. Admr.: Mary Bateman. (Inv.: 15.552; 30 April 1730; 24 June 1730)

BATEMAN, Mary. Next of kin: John Bateman, Thomas Bateman. Admr.: Benjamin Bateman. (Inv.: 21.243; 27 Feb 1735; 4 March 1735)

BATEMAN (BATON), Murdoe (Murdo). Admr.: Matthew Barnes. (Inv.: 28.498; 30 Jan 1743; 23 March 1743)

BATHERTON, John, age 12 yrs. Servant of Edward Price, 1673.

BATTIN (BATTEN), William (Capt., merchant), age ca. 43 yrs., testified on 22 April 1662. (Ct.&Land: A#1.204) Died ca. last of Oct 1662, leaving widow Margery who married John Bowles. (Arch. of Md.: LI.70) Margerie, relict of Capt. William Battin (merchant), appointed an attorney 4 Nov 1662. (Ct.&Land: A#1.259) [NOTE: William Sanford is above subject's son in law.]

BATTLE, Anthony, age 16 yrs. Servant of John OKeane, 8 March 1669/70. (Ct.&Land: D#1.127)

BAWLDING. (See BOWDER/BOWDEN.)

BAYLEY/BAYLIE/BAYLY. (See BAILEY.)

BAYNE, John of St. Mary's Co. Indenture 9 Nov 1691, to his dau., Anne Bayne; half of parcel called *Locust Thickett*, cont. 1060 acres. (Ct.&Land: R#1.281)

BAYNE, John (Capt.). In his will he mentioned Bayne Smallwood, Bayne Griggs. To wife Ann, extx., life interest in 150 acres on Piscataway on northeast side *Locust Thicket*. To son Ebsworth, 800 acres, *Brathwood*; 200 acres, *Indian Cabin*; 200 acres, *Nevett's Desire*, two tracts bought of Benj. Posey, 100 acres, *Muddle's Branch*. To dau. Ann, 300 acres lying on s. side *Locust Thicket*, and 1/2 of *Locust Thicket*. To son Walter, residue of sd. warrant lying on the n. side of *Locust Thicket* and residue of all lands at decease of wife Ann except *The Meadows*, which already belongs to son Ebsworth. (Will: 11.217; 5 Oct

1700; 25 Oct 1701) Mentioned Benjamin Warren, John Warren, Pry: Smallwood. (Inv.: 22.32; 10 July 1702; ----)

BAYNE, Ellinor (Elinor). In her will she mentions Walter and Ebsworth Bayne, Ellinor Hubbard, Eliza: Stone, Ellinor Stone, Eliza: Dutton and each of her child. and sister (unnamed) in England, Mrs. Charity Courts, and to daus. Ellinor Beale and Ann Bayne, personalty. Ex.: Son John Bayne in event of his return from Eng.; otherwise grandson Walter Bayne to be ex. at 21 yrs. of age and to be advised by his father (unnamed), or Col. John Courts. (Will: 11.298; 5 Nov 1701; 11 Nov 1701) Items in possession of Walter Bayne. (Inv.: 21.364; ----; [c1702])

BAYNE, Anne, Madam. Mentions: estate of Capt. John Bayne. (Inv.: 24.134; 15 July 1703; ----) (Inv.: 24.140; 15 July 1703; ----)

BAYNE, Walter (Gent.) of Prince George's Co. and his wife Martha on [12] March 1706, conveyed a tract called *Speakes Inclosure*, cont. 283 acres. Indenture, 3 Oct 1709, conveying a parcel of land nr. Wicomico R., 500 acres, originally granted to William Marshall (1650), sold by Marshall to Walter Bayne, grandfather of afsd. Walter, 29 Sept 1660. On 4 March 1716, Walter and Martha Bayne conveyed parcel called *Grubs Venture*, 83 acres. (Ct.&Land: C#2.39, 146; H#2.143)

BAYNE, Ebsworth and Katherine his wife on 28 Jan 1715 conveyed 100 acres of land, part of a tract called *Brotherwood*. On 22 Feb 1715, they conveyed three tracts called *Brotherwood, The Indian Cabbin*, and *Nevill's Desert*. (Ct.&Land: F#2.86, 91)

BAYNE, Ebsworth, son of John Bayne, son of Walter Bayne, conveyed in 1716 a parcel called *Partner's Purchase*, pt of *Nevils Desire*, cont. 50 acres. (Ct.&Land: H#2.27)

BAYNE, Ebsworth. Deed of gift, 14 July 1716, to his dau. Burditt Bayne, a mulatto girl, age 13 months. (Ct.&Land: H#2.14)

BAYNE, Ebsworth and his wife Kindrick (Kendrick) conveyed on 13 Jan 1718 a parcel called *The Meddows* at head of Wicomico R., cont. 400 acres and on 16 Sept 1719 they conveyed a tract called *Brothwood*, cont. 480 acres. (Ct.&Land: H#2.248, 281)

BAYNE, Walter, assigns his right to a mark belonging to his grandfather, old Walter Bayne on 15 Sept 1715; recorded 7 May 1731 at the request of Col. John Fendall. (Land: M#2.245)

BEADE, Nicholas. Cattle marks recorded for his daus., Mary and Sarah Beade, 20 Jan 1679. (Ct.&Land: H#1.252)

BEAD, Nicholas, and his wife Elizabeth, defendants with Henry Hyde, to answer George Monroe, complainant. 1668. (Arch. of Md., v. LVII, p. 411)

BEAD (BEADE), Nicholas. In his will he mentions daus. Susanna and Mary; son John. Garret Fookes appointed guardian of son John. (Will: 6.92; 18 Jan 1696; 25 Jan 1697) (Inv.: 16.39; ----; [c1698]) Ex.: John Bead. (Acct: 20.268; ----; 8 Feb 1700)

BEAD, John. (Inv.: 27.226; 23 Oct 1707; ----) Admr.: Susanna Keen (relict of John Shareman who was administrator of deceased), now wife of James Keen. (Acct: 28.343; ----; 30 Sept 1708)

BEADON, Daniel (planter), and his wife Jane, leased on 8 June 1737 from a tract called *Simpsons Supply*. (Land: O#2.206)

BEALE, John and his wife Jone, in court case against John Allen of Charles Co. That John Allen bound himself to said Jone on 20 July 1674. (Arch. of Md.: LXV.519)

BELL, Elizabeth, age 21 yrs. Servant of Robert Henley, 11 June 1678. (Ct.&Land: G#1.157)

BELL, Bridgett, age 16 yrs. Servant of Maj. John Wheeler, 10 June 1679. (Ct.&Land: H#1.134)

BELL (BEALE), Charles, son of Maj. Ninian Bell. Cattle mark, 1 March 1687. (Ct.&Land: N#1.329)

BEALL, Ninian and Ruth his wife. Indenture, 15 Sept 1694, conveyed the tract called *Foxhall* on s. side of the Oxon Run in Manor of Zachia, 150 acres. (Ct.&Land: Q#1.69)

BEALE, Jeoffrey. Next of kin: Joanah Denego, William Denego. (Inv.: 35A.144; [c1713]; ----)

BEALE, Richard, son of John Beale by Eleanor Bean, dau. of Walter Bean. Conveyance dated 19 Sept 1723, of two tracts, one called *Durham*, granted in 1666 to Walter Bean, dec'd., on e. side of the Fresh Run of Portabacco, 750 acres; and one other tract called *Durham*, also granted in 1676, bounded by Indian Path, to Eleanor Bean, dau. of said Walter Bayne [Bean] and mother of Richard, 400 acres. (Land: L#2.117)

BEALE, Richard (planter) son of John Beale, conveyed on 25 Dec 1724 a parcel called *His Lordships Favour*, bounded by Dressing Branch; cont. 300 acres. (Land: L#2.185)

BEALE, Richard, now a resident of Essex Co., Virginia, son of John Beale, conveyed on 20 Sept 1728, remainder of tract called *His Lordships Favour*, 340 acres. (Land: L#2.452)

BELL, Richard. Admr.: Samuell Hanson. (Inv.: 20.486; 27 May 1735; 17 June 1735)

BELL, Moses (planter) and his wife Katherine conveyed on 10 Aug 1732, to Thomas Milstead a tract called *Mountain*. (Land: M#2.312)

BEALE, John Sr. Recorded 14 Jan 1736/7, to his son, John Beale Jr., a tract called *Durham*, 100 acres. In subsequent deed, John Beale Sr., gives his youngest son John Beale Jr., remaining part of tract *Durham*, 275 acres, after the deaths of John Beale, Sr. and his wife Johanna Catherine Beale. (Land: O#2.184)

BELL, Moses. In the inventory is mentioned William Bell. Admr.: Catherine Bell. (Inv.: 27.448; 27 May 1743; 7 June 1743)

BEAMONT. (See BEAUMONT.)

BEANE, Walter and his wife Elenor. Assign their rights in a patent, 13 Oct 1663. (Ct.&Land: B#1.186) In his will Walter Beane left to wife Ellinor, extx., home plantation, 450 acres. To son Thomas, sd. plantation at death of mother, and 1,000 acres in St. Mary's Co., at 21 yrs. of age. To eld. dau. Edith, wife of Mathew Hill, 300 acres. To dau. Eliza:, 300 acres. To 3rd and young. dau. Ellinor, 750 acres nr. Portobacco Ck. (Will: 1.386; 12 April 1670; 28 May 1670)

BEAUMUNT, James. (Inv.: 7C.131; 20 March 1682; --)
BEAMONT, John, son of Thomas Beamont. Received mare from John Lemaire (surgeon), 28 Sept 1686. (Ct.&Land: M#1.131)
BEAUMOUNT, Richard. Admr.: Mary Burgess (relict). (Acct: 16.96; ----; 11 July 1695)
BEAUMONT, Anne. Binds her child, Elizabeth Kittes, age 4 yrs. on 11 Oct past, to Josias Cuttance, 10 Dec 1712. (Ct.&Land: D#2.27)

BECK, Elizabeth, dau. of Richard and Elizabeth Beck, born 2 Oct 1669. (Ct.&Land: P#1.206; QRev.3)
BECK (BECKE), Margarett, dau. of Richard and Elizabeth Beck, born 1 May 1674. (Ct.&Land: P#1.206; QRev.5)
BECK, Mary, dau. of Richard and Elizabeth Beck, born 15 Nov 1673. (Ct.&Land: P#1.206; QRev.4)
BECK, Lewis. Mentions: Richard Beck (brother). (Acct: 4.246; ----; 18 Sept 1677)
BECK, Richard. Admr.: Elisabeth Beck (widow). (Inv.: 5.211; ----; 27 May 1678. Acct: 5.212; ----; ----)

BEE, Thomas. Judged to be 20 years old, presented by James Bowlin, 8 Nov 1664. (Ct.&Land: B#1.384)

BELAYNE, John. Deed of gift dated 30 Sept 1662 to his son, Nicholaus Belayne, a cow. (Ct.&Land: B#1.29)
BOLAYN, John. In his will he mentions wife and her children and his children (all unnamed). (Will: 1.205)
BELAYNE, Elisabeth, relict of John Belayne (Belaine); swore in court 3 Nov 1663, that she was a witness to her husband's will. (Ct.&Land: B#1.188)
BELAYNE (BELAINE), Nicholas and Mary, of head of Wicomico River. Their children: Jemima, born 25 March 1686; Elizabeth, born 25 Feb 1688. (Ct.&Land: P#1.211; QRev.12, 14)

BELL. (See BEALE/BEALL.)

BELLINGHAM. (See BILLINGHAM.)

BELLOWS (BELOWS), George. To god dau. Elizabeth (wife of John Shaw Jr.), personalty. To Hannah Dixon, Charity Story and John Dixon, residue of estate when of age. Ex.: Walter Story. (Will: 18.338; 28 Dec 1724; 13 Jan 1724) (Inv.: 10.346; 13 Jan 1724; 20 April 1725)

BENATHON, Christian. Servant, judged to be 19 years old, presented by Richard Foxton, 10 Feb 1662. (Ct.&Land: B#1.62)

BENJAR, Robert. Appraisers: Thomas Chapman, Evan Jones. (Inv.: 19½B.136; 3 April ----; 21 May 1700)

BENNAM, Margaret, age 20 yrs., testified 2 July 1661 (Ct.&Land: A#1.143)

BENNETT, Mary, age 20-21 yrs. Servant of Edward Price, 10 March 1673. (Ct.&Land: E#1.155)
BENNETT, John, age 20 yrs. Servant of Hugh French, 9 March 1674. (Ct.&Land: F#1.69)
BENNETT, Mary, age 22 yrs. Servant of Henry Hardy, 10 June 1679. (Ct.&Land: H#1.134)
BENNITT, John (planter) and Mary his wife, conveyed on 12 March 1705, to William Smoot and John Nathan Smoot. William and John Smoot received tract called *Skipton*, from will of Capt. Thomas Smoot. Recorded by request of bro. Barton Smoot (Ct.&Land: Z#1.256)
BENNET (BENET), Isaac. Admr.: Susanna Bennet. (Inv.: 23.168; 24 Aug 1737; 1 May 1738)

BENSON, Robert. Servant man, judged to be 18 or 19 yrs. old, presented by Edward Richardson, 8 Aug 1665. (Ct.&Land: B#1.472)
BENSON, John, age 11 yrs. Servant of Mr. Prouce, 14 June 1670. (Ct.&Land: D#1.154)
BENSTONE (BENSON), Patrick. Admr.: Charles Cartee. (Inv.: 8.59; 27 Jan 1682; ----. Acct: 8.80; ----; 28 June 1683)
BENSON, Robert (nunc.). Son William, ex. and sole legatee of estate, except certain personalty belonging to testator's dec'd wife, is devised to her dau. Mary, wife of Michael Lynn. (Will: 6.369; 16 March 1699; 3 April 1700)

BERRY, Elizabeth, age 14 yrs. Servant of Thomas Baker, 14 March 1681. (Ct.&Land: I#1.258)
BERRY, John, age 17 yrs. Servant of Ralph Shaw, 11 Aug 1685. (Ct.&Land: L#1.161)
BERRY, Allice. Appraisers: Barton Smoot, John Marten. (Inv.: 8.338; 16 Sept 1723; ----)
BERRY, William. Next of kin: Abel Wakefield, John Wakefield. Admr.: Esther Berry. (Inv.: 17.125; 19 Feb 1732; 5 May 1733)
BERREY, Samuel, surgeon. On 30 Nov 1734, he conveyed to his son in law, John Robey, furniture and other items. (Land: O#2.75)

BEVAN, Charles, Sr. (planter) of Prince George's Co., and his wife Mary. On 22 June 1738 they conveyed to Basil Bevan (planter), of Prince George's

23

Co., a tract called the *Hicory Thicket*, 200 acres, and a tract called *Bevans Addition*, 100 acres; also 1/3 to his wife Martha Bevan. Provisos for Basil Bevan, his bro. Henry Bevan, his bro. Blanford Bevan, his bro. Richard Bevan, his bro. Charles Bevan. (Land: O#2.332)

BIAS, Elizabeth. Deed of gift 8 Aug 1714, to her daughter, Mary. (Ct.&Land: D#2.56)

BIGGS (BIGS), Ambros, age 19 yrs. Servant presented by Thomas Baker, 8 March 1663/4. (Ct.&Land: B#1.259)

BIGGS, John and his wife Ruth. On 11 Nov 1736 they purchased from Marmaduke Simms, part of tract called *St. Georges*, 93 acres and 78 perches. (Land: O#2.176) Children of John and Ruth Biggs: Sarah, born 14 May 1735; Elizabeth, born 12 July 1737; Priscilla, born 18 Feb 1738; Charity, born 9 June 1741; Eliner, born 24 Jan 1745. (Trinity: 105—rev.)

BILE, James. Admr.: Philip Hoskins. (Acct: 18.59; ----; 6 Nov 1698)

BILLINGHAM, Mary, age 12 yrs. Servant of Matthew Hill, 12 Jan 1674. (Ct.&Land: F#1.41)

BELLINGHAM, Alice, age 16 yrs. Servant of Robert Henley, 12 Jan 1674. (Ct.&Land: F#1.41)

BINNS(?), James, age 17 yrs. Servant of Thomas Gerrard, 13 Jan 1679. (Ct.&Land: H#1.242)

BIRD, John. In his will he left to sister Elizabeth Flye of London, and godson Isaac, son of Joshua Cecil of Prince George's Co., jointly, entire estate, in England and Maryland. Ex.: Joshua Cecil. (Will: 3.638; 26 May 1704; 10 June 1705)

BIRD, Mary, age 19 yrs. Servant of John Speake, Nov 1710. (Ct.&Land: D#2.5)

BIRTCH/BIRTH. (See BURCH.)

BISHOP, Will, age 15 yrs. Servant of James Walker, 12 March 1672. (Ct.&Land: E#1.54)

BISHOP, Archibald. (Inv.: 31.145; 1 Feb 1709; ----) Admr.: Elisabeth Raay, wife of James Raay (Acct: 32B.240; ----; 5 March 1710)

BISHOP, William. (Inv.: 29.333; 19 April 1709; ----) Admr.: Elisabeth Bishop. (Acct: 31.283; ----; 20 April 1710)

BLACKBEARD, Peeter. Judged to be 17 yrs. old, presented by James Bowlin, 8 Nov 1664. (Ct.&Land: B#1.384)

BLACKFAN, John, of Nanjemy. In his will he mentions wife Mary, extx., entire estate, with provision in event of birth of child. Mentions bro. Richard and sisters Mary and Eliza:, William and Richard Stone. (Inv.: 4.595; 25 March 1676; ----) (Acct: 7A.239; ----; [c1680]). Admr.: Joseph Manning. (Will: 5.234; 31 Jan 1676; 12 March 1676/7)

BLADEN, William of Annapolis, and his wife Ann, conveyed on 3 July 1716, part of *Beach Neck*, cont. 480 acres. (Ct.&Land: H#2.24)

BLADEN, Thomas, son of William Bladen, late of the city of Annapolis, dec'd. Lease dated 13, 14 Feb 1723, to Thomas Cowper (Gent.) of the Parish of St. Paul Covent Garden in the county of Middlesex, messuages and tenements in Chas. Co. on the s. side of Piscattaway River called *The Doeg's Neck*, 450 acres. Also a tract of 200 acres, patented to Walter Hall 26 April 1658 and a tract called *Christian Temple Manor* alias *Allisons Manor*, 800 acres. Recorded 12, 13 April 1727. (Land: L#2.339. See also L#2.343.)

BLADEN, Thomas of Annapolis, and his wife Barbara, conveyed on 25 May 1744 tract called *River Spring*, on s. side of eastern most branch of Nanjemy Ck., 207 acres; also land called *Albergirn*, 100 acres. (Land: X#2.130)

BLAKWOOD, John, age ca. 33 yrs. Swore in court, 6 June 1660. (Ct.&Land: A#1.94)

BLANCH, John, age 14 yrs. Servant boy presented by William Barton Jr., 8 March 1663/4. (Ct.&Land: B#1.258)

BLANSHAT, Henry. (Inv.: 4.87; 23 March 1720; ----)
BLANCIT (BLANCHET, BLANSHET), Henry. In his will he mentions god dau. Susannah Breeding and Matthew Breeding Sr., ex. (Will: 23.445; 8 April 1740; 6 May 1743) Next of kin: John Blanshet. (Inv.: 29.179; ----; 12 June 1744)

BLEE, John, planter. In his will he mentions Susannah Baker, godson John (son of James Elery) and god-dau. Anne (dau. of Mark Penn). Wife Margaret, extx. To Margaret Holt [minor] 2/3 estate (Capt. John Fendall to act as her guardian). (Will: 16;126; 14 Nov 1718; 15 June 1720) Admr.: Cleborne Lomax. (Inv.: 4.240; 20 Aug 1720; 9 Nov 1720)

BLEE, Margaret (widow). To Elizabeth Jr., and Mary Fendall, Sarah, wife of John Cox; Rose Law; Thomas Lomax; god-dau. Susannah, dau. of John Baker; Eliza, wife of Phillip Snivens, and Susannah Maud, personalty. To Margaret Holt, an orphan girl brought up by testator, residue of estate. Ex.: Capt. John Fendall. (Will: 16.122; 2 April 1720; 15 June 1720) (Inv.: 4.242; 20 Aug 1720; 9 Nov 1720)

BLYZARD, Gyles. To wife Mary, *Cane's Purchase*, and part of *Buplaine*.
To dau. Susanna, *Cane's Purchase*, at death of wife, and residue of
Buplaine. To dau. Ann, *St. James*. To Thomas Lewis and Katharine,
his wife, and their son Richard, a lease of 200 acres. To Eliza: Gambral,
100 acres. Wife Mary, extx. (Will: 6.27; 6 Dec 1678; 17 May 1688)

BLIZARD, Giles. Indenture 4 Aug 1684, to Giles Blizard of London, whereas
marriage is intended between Giles Blizard and Susanna Cane, dau. of
John Cane; parcel called *Blew Plane*, cont. 1000 acres. (Ct.&Land: L#1.1)

BLIZARD, Anne, dau. of Giles and Mary Blizard. Robert Thompson binds
himself to Anne for 20,000 lbs. of tobacco, 8 March 1691. (Ct.&Land: Q#1.54)

BLIZARD, Susannah, dau. of Giles Blizard, dec'd. To remain in custody of
her mother in law [step-mother] Mary Thompson, 21 Feb 1693. (Ct.&Land: S#1.242)

BOARD, Jane, age 17 yrs. Servant of John Wood, 11 March 1678. (Ct.&Land: H#1.130)

BOREMAN, William, age 20. 28 May 1650. (Arch. of Md., v. X, p. 12) St. Mary's Co.

BOREMAN, William, confesses he is a Roman Catholic and that he was born and bred so. 1655. (Arch. of Md., v. X, p. 425)

BOREMAN, Capt. William, records cattle mark of his dau Sarah. 17 July 1668. (Arch. of Md., v. LVII, p. 345) St. Mary's Co.

BOREMAN, William (Gent.) and Mary his wife conveyed on 22 March 1704 tract called *Wardle*, 780 acres. (Ct.&Land: Z#1.183)

BOARMAN, Maj., age ca. 80. Made oath on 15 Sept 1707, regarding a landmark of *Westwood Lodge* 40 years ago. (Ct.&Land: C#2.158)

BOARMAN, William, Major. To wife Mary, extx., personalty and 1/2 dwelling plant., *Boarman's Rest*; wife to pay dau. Clare certain money due by debt of Ephram Leverton, of North Carolina. To son Benedict, dwelling plantation, *Boarman's Rest*, provided he keep in repair the Chapell (Catholic). To son John Baptist, tract *Lanterman*. To son Francis Ignatius, part of *St. George's Rest*. To daus. Mary and Clare, about 400 acres. To dau. Ann Brooks, 500 acres. (Will: Part 2-12.108; 16 May 1708; 17 June 1709) Next of kin: William Boarman, Benedict Boarman. (Inv.: 30.60; 11 July 1709; ----) Extx.: Mary Sanders, wife of John Sanders. (Acct: 32B.247; ----; 4 Sept 1711) Legatees: John Baptist Boarman, Douzabella Semmes, Robert Green, Mary Boarman now Sanders, widow (unnamed), Benjamin Boarman, Baptist Boarman. Extx.: Mary Sanders, wife of John Sanders. (Acct: 33A.158; ----; 7 April 1711)

BOARMAN, William and his wife Mary conveyed on 10 June 1713 a parcel of land part of *Content* on Joseph's Branch, cont. 60 acres. (Ct.&Land: D#2.54)

BOARMAN, John Baptista and Elizabeth his wife on 12 Nov 1717 conveyed parcel called *Lanternam*. (Ct.&Land: H#2.117)

BOARMAN, William Sr. and his wife Mary conveyed on 6 Oct 1719 parcel called *Baltimores Kindness*, cont. 100 acres. Indenture, 13 Nov 1719, to Benedict Boarman; tract of 115 acres called *Hard Shift*. (Ct.&Land: H#2.292, 315)

BOARMAN (BOARDMAN), William Sr. To son William, personalty and land, reserving to use of wife Mary, dwelling plantation. To son Joseph, tract bet. lines of son in law Marsham Warran and son Josua Giurbert. To son Thomas James, a tract of land. To dau. Sarah, use of orchard with 60 acres where Betty Prockter lives, while unmarried. To dau. Jean (Jane), 30 acres in hands of cousin Thomas Turner, and use of 60 acres from her bro. Joseph's tract, while unmarried. To dau. Mary, use of 60 acres of her bro. Thomas James' tract, while unmarried. To sons Joseph and Thomas James, tract betw. son in law Josua Giurbert's and Joseph's great run. The upper pt. of plantation where John Glass lives to son Joseph. Wife Mary, extx. (Will: 16.67; 8 April 1720; 23 May 1720) Next of kin: John Pile, Benjamin Boarman. Ex.: Mary Boarman. (Inv.: 4.235; 27 June 1720; 18 Aug 1720) Next of kin: Benedict Boarman, Francis Ignatius Boarman. (Inv.: 5.101; ----; [c1721])

BOARMAN, William. To son William, *St. Dorrothys*, Clement's Bay, St Mary's Co.; pt. of tract had from father. To son James, pt. of tract had from father; 50 acres *Coventry*. To dau. Elizabeth, personalty. Tract nr. uncle Benjamin's to be sold. To cousin Raphael Neal Jr., personalty. Exs.: Sons. (Will: 19.727; 26 Feb 1728/9; 30 June 1729) Next of kin: Joseph Boarman, Francis Ignatius Boarman. Exs.: William Boarman, James Boarman (Inv.: 15.149; 28 Aug 1729; 10 Nov 1729) Next of kin: Francis Ignatius Boarman, Thomas James Boarman. Exs.: William Boarman, James Boarman (Inv.: 16.108; 6 Nov 1730; 26 Feb 1730)

BOARMAN, Joseph. To bro. Thomas James Boarman, entire real estate. To Thomas Bucknan and Peter Attwood, personalty. To mother Mary Boarman, extx., residue of personal estate. (Will: 19.891; 26 Dec ----; 13 April 1730)

BOARMAN, Mary. To daus. Jane Neale and Mary Gardiner, Thomas Leckonby, personalty. Son Thomas James, ex. and residuary legatee. (Will: 20.842; 20 Feb 1732/3; 27 Nov 1733)

BOARMAN, John Baptist and his wife Elizabeth. Sold the following land: 10 Feb 1736/7, part of the tract called *Lyons Den*, lying on w. side of Zachia Swamp, 140 acres; tract adjoining called *Wood's Addition*, 38 acres, parcel being part of two tracts called *Calverts Hope* and *Georges Rest* on e. side of Zachiah Swamp, 291 acres+; 23 May 1745, part of tract called *St. Georges*, 59 acres+. (Land: O#2.186; X#2.11; Z#2.71. See also Land: O#2.201, 206)

BOARMAN, Elizabeth, dau of William Boarman, Jr. Indenture tripartite dated 23 May 1737 betw. John Baptist Boarman and Francis Hall of

Prince George's Co. and John Parnham of Chas. Co., merchant. Reference is made to a parcel of land sold out of *Calverts Hope* to Major William Boarman by James Bowling for about 130 acres by deed which land is since bequeathed to Elizabeth Boarman, dau of William Boarman, Jr. Acknowledged by Elizabeth, wife of John Baptist Boarman. (Land O#2.201)

BOARMAN, Thomas James (Gent.), and his wife Jean (Jane), conveyed on 31 Aug 1741, part of a tract *Coventry*, lying on e. side of Zachia Swamp, 17 acres. (Land: O#2.520. See also Land Z#2.4.)

BOARMAN, Ignatius, (gent.), To sons Gerard, William, Francis, and John, entire estate at 18 yrs. Ex.: Richard Brook, Willeford Gremer. (Will: 23.446; 19 June 1743; 15 March 1743)

BOARMAN, Francis Ignatius. Next of kin: John Boarman, Benedict Boarman. Ex.: Richard Brooke (surviving ex.). (Inv.: 29.347; 27 April 1744; 13 July 1744)

BODKIN, James. To bro. Dominick, rights of 250 acres, *Saturday Work*. Mentions bro. Edward; young. bro. Augustine; cous. Andrew, son of uncle Dominick Bodkin; sisters Anne, Jane, and Ellinor; father Patrick and mother Anasta. Mentions cous. James Bodkin, Major William Boarman and Mary his wife, Michael Foster, Thomas Gavan, Francis Pennington, Thomas Massey, Richard Hubbard, Charles Quigley and James Ellis. Exs.: Clement Hill, Robt. Carville, St. Mary's Co. (Will: 4.184; 23 Aug 1683; 12 Dec 1683)

BOLTON (BOULTON), Mary. Indenture, 5 Jan 1714, binds her son James Bolton, age 3 years on 6 Sept last to serve John Browne and his wife Mereon to age 21. (Ct.&Land: F#2.71)

BONE, Isabell. Judged to be 24 years old, presented by Peeter Car, 14 March 1664. (Ct.&Land: B#1.436)

BONNER, Henry. Deed of gift dated 1 Sept 1674, from Henry Bonner and Elizabeth his wife, to her natural born sons, John Taylor and Thomas Taylor, a parcel of land surveyed for John Taylor, father of the sons and granted by patent to Elizabeth Taylor, relict of John Taylor, 21 Aug 1658; lying on n. side of Petit's Creek, cont. 450 acres. (Ct.&Land: F#1.4)

BONNER, Henry (gent.) and his wife Elizabeth. Indenture 10 May 1681, to James Tyer; parcel called *Bonners Retirement*, cont. 200 acres. (Ct.&Land: I#1.164)

BONNER, Henry. Items in the possession of Elisabeth Bonner (widow). (Inv.: 24.71; 13 Sept 1703; ----)

BONNER, Elizabeth, age 63. Made oath, 9 June 1705, that Catherine Worly, formerly her servant, had a bastard child by a Negro in Ann Arundel Co. which by law belongs to Henry Haule, minister of the Parish; Haule sold the mulatto boy to her husband Henry Bonner until age 31; Bonner had him bound in Anne Arundel Co. by name of William Worly; deponent gave the boy to Benjamin Warren who sold him to William Penn. (Ct.&Land: Z#1.210)

BOOKER, John, age 18 yrs. Servant of Alexander White, 11 Aug 1674. (Ct.&Land: E#1.181)

BOOKER, John. Deed of gift 1 June 1710 or 1711, to his grandson, John Wright. (Ct.&Land: C#2.250)

BOOKER, Elizabeth, Nangemy. To son William Brett and daus. Mary Gray and Margrett Duninton, personalty. To rest of child., viz., George and Henry Brett, Richard, Susanna and Martha, residue of estate. Exs.: Sons George and Henry afsd.. (Will: 13.512; 20 June 1713, 9 July 1713) Next of kin: William Britt, Martha Barker (Inv.: 35A.293; 10 July 1713; ---) Legatees: William Britt, Martha Barker, Margret Dunnington. Ex.: George Britt (Acct: 35A.295; ---; 19 March 1713)

BOOKER, John, of Nangemy. Mentions wife Eliza: (extx.), son John. To Thomas Price, £5. Mentions son in law Thomas Wise, and Mary, his wife and rest of child., viz., Sarah, John and Ann, residue of personal estate. (Will: 13.587; 14 Oct 1712; 25 March 1713) Next of kin: Henry Brett, John Booker (Inv.: 34.43; 2 April 1713; ----) Payments to: Richard Britt, a legacy from his father George Britt, which fell to hands of deceased by marriage, William Britt, Henry Britt, Gabriell Bobo. Legatees: executrix, Thomas Price John Brooke, Thomas Wright and his wife Mary Ann Booker (dau.). Ex.: George Britt (Acct: 35A.62; ----; 30 Dec 1713)

BOOKER, Martha, widow. To Elizabeth Noble, Ann Booker, Rebecca Dunington, Elizabeth Whartown and George, son of Henry Britt, personalty. To Francis Dunington, personalty, with proviso that he put his dau. Rebecca at school for two yrs. To son William Barker, dwelling plant., 100 acres, *Stepney*, being that testatrix had from his father, John Barker; not to sell anything without consent of his uncle, Henry Britt. Mentions Mary Godfry and Richard and George, sons of Henry Britt, and Elizabeth Noble and Rebecca and Ann, daus. of Francis Dunington. Ex.: Henry Britt. (Will: 14.496; 8 April 1718; 21 April 1718) Next of kin: George Brest, Richard Brest. (Inv.: 1.65; 23 April 1718; ---)

BOOTH, John, age 13 yrs. Boy servant presented by Thomas Mathews, 8 March 1663/4. (Ct.&Land: B#1.258)

BOOTH, Mary, wife of John Booth. Mentioned in open court 10 Aug 1680. (Ct.&Land: I#1.12)

BOREMAN. (See BOARMAN.)

BOSWEL, Marie widow of John Boswell. Gift of goods and cattle, 1 May 1686; to her six children: Marie: Mathew, Michael, William, John, Marie and Martha Boswel. (Ct.&Land: N#1.137)

BOSWELL, Marmaducke, age 12 yrs. Presented by Richard Fouke, 8 March 1663/4. (Ct.&Land: B#1.258)

BOSWELL, Mathew, son of John Boswell. Cattle mark recorded, 10 Sept 1672. (Ct.&Land: E#1.72)

BOZWELL, John. Appraiser in the estate of Edward Abbott; died before inventory was proved. (Inv.: 9.194; ----; 4 March 1684)

BOSWELL, William, age 38. Deposition, 6 Dec 1720, regarding tract called *Friendship* (petition of William Hopkins {Hoskins?}). (Chas LandComm: M2.107)

BOSWELL, John, son of William Boswell. Cattle mark recorded 20 April 1726. (Land: L#2.270)

BOSWELL (BOSSELL), William Sr. To son George, at 19 yrs. *The Desert* and *Mary's Delight*. Mentions sons: George, William, Mathew, Thomas and John. Exs.: Wife Mary and son William. (Will: 22.384; 3 June 1741; 9 Sept 1741) Next of kin: John Bosell, John Bosell Jr. Admr./Exs.: Mary Boswell, William Boswell. (Inv.: 26.553; 11 Dec 1741; 28 April 1742)

BOUGHTON, Richard. In June 1668, "about to marry," Verlinda (Eaton), widow of Thomas Burdit. (Arch of Md: 60.133)

BOUGHTON, Samuell, son of Richard Boughton. Cattle mark recorded ca. Aug 1680. (Ct.&Land: H#1.319)

BOUGHTON, Richard. Deed of gift 20 April 1686, to Sarah Pigott, dau. of Bartholomew Pigott (physician), dec'd. (Ct.&Land: M#1.32)

BOUGHTON, Richard. (Inv.: 26.142; 25 June 1706; 7 July 1706) Admr.: Samuell Boughton. (Acct: 28.97; ----; 25 Feb 1707)

BOUGHTON, Samuel. Next of kin: Katherine Thomas, Virlinda Boughton (Inv.: 36A.55; -- June 1714; 29 June 1714)

BOWLD, John and Jane, of Pickawaxon. Their children: John, born 25 June 1686; Elizabeth, born 27 October 1690; Mary Anne, born 3 April 1694. (Ct.&Land: QRev.12, 16, 23)

BOULD, John. (Inv.: 13A.16; 30 May 1694; ----) Admr.: Mrs. Jane Bould. (Inv.: 13A.260; 27 Dec 1694; ----) Payments include Admr.: Jane Danivan wife of Cornelius Dunivan. (Acct: 13B.6; ----; [c1695])

BOWLES, Edward, of Pickiawxen. To son William Bowles, ex., entire estate, he is to maintain his mother, Isabel Bowles. (Will: 1.87; 6 Nov 1659; 14 Nov 1659)

BOWLES, William, Pickiawaxen. Wife Sarah, extx. Mentions Robert Robbins; Uncle John Bowles and kinsman James Tyre. (Will: 1.171; 15 April 1662; 27 Feb 1662)

BOULS, Margaret, age ca. 30. Swore in court 30 July 1663. (Ct.&Land: B#1.166)

BOULES, John and his wife Margery. Demanding warrent; they are admrs. to estate of Capt. William Batten, 8 Nov 1664. (Ct.&Land: B#1.394)

BOWLES, John. To nephew James Tyer, ex., 500 acres, *Bowles' Purchase*, plantation, 700 acres, *O'Neal's Desert* in St. Mary's Co., and 500 acres, *Bowlstone*. Mentions George Newman Jr., son of George Newman. (Will: 5.39; 8 April 1675; 25 April 1676)

BOULES, James. (Inv.: 17.4; 9 Aug 1698; ---)

BOURNE, Jesse Jacob and Hannah Nellis, both of Patuxent Meeting, announced their intentions to marry on 12th of 1st month, 1713/14; he produced a certificate from meeting in London for clearness in marriage. (Quaker Records of So. MD, p. 74)

BOURN, James (planter) and Elizabeth his wife, (eldest dau. of Dennis Connell, late of Chas. Co., dec'd.), of Stafford Co., Virginia. Deed of gift dated 5 Feb 1721/2, to George Mason, of Stafford Co., two tracts: one called *Fernes* on s. side of Mattawoman, cont. 300 acres, and a tract nr. the head of Mattawoman Creek, called *Nowlan[d]*, 200 acres. (Land: L#2.5-6)

BOURNE (BRUCE?), Daniel (planter), and his wife Mary, conveyed on 9 Aug 1737, part of the tract called *Tower Hill*, 150 acres. (Land: O#2.224)

BOUTCHER, Francis. Next of kin: Richard Davis, Mathew Mansell. Admr.: Elisabeth Boutcher. (Inv.: 13.351; ----; 6 Nov 1728)

BAWLDING, Robert, age 21 yrs. Servant of Robert Henly, 2nd Tues in April 1669. (Ct.&Land: D#1.62)

BOWDER (BOWDEN), Roger. Admr.: Thomas Clypsham. (Inv.: 4.27; 4 Sept 1676; ----)

BOWING, William, age 16 yrs. Servant of Archiball Wahob (Waahob), 10 March 1667/8. (Ct.&Land: C#1.256)

BOWLES. (See BOULES.)

BOWLING, James. Payments include Thomas Bowling. Legatees: Bowling Speake, Millsant Hiton. Extx.: Mary Hall (relict), wife of Benjamin Hall. (Acct: 14.105; ----; 23 Feb 1696)

BOWLING, Thomas. (Inv.: 20.134; 5 Aug 1700; ----)

BOWLING, John and his wife Mary. Conveyed on 19 Aug 1703 land called *Bowling Plains*. (Ct.&Land: Z#1.57)

BOWLING, Thomas. Ex.: John Bowling. (Acct: 3.33; ----; 30 Sept 1703)

BOWLIN, Mary, dau. of John Bowlin, recorded cattle mark, 28 March 1710. (Ct.&Land: (C#2.161)

BOWLING, John. (Will: 13.301; 30 April 1711; 9 June 1711) (Inv.: 32C.169; 1711; ----) Extx.: Mary Boullin. (Acct: 33B.133; ----; 19 Sept 1712)

BOWLING, William and his wife Mary. On 27 Feb 1733/4 conveyed part of a tract called *St. Thomas'*, lying on w. side of Piles Fresh, 50 acres. (Land: O#2.31)

BOWLING, John. Next of kin: John Bowleing, William Bowling. Admr.: John Parnham. (Inv.: 21.49; 7 June 1735; 29 Aug 1735)

BOWLING, Thomas (planter), and his wife Mary. Conveyed on 14 June 1736 part of a tract called *Boarmans Rest*, 135 acres. Conveyed on 14 June 1737, part of a tract called *Charly*, 20 acres, lying on w. side of Horse Run. (Land: O#2.210, 222)

BOWMAN, John. Servant, judged to be 17 yrs. old, presented by John Duglas on behalf of Robert Hundly, 27 March 1662. (Ct.&Land: B#1.101)

BOYCE, William, son of John and Elinor Boyce. Cattle mark recorded 1680. (Ct.&Land: H#1.329) Cattle mark recorded, 9 Dec 1680. (Ct.&Land: I#1.58)

BOYCE, John, son of John Boyce, dec'd. Deed of gift 12 June 1686, from Eleanor Boyce, to William Boyce, son of John Boyce; gift to James Boyce; heifer to William Boyden, son of John Boyden, dec'd.; and two cows and calves to Mary Boyden. (Ct.&Land: M#1.115)

BOYCE, James (planter) of parish of Port Tobacco. To daus. Elizabeth and Helenor and Solomon Nicholls, exs., entire estate, sd. Solomon to have care of afsd. daus. during their minority. (Will: 21.729; 8 April 1735; 2 Feb 1736) Next of kin: Mary Smallwood, Mathew Smallwood. Ex.: Solomon Nicholls. (Inv.: 22.277; 23 April 1737; 4 May 1737)

BOYDE, James (yeoman) of St. Mary's Co., and his wife Katherine Boyd. Mentions his son in law Richard Leake. To his wife, goods and chattels, three lots in Leonard Town and two houses on them, Negro child, called Cassine, cows, mares, and other. 30 April 1734. (Land: O#2.60)

BOYDEN, William. Deed of gift dated 28 May 1668, to his bro. John Boyden; tract of land in Mattawoman or St. Thomas Creek where William now lives. Later dated 11 March 1672, part of the same land to his bro. William. (Ct.&Land: D#1.26; E.113)

BOYDEN, Mary, dau. of John Boyden. Cattle mark recorded, 14 Jan 1673. (Ct.&Land: E#1.146)

BOYDEN, William (planter) and his wife Elizabeth. Conveyed on 8 June 1675, parcel on s. side of Piscataway River and e. side of Mattawoman Creek, cont. 200 acres. (Ct.&Land: F#1.102)

BOYDEN, Roger and Susanna Clarke. Not lawfully joined in matrimony at Robert Thompson's house by Robert Barrott on 1 Jan 1675. (Ct.&Land: F#1.cover page)

BOYDEN, John. Deed of gift in 1678, to Mary Boyden, natural born dau. of his now wife Elinor; and to Elizabeth, dau. of John and Elinor. (Ct.&Land: G#1.164)

BOYDEN, William (planter) and his wife Elizabeth. Indenture 30 June 1682, to Thomas Gibson; parcel called *Maysemow*, cont. 100 acres. (Ct.&Land: I#1.318)

BOYE (BOY), Jane (widow). Mentions dau. Elizabeth; five sons, Pigeon, John, Thomas, Abraham and Bowman. (Will: 15.200; 28 July 1719, 21 Sept 1719) Next of kin: John Taylor. (Inv.: 3.254; 3 Nov 1719; ----)

BOYNE, Elizabeth and Mary, daus. of John Boyne. Cattle mark recorded, 9 Aug 1682. (Ct.&Land: I#1.343)

BRACHER, John and his wife Jane. Plaintive in court case 10 June 1690; Jane being admr. of goods and chattels of John Pembrooke who died intestate. (Ct.&Land: R#1.8)

BRADSHAW, Thomas, age 20 yrs. Servant of John Paine, 11 Jan 1669/70. (Ct.&Land: D#1.117)
BRADSHAW, John, Servant of Phillip Lynes, age judged to be 17-18 yrs. old, 8 June 1686. (Ct.&Land: M#1.221)

BRANDT, Randolph and his wife Mary. Deed of gift 12 Oct 1685, to their son in law Joseph Bullett and their dau. Elizabeth, his wife; tract called *Thomas Town* on s. side of St. Thomas Creek, cont. 200 acres. (Ct.&Land: M#1.8)
BRANDT (BRAND, BRANT, BRENDT), Randolph (Capt.). To son Marcus, now residing in Island of Barbadoes, cont. 500 acres, *The Expectation*; also real estate in Barbadoes formerly belonging to dec'd father. To son Randolph, ex., 200 acres, *Hammersmith* on Potomac R. To 2nd dau. Mary, wife of James Lattimore, two tracts, of 85 and 110 acres, *Butney*. To dau. Margaret, wife of Francis Hammersley, one island, *Barbadoes*, nr. falls of Potomac R., 175 acres. To son Charles, 1/2 of dwell. plantation, *Ashar*, 450 acres on e. side Pickiawaxen Ck., lately leased by Peter Carr, and 1/2 of *Greenwigh*. To son Jacob, 1/2 of *Ashar* and residue of *Greenwigh*. Mentions son Joseph Bullett and son James Lattemore afsd. To Susanna and Ann Skeenes, personalty. Testator desires that sons Charles and Jacob be brought up in Roman Catholic faith. (Will: 6.222; 29 Dec 1697; 10 Feb 1698) (Inv.: 19.31; 11 May 1699; ---) Legatees: Mary Lattemore, John Mosse who married Margrett Hamersly, Charles Brendt, William Hunter. Ex.: Randolph Brendt (also Randolph Brandt). (Acct: 20.50; ----; 2 Oct 1700) Legatees: James Latimer, Charles Brand (brother of his brother Jacob Brandt (dead)), John Murrey. Ex.: Randolph Brandt. (Acct: 23.97; ----; 10 Oct 1702)
BRANDT, Randolph, eldest son of Capt. Randolph, left for the island of Barbados to receive the estate left him by his brother Marcus Brandt. Letter dated 29 Aug 1700, Barbados mentions uncle Jacob Brandt who died leaving a widow and dau, now grown, whom he is assisting. -- Aug 1700. (Ct.&Land: C#2.31)
BRANDT, Marcus of St. Michaels, Barbados. Will, 23 July 1705, mentions brother Charles Brandt; sister Margarett Manzey; sister Mary Lattemore;

cousin Rebekah Dunckly; godson Bassill Dunckly; Madam Frances Collins, widow and her sister Mrs. Margarett Tyrwhitt, widow; Charles Tyrwhitt and Frances his wife, godson Richard Farrell; Mrs. Elizabeth Beachfield and her sister Anne Tyrwhitt, spinster; wife of John Jordan; to her dau. Mrs. Elizabeth Mills; Mary Morgan, spinster, dau. of Anne Morgan, since married; friend Isiah Davis; brother Randolph Brandt of Maryland, exr., remainder of estate; friends John Barry, John Jordan and Bassill Dunckly Sr. (Ct.&Land: C#2.34)

BRANDT, Randolph. Barbados—Letter from Bassill Dunckly to Randolph Brandt; states he married one of Randolph's nieces and was well acquainted with Marcus who is lately deceased; Marcus lived in the country for many years at Madam Collins. 20 Oct 1705. (Ct.&Land: C#2.31)

BRANDT, Randolph (gentleman). Mentions son Randolph. To daus. Katharine, Ann and Mary, certain stock at brother's. To wife Ann, extx. Mentions estate devised by bro. Marcus Brandt, of Barbadoes. (Will: 13.506; 12 Dec 1711; 26 May 1716) (Inv.: 34.23; 6 Aug 1713; ----) Extx.: Anne Brandt. (Acct: 34.26; ----; 21 Sept 1713)

BRANDT, Charles. Mentions Jacob, daus., Eliza: and Sarah; wife Eliza:, extx. (Will: 13.692; 12 Feb 1713/14; 10 March 1713/14) Next of kin: Benjamin Douglas, Joseph Douglass. (Inv.: 35A.363; 28 April 1714; --)

BRANDT, Charles, of Prince George's County. Ex.: Elisabeth Howard (relict), now wife of Thomas Howard. (Acct: 36B.97; ----; 31 Jan 1714)

BRANDT, Ann. Deed of gift, 26 March 1715, to her 4 children, Randolph Brandt, Catherine Brandt, Ann Brandt and Mary Brandt; half of her estate left her by her husband, Randolph Brandt. (Ct.&Land: H#2.6)

BRANDT, Jacob. Next of kin: Francis Hamersley, Mary Lattmer. (Inv.: 3.175; 14 Aug 1719; 29 Oct 1719)

BRANDT, Randolph. Creditors: Mary Hamerly, Jacob Brandt. Next of kin: Anne Smoot, Catharine Hawkins. Admr.: Anne Brandt. (Inv.: 31.127; 23 March 1744; 29 May 1745)

BRANSON, Michael and his wife Rebecca conveyed on 15 May 1744 tract called *Canterbury*, formerly in St. Mary's Co., 200 acres. (Land: X#2.109)

BRANNER, Edward, son of Henry Branner. Gift 14 Sept 1686, from Peter Farnandis (cooper), a mare. (Ct.&Land: M#1.194)

BRAWNER, John, son of Henry and Mary Brawner of Mattawoman, born 2 April 1693. (Ct.&Land: QRev.19)

BRAWNER, Henry. In his will he left to sons Edward, Henry, William and John, all lands equally. To dau. Mary, personalty. (Will: 7.387; 19 Feb 1697; 2 April 1698) (Inv.: 18.65; 23 April 1698; ----) Ex.: Mary Brawner. (Acct: 19.48; ----; 20 June 1699)

BRAWNER, Edward. Recorded cattle marks, 1 Aug 1726 for his sons Henry, William and Thomas Brawner. (Land: L#2.300)

BRAWNER, Henry. Next of kin: Edward Brawner, William Brawner. Admr.: Elisabeth Brawner. (Inv.: 29.349; 5 June 1744; 21 July 1744)

BRAWNER, Edward Jr. (planter), and his wife Elizabeth, conveyed 10 June 1741 part of two tracts, *Wheelers Delight* and *Wheelers Rest*, 120 acres; also a tract called *Lisbon*, 50 acres and on 6 June 1745, parcel called *Fountain Head*, 100 acres. (Land: O#2.512. Also see Land Z#2.45.)

BRAYFIELD, John. In his will he left to son John, dwelling plantation. Mentions daus. Mary and Margaret. Mentions Hudson Wathin, ex., and Edward Fillpot. (Will: 16.129; 13 May 1720; 5 July 1720) Next of kin: John Philpot youngest, Basil Wather. Admr.: Elisabeth Brayfield. (Inv.: 29.340; 3 May 1744, 9 July 1744)

BRAYNE, Jane, dau. of John Caine. Cattle mark recorded, 1680. (Ct.&Land: H#1.292)

BRAYSALE, Agnes, age 19 yrs. Servant of Robert Hanson, Nov 1710. (Ct.&Land: D#2.5)

BREADE, John (Gent.). Deed of gift, 9 Sept 1678, to his wife Jane Breade, and Ignatius, William, Victoria, Jane and Anne Matthews, sons and daus. of "my wife Jane and Thomas Matthews, her last husband." (Ct.&Land: H#1.45)

BREEDEN, Gerrard and Elizabeth his wife. Conveyed on 2 June 1671 parcel called *River's Spring* granted Christopher Rivers; located on Nangemy Creek. (Ct.&Land: E#1.58½)

BREEDING (BREDING), William. (Inv.: 26.80; 17 Sept 1706; ----) Admr.: Justinian Aylmer for Isabella (no surname given). (Acct: 28.96; ----; 16 Feb 1707)

BREEDING, Matthew. Lease, 16 Nov 1744, of 50 acres in St. Thomas Manor, for the life of Matthew Breeding, his wife Mary, and his son John Breeding. (Land: X#2.164)

BRENT, Margaret. Age ca. 20, servant of William Marshall, swore in court 10 March 1658. (Ct.&Land: A#1.44)

BRENT, Henry. Next of kin: William Chandler (brother), Martha Brent (sister). (Inv.: 31.329; 20 June 1710; ----) Mentions: son (unnamed), Nicholas Brent. Extx.: Jane Brent (Acct: 32A.75; ----; 19 Oct 1710)

BRENT (BENT), Martha, Mrs. To brother William Chandler, ex., sister Mary Neale, nephew William Brent, personalty. To brother Robert Brent, personal estate, including that due from brother Nicholas Brent and deceased father, Capt. George Brent. Gift to poor Catholics. (Will: 14.63; 7 April 1715; 12 May 1715) Next of kin: Oswald Neale, Jane Brent. (Inv.: 36B.172; 20 July 1715; ----) Legatees: William Bent delivered to his

mother Mrs. Jeane Bent. Ex.: William Chandler, brother. (Acct: 37A.92; ----; 21 June 1716)
BENT, Robert. Admr.: Mary Bent (Acct: 37A.93; ----; 6 April 1716)
BRENT, George, late of Stafford Co., Virginia, dec'd. and his wife Mary, sole heiress of Nathaniel Vecen of New England, (merchant), conveyed land called *Woodberrys Harbour*, by deed of 3 June 1697 (recorded in Provincial Court). Land was conveyed in 1697 to Mark Lampton, dec'd., and the lands descended to his son Mark Lampton and when he died the lands descended to his son Mark Lampton of St. Mary's Co. who now conveys said land called *Woodberry Harbour*, cont. 300 acres, to John King. Conveyance dated 24 Dec 1728. (Land: L#2.456)
BRENT, Robert and Mary Wharton, married 6 May 1729. Their children: Mary, born 1 Sept 1731; Robert, born 6 May 1734; Jane, born 2 Jan 1736; George, born 3 May 1737; he died 16 Dec 1745; Susanna, born 2 Jan 1739; she died 4 March 1739; Elizabeth, born 4 March 1740; she died 17 Oct 1740; Nicholas, born 1 Nov 1741; he died 1 Aug 1741(?); Francis, born 7 July 1745; he died 17 Dec 1745. (Trinity: 105)
BRENT, William (Gent.). 17 Oct 1740. To his mother, Jane Watts (widow), the lease of part of the tract called *Goose Creek*, 100 acres. (Land: O#2.489)

BRIDGETS, Elizabeth, being nine yrs old. Servant (to age 18) of mother Michle, 10 Aug 1669. (Ct.&Land: D#1.99)

BRETT, Elizabeth (widow). Deed of gift, 10 Dec 1705, to dau. Margarett Dunnington's three children, Elizabeth, Francis and Rebekah Dunnington. (Ct.&Land: Z#1.229)
BRITT (BRETT), George. Mentions wife Eliza, extx., dau. Susanna Noble, sons William, George, Henry and Richard and dau. Martha Baker; Mary Hewlitt. (Will: 3.485; 26 Feb 1704; 26 May 1705) (Inv.: 3.682; 2 July 1705; ---) Payments include George Brett Jr. (son). Legatees: William Brett, Martha Barker, wife of John Barker. Extx.: Elisabeth Brett (relict). (Acct: 26.31; ----; 21 May 1706)
BRETT, William. Mentions Eliza: Nobell. To the younger son of Mary Harper, otherwise called Henry Brett, 100 acres, *Chosen*, and 150 acres. Mentions three children of testator's sister Martha, viz.: George, William and Elizabeth Barker. Ex.: George Brett. Witnesses included Henry Brett. (Will: 14.509; 12 Feb 1717; 8 March 1717) Approver: Charles Britt. Next of kin: Henry Brett, Sarah Brett. (Inv.: 1.71; 10 April 1718; ----)
BRETT, Henry. To Ann Booker and Elizabeth Noble, personalty. To son Richard, *The World's End, The Addition*. To son George, *Southrich, Bretts Addition*. Wife, extx. Bro. George guardian. (Will: 15.297; ----; 8 Dec 1719) Next of kin: Mary Gray, George Brett. (Inv.: 3.255; [c1719]; ----)

BRETT (BRITT), Henry and Sarah his wife conveyed on 29 Sept 1719 tract called *Britts Adventure*, cont. 42 acres. (Ct.&Land: H#2.289)

BRETT, George (planter) and Susannah his wife on 23 April 1722 conveyed 50 acres, taken out of a tract called *Westwood Manor*. (Land: L#2.33)

BRETT, George (planter). To wife Susanna, extx., dwelling plantation, being part of *Wistwood Mannor*; sd. wife to pay for schooling of one of William Johnson's child. and one of Francis Parker's. In his will George Brett mentions George, son of Henry Brett, when he arrives at age of 21; and William, son of Richard and Elizabeth Wainwright. To Richard, son of Henry Brett, *Brett's Discovery*. To William Wainwright afsd., 100 acres. To George Brett afsd., *Chosan*, 100 acres where John Webb lives. To brother Richard, Susannah Hoult, John Roase, John son of John Haw, personalty, some of which is in possession of Charles Apleby. Brother Richard to be guardian to Richard and George Brett; Francis Meek is to have nothing to do with their portion of the estate. Test: Dr. John Haw, Robert Hoult, Ann Hoult (Robert and Ann Holt deceased at date of probate). (Will: 21.523; 31 Jan 1732/3; 14 Feb 1735) Next of kin: Richard Wanright. Admr./Ex.: Susanna Brett. (Inv.: 21.292; 2 March 1735; 3 May 1736)

BRETT, Richard (planter). Bound to Adam Crump of Stafford Co., Virginia, 6 Oct 1737, that Sarah Brett, wife of sd. Richard Brett shall acknowledge her right of dower to parcel called *Addition*, when she arrives at age 21 years. (Land: O#2.300)

BRETT, Richard. In his will he left to wife, Sarah, 1/3 estate. To sons Henry and John, dwell plan. and *Brett's Discovery*. To dau. Anne, personalty and land where Mary Johnson lives for which bro. George Brett gave his bond. To John Thompson and Alexander Hunter rents of plan. on which they dwell. To Mary Noble, servant, two yrs. time. George Brett to have authority to carry child. to Va. and to see that they have at least three yrs. schooling. Exs.: Wife and George Brett. (Will: 23.298; 11 Oct 1743; 13 Dec 1743)

BRITT (Brett), Richard. Next of kin: Richard Price, Richard Womright. Ex.: George Brett, Sarah Moore, wife of Henry Moore. (Inv.: 29.173; 18 --- 1743; 2 June 1744)

BRETT, George and his wife Contant. Wife releases her right of dower to a tract called *Chosen*, signed 14 Nov 1744. (Land Z#2.11)

BRIDGES, Steaphen, age 25 yrs. Servant of John Court, 9 March 1685/6. (Ct.&Land: M#1.90)

BRIGHT, Thomas, age 21 yrs. Servant of Mr. Young, 8 March 1669/70. (Ct.&Land: D#1.127)

BRIGHT, Edward, age 12 yrs. Servant of James Smallwood, 11 June 1678. (Ct.&Land: G#1.158)

BRIMBLECUM, John. Accidently killed by John Glover of Chas. Co. 1671/2. (Arch. of Md.; LXV.29)

BRISCOE, John (Capt., Gent.) and his wife Eleanor on 12 June 1722 conveyed tract called *Baltimores Gift*, cont. 543 acres. (Land: L#2.24) In his will John Briscoe left to wife Eliner, dwelling plantation. To son John, *Baltimore's Gift*, on condition he make over his right in the third part of land belonging to father Williamson to sons Samuel and Hesekiah. To son James, tract where mother Susanna dwells. To dau. Mary Haw, 134 acres in St. Mary's Co. To son Samuel and grandson Williamson Briscoe, personalty. Mentions five child.: Samuel, Philip, James, Hezekiah and dau. Martharn Briscoe, and Elizabeth Briscoe. (Will: 21.59; 13 Jan 1733; 8 April 1734) Creditors include Samuell and Williamson Briscoe. Next of kin: Samuell Williamson Briscoe, John Briscoe. Extx.: Mrs. Eleanor Briscoe. (Inv.: 18.275; 10 May 1734; 14 June 1734)

BRISCOE, Philip Sr. To wife Susannah, dwelling plantation *Morris's Venture*; at her decease to son John, ex. To son Philip, 80 acres had of Father Swann. To son Edward, tract *Hitchin*; 111 acres of *Loves Enjoyment*. To grandson Leonard (son of son George, dec'd), pt. of *Chaptico Manor* during term of lease. To daus. Sarah Leonard, Judith Ashcom, Susannah Compton and Ann Wood, personalty. To son James, 200 acres of *Loves Enjoyment*. Witnesses included John Briscoe Jr. (Will: 18.339; 25 April 1724; 29 Jan 1724) Next of kin: Philip Briscoe Jr., Edward Briscoe. Ex.: John Briscoe. (Inv.: 10.341; 4 Feb 1724; 11 April 1725)

BRISCOE, Philip (physician) and his wife Elizabeth conveyed on 19 June 1725 to Samuel Swann (carpenter), tract which formerly belonged to Edward Swann Sr., being part of tract called *Egglestone*, in a deed of gift to his dau. Susannah, in consideration of her marriage, cont. 80 acres. (Land: L#2.227)

BRISCOE, Edward. To sons Philip, Robert, Edward, John and George and two daus. Lydda and Priscilla and posthumus child, personalty. To son Robert, *Love's Injoyment*. To son Edward, *Hitchin*. Wife Susannah, extx. (Will: 18.444; 7 Dec 1725; 19 Feb 1725) Next of kin: John Briscoe Sr., Susanna Briscoe Sr., John Briscoe Jr. (Inv.: 11.424; 17 March 1725; 11 July 1726)

BRISCOE, James, of St. Mary's Co. and his wife Anne, conveyed on 25 March 1730 part of tract called *Loves Enjoyment*, on n. side of White Oak Swamp, cont. 100 acres. (Land: M#2.198)

BRISCOE, John (Capt.). Lease, 14 March 1738/9, on part of a tract called *West Wood Manor*, during the lives of John Briscoe, Mary, wife of sd. John Briscoe, and Samuel Briscoe, son of sd. John. Lease, 26 June 1740 of tract called *Marsh Land* in *His Lordships Manor* of Chaptico called *West Wood Marsh*, 40 acres. (Land: O#2.387, 469)

BRISCOE, Susanna. Mentions bro. Samuel Swann; dau. Elizabeth; children of son John, dec'd., viz.: Samuel Williamson (Briscoe), Philip, James, Hezikiah, John and Martha Willson; dau. Ann Wood and her dau. Mary; granddau. Elizabeth Garner; grandson William Howard; and remaining children of dau. Sarah Howard; granddau. Sarah Parker; granddau. Susanna Whitely; remaining children of dau. Susanna Comton; grandsons Briscoe Davis and George Davis; grandson Robert, son of son Edward, dec'd. and other child. of sd. son; grandson Leonard; children of dau. Judith Brook, dec'd.; granddau. Rebecca Briscoe; grandsons Williamson (Briscoe) and Henry Smoot; sons Philip and James, exs. Test: John Briscoe Jr., John Briscoe, minor, Philip Briscoe, minor. (Will: 22.212; 5 Feb 1739/40, 24 July 1740)

BRISCOE, John, Capt. (planter). Wife Mary, extx. Mentions children Samuel, Eleanore, Elizabeth and unborn child and his bros. Samuel and Philip [Briscoe]. (Will: 22.424; 30 Dec 1741; 15 Feb 1741) (Inv.: 27.299; 4 Dec 1742; 3 Feb 1742)

BRISON, John, son of Ann Brison, to receive schooling, as an obligation of Robert Sennit (planter) to Anne Cockin, 2 June 1729. (Land; M#2.168)

BROGDEN, William. Next of kin: T. T. Russell, Susanna Russell. Mentions: Eliza Brogden. Admr.: George Plater, Esq. (Inv.: 20.332; 27 Jan 1734; 24 March 1734)

BROMLEY, Mile (Mich:, Michaell), (nunc.). To boy Jno. Hall, personalty at 21 yrs. To John Penn, residue of estate (personal). (Will: 24.636; ----; 6 Nov 1713) (Inv.: 35A.51; [c1713]; ----)

BROOKES, Henry, age 19 yrs. Servant of Mrs. Beane, 10 June 1673. (Ct.&Land: E#1.132)

BROOKE, Thomas, age 11 yrs. Servant of John Lambert, 10 March 1673. (Ct.&Land: E#1.153)

BROOKES, Nathaniel. (Inv.: 1.124; 6 Nov 1674; ----)

BROOKES, William. Giles Tomkines and John Newton, sole legatees. (Will: 9.83; 16 Nov 1678; 11 Feb 1678)

BROOKE, John. Servant of Henry Hawkins, age judged to be 21 yrs., 12 Jan 1685. (Ct.&Land: M#1.67)

BROOKE, Baker, Esq. Legatees: Henry Carew. Distribution to: executrix (widow). Extx.: Ann Brent, wife of Henry Brent. (Acct: 9.390; ----; 4 Aug 1687) (Acct: 10.9; ----; 9 Dec 1687)

BROOKE, Mathew. To William Hunter of St. Mary's Co., ex., entire estate, including that bequeathed testator by his father. (Will: 11.363; ----; [c1702])

BROOKS (BROOKES), John Sr. Mentions eld. son John, young. son Matthew, dau. Eliza:, wife of Abel Wakefield, dau. Sarah Brook and dau. Mary Tennisson. To dau. Jane (Brooks), personalty. To son [son-in-law]

William Gody, ex., and dau. Margaret, his wife. (Will: 13.690; 30 June 1712; 30 March 1714) Next of kin: Abell Wakefeild, Elisabeth Wakefeild. (Inv.: 36A.43; ----; 3 April 1714) Ex.: William Godey (Acct: 36A.42; ----; 14 June 1714)

BROOKE, Clare of St. Mary's Co., dau. of Maj. Wm. Boarman. Conveyed on 30 Jan 1721 parcel of land called *Boarmans Reserve*; bequeathed by will of Maj. Wm. Boarman; cont. 200 acres. (Ct.&Land: H#2.480)

BROOKS, William. Next of kin: Susanna Goodrick, Sarah Timms. Admr.: Margaret Brooks. (Inv.: 25.60; ----; 17 May 1740)

BROONELY, Thomas, age 21 yrs. Servant of Edmond Lindsey (Lynsy), 2nd Tues Nov 1670. (Ct.&Land: D#1.169)

BROWNE, Joane. Age judged to be 18 yrs., presented for James Neall, Esq., by his overseer Thomas Carnell, 16 Dec 1662. (Ct.&Land: B#1.28)

BROWNE, John. Age ca. 26 yrs, swore in court 30 July 1663. (Ct.&Land: B#1.163)

BROWNE, Thomas. Servant, judged to be 20 yrs. old, presented by Thomas Lomax in behalf of Mr. Weekes, 12 July 1664. (Ct.&Land: B#1.314)

BROWNE, Elisabeth. Judged to be 20 yrs. old, presented by William Marshall, 10 Jan 1664. (Ct.&Land: B#1.397)

BROWNE, Ales. Judged to be 22 yrs. old, presented by William Smoote, 10 Jan 1664. (Ct.&Land: B#1.398)

BROWNE, John, son of Elizabeth Browne, born 5 July 1666. (Ct.&Land: C#1.252 (gives date as 5 June 1666); P#1.204; QRev.2)

BROWNE, John, died 7 Nov 1666. (Ct.&Land: C#1.253; P#1.204; QRev.2)

BROWNE, John. To wife Eliza:, 100 acres, (unnamed). To son John, minor, and bro. Gerrard Browne, residue of lands jointly. (Will: 1.270; 2 Nov 1666; ----)

BROWN, Gerrard (Gerrit). Married by Oct 1674, Martha, relict of William Allen of Charles County (Arch of Md: 60.588) In his will he left to wife Martha, plantation. To son John, 100 acres in *Cristen Tempellman*. To dau. Jane, personalty. To dau. Mary, 150 acres, *Merchant Tailor's Hall*. (Will: 9.73; 11 July 1676; 3 Jan 1677)

BROWNE, Thomas, age 18 yrs. Servant of John Fanning, 8 June 1675. (Ct.&Land: F#1.101)

BROWNE, Philip. Admr.: John Wood. (Acct: 4.587; ----; 9 Feb 1677)

BROWNE, William and Mary his wife, relict of Walter Davis, and admr. of Richard Smoote, presented estate of the orphans of Richard Smoote; 10 Aug 1680. (Ct.&Land: H#1.330)

BROWNE, Thomas, age 16 yrs. Servant of Peter Car, 10 Jan 1681. (Ct.&Land: I#1.224)

BROWNE, James. Servant of Domindigo Agambrah, age judged to be 15 yrs., 12 Jan 1685. (Ct.&Land: M#1.67)

BROWNE, William and Elizabeth, children of William Browne, recorded cattle mark, 12 Feb 1690. (Ct.&Land: P#1.203)

BROWNE, Thomas (planter) married Alice Horton, 26 July 1692. (Ct.&Land: P#1.210; QRev.17)

BROWNE, Thomas, son of Thomas and Alice Browne of Pickawaxon Parish, born 21 Dec 1693. (Ct.&Land: QRev.21)

BROWNE, Ann, widow of James Brown. Patrick MackAtee, ex. and sole legatee. (Will: 7:377; 17 Jan 1697; 5 Feb 1697)

BROWN(E), Mary, widow, (nunc.). To son William, personalty. To son in law Samuel Feirson, residue of estate in trust for sons John and Francis. Testatrix' daus. Sarah and Ann were the wives of John Shaw and Giles Tompkins, respectively. (Will: 11.199; ----; 21 Jan 1701) (Inv.: 21.369; 16 Feb 1701; ----) Legatees: Joseph Lewin. Ex.: Samuell Fairson. (Acct: 24.10; ----; 3 March 1702)

BROWNE, Henry, age 18 yrs. Servant of Capt. William Harbert, Nov 1710. (Ct.&Land: D#2.7)

BROWN, John (joiner) and his wife Virlinda, dau. of Robert Doyne, dec'd., conveyed on 21 Oct 1715, parcels called *Rotterdam*, 550 acres and *The Indian Town*, 600 acres. (Ct.&Land: F#2.76)

BROWN, John of Prince George's Co. and Verlinda his wife, one of the daus. of Robert Doyne, conveyed land on 25 Nov 1720, two tracts: *Lyons Denn*, and *Fendalls Delight*, together cont. 450 acres, to John Hutchinson, eldest son of William Huchinson of Prince George's Co., dec'd. Robert Doyne died intestate, seized of several parcels of land; his six children, were Wharton, William, Sarah, Virlinda, Elinor and Mary Doyne. (Ct.&Land: H#2.415)

BROWNE, John and his wife Mary Anne, conveyed on 25 Jan 1724 part of a tract called *Thomas' Choice*, 100 acres. (Land: L#2.222)

BROWN, John, of Chandler Town, and his wife Mary, conveyed on 10 March 1724, Lot #49 in Chandler Town at Portobacco. (Land: L#2.210)

BROWN, Stephen. In his will he left to wife Ann, extx., entire estate. (Will: 19.549; 29 Feb 1727/8; 25 Nov 1728) Creditors include Gustavus Brown. Exs.: Daniel MacDonnald and his wife, Ann MacDonnald. (Inv.: 14.32; 13 Dec 1728; 6 May 1729)

BROWN, Francis (nunc.). To son William and daus. Frances and Penelope, personalty, some of which desc. as had of William Cage. Test: John Brown, Penelope Brown, William King. (Will: 21.335; 25 Dec 1734, 5 April 1735) Next of kin: Ann Shaw, John Brown. (Inv.: 21.32; 8 April 1735; ----)

BROWN, Penelope, widow of John Brown. Deed of gift signed 3 Oct 1745, to her dau. Diana Wilder, wife of John Wilder Jr., and with consent of her dau. Mary Brown, a tract called *Bergen ap Zoen*. (Land: Z#2.73)

BRUCE, John. Next of kin: John Vinten, Tounley Bruce (minor), "no other kin at age." Admr.: Mrs. Sarah Bruce. (Inv.: 22.280; 8 April 1737; 2 May 1737)

BRUCE, Charles. Signed deed of gift 20 Feb 1743/4 to his bro., Townley Bruce, a tract called *Chesnutt Point*, lying on w. side of Wicomico River, 200 acres. (Land: X#2.90)

BRUMLEY, Elizabeth, age 24. Deposition on 27 Sept 1665 re the attack of four Indians. (Arch. of Md.: XLIX.483)

BRUXBANKE, Abraham, age 15 yrs. Servant of William Hatch, 10 June 1679. (Ct.&Land: H#1.134)

BRYAN, Daniel. Next of kin: Daniel Bryan, William Bryan. Admr./Ex.: Frances Bryan. (Inv.: 27.47; 29 May 1742; 21 Jul 1742)

BRYFIELD, John. Next of kin: Edward Phillpott, Margrett Phillpott. Ex.: Hudson Wathen. (Inv.: 4.241; 27 July 1720; 11 Oct 1720)

BUCKLOW, Benjamin, age 9 yrs. Servant of Thomas Mitchell, 10 Jan 1681. (Ct.&Land: I#1.224)

BULL, Thomas. Mentions: orphan of Thomas Bull. Admrs.: John Baild, John Courts. (Acct: 1.294; ----; 22 April 1675)

BULL, William, age 18 yrs. Servant of John Goosh, 10 June 1679. (Ct.&Land: H#1.134)

BULLOTT, Joseph, son of Joseph and Elizabeth Bullott of Mattawoman, born 8 Feb 1688. (Ct.&Land: P#1.212; QRev.14)

BULLETT, Benjamin, son of Joseph and Elizabeth Bullett of Mattawoman, born 28 April 1693. (Ct.&Land: P#1.212)

BULLIT, Elizabeth. In her will she left to son Joseph at 19 yrs. of age, *Bullit's Folly* and dwelling plantation. To son Benjamin, all personalty. Peter Mackmillion, ex. and to have charge of children. (Will: 2.270; 12 Jan 1693; 14 March 1693/4)

BOLLETT, Elisabeth (13A.117; 12 June 1694; ----)

BULLOTT, Benjamin, son of Joseph and Elizabeth Bullott of Mattawoman, born 28 April 1693. (Ct.&Land: QRev.21)

BULLIT, Joseph. In his will he left to brother Benja: Bullit, ex., 200 acres, *Joseph Bullit's Folly* and 30 acres taken up by father. Mentions cousin Randle Brent and Ann, dau. of Randle and Anne Brent. To cousin Katharine Brent, dau. of afsd., 100 acres. (Will: Part 2—12.209; 3 Sept 1709; 23 Nov 1709)

BUMPUS, Thomas. (Inv.: 29.61; 4 Feb 1707; ----) Admr.: John King. (Acct: 29.68; ----; 13 Dec 1708)

BUNCRAFT, Thomas. Next of kin: Richard Baarns, Sarah Hall. Admr.: Elenor Bencraft. (Inv.: 15.466; 18 April 1730; 30 --- 1730)

BIRTH, Robert. Judged to be 14 yrs. old, servant of Mr. Addames, 22 April 1662. (Ct.&Land: A#1.201 See also Ct.&Land: A#1.204 which shows Robert Birtch, judged to be 16 yrs. old, servant boy of Henry Addames, also on 22 April 1662.)

BURCH, Oliver. Deed of gift, 13 Jan 1713/14, to his son Justinian Burch; tract one half of *Boulins Plaine*, cont. 150 acres. (Ct.&Land: F#2.2)

BURCH (BIRCH), Oliver, of King and Queen Parish. To son Benjamin, 75 acres of *Bowling's Plains*. To son Edward, personalty. To son Jonathan, *Lumley* (*Lombey*) and *Penrick* (*Penray*). To sons Thomas, John, Justinian and daus. Katherine Swan, Ann Swan, Barbary Allison, Ellinor Burch and Elizabeth Cade, 5s. each. Wife Barbary, extx. Test: George Brett, James Phillips and Anne Phillips, his wife. (Will: 19.725; 15 Feb 1726/7; 27 May 1729) Next of kin: Elisabeth Owen, Jonathon Burch. Admr./Ex.: Barbara Birch. (Inv.: 15.76; 8 June 1729; 16 Aug 1729)

BURCH, John. Next of kin: Edward Burch (brother), Elisabeth Burch (daughter). Admr.: Mary Birch. (Inv.: 20.311; ----; 5 March 1734)

BURCH, Justinian Sr., and his wife Susana. 4 Aug 1743. Gives to his son Justenian, part of a tract on e. side of Piles Fresh called *Lumley*, 112.5 acres; and a tract called *Devray*, 46 acres. Reserving to Justinian Sr., one acre out of the tract called *Lumley Round*, the place where his father and mother are interred for a graveyard. (Land: X#2.20)

BURDIT, Thomas, age ca. 27 yrs., in court 28 July 1663. (Ct.&Land: B#1.133)

BURDIT, Thomas, married by June 1668, Verlinda Eaton, sister of Nathaniel and Samuel Eaton. (Arch of Md: 60.133)

BURDIT, Verlinda, admx. of Thomas Burdit, dec'd. Before her marriage to Richard Boughton, a trust is to be established for the children, Elizabeth Burdit, Francis Burdit, Parthenia Burdit and Sarah Burdit; her bros., Samuel Eaton and Nathaniel Eaton to be trustees. Including her late husband's 1000 acre land called *Burdit's Rest* and *Burdit's Ne(a)st*. 24 June 1668. (Ct.&Land: C#1.270)

BURDITT, Parthenia, Mrs., of Nanjemy. In her will she left to John Hamilton, son of testatrix' sister, all lands. To sister Catherine Boughton, personalty. (Inv.: 16.18; 4 April 1698; ----) (Will: 6.75; 17 Feb 1697; 13 March 1697)

BURFORD, Elizabeth, dau. of Thomas Burford. Cattle mark recorded, 9 Aug 1682. (Ct.&Land: I#1.342)

BURFORD, Thomas. In his will he left to son Thomas, dwelling plantation. Wife Anne, extx., 500 acres in Dorchester Co. to be sold for benefit of all children. (Will: 4.235; 13 March 1686; 24 March 1686) (Inv.: 9.384; 27 June 1687; ----)

BURFORD, Thomas. In his will he left to sons Benjamin and Charles Warren, personalty at 21 yrs. of age. To Notley Warren, sisters Eliza: Cattle and Jane Dodd and bros. in law James Cattle and Richard Dodd, and to godson Humphrey Warren, personalty. Ex.: Walter Story. (Will: 6.93; 4 Feb 1697, 1 March 1697) (Inv.: 16.22; 14 March 1698; --)

BURFORD, Ann, Mrs. (Madam). (Inv.: 25.14; 30 May 1700; ----) States Ann a widow. Servants mentioned: Edward Flinn, Sarah Redman. (Inv.: 20.102; 3 July 1700; ----) Second inventory made in Calvert County is cited. Admr.: George Plater. (Acct: 25.57; ----; 25 May 1705)

BURGESS, Benjamin, planter. In his will he mentions sons Samuel and John, and dau. Eleanor, wife of Benjamin Gardiner. Wife Anne, extx. (Will: 22.513; 31 March 1742; 1 Oct 1742) Next of kin: Samuel Burgess, John Burgess. Admx.: Ann Burgess. (Inv.: 27.293; 10 Jan 1742; 16 Jan 1742)

BARGESS, Samuel. A lease, 30 Dec 1743, on 102 acres in St. Thomas' Manor, for the term of three lives of Samuel Bargess, Elizabeth his wife and Thomas his son. (Land: X#2.122)

BURKHAINE, John, age 15 yrs. Servant of Jeremiah Dickinson, 10 Jan 1670. (Ct.&Land: E#1.1)

BURNAM, William. To wife Alice, plantation. To sons Samuel and John, land equally at majority of son John. (Will: 7.71; 11 Dec 1694; 20 April 1695)

BURNS. (See BYRN.)

BUROS (BURROWS), Paull. (Inv.: 25.346; [c1705]; ----) Admr.: Jane Brookes, wife of John Brookes. (Acct: 27.109; ----; 26 Sept 1707)

BURRUS (BURROUGHS) Thomas. Next of kin: John Brooke, Saragh Timeus. Admr.: Mary Burroughs. (Inv.: 20.377; 8 March 1734; 7 May 1735)

BUTCHER. (See BOUTCHER.)

BUTCHER, John and Mary his wife conveyed on 26 Dec 1684 parcel called *Talshell*, cont. 60 acres. (Ct.&Land: L#1.51)

BUTLER, John (planter). A lease, 15 Dec 1743, for 120 acres, for the term of the four lives of sd. John Butler, Elizabeth Butler, his wife, Lydia his eldest dau., and James Capshaw. (Land: X#2.88)

BUTLER, John. Mentions: Margaret Ward, Richard Edelen, Elisabeth Lewis. Admr.: William Butler. (Inv.: 30.149; 2 Oct 1744; 18 Dec 1744)

BUTTERY, John, age 46. 14 Mch 1658. (Arch. of Md., v. XLI, p. 395)

BUTTERY, Francis. Exs.: John Wood, Michaell Martin. (Acct: 19.43; ----; 20 June 1699)

BUTTRUNE, William. In his will he left to kinswoman Charity Courts, 400 acres on Patuxent R. in Calvert Co., with which testator is possessed in right of his father. (Will: 6.66; 3 June 1692; 16 Dec 1692)

BUTTS, Richard (carpenter) of Stafford Co., Virginia and Mary his wife, conveyed on 12 Dec 1717, a parcel called *Muckhaddam*, about a mile from the w. side of Portobacco Creek, cont. 50 acres, and a tract on the w. side of Portobacco Creek, cont. 50 acres. (Ct.&Land: H#2.120)

BYRN, James and Elizabeth his wife and William Connell (planter), conveyed on 27 April 1714, a parcel of land formerly conveyed from Eleanor Obryan, dec'd, to Mary Connell, mother of William Connell and Elizabeth Byrn; two tracts: *Freshes* nr. head of Mattawoman Creek cont. 300 acres; also *Clahammond* cont. 200 acres. (Ct.&Land: F#2.31)

BURNS(?), Matthew, age 49. Deposition in 1721 regarding tract called *Linsey*. (Chas LandComm: M2.146)

BYRN(E), Charles (planter) and his wife Margery. Recorded 24 May 1727, John Coffer Jr. (planter), binds himself whereas said Coffer, and Charles Byrne and Margery his wife have equal right to two tracts nr. Zachia Swamp; *Fortune*, cont. 100 acres, and *Nonesuch*, cont. 50 acres. Deed dated 1 June 1737; to Edward Sanders (Saunders), a tract called *Eatons Delight*, 200 acres. (Land: O#2.228; L#2.353)

CABLE, John, age ca 24. Swore in court 23 Oct 1660. (Ct.&Land: A#1.108)

CADELL, John. Next of kin: Edward Turner, Samuel Turner Jr. Admr.: Robert Cadell. (Inv.: 25.64; 19 March 1739; 16 June 1740)

CADEL, John, and his wife Anna. Conveyed on 10 Feb 1743/4, 100 acres, part of a tract called *St. Stephen Coleman*, formerly granted to Philip Combes. (Land: X#2.59)

CADLE, John (planter). In his will he left to son Robert, *Evans Reserve* where he now lives. To wife Anna, extx., dwelling plantation. At her death to pass to daus. Mary, Elizabeth and Abigail. At their marriages sd. plantation to go to testator's sons Robert and Edward. (Will: 23.545; 4 July 1744; 14 Aug 1744)

CADY, Robert, married by March 1670/1, Ellenor, widow of ---- Corner or Conner. (Arch of Md: 60.328)

CAGE, John. To wife Susanna, extx., plant., 300 acres. Mentions son John, younger son William, dau. Margery Rowland, dau. Anna when age 16. (Will: 5.289; 12 Feb 1676; 9 July 1676) (Inv.: 5.319; 21 Sept 1678; ----) Extx.: Susannah Clipsham (relict) married Thomas Clipsham immediately after deceased's death). (Acct: 7A.151; ----; 21 July 1680) On 16 Dec

1685 son John and his mother, Susannah Clipsham, sold some of above land. (Ct.&Land: M#1.190)

CAGE, John. In his will he mentions cousins Benjamin and William Ward, Nathaniel Eaty, Henry Franklin, Benjamin Flannin, John Warren, Benjamin Warren, and John Worland Sr. and cousins Richard Morris, ex. Legatees: Benjamin Ward, Benjamin Fanning, Nathaniell Eaty, Henry Frank, Arthur Eaty, executor. Ex.: Robert Norrice. (Will: 11.92; 2 Feb 1700; 13 Feb 1700) (Acct: 22.22; ----; 6 Dec 1701)

CAGE, William and Margaret(t) his wife, conveyed on 5 Dec 1719, a parcel formerly taken up by Thos. Michell, dec'd, cont. 150 acres; on 5 Dec 1719 a part of *Mitchell Platt*, cont. 108 acres; on 22 Aug 1726, tract cont. 170 acres; on 28 April 1727, part of *Mitchel Platt*, cont. 58 acres; on 11 Feb 1729/30, laid out for Thos. Mitchell, cont. 40 acres; on 9 March 1735, remaining part of 300 acres, as by deed granted to John Cage on 19 Aug 1658. (Land: H#2.328, 342; L#2.309, 349; M#2.228; O#2.123)

CAINE, John, age 40. Deposition. 1658. (Arch. of Md., v. XLI, p. 138)

CAINE, John, age ca. 40 yrs. Swore in court 4 Sept 1660. (Ct.&Land: A#1.100)

CAYNE, James, age 12 yrs. Servant of Richard Beck, 10 June 1674. (Ct.&Land: E#1.171)

CANE, John. Indenture 28 April 1684, to his dau. Susannah Cane; [appears to be part of] a tract called *Blowplaines*. (Ct.&Land: K#1.370)

CAINE, John (Gent.). Indenture 4 Aug 1684, to Giles Blizard of London, whereas marriage is intended between Giles Blizard and Susanna Cane, dau. of John Cane; parcel called *Blew Plane*, cont. 1000 acres. (Ct.&Land: L#1.1)

CAINE, John and his wife Elizabeth. Deed of gift, 5 Oct 1713, to his dau. Elizabeth and her husband Francis Oden. (Ct.&Land: D#2.59) and deed of gift, 5 Oct 1713, to his son, Thomas Caine. (Ct.&Land: D#2.60)

CALLIHON, Patrick and Ann his wife, on 11 Jan 1710 conveyed part of tract called *St. Mathew's* on w. side of Mattawoman Run, cont. 200 acres. (Ct.&Land: C#2.234)

CALVERT, Charles of St. Mary's Co, son of William Calvert, dec'd., and Elizabeth conveyed on 26 Sept 1688, 600 acres at Nangemy, part of 5000 acres taken up by William Stone, dec'd, father of Elizabeth. (Ct.&Land: P#1.35)

CALVERT, William, son of Charles Calvert, of St. Mary's Co. Indenture, 14 Jan 1689, upon marriage of his dau. Elizabeth with James Neale (Gent.), cont. 600 acres. (Ct.&Land: R#1.134)

CALVERT, Ann. Recorded 21 June 1732, to her son William Calvert, aged 4 years Jan 6 last, a young steer(?). (Land: M#2.288)

CALVIN, John. Mentions: Henry Tren, Jam. Parandier, Dan. Jenifer. Next of kin: Lawrence Androsie. Admr.: Elisabeth Calvin. (Inv.: 11.11; 1 July 1725; 20 Sept 1725) (Inv.: 11.351; 22 April 1725; 14 May 1726)

CAMPBELL, Martin (barber) and Mary his wife, dau. of Elizabeth Dermont, wife of John Dermont and sister of Robert Downes Jr., son of Robert Downes Sr., dec'd. Indenture in 1702 to Nicholas Cooper; land descended to Mary by inheritance, 100 acres called *Coldspring*. Indenture to Ralph Williamson of Liverpool, England, 14 Dec 1703; tract called *Cow Spring* at Nanjemy on the Potomac River, 100 acres. (Ct.&Land: Z#1.1, 86, 253)

CAMPBELL, John, age 14 yrs. Servant of Edward Chapman, Nov 1710. (Ct.&Land: D#2.7)

CAMPBELL (CAMBELL), Martin. (Inv.: 33B.37; [c.1712]; ----) Admr.: Robert Sanders. (Acct: 34.217; ----; 8 June 1713)

CAMPTON (See COMPTON).

CANLAND, John, age 16 yrs. Servant of Capt. John Wheeler, 11 June 1678. (Ct.&Land: G#1.158)

CANTWELL, Thomas. In his will he mentions William Hunter, Edw. Anderson, Wm. Green, Jno. Hause, Hassey Luckett and Elizabeth Price. Mrs. Juliana Price ex. (Will: 14.337; 19 Jan 1716; 6 Feb 1716) (Inv.: 37B.91; 23 July 1717; ----) (Acct: 37B.91; ----; 21 Aug 1717)

CAPSHAW, Francis, age 15 yrs. Servant of Alexander Smith, 10 Nov 1674. (Ct.&Land: F#1.13)

CAPSHAW, John. Next of kin: Stephen Mankin, Francis Capshaw. Admr.: Ann Capshaw. (Inv.: 21.503; 17 April 1736; 28 Aug 1736)

CAREADALE (CARREDALE), Thomas, age betw. 16-17 yrs. Servant of Capt. Boareman, 11 Jan 1669/70. (Ct.&Land: D#1.117)

CAREY (CARY), Philip and Susan ———. Charged with living together as man and wife for ca. 12 months, and he now disclaiming the said Susan for his wife. 1670. Mattawoman, Chas. Co. (Arch. of Md.: LVII.616) In his will Philip Cary left to Susanna Dunn, his entire estate, in trust for her dau., Mary Dunn (4 yrs. of age). (Will: 5.181; 25 Nov 1676; 9 March 1676/7)

CAREY, Cornelius, age 18 yrs. Servant of Justinian Dennis, 12 March 1677. (Ct.&Land: G#1.119)

CAREY, Hugh, age 14 yrs. Servant of Edward Price, 11 June 1678. (Ct.&Land: G#1.157)

CARY, Adam. Admr.: Charles Jones. (Acct: 3.97; ----; 1 March 1703)

47

CARLETON, Bostock (Gent.), of Blackheath, county of Kent, makes oath that Thomas Carleton, his father, had six sons and one dau., to wit, Thomas Carleton, eldest son; Edward Carleton, 2nd son; Matthew Carleton, 3rd son; the deponent, 4th son who was born in 1644, Dudley Carleton, 5th son; John Carleton; 6th son and Margaret Carleton, his dau. Said Thomas Carleton, the deponent's eldest bro., had issue three children, to wit, Thomas his son who died several years ago without issue, Margaret his eldest dau. who died very young in the lifetime of her father, and Catherine, his youngest dau., now Catherine Markwich (widow), who is now living. Said Edward Carleton, the deponent's 2nd bro., had issue five children, to wit, Josiah Carleton, his eldest son, Arden Carleton, his 2nd son, and Theodosia, Mary, and Theodore, his daus.; sd. Josiah died without issue in the lifetime of sd. Edward his father, and sd. Arden Carleton had three children, and sd. Arden and his three children died in the lifetime of sd. Edward Carleton, father of sd. Arden and without issue, and Theodosia, Mary, and Theodore died without issue in the lifetime of their father, Edward Carleton. Said Edward Carleton, this deponent's bro., died about nine years ago, leaving sd. Catherine Marwick, his niece and heir at law. Signed 27 June 1741. Other deponents: Charity Stacy of Carshelton, county of Surrey, England (widow), aged 64 years, she lived with sd. Edward Carleton as a servant while he lived at Carshalton, and afterwards of Newington in the county of Middlesex (merchant), dec'd., for about 16 years, 1691-1707; George Markinfield of Blackheath in the Parish of Lewisham, county of Kent (Gent.), age 50 years; (Land: O#2.455, 456)

CARLILE, Charles. (Inv.: 8.324; 25 April 1685; ----)

CARNAGGEY, James, age 16 yrs. Servant of John Manning, Nov 1710. (Ct.&Land: D#2.5)

CARNELL, Joseph of Pyckyawaxen. In his will he left to dau. Margaret at majority, 200 acres, part of *Dover*; also two tracts, viz., *Hopewell* and *Batten's Clifts*. Mentions son in law William Worrell at majority, and dau. in law Mary Lovett alias Herbert, wife of William Herbert. Ex. Wm. Herbert, who is to have care of sd. William Worrel during minority. (Will: 2.248; 16 Dec 1693; 30 Jan 1693/4)

CARNER, Richard. Admr.: Richard Harrison. (Acct: 14.71; ----; 2 Nov 1696)

CARNEY, Thomas. (Inv.: 33A.40; 17 Dec 1711; ----) Admr.: Capt. William Harbert. (Acct: 33B.175; ----; 30 Dec 1712)

CARPENTER, Henry, age 16 yrs. Servant of William Porfit, 11 April 1676. (Ct.&Land: F#1.173)

CARPENTER, Christopher, age 12 yrs. Servant of James Smallwood, 14 March 1681. (Ct.&Land: I#1.258)

CARR, Peter, age 33. 12 Jan 1657. (Arch. of Md., v. XLI, p. 27)
CARR, Peter, age ca. 34. Deposition 10 March 1658 (Ct.&Land: A#1.44)
CARR, Peter. In his will he left to Robert, Charles, Joseph, Eliza: and Sarah Douglass, sons and daus. of Col. John Douglass, late of Chas. Co., personalty; part of same being a debt due testator by Sarah Douglass, now wife of Ralph Smith, and mother of sd. legatees. Mentions Peter, son of George Mackmillion, at 16 yrs.; Jane, wife of John Smith; James, son of James Tyer, and child. of George Newman, personalty. Ex. Jas. Tyer. (Will: 4.12; 21 Sept 1680; 19 April 1683) (Inv.: 8.50; 16 May 1683; ----) Legatees: Mary Newman, Elisabeth Newman. Ex.: Rebocah Yeates (relict) (executrix of James Tayer), wife of Robert Yeates. (Acct: 10.324; ----; [c1692?])
CARR, Arthur. Received from: Edward Smoote who married widow Newman, James Heath. Legatees: Arthur Mackmillion paid to Joseph Bullot, William Newman, Lydia Newman, John Newman, George Newman, John Smith. Ex.: Rebecca Yates, wife of Robert Yates (executor of James Tyre). (Acct: 9.474; ----; 3 April 1688)

CARRICO, Abel and his wife Elizabeth. Deed dated 11 Nov 1736, from Marmaduke Simms and his wife Mary, part of a tract called *St. George's*, 93 acres. (Land: O#2.177. Also see Land O#2.375 recorded 4 Dec 1738.)
CARICO, Mary Ann, dau. of Abel and Elisabeth Carico, born 4 July 1737. (Trinity: 107—rev.)
CARRICOE, James (planter). Lease on 9 March 1742, of 104 acres, for lifetimes of sd. James Carricoe, Catherine Carricoe his wife, and Sarah Carricoe his dau. (Land: O#2.435)
CARICO, Abel, son of Abel and Elisabeth Carico, born 21 Jan 1744. (Trinity: 107—rev.)

CARRE? (CARYL?), Richard, age 17 yrs. Servant of Richard Wade, 11 Aug 1685. (Ct.&Land: L#1.161)
CARROLL, John (carpenter) and his wife Jane conveyed on 25 Aug 1724 to John Dagg (shipwright) of Stafford Co., Virginia, tract called *Galeys Discovery*. (Land: L#2.163)

CARTER, William, age 60. Deposition on 24 Sep 1719, regarding the tract *Tryal*, 300 acres. (Chas LandComm: M2.72)
CARTER, Timothy. Admr.: Richard Parnham. (Inv.: 11.419; 28 Feb 1725; 9 July 1725)
CARTER, William, Sr. (planter) and his wife Sophania conveyed on 23 Nov 1736 part of tract called *Bridge Town*, 101 acres. (Land: O#2.195)

49

CARTER, William. In his will he left to wife Sophia, sole ex., dwell. plantation. To dau. Jane Birkhead, pt. of *Bridge Town* for life, then to son William. To dau. Elizabeth, wife of late Thomas Thomas, personalty. (Will: 23.625-628; 12 Feb 1743; 10 March 1743) Next of kin: Jane Dirkhead, Rachel Horduilt. Admr.: William Carter. (Inv.: 31.120; 27 May 1745; 5 June 1745)

CARTIE, Demund Mack, age 13-14 yrs. Servant of Rice Jones, 11 June 1667. (Ct.&Land: C#1.164)

CARY. (See CAREY.)

CASELTON. (See CASSELTON.)

CASH, William and Rebeckah his wife of Westmoreland Co., Virginia, on 1 July 1692, conveyed 25 acres to Henry Key, part of tract called *Dorey Lane* in possession of Thomas Maris at his decease, now in possession of Henry Key, land belonging to the four daus. of Thomas Maris. (Ct.&Land: R#1.432)

CASHE (CASH), James and his wife Mary, of Westmoreland Co., Virginia, grant Benjamin Posey (carpenter) power of attorney to lease to Susanah Lomax (spinster), tract called *Promise* that has not been formerly sold to John Ralley (Railey), until Thomas Ashman, son of said Mary Cash arrives at age 21. Recorded 7 March 1729. (Land: M#2.190)

CASSELTON (See COSTLETON)

CASSOCK, Benjamin, son of John Cassock. Cattle mark recorded 8 9 Dec 1687. (Ct.&Land: N#1.204)

CASSOCK, Sarah, dau. of John Cassock. Cattle mark recorded 8 Nov 1692. (Ct.&Land: R#1.541)

CASSICK (CASSCOK), Benjamin. Mentions: dec'd. received one half estate of John Cassick (father, dead). (Inv.: 25.29; [c1704/5]; ----) Admr.: Sarah Miller, wife of John Miller. (Acct: 26.36; ----; 7 June 1706)

CATHEW, Christohper, age 14 yrs. Servant of Philip Lines, 13 June 1682. (Ct.&Land: I#1.293)

CAWSINE, Nicolas, age 40. 13 June 1648. (Arch. of Md., v. IV, p. 421)

CAUSINE, Nicholas. His will, written 26 Feb 1653, mentions his wife Jane Cawsine, and sons Ignatius (when he shall come to the age of nineteen, being aged ... years 14 July next) and Nicholas Cawsine (being 7 yrs. old the sixth of this month). [*This will is not recorded in Baldwin's Calendar of Wills.*] (Arch. of Md., v. XLI, p. 54)

CAUSINE, Ignatius, son of Nicolas Causine, a subject of France; born at the house of his father in St. George River of an English mother; holding

lands by descent from mother. Declaration of citzenship, 7 April 1671.
(Ct.&Land: E#1.49)

CAUSIN, Ignatius and Jane, of Portobacco. Their children; Jane, born 11 July 1682; Ignatius, born 10 Sept 1685; John, born 12 April 1690; William, born 20 Feb 1692. (Ct.&Land: QRev.9, 11, 15, 20)

CAUSINE (CAUSIN, CUSSINE), Ignatius. In his will he left to three sons, Ignatius, John, and William, 1700 acres, *Cusine's Manor*; division to be made at majority of eld. son Ignatius. Mentions dau. Jane. Wife Jane. (Will: 7.93; 4 May 1695; 11 June 1695) Extx.: Jane Causin (relict). (Inv.: 13A.368; 17 July 1695; ----) Mentions: four children (unnamed). Extx.: Jane Reeves, wife of Ubgatt Reeves. (Acct: 14.56; ----; 1 Oct 1696) (Acct: 16.66; ----; [c1698]) Extx.: widow, now wife of Ubgatt Reaves. (Acct: 25.244; ----; 17 May 1706)

CAUSINE (CAUSONE, CAUSOON), Ignatius, Port Tobacco. In his will he left to two brothers John and William, 300 acres, testator's part of *Causin's Manor*. Test: Mary Dawson, Thos. Reeves Jr., Eliza: Hope, Ubgate Reeves. (Will: 13.629; 25 Dec 1713; 25 Jan 1713) Next of kin: Victoria Thompson, William Matthews. (Inv.: 35A.243; 10 Feb 1713; ----) Legatees: Thomas Reeves. Exs.: John Causoon, William Causoon. (Acct: 36B.26; ----; 4 Jan 1714)

CAUSONE (CUSSEEN), William. Approvers: John Cusseen, Thomas Reeves. (Inv.: 1.358; 27 May 1718; ----)

CAUSEEN, John and his wife Mary, conveyed on 20 April 1730, a parcel of land, nr. the mouth of Portobacco Creek, 169 acres. (Land: M#2.202)

CAVE, Thomas. Next of kin: Elisabeth Oden (sister). Admr.: Mary Cave. (Inv.: 15.592; 18 April 1730; 7 July 1730)

CAVENOUGH, William, of St. Mary's Co., and his wife Mary, on 15 June 1737, conveyed part of tract called *Thompsons Humour*, 127 acres. (Land: O#2.213)

CAWOOD, Stephen and Mary his wife, conveyed on 2 Oct 1704, parcel called *Hopewell*, cont. 100 acres. (Ct.&Land: D#2.74)

CAWOOD, Stephen Sr. In his will he left to son John, part of *Hull*. To wife Mary, ex., part of *Hull*. Mentions his children: Stephen, Thomas, William, Ann Thomas, Mary Willet, Hester Robinson and Penelope Robey. After decease of dau. Ann Thomas her portion of estate to be divided amongst grandchildren (the childrem of her former husband, William Atchison). (Will: 21.439; 9 Sept 1735; 15 Oct 1735) Next of kin: Thomas Cawood, William Cawood. Ex.: Mary Cawood. (Inv.: 21.241; 19 Dec 1735; 4 Feb 1735)

CAWOOD, Mary (widow). Deed of gift signed 25 May 1737 to her son in law, Ralph Roby and Penelope his wife; gives Negro girl called Jenny, about 8 years old; her first child to be given to Mary's dau. Ann Thomas, wife of

John Thomas; and her second child to be given to Mary's dau. Mary Villett, wife of Charles Villett. (Land: O#2.200)

CAYTON, Charles (nunc.). In his will he left to Mary Mankin and brother John, personalty, some of which is due from Henry Haslip and James Ross. Test: Stephen Mankin and Marg't., his wife. (Will: 21.143; 25 March 1733/4; 3 July 1734)

CERICK, Patrick. Mentions: Thomas Pulton, John Cerreck, Thomas Realey. Admr./Ex.: Mary Kerrick. (Inv.: 27.189; ----; 17 Sept 1742)

CHAMBERS, Christopher. Admr.: William Hawton. (Accts. from Wills: 3.29; ----; 26 June 1703)

CHAMBERS, Joseph. To son Joseph, all lands in Virginia. To dau. Elizabeth, tract *Tomkisens*. To son Daniel, residue of land in Maryland. To Elizabeth Parrander (widow), personalty. Exs.: Sons Joseph and Daniel. (Will: 22.174; 27 Dec 1732; 6 May 1740)

CHAMBERS, Joseph of Durham Parish. To son Joseph, all real estate in Virginia. To dau. Elizabeth, *Thompkinson's Longlook For*. To son Daniel, residue of lands in Maryland. To Elizabeth Parrandier, personalty. Exs.: Sons Daniel and Joseph. Witnesses include William Williams, age 48 yrs. Note: William Williams testifies to having written a will for Joseph Chambers in which testator disposed of his real and personal estate in above manner; sd. will was signed, sealed, witnessed and delivered to the sd. Daniel Chambers. A few days later the sd. Joseph the elder died, and the sd. Joseph the son died within three or four days after his father without issue and intestate. (Will: 20.839; 27 Dec 1732; 1 Oct 1733) Next of kin: Elisabeth Chambers, Virlinda Grinan. Admr.: Daniel Chambers. (Inv.: 17.481; 12 Sept 1733; 1 Oct 1733)

CHAMBERS, Elizabeth. On 1st of April 1740, Thomas Douglas and his wife Elizabeth state they heard Elizabeth Chambers (spinster) say that she wished her entire estate to pass to William Chandler. (Will: 22.156; ----; ----)

CHAMPE, Stephen, age 14 yrs. Presented by William Marshall, 8 March 1663/4. (Ct.&Land: B#1.259)

CHANDLER, Job, gives testimony regarding the death of Negro called Antonio belonging to his brother Symon Overzee. That Overzee brought said Negro ca. March 1656 to his plantation in Portoback Creek and there left him with his overseer Clement Theobalds to work with his other servants. (Arch. of Md., v. XLI, p. 205)

CHANDLER, Jobe, Portobacco. In his will he left to wife Anne, ex., home plantation, consisting of 1,5000; also 500 acres on Goose Ck. To son William, plantation afsd. To son Richard, 500 acres on Goose Ck. and a possible survey on Nangemy Ck. To dau. Anne Chandler, personalty, including that given her by her grandmother, Sarah Yardley. To kinsman Thomas Maris, personalty. Children to be sent to testator's brothers in England, if sd. brothers so desire. Overseers: Capt. Wm. Stone, brother in law Symon Oversees, and brother Robert Slye. (Will: 1.97; ----; 27 April 1659) Ann, widow of Jobe Chandler, of Portobacco, nominates Edmond Lindsey, for her attorney; regarding 125 acres on w. side of St. Thomas' Creek, sold by her dec'd. husband and Symon Oversee. (Ct.&Land: A#1.181, 182) Children of Jobe Chandler, dec'd., Nancie, William and Richard Chandler, to have a share of his estate; Col. Gerrard Fouke of Westmoreland Co. [Va.], recently married their mother. Ca. date of court - 8 July 1662. (Ct.&Land: A#1.216. Note: during the colonial period Nancy (Nancie) was a nickname for Anne.)

CHANDLER, Anne, wife of Jobe Chandler and sister of Symon Oversee, acknowledged sale of land to John Greenhill, 25 May 1659. Court held 8 March 1663/4. (Ct.&Land: B#1.275)

CHANDLER, William, son of William and Mary Chandler of Portobacco, born 13 Oct 1678. (Ct.&Land: QRev.6)

CHANDLER, William, son of William and Jane Chandler of Portobacco, born 13 Oct 1678. (Ct.&Land: P#1.206)

CHANDLER, William, son of Job Chandler. Cattle mark recorded 1680. (Ct.&Land: H#1.349)

CHANDLER, Mary, wife of Col. William Chandler. Acknowledges indenture dated 29 Nov 1681, to Richard Chandler; parcel called *Cheshire* on the Avon River, part of *Poynton Manor*, cont. 500 acres. (Ct.&Land: I#1.184)

CHANDLER, Anne, dau. of William Chandler. Gift dated 9 Jan 1682, from Richard Chandler, of mulatto girl named Susanna. (Ct.&Land: K#1.83)

CHANDLER, William, Col. (Inv.: 14.124; 19 June 1695; ----) Ex.: Mary Brent (relict), wife of Capt. George Brent of Virginia. (Acct: 14.127; ----; 21 May 1697)

CHANDLER, William. Appraisers: James Smallwood, John Hanson. (Inv.: 18.23; [c1698]; ----)

CHANDLER, Richard. In his will he mentions mother Mrs. Anne Fowke; bro. Gerard Fowke; sisters Mary Fowke and Eliza. Dent; Parthenia Burditt; John Hamilton (at age of 21); Anne Burford Jr.; nephew William Chandler and niece Jane Chandler; nephew Richard Chandler (minor). Parthenia Burditt testifies she heard Richard Chandler say that shd. Mrs. Jane Brent, his niece, marry against his liking she shd. have no share in his estate. 26th Aug 1697, appears Nicholas Cooper, aged 50. (Will: T.P. 17.95; 14 Oct 1686; ----) (Inv.: 16.6; 4 Nov 1697; --)

CHANDLER, William, age 42 yrs. Deposition re *Lynes Delight*, 22 Dec 1718. (Chas LandComm: M2.41)

CHANDLER, William, age 42 yrs. Deposition, for Elizabeth Rogers (widow), 28 April 1719, re *Her Excellency's Gift*. (Chas LandComm: M2.45)

CHANDLER, William (Gent.), grandson of Job Chandler. Conveyed on 12 Nov 1720 part of a parcel on the w. side of Portobacco Creek called *Chandler Hill*; originally patented by Job Chandler for 300 acres; cont. 69 acres. (Ct.&Land: H#2.398)

CHANDLER, William. In his will he left to nephew William, (son of bro. Henry Brent, dec'd), 900 acres, *Goose Creek*, with 100 acres, *Chandler's Addition*, at age 21 yrs. To nephew William (son of sister Mary Neale, dec'd), 1,000 acres *Chandler's Hope* at age of 21 yrs. To nephew Henry (2nd son of sister Mary Neale), 600 acres *Green Spring*, 200 acres *Chandler's Hills*, where Patrick Conneley now lives, at age of 21. Mentions uncle Nicho. Sewall, aunt Eliz. Digges, aunt Rozers and Alice Pyes children; sister Jane, relict of bro. Henry Brent. Mentions George Thorold; goddau. Katrine Rozer; niece Mrs. Ann Rozer; goddau. Mrs. Jane Pye; George Thorold and his successor. To the poor Roman Catholics certain personalty. Mentions two nephews Edward and Charles Neale. Exs.: three nephews: William Brent, William Neale and Henry Neale. Codicil: 15 Jan 1726/7. To John Parnham land on which stone house stands. (Will: 20.75; 19 Aug 1725; 17 Sept 1730) Next of kin: Gerard Fowke, George Dent. Exs.: William Brent, William Neale, Henry Neale. (Inv.: 16.100; 18 Nov 1730; 4 Jan 1730) Exs.: William Brent, William Neale, Henry Neale. (Inv.: 16.325; 6 Oct 1731; 4 Dec 1731)

CHANDLER, John, Portobacco. In his will he left to wife Ann, 301 acres, *Chandler's Purchase*. To son John, 100 acres *Macton*, 74 acres *Debt*, 100 acres of *Chandler's Addition*. To son William, 144 acres, the residue of *Chandler's Addition*. To son Stephen, *Greenbank*, *Marrowbone*. To daus. Ann and Mary, and dau. Sarah Hamill, personalty. Exs.: Wife and son John. (Will: 21.520; 17 Nov 1735; 19 Jan 1735) Next of kin: William Penn, Mary Penn. Ex.: Ann Chandler, John Chandler. (Inv.: 21.287; 26 Feb 1735; 24 April 1736)

CHANDLER, John, son of John Chandler, dec'd. 15 April 1738. To William Chandler, son of sd. dec'd. John Chandler, and bro. of John Chandler, part of tract called *Chandlers Addition*, 144 acres. (Land: O#2.328)

CHAPLIN, Thomas, age 11 yrs. Servant of Garratt Sinnett, 11 Jan 1675. (Ct.&Land: F#1.163)

CHAPMAN, Thomas, age ca. 21 yrs. States he was hired in Virginia by Mr. Pinner to serve at Portobacco with Edmond Lindsey; Lindsey sent him to Clement Theoballs, 10 Feb 1662. (Ct.&Land: B#1.67-71)

CHAPMAN, George, age 22 yrs. Servant of Benjamin Rozer, 9 Jan 1671/2. (Ct.&Land: E#1.52)

CHAPMAN, Richard and wife Barbara conveyed on 11 June 1672 a parcel called *Byfield Close*, on e. side of Avon River, cont. 150 acres. (Ct.&Land: E#1.64½)

CHAPMAN, Richard. Admr.: Barbary Chapman (relict). (Inv.: 8.341; 13 July 1685; ----) Admr.: Barbary Chapman (relict), wife of John Gorly. (Acct: 9.54; ----; 9 July 1686)

CHAPMAN, Thomas, son of Thomas and Elizabeth Chapman of Nanjemy, born 26 March 1690. (Ct.&Land: QRev.16)

CHAPMAN, Mary, dau. of Thomas and Elizabeth Chapman of Nanjemy, born 19 Aug 1693. (Ct.&Land: QRev.21)

CHAPMAN, Thomas. (Inv.: 21.269; 9 Feb 1701; 7 March 1701) Admr.: Elisabeth Chapman (relict). (Acct: 23.71; ----; 15 Dec 1702)

CHAPMAN, Thomas. Admr.: Elisabeth Chapman. (Acct: 3.391; ----; 1 June 1704)

CHAPMAN, Edward. Next of kin: Joseph Manning. (Inv.: 35A.151; 15 Feb 1713; ----)

CHAPMAN, William. Next of kin: John Chapman, Thomas Gloverly. (Inv.: 29.330; 27 June 1709; ----) Admr.: Evan Jones. (Acct: 31.77; ----; 31 March 1710)

CHAPMAN, Edward. Admr.: Hester Matthews, wife of Thomas Matthews. (Acct: 36B.330; ----; 31 May 1715)

CHAPMAN, Edward. In his will he mentions mother; nephew Thomas Goley; nieces Ann Goley and Elizabeth Warner, Susanna Goley; Elizabeth Warner. Ex.: Father Richard Chapman. (Will: 20.139; 19 Oct 1730; 23 Feb 1730) Next of kin: John Craxson, Elisabeth Burges. (Inv.: 16.158; 4 March 1730; 26 April 1731)

CHAPMAN, John, son of John Chapman. Cattle mark recorded 28 Feb (1730). (Land: M#2.242)

CHAPMAN, William. In his will he left to wife Jane, extx., entire estate. (Will: 22.276; ----; 1 Oct 1740) Next of kin: Edward Murphy. John Danel, Ann Murphy. Admr.: Jane Chapman.. (Inv.: 25.397; 5 Dec 1740; 1 March 1740)

CHAPMAN, Jane, (widow). Signed 12 May 1744. To her son, William Chapman; his sister Nanny(?)'s children, Ann and Zachariah; his sister Elizabeth's children, Jane and Lucretia; his sister Lucretia's daus., Elizabeth, Jane and Chloe; his sister Jane's daus., Mary, Ann and Lucretia; his sister Sophia's sons, William and John: cattle, furniture, &c. (Land: X#2.107)

CHAPMAN, Richard. Lease, 16 Nov 1744, of 128 acres, in St. Thomas Manor, for the life of Richard Chapman, Mary Chapman and Elizabeth Reagin (Riagon) (Land: X#2.166)

CHAPMAN, John. Lease, 13 June 1745, to John Chapman Sr., in St. Thomas' Manor, of 203 acres for the term of the lives of afsd. John Chapman, his present wife Margaret Chapman, and his son John Chapman. (Land: Z#2.40)

CHARLESON, Charles married Dorothy Musgrove (widow), 14 Nov 1689. (Ct.&Land: P#1.208; QRev.15)

CHARLESON, Charles and his wife Dorothy. Defendants, dated 10 June 1690. (Ct.&Land: R#1.25)

CHARLESWORTH, Robert and his wife Ellinor, extx. of George Eyres. Sale of goods, 3 April 1704. Indenture, 7 April 1704, to Cornelius White, for the maintenance of Elinor, a plantation of 125 acres, nr. Bird's Creek, formerly granted by two patents: 50 acre *Batchelor's Hope* in the *Manor of West St. Mary's*; and 75 acres called *Morris His Hope* in *Manor of Chaptico*. (Ct.&Land: Z#1.92, 234)

CHASE, Richard Sr. Next of kin: J. Chase, Thomas Chase. Admr.: Richard Chase.. (Inv.: 30.254; 26 July 1742; 8 March 1744)

CHATTAM, Joseph. Cattle marks recorded 28 Oct 1731, for his three children, Phillis Chittam, Isaac Chittam and Rebeckah Chittam. (Land: M#2.266)

CHERRYBUB, John and Mary of Pickawaxon. Their children: Elizabeth, born 28 March 1687; John (twin), born 20 March 1690; William (twin), born 20 March 1690; Walter, born 25 Feb 1693. (Ct.&Land: P#1.212; QRev.13, 16, 22)
CHERIBUB (CHERRIBIB), John. In his will he left to wife Mary, 1/3 of estate. Children, John, William, and Eliza:, to be under the charge of William Herbert, who is appointed ex. and to whom is left residue of estate in trust. (Will: 7.9; 6 Jan 1694; 22 Jan 1694) Ex.: William Herbert. (Inv.: 13A.362; -- Jan 1694; ----) Ex.: William Harbert. (Acct: 13A.363; --; --; [c1695])

CHERMAN, Elisabeth. Age ca. 32 yrs. Swore in court 30 July 1663. (Ct.&Land: B#1.164)

CHESSON, John. Judged to be 14½ yrs. old, presented by John Meekes, 10 May 1663. (Ct.&Land: B#1.114)
CHESSON, Barbary of St. Thomas Manor, relict of John Chesson. Deed of gift, 11 Nov 1678, to dau. Mary Chesson. (Ct.&Land: H#1.58)

CHEW, Edith, age 14 yrs. Servant of Garrett Synet, 14 Jan 1667. (Ct.&Land: C#1.251)

CHILDMAN, Joane. Servant maid, judged to be 20 years old, presented by Edmond Lindsey, 8 Aug 1664. (Ct.&Land: B#1.472)

CHING, John, age 36. Deposition on 12 xber 1719, regarding tract called *Salisbury*. (Chas LandComm: M2.75)
CHING, John. (Inv.: 7.145; 28 Feb 1720; ----)
CHING, John, and Mary Farr, married 9 July 1738. Their children: John, born 12 Oct 1745; Mary, born 21 June 1748; Elinor, born 15 May 1739. (Trinity: 109)

CHISELDYNE, Kenelm (Gent.) of St. Mary's Co., conveyed on 28 Sept 1712 land which Thomas Garrard, formerly of Manchester in Westmoreland Co., Virginia, by his will ca. 5 Feb 1672, devised to Mary his dau., who married Kenelm Chiseldyne, 100 acres called *Westwood Lodge*. (Ct.&Land: D#2.24)

CHOMLEY, Francis, age 16 yrs. Servant of Henry Adames, 11 June 1669/70. (Ct.&Land: D#1.117)

CHRISMOND, Joseph. Next of kin: "minors." Admr.: Joseph Crisman. (Inv.: 11.352; 24 April 1726; 5 May 1726)

CHUNN, Samuel and Susanna Love, married 20 Jan 1731. Their children: Cassandra, born 26 Nov 1732; Aquila, born 15 March 1734; Mary, born 11 May 1737; Mersilva, born 8 July 1739, died 18 May 1743; Elizabeth, born 26 Jan 1741, died 2 Sept 1744; Samuel, born 29 June 1744, died 1 Jan 1744. (Trinity: 105—rev.; 109—rev.)

CHUNN, John Sr. To his son Andrew Chunn, all his personal estate; must agree to allow his father and his wife Muriel Chunn, maintenance during their lifetimes. Signed 13 March 1731. (Land: M#2.282)

CHUNN, John. Signed 11 March 1734/5. By request of his dec'd. father, he gives his bros.: Joseph Chunn, a tract called *Muriells Choice*, 50 acres; Benjamin Chunn, 50 acres of tract called *East Marling*; to Andrew Chunn, 50 of tract *East Marling* and by agreement with his bro. Samuel Chunn, 50 acres of a tract called *Partnership*. (Land: O#2.113)

CHUNN, Samuel (planter), and his wife Susanna. Deed dated 12 Aug 1735. To William Warder (planter), tract called *Lumber Street*, 100 acres. Samuel Chunn leases from John Lewellin of St. Mary's Co., part of a tract called *West Wood Manor*, 154 acres for lifetime of himself, his wife Susanna and his son Aquila, lease recorded 30 April 1739. (Land: O#2.126. See also Land: O #2.395.)

CHUNN, John. In his will he left to eldest son Richard, 112 acres, pt. of *Morrises Mount*, bought from Wm. Coode and Joseph Allen. To third son Andrew Chun, ex., 1/3 of *Brotherood*, land given to John Chunn. To fourth son Peregrine Chunn, 1/3 of *Brothwood*. To sons Richard, John, Andrew, Peregrine; to daus. Mary Ann, Elizabeth, Lydia, Judith and Dorothy, personalty, residue of estate. (Will: 23.628-631; 29 Dec 1743; 25 Oct 1744) Mentions: John Chunn, John Burch, Francis Parnham, James Nivison. Ex.: Rachel Chunn. (Inv.: 30.145; 4 Jan 1744; 22 Jan 1744)

CHUNN, Chloe, dau. of Benjamin and Rebeckah Chunn, born 4 Jan 1744. (Trinity:)

CHURCHYARD, Harman (planter). 7 April 1735. To Randolph Morriss of Charles Co., merchant, a tract in *his Lordships Manor* of Calverton, 37 acres, and other, for which he promises to support Elizabeth Churchyard, now the wife of sd. Harman Churchyard, for her lifetime. (Land: O#2.106)

CLARKE, John, son of Robert Clarke. Sells his right to parcel of land formerly surveyed by his father, at head of the Wicomicco River, 4 March 1661/2. (Ct.&Land: A#1.189)

CLARKE, Thomas and his wife Jane Clarke. Deed of gift dated 8 July 1662; Thomas gives his wife a mare. (Ct.&Land: A#1.215)

CLARK(E), Robert and John, sons of Robert Clark. Indenture, from William Marshall, 5 Sept 1662; parcel sold by Walter Beane. Recorded date 23 Sept 1719. (Ct.&Land: H#2.284)

CLARKE, Nicholaus. Judged to be 16 yrs. old, presented by Robert Hendley, 10 Jan 1664/5. (Ct.&Land: B#1.397)

CLARKE, John. Judged to be 12 yrs. old, presented by Zachery Wade, 15 Nov 1665. (Ct.&Land: B#1.495)

CLARKE, Ambros, son of John Clark(e), born 13 Sept 1666, buried 18 Feb following. (Ct.&Land: C#1.252; P#1.204; QRev.2)

CLARKE, James, age 13 yrs. Servant of Richard Edelen, 9 Jan 1671/2. (Ct.&Land: E#1.52)

CLARKE, Beteres (Veteres?), dau. of Robert and Mary, to age 16 yrs. old. Servant of Richard Midgeley, 11 Jan 1675. (Ct.&Land: F#1.163)

CLARKE, Anne, dau. of Robert and Mary, to age 16 yrs. old. Servant of Mathew Stonehill, 11 Jan 1675. (Ct.&Land: F#1.163)

CLARKE, Susannah, dau. of Robert and Mary, to age 16 yrs. old. Servant of Robert Thompson, 11 Jan 1675. (Ct.&Land: F#1.163)

CLARKE, Mary, dau. of Robert and Mary, to age 16 yrs. old. Servant of Henry Hawkins, 11 Jan 1675. (Ct.&Land: F#1.163)

CLARKE, Robert, son of Robert and Mary, to age 21 yrs. old. Servant of John Allward, 11 Jan 1675. (Ct.&Land: F#1.163)

CLARKE, Samuel, left his estate to brother John and sisters Abigail and Esther. Ex., Col. Jno. Douglass. (Will: 5.154; 7 Nov 1676; 30 Nov 1676)

CLARKE, Thomas (gent.). Indenture 9 Jan 1681, to Thomas Clarke (gent.) of St. Mary's Co., for "brotherly love," a parcel called *Clarke's Inheritance* lying on n. side of main fresh run, at head of Mattawoman (St. Thos:) Creek, cont. 500 acres. (Ct.&Land: I#1.225)

CLARKE, George. In his will he left to godson Richard, son of Richard and Mary Hall, William Frost, and Francis Adams, personalty. John Godshall, ex. and residuary legatee. (Will: 4.68; 30 July 1683; 22 Nov 1684) Mentions: John Goodhall. (Inv.: 8.135; 20 Feb 1684; ----)

CLARKE, Andrew. Mentions: William Smith. (Inv.: 10.11; 18 Feb 1687; ----) Admr.: James Thompson. (Acct: 10.228; ----; 6 April 1689) Admr.: James Tompson. (Acct: 17.112; ----; 31 Oct ---- [c1698])

CLARKE, John. In his will he mentions sons John and Thomas at age 18 yrs. Other child.: Mary, Sarah and Ann. (Will: 6.177; 17 April 1698; 12 Aug 1698) (Inv.: 18.61; 20 Oct 1698; ----)

CLARKE, Gilbert. Admr.: Mrs. Fantalona Clarke (relict). (Acct: 20.261; ----; 10 July 1701)

CLERK, John. Extx.: Cosimer Clerke. (Acct: 23.58; ----; 31 Oct 1702)

CLARK(E), Thomas and Juliana his wife of St. Mary's Co. conveyed on
March 1709, tract, part of *St. Mary's Manor*, cont. 220 acres. (Ct.&Land:
C#2.166)

CLARK, Thomas. Next of kin: Fantolena Benn, Mary Jenkinson. (Inv.:
4.81; 26 June 1720; ----)

CLARK, Thomas. Admr.: John Phillpot. (Inv.: 18.41; 2 Feb 1733; 14 May
1734)

CLARK (CLARKE), Carter. Admr.: Randall Morrice. (Inv.: 21.193; 21 Oct
1735; 6 Dec 1735)

CLARK, Thomas. In his will he mentions Jean Usher, Jacob Payn and
William Lovly when he has served to age of 20. Wife Mary, extx. (Will:
22.473; 13 April 1742; 20 April 1742) Next of kin: Francis Posey, Ann
Posey. Ex.: Mary Musgrave, wife of Benjamin Musgrave. (Inv.: 27.49; 24
April 1742; 4 Aug 1742)

CLARK, Thomas, son of Luke Clark, conveyed on 22 May 1745 tract called
Bowlings Reserve, 100 acres. (Land: Z#2.50)

CLARY, Morris, age 18 yrs. Servant of Owen Newen, 10 Jan 1681.
(Ct.&Land: I#1.224)

CLASH, John, son of Nicholas and Mary Clash of Portobacco, born 20 Sept
1693. (Ct.&Land: QRev.21)

CLEMENCE, Nicholaus. Servant judged to be betw. 11-12 yrs. old,
presented by Marshall William, 3 Feb 1663/4. (Ct.&Land: B#1.244)

CLEMENT, John (tailor) and his wife Elizabeth on 14 Jan 1695 conveyed a
parcel called *Middletons Kindness* on the s. side of Mattawoman Run,
60 acres in Manor of Zachia. (Ct.&Land: Q#1.77)

CLEMENS, John Jr., age 40. Deposition, 6 Dec 1720, regarding tract called
Friendship. (Chas LandComm: M2.107)

CLEMENTS (CLEMENS), John Sr. (planter). In his will he left to eld. dau.
Jean Stone, 2nd dau. Elizabeth Cofer, 3rd dau. Ann Thompson, 4th dau.
Barbary, 5th dau. Agnes, 6th dau. Mary Ann, 2nd son Benjamin, 3rd son
George, 4th son Samuell, 7th dau. Lydia, 5th and young. son Francis,
brother William and Rev. Robert Harding, personalty, some of which
described as in hands of Joseph Adams, mcht., in England. To eld. son
John, dwelling plantation after decease of wife Rosamond. Exs.: Wife and
brother Jacob; sons to be of age at 19. Witnesses included William
Clements Sr. Codicil 13 Feb 1732-3. (Will: 21.2; 31 Jan 1732/3; 13 Feb
1732/3) Next of kin: Edward Clements, Francis Clements. Exs.:
Rosamond Clements, Jacob Clements. (Inv.: 18.140; 17 April 1734; 5 June
1734)

CLEMENTS, George, son of Francis and Elizabeth Clements. Lease, 25 Dec
1743, to Edmund Maggottee, of 114 acres, for the term of the lives of
George Clements, son of Francis and Elizabeth Clements, Bennet Neal
and Edward Neal, sons of Edward and Martha Neal. (Land: Z#2.27)

CLEMENTS, John Sr. and his wife Elizabeth. To his son Jacob Clements, tract called *Wickham*, 112 acres; Jacob to pay Samuel Clements, another son of said John, 5000 lbs. of tob.; recorded 10 Aug 1728. (Land: L#2.426)

CLINKSCALES, Adam. Admr.: Mary Clinkscales. (Inv.: 15.591; 2 March 1729; 7 July 1730)

CLIPSHAM, Thomas (Gent.) and Susannah his wife conveyed on 4 June 1683 a parcel called *Mount Clipsham*, bounded by Potomac River, cont. 68 acres. (Ct.&Land: K#1.253; Z#1.240)
CLIPSHAM, Thomas. (Inv.: 8.414; 30 Oct 1684; ----)
CLIMPSON, Ignatius. Next of kin: John Howard, Peter Attwood. Admr.: William Addison. (Inv.: 15.81; 16 June 1729; 27 Aug 1729)

CLOWTER, Temperance, wife of Richard Clowter. Ordered to testify in court 29 Nov 1681; mentions her son in law James Ashbrooke. (Ct.&Land: I#1.170-171, 181)
CLOWTER, Elizabeth, dau. of Richard Clowter. Cattle mark recorded 29 Nov 1681. (Ct.&Land: I#1.217)
CLOUDER, Richard and his wife Temperance conveyed on 10 Nov 1696 a parcel called *Bastable* at Nanjemy, cont. 100 acres. (Ct.&Land: Q#1.110)

CLUBB, Matth: and Philip, sons of John Clubb. Cattle marks recorded 3 March 1724. (Land: L#2.204)
CLUBB, John (planter) and his wife Anne conveyed on 15 Nov 1727 to John Wedding and Elizabeth his wife, natural dau. of said John Clubb, that tract called *Maidens Pleasure*, 95 acres; adjoining the land sd. John Clubb now lives on, called *Hopewell*. If Eliza: should die without male issue then to descend to Anne Wedding, dau. of said John Wedding and Elizabeth. (Land: L#2.405)
CLUBB, John. Wife Anna, coex. To son, Philip, 100 acres., pt. of *Hopewell*. To son, Matthew, 100 acres, residue of *Hopewell*, coex. To dau. Elizabeth Wedding, 95 acres *Maiden's Pleasure*. (Will: 23.660-662; 25 June 1737; 18 Dec 1744) Next of kin: Mary Cawood, William Cawood. Ex.: Matthew Clubb (surviving executor). (Inv.: 30.293; ----; 26 March 1745)

COATS, John. His son Hewgh Coats, mentioned in orphans court records 9 Aug 1664. (Ct.&Land: B#1.356)
COATES, Thomas, Portobacco. Gilbert Clarke, sole legatee. Mentions cous. Conyers Clarke. Ex. John Clarke, father of Gilbert afsd. (Will: 2.169; 23 June 1681; ----) (Acct: 8.255; ----; 12 Oct 1682) Ex.: John Clarke. (Inv.: 7C.4; ----; -)

COBB, Samuel, age 15 yrs. Servant of Thomas King, 2nd Tues in June 1669. (Ct.&Land: D#1.88)

COCKRIN, John. Admr.: Ann Cockrin. (Inv.: 14.34; 7 March 1728; 8 May 1729)

CODDINGTON, Elizabeth. Servant of Henry Hawkins, age judged to be 14 yrs., 12 Jan 1685. (Ct.&Land: M#1.67)

CODWELL, William, age ca. 30 yrs. Gives an oath in court on 28 Jan 1661. (Ct.&Land: A#1.178)
CODWELL, William Sr. Deed of gift on 7 May 1661 from Alexander Smith to William Codwell Jr., minor, son of William Codwell Sr. (Ct.&Land: A#1.137)

COE, Richard. (Inv.: 10, 394; 1 May 1725; 23 June 1725)

COFER (COFFER), Thomas, son of John Cofer, born 25 Nov 1667. (Ct.&Land: C#1.253 (gives date as 15 Aug 1667); P#1.204; QRev.3)
COFER, John, son of John and Elizabeth Cofer of Portobacco, born 5 March 1694. (Ct.&Land: QRev.25)
COFER, Sarah, dau. of Thomas and Mary Cofer of Portobacco, born 28 Oct 1694. (Ct.&Land: QRev.24)
COFFER (COFER), Thomas. Admr.: Francis Coffer (Inv.: 17.118; 4 Sept 1698; ----) (Acct: 19½A.119; ----; 28 July 1699)
COFFER, John, son of Elizabeth Coffer, dau. of Hugh Thomas, dec'd. Deed dated 16 March 1724, to Mary Smallwood, widow, extx. of the will of James Smallwood, and to the devisees of the said James Smallwood (according to Smallwood's will), 100 acres called *Friendship*. (Land: L#2.217)
COFFER, John Sr. Next of kin: Matt: Barns Sr., Joseph Thomas. Extx.: Elisabeth Coffer. (Inv.: 16.65; 7 Nov 1730; 12 Nov 1730)
COFFER, John. In his will wife Elizabeth is extx. He mentions son John; son Gerrard to whom he leaves, 100 acres *Coffer's Chance*, at Portobacco; son Richard to whom he leaves *St. Michals*; son Henry; son Gerrard; son Richard; son Mathew. (Will: 20.46; 11 Oct 1724; 9 July 1730)
COFER, John. In his will he mentions children, Elizabeth, Sarah, William and Henry. He mentions Charles, son of William Cox; dau. Violata Cofer; bros. Mathew, Henry, Richard and three sisters (unnamed). Also mentioned are William and Mary Cox and Zephaniah Garner, son of John. Ex.: Robert Hanson. Next of kin: Matthew Coffer, Henry Coffer. Admr./Ex.: Col. Robert Hanson. (Will: 22.312; 10 Feb 1740; 1 April 1741; Inv.: 25.498; 10 April 1741; 23 May 1741)
COFFER (COFER), John. (Inv.: 27.47; ----; 14 June 1742)
COFFER, Elizabeth, widow. Deed of gift signed 3 May 1744, to Sarah and Richard Coffer, 1/3 of her dec'd. husband's estate. (Land: O#2.44)

COGHILL, James, son of William and Christian Coghill of Portobacco, born 10 Jan 1692. (Ct.&Land: P#1.212)

COGGHILL, Anne. In her will she left to son Smallwood, personalty at age of 16, but not to make sale thereof without consent of her mother Mary Smallwood or his uncle Mathew Smallwood until of age at 21; daus. Mary and Lidia, personalty at 16 or marriage. Ex.: Mother Mary Smallwood; if dec'd., then bro. Mathew Smallwood to act. (Will: 20.13; 24 Nov 1729; 18 March 1730)

COGWELL, James, son of William Cogwell and Christian Cogwell of Portobacco, born 10 Jan 1692. (Ct.&Land: QRev.19)

COGWELL, James, son of James and Anne Cogwell of Nanjemy, born 11 July 1693. (Ct.&Land: QRev.21)

COLE, William, age 28. Deposition re an attack on George Thompson by Thomas Oakley. 1669. (Arch. of Md.: LVII.428)

COLE, Giles. Mentions Stephen Coward and John Lemare; John Hawkins Jr., and his bro. Henry, and their sister Eliza: Hawkins; and Thomas Hawkins. Henry Hawkins, ex. (Will: 2.358; 7 Oct 1675; 27 Oct 1675) (Inv.: 3.108; [c1676]; ----) Legatees: John le Mare, Henry Hawkins (son of ex.), Elisabeth Hawkins (dau. of ex.), Thomas Hawkins (son of ex.), widow of Stephen Cawood, Joseph Jessop (shoemaker). Ex.: Henry Hawkins. (Acct: 4.340; ----; 9 Oct 1677)

COLE, Philip and Mary, of head of Wicomico River. Their children: John, born 10 Jan 1678; Philip, born 4 Dec 1680. (Ct.&Land: P#1.206; QRev.6, 7)

COLE, Philip, son of Philip Cole. Deed of gift 20 Jan 1684, from George Graves (planter), a cow. (Ct.&Land: L#1.48)

COLE, John. Servant to Robert Benson, age judged to be 18 yrs. old, 16 June 1693. (Ct.&Land: S#1.129)

COLE, Jeffrey and Linas his wife. Indenture to Joane Decregoe (widow), 26 Feb 1707. Parcel called *Harrisons Venture*, 50 acres. (Ct.&Land: C#2.97)

COLE, John. Next of kin: Mark Askins, Mary Askins. (Inv.: 30.5; 28 May 1709; ----) Admr.: Henry Taylor. (Acct: 30.307; ----; 30 Jan 1709)

COLE, John (carpenter) and Elizabeth his wife, conveyed on 25 April 1710, 100 acres being part of 300 acres called *Bartoyne Hill* on w. side of Wicomico R., and part of a tract called *Belaynes Addition*. (Ct.&Land: C#2.179)

COLE, Mary, dau. of Jeffery Cole. Recorded cattle mark, 20 July 1710. (Ct.&Land: C#2.185)

COLE, Sina. Her daus. Elizabeth and Mary, recorded cattle marks, 26 April 1714. (Ct.&Land: F#2.12)

COLE, Jeoffre. Admr.: Sina Cole, relict. (Acct: 36A.44; ----; 16 June 1714)

COLE, Edward Jr. of St. Mary's Co. Contract of marriage with Ann Neale, dau. of James Neale, 10 Jan 1715. (Ct.&Land: F#2.85)

COLE, John, carpenter. In his will he left to three sons William, John and Benjamin, real estate. Son Wm. to have dwell. plan. after his mother's decease. To daus. Jemima, Elizabeth amd Mary, personalty at age of 16 or marriage. Wife, extx. (Will: 18.287; 28 May 1724; 18 June 1724)

COLE, John (carpenter). Next of kin: Benjamin Posy Jr. (brother), Belaine Posy (brother). (Inv.: 10.122; 19 Aug 1724; 19 Sept 1724)

COLE, Edward, the Younger (Jr.), of St. Mary's Co. Acknowledges debt to his father in law, James Neale Sr. of 50,000 lbs. of tobacco. Recorded bond 17 April 1725. (Land: L#2.216)

COLE, William and his wife Ann, heir to James Tyer, conveyed on 22 Feb 1732/3; tract called *Bonner's Retirement*. Bill of sale recorded 4 April 1733 re tract called *Bonds Purchase*, cont. 75 acres. (Land: M#2.314, 332)

COLE, William. Next of kin: Margaret Waters, Rebecca Tyre. Admr.: Ann Cole. (Inv.: 18.302; 28 June 1734; 10 July 1734)

COLEMAN, Richard, planter. In his will he mentions Elizabeth Osborne (wife of Thomas Osborne, smith); Thomas Mitchell and Archibald Johnstone, joint exs. (Will: 14.666; 19 May 1718; 27 June 1718)

COLEMAN, Thomas, age 58. Deposition on 24 Sep 1719, regarding the tract *Tryal*, 300 acres. (Chas LandComm: M2.72)

COLEMAN, Thomas Sr. Mentions son Thomas, to whom he leaves tracts, *Redding* and *Homely*; dau. Catharine Samways Coleman, to whom he leaves part of tract *Homely*; Thomas Coleman, son of John Brightwell. To dau. Martha, 6 acres and dwell. house and remaining part of tract *Redding*, also remaining part of *Homely*. Slaves to be divided betw. his six child.: Thomas, Ursilla, Elizabeth, Martha, Martha, and Catharine. Ex., Thos. Coleman, Martha Coleman. (Will: 24.16; 19 Feb 1743; 2 Oct 1743) Next of kin: Catharine Bowen, Elisabeth Brightwell. Ex.: Thomas Coleman. (Inv.: 31.122; 20 April 1745; 13 June 1745)

COLLIER, William (planter), and his wife Barbara, conveyed on 17 Jan 1740/1, a parcel on s. side of St. Thomas Creek, 100 acres. (Land: O#2.481)

COLLINGWOOD, Robert, age 21 yrs. Servant of Robert Clarke, 12 March 1672. (Ct.&Land: E#1.54)

COLLINS, Alice, age 21-22 yrs. Servant of Robert Robins, 2nd Tues in Aug 1673. (Ct.&Land: E#1.135)

COLLSON, Robert, gent. In his will he left to daus. Eliza: Connill, Francis Daniell, wife of Wm. Daniell, and Eleanor Collson, personalty. To wife Ann, residue of estate. (Will: 14.50; 28 March 1715; 20 April 1715)

COLLSON, Ann. In her will she left to Isabella Dryden, Elizabeth Trimble, Faith Alavery, Mary Davis, personalty. To son George, residue of estate. Ex.; Joseph Harrison [refuses]. (Will: 14.717; 30 July 1718; 28 Aug 1718)

COLTON, Ann. (Inv.: 1.295; 14 Nov 1718; ----)

COMBES. (See COOMBES.)

CUMPTON, William, age 17 yrs. Servant of John Hatch, 11 Jan 1675. (Ct.&Land: F#1.163)

CUMPTON (CAMPTON), Christopher, age 16 yrs. Servant of Philip Lines, 14 June 1681. (Ct.&Land: I#1.124)

COMPTON, Mathew (cooper) and his wife Susannah on 14 May 1702 conveyed part of tract called *Manchester* on the Wicomico River. (Ct.&Land: (C#2.117)

COMPTON, Samuell. (Inv.: 3.52; 12 July 1703; 27 Sept 1703) Admr.: Anne Dixon (relict), now wife of Thomas Dixon. (Acct: 25.123; ----; 6 March 1704)

COMPTON (CAMPTON), John. He left to eldest son John, 2/3 of patented land, in Charles and St. Mary's Counties. To son Mathew, real estate. (Will: 15.8; 29 May 1713; 5 March 1718)

COMPTON, John Jr. Admr.: John Compton Sr. (Inv.: 36A.242; 20 May 1714; ----) Next of kin: John Compton Sr. (Acct: 36A.235; ----; 27 Aug 1714)

COMPTON, Mathew and Rachel Compton: Their childen [dates of birth unreadable in original manuscript]: Barton; Susanna; Mathew, born 31 Dec 174-; Elizabeth, born 21 May 1742. (Trinity: 114B)

COMPTON, John. Next of kin: William Compton. (Inv.: 2.135; 18 May 1719; ----)

COMPTON, William (planter) and his wife Mary conveyed on 8 March 1721 a parcel, *Brotherhood*, cont. 800 acres. (Ct.&Land: H#2.486)

COMPTON, William Sr. Next of kin: Adam Weaver, William Compton. (Inv.: 10.366; 20 March 1725; 17 May 1725)

COMPTON, William. Next of kin: George Thomas Sr., George Thomas Jr. Admr./Ex.: Elisabeth Compton. (Inv.: 20.240; 11 May 1734; 16 Jan 1734)

COMPTON, Matthew (planter), and his wife Rachael, conveyed on 3 Feb 1737/8, to Matthew Compton Jr. (planter), land which formerly belonged to John Compton, one tract called *Boswell* and the other, *Boden*, 90 acres. (Land: O#2.319)

CONNELL, William, son of Dennis and Mary Connell, born in Mattawoman, 2 April 1693; recorded 16 July 1723. (Land: L#2.96)

CONNELL, Dennis. (Inv.: 25.345; 6 Aug 1705; ----) Ex.: Mary Connell (relict). (Acct: 25.347; ----; 27 July 1706) Admr.: Mary Knowland (relict), now wife of Stephen Knowland. (Acct: 28.119; ----; 31 March 1708)

CONNELLY (CONNELLEY), Patrick (blacksmith) and wife Anna Statia conveyed on 2 Oct 1733 a tract called *Phillips Town*, cont. 100 acres. (Land: O#2.13) Patrick Connelly left to wife Annastasia, extx., entire estate, including dwelling plantation and 50 acres *Lisbon*, adjoining thereto. (Will: 21.298; 25 Jan 1734/5; 19 Feb 1734) (Inv.: 20.368; ----; 16 April 1735)

CONER, John. Next of kin: Robert Yates, Charles Yates. (Inv.: 35A.362; [c1714]; ---) Admr.: Margrett Walters, wife of James Walters. (Acct: 38B.28; ----; 2 Oct 1716)

CONNERY, Elizabeth (wife of Thomas Connery, late Elizabeth Waters). William Waters bound himself on 28 March 1741 to Elizabeth Waters (widow), to warrant that he will allow her to enjoy part of the tract called *Dover*, 66 acres during her lifetime. 28 March 1741. (Land: O#2.541)

CONSTABLE, John. A jury impaneled July 1664 to determine if John Constable, servant to William Heard, drowned himself. (Ct.&Land: B#1.342)

CONTEE, John, Col. (gentleman). Mentioned in his will are nephew John, son of brother Peter; son in law John Coates, to whom he left land, which was left to him by his father, John Coates; mother Grace Contee and sister Agnes Berry, of England, to whom he left *Effton Hills* and *Rozenbury* in Chas. Co., and money to purchase rings for relatives in England; brother Peter, of Barnstable, England, to whom he left plantation nr. Pope's Ck.; nephew Alexander, son of sd. brother Peter, 327 acres, part of *Walberton Manor* at Piscataway, Chas. Co.; three children in law (by marriage with Mrs. Charity Coates, widow of John Coates), viz., Charity, Charles and William. Wife Mary, extx. and residuary legatee of estate, including 1000 acres, *Baltimore's Bounty*, 1000 acres, *Rozer's Refuge* on Port Tobacco Ck., two tracts in Chingumuxon, and *Buck Range* in Balto. Co. Deposition of Eliza: Berry, spinster, aged 30 yrs., Alex Contee, gent., aged 17 yrs., John Courts, gent., aged 17 yrs., John Warren, aged 21 yrs. (Will: 12.276; -- --- 1708; 21 Aug 1708) Legatees: Alexander Contee stock bought of Samuel Fearson. Extx.: Mary Hemsley, wife of Philemon Hemsley (gentleman). (Acct: 33B.123; ----; 4 Aug 1712)

CONTEE, John. Request dated 2 Feb 1711/12. He left his nephew Alexander stock purchased from Samuel Fearson; to be delivered by Mary, relict of John Contee and now wife of "me the subscriber." (Ct.&Land: C#2.268)

CONTEE, Alexander (scrivener) of Prince George's Co. and Jane his wife conveyed on 26 April 1726 part of a tract called *Bakers Addition*, 118 acres, and on 27 April 1726, a parcel of land on Zachia Swamp, called *Saturday's Work*, cont. 250 acres. (Land: L#2.270, 272)

CONTEE, Alexander and his wife Jane on 9 Jan 1729/30 leased part of a tract called *Baltemore Bounty*. (Land: M#2.195. See also Land: M#2.196)

CONTEE, Alexander, Prince George's Co., by his will dated 4 July 1739, bequeathed to his son, John Contee, his tract at Portobacco, called

Rogers Refuge which John Contee conveyed to John Hanson, youngest son of Samuel Hanson, dec'd., 1164 acres. Recorded 11 March 1744/5. (Land: Z#2.14)

COODY, William, son of William Coody. Cattle mark recorded 11 Feb 1725. (Land: L#2.248)

COODE, William Gerard (Gent.), of St. Mary's Co. Recorded 27 June 1742. Binds himself to Joseph Allen (planter) to warrant that Coode will indemnify Allan from the claim of dower of Sarah, his now wife, to part of a tract *Morris his Mount*, formerly of St. Mary's Co., now Charles Co. (Land: O#2.566)

COOKE, John, age 14 yrs. Servant of Richard Newman, 9 Feb 1685/6. (Ct.&Land: M#1.89)

COOKE, Thomas (planter). Mentions James Haddock, priest; wife Sarah, extx. (Will: 13.481; 29 Oct 1712; 8 Dec 1712) (Inv.: 34.150; 19 Feb 1712; ---–) Extx.: Sarah Cooke. (Acct: 34.53; ----; 7 July 1713)

COOK, Henry and his wife Eleanor, conveyed on 1 April 1735, tract called *St. Georges*, lying on n. side of Gilberts Swamp, formerly in possession of Marmaduke Sims, which he left to afsd. Eleanor, his dau.; afterwards, John Sims, uncle to the afsd. Eleanor, imagining that his brother's right vested in him, left afsd. land by his will to dau. Eleanor, 106 acres. (Land: O#2.103)

COOK, Thomas. Admr.: James Topping. (Inv.: 27.296; ----; 16 Jan 1742)

COOKSEY, Phillip. Admr.: Sarah Cooksey. (Acct: 16.91; ----; 28 June 1697)

COOKSEY, Sarah. (Inv.: 17.22; 26 April 1698; ----)

COOKSEY, Samuell. In his will he left to three sons, Jestinian, John and William and their hrs., 400 acres, *Coate Back* and 70 acres, *Prevention*, equally. To dau. Priscilla, personalty. To son Samuel and daus., Mary and Elizabeth, personalty to be paid out of a judgment of Capt. Jerratt's estate. To wife Christian, extx., plantation. (Will: 12.330; 8 Jan 1708/9; 7 Feb 1708/9) Approvers: James Williams, Elisabeth Cooksey. (Inv.: 29.245; 14 Feb 1708; ----. Shown as Samuel Cooke in abstracts by Skinner.)

COOKSEY, Samuell. Legatees: Mary Short (daughter) wife of George Short, Elisabeth Cocksey [sic]. Extx.: Christian Lemaster, wife of John Lemaster. (Acct: 32B.267; ----; 30 July 1711)

COOKSEY, Samuell. [no county given]. (Inv.: 36A.101; 20 July 1714; ----)

COOKSEY, Justinian and Sarah. Their children: Christian (dau.), born 9 Feb 1728; Justinian, born 8 May 1731; Samuel, born 16 July 1733; Mary, born 25 Sept 1735; John, born 21 March 1738; Sarah, born 21 March 1740; Elizabeth, born 8 Feb 1744; Susanna, born 2 March 1746. (Trinity: 108)

COOMES, Elizabeth, dau. of Philip Coomes. Cattle mark recorded, 9 Aug 1682. (Ct.&Land: I#1.342)

COMBES (COOMBES), Richard, age 63. Deposition, 4 Nov 1719, regarding part of tract called *Christian Temple Manor*, on the s. side of Mattawoman (petition of John Sanders); stated that Joseph Manning being appointed at the request of Thomas Wicherly to run out a tract of land called Christian Temple Mannour afsd. and that Thomas Wicherly who married the relict of Edward Ford which Ford had some pretention to the manor. (Chas LandComm: M2.66)

COOMES, Thomas, and his wife Elizabeth leased to Thomas Kelly on 13 Sept 1744, of part of tract called *Christian Millford*, for the term of the lives of Thomas Kelly and his wife Mary. (Land: Z#2.28)

COOPER, Thomas, age 15 yrs. Servant of Richard Randall, 11 June 1667. (Ct.&Land: C#1.164)

COOPER, Mary, dau. of Joseph Cooper. Cattle mark recorded, 8 Sept 1668. (Ct.&Land: D#1.5)

COOPER, Walter. (Inv.: 2.259; 16 Dec [c1676]; ----)

COOPER, Roger, age 16 yrs. Servant of William Hinsey, 11 March 1678. (Ct.&Land: H#1.129)

COOPER, John, age 15 yrs. Servant of Capt. William Barton, 1678.

COOPER, Robert. (Inv.: 8.230; 1 April 1682; ----) Admr.: John Faning. (Inv.: 8.278; 2 Oct 1682; 14 Oct 1682) (Acct: 8.228; ----; 23 Oct 1684) (Inv.: 7C.43; 23 April 1682; ----)

COOPER, Joseph. (Inv.: 30.59; 19 Aug 1709; 30 Aug 1709) Admr.: Susanna Brett, wife of George Brett. (Acct: 32C.65; ----; 9 July [c.1711])

COOPER, Nicholas and Penelope "of the River side." Their children: John, born 14 Dec 1686; Anne, born 15 March 1688; Prudence, born 11 April 1692. (Ct.&Land: P#1.208; QRev.12, 14, 20) In his will Nicholas Cooper left to sons Jno. and Philip, *Wattson's Purchase, Cowsking* and personalty. To son William, *Middle Green* and personalty; to be under the charge of Jos. Harrison until age at 21 yrs. Mentions daus. Prudence Sanders, Ann King; wife Penelope. To trustees, Mr. Gerard Fooke, 20s., and Jos. Harrison (son of Rich.), real estate in Durham Town. (Will: 14.193; 7 Nov 1716; 4 Dec 1716) Next of kin: John Cooper, Ann King, daughter. (Inv.: 37B.219; 10 June 1717; ----) Ex.: Philip Cooper. (Acct: 37B.94; ----; 31 Aug 1717)

COOPER, Philip. Next of kin: William Cooper, John Cooper. Admr.: (name not given). (Inv.: 10.106; 28 Sept 1723; 31 Aug 1724)

COOPER, Richard (planter) of Stafford Co., Virginia and his wife Sarah, heiress to William Hargis, (late of Chas. Co. eldest son to William Hargis of Chas. Co., dec'd., the original patentee), and Samuel Noe of Stafford Co., Virginia, and his wife Helena, joint heiress with sd. Sarah — deed dated 18 Nov 1728, to Alexander Adair (practitioner in Physick) — tract called *Hargis Hope*, 200 acres. (Land: L#2.454)

COOPER, John. Next of kin: William Cooper Sr., William Cooper Jr. Admr.: Elisabeth Cooper. (Inv.: 20.443; 13 March 1734; 26 May 1735)

COUPPER, William and his wife Mary Ann. 23 Sept 1734. To John Smith, 90 acres, a tract called *Morrises Discovery*, lying on s. side of the great Beaver Dam in Durham Parish. (Land: O#2.50C)

COOPER, William Jr., son of John Cooper of Chas. Co., conveyed on 19 May 1741, 100 acres, part of tract on Potomack, *Cow* or *Cold Spring*, sold by Martin Campbell and his wife Mary, to Nicholas Cooper, grandfather of sd. William Cooper Jr. (Land: O#2.505)

COOPER, William Sr. (planter) and his wife Mary Anne on 7 July 1741 conveyed a tract *Waples Chance*, 100 acres. (Land: O#2.516)

COWPER, Isaac. Creditors: Anthony Suple, Margaret Hayes. Admr.: Alwicks Ferson. (Inv.: 27.440; 11 Feb 1742; 11 May 1743)

CORKER, Thomas. In his will he left to Penelope Rigge, Thomas Rigge, George Langham, Benjamin Roger, William Chandler, Richard Chandler, Clement Theobald and John Theobald, personalty. Wife Eliza: extx. and residuary legatee. (Will: 5.286; 17 Nov 1676; 12 May 1677) (Inv.: 5.153; 19 May 1677; ----)

CORNALL. (See CARNALL, CORNWALL, CORNWELL.)

CORNALL, Joseph and his wife Margaret, conveyed on 2 June 1687, a parcel called *Moore's Fishing Place*, 284 acres; and on 2 June 168[8], 234 acres of tract *Moore's Fishing Place*. (Ct.&Land: N#1.209; P#1.5)

CORNELL, Joseph. Ex.: William Herbert. (Inv.: 12.73; 31 Jan 1693; ----) Ex.: William Herbert. (Acct: 13A.366; ----; [c1695])

CORNISH, John and Martha of Mattawoman. Their children: Elizabeth, born 18 Aug 1678; Richard, born 11 Dec 1679; Edward, born 10 Oct 1682; Martha; born 4 May 1687; Margarett, born last day of Nov 1690; John, born 27 May 1693; (Ct.&Land: P#1.209; QRev.6, 8, 13, 16, 21) In his will John Cornish left to sons Richard and Edward, 200 acres adjoining Jno. Ward's. To son John, home plantation at decease of wife Martha, extx. (Will: 7.320; 4 Feb 1697; 14 Aug 1697) (Acct: 18.76; ----; 19 Nov 1698)

CORNISH, John (surgeon) and Martha his wife, and Robert Smallpage (planter) and Elinor his wife, on 9 June 1691, conveyed tract called *Moore's Fishing Place* in *Zachia Manor*, cont. 254 acres. (Ct.&Land: R#1.194)

CORNISH, Edward. (Inv.: 34.49; 17 July 1713; ----) Admr.: Jane Cornish. (Acct: 35A.58; ----; 11 Dec 1713)

CORNISH, John, age 26. Deposition, 9 Aug 1721; refers to statements of his mother Martha Cornish and James Tilleson in which they discussed the division of the land called *Simpsons Reply* between this deponent's father and William Collier. (Chas LandComm: M2.123)

CORNOR, Job. In his will he mentions Thomas Rigg and Eliza:, wife of Thomas Corker. Wife Anne, extx. To Thomas Corker, plantation, 300 acres, at death of wife Anne. (Will: 5.194; 9 Nov 1676; 16 April 1676-7)

CORNUTE, Hendrick, age 20 yrs. Servant of John Okeane, 14 June 1670. (Ct.&Land: D#1.154)

CORNWALL (See CARNELL, CORNELL.)

CORNWALL, Francis, age 20 yrs. Woman servant of Thomas Jenkins, 14 March 1681. (Ct.&Land: I#1.258)

CORNWELL (CORWELL), Joseph. Ex.: William Herbert. (Acct: 25.333; ----; 26 July 1706) Distribution to: James Tyer who married a daughter of deceased. (Acct: 26.108; ----; 28 Nov 1706)

CORRICKE, Patrick. In his will he mentions dau. Jone and sons James and Patrick Corricke, exs. (Will: 19.411; 10 Feb 1727-8; 3 May 1728)

COSTEKIN, Daniel. (Inv.: 29.329; 6 July 1709; ----)

CASELTON (CASSELTON), Robert. In his will he left to wife Mary, extx., plantation *Naping*. To son Robert, 150 acres called *Yorke*. Mentions son John and dau. Mary. Mary Herman, guardian of children during minority. (Will: 9.23; 6 Jan 1674; 21 May 1678) Extx.: Mary Casleton (widow). (Inv.: 5.218; 27 May 1678; ----) (Acct: 5.219; ----; 16 July 1678) (Inv.: 8.478; 13 April 1686; ----)

COSTLETON, Mary, dau. of Robert Costleton. Deed of gift to Mary dated 10 Jan 1670, from Ellenor Lambert, wife of John Lambert of Portobacco. (Ct.&Land: E#1.34)

COSSLETON, Robert (cooper) and his wife Mary. Indenture 10 Oct 1673; a parcel called *Skipton*, cont. 200 acres. (Ct.&Land: E#1.34)

COTTWELL, James, age 16 yrs. Servant of Thomas Gerrard, 13 March 1676. (Ct.&Land: G#1.16)

COTTERELL, James and Elizabeth of head of Wicomico River. Their children: Elizabeth, born last day of April 1689; Jane, born 15 Aug 1690; James, born 7 Sept 1694. (Ct.&Land: QRev.15, 17, 23)

COTTRELL, James (Gent.) and Elizabeth his wife, one of the daus. and co-heirs of Thomas Burford, conveyed land on 2 Nov 1705. Thomas Burford bought a parcel *Clipsham* at the mouth of Baker's Ck., 68 acres. Thomas Burford by his will dated 13 March 1686 devised to his son, Thomas Burford the aforementioned land; the son Thomas died intestate and the land fell to Ann Plater wife of George Plater, Elizabeth Cottrell, wife of James Cottrell, Jane Dod, wife of Richard Dod, and Frances Burford. (Ct.&Land: Z#1.240)

69

COTTRELL, James (planter). Mentions bro. Thomas; nephew James, son of Thomas Swan; son of Richard Cox; mother in law Ann Cottrell; sister Ann, wife of John Philpot, extx. (Will: 18.54; 21 March 1722; 20 April 1723)

COTTRELL (COTTRILL), James Jr. In his will he mentions sons Thomas and James; grand-children Eliza:, James, Mary and Judith (children of Thos. Swan); dau. Anne (wife of John Philpot); wife Ann. To wife Ann, estate in Barbadoes had by sd. wife. To children, viz. James, Thos., Jane (wife of Mark Penn) and Hannah Lattimore, residue of personalty. Exs.: Wife Anne and son James, the latter guardian to son Thomas. (Will: 18.63; 17 Feb 1722; 9 March 1722) Next of kin: Jane Penn, Thomas Cottrell. (Inv.: 8.218; 23 May 1723; ----) (Inv.: 8.140; 27 May 1723; ----)

COTTINGTON, Edward Cottington, age 50 yrs. Deposition, 4 Nov 1719, regarding tract called *Christian Temple Manor*. (Chas LandComm; M2.65)

COTTWELL. (See COTTERELL.)

COTTON, William. (Inv.: 1.28; 13 April 1674; ----) Admr.: Thomas Gibson. (Acct: 1.28; ----; [c1674])

COULSON, Robert. Extx.: Anne Coulson. (Acct: 37C.138; ----; 1 Sept 1716)

COURT, John, son of John Court, born 19 Feb 1655. (Ct.&Land: D#1.108; P#1.205; QRev.1)

COURTS, John. Enters his mark of hogs and cattle and gives it to his son Hugh Courts, recorded 12 May 1663. (Ct.&Land: B#1.111)

COURT, Elizabeth, dau. of John Court, born 16 May 1663. (Ct.&Land: P#1.205)

COURTS, Elizabeth, dau. of John and Margarett Courts, born 15 May 1663. (Ct.&Land: QRev.1)

COURT, Margarett, dau. of John and Margarett Courts, born 15 Jan 1665. (Ct.&Land: D#1.108; P#1.205; QRev.2)

COURTS, John. John Nevill (planter) grants to John Courts Jr., son of John Courts Sr., a heifer; or to Elisabeth Court, sister of John Court Jr., if Jr. should die; 3 Feb 1663/4. (Ct.&Land: B#1.257)

COURT, Cleat:, age 17 yrs. Servant of Daniell Johnson, 2nd Tues in April 1669. (Ct.&Land: D#1.62)

COURTS (COURTES), John and Charity, of Pickawaxon. Their children: Charity, born 4 Oct 1680; John, born 3 March 1691; Anne, born 29 Aug 1693. (Ct.&Land: QRev.7, 17, 22)

COURTE, John Sr. Deed of gift 13 March 1682/3, to John Courte Jr.; parcel called *Barnehill*, cont. 150 acres. (Ct.&Land: K#1.128)

COURTE, John Sr. In his will he left to dau. Eliza: and her husband James Keech, dwelling plan, and other lands. To son John Courte, 150 acres, *Martin's Freehold*. (Will: 11.246; 27 Jan 1697; 15 Dec 1702)

COURTS, John. To son Henley, 500 acres, *Croutches Gift*, in Prince George's Co. at hd. of Mattawoman Ck., and personalty including a silver

COURTS, John. To son Henley, 500 acres, *Croutches Gift*, in Prince George's Co. at hd. of Mattawoman Ck., and personalty including a silver flagon marked "R. M." To son John, 107 acres, *Chance* on e. side Patuxent R., Calvert Co. To son Charles, 300 acres, *Rich Hill*, 83 acres (unnamed), 60 acres, *Courts' Discovery*, 150 acres, *Barn Hill*, and 60 acres (unnamed) adjoining *Barn Hill*, given testator by his father; also personalty including one silver tankard marked "I.C." To son, William, 200 acres, *Wiccocomico Fields* on Wiccocomico R. To dau. Ann, 700 acres, *Clean Drinking*, nr. the first falls of the Potomac on the Rock Ck. branches. To dau. Charity, two tracts on Potomac R., one unnamed and the other, *Martin's Freehold*, 100 acres. To wife Charity, personalty. (Will: 11.381; 15 March 1702; ----)

COURTS, John, Col. Received from: Hannah Wilson, John Bowling. Legatees: John Courts, Henly Courts, Charles Courts, William Courts, Ann Courts, Charrity Courts. Extx.: Charity Contee (widow), now wife of John Contee. (Acct: 3.386; ----; 16 Oct 1704)

COURTS, John. (Inv.: 33A.59; 26 Jan 1711; ----) Mentions: Hannah Wilson, John Rowling, Charity Contee wife of Col. John Contee. Admr.: Mary Hemsley, wife of Phil: Hemsley. (Acct: 33A.60; ----; 8 Feb 1711) Payments to: widow (unnamed, 1/3). Legatees: widow (unnamed), Henly Courts (child), John Courts (child), Charles Courts (child). Mentions: Hery Courts (also Henry Courts) (child, dead) and his mother Madam Charity Courts. Admrs.: Philemon Hemsley and his wife Mary Hemsley. (Acct: 34.75; ----; 5 Sept 1712) Mentions: John Rogers who married Anne Courts (daughter), John Courts (son), William Courts (son). Admrs.: Philemon Hemsley and his wife Mary Hemsley. Unadministered by Col. John Contee (dead). (Acct: 34.210; ----; 27 July 1713)

COURTS, Charity. Appraisers: Walter Story, Samuell Hanson. (Inv.: 35A.109; 23 April 1713; ----)

COURTS, John. Recorded 7 May 1720 at request of John Maddocks, (planter). Granted land, 20 Oct 1650, for transporting Margaret his now wife and Joseph Letton his servant into the Province in 1649; land on the w. side of Wicomico River adjoining *Courts Marsh*, cont. 200 acres. (Ct.&Land: H#2.336)

COVERT, Robert and Christian his wife conveyed on 28 Feb 1721, 272 acre tract called *Partner Content*. (Ct.&Land: H#2.485)

COWPER. (See COOPER.)

COX, James and Margarett Cox of Pickawaxon. Their child: Margarett, born 2 Nov 1680. (Ct.&Land: QRev.7)

COX, Thomasine, dau. of James Cox. Cattle mark recorded, 13 Sept 1681. (Ct.&Land: I#1.170)

COX, James and Anne Cox of Pickawaxon. Their child: Thomasine, born 27 Dec 1690. (Ct.&Land: QRev.16)

COX, James. Admr.: John Russell. (Acct: 20.269; ----; 13 May 1701) Admr.: John Russell. (Inv.: 20.133; 17 Aug 1700; ----)

COX, John (planter), and his wife Sarah. 8 Aug 1738. To Benjamin Wood (carpenter), tract called *Keets Purchase*, lying on s. side of Piles fresh main swamp, 50 acres. (Land: O#2.344)

CRABB, Thomas, Col. He left to daus. Eliza. and Margt., tract called *Wardle*. To son in law, Charles Sommersett Smith (husband of dau. Jane), *Willshins Plains*. To wife Eliza., extx., dwelling plantation and 100 acres adj. (Will: 16.20; 3 Jan 1719; 8 March 1719) Next of kin: Ralph Crabb (brother), Charles Sommersett Smith (who married a dau.). (Inv.: 4.83; 24 May 1720; ----)

CRAIN. (See CRANE.)

CRAKSON (See CRAXON.)

CRANE, John and his wife Dorathy on 11 Nov 1730 conveyed part of tract called *Cranes Low Grounds*, cont. 25 acres. (Land: M#2.239)

CRANE (CRAIN, CRAEN), John (planter). To son John, 110 acres out of *Crane's Low Grounds*. Mentions dau. Elizabeth Murphey; granddau. Mary Murphey and dau. Monica Murphey; son in law James Murphey. Son John, ex. (Will: 21.52; 24 Dec 1733; 22 April 1734) Next of kin: Elisabeth Murphey, Monachy Murphey. Ex.: John Craen. (Inv.: 18.304; 18 April 1734; 13 July 1734)

CRAIN, Dorothy (widow). Deed of gift dated 1 Jan 1740/1 to her granddau., Dorothy Usher, dau. of Edward Usher and his wife Jane. (Land: O#2.365)

CRAKSON, Thomas, age ca. 22 yrs. Swore in court on 24 Sept 1661; and on 19 Nov 1661. (Ct.&Land: A#1.156, 168)

CRAXSON (CRAXO), Thomas. In his will he left to sons John and Thomas jointly and their hrs., 150 acres, *Field Close*. To Edward and Ann, eldest child. of Edward Till; to Thomas, eldest son of Thomas Chapman; and to Mary, dau. of sd. Thomas, personalty. Wife Ann, extx. (Will: 11.387; 27 Aug 1694; 31 Dec 1702) (Inv.: 22.92; 16 Jan 1702; ----) Extx.: Ann Craxon. (Acct: 25.166; ----; 8 June 1704)

CRAXSON, Thomas. Next of kin: Richard Chapman, Elisabeth Chapman. (Inv.: 39C.76; 23 Sept 1717; ----)

CRAXSON, John. Mentions cousin John Burgess, son of Samuel Burgess and Elizabeth, his wife; cousin Susanna Haislip, wife of Henry Haislip; cousin John Burgess and Thomas Burgess, his brother. Ex.: Samuel Burgess. (Will: 24.231; 16 April 1744; 19 Nov 1745) Next of kin: Henry Haistings, Thomas Jackson. Ex.: Samuel Burgess. (Inv.: 32.41; ----; 31 Jan 1745)

CRAYCROFT, John of Prince George's Co., Gent., and Jane his wife, on 9 May 1720, conveyed parcel called *Inclosure* at Patuxent, cont. 600 acres. (Ct.&Land: H#2.372)

CRAYCROFT, Charles (planter) and his wife Susanna on 5 Aug 1734 conveyed tract *Allens Addition*, 100 acres; on 12 July 1735, 500 acres of tract *Trumans Place*, devised by Ignatius Craycroft in his will dated 9 Aug 1704 to afsd. Charles Craycroft along with tract called *Denyal*, 100 acres. (Land: O#2.50E, 110)

CREADWELL, George. (Inv.: 5.152; 23 Oct 1677; ----)

CREDWELL, George. Admr.: Mary Ward, wife of William Ward. (Acct: 6.308; ----; 21 Aug 1679)

CRESSEY, Mary, dau. of Samuel Cressey. Deed of gift, 8 Aug 1670, from John Grubb. (Ct.&Land; F#1.204)

CRESSY, Samuel. Died seized of land in right of his wife Susanna, formerly Susanna Robinson, relict of William Robinson. Susanna died 20 Jan 1675. George Robinson, son and heir of William Robinson died 26 Jan 1675 without heirs. (Arch. of Md., :LI.181, 184) Reference to two poor orphans Mary and Susanna by the ex. of Samuel Cressey's estate, Richard Edelen. 1679. (Arch. of Md.:LI. 237, 478)

CRESSEY, Samuel. Mentions: children (unnamed), Mary Cressey. Ex.: Richard Edelen (gentleman).l (Acct: 4.171; ----; 12 July 1677)

CROOKSHANKS, Christopher. Creditors: Sharp Balliys. Admr.: William Waters and his wife Susannah Waters. (Inv.: 27.212; 27 Aug 1742; 10 Nov 1742)

CROPPER, Phillip. Admr.: Hugh Mee. (Acct: 31.79; ----; 3 March 1709)

CROSON, Thomas and his wife Mary, and James Ludwell and his wife Martha, on 27 July 1739 conveyed a tract called *Keeths Purchase*, now in Charles Co., formerly in St. Mary's Co., originally surveyed for William Keete, the father of Mary Croson and Martha Ludwell, 50 acres. (Land: O#2.408)

CROUCH, Anne, age 18 yrs. Servant of John Coll, 9 Feb 1685/6. (Ct.&Land: M#1.89)

CRUMMY (CRUMMEY), John, on 29 Jan 1727/8, bound his son, Thomas Crummey, aged seven years on 19th Dec last, to serve Edward Anderson (blacksmith), to age of 21 yrs and bound his son Oliver Crummey, aged five years, on 1 March next, to serve John Brown (planter) to age of 21 yrs. (Land: L#2.411)

CRUMPTON (CROMPTON, CRUMPTIN), Francis. To wife Johanna, extx., entire estate. (Will: 14.520; 13 Nov 1717; 13 Feb 1717/8) Mentions: John Beale, who married the executrix. (Inv.: 1.488; 12 May 1718; ----)

CRY, Patrick. Admr.: Peter Fardinando Jr. (Inv.: 16.447; 18 March 1732; 27 May 1732)

CULLES. (See CULLIS.)

CULLINS (CULLINGS), Peter. Admr.: James Waters. (Inv.: 12.384; 21 Jan 1726; 14 Oct 1727)

CULLIS, James. Mentions eldest dau. Barbara and youngest dau. Mary, wife Barbara, extx. Test: Francis Cholmly. (Will: 4.128; 28 Jan 1684; 24 April 1685)
CULLES, Charles. Extx.: Barbara Chumbly (widow), wife of Frances Chumbly. (Acct: 9.6; ----; 11 May 1685)

CULVER, William. Mentions wife Mary, extx. and daus. Ann and Cathrine. (Will: 22.295; 27 Sept 1740; 21 Feb 1740) Next of kin: Basil Beawan, Charles Blanford. Admr./Ex.: Mary Culver. (Inv.: 26.214; 18 June 1741; 10 Sept 1741)

CUMBER, Catherine. Judged to be 17 yrs. old, presented by George Newman, 14 March 1664. (Ct.&Land: B#1.436)

CUMPTON. (See COMPTON.)

CUNNINGHAM, George, age 16 yrs. Servant of Alexander Smith, 9 Jan 1671/2. (Ct.&Land: E#1.52)
CUNNINGHAME, John, and his wife Mary (nee Hoskins), on 7 March 1744 leased to Thomas Hurrie and his wife Mary, 133 acres. (Land: Z#2.29)

CURRICK, Patrick. Next of kin: Hugh Currick, Joan Currick. Admr.: Patrick Currick. (Inv.: 13.196; 25 June 1728; 24 Aug 1728)
CURRICK, James. Next of kin: Patrick Currick. Admr.: Mary Currick. (Inv.: 13.198; 1 Aug 1728; 23 Sept 1728)

CURRY, Andrew. Admr.: Robert Sennet. (Inv.: 27.305; 1 Jan 1742; 6 March 1742)

CURTIS, John, age 16 yrs. Servant of Francis Wine, 10 Nov 1674. (Ct.&Land: F#1.13)

CUTTLER, Margaret, dau. of Margaret Cuttler. Cattle mark recorded 17 Jan 1677. (Ct.&Land: G#1.84)

CUTTANCE, Josias. (nunc.) Mentions John (son of John Chandler) and wife. (Will: 19.304; 13 Jan 1727; 20 Jan 1727)

DAGG, John (shipwright), Stafford Co., Virginia, and Sarah, his wife, conveyed on 30 Oct 1733, a tract called *Galleys Discovery*, lying on n. side of Potomack River, cont. about 100 acres. (Land: O#2.18)

DAINE, Charles, who married the widow of John Thompkins. Inventory of the plantation of John Thompkins, dec'd., now in possession of Charles Daine; 7 March 1719. (Ct.&Land: H#2.333)

DAMER, Thomas, age 17 yrs. Servant of John Cage, 12 Jan 1668/9. (Ct.&Land: D#1.42)

DAMES, John. (Inv.: 1.72; 6 June 1718; ----)

DANSEY, John. Deed of gift 16 July 1689, to his wife Jane Dansy and her children by her former husbands, Richard Flower and Edward Knight: Elizabeth Flower, Elinor Knight, John Knight, Rebecca Knight. (Ct.&Land: P#1.180)

DARNELL, Elizabeth, dau. of Edward Darnall, at Zachia. Cattle mark recorded 9 Sept 1707. (Ct.&Land: Z#1.260)

DARNALL, John, son of Edward Darnall. Cattle mark recorded 8 July 1714. (Ct.&Land: F#2.17)

DARNELL, Sarah, dau. of Edward Darnell. Cattle mark recorded Dec 14, 1726. (Land: L#2.312)

DARNELL, Thomas, son of Edward Darnell. Cattle mark recorded Dec 14, 1726. (Land: L#2.312)

DARNALL, John. Next of kin: Edward Darnall, Thomas Darnall. Admr.: Rushell Darnall. (Inv.: 21.31; ----; 16 July 1735)

DAVERILL, Thomas, age 20 yrs. Servant of Thomas Dent, 11 Jan 1669/70. (Ct.&Land: D#1.117)

DAVID, William and Priscilla his wife on 27 May 1720 and 17 June 1720 conveyed parts of tract called *Burloyns (Burloyned) Hill*, laid out for Richard Trew, father of Priscilla; located on n. side of the Potomac and w. side of Wicomico River. (Ct.&Land: H#2.361, 375)

DAVID, Thomas, and his wife Ann acknowledged a deed on 15 Dec 1744. (Land: Z#2.6)

DAVIES. (See also DAVIS.)

DAVIES, James, age 16 yrs. Servant of John Ward, 8 March 1669/70. (Ct.&Land: D#1.127)

DAVIES, Alise, age 19 yrs. Servant of Thomas Howell, 8 June 1675.
(Ct.&Land: F#1.101)
DAVIES, Griffith, age 17 yrs. Servant of Nicholas Prodday, 8 June 1675.
(Ct.&Land: F#1.101)
DAVIES, Allen and his wife Martha conveyed on April 29, 1727 two tracts called *Allens Grove* and *Allens Addition*, cont. 200 acres. (Land: L#2.358)
DAVIES, James. Next of kin: James Davies Sr., Allen Davies. (Inv.: 20.350; 15 Jan 1734; ----)
DAVIES (DAVIS), Edward Sr. Deed of gift signed 14 Feb 1734/5. To his son, Henry Davis, part of tract, *Davis' Hazard*, 60 acres. (Land: O#2.100)
DAVIES, Allen. Signed 10 March 1734/5. To his children: Deborah Davies, Negro girl Beck, about 11 years; Mary Price Davies, Negro girl named Sue, about 2 years; Jon: Davies, Negro boy named Charles, about 2 years old. (Land: O#2.86)
DAVIES, Allen (Capt.). On 25 July 1742 leased 273 acres in *his Lordships Manor* called *The Discovery*, during the lifetimes of sd. Allen Davies and his sons, Jonathan Davies and James Davies. (Land: O#2.59)

DAVIS, John, age 13 yrs. Servant of Humphry Warren, 10 June 1674.
(Ct.&Land: E#1.171)
DAVIS, John and Elizabeth, of Pickawaxon. Their children: Elizabeth, born 15 Jan 1688; Mary, born 25 Dec 1685. (Ct.&Land: QRev.11, 14)
DAVIS, Thomas (tailer), married Elizabeth Clouder, dau. of Richard and Temperance Clouder of Nanjemy, in 1693. (Ct.&Land: QRev.21)
DAVIS, Elizabeth, dau. of Griffith Davis. Cattle mark, 25 Aug 1694.
(Ct.&Land: S#1.334)
DAVIS, Thomas and Elizabeth his wife conveyed on 9 Feb 1705, a parcel of land called *Bastable*, cont. 100 acres. (Ct.&Land: Z#1.262)
DAVIS, Thomas and wife Mary, of St. Mary's Co., conveyed on 4 Nov 1706, a parcel of land called *Hitchin*, 100 acres. (Ct.&Land: C#2.26)
DAVIS, Thomas. (Inv.: 26.11; 7 June 1706; ----) Admr.: Honner Hagerty, wife of John Hagerty. (Acct: 28.119; ----; 5 May 1708)
DAVIS, William (planter) of Prince George's Co. and Priscilla his wife, dau. and surviving heir of Richard True, dec'd., conveyed on 9 March 1708 parcel formerly patented by William Boarman and alienated to True, cont. 150 acres, being part of 300 acres. (Ct.&Land: C#2.141)
DAVIS, Thomas. To son William, 150 acres adjoining dwell. plant. To daus. Rachell and Margaret, 64 acres, *Wanister*, Prince George's Co. Mentions unborn child, and tract *Hardshift*; dau. Onor. To wife, dwell. plan.
(Will: 14.338; ----; 14 March 1716) (Inv.: 37B.87; 19 March 1716; ----)
Admr.: Margret Davis. (Acct: 39C.103; ----; [c1717])
DAVIS, Edward. Deed of gift, 12 Dec 1716, to his son Henry Davis; parcel of land called *Davises Hazard*, bounded by Ferney Branch. (Ct.&Land: H#2.23)
DAVIS, Thomas. (Inv.: 39A.39; 27 June 1717; ----)

DAVIS, Edward Sr. (planter) and his wife on 4 Oct 1729 conveyed half of tract called *the Good Will*, cont. 50 acres. (Land: M#2.182)

DAVIS, William Sr. and his wife Priscilla. Deed dated 20 Dec 1729; to Richard and Benjamin Davis, their two youngest sons, tract called *Breels(?) Beginning*, 100 acres. (Land: M#2.194)

DAVIS, John. Next of kin: "no kin in Maryland." Admrs.: William Smith and his wife, Catherine Smith. (Inv.: 16.107; 29 Aug 1730; 15 Feb 1730)

DAVIS (DAVIES), Thomas Sr. and his wife Anne, on 14 Nov 1733 conveyed half tract called *The Remainder*, cont. 187½ acres. (Land: O#2.20)

DAVIS, William. Admr.: Barton Hungerford. (Inv.: 18.280; 31 May 1734; 22 June 1734)

DAVIS, William. Next of kin: Thomas Davis, Elisabeth Davis. Admr.: Priscilla Davis. (Inv.: 20.242; ----; 13 Jan 1734)

DAVIS, Edward Sr. (planter). To son Henry, 10 acres of *Davises Hazard*. To son Edward, the elder, land where he now lives, being pt. of *Davises Hazard*, and *Birds Head*. To son David, 50 acres of *Davises Hazard* and *Davises Addition*. To sons John and Richard, each 50 acres where they live. To son Peter, 50 acres of *Birds Head*. To son William, 50 acres of *Birds Head*. To son James, pt. of *William Inlarged*. To son Edward, the younger, 50 acres of *William Inlarged*. To son Thomas, residue of *William Inlarged*. To son Luke, 100 acres of dwell. plant., *Birds Head*, with plantation after decease of wife; and personalty. Mentions daus. Anne and Elizabeth. Mentions daus. Susannah Burch (Birch) and Mary Gardiner. Wife Mary, extx. (Will: 21.635; 9 June 1736; 21 July 1736) Next of kin: Henry Davis, Edward Davis. Extx.: Mary Davis. (Inv.: 22.71; 14 Aug 1736; 6 Oct 1736)

DAVIS, James (planter), of Prince George's Co., and his wife Ann, on 3 March 1737/8 conveyed tracts, lying on e. side of Piles Fresh main swamp, one called *The Good Will*, and the other called *William Inlarged*, 87 acres. (Land: O#2.338)

DAVIS, Luke, and Ann Hunt, married 26 Feb 1737/8. Their children: Mary, born 25 Nov 1738; Elizabeth, born 26 Oct 1740; Priscilla, born 20 Dec 1742; Cornelious, born 7 Dec 1744; Barton, born 6 Dec 1746. (Trinity: 109)

DAVIS, Joseph and Mary Barker, married 2 Oct 1744. (Trinity: 107)

DAVIS, Randolph, son of Peter and Charity Davis, born 21 Oct 1744. (Trinity: 110)

DAVIS, Salome, dau. of Joseph and Mary Davis, born 28 March 1746. (Trinity: 107)

DAWSON, John, married Elizabeth Thirst, 16 Sept 1692. (Ct.&Land: P#1.210; QRev.18)

DAWSON, Mary, dau. of John and Elizabeth Dawson, born 22 Sept 1692. (Ct.&Land: P#1.210; QRev.18)

DAWSON, Nicholas (Gent.) of Prince George's Co. and Mary his wife on 7 April 1710, conveyed 100 acres called *Lyons Denn*, w. side of the main fresh of Wicomico River. Also 50 acres being 1/3 part of *Fendalls Delight*. (Ct.&Land: C#2.200)

DAWSON (DORSON), Nicholas of Prince George's Co., and Mary his wife, one of the daus. of Robert Doyne, dec'd., conveyed land on 8 March 1714. Robert Doyne at the time of his decease was seized of diverse tracts of land particularly a parcel on Nanjemy Ck. called *Rotterdam*, patented 9 June 1676, adjoining a tract called *Indian Town* conveyed by William Whittington then of Accomack Co., Virginia, now of Somerset Co., Maryland, dated 11 March 1685. Robert Doyne died intestate and his six children were Wharton Doyne, William Doyne, Sarah, Virlinda, Elinor and Mary Doyne. Wharton Doyne eldest son died in infancy (not yet 21); his brother William also died in infancy; Elinor died 1705; Mary wife of Nicholas Dawson inherited 1/3 of the lands. *Rotterdam*, cont. 550 acres and *Nanjemy Indian Town*, cont. 600 acres. (Ct.&Land: F#2.59)

DEAKONS, Thomas, age 11 yrs. Servant of Henry (Hamy) Bonard, 2nd Tues in April 1669. (Ct.&Land: D#1.62)

DEALE, Thomas. (Inv.: 7.230; ----; [c1722])

DEALE, James. Admr.: John Barker. (Inv.: 20.446; 18 April 1735; 26 May 1735)

DEANE, Edward, age ca. 43 yrs. Deposition on 12 July 1664, regarding a Thomas Stone and his bro. John [Stone]. (Ct.&Land: B#1.328)

DEANE, Edward. He left to Eliza: Lindesay, dau. of James and Mary Lindesay, his estate, to inherit at marriage or majority. (Will: 1.416; 6 April 1670; 8 Sept 1671)

DEANE, Charles. Next of kin: Samuel Farson, John Newman. Admr.: Sarah Dean. (Inv.: 11.256; ----; 12 April 1726)

DECREGOE, William (carpenter) and Elizabeth his wife on 23 Oct 1722 conveyed a tract formerly granted to Richard Harrison, called *Harrisons Venture*, cont. 50 acres. (Land: L#2.50)

DECRAGOE, ——, born 23 Feb 1723, dau. of William and Elizabeth Decragoe. (King George's Parish: p. 259)

de CREYGER (DECREVEIR), John. Declaration read in court on 12 Sept 1671, that an indenture was made in Holland (ca. 1663) betw. De Creyger and Capt. James Neale; sd. John to serve Neale for 8 yrs. De Creyger has been free from aforesd. service for three yrs., the first of Feb next, and sd. Neale did not pay him "his Corne & Cloaths." (Ct.&Land: E#1.46)

DELAHAY, John, age ca. 36 yrs. and Jane Delahay, age ca. 30 yrs old. Swore in court 12 May 1659. (Ct.&Land: A#1.57)

DELAHAY, Jane, age ca. 33 yrs. old. Swore in court 22 April 1662. (Ct.&Land: A#1.205)

DELAHAY (DELAHAI, DELAHAYER), George. Wife Susanna, extx. Estate to pass to children of sister Jone Harrison. (Will: 6.221; 25 Sept 1698; 24 Dec 1698) (Inv.: 19.37; 22 April 1699; ----) Admr.: Susan Delahai. (Acct: 19½A.103; ----; 26 Oct 1699)

DELL, Henry. Admr.: Mary Stigelare for her daughter Margret Dell. (Acct: 26.186; ----; 21 March 1706)

DELOZER, Daniel of Prince George's Co., and Mary his wife, dau. of John Cable (planter), dec'd., conveyed on 14 Sept 1708, parcel called *Batchelor's Agreement*, cont. 100 acres. (Ct.&Land: (C#2.111)

DELOZIER, Daniel (tailor) of Prince George's Co. 7 April 1722. Binds his son, John Delozer, to Patrick Connally (blacksmith), as apprentice for seven years. (Land: L#2.8)

DELOZEAR, Thomas, born 2 June 1724, son of Daniel Delozear. (King George's Parish: p. 257)

DELOZIER, William. Next of kin: George Delozier. Admr./Ex.: John Delozier. (Inv.: 26.143; ----; 15 June 1741)

DEMENT (DENNENT), George Sr. Deed recorded 10 Sept 1728. To his son George Dement Jr., a tract called *Crabbtree*, patented to George Dement, father of afsd. George Dement Sr., dated 15 May 1676. (Land: L#2.434)

DEMENT, George. (Inv.: 23.186; 15 March 1703; ----) Payments include George Dement (son). Admr.: Edward Davise. (Acct: 3.64; ----; 27 Aug 1703)

DEMENT, John, Margaret and George, are bound to John Moreland, Philip Moreland, Mary Moreland, Patrick Moreland, William Moreland and Jacob Moreland in sum of £104.3.2; remainder due the Morelands of £52.1.7 for balance of their deceased father's estate from their guardians. Dated 15 June 1719. (Ct.&Land: H#2.262)

DEMENT, George. To son George, *Crabbtree*. To son William, pt. of *Miles End*. To son John, pt.of *Miles End*. Mentions dau. Mary Jonson. Refers to six youngest children. To wife Elizabeth, £15 out of estate of Benjamin Word. Ex.: William Dement. (Will: 19.726; 2 March 1728/9; 31 May 1729) Next of kin: John Hunt, Edward Davis. Ex.: William Dement. (Inv.: 15.78; ---- 19 Aug 1729)

DEMENT, William and Mary. Their children: Elizabeth, born 20 May 1731; Mary, born 7 May 1733; Anne, born 15 Nov 1735; Benajah, born 17 Aug 1738; Jesse, born 10 Oct 1740; George, born 10 Jan 1742; Susanna, born 20 March 1745. (Trinity: 106—rev.)

DEMENT, George. Next of kin: William Dement, John Dement. Admr.: Ann Scallon, wife of Peter Scallon. (Inv.: 18.469; 27 April 1734; 31 July 1734)

DEMSEY, Allicen, dau. of John Demsey. Cattle mark recorded 24 Oct 1726. (Land: L#2.317)

DEMPSIE, John, planter. Mentions dau. Ellisa Down; wife Mary, extx.; Mary, dau. of Wm. Connett; and John Dowen, son of Dennis. (Will: 23.300; 12 Nov 1743; 9 Jan 1743)

DENEGOE, John. Mentions: Jurat Coram, George Dent. Next of kin: Anna Vincent (daughter and only surviving relation), wife of John Vincent. Admr./Ex.: John Smoot. (Inv.: 2.222; 29 April 1719; ----)

DENT, William and Elizabeth Fowke, dau. of Mrs. Anne Fowke, were joined together in marriage on 8 Feb 1684 by John Turlinge, at the home of said Anne at Portobacco. Witnesses: Mrs. Anne Fowke, Col. William Chandler, Madm: Mary Chandler, Gerard Fowke, Mrs. Mary Fowke, Owen Newen and diverse others. (Ct.&Land: P#1.208)

DENT, William and Elizabeth Fowke, dau. of Mrs. Anne Fowke of Portobacco married by Mr. John Turling on 8 Feb 1684. Children of William and Elizabeth Dent of Nanjemy: Thomas, bapt. 19 Dec 1685 at home at Portobacco by John Turlinge; William, born 1687; bapt. 25 Dec 1687 at Portobacco by John Turlinge; Gerrard, born 1688, bapt. 3 Feb 1688 at home at Portobacco by John Turlinge; George, born 27 Sept 1690, bapt. 16 April following at Christ Church; Anne, born 1692; bapt. 16 March 1692; Peter, bapt. 13 Jan 1694. (Ct.&Land: P#1.208, 209; QRev.10, 11, 13, 14, 16, 24)

DENT, Thomas, late of St. George's Hundred, St. Mary's Co. Division of land from will of Thomas, to his sons Peter Dent now age 21 yrs., and his bro. George Dent, now 14 yrs., 8 Jan 1688. Tract called *Gisbrough*; mentions his mother Rebecca Addison as extx. of will of Thomas Dent. (Ct.&Land: P#1.89)

DENT, William (attorney) and Elizabeth his wife on 20 Feb 1690 conveyed 200 acres at Pope's Ck., tract of 70 acres bounded by Queen's Ck. Branch; a parcel *Baltimore County*, cont. 70 acres; and one called *Boatsail*, cont. 200 acres. (Ct.&Land: R#1.538)

DENT, William. In his will he left to wife Elizabeth, plantation and mill, 500 acres, *St. Barbary's*, 15 acres, *Wheeler's Palme* and 200 acres, *Thomkinson's Long Lookt For*. To son Thomas, dwelling plantation afsd. at decease of mother, also 894 acres, *Whitehaven* and the lodge where Thomas Perry lives. To son George, plantation at Portobacco (300 acres), part of *Harrison's Gift*, 118 acres (unnamed), two tracts 118 acres and 125 acres (unnamed), and residue 888 acres of *Harrison's Gift* at Pope's Ck. To sons Thomas and George afsd., residue of land *Lawrell Branch* at Mattawoman. To son Peter, 1/3 of tract of 1569 acres, *Friendship*, also *Ginsbrough* 400 acres, inherited by testator at death of brother George Dent. To "little" dau. Elizabeth, plantation at Mattawoman and 500 acres adjoining. To young. son Philip, *St. Barbary's, Wheeler's Palme* and *Thomkinson's Long Lookt For*. Jonathan Matthews to dispose of ships, cargoes, etc. Sons to have their estates in this country at 17 yrs. and money in England at 21 yrs. Daughters at marriage or majority. In codicil he mentions Mrs. Ann Fowke, mother of wife Elizabeth. (Will: 3.475; 2 Oct 1702; 17 Feb 1704/5) Next of kin: Edmond Howard, Gerard Fowke. (Inv.: 3.718; 5 Aug 1703; -- --) Second inventory was cited. Ex.: Thomas Dent (gentleman). (Acct: 26.42; ----; 27 Sept 1706) Payments to Henry Boteler who married Katherine Linggan for legacy due from Christopher Gregory who executor was the deceased, Thomas Bordley. Ex.: Thomas Dent (gentleman). (Acct: 27.35; ----; 17 July 1707)

DENT, Thomas, heir of Philip Dent his brother, a minor, dec'd., son of William Dent (Gent.). On 9 Oct 1707, from Philip Lynes, two adjacent tracts at head of Burdicts Creek called *Roseberry*, 287 acres; also *Esston Hills*, 500 acres. (Ct.&Land: C#2.73)

DENT, Thomas (Gent.), conveyed on 3 Feb 1710, to James Moncaster (planter), parcel of land on Burditts Ck., which William Dent, father of Thomas Dent bought of Peter Achilles; during the life of James and the life of Mary his wife, and the life of James, son of James and Mary Moncaster. (Ct.&Land: C#2.229)

DENT, Thomas and Ann his wife, conveyed on 14 March 1709, a parcel of land earlier sold to William Dent, father of said Thomas, called *Tomkinsons Long Looked For*, 200 acres, and on 2 Dec 1717, a parcel called *Lawrel Branch* on Mattawoman Fresh, bounded by Elizabeth Dent, 192 acres. Deed of mortgage dated 4 Sept 1722, for £80, on a tract of Thos. Dent at Nanjemy, lying on w. side of Nanjemy Creek, 650 acres. Conveyed on 14 March 1709 a tract called *Wheelers Paltrie*, lying on Piscattaway above Maryland Point, 150 acres. (Ct.&Land: C#2.182; H#2.107; Land: L#2.47, 318)

DENT, Mr. Admr./Ex.: John Scott. (Inv.: 36B.62; 13 Oct 1714;----)

DENT, Thomas. Indenture, 18 Feb 1717 or 1718, to Joseph Harrison, the younger, a parcel being part of a tract *Cow Spring* on Portobacco River, nr. mouth of Nanjemy Ck., one acre; purchased from Martin Campbell, dec'd., by William Dent, father of Thomas Dent, Richard Harrison, father of Joseph Harrison and Benony Thomas, dec'd. (Ct.&Land: H#2.127)

DENT, Thomas, brother of Peter Dent. Assignment of personal estate at Nanjemy to his brother, 4 Aug 1718. (Ct.&Land: H#2.201)

DENT, George and Elizabeth his wife conveyed on 12 March 1721, a parcel called *Haphazard*, cont. 50 acres. (Ct.&Land: H#2.483)

DENT, Mrs. Anne Dent. Release of dower dated 6 Dec 1722. See Liber H#2.184-186, 187-188. (Land: L#2.61)

DENT, Thomas. Deed dated 4 Dec 1724. To Anne, wife of sd. Thomas Dent, tract on w. side of Nanjemy Ck., 650 acres, including bro. or sister (born of sd. Anne's mother), and failing such, to heirs of John Bayne, late of Chas. Co., dec'd. (Land: L#2.189)

DENT, Mary. Next of kin: George Dent, Samuel Turner. Admr.: John Dent. (Inv.: 11.256; 2 June 1726; 22 June 1726)

DENT, George. To William Dent, son of Thomas and Anne Dent, several articles valued at £7.12.2, now on the plantation of Anne Dent (widow), at Nanjemy. Signed 23 Nov 1726. (Land: L#2.321)

DENT, Hatch and Ann. Their children: John, born 2 Dec 1729; Mary, born 13 April 1732; Catherine, born 4 Nov 1734; Ann, born 7 May 1737; Lydia, born 22 Dec 1739; Esther, born 10 May 1742; Rhoda, born 4 Nov 1744. (Trinity: 107—rev.)

DENT, Hatch and his wife Anne conveyed on 10 May 1730 [1731] a tract called *St. Edmonds Bury*, cont. 100 acres. (Land: M#2.243)

DENT, John. Deed dated 10 March 1732/3; to his brother Hatch Dent, a tract called *Dents Inheritance*. Deed dated 14 Aug 1732; to his bro., Benjamin Dent, part of tract called *Dents Inheritance*, cont. 143 acres. Deed dated 14 Aug 1733; to his bro. Michael Dent, part of a tract called *Dents Inheritance*, on n. side of a branch called Piles fresh, cont. 144 acres. (Land: M#2.322; O#2.1, 3)

DENT, John. Next of kin: George Dent, Edward Turner. Admr.: Catherine Dent. (Inv.: 17.243; 8 June 1733; 12 June 1733)

DEVENE, Edmund. Next of kin: Thomas Skinner. Admr.: John Reyley. (Inv.: 28.338; 16 Nov 1743; 1 Dec 1743)

DEVERELL, Elizabeth, dau. of Thomas and Anne Deverell, born 1 Jan 1679. (Ct.&Land: P#1.207; QRev.6) Cattle mark recorded for her on 7 Dec 1682. (Ct.&Land: K#1.83)

DEVINCK (DEVINK), Cornelius John. (Inv.: 35A.53; ---- 1713; ----) Mentions: wife (unnamed) of the deceased died one week prior to the deceased). Admr.: George Shenston. (Acct: 35A.57; ----; 31 Oct 1713)

DYAMEND (DIAMONDS), George (planter) and Mary his wife conveyed on 20 April 1712 a tract called *Miles End* of 100 acres for a tract called *Putney*. (Ct.&Land: D#2.15)

DICKINSON (DICKESON), Jeremiah (Jeremy). In his will he left to Nicholas Proddy, Lewis Green and goddau. Eliza: Harrison, personalty. Son Thomas at 23 yrs. of age, residuary legatee of estate. To Thomas Dent and Nicholas Proddy, exs., personal estate. (Will: 2.78; 29 Sept 1673; 20 April 1675) (Inv.: 1.358; ----; 11 June 1675) Payments include Dr. Maddox for caring for Thomas Dickinson, Robert Thompson. Admr.: John Addison (gent.) of St. Mary's County. John Addison is the administrator of Nicholas Proddy the surviving executor of deceased. (Acct: 5.424; ----; [c1678])

DICKESON, Thomas, age 18-19 yrs. Servant of Thomas Harrison, 13 March 1676. (Ct.&Land: G#1.16)

DICKASON, Thomas, son of Jeremiah Dickason. Chose John Cable as his guardian, 13 Aug 1678. (Ct.&Land: H#1.1)

DICKINSON, Thomas of Nanjemy and Anne his wife conveyed on 23 Nov 1681 a parcel of land on e. side of Dickinson's land in Nanjemy Creek. (Ct.&Land: I#1.188)

DICKISON, Mary, dau. of Thomas Dickison of Piscataway. Cattle mark recorded, 9 June 1691. (Ct.&Land: R#1.234)

DICKASON, Charles. Admr.: John Craxon. (Inv.: 16.158; 3 April 1731; 26 April 1731)

DICKSEY, John. Judged to be 16 yrs. old, presented by Edward James, 10 Jan 1664. (Ct.&Land: B#1.397)

DIGGES, William. In his will he left to wife Eliza:, *Digges' Purchase*, and 200 acres, *Digges' Addition*. To son Charles, sd. estate at death of wife; to pass successively to sons Nicholas and Edward Digges. To son William, 115 acres, *Baltimore's Gift*. To sons Dudley and John, 1000 acres, *Pierce's Encouragement*, in Balto. Co. To son Nicholas, 1000 acres, *Elizabeth's Delight*. Plantation on York R. for daus. Jane, Eliza:, Ann, and Mary. Exs.: Wife Eliza: and son Edward. (Will: 7.292; 19 Sept 1695; 24 July 1697)

DIGGS, Elizabeth (widow). Mentions son Henry Wharton; sons Edward, Charles and William Diggs; son Dudley George Diggs and his wife and children; son John Nedd Diggs and his wife; daus. Jane Rozer; Mary Okey; Eliza: Neale and Anne Darnall. Ex.: Son Edward afsd., and in event of his death, sons Charles Diggs and Anthony Neale. (Will: 13.96; 30 Sept 1705; 17 June 1710) Next of kin: Charles Diggs, Henry Wharton. (Inv.: 32C.124; 20 Nov 1710; ----)

DIGGS, William, Col. Exs.: Mrs. Elisabeth Diggs, Edward Diggs. Accounts filed by William Diggs (brother & executor of Edward Diggs (surviving executor)) of Prince George's County. (Acct: 36C.44; ----; 1 Sept 1715)

DIGGES, William, of Prince George's Co., and Elinor his wife, conveyed on 24 June 1719, tract called *Baltimore's Guift* in St. Mary's Co.; cont. 543 acres, and 134 acres called *Digges Baltimore's Guift's Addition*. (Ct.&Land: H#2.275) and on 27 Sept 1728, to John Parnham (merchant) which land was granted on 10 March 1673, to Elizabeth Wharton, called *Barbadoes*; she by the name of Elizabeth Digges on 4 Oct 1697 conveyed said land to Edward Digges, her son, who by his will, devised said land to afsd. John Digges; and on 16 May 1729 to Henry Darnall of Prince George's Co. and his wife Anne, a tract *Barbadoes* in Chas. Co., 1500 acres, in exchange for 1500 acres in Baltimore Co. (Land: M#2.165) (Land: L#2.450. See also Land: M#2.216)

83

DIGGES, William (Gent.) of Prince George's Co., and his wife Anne on 12 March 1744/5 conveyed a parcel called *Peer (Peir)*, lying on s. side of Popes Creek, 291 acres. (Land: Z#2.20)

DIKE, Mathew, age 20 yrs. Servant of Mathew Stone, 12 March 1671/2. (Ct.&Land: E#1.54)

DIKE, Elizabeth, dau. of Matthew and Mary Dike. Cattle mark recorded 14 Jan 1689. (Ct.&Land: P#1.190)

DIKE, Matthew. Regarding his wife administration of estate of her late husband, Thomas Allcocks, 10 Jan 1692. (Ct.&Land: Q#1.62)

DIKE (DYKE), Mathew. In his will he left to dau. Eliza: tract called *Wood's Folly* in Stafford Co., Virginia. To Edward, son of Edw. Rockwood, William Thomas, and son in law Thomas Allcoke, personalty. Wife Mary, extx. (Will: 6.91; 28 May 1697; 3 March 1697) (Inv.: 16.1; 4 June 1698; ----)

DILLAHAY, Thomas. Married Elizabeth Hastead, relict of Michaell Hastead. Petition, 11 Aug 1691. (Ct.&Land: Q#1.40)

DINES, Thomas. Distribution to: orphans (unnamed). Admr./Ex.: Mary Roberson (relict). (Inventories/Accounts: 7A.305; ----; 16 Feb 1679)

DIVELL, James, age 14 yrs. Servant of Thomas Stone, 10 Jan 1670. (Ct.&Land: E#1.1)

DICKSON, Elizabeth, age 20 yrs. Servant of Cleborne Lomax, 10 June 1679. (Ct.&Land: H#1.134)

DIXON, Thomas, son of Thomas Dixon of Pickawaxen, born 8 June 1692. (Ct.&Land: P#1.210; QRev.18)

DIXON, Thomas. Recorded 19 March 1718, at the request of Col. Walter Story on behalf of Ann Dixon (widow); John Gwinn, age 46, and Mary Story, age ca. 37; made a deposition dated 6 Feb 1718, that they heard Thomas Dixon, dec'd., say on his death bed that his dau. Mary Dixon was to receive a Negro girl. (Ct.&Land: H#2.219)

DIXON, Thomas (gentleman). Next of kin: John Gwinn, James Baley. Admr./Ex.: Ann Dixon. (Inv.: 3.237; 4 Dec 1719; 19 Feb 1719)

DIXON, John (nunc.). In his will he left to sister Sarah, entire estate, except a legacy to brother-in-law Robert Mastin. (Will: 20.880; 6 Feb 1733; 7 Feb 1733) Next of kin: Ro. Mastin. Admr.: Sarah Dixon. (Inv.: 18.471; 17 April 1734; 3 Aug 1734)

DOBSON, Samuell. Deed of gift, 22 April 1662; gives a heiffer and calf to his wife's dau., Mary Stratton. (Ct.&Land: A#1.210)

DOD, Anne, dau. of Richard and Jane Dod, of the head of Baker's Creek, born 24 Sept 1692. (Ct.&Land: P#1.210, QRev.18)

DOD, John, son of Richard and Mary Dod, born 2 July 1666. (Ct.&Land: P#1.206; QRev.2)

DOD, Mary, dau. of Richard and Mary Dod, born 25 Feb 1666. (Ct.&Land: P#1.204; QRev.2)

DOD, Richard, son of Richard Dod, born 4 Jan 1662. (Ct.&Land: P#1.204; QRev.1)

DOD, Richard, son of Richard and Mary Dod of Potomack River, born 13 Jan 1670. (Ct.&Land: P#1.206; Rev.4)

DOD, John, of Hanover Co., Virginia, and Anne his wife; John was son of Richard Dod of Maryland, dec'd. Indenture, 22 Aug 1721, to George Dent; a parcel of 40 acres. (Ct.&Land: H#2.456)

DOD, Mary (widow) relict of Richard Dod. Deed of gift, 11 Sept 1679, to John Baker (son of Thomas Baker); a heifer. (Ct.&Land: H#1.186)

DOD, Mary, dau. of Richard Dod, born 25 Feb 1656. Entered in orphan court held 9 Aug 1664. (Ct.&Land: B#1.357)

DOD, Richard, age ca. 26 yrs. Swore in court 9 July 1662. (Ct.&Land: A#1.233)

DOD, Richard, son of Richard Dod, born 4 Jan 1662. Entered in orphan court held 9 Aug 1664. (Ct.&Land: B#1.357)

DODS, Thomas, age 12 yrs. Servant of Robert Henley, 12 Jan 1674. (Ct.&Land: F#1.41)

DODD, Richard. Next of kin: Jane Jenckins, James Cottrell Jr. (Inv.: 35A.292; 3 March 1713; ----) Admr.: Elisabeth Miles. (Acct: 36B.102; ----; 31 Jan 1714)

DODE, Richard, age ca. 25 yrs. and his wife Marie Dode, age ca. 21 yrs. Statements in court, 26 Jan 1658. (Ct.&Land: A#1.38)

DODSON, Walter, son of John Dodson. Cattle mark recorded 7 April 1727. (Land: L#2.338)

DODSON, John, to his dau., Frances Hewton and Allen Hewton her husband, part of a tract called *Dodsons Courage*, 20 acres. Deed signed 18 Aug 1730. (Land: M#2.236)

DODSON, John Sr.. In his will he left to wife Leaticia and son Walter, ex., personalty. To son John, 50 acres of *Dodson's Courage*. Personal estate to be divided between wife, sons Walter and John and dau. Frances Hewton. (Will: 21.341; 26 Jan 1734/5; 16 April 1735) Mentions: Lettisha Dodson, John Dodson, Peter Mitchel, Ann Ebernathy. Ex.: Walter Dodson. (Inv.: 20.449; ----; 4 June 1735)

DOLTON, Richard, age 18 yrs. Servant of Richard Chandler, 11 March 1678. (Ct.&Land: H#1.129)

DONAHAU, Fincene [no age given]. Man servant of Thomas Hussey, "Who: was Judg.-d invalid:—," 11 Aug 1685. (Ct.&Land: L#1.161)

DONOHAU, Cornelius, age 19 yrs. Servant of Thomas Hussey, 11 Aug 1685.
(Ct.&Land: L#1.161)

DONALDSON, Daniel, age 69. Deposition on 24 Sep 1719, regarding the tract *Tryal*. (Chas LandComm: M2.72)

DOOLEY, James and Elizabeth. Their children: John, born 8 Jan 1739; Thomas Read, born 25 Nov 1740; James, born 20 Jan 1742; Elizabeth, born 4 July 1745. (Trinity: 105—rev.)

DORROSELL, Joseph, age ca. 40 yrs. Swore in court 10 May 1663.
(Ct.&Land: B#1.115)

DOSETT, Edward, age 21 yrs. Servant of Humphrey Warren, 11 April 1676.
(Ct.&Land: F#1.173)

DOUGHTY, Enock, age ca. 22 yrs. (son of Francis Doughtie). Swore in court 25 Sept 1661. (Ct.&Land: A#1.157)

DOUGHTIE, Enock. On behalf of his brother in law Hew Oneal, demands warrent, 22 April 1662. (Ct.&Land: A#1.213)

DOUGHTIE, Enock, son of Francis Doughtie (minister) of Rapahannock Co., Virginia. Letter dated 4 June 1662, appointing Enock as his father's attorney. (Ct.&Land: A#1.222)

DOUGHTY, Ane, age ca. 42 yrs. Swore in court 5 Nov 1662, that some spoons she sent home (from London) by Richard Rich for her son Burdit's use. Thomas Burdit (Burdett), plt., did not receive items. The spoons were marked with "EB" of deponents daughter's child's name (affirmed by her cousin Elisabeth Calvert). (Ct.&Land: B#1.10-11)

DOUGHTY (DOUGHTI), Francis Sr. (minister) and his wife Anne. Court records 13 Oct 1663, assign rights to a parcel of land dated 9 Feb 1662; signed in the presence of Francis Doughty Jr. and Hugh Oneall. (Ct.&Land: B#1.173-175)

DOUGHTY, Enock. Deed of gift 20 Nov 1663; delivers to Joye Oneale, his bro. Heugh Oneale's dau., a black heifer. (Ct.&Land: B#1.243)

DOUGHTY, Robert, age 15 yrs. Servant of John Ward, 2nd Tues in June 1669. (Ct.&Land: D#1.88)

DOUGLAS, John, age ca. 25 yrs. Swore in court 19 Nov 1661. (Ct.&Land: A#1.169)

DUGLAS, Sarah, dau. of John Douglas. Cattle mark recorded, 11 March 1672. (Ct.&Land: E#1.126)

DUGLAS (DOUGLAS), Elizabeth, dau. of John Duglas, born 26 April 1673.
(Ct.&Land: E#1.126; P#1.205; QRev.4)

DOUGLAS, John. To wife Sarah, extx., 450 acres, dwelling place of testator at Pickiawaxen. To son John, 550 acres, part of *Cold Spring Manor*, at

21 yrs. of age. To son Robert, *Blithwood* at 21 yrs. of age. To sons Charles and Joseph, 500 acres, residue of *Cold Spring Manor*, at 21 yrs. of age. (Will: 9.97; 14 Dec 1678; 27 Jan 1678)

DUGLAS, John, son of John (cooper) and Mary Duglas of Pickawaxen, born 29 Oct 1686. (Ct.&Land: P#1.210)

DUGLAS, John, son of John (a cooper) and Catherine Duglas of Pickawaxon, born 29 Oct 1686. (Ct.&Land: QRev.12)

DUGLAS, Benjamin, son of John Duglas (planter). Cattle mark recorded 11 Aug 1691. (Ct.&Land: R#1.267)

DOUGHLASS, Robert. Admr.: Mary Dauglas. (Inv.: 13A.155; 29 Sept 1694; ----) (Inv.: 13A.351; 24 July 1695; ----)

DOUGLAS (DUGLAS), Mary. Items in the possession of John Compton. (Inv.: 20.27; 1 April 1700; ----) Payments include Kenelme Cheseldyne, Esq. due on administration of estate of Robert Duglas. Admr.: John Compton Jr. (Acct: 20.197; ----; [c1701])

DOUGLIS, Charles. (Inv.: 24.118; 1 May 1703; ----)

DUGLAS(S), John. (Inv.: 25.215; 21 Jan 1705; ----) Payments include Joseph Duglass. Admr.: Benjamin Duglass. (Acct: 28.101; ----; 15 March 1707)

DOUGLAS (DAUGLAIS), Gilford (Inv.: 6.16; 3 Feb 1720; ----)

DOUGHLASS, John, son of Benjamin Doughlass. Brand mark of a mare given by Thos: Hole, recorded 10 Sept 1722. (Land: L#2.46)

DOUGLASS, Joseph. Approvers: Joseph Douglass, Benjamin Douglass, James Rutherford, Thomas Douglass. (Inv.: 9.217; ----; 3 Nov 1723)

DOUGLASS, Benjamin and his wife Elizabeth conveyed on 20 April 1730 part of two tracts *New York* and *Duck Marsh*, cont. 175 acres. (Land: M#2.229) and on 28 Aug 1732 a tract called *New York*, cont. 188 acres. (Land: M#2.306)

DOUGLASS, Joseph. 16 Jan 1740/1. To his eldest son, William Douglass, a tract upon St. Raphaels Creek called *Maidens Point*, 30 acres; tract of 200 acres. Mentions son John Douglass. (Land: O#2.365)

DOUGLASS, William, and his wife Sarah conveyed on 17 Jan 1740/1 a tract called *Maidens Point*, 30 acres. (Land: O#2.366)

DOUGLASS, Joseph. 6 Sept 1744. To his son John Douglass, tract called *Bowles Land*, now called *Douglass' Clame*, 514 acres; and the tract where he lives, 60 acres, and a Negro boy called Jack. (Land: X#2.149)

DOVE, Phillip, age 45. Deposition, 6 Dec 1720, regarding tract called *Friendship*. (Chas LandComm: M2.107)

DOVE, Phillip. (Inv.: 9.218; ----; 23 Nov [c1723])

DOVER, Christopher, age 20 yrs. Servant of Thomas Mathewes, 10 June 1674. (Ct.&Land: E#1.171)

DOWIN, John (planter) and Sarah his wife conveyed on 9 Nov 1709 a parcel called *Partnership*, on e. side of Portobacco Creek. (Ct.&Land: C#2.149)

DOWNES, Robert, son of Robert Downes (decd:), born 4 Feb 1670. (Ct.&Land: P#1.207; QRev.4)
DOWNES, Robertt. (Inv.: 1.505; 24 Jan 1675; ----)
DOWNES, Robert, son of Robert Downes, dec'd., conveyed on 8 Jan 1677 parcel called *Cow Springs* nr. mouth of Nangemy Creek, cont. 400 acres. (Ct.&Land: H#1.88)
DOWNES, Elizabeth, dau. of Robert, age 10 yrs. Servant of John Wright, 1678.
DOWNES, Robert. Mentions: John Morreing, Mr. Featherston, wife (unnamed) of John Morreing, Richard Carver (aged 50 years), John Shearman (aged 25 years). Admr.: Nicholas Cooper. (Acct: 10.480; ----; 8 June 1695) Admr.: Nicholas Cooper. (Acct: 13A.255; ----; 26 March 1695)

DOWNING, Denis. Date recorded 20 June 1728. At the request of Thomas Mooney, of St. Mary's Co., guardian of Denis Downing, son of John Downing, late of St. Mary's Co. Land of the orphan, the two parcels lying at Mattawoman, *Moores Fishing Place*, 234 acres, and *Combes Chance*, 39 acres, was viewed by court appointees. (Land: L#2.425)
DOWING, Dennis Nicodemus (planter), and his wife Ellis, conveyed on 11 May 1737 a tract on s. side of fresh run called *St. Thomas'*, 234 acres. (Land: O#2.196)

DOYNE, Robert. Wharton Doyne and William Doyne, two orphans of Robert Doyne, 14 June 1692. (Ct.&Land: Q#1.54)
DOYNE, Joshua. Deed of gift, 17 June 1697, to his eldest son Dennis Doyne. Plantation where he now lives, 200 acres on Nanjemy Creek. (Ct.&Land: C#2.239)
DOYNE(S), Dennis, Nanjemy. In his will he left to wife Jane, ex. plantation at Nanjemy; also 200 acres (unnamed). Mentions brothers William, Jesse and Ethelbert. (Will: 6.81; 23 Feb 1697; 6 April 1698) (Inv.: 17.18; 4 June 1698; ----) Legatees: William Doyne, Ethelbert Doyne. (Acct: 18.163; ----; [c1699])
DOYNE, Mary of Prince George's Co., dau. of Robert Doyne, on 17 April 1702, conveyed two tracts, *Rotterdam* and *The Indian Town*. (Ct.&Land: Z#1.19)
DOYNE, Robert. Robert Doyne died intestate and his children were Wharton, William, Sarah, Virlinda, Ellinor and Mary; estate descended to Wharton as eldest son. William inherited this land at the death of Wharton; William died intestate and Virlinda who married Samuel Taylor inherited 1/4 of the land. 9 Jan 1702. (Ct.&Land: Z.8)
DOYNE, Jesse, age 44. Deposition in 1721 regarding tract called *Paynton Manor*. (Chas LandComm: M2.138)

DOYNE, Jesse, of Pointon Manor, Chas. Co. To his son Joseph Doyne, tract *Josephs Lott*, 306 acres being pt. of 600 acres purchased by Joshua Doyne, late of St. Mary's Co. (dec'd.), of Madam Elizabeth Calvert. 6 April 1727. (Land: L#2.338)

DOYNE, Jesse(e). In his will he left to son Robert, 100 acres, including dwell. plan., being pt. of 200 acres formerly belonging to bro. William, dec'd.; 1,000 acres *Timnah Sarah* left by father Joshua Doyne betw. testator and bro. Ethelbirth, dec'd.; 200 acres. To son Joseph, 100 acres of dwell. plan.; 170 acres formerly belonging to bro. Dennis, dec'd.; 550 acres *Rause* left by father to bro. William, dec'd. To Peter Atwood, personalty. Exs.: Sons Robert and Joseph, to be of age at 18 yrs. (Will: 19.185; 14 Dec 1726; 26 June 1727) Next of kin: Thomas Jameson, Mary Jameson. Ex.: Robert Doyne. (Inv.: 12.340; 1 Sept 1727; 29 Sept 1727)

DOYNE, Jane (widow) of St. Mary's Co., to her son Ignatius Doyne, land in Charles Co. called *St. Bernard*, cont. 200 acres. Deed of gift recorded 15 Oct 1731. (Land: M#2.265)

DRAPER, Railph, age 16 yrs. Servant of Philip Lines, 14 June 1681. (Ct.&Land: I#1.124)

DRAYDEN, Isabella. In her will she left to dau. Susanna Yopp and William, son of Thomas King, personalty. To son Mathew Breeding (Breed), residue of personal estate at age of 18. Extx.: dau. Susanna Yopp. (Will: 15.1; 19 March 1718/9; 1 July 1719)

DRINKING, Nimrod, orphan child. Age 9 yrs. last March, bound to John Sanders to age 21, 13 March 1710. (Ct.&Land: D#2.141)

DROYDEN, George. Next of kin: Charles Yates, Susanna Yates. (Inv.: 1.296; 26 Aug 1718; ----)

DUELY, John. Next of kin: Barton Warren, John Harris. Administratrix: (name not given). (Inv.: 10.253; 22 Oct 1724; 22 Dec 1724)

DUFFEY, Patrick and Martha McHon, married 27 Feb 1737. Their children: Elizabeth, born 23 Sept 1738; Leonard, born 3 Dec 1740; Anne, born 28 Dec 1742; Cassandra, born 4 Aug 1744. (Trinity: 105, 105Rev.)

DUGLAS. (See DOUGLAS.)

DUNN, Isaac, age 14 yrs. Servant of John Hatch, 10 March 1673. (Ct.&Land: E#1.153)

DUNN, Susanna. In his will he left to Samuel Barret and Thomas Polton jointly, 100 acres, *Atheshoop*. To Susanna, Mary, and William Thomas,

George Barton, Thomas Allcock, and Edward Maddock, personalty. Ex.: Thomas Polton. (Will: 5.182; 19 Jan 1676; 9 March 1677)

DUNNAK, Danniell. (Inv.: 21.33; 12 May 1735; ----)

DUNNAWAY, Mary. In Nov 1710 she bound her son Richard to Edward Cornish, to age 21 yrs. and her son Francis to Thomas Austin to age 21 yrs. (Ct.&Land: D#2.10)

DUNNINGTON, Francis. Servant of Mary Chandler, age judged to be 20 yrs., 12 Jan 1685. (Ct.&Land: M#1.67)
DUNNINGTON, Francis and Margaret his wife on 4 April 1704 conveyed a tract *Howland* on the n. side of Piscataway R. and s. side of Mattawoman Ck., 200 acres. (Ct.&Land: Z#1.96)

DUPPE, Thomas, age 15 yrs. Servant of Alexander Smyth, 11 June 1667. (Ct.&Land: C#1.164)

DUTTON, Thomas and Elizabeth, of Wicomico. Their children: Mathew, born 28 Sept 1692; Notley, born 19 Dec 1694. (Ct.&Land: P#1.211; QRev.18, 24)
DUTTON, Nottley. (Inv.: 39C.80; 11 Oct 1717; ----)
DUTTON, Mathew (Matthew). In his will he left to sons Notley, Thomas and Garratt, dwelling plantation. Wife Judith, extx. (Will: 21.61; 26 Jan 1733/4; 9 May 1734) Next of kin: William Penn Jr., Elisabeth Joy. Extx.: Judith Dutton. (Inv.: 19.59; 16 June 1734; 30 Aug 1734) (Inv.: 21.295; 8 Oct 1734; 13 May 1736)
DUTTON, Judith (widow). Signed 27 Feb 1734/5. Releases for 15 yrs., part of a tract called *Poppleton*, 100 acres, being left by Matthew Dutton, dec'd., to his youngest son, Gerard Dutton. (Land: O#2.105)

DYSON (DISON), Thomas Sr. To son Thomas, 55 acres lying within St. John's, and part of *Dison's Chance* divided by Spring Branch to n. line of *Swan Hill*. To son John, 100 acres, *Swan Hill*, and residue of *Dison's Chance* afsd. To wife Ann, personal estate. (Will: Part 2-12.213; 14 Oct 1702; 17 Feb 1709/10) (Inv.: 31.146; Feb 1709; ----) Extx.: Ann Dyson. (Acct: 32C.129; ----; 24 June 1711)
DYSON, Thomas and his wife Sarah on 10 June 1729 conveyed part of tract called *Lemly*, formerly in St. Mary's Co., lying on the s. side of the main swamp that falls into Piles' Fresh, cont. 125 acres. (Land: M#2.167)
DYSON, Maddox, son of Thomas, Junr., and Mary Dyson, born 25 Nov 1743. (Trinity: 110)
DYSON, James and Abigall Swann, married 17 Jan 1744/5. (Trinity: 110—rev.)
DYSON, Bennet, son of John Bapt. and Ann Dyson, born 13 Aug 1745. (Trinity: 109—rev.)

DYSON, Sarah, dau. of James and Abigall Dyson, born 15 Oct 1745. (Trinity: 110—rev.)

ETTYE, Rachell, dau. of Arthur and Elizabeth Ettye of Wicomico, born 30 July 1694. (Ct.&Land: QRev.23)

EATIE (EATY), Nathanell and Elizabeth his wife, and Benoni Fanning, on 26 April 1703, conveyed a parcel called *Fanning's Adventure*. (Elizabeth is sister of Benoni Fanning. See Ct&Land A.35.) (Ct.&Land: Z#1.188)

ETY, Nathaniell. Admr.: Elisabeth Ety (relict). (Acct: 25.257; ----; 8 Nov 1705)

EADY, Elizabeth, age 21 yrs. Servant of John Rogers, Nov 1710. (Ct.&Land: D#2.6)

EARL (EARLES, ERLE), William. Admrs.: Elisabeth Hanson (wife of John Hanson Jr.) and Samuell Lucket (executors of Samuell Lucket (admr. of deceased)). (Acct: 25.255; ---- 6 Nov 1705)

EASON, John, age 11 yrs. Servant of Humphrey Warren, 11 March 1678. (Ct.&Land: H#1.130)

EATIE/EATETY. (See EADY.)

EATON, Thomas, age 18 yrs. Servant of Thomas Clipsham, 10 June 1679. (Ct.&Land: H#1.134)

EBURNATHY, John. To wife Ann 1/2 real estate. To father John Eburnathy in or near Armagh in the Kingdom of Ireland, other half of real estate. Mentions three bros. Thomas, James and William, in or near Armagh. Exs.: Wife Ann and Col. Robert Hanson. (Will: 20.608; 11 March 1733; 21 April 1733) Exs.: Robert Hanson, Anne Eburnathy. (Inv.: 17.578; 4 May 1733; 27 Nov 1733)

EBURNATHY (ABERNATHY), John, of Grange Oneland in the county of Armagh [Ireland], has sold to Thomas Abernathy (Eburnathy) of Grange Oneland, his oldest son now living, land that was left him by the will of [his son] John Abernathy of Portobacco in Maryland. Signed 24 March 1733/4. James Delap of Ballihaden and Alexander Gray of Drummanon in County of Armagh state that John Abernathy Jr., late of Grange Oneland of sd. county, son of John Eburnethy, now of the same, until about Dec 1712 — that sd. John Abernathy Jr., left his country in order to go to America, and that the sd. John Abernathy, the father, had then four sons, viz., Thomas, James, William, and John Jr., whom these deponents often heard settled in Portobacco in Maryland. William Abernathy of Grange Oneland, sold to James Abernathy of Grange Oneland, his bro., all the estate left to him by the will of John Abernathy of Portobacco, his bro. 15 Nov 1734. (Land: O#2.64-69)

EBURNATHY (ABERNATHY), Thomas and James Eburnathy, husbandman, of county of Armagh and Parish of Kilmore in Ireland, bros. of John Eburnethy, (innkeeper) of Charles Co. on 12 March 1734/5 convey to William and James Middleton, part of a larger tract called *His Lordship's Favour*, 349 acres. Ann Eburnethy, relict of dec'd. John, is now possessed of part of a tract called *Jordan*. (Land: O#2.90. See also pp. 105, 109, 112)

EBERNETHY (EBURNATHY), Anne (widow). To grandson Peter White, son of testatrix dau. ———, to Sarah wife of Mr. Francis Ware, to Mary Manarel, wife of John, to Susannah, Sarah and Elizabeth daus. of Francis Ware, Francis, Sarah and Mary Brown, daus. of Dr. Brown, to James Adams and Jno. Neale, personalty. To grandson Thomas Ryan and J. Doncastle. Exs.: Francis Ware and Jno. Doncastle. (Will: 22.455; 23 Dec 1737; 31 March 1742) Next of kin: "no kin at age." Admr./Exs.: Francis Ware, John Doncastle. (Inv.: 27.191; 11 Sept 1742; 11 Oct 1742)

EDELEN (EDLEN), Richard. In his will he mentions sons Richard, Edward, Christopher and Thomas; and dau. Catharine. (St. Mary's Co. Will: 7.84; 5 March 1694; 31 July 1694) (Inv.: 13B.55; 10 Dec 1696; ————) Ex.: Richard Edlen (son). (Acct: 14.63; ————; 30 Sept 1696) Ex.: Richard Edlen (son) of Chas. Co. (Acct: 14.144; ————; 14 May 1697)

EDELEN, Richard, age 50. Petition of Richard Edelen on behalf of John Parnham of Virginia, 12 xber 1719, regarding tract called *Salisbury*. (Chas LandComm: M2.77)

EDELEN, Thomas, age 48. Deposition, 6 Dec 1720, regarding tract called *Friendship*. (Chas LandComm: M2.107)

EDELEN, Richard (Gent.) and Sarah his wife on 13 Nov 1722 conveyed part of a tract called *Westwood Manor*. (Land: L#2.54)

EDELIN, Richard Sr. To his sister in law, Mrs. Elizabeth Neale, wife of James Neale Sr., four Negroes: Judith, Natt, Dick and Frank; their increase to be divided between the two young. sons and the two young. daus. of above sd. James Neale Sr. Signed 2 April 1725. (Land: L#2.212)

EDELIN, Richard (planter) and wife Sarah on 11 Nov 1727 conveyed part of tract called *Assentons*, lying on e. side of Zachia Swamp. (Land: L#2.391)

EDELEN, Richard conveyed on 27 Oct 1735 to his son in law, Benjamin Neale, tract called *Lawrells Branch*, 192 acres. (Land: O#2.140)

EDELEN, Richard, and his wife Ann conveyed on 27 Nov 1735 part of a tract called *St. Thomas'*, 218 acres. (Land: O#2.132)

EDGAR, Richard and Joanna. Their children: William, born 24 June 1693; John (third son) born 30 Aug 1699; Sarah and Elizabeth, twin daus., born 28 Oct 1706. (Ct.&Land: QRev.19, 26)

EDGE, Thomas, age 17-18 yrs. Servant of Zachary Wade, 10 March 1673. (Ct.&Land: E#1.153)

EDWARDS, John, age 12 yrs. Servant of Margarett Mack Cormack [McCormick], 13 March 1676. (Ct.&Land: G#1.16)

EDWARDS, Katherine. Next of kin: Elinor Mackeny. (Inv.: 10.398; 19 March 1724; 26 June 1725)

EDWARDS, John. Next of kin: Joseph Allen, Ann Eburnathy. Admr.: Randolph Morris. (Inv.: 20.36; 3 May 1734; 16 Nov 1734)

EDZARD, Esdras Theodore (Rev.). Creditors: Barton Waring, William Warder. Admr.: John Phillpott. (Inv.: 20.310; 5 Dec 1734; 1 Feb 1734)

EGLIN, Richard, son of Richard Eglin. Cattle mark recorded 28 June 1689. (Ct.&Land: P#1.36)

ELDER, John. In his will he left to goddau. Mary Sanders, dau. of John Sanders, of Mattawoman, entire estate; mentions her eld. sister, Sarah Sanders, Ex.: John Sanders afsd. (Will: 13.511; 13 June 1713; 20 June 1713) Ex.: John Sanders. (Acct: 35A.359; ----; 7 May 1714)

ELERY (ELLERY), James. In his will he left to son in law John Gates, personalty at age of 18. Shd. sd. John Gates demand any dues by being bound to Wm. Godah by the justices of Chas. Co. court, sd. legacy to revert to dau. Elizabeth To Wm. Coe, personalty. Dau. Elizabeth residuary legatee. Robert Yates, ex. (Will: 18.446; 20 Feb 1725/6; 5 March 1725) Ex.: Robert Yates. (Inv.: 11.427; 1726; 3 Aug 1726)

ELLIOTT, William, son of William and Joan Elliott, of head of Wicomico River, born 10 Aug 1682. (Ct.&Land: QRev.9)

ELLIOTT, William. To son William and to Susannah Judd, personalty. To wife Joane, extx., residue of estate. (Will: 13.505; 15 April 1713; 25 May 1713) Extx.: Jone Elliot. (Acct: 34.41; ----; 25 Sept 1713)

ELLIOTT, William. Next of kin: Thomas Martin (father-in-law), Joane Martin (natural ?). Admr.: William Stone Sr. (Inv.: 6.225; 16 Aug 1721; ----)

ELLIS, Hugh, age 13 yrs. Servant of Francis Goodricke, 12 Jan 1674. (Ct.&Land: F#1.41)

ELLIS, John. Next of kin: William Throne, Richard Suite. Admr.: John Higton. (Inv.: 10, 364; ----; 30 April 1725)

ELLISON, John, age 16 yrs. Servant of Samuel Cressey, 11 Jan 1675. (Ct.&Land: F#1.163)

ELLITT, William and Ann his wife conveyed on 8 Aug 1717 part of a tract patented for 300 acres at head of Nanjemy Ck., 42 acres. (Ct.&Land: H#2.114)

ELLIXSON, Haines. Next of kin: Henry Ward, Robert Covart. Admr.: Margaret Hyde, wife of Joseph Hyde. (Inv.: 15.554; 27 Nov 1729; 4 July 1730)

ELLSON, Anne (spinster) of St. Mary's Co. Indenture, 25 Dec 1706, to John Briscoe of St. Mary's Co. Anne apprentices to age 21 her only son, Nicholas Ellson, age 3 years and 9 months, as a servant to Briscoe, one of the Justices of St. Mary's Co. (Ct.&Land: (C#2.79)

EMANSON, Nicholas and Elizabeth Emanson alias Beake. Charged with having children by Nicholas Emanson and he now disclaiming to be her husband. 1670. Portobacco, Charles Co. (Arch. of Md.: LVII.616)

EMANSON, Nicholas. Mentions dau. Phebe, wife Eliza: and dau. Mary Emanson [minor], residue of estate. (Will: 1.415; 20 March 1670; 8 Sept 1671)

EMANSON, Elizabeth, late husband of Nicholas Emanson. Indenture 13 June 1671; land *Glover's Point*, in Nangemy Ck., 200 acres. (Ct.&Land: E#1.45)

EMERSON, Anthoni, age 17 yrs. Presented by Thomas Gibson, 10 Jan 1664. (Ct.&Land: B#1.397)

EMERSON, William, son of Nicholas Emerson, born 17 Nov 1666. (Ct.&Land: C#1.222; P#1.204; QRev.2)

EMMETT, John. In his will he left to brother Abraham, personalty. Wife Hannah, ex., dwelling plantation on Eastern Branch in New Scotland. (Will: 6.133; 13 April 1695; 21 July 1698)

EMPSON, William, age ca. 28 yrs. Swore in court, 23 Nov 1658. (Ct.&Land: A#1.31)

EMPSON, Elenor, late wife of William Empson, dec'd.. sold to Richard Dod, cattle for nursing and keeping Mary Empson, dau. of William Empson. Mary was taken in by Thomas Baker to raise. Also from said Thomas Baker (planter); an indenture dated 23 April 1660, to Wm: Empson; parcel of land on Baker's Creek. (Ct.&Land: A#1.145-146)

EMPSON, Elinor, now Elinor Morris, age ca. 26 yrs., 4 March 1661 (Ct.&Land: A#1.195)

EMPSON, Elinor, now Elinor Morris, wife of John Morris. Richard Watson requests attachment for debt in court dated 22 April 1662. (Ct.&Land: A#1.210)

ENIBURSON, Christopher, age 16 yrs. Servant of Capt. James Neale (Neile), 2nd Tues in April 1669. (Ct.&Land: D#1.62)

ENIBURSON, Derick, age 14 yrs. Servant of Capt. James Neale (Neile), 2nd Tues in April 1669. (Ct.&Land: D#1.62)

ENNIS. (See INNIS.)

ENSEY, Winifrit, dau. of John Ensey. Cattle mark recorded 11 Feb 1722. (Land: L#2.72)

ENSEY, John. Next of kin: William Coomes, William Ensey. Admr.: Catherine Ensey. (Inv.: 18.145; 2 May 1734; 5 June 1734)

ENSEY, (Elisabeth) Catherine, spinster. Mentions son Dennis; dau. Mary; child of dau. Margaret; four grand-children born of dau. Winifred, one of dau. Margaret, and dau. of son John. Son Dennis to live with William Coomes until 21 years; dau. Mary to the care of her sister Winnifred. Exs.: William Coomes and William Mookatee. (Will: 21.549; 4 Jan 1735/6; 5 May 1736) Next of kin: John Ensey, Margaret Mackaley. Exs.: William Ceecubes (Coomes), William Maggatee (Mookatee). (Inv.: 21.434; 3 June 1736; 2 Aug 1736)

ESKRIDGE, Col. George (planter), late of Westmoreland Co., Virginia. 19 Jan 1737/8. His children and devisees: William Eskridge, Samuel Eskridge, Robert Eskridge, Willoughby Newton and Sarah his wife, Hawson Kenner and Margret his wife, William Aylet and Elizabeth his wife. To John Lewellin of St. Mary's Co., a tract called *Westwood* and a tract called *Bastford manor* in St. Mary's Co. (Land: O#2.362)

ETTYE/ETY. (See EADY, EATIE.)

EURE, Christopher, age 19 yrs. Servant of William Marshall, 12 June 1668. (Ct.&Land: D#1.42)

EVANS, Roger. Bones of a dead man adjudged to be Roger Evans, servant of Thomas Baker, 24 Sept 1661. (Ct.&Land: A#1.149)

EVANS, John. (Inv.: 5.6; 3 May 1677; ----)

EVANS, Edward (planter) and his wife Elizabeth, of St. Mary's Co., conveyed on 10 May 1686, a parcel called *Lower Poole*, cont. 250 acres. (Ct.&Land: N#1.28)

EVANS, Joanne. Indicted for having a bastard child, living at Ralph Lomax, 13 March 1710. (Ct.&Land: D#2.136)

EVANS, Edward. (Inv.: 39C.78; 2 Nov 1717; ----) Admr.: Mary Posey. (Acct: 39C.94; ----; 17 Feb 1717)

EVANS, Henry. Mentions: Francis Ware. Admr.: Henry Barnes. (Inv.: 11.347; 20 March 1726; 4 June 1726)

EVANS, Stephen. On 9th of May 1741, James Muncaster took oath that he heard Stephen Evans declare that he willed Joseph Hanson Harrison to be his sole ex. This was verified under oath on June 30th by Richard Harrison. (Will: 22.377; ----; ----)

EVANS, Rowland. He left to wife Ann, extx. and children, viz.: John, Ann, Mary and Sarah, entire estate. (Will: 22.378; 15 April 1741; 15 July 1741)

EVANS, Sarah (Mrs.). Admr./Ex.: Joseph Hanson Harrison. (Inv.: 26.374; 27 Aug 1741; 17 Oct 1741),

EVERAD, Francis. At the house of Ralph Bartton. (Inv.: 8.422; 22 April 1685; ----)

EYRES. (See AYRES.)

FAIRFAX, John and Mary his wife on 14 March 1720 conveyed a parcel called *Scotts Folly* in Baltimore County. (Ct.&Land: H#2.420)

FAIRFAX (Farfax), John, planter. He left to daus. Catarn, Elizabeth, Mary and Anne and son William, estate. Son William to live with James Latemere until 18, and dau. Anne until 16 yrs. of age. Ex.: John Phillpot. (Will: 21.519; 28 Dec 1735; 13 Jan 1735) Next of kin: Catorn Farfax, Mary Fairfax. Ex.: John Philpot. (Inv.: 22.74; 16 Jan 1735; 12 Oct 1736)

FANNING, Benoni (planter) and Hannah his wife on 4 Oct 1674 conveyed land at City of St. Mary's, 500 acres. (Ct.&Land: Z#1.153)

FANNING, John. Three children: James, Elizabeth, and Mary; Thomas Willson recorded this entry 13 Sept 1681. (Ct.&Land: I#1.170)

FANING, John. Deed of gift, 1 April 1681, to Randll. Brandt, to son John Faning and daus. Elizabeth Faning and Mary Faning. (Ct.&Land: I#1.115)

FANNING, Benoni. Indenture 9 March 1702, to Elizabeth Etie, wife of Nathan Etie (planter). James Walker willed the land to Alice his relict on 31 Oct 1673; Alice married John Fanning; their only son Benoni then possessed the land, who conveyed the land to his sister Elizabeth, wife of Nathaniell Etie, then to Elizabeth's dau., Mary Etie. (Ct.&Land: Z#1.35)

FANING (FANNING), John. To child. of James and Alice Walker, land. To son Benonie at 18 yrs. of age, 350 acres, part of a tract in Balto. Co. To daus. Eliza: and Mary at 16 yrs. of age, residue of sd. tract. To wife Jane, extx., 100 acres, *Faning's Venture*; 60 acres *Ocbridge*, and 200 acres *Mole's Venture*. (Will: 4:98; 9 Dec 1684; 16 April 1685) (Inv.: 8.329; 12 May 1685; ----) Extx.: Jane Faning. (Acct: 9.133; ----; 4 Aug 1686) Extx.: Jane Whitchaly, wife of Thomas Whitchaly. (Acct: 9.448; ----; 29 Sept 1687)

FANING (FANNING), Benony. (Inv.: 34.40; 11 May 1713; ----) Admr.: Hanna Fanning. (Acct: 35A.194; ----; 10 April 1714)

FANNING, John (cordwainer), of St. Mary's Co., and his wife Mary on 8 Oct 1737 conveyed a tract called *Dockers Delight*, lying in William and Mary's Parish 150 acres. (Land: O#2.301)

FARDINANDO. (See FARNANDIS.)

FARFAX (See FAIRFAX).

FARLOWE (FARLOE), William, son of Ambros Farlowe, born 15 Feb 1671. (Ct.&Land: E#1.166; P#1.205; QRev.4)

FARLUN (FARLUM, FARLOE), Patrick (nunc.). Charles Casey of Chas. Co., sole legatee of estate. (Will: 5.56; 19 May 1676; 17 July 1676) (Inv.: 2.207; 12 Aug 1676; ----) Ex.: Thomas Casey. (Acct: 4.322; ----; [c1677])

FARMER, Rice, age 16 yrs. Servant of John Allen, 10 June 1673. (Ct.&Land: E#1.132)

FAARNANDEZ (FERNANDEZ), Pedro, age 17 yrs. Servant of Capt. James Neale, 2nd Tues in April 1669. (Ct.&Land: D#1.62)
FERNANDOS, Winefrett, dau. of Peter Fernandos. Cattle mark recorded 15 March 1681. (Ct.&Land: I#1.293)
FARNANDIS, Elizabeth, dau. of Peter Farnandis (cooper). Gift 24 Sept 1686, from Henry Branner, a cow. (Ct.&Land: M#1.194)
FORDINANDOE, Agatha, dau. of Peter and Elinor Fordinandoe of Portobacco, born 8 Nov 1694. (Ct.&Land: QRev.24)
FARDINANDO, Peter, age 67. Deposition in 1721 regarding tract called *Linsey*. (Chas LandComm: M2145)
FERNANDRIS, Peter Sr. (planter). In his will he left to grandchild Peter Jr., entire real estate. (Will: 21.664; 18 Jan 1733/4; 18 Aug 1736)

FARRAND, John and Mary Stonestreet, married 2 May 1743. (Trinity: 109)
FARRAND, Thomas, son of John and Mary Farrand, born 12 June 1744. (Trinity: 109)

FARROWS, James, 15 yrs. Servant of Richard Book, 1674. (Ct.&Land: F#1)
FARROW, James, age 15 yrs. Servant of John Ward, 10 June 1674. (Ct.&Land: E#1.171)

FARTHING, William Maria (Marcio) of St. Mary's Co. (innholder), and his wife Anne conveyed on 8 June 1720 a tract called *Farthings Discovery*, cont. 520 acres; located on n. side of the main branch of Indian Creek. (Ct.&Land: H#2.354) and on 5 June 1722 conveyed tract called *Farthings Penny Worth*, cont. 790 acres. (Land: L#2.39. See also L#2.69)

FEARSON. (See FERSON.)

FENCOKE, Ane. Servant, judged to be 18 yrs. old, presented by Richard Dod, 10 Feb 1662. (Ct.&Land: B#1.62)

FENDALL, Josias (Gent.) and Mary his wife, on 28 April 1683, conveyed 14000 acres on Wicomico River. (Ct.&Land: K#1.170)
FENDALL, John and Elizabeth his wife, conveyed on 4 Feb 1718, part of a tract on n. side of Piscataway River called *St. Johns*, cont. 800 acres. (Ct.&Land: H#2.236)

FENDALL, John, age 46. Deposition, 24 Sep 1719, regarding the tract *Baynes*; made remarks regarding land conveyed to Walter Bayne, now in the possession of Philemon Hemlsey by right of his wife Mary. (Chas LandComm: M2.53)

FENDALL, John (Gent.) and his wife Elizabeth, formerly the wife of William Marshall, dec'd. Deed dated 3 May 1728. To William Marshall of Prince George's Co. (Gent.), son and devisee of sd. William Marshall. William Marshall by his wife dated 2 Nov 1697, bequeathed to afsd. Elizabeth his then wife land called *Piscattaway*, commonly called *Paquescoe*, and 100 acres after her decease, to his son, the afsd. William Marshall. To prevent any controversy, an agreed division line was drawn. [In the subsequent deed the same as above was acknowledged by William Marshall and his wife Rebecca.] (Land: L#2.413, 415)

FENDALL, John (Gent.) and his wife Elizabeth. Deed dated 22 Nov 1729, to his son Benjamin Fendall; a tract of land. Deed dated 26 Feb 1729/30, to Samuel Hanson (son of Robert Hanson), and Mary his wife, dau. of sd. John Fendall; tract lying on n. side of Piscattaway River called *Saint Johns*. (Land: M#2.185, 192)

FENDALL, John, Col. and his wife Elizabeth on 28 July 1732 conveyed land called *Little Worth*, cont. 112 acres. (Land: M#2.292)

FENDALL, John. To his granddau., Elizabeth Hanson, dau. of Samuel and Mary Hanson, a Negro girl named Pegg, to be delivered at age 16 or date of marriage. Deed of gift dated 30 July 1733. (Land: M#2.351)

FENDAL(L), John, Col. Mentions wife Elizabeth; daus. Elizabeth Beall and Mary Hanson; sister Mary Barnes and son in law Richard Marshall. To grandson John, lands on w. side of Wiccocomico R. (after decease of his father Benjamin). To son Benjamin, residue of estate. Exs.: Wife and son Benjamin. (Will: 21.219; 25 Sept 1734; 28 Oct 1734) Next of kin: S. Hanson, Richard Marshall, William Theobalds. Ex.: Benjamin Fendall, surviving executor. (Inv.: 20.361; 5 Feb 1734; 9 April 1735) Admr./Ex.: Mr. Benjamin Fendall. (Inv.: 23.234; ---- 1737; 3 Aug 1738)

FENDAL(L), Elisabeth, Madam. Next of kin: Benjamin Fendall, Richard Marshall. Admr.: Thomas Marshall. (Inv.: 20.438; ----; 26 May 1735) Next of kin: Benjamin Fendall, Richard Marshall. Admr.: Thomas Marshall. (Inv.: 22.75; ----; 21 Oct 1736)

FENDALL, Benjamin, with release of dower of his wife Ellen on 6 April 1745 formed a partnership with Robert Yates, to build and maintain a water mill across the Fresh Run of Allens Fresh. (Land: Z#2.46)

FENNELL, Mary. Gives her son Joseph Fennell, to serve as apprentice to Leonard Wheeler, 17 May 1721. (Ct.&Land: H#2.452)

FENNER, Thomas, age 19 yrs. Servant of Samuel Eaten, 11 Jan 1669/70. (Ct.&Land: D#1.117)

FERNANDEX/FERNANDRIS. (See FARNANDIS.)

FERNLY, Ann (widow). Signed 31 March 1743. To her son and dau., Thomas Fectrer and Mary Crown, goods and chattels. (Land: X#2.118)

FERRALL (FERRILL), Mat(t)hew. In his will he left to wife Fran., ex., entire estate. (Will: 14.508; 12 Feb 1717/8; 29 March 1717) (Inv.: 1.69; 12 Feb 1717; ----)

FERRALL (FERRIL), John. Mentions: John Parnham, James Gow. Admr.: Ann Brittain, wife of Thomas Brittain. (Inv.: 23.452; ----; 3 Oct 1738)

FEARSON, John. In his will he left to son Samuel at age, 100 acres in St. Mary's Co. To son Perry at age, 150 acres. Wife Grace, ex. (Will: 4.23; 22 July 1683; 9 Oct 1683)

FERSON, Samuel. Next of kin: Perseful Ferson, Grace Snowman. Admr.: Jane Ferson. (Inv.: 11.428; 16 March 1725; 5 Aug 1726)

FERSON, Percy. In his will he left to three child. Eliza., Sarah and Sophia, exs., personal estate equally. To dau. Elizabeth, residue of lease. Overseer: Raphael Neale. (Will: 19.126; 20 Jan 1726; 18 April 1727) Next of kin: Elisabeth Newman, "minors." Ex.: Elisabeth Ferson. (Inv.: 12.118; 30 April 1727; 4 July 1727)

FIELD, Enoch. In his will he left to John Cooche, ex., right in certain land assigned by George Bradshaw. To Jane, dau. of Capt. Josias Fendall, 250 acres at Piscataway. (Will: 5.122; 26 Nov 1675; 15 Dec 1675)

FIELD, Charles, age 20 yrs. Servant of Maj. William Boareman, 10 Aug 1680. (Ct.&Land: H#1.330)

FINLEY, James. In his will he left to godson James Hickson, 1/2 of estate. Residue to school in Parish. Exs.: Vestry of Parish afsd. (Will: 6.342; ----; 23 Dec 1699) (Inv.: 20.136; 20 Jan 1699; ----) Legatees: Temperance Clouder. Admr.: Francis Harrison. (Acct: 20.266; ----; 21 May [c1701])

FIRE, Ralph, age 20 yrs. Servant (bound to age 21) of Thomas Taylor, 11 March 1678. (Ct.&Land: H#1.130)

FISH, Elinor, age 3 yrs. (bound to age 21) Servant of Seabright Maycocke, 1674. (Ct.&Land: F#1)

FISHER, Elisabeth, age 16 yrs. Servant of James Smallwood, 12 June 1676. (Ct.&Land: G#1.37)

FITZGERRALD (FITZGERRETT), Edward. (Inv.: 19.39; 11 May 1699; ----) Admr.: Randolph Brandt. (Acct: 19½A.115; ----; 11 Aug 1699)

FITZGERALD, Morrice, son of Morrice Fitzgerald. Cattle mark for cattle given by Daniel Delozer, 17 Oct 1709. (Ct.&Land: (C#2.148)
FITZGARRALD (FITGARELL), Morris. Next of kin: only young children (unnamed). (Inv.: 33A.41; 22 Sept 1711; ----) Admr.: Rachell Smith, wife of William Smith. (Acct: 33A.189; ----; 5 May 1712)
FITZGERRALD, Morris, and Elizabeth his wife on 23 Sept 1734 conveyed 90 acres, a tract called *Morrises Discovery*, 100 acres. (Land: O#2.82)

FLETCHER, Henry. In his will he left to brother Capt. Henry Aspinall and sister Mary Aspinall, John Busby, Thomas Allcox, and Eliza: Arcelis, personalty. David Towell and Robert Wheeler, exs. (Will: 5.138; 9 Dec 1676; 15 Jan 1676) (Inv.: 3.72; 18 Jan 1676; ----)

FORBIS, William. Servant to William Dent, judged to be age 17 yrs. old, betw. June-Aug 1694. (Ct.&Land: S#1.319)

FORD(E), Edward. In his will he left to wife Eliza: *Dog's Point* and 200 acres. To son Edward sd. *Dog's Point* at death of wife afsd. To unborn child, land. To brother Charles, 200 acres. (Will: 2.246; 16 Jan 1693; 19 Jan 1693) (Inv.: 13A.114; 11 April 1694; ----) Ex.: (unnamed relict), wife of Thomas Whicheley. (Acct: 10.416; ----; [c1695])
FORD, Edward of Chingamuxon, died 6 Jan 1693. (Ct.&Land: QRev.22)
FORD, Posthuma, dau. of Edward and Elizabeth Ford of Chingamuxon, born 29 July 1694. (Ct.&Land: QRev.25)
FORD(E), Christopher. (Inv.: 29.205; 12 March 1708; ----) Admr.: Temperance Ford. (Acct: 32C.115; ----; 27 April 1711)
FORD, Edward (cordwinder) and his wife Elizabeth conveyed on 6 Feb 1710, to William Bladen, London, now of Annapolis, tract called *Christian Temple Manor* in Mattawoman, cont. 1000 acres. (Ct.&Land: C#2.216)

FORDINANDOE. (See FARNANDIS.)

FORSTER, William and Dorothy his wife, extx. of Michaell Minoake, conveyed on 26 Dec 1695 a parcel called *St. Edmonds* at the head of Portobacco Creek, 150 acres, lately in tenure of Michaell Minoake, dec'd., given to his wife Dorothy by his last will. (Ct.&Land: Q#1.74)
FOSTER, Leonard, age 12 yrs. Servant of William Smith, 11 June 1678. (Ct.&Land: G#1.157)
FORSTER, William, gent. In his will he left wife Ann, extx., 150 acres, *St. Edmonds*. (Will: 14.334; 17 April 1717; 25 May 1717) (Inv.: 39C.68; 24 June 1717; ----)
FORSTER (FOESTER), Ann, widow. She left to son John Ashman and to dau. Mary, wife of Richard Ankrum, 150 acres, *St. Edmonds*, lying at Portobacco. Mentions son Richard Ashman; granddau. Ann Ollover; James Penny; children of Mary Ankrum. Testator's three sons, John and

Rich: Ashman and Rich: Ankrum, are exs. Whatever is due to Henry
Hardy, a legatee under will of her former husband, Henry Hardy, shall
remain in hands of her son Rich: Ashman till sent for. (Will: 14.424; 10 Oct
1717; 13 Dec 1717) (Inv.: 39A.37; 2 Jan 1717; ----)

FOWKE, Gerard. Court held 22 April 1662, about to marry, Anne, widow of
Job Chandler. (Ct.&Land: A#1.217)

FOWKE, Richard, having married the widow of Humphrey Haggett. 1663.
(Arch. of Md.: XLIX.165)

FOULKE (FOUCKES), Richard. John Meekes demands warrant against
Richard Fouke, the husband of Anne Haggat, the relict and admx. of
Humphery Haggat, 8 March 1663/4. (Ct.&Land: B#1.280, 306)

FOWKE, Ann. Deed of gift 2 Oct 1672, to her son Richard Chandler, (hogs
and cattle on *Goose Creek* plantation); and on 11 March 1672 to her
three child.: Gerrard Fowke, Maryland Fowke and Eliza: Fowke, ten head
of cattle. (Ct.&Land: E#1.101)

FOULKE (FOUKE), Richard. (Inv.: 5.154; 23 Oct 1677;----) Distribution to:
orphans (unnamed). Admr.: Mary Warde. Her now husband is William
Ward. The deceased is her bro. in law. Estate is unadministered by
George Credwell (alias George Grodtwell) whose widow is administratrix.
(Acct: 5.322; ----; 10 Sept 1678) Admix.: Mary Ward. (Inv.: 6.615; ----;
11 Nov 1679)

FOUKES, Roger. Admr./Ex.: Col. William Chandler. (Acct: 7C.219; ----; 4
Aug 1682)

FOWKE, Hallilujah, age 15 yrs, and Richard (runaway), age 18 yrs., both
orphans of Richard Fowke. Both bound to Henry Hardye, to age 21, 8
June 1686. (Ct.&Land: M#1.220)

FOWKE, Gerrard of Portobacco, married Sarah Burdett, the youngest dau. of
Thomas Burdett (late of this county, decd:), 31 Dec 1686. Children of
Gerrard and Sarah Fowke of Nanjemy: Gerrard, born 16 Oct 1687; Anne,
born 30 Jan 1689; Frances, born 2 Feb 1691; Katherine, born 8 April
1694. (Ct.&Land: QRev.12, 13, 15, 17, 23)

FOWKE, Gerrard, and his wife Sarah on 18 Dec 1725 conveyed to their son,
Roger Fowke; pt. of tract called *Burditts Rest*, 329 acres; also pt. of
tract called *Birds Nest*, 226 acres; both tracts lying nr. head of Burditts
Creek. (Land: L#2.248)

FOWKE, Roger. Next of kin: Gerard Fowke, Gustavus Brown. Admr.: Ann
Fowke. (Inv.: 13.39; 31 Jan 1727; 11 April 1728)

FOWKE, Anne, to her son Gerrard Fowke [Jr.], son of her husband, Roger
Fowke, dec'd, now living in Chas. Co., gives Negro boy named Billie.
Deed of gift recorded 22 Nov 1731. (Land: M#2.270)

FOWKE, Gerard (Gerrard). In his will he left to wife Sarah, ex., plantation,
being 500 acres of *Poynton Manor*. To son Chandler, plant. in Virginia
where he now lives. To dau. Frances, wife of Doctor Gustavus Brown, lot
at Nanjemy. To dau. Ann, wife of Robert Alexander, grandsons Gerard

and William Chandler, sons of son Chandler Fouke, and granddau. Jane, dau. of son Roger, personalty. To grandson Gerard, son of son Roger, 500 acres. Also *Boughton's Disappointment*, Burdetts Creek. Residue of estate to wife Sarah. (Will: 21.269; 6 Aug 1734; 20 Jan 1734) Next of kin: Robert Alexander, Gukstavus Brown. Ex.: Sarah Fowke. (Inv.: 21.92; ----; 16 Oct 1735)

FOWLER, William, age 14 yrs. Servant of William Boarman, Jr., 8 Jan 1677. (Ct.&Land: G#1.85)

FOWTRELL (FOWKELL?) George, age 22-23 yrs. Servant of Richard Edelen, 1676. (Ct.&Land: F#1.173)

FOX, Edward. (Inv. & Acct.: 4.6; ----; 20 March 1676)

FRANCAM. (See FRANCUM.)

FRANCIS, John, age 21 yrs. Servant of Alexander Smith, 14 June 1681. (Ct.&Land: I#1.124)
FRANCIS, John. (Inv.: 10.200; 30 Dec 1688; ----)

FRANCISSON, Francis, age 10 yrs. Servant of Benjamin Rozer, 2nd Tues in April 1669. (Ct.&Land: D#1.62)

FRANCKLIN, Henry, son of Henry Francklin, Charles Co. chooses for his guardian his brother in law, Richard Williams of the same county. 1683. (Arch. of Md.: LXX.457)
FRANCKLIN, Henry and Mary, of Wicomico. Their children: Mary, born 12 Oct 1689; Jane, born 31 Jan 1692. (Ct.&Land: P#1.212; QRev.15, 19)
FRANKLIN, John, age 47. Deposition, 20 Aug 1719, regarding tract called *Saint Davids*. (Chas LandComm: M2.50)

FRANCUM, Amey, widow and admx. of Henry Francum. Deed of gift 22 March 1668/9; gives stock to her children, Henry Francum and Elizabeth Francum. (Ct.&Land: D#1.56)
FRANCKUM, Francis, age 16 yrs. Servant of William Barton, 11 April 1676. (Ct.&Land: F#1.173)
FRANKAM (FRANCUM), Henry. Admr.: Annah Maddock, wife of Edward Maddock. (Inv.: 5.285; ----; 27 Sept 1678) Admr.: Anne Maddock (relict), wife of Edward Maddock. (Acct: 7C.95; ----; 30 May 1692)
FRANCKUM, Henry, orphan son of Henry Franckum, dec'd. To remain with his father in law Edward Maddock, dated 14 Nov 1682. (Ct.&Land: K#1.32)
FRANKAM, Henry (planter), father of Henry Frankam, conveyed on 11 June 1688, land located above Nangemy. (Ct.&Land: P#1.174)

FRANCKUM, Henry, son of Henry, dec'd. Petition against Col. Wm. Diggs, exr. of his father's estate, 9 June 1691. (Ct.&Land: Q#1.31)

FRANKBURN, Henry. (Inv.: 3.277; 19 Feb 1719; ----)

FRAWNER, Edward. (Inv.: 13A.141; 30 July 1694; ----)

FRAWNES, Ellinor. Indicted for having a bastard child, 13 March 1710. (Ct.&Land: D#2.136)

FRAZER, John and Anne his wife. Bind themselves to Col. James Smallwood, Gent. for £500, 4 May 1710. Condition of obligation regarding deed of gift from James Smallwood and Mary his wife to John Frazer and Anne his wife and Mary dau. of John and Anne. Parcel in Prince George's Co., part of *Rolen Plaine*, cont. 100 acres. (Ct.&Land: C#2.205)

FRAZIER, Owen. Next of kin: Mary Bird. Admr.: Jane George (surviving admr.). (Inv.: 27.390; 11 Jan 1742; 20 April 1743)

FREETE, Teague, age 13 yrs. Servant of John Courte, 13 March 1682. (Ct.&Land: K#1.124)

FREMAN, Nathaniell. Next of kin: Thomas Morris. (Inv.: 1.60; 18 Dec 1717; ----)

FREEMAN, Anne, widow of Nathaniel Freeman. Deed of gift, 19 Feb 1721, to John Wilder, all her goods and chattels who will provide for the two children of Anne and Nathaniel Freeman: James Freeman and Anne Freeman, wife of Thomas Hanson. (Ct.&Land: H#2.478)

FRISSEL(L), Thomas and his wife Hannah Glossington. Court dated 23 Nov 1658; both servants of Simon Oversee. (Ct.&Land: A#1.33)

FRYE, John. Admr.: Constance Frye. (Inv.: 19½B.39; ----; 20 Oct 1699)

FURNIS, Francis (a cooper) and his wife Mary conveyed on 11 Jan 1674 a parcel called *Colchester*, cont. 200 acres. (Ct.&Land: F#1.49)

FURTH, Joseph, age 17 yrs. Servant boy presented by John Clarke, 8 March 1663/4. (Ct.&Land: B#1.258)

GABRIELL, Bartholome, age ca. 28 yrs. Swore in open court 12 May 1659. (Ct.&Land: A#1.56)

GALEY, Lorance, age 14 yrs. Servant of Capt. James Neale, 8 June 1675. (Ct.&Land: F#1.101)

GAILY, Thomas. To Thomas Lieuger, 300 acres, *Hardshift*, at mouth of Nanjemy, and 100 acres, part of *Gaily's Discovery*. To Eliza: Midgely, personalty. To John Wright, ex., 100 acres, part of *Gaily's Discovery*. (Will: 5.206; 25 Nov 1676; 9 March 1676/7)

GAILE, Edward. To each priest in the county and to Thomas Gavin, personalty. Wife Ruth, extx. (Will: 4.160; ----; 1 Feb 1685)

GALBREATH, George. Admr.: Daniell McDaniell. (Inv.: 21.284; ----; 21 April 1736)

GALWITH, James (planter). Mentions daus. Mary, Elizabeth, Sarah and Tamer, and son Jonas. (Will: 20.164; 8 March 1730/1; 21 April 1731) Next of kin: Thomas Lawson, James Davies, John Galwith. Ex.: William Lawson. (Inv.: 16.319; 24 April 1731; 9 Nov 1731)

GALWITH, John and wife Elizabeth. Lease dated 7 June 1739, tract called *Hills and Dales*, being part of *his Lordships Manor of Calvert*, 180 acres, during the life time of Elizabeth Galwith, wife of sd. John Galwith, John Galwith and Ignatius Galwith, sons of sd. John Galwith. (Land: O#2.346C.)

GAMBILL, William. Admr.: Mary Holland, wife of Richard Holland (or Richard Pollard). (Acct: 9.473; ----; 2 April 1688)

GAMBELL, William. (Inv.: 37B.86; 15 June 1717; ----)

A'GAMBRA, Richard, admr. of Domindigue A'Gambra. An account, 9 June 1691. (Ct.&Land: Q#1.34)

GAMBRA, Domingo (Dominoigo). (Inv.: 10.233; 8 Feb 1688; ----) Admr.: Richard Gambra. (Inv.: 10.242; ----; [c1689]) (Inv.: 22.96; 7 Dec 1702; 18 Jan 1702) (Acct: 27.262)]

GAMBRA, Richard (planter), and his wife Elizabeth, on 14 March 1743 conveyed part of a tract called *Maiden Fair*, 400 acres. (Land: X#2.79)

GANDI, William, age 17 yrs. Servant presented by John Cage, 10 Feb 1662. (Ct.&Land: B#1.61)

GANT(T), Thomas (Gent.), Prince George's Co., and his wife Magery, on 21 Aug 1738 conveyed part of a tract called *The Maze*, cont. 249 acres. (Land: O#2.354)

GARDNER, Luke and his wife Elizabeth, acknowledged the Manor of St. Richards, 100 acres, to be the right of said Luke Barber. 23 Sept 1662. (Arch. of Md.: XLIX.33, 588)

GARDINER, John. A mulatto boy belonging to Richard Chandler, had a bay filly given him by Edmund Tayler, admr. of William Gardiner, dec'd., 13 Sept 1681. (Ct.&Land: I#1.170)

GARDINER, Edward, son of Hugh Gardiner. Cattle mark recorded 12 Feb 1690. (Ct.&Land: P#1.203)

GARDINER, Hugh. (Inv.: 13A.352; 24 May 1695; 26 June 1695) Mentions: one orphan (unnamed). Admr.: Henry Gifford. (Acct: 13B.9; ----; 15 May 1696)

GARDINER, Luke and Ann his wife of Prince George's Co. and William Godfrey and Jannet his wife. Indenture, 12 Nov 1717, to Anthony Collings; 100 acres part of a tract called *Partner's Content*, cont. 302 acres by patent; bounded by a branch of Chingamoxon Creek. Indenture, 12 Nov 1718, to Robert Covent of Westmoreland Co., Virginia; part of a tract called *Partner's Content*, cont. 272 acres. (Ct.&Land: H#2.155, 245)

GARDNER, Joseph. In his will he left to wife Elizabeth, extx., 100 acres lying on Dressing Branch, part of a tract of 300 acres. To sons Biningman and Samuel, 100 acres each of afsd. tract. To son Ralph, 54 acres on Dressing Branch. To son Luke, 100 acres afsd. at decease of wife. (Will: 14.611; 9 March 1717; 10 June 1718)

GARDINER, Joseph. (Inv.: 1.291; 7 Oct 1718; ----)

GARDNER, Bullat and Mary, son and dau. of Edward Gardner. Cattle mark recorded 9 Feb 1719. (Ct.&Land: H#2.313)

GARDINER, Ignatius, of Prince George's Co., son of Luke Gardiner, acquired on 5 June 1722 of Prince George's Co., tract called *Farthings Penny Worth*, cont. 790 acres. (Land: L#2.39)

GARDNER, Edward. Next of kin: Mary Latimar, James Latimar. Admr./Ex.: Mary Gardner. (Inv.: 10.12A; 19 May 1724; 28 May 1724)

GARDINER, Hugh (nunc.). To bros. Douglas Gifford Gardiner and Bullet, personalty. (Will: 19.729; 15 June 1729)

GARDNER, Benjamin. Next of kin: Thomas Owen, Michael Gardner. Admr.: Wife (unnamed) of William Beck. (Inv.: 20.315; 6 Jan 1734; 15 Feb 1734)

GARDNER, Joseph. Next of kin: Michael Garner, Samuell Garner. Admr.: Mary Gardner. (Inv.: 20.313; ----; 19 Feb 1734)

GARDNER (GARNER), Francis (planter), of Mattawoman. To wife Ann, extx. Mentions dau. Eliner [minor], dau. Annastasia. (Will: 21.539; 13 Feb 1735/6; 17 March 1735/6) Next of kin: John Garner, Joseph Garner. Extx.: Ann Gardner. (Inv.: 21.285; 15 April 1736; 21 April 1736)

GARDINER, Benjamin. Leased on 13 March 1739/40, 100 acres, called *Mount Pleasant* in Mattawoman Neck, for the lifetime of Benjamin Gardiner and his wife Eleanor. (Land: O#2.433)

GARDINER, Joseph (planter), and his wife Martha. Deed dated 11 June 1741; from John Sanders (planter), part of a tract cont. 100 acres, on the s. side of Colters Branch called *Wood Stock Bower*, bequeathed by the will of John Sanders to Martha Sanders, his dau., now wife of afsd. Joseph Gardiner, and a tract called *Williams Purchase*, lately conveyed by William Smallwood Taylor and his wife Mary to afsd. John Sanders, 195 acres. Deed dated 11 June 1741; to John Sanders, son of John Sanders. (Land: O #2.509, 514. See also Land: O#2.209.)

GARDINER (GARDNER), John Sr. To wife Constant, entire estate, at her death to be divided between children: John Jr., Benjamin, and Elizabeth, wife of Thomas Douglas. To son Joseph and dau. Ann, wife of John Wright of Nanjemy Parish, personalty. Exs.: Son Benjamin, Thomas Douglas. (Will: 22.526; -- July 1742; 16 Nov 1742) Next of kin: Benjamin Garner, John Garner. Ex.: Thomas Douglass. (Inv.: 27.298; 16 Dec 1742; 1 Feb 1742)

GARFORTH, Richard. (Inv.: 8.502; 20 Aug 1685; ----) (Inv.: 10.97; 23 Oct 1688; ----)

GARLAND, Randolph. To dau. Mary, granddau. Charity Smallwood, dau. Elizabeth Smallwood, grandchild. Ann, Mary, Henrietta and Lodstone Smallwood and grandson William Smallwood, personalty. To wife Ann, personalty, extx. with dau. Mary. Thomas Gant to be guardian to dau. Mary. (Will: 17.299; 27 Aug 1722; 27 Sept 1722)

GARRARD. (See Gerrard.)

GARRET, James, son of James, age 7 yrs (to serve until age 21) Servant of Thomas Clipsham, 8 June 1680. (Ct.&Land: H#1.299)

GARRETT, Charles, son of Charles and Joyce Garrett of head of Wicomico River, born 7 May 1684. (Ct.&Land: P#1.208; QRev.10)

GARRETT, Ann. Next of kin: "none capable of signing." Admr.: (name not given). (Inv.: 10. 393; 22 March 1724; 11 June 1725)

GARRET, John. Next of kin: John Waple, George Waple. Admrs.: James Lutwidge, John Barker. (Inv.: 11.918; 25 March 1727; 8 May 1727)

GARTHERELL, Bartholme, age ca. 27 yrs. Swore in court 10 July 1662. (Ct.&Land: A#1.236)

GARY, Jephari. Judged to be 13 yrs old, presented by George Thompson, 12 July 1664. (Ct.&Land: B#1.314)

GASKOYNE, Samuel, age 17 yrs. Servant of John Wheeler, 2nd Tues in June 1669. (Ct.&Land: D#1.88)

GATELEY, Edward, age 13 yrs. Servant of Thomas Harris, 11 March 1678. (Ct.&Land: H#1.129)

GATES, Robert. (Inv.: 17.26; 18 July 1698; ----)

GATES, John, age 39. Deposition, 1 March 1720, regarding tract called *Canterbury* (petition of Joseph Gates). (Chas LandComm: M2.116)

GATES, Robert. To eld. son Robert, 50 acres. Sons Joseph and Peter to care of bro. Joseph until 18 yrs. of age. Witnesses include Joseph Gates. (Will: 20.880; 16 Jan 1733/4; 4 Feb 1733)

GATES, Robert Sr. Next of kin: George Heeth, John Gates Jr. Admr.: Robert Gates. (Inv.: 17.715; 25 March 1734; 17 April 1734)

GATES, John (planter), and his wife Mary. Bill of sale March 1734/5. To John Parnham (merchant), 91 acres, part of the tract *The Loving Brothers*. (Land: O#2.95)

GATES, John. Deed dated 11 March 1740, to Philip Key (Gent.) of St. Mary's Co., part of a tract called the *Loving Brothers*, granted 10 Sept 1716 to John Gates and Robert Gates, his bro., dec'd. (Land: O#2.486. See also 226, 539, 588)

GATES, John, Prince George's Co. (carpenter) and his wife Elizabeth conveyed on 10 Nov 1742 part of a tract called *Loving Brothers*, formerly granted to John Gates, uncle to the same John, and Robert Gates, father of the present seller; Philip Key lately bought an adjoining part from Joseph Gates, bro. to the sd. John. (Land: O#2.588)

GATES, Joseph (planter), fourth son of Robert Gates, dec'd., conveyed on 18 Dec 1741, to Philip Key of St. Mary's Co. (merchant), part of a tract called the *Loving Brothers*, formerly granted to John Gates, uncle to sd. Joseph Gates and Robert Gates, father of sd. Joseph, which part hereby sold to sd. Philip adjoins to that part which sd. Philip lately purchased of sd. John Gates, containing on a survey for the dividing of the land between the six children of Robert Gates, one of the patentees, about 43 acres. (Land: O#2.539. See also O#2.589).

GAZEY, Jonathon. Legatees: executrix. Extx.: Martha Gazey (also Martha Goosey). (Acct: 11B.72; ----; 13 July 1701)

GEDDES, George. (Inv.: 9.62; 25 May 1721; ----)

GEE, John, age 27. Deposition on 8 Jan 1660. (Arch. of Md.: XLI.431)

GEE, John and Hen: MacDonall, married without a license by John Legatt, minister. Warrant, 1663. (Arch. of Md.: XLIX, p.42)

GEE, John, age 40. Deposition on 12 Oct 1665. (Arch. of Md.: XLIX.480)

GEER, James. Servant to Capt. William Barton, age judged to be 12 yrs. old, 26 April 1694. (Ct.&Land: S#1.284)

GENTS, Elisabeth. (Inv.: 8.427; 6 July 1685; ----)

GERMAN, George, age 21 yrs. Servant of William Barton, 11 Jan 1669/70. (Ct.&Land: D#1.117)

GERRARD, Daniell. Admr./Ex.: Samuel Cooksey. (Acct: 26.57; ----; 14 Sept 1706)

GARRARD, Jane of Cople Parish, Westmoreland Co., Virginia, conveyed on 20 Dec 1712, a tract first granted to Thomas Garrard, and from him to his son John Garrard, husband to Jane Garrard; tract called *Westwood Mannor*. (Ct.&Land: D#2.20)

GES, Ane, relict of Walter Ges, dec'd. Court held 28 Jan 1661, binds her dau. Mary Ges, as servant until 28 Jan 1667 (for six yrs.) to Thomas Baker; and her 3-yr. old son Lewis Ges, for 18 yrs., to Henry Addames. (Ct.&Land: A#1.185)

GES, Ane, age ca. 26 yrs. Swore in court 28 Jan 1661 and 4 March 1661. (Ct.&Land: A#1.178, 195)

GEY, Anne, age ca. 50 yrs. Swore in court 26 Jan 1658. (Ct.&Land: A#1.37)

GHOUGH, Jane, age 20 yrs. Servant of Wm: Harguess, 11 June 1678. (Ct.&Land: G#1.157)

GIBBENS, Thomas, age 14 yrs. Servant of William Barton Jr., 9 Feb 1685/6. (Ct.&Land: M#1.89)

GIBBS, John, age 19 yrs. Servant of Peter Carr, 2nd Tues in April 1669. (Ct.&Land: D#1.62)

GIBSON?, Dorothy, age 22 yrs. Servant of Benjamin Rozer, 1673. (Ct.&Land:-)
GIBSON, William, age 11 yrs. Servant of Henry Adams, 1680. (Ct.&Land H.242)
GIBSON, Thomas. To son Thomas, 300 acres, *Northwick*, Balto. Co. To dau. Eliza:, all land in Chas. Co. at marriage. To Katharine Hogan, personalty. Exs.: Geo. Newman, Jno. Gooch. Test: Hugh Gardiner, Mary Gardiner, Lidia Mannoth. (Will: 4.189; 7 Sept 1675; 30 Jan 1685) Exs.: George Newman, John Gooch. (Inv.: 9.35; 30 Jan 1683; 1 May 1686) Legatees: Francis Pollett paid to James Turner, Thomas Gibson Jr. (son). Ex.: George Newman. (Acct: 9.388; ----; 3 Aug 1687)
GIBSON, Thomas, son of Thomas and Elizabeth Gibson of Pickawaxon, born 30 May 1694. (Ct.&Land: QRev.23)
GIBSON, John. (Inv.: 3.281; 3 Feb 1703; ----)
GIBSON, John. Admr./Ex.: Mary King, wife of Robert King. (Acct: 25.146; ----; 13 June 1704)
GIBSON, John. Next of kin: John Shaw Sr., John Shaw Jr. Admr.: Raphael Neale. (Inv.: 10.368; 19 Feb 1724; 25 May 1725)

GIFFORD, Douglas. Cattle mark registered 22 March 1703/4 by his father, Henry Gifford. (Ct.&Land: Z#1.80)
GIFFORD, Henry. Next of kin: Joseph Douglasse, Benjamin Douglasse. (Inv.: 36B.214; 6 Dec 1714; ---)

GIFFORDE, Douglass. Mentions Howard Gardiner. To wife Roseaman, extx., dwelling plantation 59 acres, *Gibson's Neck*, and 115 acres, *Gibson Close*. (Will: 16.157; 23 May 1720; 6 Sept 1720)

GILBARD, James, age 21 yrs. Servant of Philip Lines, 10 June 1679. (Ct.&Land: H#1.134)

GILBERT, Jane, age 20 yrs. Servant of William Hatch, 9 March 1685/6. (Ct.&Land: M#1.90)

GILLCHRIST (GILGREST, GILLEAST, GILCHREST), Samuel (planter). To William Monrow, ex., entire estate. (Will: 20.878; 17 Oct 1733; 29 Jan 1733) Ex.: William Munroe. (Inv.: 20.37; 16 Feb 1733; 16 Nov 1734)

GILPIN (GILPING), Sylvanus. To wife of Thomas Warton, and Eliza: and John, children of sd. Thomas, personalty. Thomas Warton, ex. and residuary legatee of estate, including 150 acres. (Will: 10.78; 12 Sept 1679; 19 Nov 1679) Admr.: Thomas Wharton. (Inv.: 7C.200; 16 Oct 1680; ----) Admr.: Thomas Wharton. (Acct: 7C.201; ----; 1 Aug 1682)

GILPEN (GILPIN), Isaac (planter), Portobacco Parish. To son Edward, 100 acres of *Thompson's Town*. To son Thomas, 170 acres of afsd. tract after decease of wife Charity. To son Isaac, 140 acres, called *Pyes Chance*. To four child. Henry, William, Mary Ann and Jane, residue of estate. Exs.: Son Edward and Thomas. (Will: 20.41; 4 May 1730; 24 June 1730) (Inv.: 16.108; 18 Jan 1730; 27 Feb 1730) Next of kin: Charity Gilpin, Edward Gilpin. Ex.: Thomas Gilpin. (Inv.: 16.280; 1731; 15 Sept 1731)

GILPEN, Charity of Portobacco Parrish. Mentions son Edward, ex.; daus. Mary Ann and Jane when of age; sons Isaac, Thomas and William; sons Isaac and William of age at 18 yrs. To children, viz. Edward, Thomas, Henry, William, Isaac, Mary Ann and Jane, residue of estate. (Will: 20.374; 5 April 1732; 6 May 1732)

GILPIN, Isaac. Next of kin: William Gilpin, Thomas Gilpin. Admr.: Eleanor Gilpin. (Inv.: 24.473; ----; 7 March 1739)

GILPIN (GILPON), Edward (planter). To wife Elizabeth, extx., use of estate. To son Benjamin, 100-acre dwelling plantation, being pt. of *Thomson Town*, residue to other five children, viz.: Mary, Elizabeth, Edward, Jane and Charety. Test: Ralph Shaw Sr., Ralph Gwinn (Guinn). (Will: 22.66; 16 Jan 1738; 17 May 1739)

GINNEY, John, age 14 yrs. Servant of John Ward, 12 March 1672. (Ct.&Land: E#1.54)

GLASCOCK, James (innholder). To son James, two lots of land and 1/3 personal estate, providing he will come to receive them within 10 yrs. after testator's death. To Ann dau. of James Lukes, Joseph Barnes, William McPherson Jr., William Peach, Joseph Chrismond, Thomas Bretton, Nathaniel Noddor, personalty. To William Ansell and James Lukes, exs., residue of estate. (Will: 22.277; 11 Sept 1740; 15 Oct 1740) Admrs.: William Ausil (Ansell), Jane Lucas. (Inv.: 25.496; ----; 1 Aug 1741) Admrs.: Stephen Mankin, Edward Walker. (Inv.: 29.163; ----; 8 April 1744)

GLASE (See GLAZE).

GLASS, John. Next of kin: Elisabeth Glass. Administratrix: (name not given). (Inv.: 10.364; 18 Feb 1724; 17 May 1725)

GLAWSHEN (GLASHEN), James. Next of kin: John Phillbunt. Admr.: Elinor Glashen. (Inv.: 11.921; 4 March 1726; 20 May 1727)

GLAZE (GLASE), John. To sons John, Thomas, Joseph, Benjamin and Samuel, and daus. Mary, Margaret, and Elizabeth, personalty. Wife Sarah, extx. (Will: 22.23; 26 Dec 1738; 7 Feb 1738/9) Next of kin: Benjamin Glase. Extx.: Sarah Glase. (Inv.: 24.97; 26 April 1739; 8 May 1739)

GLOSSE, George. Binds his son John Glosse to Owen Jones until the age of 21 yrs, 8 Jan 1666/7. (Ct.&Land: C#1.112)

GLOVER, Mary, age 20 yrs. Servant of Thomas Hussy, 10 June 1679. (Ct.&Land: H#1.134)
GLOOVER (GLEEVES?) George, age 21 yrs. Servant of Capt. James Neale, 10 Aug 1680. (Ct.&Land: H#1.330)

GOADY (GODY), William. Next of kin: Samuel Gody, William Plunkett. Admr.: Matthew Gody. (Inv.: 27.300; ----; 6 Feb 1742)

GODFRY, George and his wife Mary. 1674. (Arch. of Md.: LXV.355)
GODFREY, Thomas, son of George and Mary Godfrey. Cattle mark recorded, 1680. (Ct.&Land: H#1.292)
GODFREY, William, son of George and Mary Godfrey. Cattle mark recorded, 1680. (Ct.&Land: H#1.292)
GODFREY, George, son of George Godfrey. Cattle mark recorded, 9 March 1680/1. (Ct.&Land: I#1.123)
GODFREY, Anne, dau. of George and Mary Godfrey. Deed of gift from Thomas Osborne (blacksmith), 12 Aug 1707. (Ct.&Land: C#2.64)
GODFREY, George. Indenture, 13 Nov 1707, to Francis Addams and his wife Mary (dau. of George Godfrey); parcel called *Troops Rendezvous*, cont. 100 acres. (Ct.&Land: C#2.89)
GODFREY, George and his wife Mary on 21 April 1713 conveyed a parcel called *Troop's Rendezvous*, cont. 150 acres. (Ct.&Land: D#2.50, 89)
GODFREY, William. (Inv.: 36C.189; 11 July 1715; ----)

GODFREY, Archibald, son of William Godfrey. Cattle mark, 24 March 1717. (Ct.&Land: H#2.152)

GODFREY, William, age 41. Deposition (at the request of Pryor Smallwood and John Woodyard), 22 Xber 1719, regarding the tract *Christian Temple Mannour*. (Chas LandComm: M2.68)

GODFREY, William, age 42. Deposition in 1721 regarding tract called *Wadestones Enlargement* in Durham Parish. (Chas LandComm: M2.130)

GODFREY, William, age 43. Deposition, 31 May 1721, regarding tract called *Christian Temple Manor*. (Chas LandComm: M2.123)

GODFREY, George. Next of kin: Francis Barnes, "no other kin of age." (Inv.: 8.61; 4 Jan 1722; ----)

GODFREY, George. To son George, ex., dwelling plantation. To dau. Ann personalty. To sons George and Stephen, residue of estate, son Stephen [minor]. Note: Adm. granted to Wm. Godfrey during minority of infant ex. (Will: 18.8; 13 Feb ----; 15 Aug 1722)

GODFREY (GODFRY), William (carpenter) and Jennet his wife and Luke Gardiner of Prince George's Co. and his wife Ann. Indenture, 12 Nov 1718, to Robert Covert of Westmoreland Co., Virginia; part of a tract called *Partner's Content*, cont. 272 acres. William Godfrey (house carpenter) and his wife Jennet, of Stafford Co., Virginia. Deed dated 11 Aug 1726; to Samuel Grey (planter); part of tract called *Partners Content*, cont. 272 acres. (Ct.&Land: H#2.245; Land: L#2.313)

GODFREY, William and his wife Jannet. Indenture, 28 Feb 1721 to Mary Godfrey, dau. of Francis Godfrey, dec'd., for love of his cousin Mary Godfrey; tract called *Raven's Denn*, cont. 140 acres. (Ct.&Land: H#2.484)

GODFREY (GODFRY), William, and Jennett his wife of Stafford Co., Virginia. Deed dated 28 Feb 1721; to Robert Covert (planter) and Christian his wife, 270 acres, being part of tract called *Partners Content*. Deed dated 4 April 1730; to Joshua Ratcliff (planter), part of a tract called *Mendment*, cont. 150 acres. (Land: L#2.41; M#2.232)

GODFREY, William (house carpenter) of Stafford Co., Virginia, and his wife Janet (Jennet). Jointly with Walter Winter (planter); deed dated 24 June 1727 and recorded 18 Nov 1728. To Thomas Millstead (planter), parcel of land called *Winters Employment*, 264 acres. (Land L#2.448)

GODFREY, William, of Stafford Co., Virginia, and his wife Jennet (Janet). Deed Dated 24 June 1728. To Thomas Davis, tract called *The Remainder*, cont. 375 acres. (Land: L#2.444)

GODFREY, William, of Prince William Co., Virginia, and his wife Jennet. Deed dated 12 Nov 1735; to Robert Covert, part of two tracts bounded by a path that goes from Robert Covert's to Nanjemy Church, a tract called *Millum*, parcel called *Amendment*, tract called *Renewment*, and tract called *Wadestone*, cont. 270 acres. Deed dated 9 Aug 1737; to his nephew, Samuel Adams, a tract called *Batchellors Hope*, 277 acres. (Land: O#2.119, 225)

GODSHALL, John and Mary his wife, on 23 Feb 1710 conveyed parcel called *St. Bridgetts* on w. side of Portobacco Creek, cont. 250 acres. (Ct.&Land: C#2.167)

GOER (GEER, GOOS), George (blacksmith) and Anne of head of Wicomico. Their children: Mary, born 12 June 1683; Sarah, born 1 May 1686; George, born 13 July 1689. (Ct.&Land: P#1.209; QRev.9, 12, 15)
GOER, George. Admr.: Ann Goer (relict). (Inv.: 10.237; 29 April 1689; ----)
GOER, Anne, relict of George Goer, dec'd. Petitions the estate for money, court held 10 June 1690. (Ct.&Land: Q#1.10)
GOER, Ami, relict of George Goer. Gifts to natural born children: Mary, Sarah, and George, dated 2 Aug 1690. (Ct.&Land: P#1.201)
GOR, George. Next of kin: John Mellar, Sarah Mellar, Alexander Standist. (Inv.: 34.127; 9 Dec 1712; ----)
GORE, George. Admr.: John Cox. (Acct: 35A.60; ----; 25 Oct 1715)

GOLEY, Thomas. Mentions: Henry Haislip, Susannah Haislip, John George, Joseph Milstead. Admr.: Elisabeth Goley. (Inv.: 28.154; 13 May 1743; 18 July 1743)

GOOCH, John (planter). Indenture 17 March 1688, to Humphrey Warren to take care of Gooch during his lifetime and provide for his niece Brigett Fendall to age 16 or day of marriage. John Gooch gives a parcel of land on the w. side of Wicomico River formerly in possession of Briget Legate, now in possession of John Gooch, 400 acres. (Ct.&Land: P#1.26)
GOOCH, John. Assigns his cousin, John Fendall, his cattle mark, 26 Nov 1704. Mark recorded ca. 1662. (Ct.&Land: C#2.233)

GOOD, Lucie. Servant, judged to be 20 yrs. old, presented by Richard Foucke, 12 July 1664. (Ct.&Land: B#1.313)
GOOD, Lewis, age 21. Deposition on 27 Sept 1665 regarding the death of the children of his mistress, Agatha Langworth on 17 Aug 1665. (Arch. of Md.: XLIX.482)

GOODALE, Isabella, servant to James Neale Sr. Her son age 5 years of age last of Oct next to serve 19 years and Elizabeth Gibbs (Goodale) to serve five years. At a court of Westmoreland 25 Aug 1669. A statement by John Quigley of the city of St. Mary's, on 13 Jan 1674 that he did in the colony of Virginia about six years past dispose of a woman servant named Elizabeth Goodale to Capt. James Neale for the term of 5 years from her first arrival in Virginia and that she had a man child with her of about 5 years of age. (Arch. of Md.: LXV.476)

GOODRICK, George of Portobacco, Charles Co., having married Ursule, relict of Capt. William Lewis, demands administration of the estate of said Lewis. 24 April 1658. (Arch. of Md.: XLI.58)

GOODRICK, Mary, dau. of Robert Goodrick, born 13 March 1673. (Ct.&Land: E#1.163; P#1.205; QRev.4)

GOODRICK, George. To sons Robert and Francis, exs., 600 acres. To dau. ——— Stapleford, grandson Charles Stapleford, dau. ——— Gunby, and granddau. Constant Gunby, personalty. (Will: 5.91; 25 July 1673; ----) (Inv.: 4.136; 30 Dec 1676; ----) Exs.: Robert Goodrick (son), Francis Goodrick (son). (Acct: 4.419; ----; 16 Oct 1677)

GUTRIDGE, James, age 15 yrs. Servant of Philip Lines, 14 March 1681. (Ct.&Land: I#1.258)

GOODRICK, Robert (planter) and wife Elizabeth on 30 July 1684 conveyed parcel called *Pomfrett*, cont. 150 acres. (Ct.&Land: K#1.424)

GOODRICK, Robert, age ca. 70. Deposition, 7 Dec 1705, regarding a conversation about 46 years earlier concerning a land boundary. (Ct.&Land: Z#1.226)

GOODRICH, Francis Jr., age 48. Deposition re *Lynes Delight*, 22 Dec 1718. (Chas LandComm: M2.41)

GOODRICK, George (planter) of Portobacco Parrish. To dau. Christian Butts, a half crown. To son Aron, dwell. plan. and personalty; to care of son William until age of 20. To sons Benjamin and Robert and dau. Ann, personalty. To five child., viz. William, Benjamin, Robert, Aron and Ann, residue of estate. Exs.: three eldest sons, William, Benjamin and Robert. (Will: 19.155; 27 March 1727; 15 May 1727) Next of kin: Mary Semmes, Julianah Simpson. Exs.: William Goodrick, Robert Goodrick, Benjamin Goodrick. (Inv.: 12.213; 25 May 1727; 8 Aug 1727)

GOODRICK, Robert. Next of kin: Benjamin Goodrick, Ralph Queen. Admr.: Theodosia Goodrick. (Inv.: 16.1069 Dec 1730; 23 Jan 1730)

GOODY, Henry. Next of kin: William Gody, Matthew Gody. Admr.: John Theobald. (Inv.: 23.453; 15 March 1736; 1 Nov 1738)

GOOLD, Margerie, wife of John Goold, 10 May 1663. (Ct.&Land: B#1.116)

GOOSEY, Jonathan. Wife Martha, extx. and sole legatee of estate. (Will: 11.53; 22 Nov 1700, 17 Jan 1700) (Inv.: 20.165; 18 Feb 1700; ----)

GORDIAN. (See GOURDON.)

GORE/GOR. (See GOER.)

GOSH, Richard, age 15 yrs. Servant of Peter Far, 8 Jan 1677. (Ct.&Land: G#1.85)

GOSLIN (GOSTING), Robert. (Inv.: 37B.88; 9 Feb 1717; ----) Admr.: Mary Hagertee, wife of Robert Hagertee. (Acct: 37B.224; ----; 13 Aug 1717)

GOULE, James. Payments to: John Gwin, Dr. Philip Briscoe. Admr.: John Glass. (Acct: 33B.175; ----; 30 Dec 1712)

GOURDON, Daniel, age ca. 34 yrs. Swore in court 17 April 1660. (Ct.&Land: A#1.86)

GOURDON, Daniel (planter) and Mary his wife convey tract lying on w. side of Portobacco Creek; by letter granted Gourdon; 27 April 1660. (Ct.&Land: A#1.111)

GORDIAN, Daniel and his wife Mary, acknowledge sale of their plantation of 100 acres on w. side of Portobacco Creek on 10 May 1663. (Ct.&Land: B#1.120)

GORDIAN, Mary, relict of Daniell Gordian. 4 Oct 1663. (Arch. of Md.: XLIX.189)

GOURELEY (GOURLEY, GOURELEG), John and Barbary, of Cedar Point Neck. Their children: Thomas, born 4 April 1686; Elizabeth, born 20 Oct 1690; John, born 23 April 1693. (Ct.&Land: P#1.212; QRev.12, 17, 21)

GOURLEY, John. (Inv.: 13B.110; 21 May 1696; ----) Admr.: Barbary Gourley. (Acct: 18.75B; ----; 1 Oct 1698)

GORLEY, John. Next of kin: Richard Chapman, John Chapman. Admr.: Dianah Gorley. (Inv.: 13.260; 22 May 1728; 12 Aug 1728)

GOYLE, Thomas. Approvers: John Goyle, Richard Chapman. (Inv.: 4.237; ----; [c1720])

GRAHAM, James (cooper) and Anne his wife on 31 Aug 1720 conveyed tract called *Thomas and James Adventure*; on e. side of Williams Branch, cont. 130 acres. (Ct.&Land: H#2.390)

GRANDSWORTH, Mary. Acknowledges age to be 22 yrs. old, servant presented by John Courts, 16 Dec 1662. (Ct.&Land: B#1.28)

GRANT, Robert, age 19 yrs. Servant of Francis Person, Nov 1710. (Ct.&Land: D#2.8)

GRAVES. (Also see GROVES.)

GRAVES, Thomas, age 16 yrs. Servant of John Vaudry, St. Mary's Co., 11 March 1678. (Ct.&Land: H#1.129)

GRAVES (GROVES), Joshua. To wife (unnamed), plantation. To son Joshua, plantation at death of wife afsd. To dau. Dorothy, 100 acres at Portobacco. To dau. Mary, 100 acres at Portobacco. To son Samuel, 100 acres, *Mattawoman* at hd. of St. Thomas's Ck. To dau. Sarah, 134 acres. (Will: 7.10; 15 Nov 1694; 20 Nov 1694) Admr.: Dorothey Graves (relict). (Acct: 13B.108; ----; 7 May 1696)

GRAVES, Dorothy (widow). Indenture, 3 July 1708, to John Wheeler (planter), her son in law. (Ct.&Land: (C#2.109)

GRAY, Joseph, age 13 yrs. Servant presented by Garrat Sennet, 8 March 1663/4. (Ct.&Land: B#1.258)

GRAY, Ruth, age 21 yrs. Servant of Richard Edelen, 1676. (Ct.&Land: F#1.193)

GRAY (GREY), John (mariner). (Inv.: 25.228; 2 Nov 1705; ----) Admr.: Nicholas Cooper. (Acct: 26.123; ----; 17 Oct 1706) Admr.: Nicholas Cooper. (Acct: 29.238; ----; 16 April 1709) Admr.: Nicholas Cooper. (Acct: 32B.256; ----; 27 March 1711)

GREY, John. To sons John, Edward, Francis, 100 acres each where they now live. To sons Richard and William, 398 acres. To son James, 1s. To Susannah Hergesson, personalty at 16 yrs. of age. Mentions son Thomas. (Will: 14.276; 23 April 1715, 20 Dec 1716) (Inv.: 38A.129; 21 Feb 1716; ----)

GRAY, John. 15 March 1717. John Gray, dec'd. (planter), to his son Edward Gray (planter), by his will, 100 acres whereon he now dwells, two tracts called *French Lewiss* and *Harrisons Land*. (Land: L#2.14)

GREY, Richard (planter) and Johannah his wife on 16 Sept 1720, conveyed a parcel which John Grey, dec'd, father of Richard, possessed, a parcel called *Ward's Runn* and by his will 23 April 1715 devised to his sons Richard and William Grey a parcel of 350 acres. (Ct.&Land: H#2.393)

GREY, William and his wife Elizabeth on 24 Nov 1725 conveyed land as described in following. John Grey, dec'd., father of sd. William Grey, owned a parcel of land on the w. side of Wards Runn, and by his will, written 23 April 1715, devised to Richard Grey and William Grey, afsd. 348 acres. (Land: L#2.253)

GRAY, Francis, and his wife Ann, eldest dau. of William Hargiss (eldest son of William Hargiss, the original patentee of the land). By deed dated 17 Feb 1733/4 conveyed the tract called *Hargisses Hope*, 200 acres. (Land: O#2.41)

GRAY, James. Leased on 20 Dec 1743, 90 acres in St. Thomas' Manor, for the term of three lives of James Gray, his son James Gray and Mary Gray his wife. (Land: X#2.124)

GRAY, Samuel and his wife Elizabeth. 14 April 1744. From Samuel Taylor, part of a tract in Durham Parish called *the Remainder*, 61 acres. (Land: X#2.111)

GREAVES, John Sr. (yeoman), of St. Mary's Co., and his wife Ann. Deed dated March 1734/5. To William Eilbeck of Prince George's Co., a parcel *Ferne*, 182 acres, on the s. side of Mattawoman Ck. or Run (sometimes called St. Thomas). (Ct.&Land: O#2.88)

GREEN, Luke. Servant, set free by Joseph Harrisson, 16 Dec 1662. (Ct.&Land: B#1.29)

GREEN, John, age 14 yrs. Servant of Benjamin Rozer, 8 Sept 1668.
(Ct.&Land: D#1.4)
GREEN, Richard, age 17 yrs. Servant of John Allen, 10 June 1673.
(Ct.&Land: E#1.132)
GREENE, James, age 15 yrs. Servant of Benjamin Rozer, 10 June 1674.
(Ct.&Land: E#1.171)
GREEN, John. To John Allen, 300 acres. To William Dean, 200 acres. To William Stanerd, 100 acres. To Richard Robinson and Joyce Borbancks, 100 acres. Exs.: Wm. Dean and Wm. Stanerd, afsd. (Will: 5.93; 27 Jan 1675; 5 Oct 1676)
GREENE, Francis and Elizabeth, of Portobacco. Their children: Leonard, born 30 May 1691; Verlinda, born 16 Aug 1692; Francis, born 23 April 1694. (Ct.&Land: QRev.20, 25)
GREENE, Leonard. Division of lots for the children of Leonard Greene: Francis Wheeler and Winnifried his wife, Thomas Greene, Mary Greene, and Margaret Greene, 4 June 1694. (Ct.&Land: S#1.288)
GREENE, William, son of Robert and Mary Greene of Portobacco, born 28 Dec 1694. (Ct.&Land: QRev.25)
GREEN, Jane, Mrs. Relict of Joshua Green, of Stafford County, Virginia. To sister Mary Brent, dau. of George and Mary Brent, to sister Martha Brent, bro. Henry Brent, and the Roman Catholic Chapel, personalty. Bro. William Chandler, ex. (Will: 6.380; 25 Nov 1699; 19 Jan 1699) Payments to: William Dent, Dr. Joseph Venner, Capt. Thomas Emms per Joseph Green (former husband of deceased), Richard Boughton, Mary Brent (sister of deceased). Legatees: William Hunger. Ex.: William Chandler (brother). (Acct: 24.186; ----; 1 Oct 1703)
GREEN, Robert. Indenture, 9 Nov 1702, in consideration of a marriage already had between Andrew Sympson (planter), and Elizabeth Green, dau. of Robert Green. (Ct.&Land: Z#1.27)
GREEN, Robert. Indenture, 8 June 1703, to Mary Thompson, dau. of Robert Green and wife of John Thompson (planter); tract called *Thompsons Rest*, part of *Green's Inheritance*, 100 acres by the main branch of Portobacco. (Ct.&Land: Z#1.24)
GREEN, Robert and his wife Mary. Indenture, 25 Aug 1703, to Richard Combs. Land left by the will of Leonard Green to each of his four children, Thomas, Winifrid, Mary and Margaret; Lot #3 to dau. Mary, now wife of Francis Marberry. Original tract patented by Leonard, Robert and Francis Green, for 2400 acres. Land called *Green's Heritance* on the main branch of Portobacco. (Ct.&Land: Z#1.70)
GREENE, Francis. To son Leonard, 100 acres bought from Leonard Brooke, part of 800 acres, *Green's Inheritance*, lying between main road of Piscataway to brother Robert Greene's Rowling Road. To son Francis, all land on *The Old Woman's Branch*. To son Giles, all land between that of sons Leonard and Francis. To dau. Claire, personalty. Exs.: Wife Elizabeth and son Leonard. (Will: 12.132; 16 Sept 1706; 7 May 1707)

GREEN, Thomas (planter) and his wife Mildred. Indenture 3 March 1713, from John Spalding of St. Mary's Co., to Thomas Greene, of St. Mary's Co., one of the sons of Leonard Greene, dec'd. Leonard Greene and his brothers, Robert and Francis Greene, were granted a tract called *Green's Inheritance*. Leonard Green by his will devised to his children: Winefred, Mary, Thomas and Margaret Greene; mentions surviving brothers Robert and Francis. (Ct.&Land: D#2.82)

GREEN, Robert and Mary his wife and Thomas Green, eldest son of said Robert Green and Mary his wife. Indenture, 25 June 1713, to William Boarman Sr., eldest son of Maj. William Boarman, dec'd., on behalf of Francis Ignatius Boarman, infant, youngest son of Maj. William Boarman, dec'd. Parcel called *Green's Rest*, being part of Wm. Boarman's Manor called *Content*, cont. 450 acres. (Ct.&Land: D#2.45)

GREEN, Leonard. To son Leonard, real estate in St. Mary's Co. To other three sons: Cudburth, John and Francis, *Green's Inheritance*. Wife Prudence, extx. One of the witnesses is Giles Green. (Will: 20.840; 11 Oct 1733; 8 Nov 1733) Next of kin: Francis Green, Leonard Green. Ex.: Prudence Green. (Inv.: 18.142; ----; 5 June 1734)

GREENE, Leonard. Petition regarding estate of Charles Evans, and Anne his wife, relict of Leonard Greene; complaint of Francis Wheeler and Winnifrid his wife, dau. of Leonard Greene. Court held 11 Aug 1691. (Ct.&Land: Q.39)

GREENFIELD, Thomas. To John Baker, personalty. Meverill Hulse, ex. (Will: 2.81; 18 April 1675; 16 May 1675)

GREENING, Jabez. (Inv.: 26.12; 7 June 1706; ----) Admr.: Susannah Greening. (Acct: 27.234; ----; 6 Nov 1707)

GREGORY, Charles (chirurgeon). (Inv.: 2.353; 2 Oct 1676; ----)
GREGORY, Charles. (Acct: 6.667; ----; 4 March 1679) Admr.: Thomas Clipsham. (Acct: 7A.155; ----; [c1680])

GREY (See GRAY).

GREYDEN, Margarett, age 21 yrs. Servant of Henry Bonner, 8 Aug 1671. (Ct.&Land: E#1.43)

GRIFFIN, Robert, age 17 yrs. Servant of Henry Goodrick, 14 March 1681. (Ct.&Land: I#1.258)
GRIFFIN, John. (Inv.: 37B.183; 9 July 1717; ----)
GRIFFIN (GRIFFETH), William. Deceased by 19 Feb 1734/5. (Will of John Smallwood, Will: 21.299; 21 Dec 1734; 19 Feb 1734)

GRIGES (GRIGS), John. (Inv.: 22.17; ----; ----) Admr.: Mrs. Margarett King. (Acct: 22.20; ----; 24 June 1702)

GROSSER, Mary, age 18-20 yrs. Servant of Peter Carr, 10 June 1674. (Ct.&Land: E#1.171)

GROVES, George, son of George and Alice Groves of head of Wicmoico River, born 2 June 1687. (Ct.&Land: QRev.13)

GROVES, George. Servant of Edward Evans, age judged to be 11 yrs. 12 Jan 1685. (Ct.&Land: M#1.67)

GROVES, William, son of George and Alice Groves of head of Wicomico River, born 24 May 1690. (Ct.&Land: QRev.16)

GROVES, Elizabeth, dau. of George and Alice Groves, of the head of Wicomico River, born 1 Feb 1692. (Ct.&Land: P#1.211; QRev.19)

GROVES, John, son of George and Alice Groves of head of Wicomico River, born 9 Feb 1694. (Ct.&Land: P#1.211; QRev.25)

GROVES, George Sr. (planter) and Jane his wife. Indenture, 16 Oct 1708, to John Miller. Grant 20 Sept 1680 to Philip Cole, tract called *Green Banck*, about two miles off head of Wicomico River, cont. 66 acres; 7 Jan 1684—Cole conveyed to Groves. (Ct.&Land: C#2.113)

GROVES, George. Mentions: wife (unnamed, dead). Admr.: George Groves. (Acct: 32C.128; ----; 1 May 1711)

GROVES, George. To sister Mary, bro. Matthew, minors, personalty, and to brother John, certain personalty belonging to deceased brother, Wm. Groves. To John Guyun, ex., residue of estate in trust for son William at majority. (Will: 13.630; 11 Nov 1713; 3 Jan 1713)

GROVES, George. Creditors & Next of kin: John Gwinn, Math. Stone. (Inv.: 35A.358; 22 March 1713; ----) Payments to: Thomas Skinner and his wife Constance Skinner, John Groves (admr. of William Groves, son of George Groves Sr., exhibited by executor George Groves Jr.), John Groves (son of George Groves Sr.). Ex.: John Gwinn. (Acct: 36B.100; ----; 6 Feb 1714)

GROVES, William. Received from: estate of George Groves Sr., Edward Forde. Payments to: John Gwinn (executor of George Groves Jr.), Matthew Stone (administrator of John Killingsworth). Admr.: John Groves. (Acct: 36B.103; ----; 26 Feb 1714)

GROVES, George. Creditors & Next of kin: George Dent, John Groves. (Inv.: 35A.367; 8 March 1713; 11 May 1714)

GROVES, William and his wife Elizabeth conveyed on 19 April 1729 tract called *Moulds Venture*, cont. 200 acres. (Land: M#2.160)

GROVES, Matthew. Next of kin: Mary Groves. Admr.: John Groves. (Inv.: 22.227; 12 Nov 1736; 11 March 1736)

GROVES, John, and his wife Possume, on 10 April 1744, leased part of a tract called *Hattens Point*, 100 acres. (Land: X#2.103)

GRUB, Mary. Court held 14 March 1664. Amy Lambert swore that Mary Grub "Sayd that if shee was with Child it was by John Grub." Brigit Philpot swore that Mary Grub "sayeth that if shee was with Child it was by John Grub[e] for nobody had any thing to doe with her but hee and her formar husband in England." William Gandie swore same. John Cage was cleared of being the father. (Ct.&Land: B#1.445-446)

GRYER, John, age 20 yrs. Servant of Rise [Rice] Williams, 14 Nov 1682. (Ct.&Land: K#1.25)

GUESSE, Richard, age 15 yrs. Servant of Henry Adams, 8 June 1686. (Ct.&Land: M#1.220)

GUIBERT, Joshua of St. Mary's Co. and Ann his wife. Articles of agreement, 1 Dec 1716, with Peter Montgomery, given to Joshua in consideration of dower with Ann his wife by her father William Boreman Sr., possession for nine years for 700 lbs of tobacco per year. Tract located on the s. side of Zachina Swamp. (Ct.&Land: H#2.45)

GUIBERT, Thomas of St. Mary's Co., by his will dated 17 March 1728/9, bequeathed to his dau., Elizabeth Guibert, a Negro wench called Lucy and her increase to his daus.: Elizabeth and Ann Guibert. Now at this day the increase of Lucy consists of a Negro girl called Nell, a Negro boy called George, a Negro girl called Terrie and a Negro boy called Ben, who are with the consent of James Neale (who married sd. Elizabeth) and Ann Guibert, as follows: James Neale has Nell and Ben, and Ann Guibert has George and Terrie. 30 Nov 1743. (Land: X#2.82)

GUIFORD, Henry. Admrs.: Matthew Barnes and his wife Sarah Barnes. (Acct: 37A.131; ----; 23 July 1716)

GUNNER, Moyses. Judged to be 19 yrs. old, presented by Thomas Gibson, 10 Jan 1664. (Ct.&Land: B#1.397)

GUTRIDGE. (See GOODRICK.)

GUY, Elizabeth, dau. of Charles and Elizabeth Guy of Wicomico, born 1 July 1693. (Ct.&Land: QRev.21)

GWIN, Richard, age 19 yrs. Presented by Francis Pope, 8 March 1663/4. (Ct.&Land: B#1.257)

GWINN, John. Admr.: Sarah Dixon, wife of Thomas Dixon. (Acct: 9.19; ----; 25 Feb 1685)

GWIN, John. (Inv.: 8.427; 16 July 1685; ----)

GWYNN, Anne, dau. of Christopher and Susanna Gwynn, born 27 July 1692. (Ct.&Land: P#1.210; QRev.18)

GWINN, Ralph, age 6 yrs., son of Ralph Gwinn. Last day of May last, bound to Ralph Shaw Jr., to age 21 yrs. old, 13 March 1710. (Ct.&Land: D#2.141)

GWINN, John and his wife Anna. Deed dated 25 April 1722, to Joseph Gwinn, eldest son of afsd. John Gwinn, tract *Essex*, nr. Cedar Point, conveyed by John Hamilton (Gent.), late of Chas. Co., to John Gwinn, above named and grandfather of Joseph Gwinn afsd., 75 acres. Also tract *Rangle*, adjoining a tract whereon Edmund Howard formerly dwelled, and conveyed by John Compton Jr., late of Chas. Co. (dec'd.), to sd. Jno. Gwinn, father of afsd. Joshu: Gwinn, cont. 140 acres. (Land: L#2.11)

GWINN, John. Mentions eldest dau. Mary Williams; eldest son Joseph; youngest son Benjamin; youngest dau. Ann; wife Ann, extx. (Will: 21.192; 29 May 1732; 28 Sept 1734) Next of kin: Joseph Gwinn, Benjamin Gwinn. Extx.: Ann Gwinn. (Inv.: 21.34; ----; 2 Aug 1735)

GWINN, Ann(e), Mrs. To eld. son Joseph, grandsons Robert Yates, Barten Hungerford Jr., granddau. Elizabeth Hungerford, and Sarah Bailey, daus. Elizabeth Hungerford and Ann Yates, personalty. To three children, Joseph, Benjamin, and Ann Yates, residue of estate. Exs.: Robert Yates Sr., Joseph and Benjamin Gwinn. Test: Dr. John Harris, Joshua Wilson. (Will: 21.686; 3 Sept 1736; 2 Oct 1736) Creditors: John Harris, Charles Jones. Next of kin: Barton Hungerford, executors. Exs.: Maj. Robert Yates, Benjamin Gwinn, Joseph Gwinn. (Inv.: 22.223; 7 Oct 1736; 8 March 1736)

GWITHER, Mary, wife of Lieut. Nicholas Gwither. 7 Oct 1650. (Arch. of Md.: X.32, 75)

GWITHER, Nicholas, age 16. 1667. (Arch. of Md.: LVII.184)

HADDOCK, Sarah, widow of William Barton, Prince George's Co. 18(?) March 1733. William Barton by his wife, devised to his son in law Basil Waring, 300 acres, part of his tract called *Hadlow*, and the rest of *Hadlow* to his wife, afsd. Sarah Haddock. Said Sarah sells the remainder to Robert Mackhorne. (Land: O#2.28)

HAGALL, Elisabeth. Next of kin: Richard Harrison (brother). (Inv.: 1.490; 16 Oct 1718; ----)

HEAGAN (HAGON), John. (Inv.: 31.335; 17 July 1710; ----) Admr.: John Gates. (Acct: 31.343; also Acct: 34.146; ----; 18 Aug 1710)

HAGAN, Thomas. Legatees: Sarah Edelen, Charity Green, Ann Smith, Elisabeth Clarkson. Extx.: Mary Hagan. (Acct: 39B.57; ----; 13 June 1717. See HAGOE, Thomas.)

HAGAN (HARGAN), Mary. To son William, ex., entire estate. (Will: 19.26; 8 April 1721; 4 Feb 1726)

HAGAN, Thomas. To son Thomas, 48 acres *Sandy Gravel*, 10 acres *Addition to Clair*. To godson Thomas, personalty. To son Ignatius, 60 acres *Clair*. To son James, 60 acres *Clair*. To bro. Ignatius, 65 acres *Lauturnan*. To daus. Mary and Rebecca, personalty. To wife Sarah, extx., her property to pass to son Basil. Shd. any of the afsd. sons die without hrs., their property to be divided among their brothers Benjamin, William, Joseph and Henry. (Will: 23.138; 22 Nov 1742; 2 June 1743)

HAGAR, William, age 14 yrs. Servant of Thomas Baker, 2nd Tues in April 1669. (Ct.&Land: D#1.62)

HAGAR, Robert of St. Mary's Co., and his wife Mary. Indenture 8 Sept 1685; parcel called *Skidmore Rest*, cont. 80 acres. (Ct.&Land: L#1.185)

HAGER, Robert Sr. Deed of gift, 16 Oct 1703, to his son Robert Hager Jr. (Ct.&Land: Z#1.69)

HAGAR, Robert Sr. (planter), Elizabeth Hagar, and Robert Hagar Jr., eldest son of said Robert Hagar Sr., conveyed on 9 Nov 1708 a parcel of land called *St. George's*, cont. 100 acres. (Ct.&Land: C#2.119)

HAGGATE, Humpherie, age ca. 33 yrs. Swore in court 20 April 1662, mentioning Ursula Lenton (widow). (Ct.&Land: A#1.204)

HAGGETT, Humphrey. Wife Anne, extx., and sole legatee. (Will: 1.777; 30 March 1663; 30 July 1663)

HAGGETT, Ann, widow of Humphrey Haggett of Charles Co., lately dead. 1663. (Arch. of Md.: XLIX.35)

HAGGIT, John. Cattle mark for cows given him by his mother, Martha Peters, 9 Sept 1707. (Ct.&Land: C#2.72)

HAGGETT, John. (Inv.: 38A.131; 1 May 1717; 28 June 1717) Admr.: Mary Haggett. (Acct: 38A.128; ----; 13 June 1717)

HAGGETT (HAGET, HAGATT), Freeman, and his wife Alice, conveyed on 9 March 1735/6 part of tract called *Duckes Delight*, cont. 40 acres. (Land: O#2.137)

HAGNER, John. (Inv.: 38A.162; 29 May 1717; ----)

HAGOE, Thomas. To wife Mary, extx., dwelling plantation, 300 acres, *St. James*. To son James, 350 acres, part of *Good Intent*, To son Ignatius, 200 acres, part of *Good Intent*. To son Thomas, 250 acres *Clare*. To dau. Mary Baggott, 100 acres, part of *Good Intent*. To sons Thos. and Ignatius afsd., 150 acres *Correck Measure*, in St. Mary's Co. To four daus., Sarah Edelen, Charity Green, Ann Smith and Eliza: Clarkson, each 10s. To wife entire personal estate to pass to son William at her decease. (Will: 14.213; 29 March 1714; 21 Feb 1716. See HAGAN, Thomas.)

HAGOE, Thomas. Next of kin: James Hagan, Thomas Hagan. (Inv.: 37A.42; 10 March 1715; ----. See HAGAN, Thomas.)

HAGON. (See HEAGAN.)

HAGUE, Elisabeth. Next of kin: Jane Evans (mother), Thomas Harrison (brother), Richard Harrison. (Inv.: 3.252; 19 May 1718; ----)

HAYLES, Mary, age 20 yrs. Servant of Mr. Wade, 10 March 1670/1. (Ct.&Land: E#1.35)

HAIL, Thomas. Admr.: James Plant. (Inv.: 27.295; 20 [?] Nov 1742; 16 Jan 1742)

HAKSON, James. Extx.: widow (unnamed), now wife of James Moncaster. (Accts. from Wills: 3.51; ----; 6 Dec 1703)

HALERD, William, age 18 yrs. Servant of Edward Price, 11 June 1678. (Ct.&Land: G#1.157)

HALEY, John. (Inv.: 1.62; 18 May 1718; ----)

HALY, Elisabeth. Admrs.: John Butts, Stephen Mankin. (Inv.: 4.238; 19 Aug 1720; 10 Nov 1720)

HALL, Walter, and his wife Margrett. Signed 11 April 1662 and recorded Sept 1725. To Thomas Allenson, a parcel of 450 acres and another for 200 acres. There was a patent, 400 acres, assigned to Walter Hall by Ralph Crouch and 250 acres as executor to Henry Fox. Land lying on the s. side of Piscataway River called *Doags Neck*. (Land: L#2.236)

HALL, Isaack, age 13 yrs. Servant of Henry (Hamy) Bonard, 2nd Tues in April 1669. (Ct.&Land: D#1.62)

HALL, Margrett, age 18 yrs. Servant of Mrs. Young, 10 June 1673. (Ct.&Land: E#1.132)

HALL, John, age 18 yrs. Servant of William Hensly, 10 June 1674. (Ct.&Land: E#1.171)

HALL, William, age 17 yrs. Servant of Thomas Speeke, 11 Jan 1675. (Ct.&Land: F#1.163)

HALL, Richard, son of Richard and Mary Hall of Portobacco, born 28 July 1679. (Ct.&Land: P#1.207; QRev.6)

HALL, Richard. William Chandler entered cattle mark for a filly given by him to William Ling, son in law of Richard Hall and natural borne son of Mary [Hall] his wife, 1680. (Ct.&Land: H#1.293)

HALL, Mary, relict and admx. of Richard Hall. Cattle mark recorded, 9 Nov 1680, given by dau. Mary Ling. (Ct.&Land: I#1.32])

HALL, Richard. Admr.: Mary Martin (relict), wife of John Martin. (Acct: 7C.163; ----; [c1682])

HALL, Charles, age 22 yrs. Servant of Edward Mings, 8 Aug 1682. (Ct.&Land: I#1.317)

HALL, Rebecca, age 18 yrs., made an indenture on 12 July [1685], with between Thomas Wyck (merchant) to serve him for five years from her arrival in Virginia. (Ct.&Land: M#1.9)

HALL, John son of William (doctor) and Mary Hall of Portobacco, born 4 Nov 1692. (Ct.&Land: P#1.211; QRev.18)

HALL, William, Dr., lately of Chichester, Sussex Co., England, being 2nd son of William Hall of afsd. city. Wife Mary, extx. and sole legatee of estate, including property in Chichester. To sons John and William, afsd. property at death of wife. (Will: 7.261; 28 Jan 1696; 6 April 1697) (Inv.: 15.166; 13 May 1697; ----) (Inv.: 16.92; 13 May 1697; ----) Extx.: Mary Hall. (Acct: 16.93; ----; 2 June 1698)

HALL, Mary. (Inv.: 19.100; 17 June 1699; ----) Ex.: Philip Hoskins. (Acct: 19½B.93; ----; [c1699/1700])

HALL, Benjamin and Mary his wife conveyed on 19 Dec 1706, a part of land called *Strife*, cont. 135 acres. (Ct.&Land: C#2.177)

HALL?, Katherine, age 22 yrs. Servant of James Semmes, Nov 1710. (Ct.&Land: D#2.7)

HALL, Benjamin of Prince George's Co. and Mary his wife, conveyed on 28 Jan 1716, 150 acres of a tract called *Calvert's Hope*. (Ct.&Land: H#2.58)

HALL, John. (Inv.: 37A.197; 19 Dec 1716; ----) (Inv.: 38A.127; 29 March 1717; ----) Admr.: Alice Hall. (Acct: 38A.171; ----; 15 June 1717)

HALL, Francis, of Prince George's Co. and his wife Dorot[h]y, conveyed on 24 June 1736 part of *Calverts Hope*, *Boarmans Rest* and *Indian Fields*, on s. side of Zachia Swamp. (Land: O#2.158. See also Land O #2.201.)

HALL, Thomas Lant, son of Ignatius and Mary Hall, born 12 March 1741/2. (Trinity: 107—rev.)

HALL, Thomas. Admr.: Sarah Hall. (Inv.: 30.288; 1 Nov 1744; 27 Feb 1744)

HALY. (See HALEY.)

HAMBLETON. (See HAMILTON.)

HAMBLIN, James. (Inv.: 30.147; 1 Aug 1744; 25 Nov 1744)

HAMBYE, Francis. Servant of Giles Blizard, age judged to be 19 yrs. 12 Jan 1685. (Ct.&Land: M#1.67)

HAMARSLEY (HAMERSLY), Francis (Frances) of Stafford Co., Virginia. Deed dated 1 June 1726. To Elizabeth Pile (widow), in consideration of a marriage to be fulfilled between said Frances Hamarsley and afsd. Elizabeth Pile, for and in behalf of several children of Joseph Pile, born of Elizabeth Pile. Joseph Pile's will dated 15 June 1724 [Liber 18, folio 312]; bequeathed to said Elizabeth, two Negroes or slaves, named Ralph and Edward, to return to the children of Joseph Pile at her death. (Land: L#2.282)

HAMERSLY, Francis. Next of kin: James Latimer. Admr.: Mary Hamersly. (Inv.: 31.131; 13 May 1745; 29 May ----)

HAMILL, John (schoolmaster) and his wife Sarah conveyed on 13 June 1727 a tract called *Wilderness*, cont. 50 acres and on 13 June 1733 a tract called *Hamills Discovery*, cont. 20 acres and on 21 Dec 1739, two lots in Charles Town. (Land: L#2.361; M#2.345; O#2.429)

HAMBLETON, John. To son John, 325 acres. To dau. Eliza:, a negro girl formerly given by Richard Harrison to his grandson, Jno. Hambleton, and land. Wife Eliza:, extx. (Will: 13.12; 18 Nov 1708; 18 Feb 1709)

HAMLETON, John. (Inv. 31.147; 16 --- 1709; ----)

HAMILTON, John. Admr.: Elisabeth Hauge, wife of John Hauge. (Acct: 33A.122; ----; 20 Feb 1711)

HAMILTON, Alexander (planter). Mentions wife, extx., dau. Mary; sons: John (eldest), William, James, Patrick and Samuel. (Will: 20.138; 14 Jan 1730/31; 20 Feb 1730) Next of kin: "minors." Extx.: Elisabeth Hamilton. (Inv.: 16.156; 20 April 1731; 15 May 1731)

HAMILTON, Alexander (planter) and his wife Elizabeth. Lease dated 10 March 1723; to Daniel Stuart (planter), part of the tract whereon sd. Alexander dwells between Portobacco Branch and William Baswell's Branch. (Land: L#2.121)

HAMILTON, John (planter), grandson of John Hamilton, conveyed on 22 Sept 1729 a parcel of land on Nanjemy Creek, 100 acres. (Land: M#2.187)

HAMBLETON, John. Next of kin: Elisabeth Wade, Charity King. Admr.: John King. (Inv.: 18.505; 4 June 1734; 14 Aug 1734)

HAMILTON, Thomas. Admr.: Capt. Joseph Douglass. (Inv.: 23.518; 2 May 1738; 9 Feb 1738)

HAMMONDS, John, age 15 yrs. Servant of Jeremiah Dickenson, 7 April 1668. (Ct.&Land: C#1.263)

HAMMON, John. Next of kin: Daniell McDaniell, Ann Pecock. Admr.: Daniel Bryant. (Inv.: 11.357; 5 April 1726; 15 June 1726)

HANBY, Francis and Alise his wife. Indenture 13 Nov 1695, Alise binds her son Samuell Barker, now age 7 yrs., to Samuell Luckett. (Ct.&Land: S#1.431)

HANCOCK, George. Admr.: Francis Butcher. (Inv.: 12.29; 7 March 1726; 26 May 1727)

HANDY, Henry (gentleman). Next of kin: Richard Ashman, John Ashman. (Inv.: 36B.84; 28 Sept 1714; ----)

HANNA, Alexander. Next of kin: Humphrey Warren, Thomas Warren. Admr.: Mary Hanna. (Inv.: 23.361; ----; 15 Aug [c1738])

HANSON, Anne, dau. of John and Mary Hanson of Portobacco, born 18 Jan 1692. (Ct.&Land: P#1.212; QRev.19)

HANSON, Samuel son of Robert and Benedicta Hanson, born 6 Dec 1705. Recorded ca. Jan 1724/5. (Land: L#2.199)

HANSON, John Jr. Married the relict of Samuell Luckett, dec'd. In behalf of Ignatius Luckett, son of Samuell conveyed on 11 March 1706, from George Askin (planter), to Ignatius Luckett. Land called *The Square Adventure* on northwest branch of Zachia Swamp, cont. 100 acres. (Ct.&Land:: C#2.45)

HANSON, Samuel and Elizabeth. Their children: Elizabeth, born 9 Nov 1707, about 1-2 a.m.; Mary, born 4 Feb 1709, about 8-9 p.m.; Walter, born 11 March 1711, about 6 a.m.; Sarah, born 29 July 1714, about 3 p.m.;

Samuel, born 20 Dec 1716, about 2-3 a.m.; William, born 18 March 1718, about 11:30 p.m.; died 2 Sept 1721; John, born 3 April 1721, 2-3 p.m.; Jane, born 18 Feb 1721/2, 2-3 p.m.; Charity, born 15 Aug 1724, about 7 p.m.; William, born 29 Sept 1726, about 6 a.m. Recorded ca. Jan 1724/5. (Land: L#2.200)

HANSON, Elizabeth, dau. of Samuel Hanson. Cattle mark recorded 6 Sept 1709. (Ct.&Land: (C#2.142)

HANSON, John. Cattle mark recorded 10 Nov 1712, for his dau. Elizabeth Hanson. (Ct.&Land: D#2.20)

HANSON, John (planter). In his will he mentions children; Robert, John, Sam'll, Benja., Mary wife of Rev. Wm. Maconchie, Ann and Sarah Hanson; grandson Samuell Hanson. (Will: 13.719; 12 Dec 1713; 5 July 1714) (Inv.: 37B.93; 15 Jan 1714; ----) (Inv.: 36A.236; 26 Aug 1714; ----) Legatees: John Hanson (son), Samuel Hanson (son), Benjamin Hanson (son), wife (unnamed) of William Maconchie, Ann Hanson, Sarah Hanson. Cites: children (unnamed) are at age. Ex.: Robert Hanson. (Acct: 37B.225; ----; 2 Sept 1717)

HANSON, John, age 31. Deposition, 28 April 1719, re *Her Excellency's Gift*. For Elizabeth Rogers, widow. (Chas LandComm: M2.45)

HANSON, Robert, age 37. Deposition, 28 April 1719, re *Her Excellency's Gift*. (Chas LandComm: M2.45)

HANSON, Benjamin. Admr./Ex.: Josh. Douglas. (Inv.: 3.177; 3 Aug 1719; ----)

HANSON, Robert, age 40. Deposition, 21 May 1720, regarding a tract called *Mattinglys Hope*. (Chas LandComm: M2.87)

HANSON, John and Elizabeth conveyed on 13 July 1721 a parcel of land called *Newport*; *The Discovery* of 150 acres; *Ingerstone* of 230 acres; also *Moores Lodge*, 150 acres.; also *Moore's Gore* of 50 acres. [See Land: H#2.449 under Thomas Hussey, father of Elizabeth.] (Ct.&Land: H#2.446)

HANSON, Robert (Gent.) and Dorothy his wife on 17 March [1720 or 21] conveyed to Thomas Parry, son of Dorothy; when her son arrives at age 20. Two tracts of land conveyed from Thomas Turner to Dorothy Turner, then the widow of John Parry, dec'd, called *Digges Baltimore Gift* and *Digges Addition*. Recorded 29 March 1721 at request of Robert Hanson and Dorothy his wife on behalf of John Parry, minor. Indenture, 13 July 1721, to Thomas Parry, son of Dorothy, at age 20. [Reference to John Parry, minor son of Dorothy.]. (Ct.&Land: H#2.4425, 42)

HANSON, Samuel and Elizabeth his wife on 23 Sept 1720 conveyed 1/3 part of *Bergen-ap-Zome* and *Gwinn's Hope*. (Ct.&Land: H#2.383)

HANSON, Robert. Cattle marks recorded on 24 April 1722 for his children: William, Dorothy and Robert. (Land: L#2.11)

HANSON, Samuel (Gent.) and his wife Elizabeth conveyed on 14 March 1722 a tract called *Tryal*. (Land: L#2.90)

HANSON, Mrs. Elizabeth, formerly wife of Samuel Luckett, now wife of John Hanson, declares that her son, Thomas Hussy Luckett on 4 June last, was age of 46 years. Deposition 27 May 1723. (Land: L#2.140)

HANSON, John and his wife Elizabeth, only dau. and sole heiress of Thomas Hussy, dec'd., conveyed on 14 June 1727 a tract called *Hussyes Addition*, 438 acres, and a tract of 100 acres; also *Hussyes Lodge*, 33 acres, *Hussyes Reserve*, 50 acres, and *Hussyes Lott*, 103 acres. On 8 Nov 1738 John Hanson and his wife Elizabeth conveyed to Jane Luckett, widow of Ignatius Luckett, dec'd., and Samuel Luckett and Ignatius Luckett, sons of afsd. Ignatius Luckett, tract called *Mores Ditch*, 500 acres, to be divided according to will of Ignatius Luckett. (Land: L#2.367; O#2.378)

HANSON, Robert and his wife Violetta. Deed of gift dated 10 Aug 1727; to his son Samuel Hanson Jr., parcel of land on the w. side of Portobacco Creek called *Lampton*, 150 acres; part of tract called *St. Patricks Hill*, 136 acres; and part of tract called *Spring Plain*. (Land: L#2.369)

HANSON, Robert. Deed of gift dated 10 Aug 1727; to his son Samuel Hanson; a Negro man named Boatswain and a mulatto girl named Catherine. (Land: L#2.371)

HANSON, Samuel Sr. and his wife Elizabeth on 15 April 1730 conveyed lot #35 in Charles Town at Portobacco. (Land: M#2.201)

HANSON, Robert and Ann Eburnethy of Chas. Co. Signed 5 Nov 1734. To Mary Hanson, dau. of sd. Robert Hanson, a Negro girl, 8 mos. of age, named Judith, dau. of Negro Sarah Rose, mentioned in the inventory of John Eburnethy's estate. (Land: O#2.93)

HANSON, Robert Jr. To brother Samuel, house and lot in Charles Town. To bro. William, *Hanson Green*. To mother Violetta and Mrs. Elizabeth Story, personalty. Bros. afsd. exs. (Will: 21.243; 25 Oct 1734; 19 Nov 1734) Next of kin: S. Hanson, Robert Hanson. Exs.: Samuel Hanson Jr., William Hanson. (Inv.: 22.76; ----; 20 Oct 1736)

HANSON, Benjamin, son of Robert Hanson. Signed 21 July 1736; received gift from Ann Eburnethy, widow, one Negro girl called Nanny, six months old, dau. of Negro woman, Kate. (Land: O#2.159)

HANSON, Robert, and his wife, Elizabeth. 29 March 1738. To William Lucket and John Lucket, sons of Ignatius Lucket, part of a tract formerly called *Hussies Addition*, but now on a resurvey called *Green Land*, on w. side of the head of Portobacco Creek, 200 acres. (Land: O#2.326) [Mrs. Jane Lucket paid the alienation fine, 25 Apr 1738.]

HANSON, John Sr. 1 May 1738. To his son, John Hanson Jr., part of the tract called *Green Land*, 555 acres. (Land: O#2.329)

HANSON, Samuel, and his wife Elizabeth conveyed on 5 Oct 1733 Lot #9 in Benedict Town. On 7 March 1738/9 they conveyed to their son, Walter Hanson, 190 acres, part of the tract called the *Hills*, whereon Samuel and Elizabeth dwelt. (Land: O#2.6A, 383. Also see Land O#2.384.)

HANSON, Robert (Col.), and his wife Violetta. William Hoskins, died intestate, leaving said Violetta his widow, and two daus.: eldest dau. Elizabeth who married Walter Hanson and Mary who married John Cunninghame. On 15 Nov 1744 Robert and Violetta Hanson, give 1/3 of the tract *Friendship*, Violetta's right of dower, to daus. Elizabeth and Mary. (Ct.&Land: X#2.162)

HANSON, Samuel, Jr., son of Robert Hanson. 28 Sept 1739. John Ashman (planter) of Princess Anne Co., Virginia, is bound to sd. Samuel Hanson, having sold to Hanson a tract called *St. Edmunds*, 150 acres. (Land: O#2.417. Also see Land O#2.385.)

HANSON, Elizabeth, relict of Samuel Hanson (late clerk of Chas. Co.). Order dated 11 Nov 1740. To deliver all county records of Samuel Hanson, late Clerk of the County Ct. (Land: O#2.487)

HANSON, Samuel Sr. (gentleman). To son Samuel, 140 acres *Greens Inheritance*, 35 acres *Addition to Hereford*. To son John, *Hereford* and residue of *Addition to Hereford*. To dau. Elizabeth Douglass, granddau. Eleanor dau. of Benjamin and Elizabeth Douglass; son Walter and daus. Charity, Joan, Chloe and Jane, personalty. To son William, *Little Wood* and 203 acres of *Wilkinsons Throne* at death of his mother. To wife Elizabeth, extx., dwelling plantation *Little Worth*, 203 acres *Wilkinsons Throne*. Son in law Benjamin Douglass and his wife to be the guardians of William Hanson, afsd. Overseer: Son Walter. (Will: 22.296; 22 Oct 1740; 5 May 1740) Next of kin: Samuel Hanson Jr., John Hanson youngest. Admr./Ex.: Elisabeth Hanson. (Inv.: 26.146; 11 May 1741; 10 July 1741)

HANSON, John, youngest son of Samuel Hanson, dec'd., and his wife Jane, on 12 March 1744/5 conveyed, 1/2 of tract called *Rozers Refuge*, 561 acres. (Land: Z#2.34)

HANSON, Robert (Col.) Hanson and his wife Violetta, relict of William Hoskins, Walter Hanson and his wife Elizabeth, eldest dau. of sd. William Hoskins and John Cunningham(e) and his wife Mary, other dau. of sd. William Hoskins requested a survey of a part of the tract called *Lindsey*, on the w. side of the eastern most branch of Avon River, formerly belonging to the sd. William Hoskins, now in the possession of Rev. Theophilus Swift. Land was divided into three parts. Signed 13 Feb 1743/4. (Land: O#2.73, 584; X#2.162, 296; Z#2.64)

HANSON, Walter, and his wife Elizabeth (nee Hoskins, dau. of William Hoskins). 6 Nov 1744. To Heloise Hanson, dau. of sd. Walter Hanson and his wife Elizabeth, 1/2 of their right to tract called *Lindsey* on w. side of eastern most fresh of Nanjemy Creek, which Archibald Wauhob made over to his dau., Elizabeth, wife of Philip Hoskins, grandfather of afsd. Elizabeth Hanson, to be delivered to sd. Helloise when she arrives to age 16. (Land: Z#2.8)

HARBERT, William (gent.). To dau. Ann (wife of George Dent), 500 acres, part of *Clarke's Purchase*; after her decease to granddau. Rebeckah Dent and unborn child of dau. Anne. To Jno: (son of John Douglass, dec'd), 150 acres, *Harbert's Chance*. Personal estate to wife Sarah and George Dent, joint exs. (Will: 14.661; 9 May 1715; 26 July 1718)

HARBERT, Sarah, Mrs. (widow). To son Joseph Douglas, dwell. plantation and 200 acres, *The Hills*. To grandsons Thomas, Benjamin, and Joseph Douglas and Douglas Giffard, personalty. To granddaus. Eliz. Howard and Mary Douglas, personalty. Son Joseph afsd., ex. and residuary legatee. (Will: 14.662; 8 July 1718; 26 July 1718) Next of kin: George Dene, Douglas Differt. Ex.: Joseph Douglass. (Inv.: 3.97; 13 Nov 1719; ----) Next of kin: George Doul, Douglas Gifferd. Admr./Ex.: Josh: Douglas. (Inv.: 3.178; 25 Aug ----; 13 Nov 1719)

HARDE (See HARDY).

HARDY, Henry. Servant, judged to be 20 yrs. old, presented by Thomas Percei, 12 July 1664. (Ct.&Land: B#1.314)

HARDY, Henry of Pickawaxon, married Elinor Compton, dau. of John Compton [Cumpton] of St. Mary's Co., 21 Aug 1694. (Ct.&Land: QRev.23)

HARDY, Henry [Capt.]. Wife Ann, extx. To dau. Ann, *Hardy's Purchase* at 16 yrs.; to be brought up in Protestant Church. Mentions kinsman Henry, son of George Hardy, of Loughborow, Leicester Co.; bro. George. Exs.: Philip Briscoe and his son John. (Will: 13.733; 21 Dec 1705; 20 Sept 1714) [Entry crossed out]. (Inv.: 38A.126; 28 Sept 1714; ----) Next of kin: Richard Ashman. (Inv.: 36B.332; 22 March 1714; 25 March 1715) Admr.: Anne Hardy. (Charles county Acct: 37A.21; ----; 29 Sept 1716) (Inv.: 39A.35; 30 Jan 1717; ----) Mentions: residuary legatee (unnamed) resident in Britain. Admr. (de bonis non): Richard Ashman. (Acct: 39C.128; ----; 26 Jan 1717)

HARDY (HARDE), William. Mentions son George, son William, dau. Elizabeth, son Ignatius 50 acres dwell. plant., at decease of wife Elizabeth, extx.; son John, 50 acres, *Dividing Run*; daus. Mary Wheatley and Martha Cohow. (Will: 14.714; 4 Jan 1717; 12 Aug 1718) Next of kin: Francis Witly, James Cahow. (Inv.: 1.295; 8 Oct 1718; ----)

HARDY, Ignatius, and his wife Rebecah Hardy. Recorded 28 Nov 1735; conveyed a tract called the *Dividing Run*. (Land: O#2.326B)

HARE, James, age ca. 30 yrs. Swore in court 27 Oct 1658. (Ct.&Land: A#1.27)

HARGAY, William. (Inv.: 8.455; 22 March 1686; ----)

HARGIS (HARGIST), William. In his will he mentions son John Draper and sons Roger and William Hargis. Wife Anne, extx. (Will: 4.188; 19 Nov 1685; 19 March 1685) Extx.: Ann Hargist. (Acct: 9.317; ----; 22 June 1687)

HARGUESSE, Ann, dau. of William Harguesse. Cattle mark recorded 4 July 1689. (Ct.&Land: P#1.201)

HARGESS (HARGNESSE), Thomas. To sons Thomas, William, Francis and Abraham, *Hargess Hope*, equally divided between them. Exs.: Wm. Williams, Timothy Carrington, Jno: Martin. (Will: 14.336; 22 Jan 1716; 8 Feb 1716) (Inv.: 37B.93; 7 March 1716; ----)

HARKLEY (HARTLEY), Robert. Mentions children: Mary Earle, Ann Wineard, Robert, Jane, Elizabeth and Richard; "as they come of age." Exs.: Henry Neale, William Neale. (Will: 22.173; 20 April ----; 5 May 1740) Next of kin: Robert Harkley, William Calry. Ex.: Henry Neal Sr. (Inv.: 25.413; 15 June 1740; 31 March 1741)

HARPER, Peter, age 13 yrs. Servant of Robert Thompson Jr, 8 March 1691. (Ct.&Land: R#1.372)

HARPER, Daniel. (Inv.: 35A.52; [c1713]; ----) Received from: estate (unnamed) exhibited by James Munkister by right of marriage. Admr.: Mary Harper. (Acct: 35A.291; ----; 19 Feb 1713)

HARPER, Mary. (Inv.: 36A.234; 3 Aug 1714; ----) Admr.: William Munkister. (Acct: 36B.334; ----; 14 July 1715)

HARRARD, William, age 15 yrs. Servant of Joseph Manning, Nov 1710. (Ct.&Land: D#2.5)

HARRINGTON, John. (Inv.: 1.184; 4 Jan 1674; ----) Admr.: Samuell Creney. (Acct: 1.474; ----; 24 Nov 1675)

HARRIS (HARRISE), Samuel and his wife Ales, "thereabouts" 40 yrs. and 48 yrs., respectively. Testified in court on the 6 April 1659 and 12 May 1659. (Ct.&Land: A#1.49, 52)

HARRIS (HARRISE), Samuel, age ca. 24 yrs. Swore in court 4 March 1661. (Ct.&Land: A#1.191)

HARRIS, Thomas. Inventory of Thomas Harris' estate (son of Thomas Harris), presented by Messrs. Pope, Marshall and Handly on 15 Dec 1662; list description of cattle only. (Ct.&Land: A#1.256-7)

HARIS, George, age ca. 30 yrs. Swore in court concerning case involving John Lumbroso and his servant named Elisabeth Wiles on 30 July 1663. (Ct.&Land: B#1.165)

HARRISE, George, age 30. Deposition. 9 Feb 1663. (Arch. of Md.: XLIX.158)

HARRIS, Jane, age 20 yrs. Servant of Richard Jones, 1676. (Ct.&Land: F#1.193)

HARRIS, Richard. Henry Henley, admr. of Richard Harris, entered a cattle mark for John Burgess, son in law of said Richard Harris. Recorded 11 Sept 1677. (Ct.&Land: G#1.66)

HARRIS, Richard. Payments include Col. Douglas, administrator from Richard Harris, William Hatton, for clothing for the children (unnamed). Admr.: Henry Henley. (Acct: 5.9; ----; 10 April 1678)

HARRIS, Susanna, dau. of Richard Harris. Chose William Browne and Mary his wife, as her guardians, 10 Aug 1680. (Ct.&Land: H#1.330)

HARRIS, Bethseba and Mary, daus. of Thomas Harris. Cattle mark recorded, 9 Sept 1684. (Ct.&Land: L#1.2)

HARRISS, Thomas & Mary. (Inv.: 9.192; 23 Nov 1686; ----)

HARRIS, Thomas. Admrs./Exs.: Thomas Harris, John Harris, Mrs. Bersheba Nicholls. (Inv.: 22.90; 13 Dec 1702; ----)

HARRISS, Elizabeth (widow). Signed 30 April 1742. To her son Samuel Lewis, a Negro boy called James, son of Negro wench called Frank, until her son Nathan Harriss arrives at age 25 years; Nathan to discharge her from any claim he may have to the estate of his late father, John Harriss. (Land: O#2.450)

HARRIS, Thomas and Mary, of Pickawaxen. Their children: Mary, born 16 Nov 1680; Thomas, born 6 Feb 1682; John, born 5 March 1684. (Ct.&Land: P#1.212; QRev.7, 8, 10)

HARRIS, Thomas (planter) of St. Mary's Co. Indenture 10 Aug 1713, to John Scott (cooper); a parcel called *Indian Quarter* by patent granted Thomas' father Richard Harris; on the s. side of Pile's Fresh, cont. 100 acres. (Ct.&Land: D#2.57)

HARRIS, John of Prince George's Co. Gift to his son John Harris, 7 Nov 1720. (Ct.&Land: H#2.386)

HARRIS, Thomas. Next of kin: John Harris Jr., Nathan Harris. Admr.: Mrs. Elisabeth Harris. (Inv.: 17.484; 25 June 1733; 11 Oct 1733)

HARRIS, Thomas. Next of kin: John Harris, Thomas Harris. Admr.: Elisabeth Harris. (Inv.: 18.468; 27 July 1734; 30 July 1734)

HARRIS, Thomas Jr. Next of kin: Nathaniell Harris, Mary Love. Admr.: John Harris Jr. (Inv.: 20.374; 6 May 1734; 3 May 1735)

HARRIS, John. Next of kin: Thomas Harris, Barton Harris. Admr.: Elisabeth Harris. (Inv.: 25.61; 30 April 1740; 20 May 1740)

HARRIS, John. Next of kin: Nathan Harris, Mary Love. Admr.: Katharine Harris. (Inv.: 27.297; 18 Dec 1742; 16 Jan 1742)

HARRISON, Joseph. Deed of gift dated 9 June 1660, Samuel Palmer gives Francis Harrison, his godson, son of Joseph Harrison of Nansemicke in Avon River; a cow calf. (Ct.&Land: A#1.110)

HARRISON, Joseph. His children: Richard, born 12 Oct 1659; Mary, born 21 Dec 1661; Elizabeth, born 11 March 1663; Catherine, born 4 Jan 1666. (Ct.&Land: C#1.252; P#1.204; QRev.1, 2; A.217. NOTE: Ct.&Land: A.217 gives date of Richard's birth as 13 Oct 1659.)

HARRISON, Joseph. To son Francis, land on the e. of Main Branch. To son Joseph, land on the w. of Main Branch. To child., viz: Richard, Eliza:, Katharine and Benjamin, and to Luke Greene, personalty. Wife Eliza:, extx. (Will: 1.589; 28 Aug 1673; 26 Dec 1673) Child.: Catherine, Joseph and Benjamin received cattle from Thomas Shuttlesworth on 8 June 1674. (Ct.&Land: E#1.155)

HARRISON, Anne, age 20 yrs. Servant of William Barton Jr., 10 Nov 1674. (Ct.&Land: F#1.13)

HARRISON, Robert, age 13 yrs. Servant of Alexander Smith, 10 Nov 1674. (Ct.&Land: F#1.13)

HARRISON, Richard. Wife Eliza:; dau. Susanna, all land at death of wife. Also mentions sons Richard, Thomas and John Burges. (Will: 5.249; -- -- -- 1676; 12 April 1677) (Inv.: 4.72; 24 April 1677; ----)

HARRISSON, Richard and Jane, of Nanjemy. Their children: Elizabeth, born 24 July 1685; Joseph, born 27 Oct 1687; Richard, born 31 Jan 1689; Tabitha, born 23 June 1693. (Ct.&Land: QRev.11, 13, 15, 22)

HARRISON, John (Gent.) and his wife Martha conveyed on 14 May 1686, to Robert Surling (mariner), of London; parcel on Wicomico River called *Rich Hill*, 600 acres; also parcel called *Thomas's Addition*, 83 acres. (Ct.&Land: M#1.154)

HARRISON, John and his wife Martha. Court case judgment in 8 June 1686/7; mentioning Robert Potts and his wife Jane. (Ct.&Land: N#1.149)

HARRISON, Oliver, son of John Harrison. Cattle mark recorded, 1687/8. (Ct.&Land: P#1.61)

HARRISON, Richard. Deposition regarding Richard Jones, orphan son of Richard Jones, 14 June 1692. (Ct.&Land: Q#1.54)

HARRISON, Thomas. Admr.: Francis Harrison. (Acct: 19.34; ----; 4 Jan 1698)

HARRISON, John. To Nathaniel Bolton and Mary his wife, 50 acres, *Haphazard* and personalty. To Martha, dau. of Gyles Wilson, Thos. Spinke and Jane his wife, personalty. John Dent of St. Mary's Co. ex. and residuary legatee of estate, including *Harrison's Adventure*, 215 acres, *Providence*. In event of sale of latter not being confirmed to Mr. Edward Greenhalge, it is devised to Mr. Dent as also all land in Corretoman, Virginia. Note — Capt. Dent in the administration of this estate showed that Mr. John Harrison removed to Virginia and had no personal estate in Maryland. (Will: 3.483; 5 Dec 1690; 30 May 1705)

HARRISON, Richard (Gent.). Deed of gift: 1 Jan 1706, to his grandson Joseph Hammilton, son of John and Elizabeth Hammilton, a slave; if he dies then to his sister Elizabeth Hammilton. (Ct.&Land: C#2.78)

HARRISON, Richard. To son Joseph, four tracts, viz., part of *Delahey's Chance*, 150 acres, *Woodberry's Hope*, 150 acres, *Holy Spring*, and 200 acres, *Carpenter's Square*. To son Richard, *Lane's Land* near Maryland Point, and sloop *Indian Princess*, jointly with his bro. Joseph. Mentions son Benjamin [minor]; grandchild. John and Eliza: Hambleton at majority; their mother, Eliza: Hambleton; dau. Tabitha (Harrison), at 18 yrs., bros. Francis and Joseph Harrison, and son Thomas at 21 yrs. To child., Eliza:, Joseph, Richard, Tabitha and Benjamin afsd., residue of estate. Exs.: Wife Jane and sons Joseph and Richard. (Will: 13.98; ----; 25 July 1710) Next of kin: Joseph Harrison, Elisabeth Hamilton. (Inv.: 32A.115; 14 Aug 1710; ----) Exs.: Joseph Harrison, Jane Harrison, Richard Harrison. (Acct: 32C.168; ----; 22 Aug 1711)

HARRISON, Francis. Mentions dau. Diana Price; dau. Violatta Harrison; wife Eliza:, extx. (Will: 13.504; 9 Sept 1712; 20 April 1713) Next of kin: Jos. Harrison. (Inv.: 34.49; 26 July 1713; ----)

HARRISON, Thomas, of St. Mary's Co, and Alice his wife convey on 22 Aug 1713 a tract called *Harrisons Venture* on w. side of Wicomico River, cont. 57 acres. (Ct.&Land: D#2.65)

HARRISON, Joseph, son of Richard Harrison acquired land on 14 Nov 1717, from John Lambetty. A parcel on the e. side of the easternmost branch of Nanjemy Creek, 100 acres, tract called *Conveniency*, and on 15 Nov 1724, from William Smith (planter), tract *Britts Adventure*, lying in Nanjemy Parish, 42 acres. (Ct.&Land: H#2.131; Land: L#2.194)

HARRISON, Cathrine. Relict and widow of Joseph Harrison (gent.), of Chas. Co., dec'd, intestate; renounces right to administer on estate of afsd. Joseph Harrison. 12 Feb 1718. (Will: 15.13)

HARRISON, Richard. Indenture, 18 Feb 1718, to John Fendall, 1/3 of *St. John's*, devolved to Richard Harrison from his mother, Mary Harrison, dec'd., dau. of Randolph Hinson, dec'd. (Ct.&Land: H#2.214 [241?])

HARRISON, Joseph, Capt. Next of kin: John Harrison, Richard Harrison. (Inv.: 2.110; 4 May 1719; ----)

HARRISON, Richard. Next of kin: Jane Evans (mother), Thomas Harrison (brother of whole blood). (Inv.: 3.256; 15 Feb 1719; ----)

HARRISON, William. (Inv.: 4.80; 4 Aug 1720; ----)

HARRISON, William. To wife Priscilla, extx., entire estate. (Will: 16.66; 9 March 1720; ----)

HARRISON, Richard and his wife Esther conveyed on 27 July 1724 a tract called *Hoggs Island*, 140 acres; tract laid out for Joseph Harrison. (Land: L#2.159)

HARRISON, Joseph, and his wife Virlinda conveyed on 11 Aug 1724 a tract called *Tabitha's Lot*, Nanjemy Parish, 130 acres. (Land: L#2. 162)

HARRISON, Joseph, Capt. [Referred to as Colonel in inventories.] To son Richard, 400 acres *Cow or Cool Spring*, 300 acres *Richard's Pleasure* and *Holy Spring*. To son Joseph, 427 acres *Amsterdam*, 300 acres *Urlinda (Verlinda)* and 200 acres *Carpenter's Square*. To dau. Tabathia, *Daniel's Quarter* bou. of John Allen, 400 acres *Land's Lane* at Maryland Point. To wife, 300 acres, *Delahayes Chance*, 150 acres *Minges Chance, Woodberries Hope*; at her decease to unborn child. To godson Hezekiah (son of Richard and Hester Harrison), 150 acres of *Christian Milford*. Mentions maintenance of son William. Exs.: wife, William Stone Sr., Thomas Mathews. Codicil: 24th Dec. 1726. To bro. Thomas, use of plantation whereon mother now lives during his life. [On 5th May 1727. Virlinda, relict of afsd. Joseph Harrison, accepts will.] (Will: 19.151; 24 Dec 1726; 5 May 1727) Next of kin: Jane Evans (mother), Thomas Harrison (brother). Extx.: Mrs. Verlinda Harrison. (Inv.: 12.207; 5 July 1727; 5 Aug 1727)

HARRISON, Thomas. To Mary Meek, personalty. Francis Meek, ex. (Will: 21.59; 24 Jan 1734; 1 May 1734) Next of kin: Charity King, Elisabeth Wade. Ex.: Francis Meeke. (Inv.: 18.500; 5 June 1734; 13 Aug 1734)

HARRISON, Richard. To son Richard, tract on n. side of Chinkamuxon Road. To son Thomas, other part of said tract on e. side of Chinkamuxon Road. To son Joseph, *Baltimore's Gift, New Street* and 50 acres *Harrison* after death of wife Ester, extx. To daus. Mary and Elizabeth, personalty. (Will: 21.136; 25 March 1733/4; 19 June 1734) Next of kin: Joseph Harrison, Benoni Harrison. Extx.: Esther Harrison. (Inv.: 20.239; 11 Dec 1734; 1 Jan 1734/5)

HARRISON, Francis. Next of kin: Charity Adams, Edmond Berry, Godfry Payne. Admr.: Joseph Harrison. (Inv.: 24.316; ----; 7 Nov 1739)

HARRISON, Virlanda (Virlinda), Madam. To sons Richard and Joseph Harrison and daus. Elizabeth and Tabitha Hoe, entire estate. That wife's dau. Elizabeth live with testator's sister Theodosia until she becomes of age or marrys. (Will: 22.136; 4 Dec 1739; 6 Feb 1739) Next of kin: Thomas Stone, Bethia Barnes. Exs.: Richard Harrison, Joseph Harrison. (Inv.: 25.4; 12 Feb 1739; 21 April 1740)

HARSTON, William, age 22 yrs. Deposition in 1710 regarding a tract on the w. side of Wicomico River, originally patented for John Courts, 200 acres. (Chas LandComm: M2.83)

HARTLEY (See HARKLEY).

HASLINGS, Thomas, age 23. Deposition on 27 Sept 1665 re the attack of Indians on the family of Agatha Langworth. (Arch. of Md.: XLIX, pp. 483)

HASLIP (HAISLIP), Richard. Thomas Chamber and his wife Ann, exs., and guardians of sons Henry and Robert till age of 18 and of son Richard till age of 21. (Will: 18.9; 11 Feb 1722/3; 15 Feb 1722) (Inv.: 8.103; [c1722]; --
--)

HATCH, John, age ca. 45 yrs. Swore in court 26 Jan 1658. (Ct.&Land: A#1.35)

HATCH, William (Gent.). Agreement and indenture betw. Sept-Dec 1686, that William Hawton maintain William Hatch for his lifetime and care for his dau. Sarah Hatch to age 18 yrs.; receiving tract on w. side of Wicomico River called *Courts Marsh*, cont. 200 acres. Other parcels totaling 600 acres; also parcel called *Waterbeech* of 50 acres on w. side of Wicomico. (Ct.&Land: N#1.10; Q.103)

HATCH, Thomas. In his will he left to wife Mary, ex., *Thomas his Purchase*. Mentions eldest son John; younger son Thomas; dau. Sarah; wife's dau. Elizabeth Marles; Thomas Standish. Residue of estate to wife, to be divided among child. after her decease. (Will: 19.607; 16 Nov 1728; 24 Jan 1728)

HATCH, Thomas. Next of kin: "minors." Exs.: Bryan Flin and his wife, Mary Flin. (Inv.: 14.160; 12 May 1729; 24 May 1729)

HATHERTON, John, age 12 yrs. Servant of Edward Price, 10 March 1674. (Ct.&Land: E#1.153)

HOTTON, William. A second inventory was cited. Mentions: no orphans. Exs.: Lydia Hatton, William Hatton. (Acct: 24.41; ----; 5 Aug 1703)

HATTON, Benoni and his wife Lidia. Deed dated 15 Feb 1732/3. To John Maddox, part of the tract called *Hattons Improvement*. (Land: M#2.321)

HATTON, George. Admr.: Elisabeth Hatton. (Inv.: 29.332; 20 April 1744; 24 Aug 1744)

HAW, John (Dr.). Admr.: Mary Haw. (Inv.: 22.275; 2 March 1736; 16 May 1737) Admr.: Mary Haw. (Inv.: 23.28; 18 Aug 1737; 15 Feb ----)

HAWKINS, Elizabeth, wife of Henry Hawkins. Cattle mark recorded 9 Aug 1682. (Ct.&Land: I#1.342)

HAWKINS (HAWKING), Henry son of Henry Jr. and Sarah Hawking of Zachiah Hundred, born 5 Jan 1689. (Ct.&Land: P#1.208)

HAWKINS, Henry, son of Henry and Sarah Hawkins Jr. of head of Wicomico River, born 5 Jan 1689. (Ct.&Land: QRev.15)

HAWKINS, Alexander Smith, son of Henry and Sarah Hawkins Jr., of head of Wicomico River, born 20 Jan 1691. (Ct.&Land: QRev.17)

HAWKINS, Henry, son of Henry Hawkins. Cattle mark recorded 14 Nov 1693. (Ct.&Land: S#1.169)

HAWKINS, Henry. In his will he left to son John, 100 acres, *Goat's Lodge*, and 1/2 of *Hawkin's Purchase*, formerly called *Fair Fountain*; also 266 acres, *Hawkin's Lot*. To wife Eliza:, extx., residue of *Hawkin's Purchase* and dwelling plantation; also 500 acres, *Jamaica*. To son Henry Holland Hawkins, residue of *Hawkin's Purchase*. To dau. Ruth and in turn to dau. Mary in event of death of son John without issue. To son Henry, 300 acres, *Stone Hill*, Prince George's Co. To dau. Ellinor Hawkins, alias Tubman, 238 acres, *Hawkin's Addition*, and 100 acres, *Come by Chance*, and 50 acres, part of *More's Branch*. To dau. Mary, 171 acres, *Hawkin's Barrens*, 50 acres, *Moore's Folly*, part of *Come by Chance*, and part of *Moore's Branch*. (Will: 6.310; 18 Oct 1698; 12 May 1699) Cites items in the possession of Elisabeth Hawkins. (Inv.: 19.127; 29 May 1699; ----) Mentions: coffin for son Thomas. Ex.: Elisabeth Hawkins. (Acct: 20.265; ----; 25 July 1701)

HAWKINS, Henry. Appraisers: Thomas Smoot, Michaell Martin. (Inv.: 3.689; 2 Dec 1702)

HAWKINS, Henry. To son Alexander, 200 acres of land belonging to plantation at Piscataway. To son Tubman, daus. Eliza: and Ellinor, personalty. Wife Sarah, extx., 130 acres called *Swney*. (Will: 11.371; 12 June 1702; 12 Jan 1702)

HAWKINS, Elizabeth. Enters Negro boy for her son Henry Holland Hawkins, 1 Oct 1707. (Ct.&Land: Z#1.276)

HAWKINS, Elizabeth. Mentions James Keech and Ruth, his now wife, dau. of Elizabeth Hawkins and John Keech, 1 Oct 1707. (Ct.&Land: Z#1.276)

HAWKINS, Henry Jr. (Inv.: 36C.46; [c1715]; ----) Admr.: Alexander Hawkins. (Acct: 37A.19; ----; 18 Sept 1715)

HAWKINS, Elizabeth [widow]. In her will she mentions three grandchildren, Francis, Eliz. and Mary Wine (son and daus. of Henry Wine, late of Gr. Britain, deceased); dau. Eliz: Lewis, wife of ――― Lewis, of Gr. Britain; granddaus. Eliz. and Martha Keech; grandson Henry Holland Hawkins, son of Henry Holland Hawkins. To granddau. Eliz. Hawkins, 500 acres, *Jamaica*, in Pr. Geo. Co. Mentions grandson John Hawkins; Richard Tubman, son of Revd. Geo. Tubman; kinswoman Eliz: Middleton (wife of Wm. Middleton). Son Henry Holland Hawkins, ex. Mentions Michael and John Martin. (Will: 14.510; 12 June 1716; 14 June 1717) (Inv.: 39C.82; 1717; ----)

HAWKINS, John of Prince George's Co. and Elizabeth his wife. A gift, 6 Jan 1721/2, to their loving bro. Thomas Hawkins. Parcel called *Goats Lodge*, bounded by *Zachia Manor*, cont. 150 acres. Also 50 acres formerly called *Fair Fountain* now called *Hawkins Purchase*. Deed of gift dated 28 March 1723, to their bro., William Hawkins; 200 acres, being part of tract formerly called *Fair Fountain*, but now *Hawkins Purchase* (250 acres) being designated for Thomas Hawkins, bro. to sd. John and William. (Ct.&Land: H#2.475; Land: L#2.81)

HAWKINS, Thomas. In his will he left to bro. Alexander, ex., personalty. (Will: 18.336; 13 Nov 1724; 18 Dec 1724)

HAWKINS, Thomas, and his wife Sarah, conveyed on 16 Nov 1734 Lot #9 in Benedict Leonard Town. (Land: O#2.74)

HAWKINS, Henry Holland and Joan his wife conveyed on 15 June 1727 the tract called *Hussyes Addition*, 438 acres; also tract of 100 acres; and three other tracts called *Hussyes Lodge*, 33 acres, *Hussyes Reserve*, 50 acres and *Hussyes Lott*, 103 acres. (Land: L#2.365)

HAWKINS, William of Prince George's Co., and his wife Sarah, conveyed on 26 June 1732 to Henry Holland Hawkins, tract called *Fair Fountain*, but now *Hawkins' Purchase*, cont. 200 acres. (Land: M#2.288)

HAWKINS, Thomas. Next of kin: Samuel Hanson Jr., John Duncastle. Admr.: Sarah Hawkins. (Inv.: 29.166; 15 March 1743; 20 --- 1744)

HAWKINS, Mrs. Elizabeth. Deed of gift, 15 Nov 1704, to her dau. Ruth, wife of James Keech Jr., a Negro girl named Elley age 13-14 yrs. (Ct.&Land: Z#1.160).

HAWLING (HAWKING), William and Mary of Portobacco. Their children: Mary, born 20 June 1687; William, born 18 March 1689. (Ct.&Land: P#1.208; QRev.13, 15)

HAWLTON, William. (Inv.: 10.207; 18 March 1688; ----)

HAWTON, William. Mentions bro. in law William Hatch; Sarah Worrell, dau. of sd. bro. in law; Richard Smoot; John Newton, godson William Oard and goddau. Mary Wilder. Wife Lydia, extx. Mentions children: John, William and Thomas. (Will: 11.377; 23 Jan 1702; 17 April 1703)

HAWTON, William Sr. (Inv.: 1.687; 23 April 1703; ----)

HAWTON, William (gentleman). To sons John, William and Thomas, all land devised them by their grandfather, deceased. To sons Joseph and Benony, *Hawton's Improvement*. Ex.: Father in law Robert Yates, and in event of his death, Robert Yates Jr., to have charge of sd. sons during their minority. (Will: Part 2-12.210; 14 Sept 1708; 4 July 1709) Next of kin: John Maddox. (Inv.: 30.255; 16 July 1709; ----) (Inv.: 32B.74; 6 May 1710; ----) Mentions: no widow (unnamed), but five children (unnamed). Ex.: Robert Yates. (Acct: 32B.248; ----; 9 April 1711)

HAWTON, John, blacksmith. In his will he left to two bros., Joseph and Benja., land devised testator by his grandfather. To grandmother Mrs. Lydia Yates, bro. Joseph afsd., Judith O'Caine and Mrs. Sarah Maddox, personalty. To John Maddox, ex., a servt. boy Richard Smoot, with what estate of the Smoots now in testator's hands, until sd. boy comes of age. To four bros., residue of estate. (Will: 14.498; 26 Dec 1717; 23 Jan 1717)

HAWTON, John. Next of kin: William Hawton. (Inv.: 39A.32; 18 April 1718; ----)

HAWTON, William (Gent.) and his wife Margaret conveyed on 7 May 1730, two parcels, one cont. 82 acres, and other cont. 73 acres. (Land: M#2.224)

HAWTON, Benoni (planter), and his wife Hannah conveyed on 14 May 1737 part of a tract called *Hawtons Improvement*, 72 acres. The tract was laid out for 172 acres and was bounded by the land of William Hawton, late of Charles Co., on the Wicomico River. On 15 Feb 1732/3 said Benoni and his wife Lydia conveyed a part of the same tract cont. 70 acres. (Land: M#2.327; O#2.204)

HAWTON, William and his wife Margret conveyed on 12 Jan 1732/3 157 acres in Stafford Co., Virginia; another 127 acres; also 30 acres. (Land: M#2.325)

HAXBY, Isabell of Beedale in the county of Yorke, widow, and Laurence Parker of Tunstall in the county of Yorke, yeoman, and his wife Anne; John Poulson of Catticke in county of York, yeoman and his wife Elizabeth, William Greyson of Seamore, of county of York, yeoman and his wife Jane—that Isabell, Anne, Margarett, Elizabeth and Jane are the surviving sisters and heirs of Richard Watson, their brother in Charles

Co., convey to Thomas Dent of St. Mary's Co. all parcels of land of their brother Richard Watson. 1676. (Arch. of Md.: LXVI, p.180)

HAYES. (See HAYS.)

HAYFIELD (HEIGHFEILD), Richard. (Inv.: 32C.63; 10 March 1710; ----) Admr.: Thomas Burch. (Acct: 33A.232; ----; 27 May 1712)

HAYS, James, age ca. 23 yrs. Swore in court 22 April 1662. (Ct.&Land: A#1.202)

HAYS, Patrick, age ca. 23 yrs. Swore in court on Oct and Nov of 1662. (Ct.&Land: A#1.242. B.5)

HAYS, James. Mentions: daughter (unnamed) of the deceased. Admr.: Charles Jones. (Acct: 31.80; ----; 14 March 1709)

HAYSE (HAYES), Peter. Admr.: Elisabeth Foxley. (Inv.: 22.344; 29 Jan 1735; 17 Aug 1737)

HAYES, Samuel (Inv.: 27.391; 18 Feb 1742; 27 April 1743) Creditors: George Dent, Benjamin Fendall. Admr.: Margaret Hayes.

HAYWARD, John, son of Phillis (bound for 21 years). Servant of William Barton, 12 Jan 1668/9. (Ct.&Land: D#1.42)

HAYWOOD, Mary, age 12 yrs. Servant of Thomas Jenkins, 10 Jan 1681. (Ct.&Land: I#1.224)

HEAGAN/HAGON. (See HAGAN.)

HEARBEN, Allen, son of Elisha and Elizabeth Hearben, born 8 Jan 1745. (Trinity: 105—rev.)

HEARD, Brigit. Account of Bridgit Heard, wife of William Heard, presented by Walter Story; John Duglas is admr. of Brigit Heard. 13 March 1665/6. (Ct.&Land: B#1.521-2)

HEARD, Bridgett. John Compton and Rob: Page (planters), Maryland, have due them 500 acres, the assignee of Bridgett Heard, relict of William Heard, and 300 acres, a parcel called *Brothwood* in St. Mary's Co.; recorded 20 Dec 1722. (Land: L#2.66)

HELGAR, Thomas (innholder). Deed of gift dated 16 Oct 1678, to his wife Anne Helgar. (Ct.&Land: H#1.57)

HELMES, John married the widow of John Mills, by 8 March 1669/70. (Ct.&Land: D#1.134)

HEMSLY, Philemon of Queen Anne's Co. and Mary his wife, on 30 April 1713, from William Bladen of the City of Annapolis, 50 acres at the head of Wicomico R. (Ct.&Land: D#2.62)

HEMSLY, Phelemon and his wife Mary. Indenture, 14 June 1713, from Abraham Lemaster. Parcel of land on the e. side of Zachia Swamp. (Ct.&Land: D#2.51)

HEMSLEY, Philemon and his wife Mary conveyed on 10 Aug 1714 part of a parcel cont. 20 acres; in Mattawoman on the n. side of Piscataway River and on 2 Nov 1714 a parcel called *Rich Hill*, cont. 300 acres. (Ct.&Land: F#2.21, 51)

HENSLEY, Philemon and his wife Mary of the City of Annapolis conveyed on 23 Feb 1718 a lot in the town at the head of Portobacco Creek. (Ct.&Land: H#2.223)

HEMSLEY, Mary, widow of Philemon Hemlsey, to be paid by Philip Lee, 354 lbs. of tobacco, damages the court judged that Philemon Hemsley sustained. 12 Aug 1719(Chas LandComm: M2)

HEMSLEY, Philemon (Phillomen), (gentleman). Next of kin: Mary Hemsley, Ann Hemsley. (Inv.: 4.38; 17 May 1720; ----) Approvers include Mary Hemsley. Mentions: Richard Willson. Admr.: Thomas Price. [no county given]. (Inv.: 5.28; 29 March 1721; 3 April 1721) (QA. Inv.: 9.181; [c1723]; ----) Creditors: William Rogers. Approvers: Mary Rogers.

HEMSLEY, Mary (widow) of Annapolis, Anne Arundel Co. To the four children of her sister, Mrs. Judith Bruce, dec'd.: Charles Bruce, her eldest son, Negro boy Toney, age about 5 yrs.; Townley Bruce, youngest son, Negro boy Nacey, age about 16 months, both the sons of Negro woman called Jeany; Francis Bruce, eldest dau., a Negro girl Bett, dau. of Negro woman Sarah, age about 2 yrs.; Elizabeth Bruce, youngest dau., Negro girl Sarah, dau. of Negro woman Dubba, age about 2 yrs. Signed 19 April 1723. (Land: L#2.84)

HEMSLEY, William, Queen Anne's Co., son and admr. of Philemon Hemsley, late of Anne Arundel Co., appoints attorney to recover money and tobacco due him on the western side of the Chesapeake Bay. Signed 2 Oct 1723. (Land: L#2.239)

HENLY, Robert, Pyckywaxen, (gentleman). In his will he left to Bethsheba and Mary, daus. of Thomas Harris, Eliza: Nichols and granddau. Charity, dau. of John and Charity Courts, personalty. To son in law John Courts, Charity, his wife, residue of estate. Ex. Son in law John Courts afsd. (Will: 4.31; 15 Feb 1683; 31 March 1684) (Inv.: 8.187; 23 April 1684; ----)

HENSEY, William. In his will he left to Susanna Abbott, John Courts Jr., Robert Powell, Thomas Harris, Richard Smith and Anne Brown, personalty. To grandson William Chapman, ex. To grandson Richard Chapman, sd. estate should sd. William die without issue. (Will: 4.138; 23 March 1684; 12 May 1685) Legatees: John Courtes, Robert Powell, Susanna Abbott, Mary Harris, Richard Smith, Ann Browne. Admr.: Barbary Chapman, now wife of John Gorly. (Acct: 9.44; ----; 9 July 1686)

HENSLEY (HENSELY), Edward, age 17 yrs. Servant of John Bowles, 10 June 1674. (Ct.&Land: E#1.171)

HENSON, William, age ca. 25 yrs. Swore in court 19 Nov 1661. (Ct.&Land: A#1.168)

HENSON, Randolph (Gent.), Barbarah his wife, and Richard Wade (planter) and Anne his wife conveyed on 10 July 1691, a tract called *Lonist Thickett*, 1060 acres. (Ct.&Land: R#1.421)

HERBERT, William, age 17 yrs. Servant of Robert Rowland, 11 April 1676. (Ct.&Land: F#1.173)

HERBERT, John, age 18 yrs. Servant of Humphrey Warren, 13 March 1676. (Ct.&Land: G#1.16)

HERBERD (HERBURD), William of John and Elizabeth Herberd of head of Wicomico River, William, born 6 July 1688. (Ct.&Land: QRev.14)

HERBERT, William, son of John and Elizabeth Herbert both of Zachia Hundred, born 6 July 1688. (Ct.&Land: P#1.208)

HERBERT, Catherine, dau. of William and Mary Herbert of Pickawaxon, born 6 Dec 1692. (Ct.&Land: P#1.211; QRev.19)

HERBERT, Sarah, Madam. Next of kin: George Dent, Douglass Grifferd. (Inv.: 1.288; 26 July 1718; 8 Oct 1718)

HERBERT, William, Capt. Next of kin: Joseph Douglass, Douglass Grifferd. (Inv.: 1.281; 26 July 1718; ----) Next of kin: Joseph Douglass, Douglass Gotfard. (Inv.: 2.233; 8 July 1719; ----)

HERMAN, Robert. Servant, judged to be betw. 17-18 yrs. old, presented by Henry Addames, 3 Feb 1663/4. (Ct.&Land: B#1.244)

HERRANT, John, son of Peter Herrant. Cattle mark, 18 Feb 1718, for heifer given him by his godfather Even Hughs. (Ct.&Land: H#2.214)

HERRICKSON, Hans, son of Hans and Judith, age 4 yrs. To serve Robert Benson to age 21, 16 June 1693. (Ct.&Land: S#1.129)

HERRINGTON, Thomas. Admr.: John Howison. (Inv.: 17.709; 23 Jan 1733; 1 April 1734)

HESELDEN, Elizabeth. Servant to Robert Thompson; had bastard child, 16 June 1693. (Ct.&Land: S#1.129)

HEUTON (HEWTON), Allen. In his will he left to son George, two lots in Portobacco, he to be under care of Walter Dodson. To dau. Mary, personalty, she to be under care of Mary Ann Boswell till age of 16. To Geo. Sinkilton use of shop and tools. Exs.: Walter Dodson and John Boswell. (Will: 22.488; 4 May 1742; 7 July 1742)

HEWS. (See HUGH/HUGHS.)

HEY, Charles, age 16 yrs. Servant of Benjamin Rozer, 7 June 1668. (Ct.&Land: C#1.268)

HEYDON, Francis (planter) of St. Mary's Co., and Thomasine his wife, conveyed on 13 Aug 1678, a tract called *Partnership*, on e. side of Portobacco Fresh; cont. 300 acres. (Ct.&Land: H#1.320)

HICKSON, Henry, Nanjemy. In his will he mentioned sons James and Edward. Richard Treie, ex. (Will: 4:140; 3 Feb 1684; 10 July 1685) (Inv.: 9.438; 17 July 1685; ----)
HICKSON, James, age 8 yrs., orphan of Henry Hickson, bound to James Finley, 8 June 1686. (Ct.&Land: M#1.220)
HICKSON, James. Wife Mary, extx. and sole legatee of estate. (Will: 11.361; 12 Jan 1702; 23 Feb 1702) (Inv.: 1.693; 15 March 1702; ----)

HIGTON, John, planter. In his will he left to sons John, Charles and Benjamin and dau. Mary Sims, personalty. To wife Menesenca, extx., residue of estate; at her decease, to sons Thomas and William. (Will: 18.108; 29 April 1723; 11 June 1723) Next of kin: John Higton, Benjamin Higton. (Inv.: 9.289; ----; 12 Dec 1723)
HIGDON, Benjamin. Mentions: John Hawsse, Mary Lommes, Charles Higdon. (Inv.: 10.363; ----; [c1725]. NOTE: Benjamin Higdon was dead as of 12 Jan 1724. See Will of John Semms: 18.368; 15 April 1723; 12 Jan 1724.)
HIGDON (HIGTON), John. Next of kin: Thomas Higdons, William Higdons. Admr.: Bathia Higton. (Inv.: 23.24; 19 March 1736; 13 June 1737)
HIGDEN, William and Jane. Their children: Benjamin, born 11 Dec 1733; William, born 21 Feb 1735; Benedict Leonard, born 6 Aug 1738; Ignatious, born 12 Aug 1740; Susanna, born 25 June 1743; Martha, born 13 Nov 1745. (Trinity: 106)

HIGONS (HIGGONS), John. (Inv.: 3.289; 8 April 1704; ----)

HILLS, William married Edith Headlow (Idy Hadlowe), in June 1667 at Mr. Montague's. (Ct.&Land: C#1.253; P#1.204; QRev.3)
HILLS, Edee, widow of William Hills, lately dec'd. Deed of gift 24 April 1669; to dau. Susanna Marea Hills; two yearling heifers. (Ct.&Land: D#1.68)
HILL, Thomas, age 16 yrs. Servant of Mr. Rozer, 14 June 1670. (Ct.&Land: D#1.154)
HILL, Vall: (Walt), age 12 yrs. Servant of William Hinsey, 12 March 1672. (Ct.&Land: E#1.54)
HILL, Onsley, son of Thomas and Mary Hill (servants to Benjamin Rozer), born 5 May 1677. (Ct.&Land: P#1.206; QRev.5) [baptized: 3 June 1677, F: 244; H#1.244]
HILL, Matthew. (Inv.: 7A.156; 21 Nov 1679; ----)

HILL, Thomas. Servant of Giles Blizard, age judged to be 13 yrs. old, 8 June 1686. (Ct.&Land: M#1.220)

HILL, Onsley, orphan son of Thomas Hill, dec'd. John Hammond charged with abusing him, 9 June 1691. (Ct.&Land: Q#1.28)

HILL, Richard. Mentions: no children. Admr.: Capt. James Bigger. (Inv.: 13A.367; 5 April 1695; ----. Acct: 14.58; ----; 8 Oct 1696)

HILL, Robert. Mentions: Mary Hill (widow, very poor) left with a great many poor children (unnamed). (Inv.: 15.242; 5 July 1697; ----) Admr.: Mary Watson (relict, now dead), formerly the wife of John Watson. (Acct: 18.78; ----; 1 Oct 1698)

HILL, Philip, son of Robert Hill, dec'd. Cattle mark recorded 9 Sept 1707. (Ct.&Land: Z#1.260)

HILL, Clement of Prince George's Co. and his wife Ann conveyed on 18 Sept 1714 a parcel on the main branch of Swanson's Creek and the w. side of *Calverton Manor*, 250 acres. (Ct.&Land: H#2.111)

HILL, Giles of St. Mary's Co., and his wife Margaret conveyed on 17 Nov 1718, a part of *Simpsons Supply*, cont. 160 acres. (Ct.&Land: H#2.210. Also see H#2.216)

HILL, John (carpenter) of St. Mary's Co. and Anne his wife conveyed on 6 Oct 1719 a parcel called *Coventry*, cont. 53 acres and on 20 Dec 1720, a parcel called *Addition*, cont. 50 acres and *Smith's Addition*, cont 50 acres. (Ct.&Land: H#2.321, 413)

HINCH, Mathew, age 21 yrs. Servant of Mr. Rozer, 2nd Tues in Nov 1670. (Ct.&Land: D#1.169)

HINCKS, Dorothy, age 19 yrs. Servant of John Wheeler, 12 Jan 1668/9. (Ct.&Land: D#1.42)

HINDE, William, age 12 yrs. Servant of Thomas Clarke, 12 March 1677. (Ct.&Land: G#1.119)

HINDLE, Joshua, age 20 yrs. Servant of Francis Gooderick, 11 June 1678. (Ct.&Land: G#1.158)

HINSLEY, Thomas, age 21 yrs. Servant of Philip Lines, 14 March 1681. (Ct.&Land: I#1.258)

HINSON, (HENSON), Randolph. To wife Barbara, extx., plantation, *St. John's*. To dau. Blanch Thompson and her son Thomas, *St. John's* at death of wife afsd. (Will: 6.235; 28 Sept 1698; 16 April 1699) Ex.: Barbara Henson. (Inv.: 19.29; 5 May 1699; ----. Acct: 20.196; ----; [c1701])

HIPKIS, Peter, age ca. 24 yrs. Swore in court 22 April 1662. (Ct.&Land: A#1.202)

HITCHINSON, John. Died 18 or 19 Dec 1668, possessed of 300 acres at Nanjemy in Charles Co. (Arch. of Md.: LI.172)

HOBART (HUBART), Richard (gentleman). In his will he left to William Hunter, Robert Brookes, John Hall, Nicholas Dewlick, Christopher Plunkett, George Tubman, each child of Maj. Wm. Boarman, to son (unnamed) of Anthony Neale, John Smith, Thomas Massey, John Bredd, Thomas Piper, Mary Benson, Leonard Brooke and his wife, Maj. Boarman, and to Ann Brookes, personalty. Exs.: Anthony Neale, Wm. Boarman, Benj. Hall. (Will: 6.181; 7 May 1698; 14 June 1698) (Inv.:17.114; [c1698]; -- --) Exs.: Benjamin Hall, William Boreman, Anthony Neale. (Acct: 19½B.112; ----; 6 May 1700)

HOBB, Thomas and his wife Isable on 18 Sept 1690 conveyed land purchased from Nicholas Proddy. (Ct.&Land: R#1.32, 97)

HOBSON, John. Servant boy judged to be 13 yrs. old, presented by Robert Hundley, 12 May 1662. (Ct.&Land: B#1.111)
HOBSON, John (brick layer), and his wife Elizabeth conveyed on 16 Aug 1739 lots in Charles Town, 3, 5 and 6. (Land: O#2.406)
HOBSON, John. In his will he left to mother Phoebe, estate; then to go to John, son of bro. Thomas. To wife Elizabeth residue of estate. Exs.: Wife, William Theobold, bro. Thomas. (Will: 22.424; 9 Sept 1741; 30 Dec 1741) Mentions: J. Hobson, John Muschett, Francis Goodrich. Admr./Ex.: Eliza Hobson. (Inv.: 27.188; ----; 17 Aug 1742)

HOCTON, Adam, son of Joseph Hocton. To serve Philip Lines until age 21 yrs., 8 June 1675. (Ct.&Land: H#1.101)

HODGINS, Charles, age 14 yrs. Servant of Archebald Wahob (Walkup), 10 March 1673. (Ct.&Land: E#1.152)
HOGDIN, Johnathan, age 18 yrs. Servant of John Redish, 9 Nov 1680. (Ct.&Land: I#1.33)

HODGLY, John, age 21 yrs. Servant of Joseph Harrison, 8 March 1669/70. (Ct.&Land: D#1.127)

HODGSON, Richard (planter). Indenture, 18 Oct 1678, to Benjamin Rozer; for love and maintenance of Johannah his wife and Elizabeth his youngest dau. in law; tract of land on the Avon R. in Nangemy or Stone's Fresh. If Eliza: has no hrs., then to his bro. William Hodgson. (Ct.&Land: H#1.91)
HODGSON, Richard and his wife Johannah, lately called Johannah King. Court held 8 Aug 1682. (Ct.&Land: I#1.321)
HOGIN (HODGEN), John. Admr.: Hugh Perry. (Inv.: 17.483; ----; 5 Oct 1733)
HODGSON, Richard. In his will he left to eld. son Richard, 2nd son Philip, young. son William, personalty; sons to be free at 18 yrs. Exs.: Wife Elizabeth and eld. dau. Johana. Witnesses: John Baker, Elizabeth

Hodgson, Elinor Hodgson. (Will: 21.342; 20 Sept 1734; 16 April 1735) Next of kin: G. Burns, Matthew Burns Jr. Ex.: Elisabeth Hodgson, Johannah Hodgson. (Inv.: 21.42; ----; 6 Aug 1735)

HOGGIN, Henry, age 21 yrs. Servant of Philip Lines, 11 Jan 1675. (Ct.&Land: F#1.163)

HOLMES, Grace, age 22 yrs. Servant of Philip Lines, 14 June 1681. (Ct.&Land: I#1.124)

HOLT, Jane, dau. of James and Margarett Holt of Pickawaxon Parish, born 19 Nov 1693. (Ct.&Land: QRev.21)

HOLT, Robert, son of William and Mary Holt of Portobacco, born 15 Feb 1694. (Ct.&Land: QRev.25)

HOLT, William, age 52. Deposition in 1720 regarding tract called *Westwood Mannor*. (Chas LandComm: M2.94)

HOLT, William. Next of kin: Francis Parker, William Holt. Admr.: Robert Holt. (Inv.: 10.218; 27 July 1724; 13 Oct 1724)

HOLT, Robert. Next of kin: William Holt. Admr.: Mary Holt. (Inv.: 20.203; 29 May 1734; 4 Dec 1734)

HOLT, John, son of William and Milicent Holt, born 17 Sept 1745. (Trinity: 114B—rev.)

HOLTON, Joseph, age 22 yrs. Servant of Mr. Rozer, 14 June 1670. (Ct.&Land: D#1.154)

HOMAN, Herbert. To Thomas Hyde and Mary, dau. of sd. Thomas, personalty. Wife Dorothy, extx. (Will: 5.161; 13 Jan 1676; 9 March 1676)

HONNKER, Elisabeth. Servant maid, judged to be 15 years old, presented by James Lee, 9 Aug 1664. (Ct.&Land: B#1.355)

HOPE, George. Admr.: James Mankin. (Inv.: 28.470; ----; 28 Feb 1743)

HOPEWELL, John. Next of kin: John Manning, Sarah Manning. Admr.: Francis Ware. (Inv.: 19.135; ----; 10 Oct 1734)

HOSKINS, Jeremi:, age 21 yrs. Servant of John Bowles, 2nd Tues in April 1669. (Ct.&Land: D#1.62)

HOSKINS, Lauran:, age 17 yrs. Servant of John Bowles, 2nd Tues in April 1669. (Ct.&Land: D#1.62)

HOSKINGS, Thomas, age 12 yrs. Servant of Robert Thompson, 11 March 1678. (Ct.&Land: H#1.130)

HOSKYNS, Philip and his wife Elizabeth. Indenture 14 Nov 1682, from Archibald Wahob (planter), for fatherly love and affection to his dau. Elizabeth Hoskyns; parcel cont. 400 acres. (Ct.&Land: K#1.26)

HOSKINS, Philip and Elizabeth of Portobacco. Their children: Jane, born 1 March 1681; Benedista, born 18 Dec 1685; Elizabeth, born 9 Feb 1687; William, born 18 March 1690; Mary, born 24 March 1692; Margarett, born 15 Aug 1694. (Ct.&Land: QRev.8, 11, 13, 17, 20, 23)

HOSKINS, Lawrence (Laurance). To James, son of Rebecca Tyer, entire estate. Extx. sd. Rebecca Tyer. (Will: 4.259; 9 Jan 1686/7; 12 June 1687) Admr.: Mrs. Rebeckah Tyer. (Inv.: 9.352; 18 April 1687; ----) (Inv.: 10.97; 23 July 1688; ----) A second inventory was filed. Admr.: Rebecca Yates (relict of James Tyre (executor of deceased)), now wife of Robert Yates. (Acct: 10.163; ----; 5 Oct 1688) Extx.: Rebeckah Yates (relict of James Tyer), wife of Robert Yates. (Acct: 12.21; ----; 8 Sept 1691) (Acct: 12.67; ----; 8 Sept 1691)

HOSKINS, Phillip, Col. He left to his son William; son Phillip, 50 acres, *Friendship*; grandchildren, personalty; son Oswald, 178 acres, dwelling plantation; son Bennett, 200 acres plus *Hoskins' Lot*; son Ballard, 190½ acres bou. of James Makey, nr. China Moxson Ck., 100 acres, *St. John's*, and 100 acres adj. *St. John's*; daus. Mary, Ann and Martha. Mentions children of former wife and children of last wife, Ann. Wife Ann, extx. To be buried in Portobacco Church. Mentions Jane Hamilton, late called Jane Booth. (Will: 14.475; 20 June 1714; 3 April 1718)

HOSKINS, Ann. Personalty of her late husband, be divided among her children; sons Oswald and Bennett Hoskins, exs., to whose care she leaves her three other child. Overseers: William Chandler, bro. William Thompson, son in law Mr. Craycroft and Mr. Brooke. (Will: 14.611; 6 May 1718; 9 May 1718)

HOSKINS, Mary. Next of kin: Phil: Hoskins, Robert Hanson. (Inv.: 1.90; 15 June 1718; ----)

HOSKINS, Philip (gentleman). Next of kin: Robert Hanson, Thomas Stone. (Inv.: 1.345; 8 Aug 1718; ----)

HOSKINS, William, age 28 yrs. Deposition, 12 Aug 1719, regarding *Glovers Point*. (Chas LandComm: M2.48)

HOSKINS, William, age 29 yrs. Deposition on 24 Sep 1719, regarding the tract *Tryal*, 300 acres. (Chas LandComm: M2.75)

HOSKINS, Philip (joyner). To bros. Oswell and Bennet, personalty. To bro. William, ex., residue of estate, with all rights in estate of father, Col. Philip Hoskins, dec'd. (Will: 16.218; 26 June 1720; 16 Nov 1720)

HOSKINS, Oswald. He left to bros., Bennett and Baylord, real estate, and sisters, Mary Ann and Martha, personal estate. Bro. Bennett ex. of this as well as will of mother. Overseers: Brother in law Thomas Stone and William Chandler. (Will: 17.79; 14 Jan 1720; 6 Sept 1721)

HOSKINS, William. Next of kin: Benjamin Hoskins, Baylard Hoskins. Admr.: Violetta Hanson, wife of Robert Hanson. (Inv.: 12.342; 21 May 1727; 26 Sept 1727)

HOSKINS, Mary Anne. Acknowledges receipt from her bro. Bennett Hoskins, exr. of Oswald Hoskins, exr. of Anne Hoskins, extx. of Col. Philip Hoskins, her part of all sd. estates; signed 18 Oct 1726. Also same for her bro. Baylord Hoskins's estate signed 15 Jan 1728/9; and both documents recorded 2 July 1729. (Land: M#2.169)

HOSKINS, Martha. Acknowledges receipt from her bro. Bennett Hoskins, exr. of Oswald Hoskins, exr. of Ann Hoskins, extx. of Colo. Philip Hoskins, of all her part of all the sd. estates, likewise her part of her bro. Baylord's estate; signed 8 July 1729. (Land: M#2.205)

HOSKINS, Bennett and his wife Eleanor conveyed on 21 April 1730 part of a tract called *New York* and tract called *Duck Marsh*, ca. 169 acres. (Land: M#2.203)

HOSKINS, Bennet (Bennett). Father Raphael Neale, ex., and directs that an agreement between himself and Edward Neale for making over two tracts, *St. John's* and *St. John's Addition* be carried out by ex. (Will: 21.53; 21 Feb 1733/4; 22 April 1734) Next of kin: John Lancaster, William Neale. Ex.: Raphael Neale. (Inv.: 18.297; 27 May 1734; 3 July 1734)

HOUGHTON, James, age 14 yrs. Servant of Capt. Henry Aspenall, 8 Aug 1682. (Ct.&Land: I#1.317)

HOWARD, Philise. Judged to be 20 yrs. old, presented by William Barton Jr., 8 Nov 1664. (Ct.&Land: B#1.384)

HOWARD, Edmund. Deed of gift, 31 Aug 1705, to dau. Elizabeth Howard; should she die before age 16, to youngest son of my now wife, Margaret Howard. (Ct.&Land: Z#1.210)

HOWARD, Margarett, dau. of William and Elizabeth Howard. Cattle mark recorded 24 Jan 1708. (Ct.&Land: C#2.125)

HOWARD, Thomas. Deed of gift: 9 May 1709, to his brother George Howard. (Ct.&Land: C#2.130)

HOWARD, Edmund (gent.). To eld. son Wm. Stevens (Howard), 100 acres. To 2nd son Thomas, dwelling plantation, 150 acres. To 3rd son John, 100 acres. To only dau. Eliza:, part of *Saturday Work*, at 16 yrs. or marriage. To young. son George at 21 yrs., residue of lands. To little granddau. Margaret Howard, mourning ring in memory of late deceased brother, Geo. Dent, and ring in memory of her grandmother, deceased, marked M. H. To brother Rich'd Eyton, merchant in London, and only sister, Mrs. Hester Tyndale, wife of Athelstand Tyndale, upholsterer in Bristol, personalty. Exs.: two eld. sons. In codicil he mentions Edmund Howard at 21 yrs., son of eld. son Wm. Stevens Howard, and Eliza:, his wife; and sister Margarett afsd., dau. of same. (Will: 13.632; 3 Dec 1709; 5 Jan 1713)

HOWARD, Elizabeth. To niece and god-dau. Elizabeth (dau. of eldest bro. William Stevens Howard), personalty. To god-daus. Rebecka, dau. of cousin Geo. Dent, and Ann dau. of Thos. Skinner, personalty. To nephew Thomas, ex. (son of bro. Thomas Howard), residue of estate. (Will: 14.187; 7 July 1716; 8 Oct 1716) Next of kin: John Howard, George Howard. (Inv.: 38A.15; 9 Oct 1716; ----)

HOWARD, Edmund (Edward). Next of kin: George Dent, John Howard, Thomas Skinner, Barton Smoot. Mentions: William Dent. (Inv.: 35A.248; 15 March 1713; ----) Exs.: William Stevens Howard, Thomas Howard. (Acct: 36B.155; ----; 12 April 1715)

HOWARD, Thomas. Next of kin: William Howard, John Howard. Admr.: Elisabeth Howard. (Inv.: 11.421; 23 March 1726; 11 July 1726)

HOWARD, John. To his cousin, William Dent, late of Chas. Co., his right to 15 ewes and ram; 14 Sept 1726. (Land: L#2.311)

HOWARD, John (Gent.). Deed of gift signed 15 Jan 1728/9; to his daughter Anne Howard, a Negro boy Basill, son of Negro woman named Doll. (Land: L#2.459)

HOWARD, Elizabeth, widow. Signed 10 June 1734; to her son Jacob Brandt, all her claim of dower, by right of his father, Charles Brandt, dec'd. Signed 29 July 1734; to her dau. Elizabeth Brandt, spinster, a Negro man named John. (Land: O#2.46, 47)

HOWARD, William Stevens (planter). Mentions eldest son Edmund; wife Sarah, extx.; youngest son William; dau. Rachel wife of Mathew Compton. Refers to four young. children: William, Elizabeth, Susannah and Sarah. (Will: 21.55; 15 Dec 1733; 29 April 1734) Extx.: Sarah Howard. (Inv.: 20.313; ----; 3 Feb 1734) Next of kin: John Howard, Edmond Howard. Extx.: Mrs. Sarah Howard. (Inv.: 18.482; 9 May 1734; 10 Aug 1734)

HOWARD, Sarah (Mrs.). To sons Henry Truman; James Truman; and William Howard; daus. Elizabeth and Sarah Howard; and grandson Henry Smoot, personalty, including silver marked T. T. Whereas husband William Stevens Howard, deceased, disposed of two horses belonging to his son Edmund certain personalty is bequeathed sd. Edmund to compensate him for any loss sustained. Sons Henry and James Truman are cautioned to behave toward sd. Edmund with tenderness. (Will: 21.344; 16 April 1735; 20 May 1735) Next of kin: Philip Briscoe, James Briscoe. Ex.: Henry Truman. (Inv.: 21.193; 29 May 1735; 28 Dec 1735)

HOWARD, John. Mentions son Thomas, *Partners Purchase*; son Baker; son John, part of *Three Brothers*; dau. Elenor, wife of John Dowglass; dau. Jane; grandson John Dawglass; wife Rebecca Brooke, extx. (Will: 23.51; 2 Feb 1742; 22 March 1742)

HOWARD, John, Capt. Mentions: Henry Truman, Stephen Chandler, Thomas Howard, John Howard. Admr.: Rebecca Howard. (Inv.: 27.441; 26 April 1743; 19 May 1743)

HOWARD, James. (Inv.: 27.444; [c1742/3]; ----)

HOWARD, Ann. Mentions children: Sarah and Mary Ann [minors]; sister Prudence Saunders; sister Mary Poore; trusty friend, Joseph Lancaster, and wife Jane. Ex. Jos. Lancaster. (Will: 24.15; 5 Oct 1744; 6 Oct 1744) Next of kin: Mary Power, William Sanders. Ex.: Joseph Lancaster. (Inv.: 31.137; 3 April 1745; 12 June 1745)

HOWELL, Thomas. (Inv.: 4.191; [c1677]; ----)

HOWES, Thomas, age 16 yrs. Servant of Capt. Josias Fendall, 12 March 1677. (Ct.&Land: G#1.119)

HOWSON, John. Admr.: James Bigger. (Acct: 14.59; ----; 8 Oct 1696)
HOWISON, John. Mentions: Francis Meek, George Medrey, James Muncaster. (Inv.: 22.141; 14 Oct 1736; 15 Dec 1736)
HOWISON, Ann. Next of kin: Robert Sennet. Admr.: John Rigg. (Inv.: 28.339; ----; 16 Dec 1743)

HOWLING, Mary, dau. of William and Mary Howling. Cattle mark, 14 Jan 1689. (Ct.&Land: P#1.190)

HOYLE, Samuell, age 21-22 yrs. Servant of Edmond Lindsey, 2nd Tues in Nov 1669. (Ct.&Land: D#1.169)

HUBBARD, Nathaniel of Goodman's Fields in parish of St. Mary White Chapel, Middlesex, Gent., and Eleanor his wife, one of the daus of Mathew Hill of Maryland, dec'd., for love and affection, to Edith Dutton, dau. of ────── Dutton, dec'd., niece of Eleanor, to use of Notley Dutton, brother of Edith Dutton and nephew of Eleanor; equal moiety to Elizabeth Penn, dau. of William Penn and Elizabeth his late wife, dec'd., formerly Elizabeth Dutton and niece of Eleanor; for default of issue then to William Penn, brother of Elizabeth Penn, nephew of Eleanor. 9 Aug 1717. A parcel belonging to Eleanor Hubbard called *Poppleton*, of 200 acres on w. side of Wicomico River (1/2 part). (Ct.&Land: H#2.88)

HUBBERTON, Mary, age 18 yrs. Servant of Bartholomew Coates, 10 March 1670/1. (Ct.&Land: E#1.35)

HUDSON, Robert, age 13 yrs. Servant of Richard Midgeley, 11 April 1676. (Ct.&Land: F#1.173)
HUDSON, Johanna(h). (Inv.: 17.20; 1 Aug 1698; ----) A second inventory was cited. Mentions: William Hudson (son, dead). Admr.: Mathew Barnes. (Acct: 19½A.111; ----; 3 Aug 1699)
HUDSON, Thomas (planter) and his wife Elizabeth on 4 April 1745 conveyed tract called *Hudsons Sinnagouge*, 30 acres. (Land: Z#2.40)

HUGH (HEWS), Even. To John (son of Peter Harrow) and to Jane Shiler, personalty. To bro. in law Josias Mankin and Peter Harrow, exs., residue of estate. Memorandum to above will states that testator Even Hugh paid for the accounts of the estate of Thos: Hawes, £2,250. tobacco. (Will: 14.426; 22 Oct 1717; 6 Dec 1717) (Inv.: 39C.81; 10 Dec 1717; ----)

HUGHS, Dorothy. Admr./Ex.: Mathew Frawner. (Inv.: 16.220; ----; 10 Aug 1731)

HUGHTON, Allen. Mentions: William Eborsell, John Singleton, Stran Goodrich, Lettica Dodson. Admr./Exs.: John Boswell, Walter Dodson. (Inv.: 27.210; ----; 3 Nov 1742)

HULSEY, Elizabeth, dau. of Menshall (Muerell?) Hulse. Cattle mark recorded by John Goomes, 1678. (Ct.&Land: H#1.185)

HULSE, James, son of Meverell Hulse. Cattle mark recorded, 9 Aug 1682. (Ct.&Land: I#1.342)

HUMBLE, Barbary, age 20 yrs. Servant of Philip Lines, 11 Jan 1675. (Ct.&Land: F#1.163)

HUNDBY, Henry. Servant, judged to be 21 yrs. old, presented by Mrs. Elisabeth Atwicks, 12 July 1664. (Ct.&Land: B#1.314)

HUNDLY, Robert, age ca. 44 yrs. Witness in court case 19 Nov 1661. (Ct.&Land: A#1.169)

HUNGERFORD, William (planter) of Stafford Co., Virginia, and Margaret his wife, dau. of William Barton, on 10 June 1688, acquired a parcel called *Barton Woodyard*, cont. 100 acres; also tract called *Capell*, cont. 100 acres. (Ct.&Land: R#1.537)

HUNGERFORD, William and Margarett, of Portobacco. Their children: Elizabeth, born 14 Feb 1691; William, born 12 June 1694. (Ct.&Land: QRev.20, 23)

HUNGERFORD, William. To four sons, viz., William, Thomas, John and Charles, jointly, two tracts, 150 acres, *Johnson Choice* and 250 acres, *Smoot's Choice*. Mentions daus. Ann, Elizabeth and Mary. To son Barton, 28 acres, *Hungerford's Choyce*. Extx.: Wife Margaret. (Will: 3.650; 22 Jan 1704; 14 March 1704/5) Admr.: Margarett Hungerford (relict). (Inv.: 3.697; 18 May 1705; ----) Extx.: Margret Miller, wife of Jacob Miller. (Acct: 32B.9; ----; 20 Nov 1710)

HUNGERFORD, Thomas. Next of kin: Margett Miller, Charles Hungerford. Administratrix: (name not given). (Inv.: 10.123; 6 Sept 1724; 22 Sept 1724)

HUNGERFORD, Charles, son of William Hungerford on 3 May 1728 conveyed part of two tracts, *Hungerford Choice* and *Smoots Choice*, devised by the will of William Hungerford to his son, sd. Charles Hungerford. (Land: L#2.423)

HUNGERFORD, Barton Sr. and his wife Elizabeth conveyed on 9 Dec 1729 a tract in Zachia Swamp, cont. 100 acres and on 26 May 1740, to their son, Barton Hungerford Jr., a tract called *Batchellers Delight*, 140 acres. They conveyed on 8 June 1743, part of tract called *Bartons Woodyard*, on w. side of Zachia Swamp, 5 acres. (Land: M#2.191; O#2.446; X#2.18).

HUNT, Mary, dau. in law of Garrett Sinnett, born two days before Easter 1665. (Ct.&Land: C#1.253; P#1.204; QRev.2)

HUNT, John, age 16 yrs. Servant of William Barton, 2nd Tues in April 1669. (Ct.&Land: D#1.62)

HUNT, John. (Inv.: 19½B.38; 18 Nov 1699; ----) Admr.: Dorothy Hunt. (Acct: 20.198; ----; [c1701])

HUNT, Thomas, age 53. Deposition, 1 March 1720, regarding tract called *Canterbury*. (Chas LandComm: M2.116)

HUNT, Thomas. To wife Anna, extx., 100 acres. dwelling plantation, *Hunt's Venture*. To grandson Thomas, son of son John, deceased, sons Thomas, Joseph and Philip, grandson, son of Elizabeth Farring, and dau. Catherine Harrold, 1s. each. (Will: 21.64; 21 April 1734; 16 May 1734) Next of kin: Philip Hunt, Joseph Hunt. (Inv.: 18.516; 8 June 1734; ----)

HUNT, Joseph (planter), of Prince George's Co., and his wife Mary, a dau. of Thomas Lewis, dec'd.; and Joseph Fry of Prince George's Co., and his wife Elizabeth, another dau. of Thomas Lewis; and William Robins of Prince George's Co. and Ann his wife, another dau. of Thomas Lewis - conveyed on 12 June 1739, a tract called *Birch Den*, 150 acres, which formerly belonged to afsd. Thomas Lewis. (Land: O#2.402)

HUNTER, Richard, age 21 yrs. Servant of Benjamin Rozer, 9 Jan 1671/2. (Ct.&Land: E#1.52)

HUNTER, William, age 14 yrs. Servant of Thomas Hussey, 11 Jan 1675. (Ct.&Land: F#1.163)

HUNTER, William (Revd.) To friend George Thorold, ex., now of St. Mary's Co., entire estate. (Will: 18.174; 16 Aug 172-; 20 Sept 1723)

HUNTINGTON, Elias, age 40. Deposition in 1720 regarding tract called *Westwood Mannor*. (Chas LandComm: M2.91)

HURRIE, George (planter), and his wife Ann. Recorded 26 Feb 1744/5. Leased 133 acres. (Land: Z#2.13)

HURST, Samuell. Admr.: Thomas Sympson Jr. (Inv.: 17.62; 18 Dec 1732; 10 March 1732)

HUS, Robert, living at Edward Tills (Tells) at Mattawoman, formerly belonging to Robert Smallpage, died 24 July 1694. (Ct.&Land: QRev.23)

HUSBAND, William, by his will in Cecil Co. dated 25 March 1717, bequeathed to his eldest son, James Husband (planter), of Cecil Co., a tract called *Canterbury*, 100 acres, which he conveyed on 10 April 1729. (Land: M#2.153)

HUSBAND, James (of Cecil Co.) and his wife Alice on 28 Sept 1727 conveyed 1/2 of a tract called *Cantibury*, cont. 100 acres. (Land: L#2.406)

HUSSEY, Thomas, age ca. 27 yrs. Swore in court 4 March 1661/2. (Ct.&Land: A#1.195)

HUSSEY, Thomas, age ca. 26 yrs. Swore in court 22 April 1662. (Ct.&Land: A#1.202)

HUSSY, Elisabeth, age ca. 20 yrs. Witness in court 9 July 1662. (Ct.&Land: A#1.227)

HUSSEY, Thomas, age 27. Deposition. 9 Feb 1663. (Arch. of Md.: XLIX.159)

HUSSEY, Thomas (Gent.). On 13 Aug 1666 William Nevill (planter), and Thomas Hussey and Johanna his wife, relict of John Nevill, dec'd., conveyed a tract on n. side of the Piscataway River called *Wheeler's Palme*, cont. 150 acres. (Ct.&Land: C#1.61)

HUSSEY, Thomas and his wife Joan(e) on 13 June 1670, conveyed a parcel called *Newport*, cont. 150 acres. (Ct.&Land: D#1. suppl. 53)

HUSSY, Johannah, [wife of] Thomas Hussy. Cattle mark recorded, 10 June 1673. (Ct.&Land: E#1.132) Also court files dated 6 Sept 1681. (Ct.&Land: I#1.166)

HUSSEY, Thomas and his wife Johannah. Indenture 10 July 1684, to Richard Harrison; parcel called *Woodberry's Hope*, cont. 150 acres. (Ct.&Land: L#1.175)

HUSSEY, Thomas, married Jane Breade, relict of John Breade, court records 11 Nov 1690. (Ct.&Land: R#1.103)

HUSSY (HUSSEY), Thomas. To grandson Thomas Hussey Lucket, 1310 acres in Chingamuxon. Dau. Eliza: Luckett, extx. (Will: 11.43; 6 Feb 1699; 14 Oct 1700) (Inv.: 20.135; 9 Oct 1700; ----)

HUSSEY, Thomas, father of Elizabeth, wife of John Hanson (Gent.). Indenture from William Wills, 14 July 1721, to John Hanson, the following tracts of Thomas Hussey, father of Elizabeth, wife of John Hanson: *Newport*, cont. 150 acres; *Discovery*, cont. 150 acres; *Ingerstone* on the e. side of Zachia Swamp., cont. 230 acres; *Moores Lodge* on the n. branch of Zachia Swamp, cont. 150 acres; *Moores Gore* of 50 acres; 880 acres which Thos. Notley sold to Thomas Hussey. (Ct.&Land: H#2.449)

HUTCHINS, Elianor, age 13 yrs. Servant of Henery Hawkins, 10 June 1674. (Ct.&Land: E#1.171)

HUTCHINSON, William (Gent.) of Prince George's Co., and Sarah his wife on 29 May 1704 conveyed parcel called *Mount Pleasant* on s. side of Piney Branch, 164 acres. (Ct.&Land: Z#1.171)

HUTCHYSON (HUTCHISON, HUTCHINSON), Thomas (merchant). Wife Ann, extx., entire estate, during minority of dau. Eliza:. (Will: 6.180; 3 Jan 1697; 23 Aug 1698) (Inv.: 18.67; 23 Sept 1698; ----) (Acct: 19½A.102; ----; 7 Dec 1699) (Acct: 28.1; ----; 21 Nov 1707) Extx.: Ann Hutchinson (widow), now wife of Alexander Magruder. (Acct: 36B.27; ----; 14 Feb 1714)

HUTCHISON, Mary married 20 Oct 1715 to John Abington. (King George's Parish: p. 248)

HUTCHINSON, John, eldest son of William Hutchison, late of Prince George's Co., on 30 Sept 1721, conveyed half of parcel called *Mount Paradise* on s. side of Mattawoman, cont. 292 acres. (Ct.&Land: H#2.473)

HUTCHESON, William. Next of kin: Mary Abington, John Howard. Admr.: Ann Hutchison. (Inv.: 16.411; -- Dec 1731; 15 March 1731)

HUTTON, John (yeoman) of Dearham, Cumberland Co., nephew to Charles Hutton, late of Patuxent, Maryland, appoints Henry Thomson of Whitehaven, sailor, as his attorney, to recover money estate of his late uncle. Signed 10 Oct 1722. (Land: L#2.88)

IBBETSON, Francis. Proved in Prince George's County. (Inv.: 1.277; 7 Oct 1718; 29 Oct 1718)

IBBETSON, Teresa. Deed of gift, 30 July 1719, to her son John Thomas (planter); tract called *Ware*. (Ct.&Land: H#2.298)

IDE, Margere, age ca. 18 yrs. Servant to Henry Addames, having five years to serve from the date of her arrival. Court held 19 Nov 1661. (Ct.&Land: A#1.167)

ENNIS, David, age 16 yrs. Servant of Thomas Hussey, 11 Aug 1685. (Ct.&Land: L#1.161)

INNIS (ANNIS), Thomas. Next of kin: William Annis, John Cooper. Admr.: John Webb. (Inv.: 19.134; 27 May 1734; 16 Oct 1734)

IRELAND, Elisabeth. Judged to be 17 yrs. old, presented by Edward Swan, 22 April 1662. (Ct.&Land: A#1.201)

IVERY, Catherine. Servant to Anne Neale, mother of Anthony Neale, age judged to be 15 yrs. old, 16 June 1693. (Ct.&Land: S#1.128)

JACKSON, Thomas. Judged to be ca. 16 yrs. old, servant to Thomas Gerrard, 22 April 1662. (Ct.&Land: A#1.201)

JACKSON, Mary, age 21 yrs. Servant of Robert Henley, 10 March 1670/1. (Ct.&Land: E#1.35)

JACKSON, James, age 19 yrs. Servant of John Wright, 8 Sept 1674. (Ct.&Land: F#1.1)

JACKSON, Elizabeth. Indicted for having a bastard child, servant of John Warren, 13 March 1710. (Ct.&Land: D#2.136)

JACKSON, William. Cattle mark recorded 14 May 1712, for heifer given to his dau. Jane Jackson by her godmother Anne Miles. (Ct.&Land: D#2.5)

JAXSON, William. Admr.: John Chapman. (Acct: ----; 20 Dec 1716)

JAMES, William, age 38. In 1669 he stated he was at Edmund Lindseys in Oct 1668 and heard Thomas Oakley striking and beating at a door of a room in which George Thompson of Charles Co. was and said Thompson had barred up the door by drawing a great chest athwart the inside of said door. (Arch. of Md.: LVII.428)

JAMESON, Henneretta, dau. of Barbarah Jameson. Cattle mark recorded for cow given to her by Henry Barnes, 9 Jan 1705/6. (Ct.&Land: Z#1.230)

JAMESON, John. Admr.: Thomas Jameson. (Acct: 37B.219; ----; 29 Oct 1717)

JAMESON, Thomas and his wife Mary. To his son Henry Joshua Jameson; deed dated 16 May 1729; part of tract called *Halls Place* and part of *Halls Lott*, 250 acres. (Land: M#2.167)

JAMESON, Henry Joshua. To sons Henry and Richard, dwell. plant. with land adjoining, being part of *Hall Lott* and part of *Hall Place*. Wife: Elizabeth, extx. (Will: 20.820; 30 Aug 1733; 6 Nov 1733) Next of kin: Thomas Jameson, Luke Mathews. Extx.: Elisabeth Jameson (widow). (Inv.: 20.72; 19 Dec 1733; 29 Nov 1734)

JAMESON, Thomas (gent.). To son Thomas, parts of the several tracts following, viz.: *Hall's Place, The Addition, Jarvis, Preston* and *Queen Mary*; after decease of son Thomas lands (300 a.) to be divided between his two sons John and Thomas. To wife of son Thomas (unnamed), and every one of her children, personalty. To son Benjamin, parts of tracts: *Hall's Lot, Hall's Place, Jarvis* and *The Addition*. Refers to dec'd. son Henry Joshua Jameson. To son Joseph, parts of tracts: *Hall's Lot, Indian Fields, Hall's Place, The Addition* and *Jarvis*, and *Spring Run*. To Henry and Richard, sons of deceased son Henry Joshua, personalty. To dau. Mary Queen and to each of her children (unnamed), son in law Marsham Queen, dau. Martha Matthews and to each of her child. (unnamed), son-in-law Luke Matthews, daus. Elizabeth and Ann, personalty. To wife Mary and four children: Benjamin, Joseph, Elizabeth and Ann, personal estate. Exs.: Marsham Queen and Luke Matthews. (Will: 21.49; 17 Nov 1733; 6 April 1734) Next of kin: Thomas Jameson, Elisabeth Jameson. Ex.: Marsham Queen. (Inv.: 18.493; 7 Aug 1734; 13 Aug 1734)

JAMESON, Thomas and his wife Frances. Recorded 26 Sept 1734. To his mother, Mary Jameson Sr., Thomas' right to lands that his father sold in Great Britain and in Lancaster Co., and in particular the lands in the possession of John Hayes that formerly belonged to his father. (Land: O#2.50)

JAMIESON, John. In letter/bill of lading to Robert Whythill, Glasgow, 21 Jan 1744/5, John Jamieson mentions his son William. (Land X#2.176, 177)

JARBO, John and his wife Mary, Portobacco. 1 Nov 1659. (Arch. of Md.: LXV.679)

JARBOE, John, of St. Mary's Co., and his wife Mary on 9 Sept 1728 conveyed moiety of 300 acres formerly taken up by Col. John Jarboe, late of St. Mary's Co., called *Thompsons Delight*, cont. 150 acres. (Land: L#2.438)

JEFFERS, Marie. Servant judged to be 14 yrs. old, presented by John Cain, 8 July 1662. (Ct.&Land: A#1.220)

JEFFERSON, Michael. To the Roman Catholic Church, entire estate. (Will: 1.417; -- June 1670; 30 Nov 1670)

JEFFERSON, James. (Inv.: 7A.344; 8 Feb 1680; ----)

JEFFS, John, age 13 yrs. Servant of John Courts, 14 June 1670. (Ct.&Land: D#1.154)

JENIFER, Daniel (surgeon) and Elizabeth his wife on 14 July 1721 conveyed parcel called *Coate's Retirement*, cont. 243 acres. (Ct.&Land: H#2.444)

JENIFER, Daniel and his wife Elizabeth leased to John Brown and his wife on 13 Sept 1725, a house at Portobacco Road, until his son in law, Rodham Rogers, arrives at the age of 21 yrs. (Land: L#2.251)

JENIFER, Daniel. Mutually agreed on 27 Oct 1726 that John Beale (Gent.), should assign Daniel Jenifer (chirurgeon), a certain tract. Said Daniel Jenifer, by his will devised said land to his eldest son, Daniel of Saint Thomas Jenifer, deed made 28 Jan 1728, 1/2 of *Durham*, of 370 acres. Acknowledged by Johanah Catherine Beale, wife of John Beale. (Land: L#2.466)

JENIFER, Daniel (chyrurgeon). To son Daniel of St. Thomas Jenifer, part of *Durham*; part of *St. Edmond's*; also land called *Betty's Delight*, *Lemaister's (Leinaster's) Delight*; and *Coates Retirement*. Children to be in care of Revd. William Maconokie, ex., until of age. (Will: 19.724; 22 Aug 1728; 4 June 1729) Next of kin: Ann Jenifer, "no other kin that can claim." Administrators: John Theobalds and his wife, Elisabeth Theobalds, Mary Jenifer. (Inv.: 15.145; 7 July 1729; 3 Nov 1729)

JENKINS, Elizabeth and Mary, daus. of Thomas Jenkins. Cattle mark recorded, 10 June 1674. (Ct.&Land: E#1.180)

JENKINS, Thomas (planter) and his wife Anne conveyed on 8 June 1675 a parcel on the Avon River, cont. 85 acres. (Ct.&Land: F#1.103)

JENKINS, Enock, son of Daniell and Elizabeth Jenkins of Pickawaxon, born "last day of July 1694." (Ct.&Land: QRev.23)

JENKINS, William. (Inv.: 23.180; 8 April 1703; ----) Admr.: Mary Bateman (relict), now wife of George Bateman. (Acct: 3.133; ----; 15 March 1703)

JENKINGS, Richard. Next of kin: none. (Inv.: 34.145; [c1712]; ----)

JENKINS, Richard. Mentions three orphans of Francis Lang: John, William and Robert; Rebecca Duphex, extx. (Will: 13.586; 18 Nov 1712; 30 March 1713)

JENKINS (JENCKINS), Abenigo (Abednego). Next of kin: Edward Miles, James Cottrell Jr. (Inv.: 35A.56; 17 Dec 1713; ----) Admr.: Jane Penn, wife of Mark Penn. (Acct: 36B.101; ----; 19 Feb 1714)

JENKINS, Philip and John, sons of Philip and Zantalina Jenkins. Philip being 5 yrs. old 7 March last; and John was 3 yrs. old 2nd of this April [1714]. To receive their father's estate at age 18 yrs. old. (Ct.&Land: F#2.10)

JENKINS, Thomas Jenkins, age 79. Deposition in 1721 regarding tract called *Linsey*. (Chas LandComm: M2.146)

JENKINS, William and Mary his wife, of St. Mary's Co., on 16 Oct 1722, leased to Edward Miles, part of tract called *Pyeshard Shift*, for 18 years and conveyed to Edward Jenkins, tract called *Batchelors Hope*. (Land: L#2.51, 83)

JENKINS, Thomas. To his son George Jenkins, one Negro lad called Peter, at the decease of Thomas Jenkins' wife, Anne Jenkins. Signed 1 July 1725. Recorded at the request of the widow of afsd. Wm. (sic) Jenkins on 19: 9ber [Nov] 1725. (Land: L#2.240)

JENKINS, Thomas. To son Edward, 160 acres, half of *Pyes Hardshift*. To son William, residue of afsd. tract. To son George, after decease of wife Ann, 150-acre dwell. plan. *Lynsei (Lindsey)*. To dau. Ann Spaulding, 100 acres called *St. Thomas*. To Peter Attwood, granddau. Sarah Simpson and Eliza. Winser, personalty. Mentions daus. Elizabeth Edlen, Ann Spaulding and Mary Norris. Exs.: Wife Ann and son George. (Will: 19.251; 1 Nov 1726; 31 Oct 1727) Appraisers: Matthew Stone, Thomas Sanders. Creditors: Will. Chandler. Next of kin: Edward Jenkins, William Jenkins. Extx.: Ann Jenkins. (Inv.: 13.42; 28 Jan 1727; 29 March 1728)

JENKINS, Ann. Mentions Elizabeth Windsor (Windzer); dau. Mary Narris; sons Edward and William, exs. (Will: 19.836; 25 June 1729; 3 Dec 1729) Next of kin: Susannah Jenkins, Henrietta Jenkins. Exs.: Edward Jenkins, William Jenkins. (Inv.: 15.394; ----; 17 Feb 1729)

JENKINS, Thomas. Next of kin: Edward Jenkins, Mary Jenkins. Admr./Ex.: Henerilla Jenkins. (Inv.: 26.438; 25 Feb 1740; 3 Jan 1741) (Inv.: 28.154; 1 Feb 1742; ----)

JENKINS, Thomas. Next of kin: Susannah Jenkins, John Jenkins. Admr.: Ann Jenkins. (Inv.: 27.218; ----; 26 Nov 1742) (Inv.: 30.145; ----; [c1744])

JENKINS, Thomas, by his will left his two sons, Edward and William Jenkins, a tract called *Pyehard(?) Shift*, 333 acres, called the *Miry Branch*. Division agreement signed 2 Nov 1744. (Land: X#2.159)

JENKINS, William. Next of kin: John Bateman, Thomas Batman. Admr.: Margaret Jenkins. (Inv.: 31.372; 25 Sept 1743; 19 Nov 1745)

JENKINSON, William (planter) and his wife Mary on 8 Nov 1675 conveyed a parcel of land formerly known at *Goate's Lodge*, cont. 150 acres. (Ct.&Land: F#1.150)

JENKINSON, Ignatius, son of William and Mary Jenkinson of Wicomico, born 2 May 1693. (Ct.&Land: QRev.22)

JENKINSON (JENKINS), Philip. (Inv.: 37A.53; 5 June 1716; ----) Admr.: William Penn. (Acct: 37C.133; ----; 13 Sept 1716)

JOANES (See JONES).

JOHNS, Hannah, relict of Abraham Johns, Baltimore Co., dec'd., on 28 Sept 1734 conveyed tract called *Black Oak Thickett*. 200 acres. (Land: O#2.70)

JOHNSON, Daniel, age ca. 22 yrs. Swore in court 26 Oct 1658. (Ct.&Land: A#1.24)

JOHNSON, Elisabeth. Jury determines that Elisabeth Johnson hanged herself with a bridle rein, 12 July 1664. (Ct.&Land: B#1.342)

JOHNSON, John. Servant, judged to be ca. 12-13 yrs. old, presented by Edmond Lindsey, 12 July 1664. (Ct.&Land: B#1.314)

JOHNSON, John, age ca. 45 yrs. Swore in court 14 Nov 1665, that Richard Smith made his will upon his death bed. (Ct.&Land: B#1.493)

JOHNSON, Thomas, age 17 yrs. Servant of Henry Adams, 11 April 1676. (Ct.&Land: F#1.173)

JOHNSON, Daniell, son of Daniell (dec'd.) chooses his guardian, Thomas Gerrard, 1677. (Ct.&Land: G#1.46)

JOHNSON, Jemima, age 13 yrs. Servant of Benjamin Rozer, 9 March 1679. (Ct.&Land: H#1.270)

JOHNSON, William. (Inv.: 36B.307; 2 Dec 1714; ----) Admr.: Alexander Willson. (Acct: 37A.13; ----; 29 Sept 1715)

JOHNSON, George. To Henry Blanchet, John Harris of Prince George's Co. and his dau. Mary, godson Thomas Williams and servant Mary Dickson, personalty. To William Munroe and Sarah Rosan, exs., and William Williams, residue of estate. (Will: 23.443; 4 Feb 1743/4; 29 Feb 1743) Exs.: William Williams, Sarah Rozar (Rosan). (Inv.: 29.164; 3 March 1743; 28 May 1744)

JOHNSON, Richard (house carpenter), and his wife Annastasia, on 9 June 1741 conveyed part of two tracts, *Wheelers Delight* and *Wheelers Rest*, 120 acres. Also a tract called *Lisbon*, 50 acres. (Land: O#2.511)

JOANES, Mary. Maid servant judged to be 20 yrs. old, presented by Walter Beane, 28 July 1663. (Ct.&Land: B#1.132)

JONES, Joanna, wife of Owen Jones. Cattle mark recorded, 12 March 1666. (Ct.&Land: C#1.163)

JONES, Owen and Joanna his wife on 20 Jan 1668, conveyed a parcel called *The Adventure*. (Ct.&Land: H#2.177)

JONES, Edward, age 14 yrs. Servant of John Lambert, 10 March 1673. (Ct.&Land: E#1.153)

JONES, Elizabeth, dau. of Owen Jones. Cattle mark recorded, 10-11 March 1673. (Ct.&Land: E#1.163)

JONES, Elizabeth, dau. of Owen Jones. Deed of gift dated 12 June 1674, from Robert Robins, a heifer. (Ct.&Land: E#1.156)

JONES, Moses, age 17 yrs. Servant of Zachary Wade, 8 June 1675. (Ct.&Land: F#1.101)

JONES, Richard and Elizabeth, of Mattawoman. Their children: Margarett, born 6 May 1673; Mary, born 27 May 1677; Elizabeth, born 27 April 1679. (Ct.&Land: P#1.206; QRev.4, 5, 6)

JONES, Philip, age 21 yrs. Servant of Robert Henly, 13 March 1676. (Ct.&Land: G#1.16)

JONES(?) Richard, age 19 yrs. Servant of William Chandler, 12 March 1677. (Ct.&Land: G#1.119)

JONES, Elizabeth. Servant of John Mun, presented for having a bastard child, 1678. (Ct.&Land: H#1.33)

JONES, Elizabeth, had a bastard child. Servant of John Munn, 9 March 1679. (Ct.&Land: H#1.270)

JONES, Robert, age 21 yrs. Servant of Thomas Hussey, 12 Sept 1682. (Ct.&Land: K#1.5)

JONES, Richard and Jane, of Cedar Point Neck. Their children: Richard, born 1 April 1680; Anne, born "at Christmas in ye yeare" 1684. (Ct.&Land: P#1.208; QRev.7, 10)

JONES, Mary, age 18 yrs. Servant of John Stone, 8 Aug 1682. (Ct.&Land: I#1.317)

JONES, Richard. Wife Jane, extx. To children: Richard and Ann Jones, at 16 yrs. of age. personalty. (Will: 4.201; 26 Jan 1685; 19 April 1686) Extx.: Jane Potts (relict of deceased), wife of Thomas Lindsey. (Acct: 10.160; ---; 1 Oct 1688)

JONES, Moses and his wife Katherin. Executors of last will of James Wheeler, court records 8 June [1686]. (Ct.&Land: N#1.33)

JONES, Katherine. Servant of Phillip Lynes, judged to be 16 yrs. old, 8 June 1686. (Ct.&Land: M#1.221)

JONES, John, son of Moses Jones. Gift dated 10 Sept 1689, from Joseph Gray and Richard Newton (planters); cattle. (Ct.&Land: P#1.184)

JONES, Richard. Petition of his two orphan children, Richard and Anne Jones, regarding the disposition of estate; mentions mother Jane Lyndsey, wife of Thomas Lyndsey. Court held 2 March 1690. (Ct.&Land: Q#1.23)

JOANES, Morgan (potter) of Dorsett Co., Maryland, and his wife Jane. Indenture 20 Sept 1690, with Edward Rookewood; parcel called *Saint Bennetts*, lying on Goose Bay, cont. 300 acres. (Ct.&Land: R#1.141)

JONES, Richard and Anne, orphans of Richard Jones and Jane, now wife of Thomas Lyndsey. Petition regarding guardianship, by Thomas Lyndsey, 9 June 1691. (Ct.&Land: Q#1.30)

JONES, Moses. Married Catherine, relict and extx. of James Wheeler. Order against him, 8 March 1691. (Ct.&Land: Q#1.53)

JONES, Richard. His estate to be taken out of the hands of Thomas Lyndsey who married Jane, relict of Robert Potts, for benefit of orphans Richard and Anne Jones, 13 Sept 1692. (Ct.&Land: Q#1.58)

JONES, Jane, dau. of Moses and ―― of Portobacco, born 4 Jan 1692. (Ct.&Land: P#1.211; QRev.19)

JONES, John. Servant to John Wilder, judged to be age 14 yrs., 2 Jan 1693. (Ct.&Land: S#1.211)

JONES, Thomas, son of Moses and Elizabeth Jones of Portobacco, born 2 March 1694. (Ct.&Land: QRev.24)

JONES (JOANES), Philip. (Inv.: 17.31; ----; 1 Aug 1698) Admr.: Mathew Barns. (Acct: 19½A.122; ----; 3 Aug 1699)

JONES, Richard. To dau. Margaret Thomas, 20 acres, *Valle*, and *Bachelor's Hope*. To daus. Eliza: and Ann, dwelling plantation. To grandson Richard Higgins, *Want Water*. Mentions Eliza: Higgins, Mary Higgins and Margaret Higgins. To daus. Margaret Thomas and Eliza: Jones, *Rich Delight*. To daus. Eliza: and Ann and to Joseph Thomas and John Higgins, residue of estate. Exs.: Joseph Thomas and John Higgins afsd. (Will: 6.368; 2 June 1698; 2 March 1699) (Inv.: 19½B.141; 25 April 1700; ----) Legatees: Elisabeth Jones, Ann Jones. Ex.: Joseph Thomas. (Acct: 20.183; ----; 12 March 1701)

JONES, Lewis. Mentions Capt. Philip Hoskins; Richard Wade; exs. (Will: Part 2-12.37; 18 Feb 1702/3; 16 March 1708/9) (Inv.: 29.141; 17 March 1708; ----) Admr./Ex.: Capt. Philip Hoskins, Richard Wade. (Acct: 29.143; ----; 4 April 1709)

JONES, Charles and his wife Elinor. -- Nov 1704. Sign lease and license from Philip Lynes, merchant, tract nr. Portobacco Creek called *Lines' Gore*, cont. 130 acres. (Ct.&Land: Z#1.174)

JONES, Charles. Next of kin: Robert Yates, Charles Yates. (Inv.: 36A.72; 3 June 1714; ----)

JONES, Charles. (Inv.: 37A.198; 23 Nov 1716; ----)

JONES, Barbara. To son Richard Chapman and to his dau., Eliza: Chapman, to son in law John Suttle, to dau. Ann Suttle and to Eliza: Suttle, personalty. To son Thos. Goletie, personalty formerly belonging to son William Chapman. Exs.: sons, Jno. Chapman and Thos. Goletie. (Will: 13.640; 1 Jan 1713; 27 Feb 1713) Next of kin: Richard Chapman, Thomas Gorly. (Inv.: 35A.145; 12 March 1713) Mentions: husband (unnamed, dead). (Acct: 36B.24; ----; 27 Dec 1714)

JONES, Jane. To son James Tyre, personalty. To other three children: Mary Jones, Eliza: Jones, and Charles Jones; share of Mr. Jones' estate. Exs.: Brothers Robert and Charles Yates. (Will: 14.161; 6 Aug 1716; 12 Sept 1716) (Inv.: 37A.199; 23 Nov 1716; ----) Ex.: Robert Yates. (Acct: 39C.111; ----; 28 Oct 1717)

JONES, Charles. Exs.: Robert Yates and Charles Yates (executors of Mrs. Jane Jones, administratrix of deceased). (Acct: 39C.112; ----; 28 Oct 1717)

JONES, Charles. Mentions: Leonard Hollyday, Samuell Wood, John Ramsey, Ann Promroy. Admr.: Mary Stone, wife of Hugh Stone. (Inv.: 11.508; -- July 1726; 12 Sept 1726)

JORDAN, Margaret. Judged to be 16 yrs. old, presented by Samuell Fendall, 10 Jan 1664. (Ct.&Land: B#1.398)

JUBB, James. Admr.: John Medly Sr. (Inv.: 3.261; ----; 6 June 1720)

KARNES, Henry, son of Robert [tailor] and Mary, of Portobacco. Their children: Henry, born 3 Sept 1688; William, born 3 April 1691. (Ct.&Land: P#1.209, 201; QRev.14, 17)

KARR, Robert. (Inv.: 39C.95; 3 March 1717; ----)

KEE. (See KEY.)

KEECH, John. Next of kin: Elisabeth Keech, James Keech. (Inv.: 32B.79; 13 July 1710; ----) Admr.: Elisabeth Midleton, wife of William Midleton. (Acct: 33B.131; ----; 14 July 1712)

KEECH, Elizabeth, of St. Mary's Co., relict of James Keech. To her son Courts Keech, a tract now in the possession of Elizabeth Keech, called *Courts Choice,* lying at head of Wicomico River, 100 acres. Deed signed 11 March 1729/30. (Land: M#2.200)

KEELBY, John, age 16 yrs. Servant of Peter Carr, 10 June 1674. (Ct.&Land: E#1.171)

KEENE, James (planter) and Mary his wife on 5 March 1709 conveyed a parcel called *Merchant Taylor Hall* on on Broad Neck Branch, cont. 150 acres. (Ct.&Land: C#2.176)

KEENE (KEEN), James (planter). Mentions sons John and James; dau. Jeane; dau. Frances; dau. Anne. Son Nicholas, ex. (Will: 21.750; 22 Oct 1735; 6 April 1737) Next of kin: Ann Rilay, Geane Stokes. Ex.: Nicholas Keen. (Inv.: 22.279; ----; 4 May 1737)

KEETE, William, father of Mary Croson, wife of Thomas Croson, and Martha Ludwell, wife of James Ludwell. (Land: O#2.408)

KEETT, William (planter) of St. Mary's Co., and his wife Elizabeth. Indenture 17 Dec 1686, tract called *Lower Poole,* cont. 250 acres. (Ct.&Land: N#1.29)

KENDALL, Francis, age 14 yrs. Servant of John Newton, 1676. (Ct.&Land: F#1.193)

KENDAY, James. Admr.: John Kennady. (Inv.: 13.171; 27 June 1728; 5 July 1728)

KENEDY, John (planter), of Prince George's Co., and his wife Elizabeth. On 16 July 1744 conveyed tract called *Turles(?)*, on w. side of Zachia Swamp, 100 acres. (Land: X#2.139)

KENT, Robert, age 12 yrs. Servant of John Dent, wnd Tues in April 1669. (Ct.&Land: D#1.62)

KERKLEY. (See KIRKLEY.)

KERSEY, Thomas and his wife Margaret. Deed of gift to their children, William and Margaret, 17 Jan 1677. (Ct.&Land: G#1.84)

KEY (See KEE).

KEE (KEY), Henry. (Inv.: 17.116; 30 Aug 1698; ----) Admr.: Sarah Kee. (Acct: 19.44; ----; 9 June 1699)

KEY, William. Next of kin: Sarah Carpenter, Thomas Barron. Admrs.: Lewis Williams and his wife (name not given). (Inv.: 11.505; 16 Aug 1726; 9 Sept 1726)

KEY, Philip (Gent.), of St. Mary's Co., and his wife Susannah on 10 March 1739/40 conveyed part of tract called *Baltimore Gift*, 32 acres. (Land: O#2.346A)

KEYBERT (KERBERT), Thomas (planter), and his wife Constant on 6 Feb 1737/8 conveyed a tract called *Quick Dispatch*, on e. side of Burdits Ck., cont. 100 acres. (Land: O#2.316)

KEYTH, George and Elizabeth his wife. Leased on 25 March 1730 tract called *Maidston*, cont. 50 acres. (Land: M#2.221)

KIDWELL, Haggit, and his wife Elizabeth(?). 12 Nov 1739. To James Kidwell Jr., part of tract called *Bridge Town*, 101 acres. (Land: O#2.438)

KIDWELL, James. Wife Anne, extx. Mentions children: John; William, Tracy, Elizabeth, Thomas and Benjamin. (Will: 22.511; 28 Sept 1740; 11 Oct 1742) Mentions: John Davis Jr., Charles Beavan. Admr.: Ann Kidwell. (Inv.; 27.439; 22 Nov 1742; 2 Feb 1742)

KILBORNE, Francis and his wife Elizabeth, guardian of Daniell Johnson, infant, defendant, 16 Sept 1672. (Arch. of Md., v. LI, p.84) Francis Kilborne and his wife Margaret, admrs. of Donnell (Daniel) Johnson, late of Charles Co., dec'd. 1672/3. (Arch. of Md.: LI.379; LXV.69) Francis and Elizabeth Kilborne present at the suit of Thomas Hussey. 1672/3. (Arch. of Md.: LXV.62)

KILINGSWORTH, John (nunc.). To Capt. John Fendall for benefit of two children, entire estate. Note — management of this estate was assigned to Matthew Stone. (Will: 13.605; ----; 27 July 1713) (Inv.: 35A.54; 25 Aug 1713; ----) Admr.: Matthew Stone. (Acct: 36B.98; ----; 24 Jan 1714)

KILLCART, John. Servant of William Hatch, age judged to be 15 yrs., 12 Jan 1685. (Ct.&Land: M#1.67)

KING, Thomas. In his will he mentions wife Joanna, extx.; unborn child; wife's eldest dau. Eliza: Jones and son Philip Jones; Mary Rider and Susanna Fogg, daus. of dec'd sister, Susanna Fogg, wife of David Fogg and their cous., Eliza: Johnes; George Newman Sr., and John Weler. (Will: 9.54; 17 Jan 1677; 15 Aug 1678)

KINGE, Thomas. (Inv.: 5.351; 3 July 1678; ----)

KING, Samuel. (Inv.: 32B.74; 13 March 1710; ----) Admr.: Mary King. (Acct: 32C.169; ----; 29 Sept 1711)

KING, Mary and Elizabeth, daus. of Robert King. Cattle mark recorded 3 Aug 1721. (Ct.&Land: H#2.452)

KING, Samuel. Mentions wife Eliza:; eldest son William; son Thomas; son Samuel; son John and son Benjamin. (Will: 18.66; 16 June 1722; 25 March 1722) Next of kin: William King, Thomas King. (Inv.: 8.220; -- ---- 1723; 14 June 1723)

KING, Thomas. Next of kin: John King, John Cooper. Admr.: Richard King. (Inv.: 17.577; 3 Sept 1733; 14 Nov 1733)

KING, Thomas. Ex.: Thomas Mitchell. (Inv.: 18.507; 1 July 1733; 21 Aug 1734)

KING, William. Next of kin: Samuell King, Catherine King. Admr.: Elisabeth King (widow). (Inv.: 21.240; 4 Nov 1735; 14 Jan 1735)

KING, Robert. Next of kin: William Kinney, Benjamin King. Admr.: Mary King. (Inv.: 21.294; ----; 17 May 1736)

KING, John. Next of kin: Richard King, William King. Admr.: Francis Meeke. (Inv.: 21.403; ----; 2 June 1736) (Inv.: 22.345; ----; 17 Aug 1737)

KING, William. To cousins Thos. King and Mary Muncaster, personalty. To sister Ann, real estate. or to bro. Richard, ex. (Will: 22.474; 28 March 1742; 3 May 1742) Mentions: Catherine Muncaster, Ann King, Thomas Jackson, William Cooper. Admr./Ex.: Richard King. (Inv.: 27.50; 25 May 1742; 6 Aug 1742) (Inv.: 28.154; 21 April 1743; ----)

KINGERSLEY, George and Elizabeth, of Portobacco. Their children: Mary, born 15 Feb 1692; Elizabeth, born 25 March 1694. (Ct.&Land: QRev.20, 25)

KINGLAND, William, age 50. Deposition re the tract *Salisbury*, 12 Xber 1719. (LandComm: M2.77)

KINGLAND, William. Next of kin: Samuel Love, Samuel Love. Administratrix: (name not given). (Inv.: 11.414; 28 April 1726; 4 July 1726)

KINGSBURY, George. Servant of Henry Hawkins, age judged to be 19 yrs., 12 Jan 1685. (Ct.&Land: M#1.67)

KINGSTONE, Thomas, age 14 yrs. Servant of James Tyre, 1676. (Ct.&Land: F#1.193)

KINIKIN, James, age 13 yrs. Servant of Ralph Smith, 9 Dec 1685. (Ct.&Land: M#1.66)

KIRBY, John, age ca. 30 yrs. Swore in court 4 Sept 1660. (Ct.&Land: A#1.100)
KIRBY, Paul, age 16 yrs. Servant of William Barton, 8 June 1675. (Ct.&Land: F#1.101)

KERKLEY, William, age 10 yrs. Servant of Richard Morris, 12 March 1672. (Ct.&Land: E#1.54)
KIRKLEY, Christopher and Catherine, of head of Wicomico River. Their children: Susanna, born 17 March 1681; Christopher, born 23 Feb 1684. (Ct.&Land: P#1.211; QRev.8, 10)
KIRKLY, Christopher (joiner). Gives all his estate to dau. Susannah, wife of John Vincent (planter), 16 Feb 1705/6. (Ct.&Land: Z#1.227)
KIRKLEY, (KIRKLY, KIRTLY), Christopher. To grandson William Vinson, son of John and Susanna Vinson, 2/3 of estate. To present wife Eliza:, residue of estate. Ex.: Son in law John Vinson. (Will: Part 2-12.132; 10 Sept 1708; 7 July 1709) (Inv.: 29.204; 24 Jan 1708) Distribution to: relict (unnamed) wife of William Crocker. Ex.: John Vincent. (Acct: 30.17; ----; 30 July 1709)

KIRTEN, Zachary, age 14 yrs. Servant of Josias Fendall, 1676. (Ct.&Land: F#1.193)

KNIGHT, Hannah, age 20 yrs. Servant of Thomas Taylor, 14 June 1681. (Ct.&Land: I#1.124)
KNIGHT, John son of Edward Knight. Thomas Smith, planter to answer court regarding estate of John Knight, 9 June 1691. (Ct.&Land: Q#1.28)
KNIGHT, Anne, dau. of John Knight. Cattle mark recorded 26 Sept 1692. (Ct.&Land: R#1.502)
KNIGHT, John and Jennett of Cedar Point Neck. Their children: Anne, born last Thursday in March 1688; John, born last day of Sept 1691; Mary, born 27 March 1694. (Ct.&Land: QRev.14, 17, 23)
KNIGHT, John. (Inv.: 15.358; 27 Nov 1697; ----) Admr.: Jennett Boy (relict), wife of John Boy. (Acct: 18.79; ----; 11 Oct 1698)
KNIGHT, James. Registers cattle mark for cows given him by his mother Martha Peters, 9 Sept 1707. (Ct.&Land: (C#2.72)

KNIGHT, John and Sarah his wife of Stafford Co., Virginia, give power of attorney, 5 Nov 1713, to Wm. Brett. Also to Wm. Brett, parcel of land *Chosen* on Chingamuxon Ck., cont. 150 acres. (Ct.&Land: D#2.72, 73)

KUE, John, age 19 yrs. Servant of Phillip Lynes, 8 June 1686. (Ct.&Land: M#1.221)

LAMASTER (See LEMASTER).

LAMBERT, Samuel. In his will he mentions John Williams, and his brother John Lambert, ex. (Will: 1.59; 14 Oct 1661; 21 Dec 1661)

LAMBER, Ami, age 20 yrs. Maid servant, presented by John Pain, 9 Aug 1664. (Ct.&Land: B#1.355)

LAMBERT, John and his wife Ellinor. Acknowledge a conveyance 27 Nov 1666 to Richard True and his wife Anne. (Ct.&Land: C#1.100)

LAMBERT, John. His children: John, born 5 Feb 1664; Elinor, born in Jan 1667; Elizabeth, born [1st] Jan 1667; William, born 27 Feb 1669; Samuell, born 10 March 1671. (Ct.&Land: E#1.72 (lists all children except Elizabeth; P#1.205; QRev.1, 3, 4)

LAMBERT, John and his wife Ellen [Ellinor], dau. of John Nevill, dec'd. Deed of gift signed 25 Nov 1670. (Ct.&Land: D#1.74)

LAMBERT, John (planter). In consideration of a marriage between John Lambert, and Sarah Barker, a half part of a parcel of land called *Simpson's Supply* dated 13 April 1676. (Ct.&Land: F#1.182)

LAMBERT, William, son of John Lambert. Deed of gift, 1 March 1680, from Lewis Jones (planter); tract on w. side of Portobacco Creek. If William shd. die without hrs., to John Lambert Jr.; if he dies, to Elinor Lambert, dau. of John Lambert Sr. (Ct.&Land: I#1.78)

LAMBERT, John and his wife Sarah. Indenture 22 Feb 1681, to Giles Collier, parcel being part of *Simpson's Supply* on e. side of Piscataway R. and s. side of Mattawoman Creek, cont. 100 acres. (Ct.&Land: I#1.261)

LAMBERT, John. Deed of gift, 9 Jan 1692, to John Allen and Ellinor his wife, dau. of John Lambert; tract of 100 acres on Nanjemy Ck. (Ct.&Land: D#2.36)

LAMBERT, John. In his will he left to Eliza:, dau. of John Gourly, Prudence, dau. of Nicholas Cooper, and to James Smoot, personalty. Thomas Witchell of Portobacco and William Dent of Nanjemy, joint exs. and residuary legatees of estate. Test: Wm. Hall, Ann Hide. (Will: 2.246; 25 Jan 1693; 7 Feb 1693)

LAMBERT, William (Acct: 22.19; ----; 27 Aug 1700) Admr.: Mary Lambert.

LAMBETH, John. (Inv.: 13A.60; 12 Feb 1693; ----)
LAMBETH, James. Exs.: Thomas Mickell, William Dent. (Acct: 13B.57; ----; [c1695])
LAMBETH, William. (Inv.: 20.27; 4 June 1700; ----)

LAMBETH, John and Sarah his wife, on June 1714, conveyed a parcel of 50 acres being part of a tract taken up by Wm. Boarman. (Ct.&Land: F#2.40)

LAMBETH, John. Mentions: James Nicoll. Next of kin: John Clarke, John Clarke Jr. Admrs.: Phillip Tippett and his wife, Mary Tippett. (Inv.: 11.864; 28 Jan 1727; 23 March 1726 [sic])

LAMPTON, Marke. Judged to be 16 yrs. old, presented by Daniell Johnson for William Robisson, 10 Jan 1664. (Ct.&Land: B#1.398)

LAMPTON, Marke and Elizabeth, of head of Portobacco Creek. Their children: Mary, born 24 Jan 1678; Marke, born 6 Oct 1680; William, born 29 April 1682; Victoria, born 29 May 1685; John, born 16 Oct 1687; Anne, born 13 Jan 1689; Elizabeth, born 8 Aug 1692; Isable, born 15 Dec 1694. (Ct.&Land: P#1.206, 207; QRev.6, 7, 8, 11, 13, 15, 20, 24)

LAMPTON, Marke (planter) and Elizabeth his wife on 11 Sept 1694 conveyed a parcel called *Jeamind*, cont. 371 acres. (Ct.&Land: S#1.348)

LAMPTON, Mark, of Anne Arundel Co. He left to his sons, William and John, 200 acres nr. Piscataway, obtained from Thos. Mitchell by exchange of land. Mentions daus. Victory, Ann, Eliza:, Isabell and Sarah and son Mark, ex. (Will: 11.186; 3 Nov 1701; 1 Jan 1701) (Inv.: 21.292; 23 Jan 1701; ----) Admr./Ex.: Mark Lampton. (Acct: 23.98; ---- 13 Oct 1702)

LAMPTON, Mark Jr. To sister Isabella, personalty which was her sister Ann's, also legacy left her by will of father. To sisters Sarah and Jane, legacies also left by will of father. To son Mark, residue of estate, he to be brought up by his grandmother, Mrs. Tante. Ex.: bro. William, who is also to have charge of "my little sisters." Mentions bro. John. (Will: 12.327; 13 Dec 1708; 7 Feb 1708) Next of Kin: John Lampton, Issabella Lampton. (Inv.: 29.367; 4 March 1709; ----) Legatees: John Lampton. Ex.: William Lampton. (Acct: 32A.36; ----; 6 Oct 17) Legatees: Isabella Lampton (from her father Mark Lampton Sr. and her brother, the deceased). (Acct: 36B.262; ----; 6 May 1715)

LAMPTON, Esther, wife of William Lampton, of King George Co., Virginia, appoints an attorney, recorded on 19 Dec 1722, to make over tract called *Lampton*, 150 acres, conveyed from her husband Wm. Lampton, by deed on 1 March 1717. (Land: L#2.65)

LAND, Philip. Mentions sons Philip, Thomas and William. Wife Anne, extx. (Will: 1.95; 1 April 1657; 8 March 1659)

LANS, William, age 14 yrs. Servant of William Perfect, 7 April 1668. (Ct.&Land: C#1.263)

LAND (LAUD?) Elinor, had a bastard child. Servant of George Godfrey, 9 March 1679. (Ct.&Land: H#1.271)

LAND, Richard. Appraisers: Ralph Smith, William Harbert. (Inv.: 10.369; 22 March 1692; ----)

LAND, Richard and Penelope, of Pickawaxon. Their children: Richard, born 8 Oct 1687; John, born 12 Jan 1689; Elizabeth, born 4 April 1691; Susanna, born 8 Nov 1694. (Ct.&Land: P#1.212; QRev.13, 15, 17, 25)

LAND, Penelope. Mentions eldest dau. Mary; son John; dau. Eliza:. Son John and dau. Eliza: to live with son in law Walter Storey and to be under his care and that of bro. John Theobald. Dau. Susanna to live with dau. Penelope and her husband, Joseph Douglase. Mentions John Scroggin and godson George Scroggin. Sons in law Walter Storey and Joseph Douglase, exs. One of the witnesses was Mary Theobalds. (Will: 11.299; 10 May 1702; 20 Oct 1702) Ex.: Walter Storry. (Acct: 3.403; ----; 29 May 1704)

LANDEN, Robert, age ca. 20 yrs. Swore in court 8 July 1662; mentions his master, Capt. Russell's demise. (Ct.&Land: A#1.220)

LONE (LANE), Elizabeth, dau. of William Lone (Lane), born last day of May 1668. (Ct.&Land: P#1.205)
LANE, Anne, age 18 yrs. Maid servant presented by William Heard on behalf of Humphery Warren, 27 March 1662. (Ct.&Land: B#1.101)
LONE, John. (Inv.: 25.217; -- Sept 1705; ----)

LANGWORTH, James, of St. John's. Wife Agatha, extx. Distribution of tract *St. John's* to heirs is described.] Mentions son William; son John; dau. Mary; dau. Eliza:; godson John Gardner, son of Luke Gardner; goddau. and niece Eliza: Johnson; goddau. and niece Mary Turner, dau. of bro. Thomas Turner; goddau. and niece Jane Constable, dau. of Marmaduke Constable; bros. and sisters Luke Gardner and Eliza: his wife, Thomas Turner and Emma his wife, of St. Clement's Bay; kinsman Robert Greene. To Roman Catholic Church, personalty. (Will: 1.33; 18 Aug 1660; ----)
LANGWORTH, Agatha, relict of Capt. James Langworth. 1663/4. (Arch. of Md.: XLIX.113)
LANGWORTH, John, son of Agatha Langworth, was killed by Maquamps alias Bennett an Indian of Mattawoman at the house of said Agatha (spinster) of St. Johns, in Charles Co. 1665. (Arch. of Md.: XLIX.481)

LANNUM, John, son of John Lannum. Cattle mark, 4 July 1689. (Ct.&Land: P#1.201)

LANS. (See LAND.)

LASTELY (LESLEY), Alexander. Admr.: Thomas Hail. (Inv.: 23.169; 20 Oct 1737; 5 May 1738)

LATTEL, Ann, dau. of John Lattel. Receives from Ann Tanner, 8 Feb 1709, a heifer and mark. (Ct.&Land: C#2.156)

LATTIMER, James. (Inv.: 1.74; 7 Feb 1717; ----)

LAURENCE, Thomas, age 12 yrs. Servant of Henry Bonner, 12 March 1672. (Ct.&Land: E#1.54)

LAWRENCE, Benjamin, has removed from Patuxent and carried records with him. 6th of 8th month, 1682. (Clifts Monthly Meetings, Quaker Records of So. MD, p. 67)

LAWSON, Thomas (planter). To wife Elizabeth, extx., 1/3 of estate. To son William, residue of estate. (Will: 14.271; 10 Dec 1716; 12 March 1716)

LAWSON, Thomas. Next of kin: William Lawson, son; Elisabeth Lawson, daughter. (Inv.: 38A.166; 22 May 1717; ----) Extx.: Elisabeth Lawson. (Acct: 39C.133; ----; 11 March 1717)

LAWSON, William. Next of kin: Thomas Lawson, John Parker. Admr.: Rachel Lawson. (Inv.: 24.315; 12 Sept 1739; 17 Oct 1739)

LAWSON, John (Gent.), and his wife Elizabeth, of Prince George's Co. on 13 Dec 1745 conveyed tract called *Batchellors Forrest*, 125 acres. (Land: Z#2.81)

LEAMER, Margret. (Inv.: 10.96; 5 June 1688; ----)

LEE, Hannah, widow and admx. of Hugh Lee. 23 Sept 1662. (Arch. of Md.: XLIX, p.34) Appoints her servant William Price as her attorney, to collect monies owned her in St. Mary's and Charles Cos., 18 Dec 1662. (Ct.&Land: B#1.56) Hannah Lee married William Price. 1664. (Arch. of Md.: XLIX.222) Court held on 6 Dec 1665, sheriff presents his "bill of charge" for Hannah Lee alias Price, and her maid Mary Marlor. (Ct.&Land: B#1.514)

LEE, James. Court held on 1 Oct 1662, charging James with having two wives, 1 Oct 1662. (Ct.&Land: A#1.243)

LEE, James. Admr./Ex.: Jane Lee (relict). (Inv.: 1.362; 22 Feb 1674; ----. Acct: 5.28; ----; 15 April 1678)

LEE, Margaret, had bastard child, servant of John Newton, 8 Nov 1681. (Ct.&Land: I#1.174) Also in court 10 Jan 1681; found guilty and given 21 lashes. (Ct.&Land: I#1.231)

LEE, Robert. Admr.: Margret Lee. (Acct: 31.82; ----; 27 Feb 1709)

LEE, Winifred (nunc.). Child. (unnamed) to care of Thomas Jameson, who is to retain personal estate of testator and her husband until children are of age. Children to be brought up Roman Catholics. (Will: 15.297; 7 Dec 1719; ----)

LEE, Roger. Mentions: Winifier Lee, Winifred Lee. Admr.: Thomas Jameson. (Inv.: 10.153; ----; 22 Oct 1724)

LEE, Philip Jr. (Gentleman). Mentions wife Bridget; son John and daus. Sarah, Elizabeth and Lettice. Exs. to recover tract known as *Lee Langly*. Ex.: Father Philip and bros. Francis, Henry and Thomas. Note — Henry and Francis Lee renounced the execution of this will as they intend to go to England. (Will: 22.91; 17 April 1739; 9 Aug 1739) Next of kin: Arthur Lee, Richard Lee. Mentions: John Wilson. Exs.: Phillip Lee, Esq., Thomas Lee Jr. (Inv.: 24.378; 20 Sept 1739; 26 Nov 1739)

LEE, Robert (planter), and his wife Frances on 14 Nov 1739 conveyed part of a tract called *Lees Freehold*, lying in Durham Parish, cont. 20 acres. (Land: O#2.326)

LEE, Philip. Next of kin: Arthur Lee, Richard Lee. Ex.: Thomas Lee. (Inv.: 29.48; 16 June 1740; 11 May 1744)

LEE, Henry. Next of kin: Philip Lee, Thomas Lee. Admr./Exs.: Francis Lee, Arthur Lee. (Inv.: 26.216; 9 June 1741; 19 Sept 1741)

LEE, Arthur. Signed 24 May 1744. To his wife Ann Lee, before marriage, and for his sons in law, Robert and Jonathan Yates, a punch bowl which belonged to his father, the late Major Robert Yates, dec'd., and to Jonathan Yates, a Negro girl about 10 years old called Judeth, dau. of Negro Moll. (Land: X#2.119)

LEECH, James, age 11 yrs. Servant of Edmund Taylor, 8 June 1675. (Ct.&Land: F#1.101)

LEECH, James (runaway). Servant of Elinor Boice, 9 Feb 1685/6. (Ct.&Land: M#1.89)

LEEDS, Robert. Servant man, judged to be 20 yrs. old, presented by Edward Richardson, 8 Aug 1665. (Ct.&Land: B#1.472)

LEEK, George. Mentions: widow (unnamed). (Inv.: 19.120; 21 April 1699; 7 May 1699)

LEETE, John, son of George and Elinor Leete of Portobacco, born 15 Jan 1687. (Ct.&Land: QRev.12)

LEET, George. Admr.: Elinor Leet. (Acct: 11B.55; ----; [c1700])

LEMASTER, Richard, son of Abraham, and Martha his wife conveyd on 4 March 1710, two tracts: one called *Georges Rest*, on w. side of a branch of Zachia Swamp; part of a tract conveyed in 1671 from William Boarman of St. Mary's Co. (Gent.) to Abraham Lemaster, father of the afsd. Richard; from Abraham to William Taylor of Anne Arundel Co., Gent.; from Taylor to Richard Lemaster afsd.; cont. 100 acres; also other tract called *Strife* conveyed to Richard Lemaster from Benja. Hall, Gent. (1706); tract *Hall* sold to Samuel Smallwood of St. Mary's Co.; cont. 100 acres. (Ct.&Land: C#2.161) Indenture 13 Aug 1713, to Thomas Hays (planter); a parcel called *Noe's Desart*, laid out for 96 acres. (Ct.&Land: C#2.161; F#2.5)

LEMASTRE (LAMASTER), John (planter). Deed recorded 25 Nov 1727, to Richard Lemastre (carpenter); tract called *Bettyes Delight*, formerly in St. Mary's Co., now Charles Co.; first granted to Edward Evans of St. Mary's Co. by patent, 1 Aug 1673 and by his deed of 10 Nov 1685, conveyed to Abraham Lamaster, father of the parties to these presents, and by sd. Abraham's will devised to afsd. John Lemaster, cont. 200 acres. Also, all that tract on the e. side of Zachia Swamp, called *Lemasters Delight*, originally granted to Abraham Lemaster, dated 1 Oct 1700, cont. 200 acres. (Land: L#2.393)

LEMAISTRE, Abraham, son of John and Sarah Lemaistre, age ca. 81, swore, 27 June 1720, he was born in the old Jerseys in the Parish of St. Maries. (Ct.&Land: H#2.415)

LEMASTER, John, age 39. Deposition, 6 Dec 1720, regarding tract called *Lamastres Delight* (petition of Abraham Lemaster). (LandComm: M2.139)

LEMASTRE, Richard, age 52. Deposition, 6 Dec 1720, regarding tract called *Lamastres Delight* (petition of Abraham Lemastre). (LandComm: M2.104)

LEMASTRE, Abraham. Deed of gift, 9 Sept 1721, to his son John Lemastre; tract called *?Bargids*. (Ct.&Land: H#2.468)

LEMASTER, Abraham. To son John, ex., dwelling plantation. To son Isaac, tract where he now lives. To daus. Sarah Teneson and Mary Barron, tract called *Berry*, equally. Wife to have use of dwell. plan. Dau. Anne to dwell on some pt. of land during her husband's absence. (Will: 18.10; 20 Sept 1722; 11 Dec 1722) Next of kin: Isaac Lemaster. (Inv.: 8.104; 21 March 1722/3; ----)

LEMASTRE, Richard (carpenter), Thomas Hayes (planter) "of the same parts," and his wife Mary. Deed dated 19 Aug 1723; to Edward Davies Jr., tract on e. side of Zachiah Swamp called *Noes Desart*, cont. 96 acres. (Land: L#2.106)

LEMASTER, John and his wife Christian. To their three sons and one dau., Justinian, John, and William Cooksey and Priscilla Barran, tract called *Simkin and Crowback*. Signed 2 Feb 1731/2. (Land: M#2.275)

LAMASTER (LEMASTER), John. Next of kin: Thomas Barron, John Cooksey. Admr.: Christian Lemaster. (Inv.: 25.7; 8 April 1740, 26 April 1740)

LENDSEY. (See LINDSEY.)

LENHAM, John, age 19 yrs. Servant of Henry Hardy, 10 June 1679. (Ct.&Land: H#1.134)

LENOIR, John (a glazier). 22 Feb 1722. Binds himself to Robt: Hanson (Gent.), in his marriage to Mary Newman (Mewman), widow. (Land: L#2.75)

LENOIR, Mary, widow. In her will she left to Robert Hanson (gent.); Anne, wife of Thomas Dent (gent.); Elizabeth, wife of Richard Tarvin (gent.); Dr. Daniel Jenifer and John Lawson, personalty. Robert Hanson afsd., ex. and residuary legatee. (Will: 19.569; 22 Dec 1725; ----) Ex.: Robert Hanson. (Inv.: 15.638; 25 Jan 1728; ----)

LENTON, Joseph. Will, 15 Dec 1660, mentions wife and child (unnamed), 22 April 1662. (Ct.&Land: A#1.205)

LYNTON, Ursuly (nunc.). Mentions Jane Thomkinson, John Delahey, wife and youngest son (both unnamed) of sd. John Delahey. Francis Polk, ex. (Will: 1.124; ----; 17 April 1661)

LEVRITT, John (planter). To wife Jane, extx., entire estate. (Will: 18.107; 12 May 1723; 15 July 1723)
LEVERETT, John. (Inv.: 8.335; [c1723]; ----)

LEWEN, Joseph. (Inv.: 39A.36; 14 Jan 1717; ----)
LEWIN (LEWEN), John. Admr.: Notley Maddox. (Inv.: 21.505; ----; 13 Sept 1736)

LEWGAR, John (gent.) and Martha his wife on 13 Aug 1666 conveyed 150 acres out of his manor of 1000 acres on n. side of a beaver dam; bounded by Deep Swamp. (Ct.&Land: C#1.61)
LEWGER, John. To two sons John and Thomas, jointly, *St. Barbary's Manor*. To dau. Eliza: 300 acres adjoining the *Manor*. Wife Martha, residuary legatee. Ex. not named. (Will: 1.356; 26 Nov 1669; 9 Dec 1669)
LUGAR, Thomas conveyed on 16 Dec 1692 a parcel on the n. side of Piscataway R. called *St. Barbaries Manor*, 1000 acres, granted to John Lugar (gent.), grandfather to Thomas Lugar, to his son John Lugar, to his son Thomas Lugar. (Ct.&Land: S#1.12)

LEWIS, William, planter. On 2 Nov 1638 he stated he was not precontracted to any woman other than Ursula Gifford (bond). Marriage license granted. (Arch. of Md., v. IV, p. 50)
LEWIS, William (Capt.). Administration of his estate. An inventory is exhibited by George Goodrick, who married Ursule, relict of Capt. William Lewis, 1658. (Arch. of Md., v. XLI, p. 58, 60, 114.)
LEWIS, William (Lieut.). Died with right to 3000 acres without heirs. 11 Sep 1674. (Arch. of Md.: LI.139)
LEWIS, James, age ca. 22 yrs. Deposition taken 11 April 1663 and presented to court. (Ct.&Land: B#1.331)
LUCE (LUES?), Thomas, age 20 yrs. Servant of Richard Edelen, 9 Jan 1671/2. (Ct.&Land: E#1.52)
LEWIS, David and Jane, of Pickawaxen. Their children: Henry, born 16 Oct 1687; Isable, born 4 Aug 1690; Mary, born 28 Nov 1692; David, born 14 Dec 1694. (Ct.&Land: P#1.211; QRev.13, 16, 18, 24)
LEWIS, Thomas. Admr.: Rebecca Lewis. (Inv.: 11.507; 19 July 1726; 10 Sept 1726)
LEWIS, Gilbert. Next of kin: Jesse Cockley, William Cockley. Admr.: Elisabeth Harris, wife of John Harris. (Inv.: 15.594; 4 April 1730; 11 July 1730)
LEWIS, Henrietta Lewis Williams, dau. of Thomas and Mary Lewis, born 8 Jan 1743. (Trinity: 107)

LEWIS, George Rogers Williams, son of Thomas and Mary Lewis, born 5 Jan 1746. (Trinity: 107)

LIGET (LEGET), Bridgett, widow of John Leget; he died without issue, possessed of 400 acres. (Arch. of Md.: LI.147)

LILLY, Elizabeth. Father in law Peter Carr, ex. and sole legatee of estate. (Will: 5.155; 15 Nov 1676; 30 Dec 1676)

LILLEY, Thomas (chirurgeon barber). Jacob Miller, ex. and sole legatee. (Will: 14.47; 25 Dec 1714; 14 March 1714/5)

LILLEY (LILLY), Thomas. (Inv.: 36B.329; 16 April 1715; ----) Ex.: Jacob Miller. (Acct: 37C.131; ----; 27 Sept 1716)

LINSEY, James and his wife Marie, of St. Thomas. Transported his wife Marie to the Province; granted parcel of land called *Linsey* on the Avon River, cont. 300 acres, dated 2 Sept 1659. Court held 19 Nov 1661. (Ct.&Land: A#1.173)

LINDSEY, Edmond, age ca. 36 yrs. Court held 17 April 1660. (Ct.&Land: A#1.86)

LINDSEY, James (gent.) and his wife Mary, on 4 Nov 1664, conveyed tract on n. side of Avon River, called *Poynton Manor*, cont. 500 acres. (Ct.&Land: B#1.510-513)

LINDSEY, Elinor, wife of Edmund Lindsey. To testify *viva voce* in court. 1665. (Arch. of Md.: XLIX.476, 505) 1666. (Arch. of Md.: LVII.99)

LENDSEY, Anne, dau. of Edmond Lendsey. Cattle mark recorded, 14 Aug 1666. (Ct.&Land: C#1.71)

LINDSEY (LYNDSEY), James, son of James Lyndsey, born 10 Feb 1666. (Ct.&Land: C#1.253 (gives date as 18 Feb 1666); QRev.2)

LINDSEY, James. To the Roman Catholic Church, personalty. Wife Mary, extx.; estate to be disposed of among children (unnamed) by her. (Will: 1.433; 21 April 1671; 3 May 1671)

LINDSEY, Edmund. Mentions: estate Darby Caneday gave him. (Inv.: 4.285; 24 Sept 1677; ----) (Acct: 4.286; ----; 4 Oct 1677)

LINDSEY, Elizabeth. To father in law Kenelme Mackloghlin and the Roman Catholic Church, personalty. Bro. James, residuary legatee. (Will: 5.342; -- ---- 1675; 2 March 1677/8)

LENDSEY, Edmond, son of Edmond Lendsey and Ellenor his wife. Assigned a heifer, court held 8 Aug 1671. (Ct.&Land: E#1.45)

LINSEY, Cornelius, age 19 yrs. Servant of William Chandler, 20 Jan 1679. (Ct.&Land: H#1.253)

LINDSEY, Henry, age ca. 19. Memorandum, 3 July 1703, between Dr. William Lock and Henry Lindsey, with John Williams and Sarah his wife, being sister of Henry who binds himself as apprentice and servant to Dr. Lock. (Ct.&Land: Z#1.60)

LINE (See LYNN).

LINEGAR, John. Items in the possession of William Penn. (Inv.: 13A.260; 30 Jan 1694; ----)

LINES (See LYNES).

LING (LYNG), Francis and Mary. Their children: William, born 11 March 1669; Michaell, born 22 Jan 1671; Mary, born born 27 March 1673; Francis, born 9 Oct 1676. (Ct.&Land: P#1.207; QRev.3, 4, 5)

LING, William, son of Francis Ling. Cattle mark recorded, Oct 1671. (Ct.&Land: E#1.49)

LINGE, Francis, age 17 yrs. Presented by Henry Adames, 8 March 1663/4. (Ct.&Land: B#1.266)

LINOE, John. Next of kin: Mary Lindar. Admr.: John Lambeth. (Inv.: 11.343; ----; 27 April 1726)

LIPSCOMB. (See LYBSCOME.)

LIUGE, Michael. Admr.: Mary Justis, wife of Henry Justis. (Acct: 31.76; ----; 10 March 1709)

LLEWELLIN, Jane, Mrs., widow. In her will she left to dau. Margaret, all real estate except *Green Spring*, St. Mary's Co., bequeathed to Richard Rodgers. Mr. Alex. Contee to take into his hands all father ——— Orrell's estate, for use of sd. Richard. Dau. Margaret to care of Mrs. Jane Doyne. Son John to be in care of Mr. Wm. Chandler, ex. Note: Codicil 27 Aug., Mrs. Ann Johnson to hold *Brambry* till dau. Margaret is of age. (Will: 18.7; 7 Aug 1722; 22 Dec 1722) (Inv.: 8.137; 1 March 1722; ----)

LLEWELLIN, Richard. (Inv.: 8.135; 25 Feb 1722; ----) (Inv.: 7.227; 7 May 1722; ----)

LOYD (LLOYD), Morris (Maurice). To Mary Gray, William Sargent, Joseph Manning, and Mary Martin, personalty. To Michael and Francis Lynge, 200 acres, *Eaton's Delight*. Michael Lynge, ex. (Will: 7.73; 20 Feb 1694; 13 March 1694) (Inv.: 13B.65; 4 May 1695; ----) Legatees: Mary Martin. Ex.: Michaell Lign (also Michaell Lynn). (Acct: 14.71; ----; 13 Oct 1696)

LOYD, Edward. Next of kin: Garrard OCane, William Cage. Admr.: Eliza Loyde. (Inv.: 15.393; 31 Aug 1729; 25 Jan 1729)

LOYD, Elisabeth. Next of kin: Roydrick Loyd, James Smith. Admr.: Richard Loyde. (Inv.: 16.624; 6 Sept 1732; 28 Oct 1732) Admr./Ex.: Richard Loyd. (Inv.: 17.484; 29 Sept 1733; 10 Oct 1733)

LLOYD (LOYD), Richard. Next of kin: Martha Lloyd, Richard Smith. Admr.: William Cage. (Inv.: 22.270; 17 March 1736; 6 June 1737)

LOFLING, John (Inv.: 1.63; 22 March 1717; ----)

LOFTON (LOFTEN), Robert Sr. (Inv.: 13A.387; 8 April 1695; ----) Admr.: Robert Loften (son). (Acct: 15.65; ----; 9 Feb 1696)
LOFTON (LOXTON), Robert Jr. (Inv.: 16.5; 23 Nov 1697; ----) Admr.: Robert Benson. (Acct: 18.74; ----; 30 Sept 1698)
LOFTEN, Frances, widow. Deed of gift, 22 June 1721, to her dau. Priscilla Loften. (Ct.&Land: H#2.430)
LOFTEN (LOFTING), Frances (widow). In her will she left to son John (at age of 18), Christopher Thompson, dau. Onah, or Oriah, and nephew Wm. Jenkins, personalty. Sons-in-law Francis Brown and John Newman, exs. (Will: 18.22; 11 Oct 1722; 20 Nov 1722) Next of kin: John Lofting, William Jenkinson. (Inv.: 8.60; 9 Nov 1722; ----)
LOFTON, John. Mentions: John Lancaster, John Harris, Parsiler Newman, Oriah Smoot. Admrs.: Francis Brown and his wife, Ruth Brown. (Inv.: 15.396; ----; 28 --- 1729)

LOFTAS, Margrett, age 19 yrs. Servant of Richard Fowke, 8 Sep 1674. (Ct.&Land: F#1.1)

LOMAX, Thomas, residing at Capt. Josias Fendall's house in Chas. Co., age 30. Deposition on 18 Feb 1660. (Arch. of Md.: XLI.448)
LOMAX, Cleborne (blacksmith) and Blanch, of head of Wicomico River. Their children: Railph (Ralph, Raiph), born last day of July 1673; Susanna, born 3 April 1675; Catherine (Katherine), born 13 May 1677; Cleborne, born 22 Jan 1678; Thomas, born 8 April 1681, bapt. 4 July following; John, born 20 Nov 1683. (Ct.&Land: F#.38; P#1.206, 207; QRev.5, 6, 8, 9)
LOMAX, Thomas. Deed of gift, 9 Jan 1676, to his bro., Cleborne Lomax; 100 acres being part of tract of 600 acres called *Rich Hills*, located on w. side of the main fresh of Wicomico River. (Ct.&Land: G#1.3)
LOMAX, Blanch. Deed of gift, 26 March 1676, to oldest son of Blanch Lomax, wife of Cliborne Lomax. (Ct.&Land: F#1.184)
LOMAX, Cleborne Jr. (Inv.: 19½B.37; 28 Dec 1699; 29 Dec 1699) Payments to: Thomas Hussey (dead) paid to Samuell Lucket who married Elisabeth the executrix. Admr.: Blanch Lomax (relict). (Acct: 20.193; ----; 7 Dec 1701)
LOMAX, John, son of Ralph Lomax. Cattle mark recorded 21 May 1707. (Ct.&Land: Z#1.267)
LOMAX, Ralph and Margaret his wife conveyed on 3 March 1710 part of a tract called *Rich Hills*, cont. 600 acres, formerly granted to Hugh Thomas, dec'd.; conveyed to Thomas Lomax, dec'd. (Ct.&Land: C#2.245)
LOMAX, Ralph. Next of kin: Cleborne Lomax, Thomas Lomax. [no county]. (Inv.: 37A.54; 28 July 1716; ----)
LOMAX, Ralph. Admr.: John Blee. (Acct: 38A.125; ----; 8 May 1717)
LOMAX, Cleborn. Cattle mark 21 June 1721, for his son Cleborn Lomax Jr. (Ct.&Land: H#2.442)
LOMAX, Thomas, son of Cleborn Lomax. Cattle mark recorded 22 Oct 1722. (Land: L#2.49)

LOMAX, Cleborn (planter) and Marjery his wife conveyed on 19 Dec 1723 1/3 of the lands lately in the possession of Richard Morris, dec'd., called *Bergen Apzome*, 300 acres and 1/3 of another tract called *Gwins Hope*, 30 acres. (Land: L#2.112)

LOMAX, Cleborn. Next of kin: Thomas Lomax, Frances Posey. Admr.: Susannah Lomax. (Inv.: 14.30; 15 April 1729; 5 May 1729)

LONE. (See LANE.)

LONG, Jemima, wife of Robert Long. Swore in court, dated 3 Nov 1665. (Ct.&Land: B#1.501)

LONG, Jemima, dau. of Robert Long, born 5 Jan 1667. (Ct.&Land: C#1.254; P#1.205; QRev.3)

LONG, John. Wife Elenor, extx. Testator desires his wife to care for Mary and Eliza: Haly, daus. of Clement Haly, dec'd., who were left in care of testator by their father. Should sd. wife die during minority of afsd. child., their grandfather, Edward Turner, to have charge of them and their estate. (Will: 7.335; 19 Nov 1697; 10 Jan 1697)

LOVE, Elizabeth, dau. of William Love, born last day in May 1668. (Ct.&Land: D#1.4; QRev.3)

LOVE (LOOFE), William. In his will he mentions godson Richard Robbins; son Thomas [minor], ex. (Will: 2.102; 28 Oct 1680; 25 Nov 1680) (Inv.: 8.258; 10 July 1682; ----)

LOOFE, William. (Inv.: 7A.384; 12 March 1680; ----)

LANE (LOVE), Florence (widdow). She desirous her son John Love be brought up by Capt Henry Aspinall, 13 June 1683. (Ct.&Land: K#1.209)

LOVE, Thomas, son of William Love conveyed on 26 April 1694, a parcel of land on w. side on Portobacco Creek, where William Love lived, cont. 100 acres. (Ct.&Land: S#1.275)

LOVE, Samuel (carpenter), and Kindrick his wife. Acknowledge indenture from Ebsworth Bayne (Gent.), 11 Nov 1718; parcel of 100 acres, part of tract *Brother Wood*. (Ct.&Land: H#2.208)

LOVE, Lucy. Next of kin: Susanna Love, Samuel Tennison. (Inv.: 8.221; 30 April 1723; ----)

LOVE, Samuel (planter), and his wife Mary on 31 Jan 1737/8 conveyed a tract *Linner Sheet*, 100 acres. (Land: O#2.315)

LOVE, Charles and Mary. Their children: Pintheselia, born 21 Dec 1742; Thomas, born 29 Nov 1745. (Trinity: 112)

LOVE, Samuel Jr. and Mary Haw, married 5 Dec 1742. Their children: Elinor, born 18 Sept 1743; Samuel, born 20 Feb 1745/6. (Trinity: 111)

LOVEDAY, William. (Inv.: 6.373; 8 Aug 1679; ----)

LOVETT, Margaret, relict of John Levett, in possession of land by virtue of a lease from James Neale. 13 Feb 1674. (Arch. of Md.: LXV.468)

LOWE, John and his wife Mary, of Prince George's Co. conveyed on 3 May 1727, tracts of land e. side of Portobacco Fresh, cont. 330 acres. Land as it was given by Henry Hawkins, late of Chas. Co., to Mary Hawkins, his natural dau. and now Mary Lowe, wife of John Lowe. (Land: L#2.355)

LOWE (LAWN), Edward. Next of kin: John Thomas, Henry Corspher. Admr.: Elisabeth Catlet, wife of Daniell Catlet. (Inv.: 20.376; 28 Jan 1734; 7 May 1735)

LOWRY (LAWREY), David. (Inv.: 26.141; 20 Nov 1706; ----) Admr.: James Wapple. (Acct: 28.98; ----; 9 March 1707)

LOXTON (See LOFTON).

LOYD. (See LLOYD.)

LUCAS, Thomas (carpenter) of Prince George's Co. and Anne his wife conveyed on 22 Nov 1721 a parcel called *Smoots Choice*, cont. 45 acres and on 13 Oct 1731 a tract called *Johnsons Choice*, cont. 50 acres. (Ct.&Land: H#2.476; Land: M#2.269)

LUCE/LUES. (See LEWIS.)

LUCK, Clark of St. Mary's Co., son of Thomas and Juliana Clark conveyed on 5 Feb 1721, tract called *Bowling*, cont. 100 acres; also tract called *Jarvis*, cont. 111 acres. (Ct.&Land: H#2.481)

LUCKETT, Samuell and Elizabeth at the head of Portobacco Creek. Their children: Samuel, born 10 Oct 1685; Thomas, born 12 Aug 1688; Ignatius, born 30 Jan 1689. (Ct.&Land: P#1.207, 208, 210; QRev.11, 14, 15)

LUCKETT, Samuell. Died on 2 April 1705. (Inv.: 3.676; 23 Aug 1705; ----)

LUCKETT, Samuell. Died on 2 April 1705. (Inv. from Wills: 3.676; 23 Aug 1705; ----)

LUCKET, Samuell Sr. Exs.: Elisabeth Hanson, wife of John Hanson Jr. and Samuel Lucket. (Acct: 29.234; ----; 28 April 1709)

LUCKETT, Samuel (planter), son of Samuel Luckett, dec'd., and Ann his wife conveyed on 11 June 1712, a parcel called *Johnson's Choice*, cont. 100 acres which William Smoot, ca. 12 Aug 1684 conveyed to Samuel Luckett the elder. (Ct.&Land: D#2.6)

LUCKETT, Samuel. To wife, 150 acres, *Smootes Chance*, at Port Tobacco. To eld. son Samuel, 200 acres, *Hussey's Discovery*, also 150 acres. To son Thomas, 500 acres in Virginia, near Quanticott. To son Ignatius, 100 acres, *Thompson's Square*. To young. son Thomas Hussey Luckett,

173

personalty. Refers to money due in England. Exs.: Wife and son Samuel.
(Will: 3.649; 5 March 1705; 18 July 1705)

LUCKETT, Samuel. Exs.: Samuel Luckett, Elisabeth Hanson, wife of John Hanson Jr. (Acct: 27.12; ----; 22 April 1707)

LUCKETT, Thomas Hussey and wife Elizabeth conveyed on 13 Oct 1719 a parcel *Doncaster*, located on Chingamuxon Creek, 200 acres, and part of *Aspinalls Chance*, 100 acres. (Ct.&Land: H#2.295)

LUCKETT, Thomas Hussey and Elizabeth his wife conveyed on 10 Aug 1725 a tract called *Milerne*, and at Chinquamuxon, cont. 200 acres. (Land: L#2.242)

LUCKET, Samuel, son of Thomas Lucket. Cattle mark recorded [ca. Feb 1726]. (Land: L#2.330)

LUCKETT, Ignatious (gent.). To wife Jane, extx., 250 acres being half of *Moore's Ditch*; at her decease to son Ignatius. To son Samuel, other half of *Moore's Ditch*. To sons William and John, 100 acres *Luckett's Level*, 100 acres *Square Adventure*, 50 acres of *Small Hope*. Mentions father in law John Hanson. Residue to be divided among all child., viz.: Samuel, Ignatius, William, John, Thomas Hussey, Elizabeth, Ann and Charity. (Will: 21.338; 29 March 1734/5; 16 April 1735) Next of kin: John Hanson Jr., Thomas H. Luckett. Extx.: Jane Luckett. (Inv.: 21.38; 19 May 1735; 6 Aug 1735) Extx.: Jane Luckett. (Inv.: 21.506; 15 Sept 1736; 15 Sept 1736)

LUCKETT, Thomas. Next of kin: Ignatius Luckett, Thomas H. Luckett. Admr.: Sarah Luckett. (Inv.: 20.201; ----; [c1734]) Admr.: Sarah Luckett. (Inv.: 21.50; ----; 3 Sept 1735)

LUCKET, Thomas Hussey and his wife Eleanor conveyed on 4 Oct 1738 to his son in law, Jeremiah Aderton and his wife Anne, dau. of sd. Thomas Hussey Lucket, part of three tracts, lying at Chinguamuxon, *Mountagues Mountains*, *Mountagues Addition* and *Aspinals Chance*, 206 acres. (Land: O#2.369. See also Land O#2.371 and Land O#2.346B.)

LUCKET, Thomas Hussey, son of Ignatius Lucket conveyed on 4 Oct 1738 part of two tracts, near Chinquamuxon, *Mountagues Mountains* and *Mountagues Addition*; also a tract called *Luckets Addition*, 250 acres in all. Mrs. Jane Lucket paid the alienation fee on behalf of her son Thomas Hussey Lucket. (Land: O#2.364)

LUCKETT, Samuel and his wife Elizabeth convyed on 28 Sept 1745 Lot #28 in Charles Town. Said lot was taken up by Archibald Campbell and Ignatius Luckett, father of sd. Samuel, and since his death, devolved to sd. Samuel. (Land: Z#2.67)

LUGAR. (See LEWGER)

LUMBROSO, John, alias Jacob Lumbroso, entered mark of hogs and cattle, 2 Oct 1662. (Ct.&Land: A#1.250)

LUMBROZO, John. To sister Ribna Lumbrozo, personalty. To Edward
Richardson, *Lumbrozo's Discovery* on Nangemy Creek. Wife Eliza:,
extx. and residuary legatee of estate. Overseers: Henry Adams and Luke
Gardner of Maryland, and Edward Richardson of London. (Will: 1.249; 24
Sept 1665; ----)

LUTIE, Nathaniel and Elizabeth his wife conveyed on 11 March 1717 a parcel
of 99 acres called *Good Fortune*, formerly in St. Mary's Co. (Ct.&Land:
H#2.147)

LYBSCOME, Dorothy, age 22 yrs. Servant of Benjamin Rozer, 2nd Tues in
Aug 1673. (Ct.&Land: E#1.135)

LYLE, John, age 17 yrs. Man servant presented by Mathias Obrian, 8 March
1663/4. (Ct.&Land: B#1.257)

LYNES (LINES), James. Items in the possession of Henry Hardy. (Inv.
21.286; 22 Dec 1701; ----) Admr.: Henry Hardy. (Acct: 22.20; ----; -- Feb
1701)

LYNES, Philip (Gent.) conveyed on 10 June 1704, to William Dent on behalf
of himself and Philip Dent his infant son, godson of Philip Lynes; parcel
called *Roseberry*, 280 acres. (Ct.&Land: Z#1.112)

LYNES, Philip of Portobacco (Gent.) and Anne his wife conveyed on 19 Sept
1704, a parcel called *Corkers Hogg Hole* on w. side of Portobacco Ck.,
100 acres. (Ct.&Land: Z#1.167) John Theobalds and Mary his wife
acknowledge right of Philip Lynes to the above 100 acres called *Corkers
Hogg Hole*. (Ct.&Land: Z#1.171)

LYNES, Philip (Hon.). To Jane Seymour, Mary Contee, bro. Capt. Thos.
Seymour, William Bladen, Mrs. Frances and Mrs. Judith Townley, James
Wooten, Amos Garrett and Col. Thomas Greenfield, personalty. To Joane,
young. dau. of Col. Greenfield, 110 acres, *Haton*, in Prince George's Co.,
adjoining *Bean's Land*. Kent Fort Manor is devised to cousin Mary
Contee, Wm. Bladen, each 1/4. To wife Ann, extx., dower rights in all real
estate in Pennsylvania, this province or in any other part of America.
Mentions cous. Mary Contee, Wm. Bladen. (Will: Part 2-12.151; 6 Aug
1709; 15 Aug 1709) (Inv.: 30.280; 16 Nov 1709; 13 Dec 1709) (Inv. 32A.113; 8
May 1710; ----) Extx.: Madam Anne Lynes. (Acct: 32C.128; ----; [c1711])

LYNES, Ann(e). To Mary Chismund, goddau. Ann, dau. of James Tyre; Ann
Hoskins, wife of Col. Philip Hoskins; Frances, wife of Col. Rice Hoe, in
Virginia; Major Walter Story; Sarah Story, dau. of sd. Walter and Mary,
his wife; Robert Yates; Mary, wife of Philemon Hensley; Rice Loe; Judith,
wife of John Warren; Eliza:, wife of Benja. Douglass; and Mary, dau. of
Joseph and Penelope Douglas, personalty. To Robert Yates, Brittish boy
John Radfield, in payment of debt due by late husband. To John, eld. son

of Col. John Seymour (late governor), and his hrs., 1000 acres, *Bellconnell*, on Elk R. Ex.: Maj. Walter Story. (Will: 13.325; 20 Nov 1711; 17 Dec 1711) Exs.: Walter Story, Michael Martin (also Michael Marten). (Acct: 33B.23; 33B.119; ----; 6 Aug 1712) Exs.: Walter Story, Nicholas Martin. (Acct: 34.58; ----; 8 June 1713)

LYNN (LINE), Francis. To son Richard, 159 acres, ──── *Choice*. To dau. Eliza: and sister Anne Martin, personalty. To wife Margery and children afsd., residue of estate. (Will: 13.628; 10 Dec 1713; 26 Jan 1713) Next of kin: Rebechak Mertin (sister), Ann Mertin (sister). (Inv.: 35A.367; 3 April 1714; ----) Extx.: Marjery ──── (no surname given), relict. (Acct: 36B.94; ----; 5 March 1714 [Note: See John Thomas, Acct: 36B.95]).

LYON, John. (Inv.: 37B.89; 27 June 1717; ----) Admr.: Mary Lyon. (Acct: 39C.132; ----; 11 March 1717)

MACDANIEL (See MCDANIEL).

MACARTIE, Denis. (Inv.: 34.210; 6 Aug 1713; ----)

MACKENEARD (MACKENDARD?) Elinor, had bastard child, servant of Robert Doyne, 9 March 1679. (Ct.&Land: H#1.271)

MACKENHINE, John, age 18 yrs. Servant of James Mackey, 2nd Tues in April 1669. (Ct.&Land: D#1.62)

MAGITTEE (MAGITEE), James, son of Patrick and Rose Magittee, of the head of Portobacco Creek; born last week of March 1695. (Ct.&Land: Q#1.26)

MACHETEE, Patrick. To sons Patrick, Edmond and James, dwelling plantation equally. Son Edmond to have northernmost part where his house is. To godson and grandson Patrick Machetee, personalty. To wife Rosomond, extx., residue of estate. (Will: 14.235; 5 Oct 1716; 26 March 1717)

MACATEE, Patrick. (Inv.: 38A.134; 25 June 1717; ----)

MACHETEE, Rosamond. To granddau. Frances, personalty. Residue of estate to be divided equally among seven child., viz.: Edmond, Patrick, James, Katherine Galahaw, Mary Boswell, Elinor Clements and Rosomond Clements. Ex.: son James. (Will: 14.236; 3 March 1716; 20 March 1717)

MACAY, John. Admr./Ex.: Benjamin Adams. (Inv.: 23.362; 28 July 1738; 16 Aug 1738)

MACCABE, Barbara (widow), only surviving heir of James McKey. Deed dated 18 June 1733. To Francis Meek, 100 acres, assigned to James McKey, grandfather to Barbara McCabe. (Land: M#2.352)

MAC DANIEL, Charles. Admr.: Joshua Ratliff. (Inv.: 21.504; ----; 1 Sept 1736)

MACDANIELL, Alexander (planter), and his wife Elizabeth. 14 Sept 1743. To Thomas Hudson, MacDaniel's right to part of a tract called *Thomas' Disappointment*, cont. 84 acres. (Land: X#2.46)

MACDANIELL (MACDONALD), Alexander (planter) and his wife Elizabeth MacDaniel conveyed to George Waple, part of a tract called *Hudsons Disappointment*, cont. 177 acres and to Archibald Philbert (planter) on 14 Sep 1743, part of a tract called *Hudsons Disappointment*, bounded by the Stable Branch, cont. 50 acres, and to Thomas Hudson, on 4 June 1745, part of tract called *Hudsons Disappointment*, cont. 30 acres. (Land: X#2.34, 36; Land Z: #2.58.)

MACDONALL, Daniel, married by John Legatt, minister, to a maid servant that Benjamin Hammond sold to the said Madonell last Spring—without a license or bann. 5 Sept 1663. (Arch. of Md.: XLIX.84)

MACHETEE. (See MACATEE.)

MACHON, Robert (planter), and his wife Elizabeth. Signed 25 March 1741; to his dau., Jane Wood, part of a tract *Hadlow*, on s. side of Piles fresh, 93 acres; recorded at the request of Jacob Wood of Chas. Co. Signed 1 April 1741; to his dau. Anne Ash, part of the tract called *Hadlow*, on e. side of Piles fresh, 94 acres, and if she dies without heirs then the land to revert to his sons, William and Robert Machon, saving to Thomas Ash, husband of Anne, sd. land during his lifetime. (Land: O#2.488, 491)

MACKDONALD (See MC DONALD).

MACKENCE, Lomax, age 46. Deposition, 31 May 1721, regarding tract called *Christian Temple Manor* (petition of Benjamin Tasker). (Chas LandComm: M2.123)

MAKEY, James, son of James Makey. Gift dated ca. Oct 1674, from James Ashton of Stafford Co., Virginia to his godson, James Makey, heifer. (Ct.&Land: K#1.113)

MAKEY, Elizabeth, relict and extx. of James Makey, and now wife of Keneline Magloughlin, 13 Sept 1681. (Ct.&Land: I#1.170)

MAKEY (MACKY), James. In his will he left to wife Elizabeth, extx., all estate including 100 acres at Maryland point called *St. Johns*. In default of issue in wife Elizabeth, to pass to cousin Francis, son of Francis Meeks,

177

(gent.), late of Charles County, deceased. (Will: 14.335; 8 Feb 1716; 18 May 1717)

MACKEY, James. (Inv.: 37B.87; 26 May 1717; ----)

MACKEY, Anguis. Admr.: Stephen Brown. (Inv.: 11.412; ----; 28 June 1726)

MACKLANAN, Margret. Indicted for having a bastard child, servant of John Speake, 13 March 1710. (Ct.&Land: D#2.136)

MACKMILLION, George married Grace Carr, in Jan 1669. Their son Peter, born in April 1670. (Ct.&Land: D#1.108; P#1.205; QRev.3)

MACKMILLION, MACKMILLIAN (See MC MILLION).

MACONCHIE, John. Next of kin: William Maconchie, Thomas Stone. Admr./Ex.: Ann Macouchie. (Inv.: 26.439; 1 June 1741; 5 Feb 1741)

MACONCHIE, William. In his will he left to nephew Alexander, son of Jno. and Anne Maconchie, parts of the tracts: *Troop's Rendesvous, The Adventure, The Addition to the Adventure, Belmont, The Addition to Belmont* and other. To nephew William, son of John and Anne afsd., parts of *Maconchie's Dale* and *A Trifle*. To Sarah, dau. of Joseph and Sarah Douglas, to vestry of Port Tobacco Parish, to vesty of Durham Parish, to father Alexander (Maconchie), personalty. To wife Mary, ex., real estate. (Will: 22.454; 2 Feb 1741; 25 Feb 1741)

MACONCHIE, William (Revd.). Next of kin: Thomas Stone, Ann Maconchie. Admr./Ex.: Rev. Mr. Theophilus Swift. (Inv.: 27.289; -- June 1742; 15 Jan 1742)

MACOY, John. Admr.: Stephen Mankin. (Inv.: 22.274; ----; 18 May 1737)

MACPHERSON, William Jr. (planter), who married Eleanor Wilkinson, dau. of John Wilkinson, dec'd. Deed of partition dated 1 April 1740. A patent was granted to Samuel Hanson (Gent.) and Eleanor called *Wilkinsons Throne*, 506 acres; half the land went to sd. Samuel Hanson and the other half to sd. Eleanor Wilkinson. On 5 May 1739 William and Eleanor acquired from Dennis Nalley (planter), tract called *Husinlows Addition*, on e. side of Zachia Swamp, 50 acres; and part of a tract called *Georges Rest*, 50 acres. (Land: O#2.399, 443. See also O#2.24)

MACQUEEN, George. (Inv.: 3.120; 28 Apr 1704; ----)

MADDOCK, Edward (apothecary) and his wife Margery, relict of Matthew Stone conveyed on 5 June 1681, a tract called *Cheshires*, being part of *Poynton Manor*; inherited by Margery from the will of William Stone; cont. 500 acres. (Ct.&Land: I#1.125)

MADDOCK, Edward (surgeon) of Stafford Co., Virginia, and Margery Maddock his wife conveyed on 19 Feb 1684, 440 aces in Stafford Co. and a tract in Nangemy of 500 acres; land that was willed by Capt. Wm. Stone to Mathew Stone, and from Mathew to Margery, his wife. (Ct.&Land: L#1.140)

MADDOCK, William, age 20 yrs. Servant of Thomas Gerrard, 9 Feb 1685/6. (Ct.&Land: M#1.89)

MADDOCK, Cornelius (merchant) and his wife Mary conveyed on 27 May 1688 a tract called *Nutshall*, cont. 60 acres. (Ct.&Land: P#1.1)

MATTOX, David. Servant to George Plater, age judged to be 15 yrs. old, 12 Jan 1691. (Ct.&Land: R#1.337)

MATTOX, Thomas. Servant of William Dent, age judged to be 12 yrs. old, 12 Jan 1691. (Ct.&Land: R#1.337)

MADDOCK, Cornelius. (Inv.: 25.222; 9 March 1705; ----)

MADDOCKS, John (planter). Deed of gift 7 July 1711, to his dau. Elizabeth Maddocks. (Ct.&Land: (C#2.250)

MADDOX, John and Sarah his wife conveyed on 19 April 1714 a parcel of land on w. side of Wicomico River, cont. 200 acres and 100 acres adjoining. (Ct.&Land: F#2.10)

MADDOX, William. (Inv.: 36A.47; [c1714]; ----)

MADDOCK (MADDOKE), James (innholder) and his wife Mary conveyed on 26 April 1731 a parcel of three acres. (Land: M#2.250)

MADDOX, James. Next of kin: Walter Maddox, Notley Maddox. Admr.: Mary Maddox. (Inv.: 20.446; 6 May 1735; 4 June 1735) Admr.: Mary Maddox. (Inv.: 21.192; 29 Nov 1735; 3 Dec 1735)

MADDOX, John (planter), and his wife Ann conveyed on 1 Aug 1737 a tract called *Carrot Bed*, cont. 117 acres. (Land: O#2.218)

MADDOX, Notley (planter), and his wife Mary conveyed on 22 June 1738. To Walter Hanson (planter), part of a tract called *The Hills*, which was made over and confirmed to Samuel Hanson and his wife Elizabeth by John Warran in 1708. (Land: O#2.371)

MADDOCK, Notly (planter), Portobacco Parish, son of James Maddock, dec'd., and his mother, Mary Maddock (widow), conveyed on 11 Nov 1741 Lots #61 and #62 in Charles Town in Portobacco. (Land O#2.531)

MADDOX, John (planter), and his wife Sarah conveyed on 17 March 1743/4 to kinsman, William Waters (planter), her right of dower, to part of tract called *Dover*, 100 acres. John Maddox acknowledged he received 500 lbs. of tobacco in consideration, from James Waters, father of afsd. William Waters. (Land: X#2.135)

MAGITTEE/MAGITEE. (See MACHETT/MACATEE.)

MAGLOCKERY, William, son of William Maglockery, dec'd. Receives heifer as gift from William Smith, 12 June 1686. (Ct.&Land: M#1.115)

MAGREGER, Dunking, age 21 yrs. Servant of Henry Holland Hawkins, Nov 1710. (Ct.&Land: D#2.7)

MAHAWNEY, Tymothy. Servant to Humphrey Warren, age judged to be 17 yrs. old, 16 June 1693. (Ct.&Land: S#1.128)

MAHONY (MAHONEY), Elizabeth of St. Mary's Co. (widow), late wife of Timothy Mahony, dec'd., and one of the daus. of John Smith, formerly of St. Mary's Co., and Dennis Mahony, son of Timothy and Elizabeth Mahony and Francis Searson, now of St. Mary's Co. (surgeon), conveyed on 4 Aug 1714 a parcel belonging to John Smith in his lifetime called *Smith's Be Served* formerly in St. Mary's before the division of the county, cont. 100 acres. Signed by Fran: Searson and Alice his wife; and by Dennis Mahoney and Elizabeth his wife. (Ct.&Land: F#2.25)

MAKEY. (See MACKEY.)

MALDEN, James. Next of kin: W. Malcom, Elisabeth Pindowell. Ex.: Elinor Dorumple, wife of John Dorumple. (Inv.: 21.277; 16 April 1735; 16 March 1735)

MANITHURB, Thomas. Judged to be 16 yrs. old, presented by Robert Hendley, 10 Jan 1664. (Ct.&Land: B#1.397)

MANKESTER (See MONKESTER, MUNKESTER, MONCESTER).

MANKIN, Stephen and Mary, of Portobacco. Their children: Elizabeth, born 22 June 1682; Stephen, born 4 July 1685; John, born 16 Jan 1686; Margarett, born 20 March 1688; Josiah, born 18 Jan 1690; Mary, born 9 Feb 1692; Hope [twin], born 9 Jan 1694; James [twin], born 9 Jan 1694; Tubbman, 9 April 1696. (Ct.&Land: P#1.207, 208, 210, 212; QRev.8, 11, 12, 14, 19. 24, 26)

MANKIN, Elizabeth, dau. of Stephen and Mary Mankin of Portobacco. Gift dated 14 Jan 1689, from Richard Hobart; a mare. (Ct.&Land: P#1.190)

MANKIN, John, son of Stephen Mankin. Cattle mark recorded, 8 March 1691. (Ct.&Land: R#1.411)

MANKIN, Margarett, dau. of Stephen and Mary Mankin. Gift dated 8 Nov 1692, from Henry Thompson (planter); a filly. (Ct.&Land: R#1.536)

MANKIN, Stephen. (Inv.: 18.58; 22 July 1698; ----) Admr.: Mary Howard, wife of Thomas Howard. (Acct: 19.35; ----; 24 May 1699)

MANKIN, Josias. Registers cattle mark for heifer given him by his brother, John Mankin, dec'd., 8 May 1705. (Ct.&Land: Z#1.188)

MANKIN, Josias (carpenter) and Margaret his wife conveyed on 8 March 1725/6 to James Mankin (carpenter); 1/3 of tract called *Ba(r)kers Rest*, 150 acres; also 1/3 of 40 acres, being part of tract called *Bakers Enlargement*. (Land: L#2.267)

MANKIN, Josiah (Josias), (nunc.). Three sons John, Stephen and William to remain with bro. Stephen; son John to be of age at 18. Son Joseph and dau. Eliza. and son John to remain with bro. in law John Chapman. Entire estate to be in hands of bro. Stephen Mankin and John Chapman afsd., and divided among child. as they come of age. (Will: 19.923; 6 March 1730; 20 April 1730) Next of kin: Jame Mankin, Tubman Mankin. Admr.: Stephen Mankin. (Inv.: 16.63; 24 Aug 1730; 2 Nov 1730)

MANKIN, Stephen and his wife Margaret conveyed on 1 Oct 1730 a parcel called *Mankins Adventure*, cont. 65 acres. (Land: M#2.237)

MANNERLEY(?) Margaret, age 9 yrs. Servant of Joshuah Doyne, 11 March 1678. (Ct.&Land: H#1.129)

MANING, Edmond (planter). Binds his son on 3 April 1713, John Maning, age 10 yrs. on 16 March last, to age 21, to William Middleton. (Ct.&Land: D#2.37).

MANNING, Joseph. In his will he left to dau. Esther Mathews, 100 acres, *Mannings Discovery*, to her and the male heirs of herself and present husband, Thomas Mathews, who shall be born after the date hereof, and personalty. To son John, ex., residue of estate. Test: John Hayes, Dunkin Cambell, Wm. Herald. (Will: 14.447; 14 Jan 1717; 4 Feb 1717) (Inv.: 39A.46; 14 April 1718; ----)

MANNING, John. In his will he left to son Joseph, 62 acres. To son John, 50 acres. To son Richard, 50 acres *Ward's Addition*. To wife Mary, extx., dwelling plantation. Sons afsd. to be for themselves at age of 18. (Will: 21.437; 4 Feb 1718/19; 3 Sept 1735) Next of kin: Thomas Stone, Richard Stone. Extx.: Mary Manning. (Inv.: 21.169; ----; 5 Nov 1735)

MANNING, John, age 40. Deposition, 2 Nov 1719, regarding tract near Nanjemy called *Moulds Adventure*. (Chas LandComm: M2.63)

MANNING, John and his wife Mary conveyed on 20 April 1721 a parcel called *Lot No. 29 (or 19)* at Portobacco for *Chandler Town* and on 18 Sept 1724 a tract called *Wards Addition*, on the e. side of Poniton Run, 50 acres. (Ct.&Land: H#2.454; Land: L#2.96, 200)

MAINSTER, Thomas, orphan of John Mainster (dec'd), 9 Jan 1683. (Ct.&Land: K#1.319)

MANNISTER, Thomas, son of Thomas Mannister. John Raines (planter), late of Mattawoman, seek disposition of orphan child Thomas Mannister, bound to him by the court, 9 June 1691. (Ct.&Land: Q#1.27)

MANNISTER, Thomas, son of John Mannister (dec'd). Bound to John Raines to age 21, 12 Jan 1691/2. (Ct.&Land: R#1.338)

MANSELL, William. Mentions William Clark; son Benjamin Clark, alias Mansell — that son Benjamin remain in care of Richard Davis. Ex.:

Richard Davis. (Will: 22.173; 9 April 1739; 6 May 1740) Ex.: Richard Davis. (Inv.: 25.334; ----; 13 Aug 1740)

MANTE, John, age 16 yrs. Servant of Philip Lines, 11 Jan 1675. (Ct.&Land: F#1.163)

MANWAREN, Walter, age 20 yrs. Servant of Richard Smoot, 11 Aug 1668. (Ct.&Land: D#1.2)

MANWARING, George. In his will he left to wife Anne, 780 acres in St. Mary's Co., and plantations in Chas. Co. To Henry Warren, Michael Foster, Bennard Haines and William Turbervill, personalty. Exs.: Henry Adams and Thomas Matthews. (Will: 1.434; 11 April 1671; 5 May 1671)

MARCHEGAY, Bennett, age 32. Deposition on 27 Sept 1665 re the attack of Indians on the family of Agatha Langworth. (Arch. of Md.: XLIX.485)

MARDEN, John, age 13 yrs. Servant of Alexander Sympson, 11 Aug 1668. (Ct.&Land: D#1.2)

MARHALL, Richard, age 14 yrs. Servant of Benjamin Rozer, 11 April 1676. (Ct.&Land: F#1.173)

MARIS. (See MORRIS.)

MARKEAT, Anthonie, age ca. 14 yrs. old. To serve seven yrs., presented by Arthur Turner, 28 Jan 1661. (Ct.&Land: A#1.183)

MARKEN, John, age 20 yrs. Servant of Maj. John Wheeler, 10 June 1679. (Ct.&Land: H#1.134)

MARLER, Mary, of Portobacco, in Charles Co., spinster, on 15 April 1665, caused the death of her child, leaving it in the cold to die. Hannah Price was found to be an accessory. (Arch. of Md.: LVII.74)

MARLOW, Anthony, age 17 yrs. Servant of Samuel Fendall, 9 Jan 1671/2. (Ct.&Land: E#1.52)

MARLER, Jonathan. In his will he left to brother John Marler, of Manchester, England, 100 acres (unnamed). To sd. brother John and to brother Samuel, all estate in England. To Thomas Wakefield, 180 acres, *Manchester*. To John Worland, 100 acres. Said Thomas Wakefield and John Worland, exs. (Will:1.561; 29 July 1673; 24 Dec 1673) Ex.: Thomas Waikfield. (Acct: 1.105; ----; 21 Oct 1674)

MARLOE, John, son of William Marloe. Cattle mark recorded, June 1678. (Ct.&Land: G#1.164)

MARLOW, Elizabeth (widow). Gift 12 June 1683, to Bur and Susanna Marlow, a black heifer. (Ct.&Land: K#1.184)

MARLOW, Bartholomew. Admr.: John Marlow. (Acct: 29.1; ----; 30 Oct 1708)
MARLER, John. Admr.: Margaret Marler. (Acct: 39C.107; ----; 13 Nov 1717)
Admr.: Margaret Marler. (Acct: 39C.110; ----; 26 Dec 1717)
MARLOW (MARLOE), William (planter). Mentions wife Ellinor, extx.; daus. Anne and Mary at age 16; sons Joseph (100 acres of *Aberdeene*), Edward, William, Richard and James, at age 20. (Will: 19.768; 13 Dec 1728; 12 Aug 1729) Next of kin: Richard Gambra, Henry Acton Sr. Extx.: Eleanor Acton, wife of Henry Acton Jr. (Inv.: 15.298; 16 Oct 1729; 11 Nov 1729)
MARLOE, Edward of South Farnham Parish in Essex Co., Virginia conveyed on 26 Nov 1731 to Daniel Bourne of Stafford Co., Virginia, tract called *Tower Hill*, 250(?) acres, first granted to William Marloe (1670), grandfather of sd. Edward Marloe. (Land: M#2.272)

MARROME, James, judged to be 17 yrs. old. Presented by Walter Beane, 14 March 1664. (Ct.&Land: B#1.436)

MARSH, William, age 18 yrs. Servant of Thomas Gerrard, 11 Aug 1674. (Ct.&Land: E#1.181)
MARSH, Thomas, son of Gilbert Marsh. Cattle mark recorded, 9 June 1691. (Ct.&Land: R#1.234)
MARSH, John, son of Gilbert Marsh. Cattle mark recorded, 9 June 1691. (Ct.&Land: R#1.234)
MARSH, John and Margaret, his wife. Lease 9 March 1724, from Thomas Allen, pt. of that tract that Philip Allen, father of sd. Thomas by his will bequeathed to said Thomas, called *Branford Enlarged*, cont. 100 acres. (Land: L#2.207)

MARSHALL, Elizabeth, dau. of William Marshall, born 15 April 1667. (Ct.&Land: C#1.252; P#1.204; QRev.2)
MARSHALL, William. In his will he left to son William, four tracts in Chas. Co. To son Joshua and dau. Eliza:, Marshall, 500 acres, *Two Friends*. To son Joshua, cattle mark, obtained by marriage of testator with Katharine Ebden. Exs.: Thos. Notely, Robt. Henley and bro. Francis Wyne. (Will: 1.592; 22 April 1673; -- Dec 1673) Ex.: Francis Wyne (also Francis Wine). (Acct: 1.212; ----; 8 April 1675) Ex.: Francis Wyne (dec'd.), by Henry Hawkins (gentleman) who married Elisabeth (Francis Wyne's widow). (Acct: 8.269; ----; [c1682])
MARSHALL, William, son of William Marshall, dec'd. William Marshall in his lifetime stood indebted to John England for transporting Wm. Marshall son of said Wm. to England and maintaining him there in England at school and transporting him again to Maryland. 20 Feb 1677. (Arch. of Md.: LXVII.158)
MARSHALL, Hugh. In his will he left to wife Mary and to Thomas Breeding, personalty. Exs.: Edw. Naper, Gilbert Clarke. (Will: 4.275; ----; 10 Nov 1687)

MARSHALL, William, son of William and Elizabeth Marshall of Wicomico, born 12 Sept 1690. (Ct.&Land: P#1.210; QRev.16)
MARSHALL, Barbary, dau. of William and Elizabeth Marshall of head of Wicomico River, born 30 Sept 1692. (Ct.&Land: QRev.18)
MARSHALL, Barbary, dau. of William and Elizabeth Marshall, born 30 Oct 1692. (Ct.&Land: P#1.210)
MARSHALL, Thomas, son of William and Elizabeth Marshall, of head of Wicomico River, born 27 Jan 1694. (Ct.&Land: QRev.24)
MARSHALL, Richard (planter) and Mary his wife conveyed on 11 Aug 1696 a parcel called *Merchant Taylor's Hall* on s. side of Mattawoman Creek, 150 acres. (Ct.&Land: Q#1.99)
MARSHALL, William. In his will he left to wife (unnamed), *Peccattoway* and 100 acres. To son William, afsd. land. To son Thomas, 100 acres. To son Richard and dau. Barbara, 200 acres. (Will: 6.152; 2 Nov 1697; 28 June 1698)
MARSHALL, William. (Inv.: 17.23; 2 Aug 1698; ----) Extx.: Elisabeth Marshall. (Acct: 19½A.97; ----; 23 Feb 1699) Mentions: four orphans (unnamed). Admr.: John Fendall. (Acct: 21.354; ----; 1 May 1702)
MARSHALL, William of Prince George's Co., and Rebeckah his wife conveyed on 29 March 1714 a tract called *Two Friends*, cont. 525 acres; it being the n. half formerly sold to Josua Marshall to John Sothoron, to Benj: Sothoron (son of John), and on 11 Jan 1719 conveyed to Richard Marshall; and 100 acres of land on the Wicomico River granted to Wm. Marshall Sr. for 200 acres. (Ct.&Land: F#1.16; H#2.308)
MARSHALL, Richard (carpenter) and his wife Mary conveyed on 30 Jan 1721 part of a tract sold by William Marshall to Richard Marshall on the w. side of the Wicomico River; bounded by *Paquaseat*, cont. 60 acres. (Ct.&Land: H#2.489)

MARSTON, Constance, relict and admx. of Robert Marston, acquired on 12 July 1711, from James Bayley; grant dated 17 Aug 1680 to John Bayley, father of afsd. John Bayley, a 187 acre tract called *Bayley's Rest*, part of tract cont. 87 acres. (Ct.&Land: C#2.255)
MARSTON (MASTON), Richard. In his will he left to eld. son Robert, 50 acres at Piccawaxen. Mentions 2nd son Henry, eldest dau. Mary and youngest dau. Eliza:. Son Robert, ex. (Will: 6.271; 3 Sept 1698; 21 July 1699) (Inv.: 19½A.71; 1699; ----)
MARSTON (MARSTIN), Robert. (Inv.: 32A.114; 6 April 1710; ----) Admr.: Constance Marstin. (Acct: 32C.126; ----; 5 March 1710)

MARTIN, Catherine, dau. of John (a smith) and Mary Martin of Portobacco, born 3 Dec 1681. (Ct.&Land: P#1.207; QRev.8)
MARTIN, James, and Elizabeth of Nanjemy. Their children: Elizabeth, born 10 April 1683; Anne, born 23 April 1686; William, born 23 April 1686. (Ct.&Land: QRev.9, 12)

MARTIN, Penelope, dau. of John (carpenter) and Demaris Martin of Wicomico, born 13 Nov 1690. (Ct.&Land: QRev.16; P.210)

MARTIN, John, son of John (boatwright) and Damaris Martin of Wicomico, born 7 Dec 1693. (Ct.&Land: QRev.21)

MARTIN, John, son of Michaell and Jillian Martin of Portobacco, born 15 March 1691. (Ct.&Land: QRev.17)

MARTIN, James, planter. In his will he left to wife Eliza., extx., dwelling plantation. Mentions children: William, Anne, Margaret and James (minor). (Will: 15.6; 18 Jan 1711/2; 10 March 1718)

MARTIN, James. Next of kin: James Martin. Executrix: (name not given). (Inv.: 2.60; 23 March 1718; ----)

MARTIN, John. (Acct: 19.46; ----; 25 May 1699) Admr.: Mary Martin. (Inv.: 19.40; 29 Oct 1698; 2 Nov 1698)

MARTIN, Michael, planter. In his will he left to grandson Michaell [minor], 250 acres called *Hab Nab at a Venture* at decease of wife. To two grandsons, John and Henry, 200 acres called *Johnson's Addition*, and 73 acres called *Nonsuch*. Mentions grand-daus. Sarah and Eliza. To wife, her thirds. To son John, ex., residue of estate. (Will: 17.8; 26 Aug 1721; 5 Sept 1721)

MARTIN, Thomas. In his will he left to wife Joan and son in law John Pigeon Boyd, exs., entire estate. (Will: 18.83; 24 April 1723; 7 June 1723) Next of kin: "one of the executors and his wife." Extx.: Joan Martin. (Inv.: 9.299; 8 June 1723; 6 Feb 1723)

MARTIN, Michael(l). (Inv.: 7.174; 20 Nov 1721; ----) (Inv.: 9.288; 13 Dec 1723; ----)

MARTIN, William and his wife Anne, and James Martin and his wife Mary, conveyed on 9 May 1728 a tract called *Hopewell*, cont. 80 acres. (Land: L#2.421)

MARTIN (MARTING), William, planter. In his will he left to wife Ann, personal estate, excepting certain personalty to son William and dau. when of age. (Will: 20.373; 23 Feb 1732; 20 April 1732) Next of kin: Margrett Woodward, John Clarke Sr. Admr.: Ann Martin. (Inv.: 16.560; 22 May 1732; 20 July 1732)

MARTEN, John, and his wife Elizabeth conveyed on 30 March 1734 a tract called *Marten's Supply*, 65 acres and tract called *Marten's Triangle*, 60 ares. (Land: O#2.35)

MARTIN (MARTEN), John Jr. and his wife Elizabeth conveyed on 10 Nov 1736 to his bro., Henry Marten, part of a tract left him (John Jr.) by his grandfather, Michael Martin, called *Johnsons Addition*. (Land: O#2.306)

MARTIN (MARTEN), John and his wife Elizabeth conveyed on 10 Nov 1737, to his son John Martin Jr., tract *Owens Purchase*, lying on s. side of a branch commonly called Holly Branch; and another *Lyons Den* and on 10 Nov 1737, to his son in law, Notley Maddox, a tract called *Troublesom*, 125 acres; also part of the tract called *Owens Purchase*. (Land: O#2.307, 308)

MARTEN, John Sr., and his wife Elizabeth conveyed on 8 Nov 1743 to his son in law, James Mudd and Mary Mudd his wife, part of tract called *Strife*, 50 acres. (Land: X#2.67)

MARWICH (MARKWICH, MARWICK), Catherine, late of Clapham, but now of Camberwell in the county of Surrey, England (widow), and dau. of Thomas Carleton, late of London and afterwards of Clapham (merchant), dec'd.; which sd. Thomas Carleton was eldest bro. of Edward Carleton, late of London, and afterwards of Never Newington in the county of Middlesex, merchant, dec'd. To Joshua Savage in a deed dated 27 Aug 1739, and for the love that sd. Catherine Markwich has for her kinswoman, Mary Savage, eldest dau. of Bostock Carleton, another bro. of sd. Thomas Carleton, now the wife of the sd. Joshua Savage, sd. Catherine has sold to sd. Joshua Savage, part of a tract called *Prior Cleve*, 400 acres, which sd. part called *Trumans Place*, 500 acres, and tract *Prior Cleve*, are in Chas. Co. Recorded at the request of Benj. Hance, attorney of Calvert Co. 21 May 1742. (Land: O#2.450)

MASON, William, age 13 yrs. Servant of Philip Lines, 13 March 1676. (Ct.&Land: G#1.16)

MASON, John, age 21 yrs. Servant of John Redish, 9 Nov 1680. (Ct.&Land: I#1.33)

MASON, Philip and Mary of Piscataway. Their children: Elizabeth, born 6 Oct 1685; Samuell, born 18 April 1687; Philip, born 2 June 1689; William, born 23 Jan 1690; John, born 19 July 1693. (Ct.&Land: P#1.207, 209, 210; QRev.11, 13, 15, 16, 21)

MASSON, Francis. Admr.: Joseph Cornell. (Inv.: 10.273; 14 June 1689; ----)

MASON, Philip (planter) and Mary his wife conveyed on 19 July 1692 1/2 of tract called *Battessey*, 250 acres bounded by Cash Creek. (Ct.&Land: S#1.48)

MASON, Mathew, age 30. Deposition on 21 Xber 1719, regarding the tract *Christian Temple Mannour*. (Chas LandComm: M2.68)

MASON, George, Col. (Gentleman). Next of kin: John Bronaugh, ------ Mercer. Admr.: Ann Mason. (Inv.: 21.89; ----; 30 Sept 1735) Admr./Ex.: Ann Mason. (Inv.: 21.407; 22 June 1736; 24 June 1736)

MASSEY, Thomas. Appraisers: Henry Neale, Thomas Sparks. Creditors: Owen McDonald, John Lancaster. Admr.: Margaret Massey. (Inv.: 17.621; 21 May 1733; 15 Jan 1733)

MASTERS, William, of Prince George's Co., and his wife Mary. 23 Aug 1737. To Thomas Farrand of St. Mary's Co., a tract called *Hopefull Blessing*, 50 acres. (Land: O#2.303)

MASTON, Robert, son of Richard Maston. Cattle mark recorded 8 June 1680. (Ct.&Land: H#1.329)

MASTON, John son of Richard and Mary Maston of Baker's Creek, "borne ye last day of Decemr:" 1693. (Ct.&Land: QRev.22)

MASTON, Mary, dau. of Richard and Mary Maston. Cattle mark recorded 25 Aug 1694. (Ct.&Land: S#1.334)

MASTIN, Charles. Next of kin: Francis Mastin, Constant Skinner. Admr.: Susanna Mastin. (Inv.: 25.338; 23 Aug 1740; 29 Sept 1740)

MATHENA, Sarah, dau. of Daniel Mathena. Cattle mark recorded, 2nd Tues in Jan 1672. (Ct.&Land: E#1.100)

MATHENA, Mary, dau. of Daniell Mathena. Cattle mark recorded 8 Aug 1676. (Ct.&Land: H#1.203)

MATHENA, Daniel. Entered cattle mark for his dau. Elizabeth, being formerly entered by him for his dau. Sarah who being now dec'd., 1680. (Ct.&Land: H#1.293)

MATHENA, Daniell and his wife Sarah, late of Chas. Co., now of Stafford Co., Virginia conveyed on 4 Dec 1682, to Nathan Barton of Stafford Co., Virginia; a 300 acre parcel of land in Mattawoman (St. Thomas Creek) called *Wentworths Woodhouse*, on the n. side of Piscattaway R. and s. side of St. Thomas Ck. Also a parcel called *Cow Land*, 28 acres. (Ct.&Land: K#1.43-44)

MATHEWS, John, age 14 yrs. Servant presented by John Lewgar, 5 Jan 1663. (Ct.&Land: B#1.213)

MATTHEWS, Thomas [Dr.]. In his will he left to wife Jane, extx., 300 acres called *Huckleberry Swamp* or *Beckley*, in Chas. Co.; 400 acres called *Matthews' Hope* at St. Helen's. To son Thomas, 700 acres, part of tract on Mattawoman Branches. To dau. Mary, wife of Capt. Boreman, part of tract given to son Thomas, and 255 acres, called *Hill Freehold* at St. Mary's. (Will: 5.83; 9 Jan 1675; 11 March 1676) (Inv.: 2.253; 11 July 1676; ----) Extx.: Jane Bread (relict). (Acct: 4.379; ----; 13 Oct 1677)

MATHEWS, Ignatius. (Inv.: 18.17; 16 Aug 1698; ----) Admr./Ex.: wife (unnamed, relict of deceased), of Thomas Jameson. (Acct: 19½A.107; ----; 9 Dec 1699)

MATHEWS, William. Recorded 27 May 1709, cattle marks of Luke, Thomas and Joseph Mathews. (Ct.&Land: (C#2.135)

MATTHEWS, William, and Jane his wife conveyed on 11 May 1717, a parcel on the s. side of Baker's Creek, cont. 100 acres. (Ct.&Land: H#2.80)

MATHEWS, William. In his will he left to son Thomas, 1/2 of *Mathew's Purchase*, cont. 460 acres. To son Joseph, s. end *Mathew's Purchase*. Sons afsd. to live with their bro. Lucas. To son Lucas, ex., *Second Addition* and land adj. (Will: 18.352; 15 Feb 1724/5; 24 March 1724)

MATHEWS, William. Next of kin: Thomas Matthews, Ignatius Doyne. (Inv.: 10.396; 26 May 1725; 23 June 1725)

MATTHEWS, William and his wife Mary, of Prince George's Co., weaver, conveyed on 28 Sept 1733 part of a tract called the *Stor plantation*, cont. 50 acres. (Land: O#2.16)

MATTHEWS, Joseph. In his will he left to two sons William and Ignatius, 230 acres, also 115 acres, the northern end of *Matthew's Purchase*. Mentions dau. Ann; wife Susana, extx. (Will: 20.925; 31 Dec 1733; 30 March 1734) Next of kin: Jonathon Doynes, Thomas Thompson. Extx.: Susannah Mathews. (Inv.: 18.289; 2 April 1734; 2 July 1734)

MATTHEWS, Luke (Lucas). In his will he left to sons Jesse, 1/2 of *Cocksetts*, 1/2 *The Addition* and personalty. Mentions unborn child. To wife, ex., part of *Matthew's Purchase*. Mentions daus. Mary, Jane. To child. of brother Joseph viz.: William and Ignatius, other part of *Matthew's Purchase*. (Will: 20.927; 3 Jan 1733/4; 2 April 1734)

MATHEWS, Lucas. Next of kin: John Cowseen (?), Ignatius Doyne. Extx.: Martha Mathews. (Inv.: 18.293; 18 April 1734; 2 July 1734)

MATTHEWS, Susanah, widow. Deed of gift signed 3 Oct 1737. To her two sons, William and Ignatius Matthews, Negro girl Catherine. (Land: O#2.229)

MATHEWS, Thomas (blacksmith), and his wife Mary conveyed on 13 March 1741/2. To William Mathews and Thomas Mathews Jr., sons of the sd. Thomas Mathews and his wife Mary, part of a tract called *Oneales Desert*, on e. side of Piles fresh, 309 acres. (Land: O#2.448)

MAUD, John. Entered cattle mark for his son in law, Leonard Smoot, 4 April 1705. (Ct.&Land: Z#1.80)

MAUD, John and Susanna his wife on 10 June 1706, to John Standbury (cordwinder), binding Leonard Smoote, son of Susanna, to age 21. (Ct.&Land: D#2.8)

MAYBANCK, Elizabeth, age 13 yrs. Servant of John Wood, 4 June 1674. (Ct.&Land: E#1.171)

MAYROOK, Mary, late of Charles Co., now Baltimore Co., widow of Seabright Mayrook conveyed on 30 Aug 1682, land called *Mayrooks Rest*, cont. 85 acres. (Ct.&Land: K#1.28)

MCCLAINE (MCCLAIN), Laughlane. Next of kin: Francis Dunnington Sr., Francis Dunnington Jr. Admr.: Elisabeth McClane. (Inv.: 18.508; ----; 21 Aug 1734)

MCDANIEL, John, and his wife Elizabeth leased on 17 May 1737 part of a tract called *Simpsons Supply*. (Land: O#2.199)

MCDONALD (MACKDONALD, MCDANIEL), Daniel, planter. In his will he left to Mary Rankin, Margret Peacock, David Cogill, Peter Cogill, William Mitchel, John Pidgon Bowie, James Mackintosh, personalty. To Ann

Rankin, extx., residue of personal estate. At her death to be divided between her sons John and Robert. (Will: 22.334; 17 Jan 1740; 15 May 1741) (Inv.: 26.211; ----; 5 Aug 1741)

MCFERSON (See MCPHERSON, MACPHERSON).

MCGRIGER (MCGRIGGER), Duncan. Admr.: Frances Magrigger. (Inv.: 15.596; 5 May 1730; 28 July 1730)

MCGRIGGER, Frances (widow). To her children, John, Anne, Elizabeth and Katherine McGrigger, horses, mares, cattle, &c. Signed 10 Jan 1731/2. (Land: M#2.275)

MCMILLION (MACKMILLION, MACKMILLIAN), Peter. In his will he left to Joseph and Benjamin Bullet, personalty at 18 yrs. of age; sd. child. to be educated in Protestant faith. Capt. Phillip Hopkins and Jno. Bullet appointed guardians. Wife Elizabeth, extx. (Will: 12.14; 22 July 1696; 27 July 1706) (Inv.: 26.188; 29 July 1706; ----) Extx.: Elisabeth Smallwood, wife of Pryer Smallwood. (Acct: 28.129; ----; 14 June 1708)

MCBRIDE, John Duncan, son of Mary McBride, born 30 March 1745. (Trinity: 107)

MCCOY (MACOY), Hugh (planter). From Matthew Coffer (planter), a lease of a tract, 5 Dec 1741, called *Coffers Chance*, lying in Portobacco Parish, 100 acres, during the terms of the lives of sd. Hugh Macoy and his wife Mary Ann and William Macoy, son of sd. Hugh. (Land: O#2.431)

MCHAN (MACCAN), Timothy, leased on 16 Dec 1743, of 186 acres, for the term of three lives of Timothy Mchan, Ann Mchan and Daniel Mchan. (Land: Z#2.6)

MCHON, William and Priscilla. Their children: Virlinda, born 21 March 1740; Prisalla, born 12 Jan 1742; Elizabeth, born 27 March 1745; Robert, died 3 Sept 1745. (Trinity: 106—rev.)

MACKHORN, Robert. In his will he mentions wife Elizabeth and child., Robert, Elizabeth, William, Martha Duffey, Jane Wood and Anne Ash; grandchild Bennett Woodson and sons in law, Jacob Wood and Thomas Ash. (Will: 24.296; 17 Oct 1745; 20 Dec 1745)

MCPHERSON, William (tailor). Cattle marks recorded for his sons, Thomas and Daniel on 17 May 1737. (Land: O#2.200)

MCPHERSON, William and Elinor Wilkinson, married 13 Aug 1737. Their children: Kerenhappuck, born 19 Dec 1739; John, born 5 April 1742; Alexander Wilkinson, born 25 Feb 1743. (Trinity: 116)

MCPHERSON (MCFERSON), Daniel, planter. In his will he left to wife Elizabeth, extx., sons Richard Bassill and Alexander at 18 yrs. and daus. Mary and Elizabeth at marriage, entire estate. (Will: 22.275; 22 May 1740; 1 Oct 1740) Extx.: Eliza McFerson. (Inv.: 25.414; 6 Nov ----; 1 Aug 1741)

MCQUEEN (MACQUEEN), William, and his wife Katherine, of Prince George's Co. 10 March 1741/2. To Humphrey Deaverson of Prince George's Co. (cordwainer), part of a tract called *Birch Den*, which fell to Katherine, she being co-heir with other sisters. (Land: O#2.464)

MECARTEE, Dennis. Admr.: Anne Brandt. (Acct: 34.27; ----; 21 Sept 1713)

MEDCAPH, Robert. Judged to be 11 yrs. old, presented by John Duglas, 10 Jan 1664. (Ct.&Land: B#1.397)

MEDLEY, George (planter) of St. Mary's Co., and his wife Anne conveyed on 10 April 1728, 400 acres of tract *Tatter Shalls Gift*. (Land: L#2.435)

MEE, Hugh (planter). Deed of gift recorded 29 Oct 1722; to his dau. Elizabeth Mee (spinster). (Land: L#2.49)

MEEKE, Francis and his wife Mary. Demands writt against Thomas Deverille and his wife Ann, dated 14 Sept 1686. (Ct.&Land: M#1.198)
MEEK(E), Francis (Inv.: 15.168; 29 June 1697; ----) Admr.: Mary Meek. (Acct: 16.89; ----; 27 June 1698) Admr./Ex.: widow (unnamed), now wife of Richard Wade. (Acct: 21.47; ----; 2 Oct 1701)

MELLOR, John (tailor), and his wife Mary conveyed on 13 Oct 1719, a parcel of 100 acres called *Cassocks Lopp* and 100 acres called *Tiverton*; also 100 aces called *Lemarr's Purchase*; and 100 acres called *Hispaniola*. (Ct.&Land: H#2.310)
MELLOR, John (tailor) and his wife Mary conveyed on 17 Dec 1720 a parcel called *Doncaster*, cont. 200 acres, and *Aspinalls Chance*, 210 acres; later conveyed to John Mellor; cont. 100 acres. (CT.&Land: H#2.410)
MELLOR, John. Gift, 5 March 1721, to his son Nathaniel Mellor. (Ct.&Land: H#2.430)
MELTON, James. Admr.: Thomas Taylor. (Inv.: 14.164; 22 March 1728; 12 June 1729)

MERCHANT, Thomasine, had a bastard child, 8 Nov 1681 and 10 June 1681, respectively. (Ct.&Land: I#1.174, 231)

MERRICK, William. Next of kin: John Filburt, Thomas Smith. (Inv.: 10.272; 21 May 1724; 25 Jan 1724)

MERICK, William, father of John Merick. 27 Aug 1742. From George Brett of Prince William Co., Virginia, to Joseph Milburn Semmes, a tract called *Mericks Chance*, which land was originally granted to William Merick, for 150 acres and by his son John, conveyed to sd. George Brett, 115 acres; 24 acres excepted until the death of Elizabeth Reynolds (Renolds, Reinolds), widow of William Merick and now wife of Edward Renolds. (Land: O#2.490)

MICANEY, Andrew, age 21 yrs. Servant of John Douglas, 10 March 1670/1. (Ct.&Land: E#1.35)

MICHELL. (See MITCHELL.)

MIDDLETON, Robert (tailor) and his wife Mary. Two indentures dated 12 and 13 March 1688, respectively: parcel called *Hardshift*, cont. 160 acres; and parcel called *Saturday's Work*, cont. 400 acres. (Ct.&Land: P#1.97, 99)

MIDDLETON (MIDDLETOWN), Robert and his wife Mary acquired on 30 Feb 1684, from John Wheeler, father of Mary Middleton; tract called *Wheeler's Hope* on Piscattaway Ck., 300 acres. Indenture 18 July 1692, to John Clement; parcel called *Wickham* in Piscataway Manor, 112 acres. (Ct.&Land: L#1.52; S.127)

MIDDLETON, Robert (Gent.) and his wife Elizabeth, dau. of John Smith conveyed 7 April 1729, tract granted by will to said Elizabeth Middleton by afsd. John Smith, part of tract *Jordan*, 120 acres. [detailed history of tract] (Land: L#2.467)

MIDDLETON, Robert, conveyed on 13 June 1722, 180 acres which on 28 Nov 1717 was laid out at the request of Jno: More, ex. of the will of John Smith, dec'd.; a parcel of land for Robert Middleton and Elizabeth his wife pursuant to said will, being part of a tract called *Jordan* on the w. side of Zachia Swamp. The land was left to Robert Middleton's wife, Elizabeth, by said will. (Land: L#2.37)

MIDDLETON, Smith, son of James Middleton. Cattle mark recorded 20 Feb 1722. (Land: L#2.75)

MIDDLETON, Thomas Jr., and his wife Ann conveyed on 2 March 1738/9 a tract called *Stevens his Hope*, 98 acres and a tract called *Norwick* near the head of Zachia Swamp, 100 acres. (Land: O#2.385)

MIDDLETON, Thomas, of Prince George's Co., and his wife Susannah conveyed on 16 Jan 1739/40 part of *West Wood Manor*, 50 acres. (Land: O#2.431)

MIDDLETON, William and his wife Elizabeth conveyed on 15 Nov 1732 part of a tract called His *Lordships Favour*, 267 acres; given by Hugh Tears, 1/2 to his wife Eleanor Tears, and the other half to his dau. Elizabeth Tears, wife of William Middleton; on 24 April 1738, they conveyed part of a tract called *His Lordship Favour*; on 16 Feb 1743/4 William Middleton assigned the bill of sale of a Negro man called Tomacoe to his son Samuel Middleton. (Land: M#2.309; O#2.323, 358, 361 and Land Z#2.23, 24.)

MIDDLETON, William. Deed dated 9 March 1735/6. To Benjamin Tyler and Eleanor his wife, dau. of sd. William Middleton. 1/2 of part of a tract *His Lordships Favour* which sd. William bought of Thomas and James Abernathy. (Land: O#2.139)

MIDGELY, Richard. In his will he left to brother in law Thomas Lewgar, personalty. To wife Eliza: and John Hanson, his real estate. Admr./Ex.: John Hanson. (Will: 5.281; 18 Nov 1676; 22 Dec 1676; Inv.: 4.247; [c1677]; ----; Acct: 5.282; ----; [c1678])

MILES, Elizabeth, age 17 yrs. Servant of William Wells, 13 Aug 1678. (Ct.&Land: H#1.1)
MILES, Nathaniel, age 14 yrs. Servant of Archibald Wahob, 9 March 1679. (Ct.&Land: H#1.270)
MILES, Henry. In his will he left to children, viz. Mary, Elizabeth and Henry and wife Mary, extx., his estate. Daus. of age at 16 and son at 18. (Will: 16.49; 25 March, 1720; 2 May 1720) (Inv.: 4.82; 9 May 1720; ----)

MILL, Isabella, age 21 yrs. Servant of Barton Hungerford, Nov 1710. (Ct.&Land: D#2.5)

MILLBORNE, Rachell. Judged to be 18 yrs. old, presented by Richard Smoot, 8 Nov 1664. (Ct.&Land: B#1.384)

MILLER, John and Grace, of Nanjemy. Their children: John, born 5 Nov 1673; Peter, born 7 July 1682. (Ct.&Land: P#1.209; QRev.4, 8)
MILLER, Francis, son of John Miller. Cattle mark recorded June 1678. (Ct.&Land: G#1.164)
MILLER, John, son of John Miller. Gift 27 Feb 1687, from Henry Bransoner (planter), a cow. (Ct.&Land: N#1.297)
MILLER, John Sr. (Inv.: 20.131; 16 Dec 1700; ----) Admr.: William Stone. (Acct: 20.267; ----; 25 Aug 1701)
MILLER, John (tailor) and Sarah his wife conveyed on 13 June 1710 a parcel called *Green Branch*, cont. 66 acres. (Ct.&Land: C#2.186)
MILLER, Andrew, age 16 yrs. Servant of Elizabeth Hawkins, Nov 1710. (Ct.&Land: D#2.5)
MILLER, Jacob. Cattle marks recorded on 9 June 1718 for his children: Jacob, Dinah and Sophia. 9 June 1718. (Ct.&Land: H#2.170)
MILLER, Sophia, dau. of Jacob Miller, Cattle mark recorded 9 June 1718. (Ct.&Land: H#2.170).
MILLER, Jacob. (Inv.: 3.328; [c1719/20]; ----)
MILLER, Margret (widow). In consideration of a marriage intended shortly between her son, Jacob Miller and Sarah Marten, dau. of John Marten, her whole estate of inheritance, provide he gives to her a complete

maintenance and support. Deed of gift signed 1 Jan 1732/3. (Land: M#2.313)

MILLER, Margaret (widow). Deed of gift dated 12 June 1733. William Barton by his deed dated June 13, 1688, granted to William Hungerford and Margret his wife, the natural born dau. of sd. William Barton, land called *Bartons Wood Yard*, 100 acres; also the tract called *Capell*, 100 acres. After execution of the deed William Hungerford died and the two tracts became the sole property of said Margret and she now gives same to her son Barton Hungerford. (Land: M#2.343)

MILLOR (MILLER), John (tailer), in Stafford Co., Virginia, appoints his two sons [in law?], Benjamin and Francis Posey (carpenters), as his attorneys, to sue anyone indebted to him on debts due his late wife Mary Miller, dec'd., and to pay her debts. Signed 9 Jan 1730. (Land: M#2.241; also see 242)

MILLER, Jacob. Next of kin: Barton Hungerford, Thomas Hungerford. Admr.: Sarah Miller. (Inv.: 23.28; 14 Dec 1737; 2 March 1737)

MILLNER, Thomas, Avon River. In his will he left to Joseph Harrison, all estate in Md. To John Thomkinson, 200 acres called *Redd Clift* in Westmoreland Co., Virginia. Ex. not named. Test: Thos. Robinson, Samuel Palmer. (Will: 1.132; 23 Feb 1659; 12 Feb 1661)

MILLNER, Madam Anne, late wife and admrix. of Isaac Miller (?Millner) and Peter Pagan, merchant of London, appoint Thomas Crabb of Maryland as attorney, 5 Dec 1715. (Ct.&Land: F#2.94)

MILSTEAD, Edward, age 19 yrs. Servant of William Chandler, 12 Jan 1674. (Ct.&Land: F#1.41)

MILLSTEADE, William, son of Edward and Susanna Millsteade, born 20 July 1685. (Ct.&Land: P#1.208; QRev.11)

MILSTEAD, William and his now wife Elizabeth. Deed dated 12 June 1733; from Thomas Milstead, 130 acres called *Winter's Imployment*. (Land: M#2.344)

MILLSTED (MILLSTEED, MILLSTEAD), Edward Sr., planter. In his will he mentions son Edward; wife Mary, extx.; John and William Milstead; James Mordock; Benjamin Shakalit; John Grew. To children not herein mentioned, 1 s. (Will: 20.876; 14 Dec 1733; 17 Jan 1733) Next of kin: Edward Millstead, William Millstead. Admr.: John Millstead. (Inv.: 18.37; ----; 9 --- 1734)

MILSTEAD (MILLSTEAD), William Jr. Mentions: John Stevenson, Elisabeth Goley, Joseph Milstead, G. Tarvire(?) (sheriff). Admr.: John Blanchet. (Inv.: 28.161; -- Feb 1742; 28 July 1743) Next of kin: Edward Milsteed, William Millsteed. Admr.: Sarah Millstead. (Inv.: 26.209; 30 May 1741; 5 Aug 1741)

MILSHAW, John, age 15 yrs. Servant of John Ward, 11 March 1678. (Ct.&Land: H#1.129)

MINGS, Edward and his wife Jane conveyed on 5 Nov 1687 a parcel granted 10 May 1671 to Edward Mings called *St. Edward*, cont. 100 acres. (Ct.&Land: N#1.302)

MINGS, Edward. In his will he left to wife Mary, ex., *Minges Chance*. (Will: 14.308; 10 March 1716; 14 July 1716) (Inv.: 37C.107; 9 Aug 1716; ----)

MING, Mary, relict of Edward Ming conveyed 26 July 1716, to Joseph Harrisson, son of Richard Harrison, tract called *Ming's Chance* in Nanjemy, cont. 150 acres. (Ct.&Land: H#2.15)

MINGOE, ~~Lewis~~ Joseph and Elizabeth, of Nanjemy. Their children: Lewis, born 12 March 1681; Charles, born 14 March 1685; Elizabeth, born 11 May 1689; Thomas, born, 18 Oct 1691. (Ct.&Land:P#1.209. Ct.&Land:Q.Rev 8, 11, 15, 17 show father as Lewis crossed through and Joseph added.)

MINOCK, Michaell, of Portobacco. Will dated 18 March 1683, proved 9 June 1691; leaves to his wife Dorothy, 150 acres called *St. Edmonds* at the head of Portobacco Creek. One of the witnesses is William Frost. (Ct.&Land: Q#1.34)

MINOCK, Michall. Ex.: Dorothy Forster, wife of William Forster. (Inv.: 13A.145; [c1693/4]; ----)

MIRES. (See MYERS.)

MIREX, Jacob son of William Mirex (planter). Cattle mark recorded 1 May 1723. (Land: L#2.85)

MICHELL, Marke, age 12 yrs. Servant boy presented by Zachery Wade, 8 March 1663/4. (Ct.&Land: B#1.258)

MICHELL, Joan(e), relict of Thomas Michell. Court 28 July 1663, demands satisfaction for 1/3 of land sold by her husband without her consent. (Ct.&Land: B#1.138)

MITCHELL, Anthony, age 18 yrs. Servant of Thomas Gerrard, 8 Jan 1677. (Ct.&Land: G#1.85)

MITCHELL, Thomas. Admr.: Mary Mitchell (relict). (Acct: 11B.53; ----; 14 June 1700)

MITCHEL(L), John. (Inv.: 17.249; 3 May 1733; 2 Aug 1733) Admr.: Esther Mitchell.

MITCHELL, Peter (innholder). In his will he mentions bro. Colline; dau. Agnes at 16 yrs. (house in Port Tobacco and 98 acres *Richard's Delight*). Wife Janet, extx. (Will: 23.211; 22 March 1742/3; 21 July 1743) Next of kin: Collin Mitchell. Admr.: Janet Mitchell. (Inv.: 28.337; -- --- 1743; 29 Nov 1743)

MITCHELL, Janet, widow of Peter Mitchell (innholder). Signed 5 June 1744. To Ann Mitchell, dau. of sd. Peter Mitchell and herself, furniture, &c., when she reaches age 16. (Land: X#2.128)

MOLLER, Jane, dau. of John Moller. Cattle mark, 3 June 1719. (Ct.&Land: H#2.253)

MONCESTER. (See MONCASTER.)

MONTAGUE, Stephen, age 28 yrs. Sworn statement in court, 4 March 1661. (Ct.&Land: A#1.191)

MONTAGUE, Stephen. In his will he left to Mary Emanson, dau. of Nicholas and Mary Emanson, tract called *Howland*, cont. 100 acres. George Godfrey, ex. (Will: 1.507; 21 June 1672; 4 Oct 1672)

MONTEAL, Richard, age 14 yrs. Servant presented by William Perfect, 10 Feb 1662. (Ct.&Land: B#1.61)

MONTREW (MUNROE), William. Admr.: Elisabeth Munroe. (Inv.: 29.180; ----; 3 July 1744)

MOOD (See MUDD).

MOODY, Anne, dau. of William and Jane Moody of head of Wicomico River, born 2 March 1692. (Ct.&Land: P#1.212; QRev.19)

MOORE, Henry (Hennerie), age ca. 22 yrs. Swore in court, 26 Oct 1658. (Ct.&Land: A#1.25)

MOORE (MORE), Henry and his wife Elisabeth conveyed on 20 Sept 1665 a parcel of land called *Moore's Branch* lying on the w. side of a branch of Zachia Swamp, cont. 50 acres; and on 17 May 1667, a parcel of land called *Moore's Rest*, cont. 150 acres. (Ct.&Land: C#1.14; D. suppl. 28)

MOORE, Elizabeth, dau. of Henry Moore, born 13 March 1664. (Ct.&Land: P#1.205; QRev.1. Date of birth is 30 March according to Ct.&Land: E#1.87.)

MOORE, Henry, son of Henry Moore, born 3 Oct 1665. (Ct.&Land: E#1.87; P#1.205; QRev.2)

MOORE, Thomas, son of Henry Moore, born 9 Oct 1667. (Ct.&Land: E#1.87; P#1.205)

MOORE, Thomas, son of Henry and Elizabeth Moore, born 9 Oct 1667. (Ct.&Land: QRev.3)

MOORE, John, son of Henry and Elizabeth Moore, born 13 March 1669. (Ct.&Land: QRev.3)

MOORE, John, son of Henry Moore, born 13 March 1669. (Ct.&Land: E#1.87; P#1.205)

MOORE, Henry. In his will he left to son Henry and dau. Eliza: home plantation; sd. Eliza: to be of age at 16 yrs. To second son John, 50 acres, *Moore's Folly*, at Portobacco. To son Thomas, part of *Wheatland*. Wife Eliza:. (Will: 1.525; 9 May 1673; ----)

MOORE, Henry (planter). Indenture 25 Dec 1685, to John Boyer; 100 of 200 acres, called *Ma*—— (left by will of dec'd. father Henry Moore), to be divided between Henry Moore and Elizabeth Moore. (Ct.&Land: L#1.139)

MOORE, Henry. Acknowledged moiety of *Maismore* sold by William Boyden, and Elizabeth Boyden alias Moore, relict of Henry Moore (dec'd.), to Thomas Gibson. 16 May 1690. (Ct.&Land: R#1.3)

MOORE, Henry, son of Henry Moore, dec'd., conveyed on 10 Nov 1691, a tract called *Maismire*, cont. 200 acres. (Ct.&Land: R#1.277)

MOORE (MORE), Hugh. Admr.: Henry Hawkins (gentleman). (Inv.: 12.78; 26 Dec 1693; ----) Admr.: Henry Hawkins. (Inv.: 13A.142; 18 Sept 1694; ----) Payments include James Knox attorney for Lilias Moore. Admr.: Henry Hawkins. (Acct: 13A.256; ----; 29 March 1695)

MORE, Christopher. Admrs.: Samuel and Mary Mason. (Acct: 19½B.68; ----; 12 July 1699)

MOORE, Henry, age 59. Deposition, 4 Nov 1719, regarding part of tract called *Christian Temple Manor*. (Chas LandComm: M2.65)

MOORE, Thomas. Admr.: Henry Moore. (Acct: 20.184; ----; 4 March 1700)

MOORE, John and Priscilla his wife conveyed on 18 June 1720 a parcel being part of 400 acres of land given by John Smith to his dau. Priscilla, wife of John Moore, called *Jordan* on w. side of Zachia Main Swamp, cont. 50 acres, and on 27 April 1724, 60 acres, being part of the same 400 acres. (Ct.&Land: H#2.357; Land: L#2.134)

MOOR, Henry (planter) and his wife Sarah, of Prince George's Co. conveyed on 11 March 1723; Thomas Morris and his wife Sophia, tract called *Smallhopes*, on the w. side of main fresh of Wicomico River, cont. 100 acres. (Land: L#2.126)

MOORE, Sarah, relict of Henry Moore. Signed 24 March 1743/4. To her son Henry Moore, all her personal estate and a Negro man named Peter. On 11 Sept 1744 the witnesses, William Winters and Daniel Bryan, stated they say Sarah Moore, now dec'd., subscribe the said deed. (Land: X#2.153)

MORAN (MORRAN), Gabriel, planter. In his will he left to wife Elizabeth, dwelling plantation; at her decease to son John and 150 acres of *Addition to Cattles Grave*, at her decease to unborn child. To four sons, viz.: John, Peter, Andrew and William, residue of real estate. Exs.: Wife and son John. Ex.: Elisabeth Moran, John Moran. (Will: 21.137; 15 March 1733; 3 July 1734) (Inv.: 18.501; 25 July 1734; 13 Aug 1734)

MORELAND. (See MOWLAND.)

MORETON, Ann, dau. of William and Margaret Moreton, born 21 Feb 1740. (Trinity: 120—rev.)

MORGAN, Frances, had bastard child, servant of Madam Rozer, 8 Nov 1681. (Ct.&Land: I#1.174) Also in court 29 Nov 1681, found guilty and given 20 lashes. (Ct.&Land: I#1.180)

MORPHEY. (See MURPHEY.)

MORRELL, Christopher, age 20 yrs. Servant of Richard Chandler, 10 June 1673. (Ct.&Land: E#1.132)

MORRICE, Richard, age ca. 24, swore in court, 24 Sept 1661. (Ct.&Land: A#1.155)

MORRIS (MAURISE), Richard and his wife Ales Morris, assign title in 350 acres to William Codwell, 30 Oct 1661. (Ct.&Land: B#1.17)

MORRIS, John of Charles County, married by March 1661/2, Eleanor, widow of William Empson. (Arch of Md: 53:196)

MORIS, John (planter), age ca. 30 yrs. Swore in court, 8 July 1662. (Ct.&Land: A#1.218)

MARIS, Sarah, dau. of Thomas Maris. Cattle mark recorded, 7 April 1668. (Ct.&Land: C#1.266)

MORRIS, John, age 16 yrs. Servant of Peter Carr, 10 June 1674. (Ct.&Land: E#1.171)

MORRIS, Annas, age 18 yrs. Servant of Richard Morris, 11 April 1676. (Ct.&Land: F#1.173)

MARIS, Elizabeth, age 4 yrs., dau. of Abice Maris. To serve John Hanson until age 16 or marriage, 10 Aug 1680. (Ct.&Land: H#1.330)

MARIS, Sarah, dau. of Thomas and Alice Maris, late of this co. Servant of Johannah Hodgson, 9 Nov 1680. (Ct.&Land: I#1.33)

MORRIS, Richard and Penelope of Cedar Point Neck. Their children: Mary, born 22 Dec 1680; Penelope, born 13 Nov 1684. (Ct.&Land: P#1.212; QRev.7, 10)

MORRIS, Ellis, age 19 yrs. Servant of James Neale, 12 Sept 1682. (Ct.&Land: K#1.5)

MORRIS, Richard. In his will he left to wife Penelope, extx. personalty. To child., viz., Richard, Christopher, Mary, and Penelope, personalty. (Will: 4.196; 22 Jan 1685; 14 May 1686) (Inv.: 9.169; 18 May 1686; ----)

MARIS, Elizabeth, one of the orphans of Thomas and Anise Maris. Petitions for her freedom, 14 Jan 1691. (Ct.&Land: R#1.372)

MORRIS, Thomas, son of Stephen and Anne Morris of Cedar Point Neck, born 9 Nov 1693. (Ct.&Land: QRev.21)

MORRIS, Elizabeth, widow of Randl: Morris. 2 Feb 1744/5. To Young Parran (planter), Lot #19 in Benedict Leonard Town. (Land: Z#2.21)

MORRIS, Randolph (Rand:), merchant. In his will he left to wife Elizabeth, entire estate. Exs.: Wife, Benjamin Hance Sr., Richard Jones. (Will: 21.815; 17 Sept 1737; 25 Oct 1737; Inv.: 23.65) Exs.: Elisabeth Morris, Mr. Richard Johns. (Inv.: 23.63; 26 Oct 1737; 28 March 1738)

MORRIS, Richard (planter), son of Richard Morris (planter), dec'd., conveyed on 8 Aug 1705, tract called *Morris, His Hope*, 75 acres on the west side of Budd's Creek, formerly in St. Mary's Co. (Ct.&Land: C#2.70)

MORRIS, Stephen. (Inv.: 1.58; 17 Dec 1717; ----)

MORRISS, Richard. Creditors & Next of kin: Wallter Story, John Douglas. (Inv.: 3.253, [c1719]; ----)

MORRIS, Richard and his wife Dinah. Their second dau. Anne Morris married Edward Anderson (blacksmith); their first dau. Penelope married John Brown (planter); their youngest dau. Margery married Cleborn Lomax. Two tracts, one called *Bergen ap Zoen*, and the other called *Gwines hope*. An agreement relating to the inheritance of afsd. land by the daus. Signed, 11 July 1724. (Land: L#2.165)

MORRISS, Thomas (carpenter) and his wife Sophia conveyed on 7 Oct 1731 half part of a tract called *Small Hopes*, lying on w. side of main fresh of Wicomico River, cont. 100 acres. (Land: M#2.267)

MORRIS, Thomas. Next of kin: Thomas Harrison, John Wilder. Admr./Ex.: James Freeman. (Inv.: 26.554; 8 Sept 1741; 20 April 1742)

MOSS, William (Gent.) son of Elizabeth Swinburne, dec'd. Grants George Mason several parcels of land, 8 June 1705. (Ct.&Land: Z#1.201)

MOSS, William. To son Edward in England, 5 shillings. To goddau. Barbary Spikman and Robert Colson, personalty. To Margarett, dau. of Walter Weate, two tracts, one near Maryland Point and the other at Gose Bay, and residue of personalty, she being of age 12th Jan 1708. Ex.: Robert Colson. (Will: 12.217; 31 Oct 1707; 8 Dec 1707) (Inv.: 28.112; 5 March 1707; ----) Ex.: Robert Colson. (Acct: 30.308; ----; 25 Jan 1709)

MOULD, Frances and Barbara, daus. of John Mould. Cattle mark recorded 8 Aug 1676. (Ct.&Land: H#1.198)

MOULTON, Margarett, age 14 yrs. Servant of Robert Greene, 11 Aug 1674. (Ct.&Land: E#1.181)

MOULDIN, John. Lancelott Wilkinson and his wife Margarett, executors of afsd. Mouldin, 8 March 1680/1. (Ct.&Land: I#1.108)

MOUNKE, Elisabeth, age 18 yrs. Servant presented by John Cherman, 10 Feb 1662. (Ct.&Land: B#1.74)

MOUNTO, Charles. Admr.: Benoni Harrison. (Inv.: 22.279; 24 March 1737; 4 May 1737)

MOW (MOVE), Peter, age 7 yrs. Servant of Christopher Brimins, 11 Jan 1669/70. (Ct.&Land: D#1.117)

MOWLAND (MORELAND), Patrick. Next of kin: none. (Inv.: 38A.138; 22 Jan 1716; ----) Mentions: orphans (unnamed). Admr.: Mary Magraugh, wife of John Magraugh (Magrah). (Acct: 39C.117; ----; 11 Dec 1717)

MUDD, Thomas. In his will he left to wife Ann, *Hall's Place*. To son Thomas, sd. plantation at decease of wife and land in dispute bet. testator and Maj. Boreman; also 650 acres, *Brierwood*. To son Henry, *Boreman's Reserve*. To son George, 400 acres, part of *Cannarvan*. To son John, 180 acres, *St. Catherine's*, and 250 acres, residue of *Cannarvan*. To dau. Julian Clarke, 120 acres, *Jarviss*. To dau. Barbara, 200 acres, *Mudd's Rest*. Sons Henry and George to be taken in charge by their brother in law, Thomas Clarke. Wife Ann and son Thomas afsd. joint exs. Residue of estate to be divided among wife and child, viz., Thomas, Henry, George, John, Barbara, Sarah, Jane, and Ann Mudd. Overseers: Son Thomas Clarke and brother William Boarman. (Will: 7.265; 12 Oct 1696; 11 March 1696/7) (Inv.: 15.127; 12 March 1696; ---) Exs.: Thomas Mudd, Ann Hoskins (widow), wife of Phillip Hoskins. (Acct: 18.126; ----; 15 Dec 1698) (Inv.: 18.139; ----; [c1698]).

MUDD, Thomas (Gent.). Indenture quadrupartite, 30 Sept 1703, from Thomas Mudd, of the first part; John Sanders (Gent.), and Sarah his wife of the second part; Thomas Simpson (Gent.), and Mary his wife of the third part; Thomas Jameson of the fourth part—to end a chancery suit concerning a tract given by Wm. Boreman to his dau. Sarah Mudd, mother of Thomas Mudd, to Sarah Matthews for her lifetime; and Sarah Saunders and Mary Simpson, co-heirs of Sarah Mudd by her former husband Thomas Matthews, dec'd. (Ct.&Land: Z#1.127)

MUDD, Thomas. Assigns on 2 March 1710 deed of gift dated 5 Aug 1678 from Maj. William Boreman to his dau. Sarah Mudd, mother to said Thomas Mudd. Tract called *Hall Place*, cont. 450 acres. (Ct.&Land: C#2.227)

MUDD, Thomas and his wife Casander, of St. Mary's Co., conveyed on 9 Aug 1715, a parcel of land called *Carnavan*, on side of Zachia Swamp, cont. 650 acres. (Ct.&Land: F#2.82)

MUDD, Thomas, Henry Mudd, John Mudd, and Thomas Mudd (son of said Henry) conveyed on 12 March 1729 part of a tract called *Carnavan* and part of *Boarmans Reserve*, 100 acres. The wives [unnamed] of said Thos:, Henry, and John Mudd relinquished their dower. (Land: M#2.193)

MUDD (MOOD), Henry. In his will he left to wife Elizabeth, extx., and four youngest child., viz.; Henry, Monaca, Bennett and Ellinder, personalty. To dau. Elizabeth Simson, son Thomas, daus. Mary Bevens, Sarah and Heneretter, personalty. Memo.: No probate to above will. (Will: 21.663; 20 June 1736; ----) Next of kin: Thomas Mudd, Ignatius Simpson. Admr.: Elisabeth Mudd. (Inv.: 22.142; 1 Nov 1736; 15 Dec 1736)

MUDD, Thomas (gent.). To wife Casandra and young. children: William, John, George, Benedick and Casandra, estate. Wife to have charge of children's share during minority. To sons Thomas, James and Jeremiah and daus. Ellen Tarain, Sarah Haggon, personalty. Exs.: Wife Casandra and son Thomas. (Will: 22:119; 25 July 1739; 23 Nov 1739) Next of kin: John Mudd, James Mudd. Extx.: Cassandra Mudd. (Inv.: 24.474; 11 Dec 1739; 2 April 1739)

MUGLESTON (MUGGLESTON), Thomas. Admr.: Barbara Muggleston. (Inv.: 28.156; ----; 18 July 1843)

MULLET, Winifrede. In his will he left to nieces Helen Spratt, Ann Knipe, and Ann Brookes, personalty. To Mary Chandler, Edward Pye, Ann Pye, and to Mary Wathan, personalty. Niece Mary Brooke, extx. (Will: 2.244; 20 April 1685; 9 Jan 1693)

MUN(N), John. Cites goods belonging to the estate of Roger Dickinson. (Inv.: 8.494; 6 Nov 1685; ----) (Inv.: 9.38; 23 June 1686; ----)

MUNKISTER, (?) of Charles County, married by September 1671, Elizabeth, widow of John Charman. (Arch of Md: 60:346)

MUNKASTER, James, son of James Munkaster. Cattle mark recorded, 1678. (Ct.&Land: G#1.156)

MUNKESTER (MUNKISTER), James. Creditors & Next of kin: William Munkester, Richard Waye, George Geddas. (Inv.: 33A.123; 18 Jan 1711; ----) Admr.: Mary Harper, of Daniell Harper. (Acct: 34.136; ----; 11 April 1713)

MUNCASTER, James. Next of kin: Will. Muncaster, Mary Muncaster. Admr.: Ann Muncaster. (Inv.: 15.643; 31 Aug 1730; 15 Sept 1730)

MONCESTER (MONKESTER, MUNKESTER), William. In his will he left to son James, dwelling plantation, 98 acres, *Mankester's Craft*. To sons James and William and daus. Prudence and Mary, personal estate. Son James and dau. Prudence to be under care of John Sudfif. Son William and dau. Mary to be under care of John Craxson. Exs.: Thos. King and Jon. Cooper. Test: Dan. Jenifer, Mary Ratfif (Ratclief), Eliza: Monkester. Two last testes. are described as being about 15 yrs. (Will: 15.30; 24 Feb 1718/9; 17 March 1718) Next of kin: Elisabeth Munkester, James Munkester. (Inv.: 2.119; 24 March 1718; ----)

MUNES (MUNS), John. Age ca. 19 yrs., swore in open court, 30 July 1663. (Ct.&Land: B#1.164)

MUNKESTER (See MASKESTER, MONCESTER).

MUNROE (See MONTREW).

MURFREY (MURPHEY), Dennis (Dennie), died 23 Sept 1667 at James Lyndsey's. (Ct.&Land: C#1.253; P#1.205; QRev.3)

MURPHY, Dan(n)iel (Daniell). To sons William, Daniel and Edward at 21 yrs., and James and John at 18 yrs., and dau. Ann at 16 yrs., or marriage, personalty. Wife Rachell, extx., residue of estate. (Will: 13.436; 26 April 1712; 21 June 1712) (Inv.: 33B.183; 21 June 1712; ----) Extx.: Rachell Fairerfax, wife of John Fairerfax. (Acct: 34.145; ----; 16 March 1712)

MORPHEY, Daniel and his wife Rachel. Rachel Morphey requests the following depositions: Thomas Dyson, aged about 41 years, 6 Nov 1729, states he saw Daniel Morphey, dec'd., and his wife Rachel with a child about one year old, which the priest then christened by name of William, and that Daniel said that he was married about 1, 2 or 3 months before that time which was in February. John Gates, aged about 49 years, 6 Nov 1729, states that Daniel Morphey, dec'd., was not married to his wife Rachell until she had a base born child which was called William and afterwards Rachell was lawfully married by common discourse to said Daniel Morphey, and after the marriage said Rachell has a son born who is now called Daniel. (Land: M#2.185)

MURPHEY, Edmond and his wife Elizabeth conveyed on 24 March 1734/5 tract called *Lomley*, 100 acres. (Land: O#2.97)

MURPHY, Zephaniah, son of Daniel and Mary Murphy, born 20 Jan 1745. (Trinity: 107)

MURRAINE, Nicholas, age 17 yrs. Servant of Ann Fowke, 12 March 1677. (Ct.&Land: G#1.119)

MUSGROVE, Cuthbert (late of Charles Co.) and his wife Dorothy. In court 9 Aug 1682, to anwser unto Roger Dickinson (plt.), plea of trespass: "Roger is now and from ye times of his nativity — hath hither to both of Kingdom of England and in this Province." Dorothy called Roger "a hogg stealing Rogue," and promise to prove it. Sd. Roger stole husband's hoggs. Roger denies. (Ct.&Land: I#1.333)

MUSGROVE, William. Appraisers: Courts Keech, John Baker. (Inv.: 3.42; 4 Sept 1719; ----)

MIRES, Christopher, age 21 yrs. Servant of Thomas Craystone, 13 June 1682. (Ct.&Land: I#1.293)

MYERS, Christopher and his wife Mary. Thomas Craxon, late of Charles Co., and his wife Anne. In 15 June 1689 Mary Myers, known as Mary Sellwood, lived in the Craxon house and in service. Mary was not a freewoman and they [Craxons] bought her into this province from London to serve five yrs. Court (11 Aug 1691) states Myers pay Craxons. (Ct.&Land: R#1.260)

MYERS, Christopher. (Inv.: 13B.101; 30 April 1696; ----)

NAILL, James, Capt. Mentions: Anthony Neale, Madam Neale, father (unnamed) of the deceased. (Inv.: 8.215; 26 Aug 1684; 18 Sept 1684)

NAILOR, George. To wife Elizabeth, extx., *Stainland* and part of *Woodborrough*. To son in law John Adams, husband of dau. Elizabeth, 164 acres called *Nailor's Range*, Prince George's Co. To grandson James, eldest son of son James, lot No. 53, Mill Town. To granddau. Priscilla, dau. of son George, personalty. To son James, real estate not otherwide bequeathed. To wife and sons George and James, residue of personal estate. Exs.: Sons George and James. (Will: 21.141; 21 Dec 1729; 11 June 1734)

NALLY (NALLEY), John (planter). To son Denis, 75 acres of two tracts, *Georges Rest* and *Huskilow's Addition*, provided sd. son make over and confirm to son Joseph, 50 acres called *Saint Vincents*. To son John, 75 acres called *Langley*. To son William, ex., 75 acres. (Will: 20.578; 6 Feb 1732; 3 March 1732) Next of kin: Dennis Nalley, John Nalley. Ex.: William Nalley. (Inv.: 17.245; 20 April 1733; 16 June 1733)

NALLY, Denis (planter), and his wife Mary conveyed on 12 Nov 1736 part of the tract called *St. Vincents*, 50 acres. (Land: O#2.172)

NALLY (NALLEY), Dennis. Mentions: John Nalley, William Nalley, Abraham Hargis, John Muschet. Admr.: Mary Nalley. (Inv.: 26.557; 26 April 1742; 2 June 1742)

NALLY, Joseph, and his wife Elianor conveyed on 1 Aug 1743 part of tract *Georges Rest* and part of *Huscullens Addition*, lying on e. side of Zachia Swamp. (Land: X#2.40)

NASH, Samuell, age 20 yrs. Servant of Philip Lines, 14 March 1681. (Ct.&Land: I#1.258)

NAYLOR. (See NAILOR.)

NEALE, Henrie, age 16 yrs. Servant of John Courts, 11 Aug 1668. (Ct.&Land: D#1.2)

NEALE, James and his wife Anna. 1675. (Arch. of Md.: LXVI.43) (Arch. of Md.: LXV.465)

NEALE, James, Capt. Deed of gift, 1 July 1681, to his son Anthony Neale; horse and mare. (Ct.&Land: I#1.143)

NEALE, James (Gent.) and Elizabeth his wife. Indenture 11 March 1683, to Giles Blizard of the City of London; a tract on Piscattaway Creek called *St. James*, cont. 700 acres. (Ct.&Land: K#1.421)

NEALE, Robert, age 20 yrs. Servant of Thomas Gerrard, 9 Feb 1685/6. (Ct.&Land: M#1.89)

NEALE, James (gentleman). Mentions sons James and Anthony; grandson Raphael Neale; grandchildren: Roger, James and Dorothy Brooke, Jane

Boarman, dau. of William and Jane Boarman, and James Lloyd. To wife
Ann, son Anthony, and daus. Henrietta Maria Lloyd and Jane Boarman,
residue of estate. Exs.: Wife Anne and son Anthony. (Will: 4.40; 27 Nov
1683; 29 March 1684) Legatees: Jane Boarman, Jane Boarman delivered to
William Boarman (gentleman), Roger Brooke, James Brooke, Dorothy
Brooke, poor of St. Gile's Parish of London paid by Mr. Henry Warren,
Mr. Hubbard, Mr. Massey, Mr. Foster paid to Mr. Gavin. Ex.: Anthony
Neale. (Acct: 10.187; ----; 23 Feb 1686) Ex.: Anthony Neale. (Acct:
10.188; ----; 10 Oct 1688)

NEALE, Ann. To sons James and Anthony and their wives, to granddau.
Mary Neale, to grandchild, viz., William Boarman's child., and to Richard
Hobert, personalty. To son Anthony, ex., and son James afsd., residue of
estate. (Will: 7.378; 28 June 1697; 3 June 1698)

NEAL(E), Ann, Madam. Appraisers: Gilbert Clarke, Joseph Wilson.
Legatees: Anthony Neale, James Neale (son of Henry Neale), Mary Neale,
James Neale, Elisabeth Neale. (Inv.: 16.15; 20 June 1698; ----) Legatees:
Henry Neal (son of James Neal), Mary Neal, Elisabeth Neal, James Neal,
(unnamed) of the accountant, children (unnamed) of the accountant.
Distribution to: James Neal, accountant. Ex.: Anthony Neal. (Acct:
19½A.117; ----; [c1699])

NEALE, Anthony, son of James Neale. Intended marriage with Elizabeth
Rosewell, dau. of William Rosewell. Marriage agreement between James
Neale (Gent.) and Wm. Rosewell of St. Mary's Co.; land called
Wolleston Manor. Dated 10 Oct 1681 and 17 Aug 1682, respectively.
(Ct.&Land: K#1.132, 173)

NEALE, Anthony, son of Capt. James Neale. Original warrant for land
bounded by land of Arthur Turner, surveyed for Anthony Neale, 1 Aug
1692. (Ct.&Land: S#1.49)

NEALE, James, Capt. Legatees: James Lloyd paid his mother Madam
Henrietta Mary Lloyd. Distribution to (equally): accountant, Henrietta
Marea Lloyd, Anne Neale, Jane Boarman. Ex.: Anthony Neale. (Acct:
26.193; ----; 18 Feb 1706)

NEALE, Raphaell and Mary his wife. Indenture, 15 April 1710, to Patrick
Callihon. Parcel on e. side of Mattawoman River, cont. 200 acres.
(Ct.&Land: C#2.181)

NEALE, James Sr. (Gent.) of *Woolleston Manor*. Deed of gift, 21 Dec 1710,
to his eight children: James, Henry, Benjamin, Joseph, Elizabeth, Ann,
Mary, Margaret. (Ct.&Land: C#2.209)

NEALE, Henry and Edward Neale, sons of Anthony Neale. Indenture, 8 Nov
1715, from William Chandler; parcel nr. Portobacco Creek, being part of a
tract called *Chandler Hill*, cont. 20 acres. (Ct.&Land: H#2.4)

NEALE, James Sr. and Elizabeth his wife. Indenture, 26 April 1716, to
James Neale Jr., son of James Neale Sr. who is seized of *Wolleston
Manor* of 1000 acres; located on Wear Ck., nr. confluence of St. James and
St. Raphael Ck. (Ct.&Land: H#2.11)

NEALE, James Sr. Indenture, 26 April 1716, to his son Henry Neale; parcel on w. side of Wicomico River called *Gills Land*, cont. 500 acres. (Ct.&Land: H#2.7)

NEALE, James Sr. and Elizabeth his wife. Deed dated 25 Feb 1724. To Benjamin Neale, son of afsd.; part of a tract called *Giles land*. (Land: L#2.211)

NEALE, Henry. Acknowledges debt to his father, James Neale Sr., of 50,000 lbs. of tobacco. Signed 25 Feb 1715 and recorded 17 April 1725. (Land: L#2.215)

NEALE, Anthony and Raphaell Neall, son of Anthony. Indenture, 13 Nov 1716, to James Neale, son of Anthony and brother of Raphael; parcel called *Neale's Gift*, a fresh of St. Raphaell Creek, Huckleberry Swamp, cont. 494 acres. (Ct.&Land: H#2.32)

NEALE, James Jr. In his will he directs 1/2 the profit from his plantation to the Roman Catholic Church. To widow Ash, John Lancaster, George Newman and bro. Roswell, personalty. Bro. Raphael ex. and residuary legatee. Next of kin: Thomas Tuther, Henry Neale. (Will: 15.32; 28 Feb 1718/9; 13 March 1719) (Inv.: 2.105; 17 April 1719; ----)

NEALE, Margaret and William, children of John Neale. Cattle mark recorded 21 June 1721. (Ct.&Land: H#2.441)

NEAL(E), Raphael (Gent.) and Mary his wife conveyed on 15 June 1723 part of a tract *St. Matthews*, w. side of the main fresh of Portabacco or St. Thomas' Creek, 200 acres. (Land: L#2.99)

NEALE, Anthony. In his will he mentions Thomas Mansell, William Hunter and John Bennett, priests; George Newman, James Gates and dau. Mary; son Raphael (tract *William's Folly*). Refers to four younger children, viz. Edward, Charles, Bennett and Mary [minor]. To son Edward, 1/2 dwelling plantation *Aquenseek*. To son Charles, residue of *Aquenseek*; sd. tract to be divided by sons Raphael and Roswell, Charles Diggs, Wm. Chandler and William Diggs. To son Bennett, in case he does not enter priesthood, lease of 200 acres. (Will: 18.163; 20 Nov 1722; 12 July 1723) Next of kin: Charles Neale, William Chandler. Admr./Ex.: Edward Neale. (Inv.: 9.327; 9 Feb 1723; 4 May 1724)

NEALE, James Jr. Acknowledges debt to his father, James Neale Sr. of 50,000 lbs. of tobacco. Signed 25 Feb 1715 and recorded 17 April 1725. (Land: L#2.214)

NEALE, James Sr. To his bro. in law, Richard Edelen, four Negroes: Judith, Natt, Dick, and Frank. Signed 1 April 1725. (Land: L#2.213)

NEALE (NEAL), James Sr. of Wolleston Manor. To eldest son James Jr., *Woolleston Mannour*. To second son Henry, deed of 500 acres, *Gills Land*. To son Benjamin, 500 acres. To son William, 500 acres and other land. To wife Elizabeth, interest in 340 acres lying at Upper Machoteck, Virginia. To daus. Mary Deaton, formerly Vanswerring, Mary Tawney, formerly Neale, Ann, now wife of Mr. Edward Cole, and Margaret, personalty. To dau. Mildred, £30 at age or marriage. Exs.: Wife and sons Benjamin and William. (Will: 19.246; 1 April 1725; 11 Oct 1727)

NEALE, James. (Inv.: 13.45; 18 March 1727; ----) Next of kin: James Neale, Henry Neale. Extx.: Elisabeth Neale. (Inv.: 12.523; 31 Oct 1727; 22 Jan 1727)

NEALE, Raphael and his wife Mary. Deed dated 7 May 1731. To Capt. John Lancaster and Elizabeth his wife, dau. of said Raphael Neale, (as by patent granted to Anthony Neale, son of James, dated 10 Oct 1695); tract of 494 acres. (Land: M#2.246)

NEALE, James. To son James, entire real estate, including *Woollestan Mannor*. Mentions wife Jane, extx.; daus. Jane and Mary Ann; dau. Eliza. (land in St. Mary's Co. had with former wife, her mother). (Will: 20.160; 7 Jan 1730/31; 8 March 1730) Next of kin: Henry Neale, Benjamin Neale. Admr./Ex.: Mrs. Jane Neale. (Inv.: 16.139; 16 April 1730; 26 June 1731)

NEALE, John (planter). To son John, 50 acres, *Neale's Chance or Choice*. To dau. Margaret Scott, sons William, Barton and Daniel at age of 18, personalty. Residue of estate to be divided among child., viz.: William, Barton, John, Charles, Daniel, Benjamin, Zachariah, Jacob and Catherine, at age of 16. Exs.: Sons William and John. (Will: 20.819; 5 Oct 1733; 5 Nov 1733) Next of kin: Margarett Miller, Barton Neale. Exs.: William Neale, John Neale. (Inv.: 17.622; ----; 30 Jan 1733)

NEALE, Elizabeth (widow). To sons Henry and Benjamin and daus. Ann Cole, Mary Tawney and Margaret Egglin, 5s. each. To son William, tract on Machodock Creek, Virginia, and personalty; to divide with dau. Mildred residue of estate; should either of them die without issue survivor to inherit portion of deceased. Exs.: Son William and dau. Mildred. Overseer: Edward Cole, of St. Mary's Co. Test: Raphael Neale, Peter Falkner, Samuel Simpson. (Will: 21.54; 17 Jan 1733; 22 April 1734) Next of kin: Henry Neale, Benjamin Neale. Exs.: William Neale, Mildred Neale. (Inv.: 18.286; 24 May 1734; 1 July 1734)

NEALE, William (Gent) and his wife Anne. 4 Nov 1738. To Ann Aburnathy (Eburnathy), Lot #41 in Charles Town, cont. (Land: O#2.374, 391, 393)

NEALE, Edward, and his wife Martha conveyed on 12 Nov 1735 to William Theobalds, tract called *St. Johns*, 100 acres, and a tract called the *Addition of St. Johns*, 100 acres. Edward Neale covenants that Theobalds may have the land, free from the encumbrances from the heirs of Bennet Hoskins, dec'd., and from the heirs of Lewis Jones, dec'd. Edward Neale received this land from Raphael Neale, exr. of Bennet Hoskins who left the land to Edward Neale — deed recorded 5 Dec 1735 at the request of Henry Neale of Charles Co. (Land: O#2.127 {both entries}. Also see Land O#2.576 recorded 25 Aug 1742.)

NEAL, Bennet and Edward Neal, sons of Edward and Martha Neal. Leased on 25 Dec 1743. Lease to Edmund Maggottee, of 114 acres, in *his Lordships Manors of Panquiah*, for the term of the lives of George Clements, son of Francis and Elizabeth Clements, Bennet Neal and Edward Neal, sons of Edward and Martha Neal. (Land: Z#2.27)

NEAL(E), Henry. To son Richard, *Gill Land*. To wife Mary, extx., life interest in *Gill Land*. To Mary afsd. and children Richard, Henry, James, Garrett, Sarah, Mary, Henrietta and Trinso, personal estate. (Will: 23.50; 3 Dec 1742; 8 March 1742) Next of kin: William Neale, H. Neale. Extx.: Mary Neale. (Inv.: 27.450; ----; 12 June 1743)

NEALE (NEAL), Raphael. To John Lancaster, land where he now dwells. Mentions hrs. of dau. Elizabeth Lancaster; dau. Mary Taney; dau. Henrietta; dau. Monica Diggs and dau. Ann Thompson. To the Hoskins, grandchild. of test. including Mary Boarman, (once Hoskins) and Anne, to grandchild. Ralph Taney, and John and Raphael Lancaster, to ——— Mullineux, personalty. Wife Mary, extx. (Will: 23.294; 20 July 1743; 10 Dec 1743) Next of kin: Henrietta Neale, Edward Diggs. Extx.: Mary Neale. (Inv.: 31.255; 11 Sept 1744; 29 Aug 1745)

NEEVES, Mary, age 17 yrs. Servant of Thomas Mudd, 8 Jan 1677. (Ct.&Land: G#1.85)

NEISBUT, Edmond. Judged to be 18 yrs. old, presented by Jeromy Dickeson for Richard Stone, 10 Jan 1664. (Ct.&Land: B#1.398)

NELSON, John. To wife Mary, entire estate, including *Danfrit* and *Gilliod*, cont. 546 acres. Exs.: Wife afsd. and father in law Griffin Davis. (Will: 6.220; 21 May 1698; 15 March 1698/9)

NELLSON (NELSON), Richard. To eld. dau. Barbary and dau. Eleanor, personalty. To dau. Margrett, 117 acres adjoining *Christian Temple Manor*, it being 1/2 of *Cole*. To dau. Alice, 117 acres, residue of *Cole*. To dau. in law Mary Beck, personalty. To sons Richard and William, jointly, 224 acres, *Howland* where George Britt lived. To son John, dwelling plantation at decease of wife, it being residue of *Howland* afsd. To wife Mary, extx., plantation afsd., and personalty. (Will: Part 2—12.33; 9 Feb 1708; 18 April 1709) Approvers: Margret Nelson (daughter), Alice Nelson (daughter). Legatees: Barbary Nelson paid to her husband Thomas Robins, Elinor Nelson, Margret Nelson, Alice Nelson. Extx.: Mary Gray, wife of John Gray. (Inv.: 30.278; 23 April 1709; ----) (Acct: 32A.35; ----; 4 Oct 1710)

NELSON, Richard. Next of kin: William Nelson, Ann Nelson. Admr.: Ann Nelson. (Inv.: 12.520; 23 Nov 1727; 3 Feb 1727)

NENAN, Dennis, age 22 yrs. Servant of William Chandler, 20 Jan 1679. (Ct.&Land: H#1.253)

NEVETT, Richard. Next of kin: John Nevett (brother). Admr.: (name not given). (Inv.: 10.120; 3 Sept 1724; 1 Oct 1724)

NEVILL, John, age ca. 35 yrs. Swore in court 26 Oct 1658. (Ct.&Land: A#1.25)
NEVILL, John, and wife Joane. Subpoenas on 6 June 1660. (Ct.&Land: A#1.97)
NEVILL, John, age ca. 44 yrs. Swore in court 4 Sept 1660, about a tract of land at Nanjemy of John Wheeler. (Ct.&Land: A#1.100)
NEVILL, Joan, age ca. 34 yrs. Swore in court 2 July 1661. (Ct.&Land: A#1.142)
NEVILL, John, age ca. 41 yrs. Swore in court 2 July 1661. (Ct.&Land: A#1.142)
NEVILL, John. Deed of gift 22 April 1662; gives his son William Nevill a cow. (Ct.&Land: A#1.210)
NEVILL, John. Deed of gift 11 Feb 1662; grants to his son in law John Lambert and his wife, cattle, hogs and mare; by 1666 to be divided equally with his son William. (Ct.&Land: B#1.78)
NEVILL, Johanna, wife of John Nevill, of Charles Co. John gives to his wife, 500 acres called *Mooredith*. 12 Jan 1664. (Arch. of Md.: XLIX.446)
NEVILL, John of Portobacco. To wife Johanna, property formerly bestowed by deed of gift. To son William, plantation. To dau. Ellen Lambert, son John Lambert, grandson John Lambert, personalty. (Will: 1.222; 15 Jan 1664; 4 Feb 1664)

NEWEN, Owen. (Inv.: 10.15; 8 Sept [c1688]; ----)

NEWITT, John, of St. Mary's Co. and his wife Melesaint conveyed on 1 Aug 1692 a parcel in St. Mary's Co. called *Newitts Desire*, adjoining land of Edward Swann. (Land: O#2.372)

NEWMAN, Ann, age 17 yrs. Servant of William Barton, 11 Jan 1669/70. (Ct.&Land: D#1.117)
NEWMAN, George. Admr.: Charles Newman. Admr.: George Newman. (Inv.: 8.101; 20 Aug 1683; ----) (Acct: 9.52; ----; 9 July 1686) (Acct: 9.363; ----; 2 Aug 1687)
NEWMAN, Hannah. Servant of Henry Hawkins, age judged to be 11 yrs., 12 Jan 1685. (Ct.&Land: M#1.67)
NEWMAN, George. Cattles marks recorded on 14 Feb 1693 for his children: Elizabeth, Mary and Sarah. (Ct.&Land: S#1.174)
NEWMAN, George and Grace his wife conveyed on Jan 1703 part of tract called *Wicomico Fields*. (Ct.&Land: Z#1.72)
NEWMAN, William. (Inv.: 24.272; 14 July 1703; ----) Admr.: George Newman. (Acct: 25.148; ----; 14 March 1704)
NEWMAN, William and Mary his wife conveyed on 13 Nov 1705, to Elizabeth Dent, dau. of William Dent, dec'd., for love and affection, a parcel called *St. Nicholls*, cont. 300 acres. (Ct.&Land: Z#1.217)
NUMAN, William. To wife Mary, extx., entire estate. (Will: 13.736; 21 Feb 1710/11; 3 Aug 1714) (Inv.: 36A.238; 5 Aug 1714; 6 Sept 1714)

NEWMAN, William. Extx.: Mary Newman. (Acct: 37A.132; ----; 23 July 1716)
NEWMAN, Mary (widow). 26 March 1722. Sundry goods and chattels assigned to Robert Hanson, for Mary Newman's use. (Land: L#2.77)
NEWMAN, George. Next of kin: Elisabeth Newman, Sarah Dean. (Inv.: 8.301; 7 April 1723; ----)
NEWMAN, Mary, dau. of George Newman. Lease dated 26 March 1729/30 to Raphel Neale, land on the e. side of land formerly belonging to her father. (Land: M#2.205)
NEWMAN, William and his wife Elizabeth conveyed on 10 Aug 1730 a tract called *Monmoth*, formerly taken up by William Newman, father of afsd. William, cont. 87 acres. (Land: M#2.233)
NEWMAN, John. Next of kin: Walker Farsen, Atwix Fersen. Admr.: Priscilla Newman. (Inv.: 22.273; 10 April 1737; 1 June 1737)
NEWMAN, Prissilla, widow of John Newman. Signed 27 April 1738. To her children: John Newman, Loften Newman, George Newman and Mary Newman - cattle, personalty. (Land: O#2.328)

NEWTON, John, age 20 yrs. Servant of Henry Hawkins, 14 June 1681. (Ct.&Land: I#1.124)
NEWTON, Richard, son of Richard and Jane Newton of Wicomico, born —— 1693 and bapt. 13 May 1693. (Ct.&Land: P#1.212; QRev.21)
NEWTON, Richard. Servant to Capt. Ignatius Causin, judged to be age 14 yrs. old, 2 Jan 1693. (Ct.&Land: S#1.211)
NEWTON, Richard. (Inv.: 29.189; 21 Jan 1708; ----) Admr.: John Woodard. (Acct: 32A.37; ----; 15 Sept 1710)

NICOLLS, Christobell, age 20 yrs. Servant of Thomas King, 12 Jan 1674. (Ct.&Land: F#1.41)
NICHOLS, Rachell, age 17 yrs. Servant of Capt. James Neale, 14 March 1681. (Ct.&Land: I#1.258)
NICHOLS, Anne, dau. of William Nichols, of Pickawaxen. Cattle mark recorded 9 June 1691. (Ct.&Land: R#1.234)
NICHOLLS, Elizabeth, dau. of William Nichols. Cattle mark recorded, 12 Sept 1693. (Ct.&Land: S#1.168)
NICHOLLS, John (carpenter) and Bathsheba his wife conveyed on 10 Sept 1706 a parcel called *Rome*, cont. 400 acres, on the e. side of Anacostia R. at the mouth of Tiber Bay or Inlet. (Ct.&Land: C#2.21)
NICHOLS (NICHOLAS, NICHOLLS), John. To dau. in law Mary Rattclif and to Richard Rattclif and to Thomas ——, personalty. To rest of child., residue of estate, plantation being already recorded between Jonathan and William [Nichols]; both dying without issue, to pass to son Solomon. Exs. and overseers: John Sanders of Mattawoman, and Thomas Harris of Patuxent. (Will: 13.539; 28 April 1713; 4 May 1713) Next of kin: only small children. (Inv.: 34.186; 25 May 1713; ----) Ex.: John Sanders. (Acct: 34.243; ----; 7 Oct 1713)

NICHOLLS, Jonathan and his wife Elizabeth conveyed on 14 March 1731/2 a parcel of land called *Massemore*, bounded Mattawoman Creek, cont. 100 acres. (Land: M#2.279)

NICHOLLS, Bathsheba, wife of John Nicholls. On 7 Dec 1706 paid alienation on moiety of 200 acres called *Masemore* for use of James Heath, farmer. (Ct.&Land: C#2.19)

NICHOLSON, Esther, age 7 yrs. Servant of Henry Hawkins, 10 Aug 1680. (Ct.&Land: H#1.330)

NICHOLSON, William, age 6 yrs. Servant of John Stone, 10 Aug 1680. (Ct.&Land: H#1.330)

NICHOLSON, John, age 10 yrs. Servant of Henry Hawkins, 10 Aug 1680. (Ct.&Land: H#1.330)

NICHOLSON, Nicholas and his wife Hester. Summoned John Wood (planter), late of Chas. Co. to court about goods and chattels of Wm: Gough, who died interstate. 1686. (Ct.&Land: M#1.60)

NICHOLSON, Margarett, age 22 yrs. Servant presented by George Plater (Gent.), 9 June 1691. (Ct.&Land: R#1.189)

NOBLE, Joseph Jr., and his wife Martha conveyed on 5 April 1744, parcel of 100 acres called *St. Marthis*, lying in Pomfret. (Land: X#2.100)

NOE, John, age ca. 21 yrs. Deposition, 14 June 1720, that he heard Justinian Tennison say he was born in Weymouth, England. (Ct.&Land: H#2.415)

NOE, John Sr. Next of kin: James Jones, Peter Noe. Admrs.: John Noe, Abell Noe. (Inv.: 11.21; 11 May 1725; 3 Sept 1725)

NOE, John and his wife Sarah conveyed on 27 Feb 1726, a tract called *Lomley*, lying on s. side of the main swamp that falls into Piles Fresh, cont. 125 acres, and on 25 Sept 1727, part of tract called *Lomley*, cont. 100 acres. (Land: L#2.335, 389)

NOE, John. Next of kin: Joseph Semson, Sarey Semson. Admr.: Sarah Noe. (Inv.: 15.80; 12 July 1729; 23 Aug 1729)

NOE, Eleanor. Signed 26 Nov 1735. To her child, Henrietta Noe, furniture, 74 acres of land, &c. (Land: O#2.131)

NOLINN, Patrick, age 20 yrs. Servant of Mr. Dickinson, 2nd Tues in April 1669. (Ct.&Land: D#1.62)

NOELAND, Stephen and Mary his wife. Leased, 27 Dec 1709, to Thomas Riggs, 200 acres called *?Hemirad* (commonly known as *Mathias OBryans Old Plantation*). (Ct.&Land: C#2.203)

NOLAND, James. Next of kin: Daniel Noland, Stephen Nowland. Admr./Ex.: John Dempsey. (Inv.: 17.480; 9 April 1733; 26 Sept 1732)

NORMAN, John, age ca. 28 yrs. Swore in court 22 April 1662. (Ct.&Land: A#1.201)

NORMAN, Thomas, age 21 yrs. Servant of Henry Adames, 2nd Tues in April 1669. (Ct.&Land: D#1.62)

NORMANSELL, Thomas, age 19 yrs. Servant of Thomas Clarke, 9 March 1685/6. (Ct.&Land: M#1.90)

NORRIS, Henry. To son in law John Fairfax, ex., to pass to grandchild, son of same, entire estate, including *Kitts Choice* in Chas. Co., nr. Gilbert's Bridges. (Will: 13.637; 5 Jan 1713; 25 Jan 1713) (Acct: 35A.357; ----; 24 April 1714)

NORTON, Amy, age 15 yrs. Servant of Thomas Mitchell, 8 June 1680. (Ct.&Land: H#1.299)

NORTON, Andrew, formerly of Fairfield Stope Parish, So. Britain (planter). To son Cornelius, ex., all estate lying in Fairfield conveyed to testator by his father; mentions kinsman Wm. Morwood, of Burbige Green, near Buxton, in Darbyshire. Refers to estate, in South Britain, Maryland, or elsewhere. To Ann Cope and goddau. Ann, dau. of Rebecca Duplex, personalty. Father in law Cornelius White of Charles Co., guardian and trustee for son during minority, he being seven yrs. old 2nd of Feb. last and in case of his death then bro. in law, Luke Barber. Test. describes himself as eld. son and heir of Andrew Norton Sr. (yeoman), of Fairfield afsd., and states that it has been 13 yrs. since his leaving Cheshire and arrival in this province. To be buried near his late wife. Note—In probate on this will Rebecca Duplex has become Rebecca Cumberbitch. (Will: 14.500; 10 Aug 1712; 1 Aug 1717) Next of kin: John Parry. (Inv.: 1.73; 24 March 1717; ----)

NORTON, Cornelius. Wife Mary, extx. Mentions cousins Baptist and Cornelius Barber; cousin Dorothy Greenfield. Note—Heir at law was in England at time of probate of above will. (Will: 22.423; 20 Oct 1741; 2 Dec 1741) Next of kin: Baptist Barber, Cornelius Barber. Admr./Ex.: Mary Norton. (Inv.: 26.555; 30 Dec 1741; 5 May 1742)

NUMAN. (See NEWMAN.)

OAKES, Francis, age 19 yrs. Servant of Henry Hawkins, 8 June 1686. (Ct.&Land: M#1.220)

OAKLEY, Giles, son of John Okeley. Cattle mark recorded 11 June 1721. (Ct.&Land: H#2.431)

OAKLEY, John. Admrs./Exs.: William Hetton, Percival Fearson. (Inv.: 11.200; 2 Dec 1725; 28 Feb 1725)

OARD. (See ORD.)

OBRIAN, Mathias, age ca. 33 yrs. Testifies in court 12 Feb 1660. (Ct.&Land: A#1.121)
OBRYAN (OBRIAN), Elinor, dau. of Matthias OBryan, born 5 Nov 1666. (Ct.&Land: C#1.222; P#1.204; QRev.2)
OBRYAN, Elizabeth, wife of Mathias Obryan, died 6 May 1670. (Ct.&Land: D#1.108; P#1.205; QRev.3)
OBRYAN, William, son of Matthias and Magdalen Obryan of Mattawoman, born 6 March 1672. (Ct.&Land: P#1.206; QRev.4)
OBRYAN, William and his wife Mary. Receives cattle mark recorded 9 Dec 1680, from his wife's father, William Tayler. (Ct.&Land: K#1.219)
OBRYAN, Ellinor, surviving heir of Matthias Obryan. Indenture, 10 Aug 1703, to Mary Connell, wife of Dennis Connell, for love and affection, then to William, Elizabeth, Mary and Angellica Connell, children of Mary Connell. Two tracts, *Fernes* on the s. side of Mattawoman, cont. 300 acres and *Howland*, 200 acres. (Ct.&Land: Z#1.53)

OCAINE (OCANE), Gerrard. Next of kin: Edward Loyd, Judeth Cain. (Inv.: 35A.246; 8 March 1713; ----) Payments to: Capt. John Vincent, Darby Ocaine, Eleanor Smoot (daughter of Edward Smoot (deceased was administrator)) paid to her husband Edward Feild, Judith Occaine (daughter). Admr.: John Smoot. (Acct: 39B.72; ----; 29 March 1717)
OCAINE, Garrat, son of Garrat Ocaine, dec'd. His guardian, Mathew Dutton, summons, 13 March 1720/1, Robert Yates and John Scrogin; after viewing orphan's land. (Ct.&Land: H#2.429)
OCANE (OCAIN), Ger(r)ard. Next of kin: Judeth Dutton, W. Cage. Admr.: Martha Ocain. (Inv.: 18.489; 21 May 1734; 12 Aug 1734) (Inv.: 21.33; 28 Oct 1734; ----)

ODEN, Francis. Mentions: Thomas Ogden, Thomas Caus. Admr.: Elisabeth Oden. (Inv.: 11.25; 20 May 20 1725; 11 Aug 1725)

OGDEN, Andrew. Admr.: Elisabeth Ogden. (Acct: 16.245; ----; 28 June 1697)
OGDEN, Mary of Charlestown, Charles County. Mentions Mary Goally, an orphan, and Penelope, wife of John Musshell; Francis Fener, gent., ex., of Prince George's Co. (Will: 23.159; 20 July 1743; 10 Aug 1743)

OGILVY, John, Dr. Admr.: John Estep. (Inv.: 16.486; 13 April 1732; 4 July 1732)

OLLARD, John. To cousin William Beeman, entire estate, he to remain with his grandmother as long as she lives and to be under the guardianship of John Stramate. (Will: 23.49; 13 Nov 1742; 7 Feb 1742)

ONEALE, Hugh, Capt. Deed of gift 16 July 1669; his children, Daniel and Joy Oneal receive gift from Francis Dowty (minister). (Ct.&Land: D#1.97)

ONEALE, Hugh, Capt. Deed of gift 10 Aug 1669; to his dau. Wenifret of a cow. (Ct.&Land: D#1.98)

ONEALE, Arthur. Admtrix.: —— (name not given, widow). (Inv.: 19½B.35; 1 Dec 1699; ----) Admrs.: William Glover and his wife Mary Glover. (Acct: 20.178; ----; 2 Oct 1700)

ORELL, Jane, dau. of Thomas and Isabell Orell. Cattle mark recorded 10 Jan 1692. (Ct.&Land: R#1.548)

ORRELL (ORRILL, ORRILE), Thomas. To dau. Jane Lewellin, son in law Richd. Lewellin, ex., grandson John Lewellin and granddau. Margtt. Lewellin, personalty. To grandson Richd. Roger, residue of estate; he dying during minority, sd. estate to grand children John and Margtt: Lewellin afsd. (Will: 16.412; 25 Aug 1719; 2 May 1721)

OARD, Peter, age 18 yrs. Servant of Robert Henley, 12 March 1672. (Ct.&Land: E#1.54)

ORD, Peter and Anne, of Wicomico. Their children: Mary, born 24 March 1683; Thomas, born 19 Nov 1686; James, born 21 April 1690; Anne, born 19 Sept 1694. (Ct.&Land: P#1.209; QRev.9, 12, 16, 23)

OARD, Peter. Next of kin (sons in law): Edward Turner, Robert King. (Inv.: 30.13; 30 July 1709; ----) Admr.: Ann Oard. (Acct: 31.289; ----; 16 June 1710)

ORSON, Bearer, age 13 yrs. Servant of Robert Clearke (Clarke), 12 Jan 1668/9. (Ct.&Land: D#1.42)

OSBURN (OSBORNE), Thomas. Mentions Elizabeth and Mary, daus. of Will Hoskins; son Joseph [minor] to be under the care of Will Hoskins, and Richd. Harrison. Wife Elizabeth, extx. (Will: 19.86; 10 Nov 1726; 20 Feb 1726) Admr./Ex.: Elisabeth Osborne. (Inv.: 11.915; ----; 25 April 1727) Exs.: Absalom Thorne and his wife, Elisabeth Thorne. (Inv.: 16.409; 19 Nov 1728; --)

OSBOURNE, Joseph (planter). To mother in law Elizabeth Thorne, extx., entire estate. (Will: 23.48; 21 June 1735; 16 Jan 1742)

OULSON, John, age 21 yrs. Servant of Robert Rowland, 9 Jan 1671/2. (Ct.&Land: E#1.52)

OVERSEE, Simon. Died in the beginning of Feb 1659 possessed of 1000 acres on e. side of Portobacco Creek and other acreage. His land called *St. John's Freehold*, and the 800 acres adj. was occupied by his widow Elizabeth for one year after his death. (Arch. of Md.: LI.12, 66, 120, 333, 370)

OWEN, Mary, dau. of William Owen and Sarah his wife. Cattle mark recorded 17 Sept 1707. (Ct.&Land: Z#1.260)

PACEY, Thomas. Jemima Long, extx. and sole legatee. In event of death of sd. Jemima without issue, estate to be used for free schools. (Will: 1.272; 3 Nov 1665; 2 May 1667)

PAGE, Margerie. Servant maid, judged to be 19 yrs. old, presented by Walter Beane, 5 Jan 1663. (Ct.&Land: B#1.213)

PAGGET (PAGETT), Benjamin. To son William, *Wallnut Thicket*. To son Benjamin, *Paggets Purches*. Wife Mary, extx. (Will: 19.184; 15 April 1727; 13 June 1727) Next of kin: Henry Stephens, John Stephens. Extx.: Mary Pagett. (Inv.: 12.252; 19 Aug 1727; 22 Sept 1727)

PAIN(E) (See PAYNE).

PALMER, Samuell, ages ca. 33 yrs. and ca. 32 yrs., in court 12 Feb 1660/1 and 28 Jan 1661/2, respectively. (Ct.&Land: A#1.121, 184)

PARANDEOR (PARANDYER, PARRANDIER, PALINTEAR), James. To bro. John, *Saint Thomas*. To goddau. Elliner Haththorne White, *Parrandyer (Parenders') Lott* and *Archibald's Desert*; and personalty. To Henry Blansett, Mathew Breding and sister; personalty, some of which in poss. of Richard White. Exs.: Bro. John and Charles Musgrave. (Will: 20.162; 20 Feb 1730/31; 6 April 1731) Next of kin: Henry Blanset, Elisabeth Palintear. Admr.: Elisabeth Parrandier. (Inv.: 16.413; 20 Nov 1731; 17 March 1731)

PARRANDYER (PARRANDIER), John. Admr.: Elisabeth Parrandier. (Inv.: 16.220; 3 June 1731; 13 Aug 1731) Admr.: Elisabeth Parrandier. (Inv.: 16.450; ----; 12 June 1732)

PARKER, Samuel, age ca. 24 yrs. Swore in court 23 Nov 1658; mentions being "at his bachelor brother's house." (Ct.&Land: A#1.31)

PARKER, Samuel, age 25. Deposition regarding John Butteris, working at the house of Capt. William Lewis. 15 Oct 1659. (Arch. of Md.: LXV.673)

PARKER, Samuell (dec'd.) and his wife Joane. Court held 17 Dec 1662; William Heard, admr. to Samuell, in reference to a bill of debt dated 6 June 1656. (Ct.&Land: B#1.42)

PARKER, William, son of Jo: Parker. Cattle mark recorded, 10 Nov 1668. (Ct.&Land: D#1.6)

PARKER, Ann, age 19 yrs. Maid servant of John Cage, 2nd Tues in June 1669. (Ct.&Land: D#1.88)

PARKER, John, age 18 yrs. Servant of Jeremiah Dickison, 8 March 1669/70. (Ct.&Land: D#1.127)

PARKER, Jonas, age 15 yrs. Servant of John Courtes, 8 June 1675. (Ct.&Land: F#1.101)

PARKER, John (planter) and Anne his wife. Indenture, 13 Sept 1695, to Thomas Chapman, planter. (Ct.&Land: Q#1.94)
PARKER, Thomas. Admr.: Sarah Powell (relict). (Inv.: 24.231; 20 Aug 1703; ----)
PARKER, Jonas, age 59. Deposition, 30 Aug 1720, regarding tract *Farthings Discovery*. (Chas LandComm: M2.99)
PARKER, Jonas. Next of kin: Abraham Parker, Jonas Parker. Admr.: Eliza Parker. (Inv.: 19.95; 12 Sept 1734; 2 Oct 1734)
PARKER, Abraham. Next of kin: Elisabeth Parker, John Parker. Admr.: Elisabeth Parker. (Inv.: 21.94; 1 ---- 1735; 17 Oct 1735)
PARKER, John (planter). To bro. Jonas and nephews Farner, Galwith and Abraham, personalty. To wife Sarah, extx., residue of estate. (Will: 22.313; 13 Sept 1738; 4 April 1741) Mentions: Jonathon Davis Jr., Jonas Parker, John Parker (son of Abraham Parker), Abraham Branson. Admr./Exs.: Allen Davis and his wife, Sarah Davis. (Inv.: 26.153; -- April 1741; 25 July 1741) (Inv.: 26.512; ----; 21 Dec 1741)

PARKES, Robert, age 18 yrs. Servant of Thomas Dent, 11 Jan 1675. (Ct.&Land: F#1.163)

PARNHAM (BARNHAM), John Jr. (merchant) and his wife Jane. From Henry Wharton (Gent.) and his wife Jane. A treaty of marriage being lately on foot betw. John Parnham and Jane Wharton, dau. of sd. Henry Wharton and Jane his wife. In consideration that sd. marriage should take effect and be solemnized by articles of agreement dated 8 Nov 1728, Henry Wharton conveys to said John Parnham (Barnham) and Jane, half part of a tract called *Baltemores Gift*, lying nr. Budds Creek, cont. 181½ acres. Sd. marriage did take place and the land is conveyed; if in default remainder to Francis Wharton, son of sd. Henry Wharton. Lease and release dated 15, 16 June 1731. (Land: M#2.258) Bill of sale recorded 17 June 1731: Henry Wharton grants John Parnham (Barnham) Jr. eight Negroes: Ignatius, Margaret, Monica, John, Jonathan, Little Bess, Jesse, and Pegg. (Land: M#2.260)
PARNHAM, John. To son John, tract bou. of John Diggs, dwelling plantation *Ferne* and *Salsbury*, three lots in Charles Town. To son Fras: Xaverius, pt. of *Calvert's Hope*. Mentions Millasaint Higton; dau. Anna Maria; (100 acres and personalty, some of which in consideration of legacy left her by William Robinson); dau. Elizabeth; Thomas Higton, William Johnson, Thomas Simpson and Ignas. Wathen. Money in England at time of death to be divided. Son John trustee for two daus. (Will: 21.884; 21 March 1737; 4 May 1738) Next of kin: Ann Parnham, Elisabeth Craycroft. Exs.: John Parnham, Francis Xavier Parnham. (Inv.: 23.358; 1 Aug 1738; 9 Aug 1738)
PARNHAM, Anna Maria. Recorded 16 July 1742. To her bro. John Parnham, all her personal estate; to her sister Elizabeth Craycroft or her

eldest dau., a tract bought of Joseph Gates; other land in Piccawaxen Neck to her bro. Francis Parnham. Mentions Clement Craycroft. (Land: O#2.570, 573.)

PARRAN, Young (planter). Lease, 25 July 1752, of a tract in *his Lordships Manor* of Calverton, 102 acres, for the lifetime of sd. Young Parran and his wife Elizabeth Parran and Francis Wilkinson, son of the sd. Elizabeth. (Land: O#2.587. Also see Land X #2.23.)

PARRANDYER, PARRANDIER (See PARANDEOR, PARANDYER).

PARRY, John (gentleman). (Inv.: 3.239; 14 Dec 1719; ----)
PARRY, Hannah, dau. of John Parry. Receipt. Recorded 8 Aug 1737. From Col. Robert Hanson, admr. of John Parry, bond of Walter Parry and Joseph Parry's dated 29 Sept 1721, payable to sd. Robert Hanson with an assignment on the back to Hannah Parry, dau. of afsd. John Parry, signed by Robert Hanson. (Land: O#2.216)
PARRY, Thomas (Gent.) of Balle Easton in Somersetshire in Great Britain conveyed on 31 Dec 1737 part of two tracts called *Digges' Baltimore Gift* and *Digg's Addition*, conveyed by Thomas Tanner to Dorothy Parry, widow, the mother of afsd. Thomas Parry, in 1719. Said Dorothy Parry later married Robert Hanson and they conveyed the lands to sd. Thomas Parry by deed dated 17 March 1720/1, 365 acres. Also all the right that sd. Thomas Parry has to two parcels at head of Budd's Creek, whereon John Parry, father of afsd. Thomas Parry, formerly dwelt, and other land—in all 680 acres. (Land: O#2.366)
PARRY, Thomas of Bath Eastone in Somerset Shire, son of John Parry. Daniel Watts acknowledges to have received from Robert Hanson of Charles Co. a bond payable to sd. Hanson from Walter Parry, dated 29 Sept 1721, for £322.10, received by virtue of a power of attorney from Thomas Parry, son of John Parry, dec'd., and is in full of the monies, profits of his lands in possession of sd. Hanson, and his filial part of sd. John Parry's personal estate. Acknowledged 4 Aug 1736. (Land: O#2.162. See also Land O#2.309.)

PARSONS, David and his son William Parsons on on 8 March 1732/3 conveyed a plantation where James Johnson lives and part of tract called *Cole*, cont. 50 acres. (Land: M#2.324)

PASTAN (PASTIN), John Sr., planter. In his will he left to sons John, Thomas and Francis, each 82 acres of tract called *Poverty*. To wife Susanna, 50 acres dwelling plantation *Goodwill*. At her death to go to son William. To children William, Edward, Mary, Susanna, Rebecca, Charity, and Jeremiah, personal estate. Edward to be of age at 18. Exs.: Wife Susanna, son William. (Will: 23.508; 12 Dec 1739; 24 May 1744)

PATRICK, Thomas. Admr.: Charles Garrett (also Jarrett). (Acct: 13A.203; ----; 10 Nov 1691)

PATRIGE, Mary. Maid servant, judged to be betw. 11-12 yrs. old, presented by John Hatch, 3 Feb 1663/4. (Ct.&Land: B#1.244)

PATTISON, John, age 13 yrs. Servant of Benjamin Rozer, 10 June 1673. (Ct.&Land: E#1.132)

PAUDING, William, age 16 yrs. Servant of Henry Adames, 2nd Tues in April 1669. (Ct.&Land: D#1.62)

PAYNE, Thomas. Judged to be 15 yrs. old, presented by William Boyden for Thomas Stone, 10 Jan 1664. (Ct.&Land: B#1.397)

PAYNE (PAINE), John married Marie (Mary) White 23 Sept 1667. (Ct.&Land: C#1.253; P#1.204; QRev.3)

PAYNE, John, son in law of George Godfrey. Cattle mark recorded, 14 Jan 1673. (Ct.&Land: E#1.152)

PAYNE, Mary, relict of Jno. Payne, dec'd., now wife of George Godfrey. Deed of gift, 9 March 1680/1, to William Ling, son of Francis and Mary Ling, one cow. (Ct.&Land: I#1.122)

PAYNE (PAIN), John. Admr.: Mary Pain. (Inv.: 15.301; ----; 7 Dec 1728)

PAIN (PAYN), Mary (nunc.). Mentions Thomas Douglas, Ann Shaw, Margery Lomax, Jane Walker and John Fearson. George Sympson, ex. (Will: 20.541; 10 Nov 1732; 30 Dec 1732) (Inv.: 17.88; 29 Jan 1732; 24 March 1732)

PAYN(E), John (planter), and his wife Eleanor on 20 Oct 1740 conveyed part of three tracts, *Raley*, *Payns First Addition* and *Payns Second Addition*, 152 acres and on 19 Jan 1743/4 part of tracts *Raly*, 100 acres, *Payn's Addition*, 140 acres, and *Payn's Second Addition*, 216 acres. (Land: O#2.479, X#2.61.)

PEACOCKE, William, age 14 yrs. Servant of Philip Lines, 13 March 1676. (Ct.&Land: G#1.16)

PEALE, Henry. Died 29 June 1662, man servant of Zacharia Wade. (Ct.&Land: A#1.240)

PEELE, James. Next of kin: "no kin at age." Admr.: John Barker. (Inv.: 20.444; ----; 26 March 1735)

PEIRCY, Thomas, died 5 Nov 1666. (Ct.&Land: C#1.252; P#1.204; QRev.2)

PEARCE, Joseph, of Dartmouth, England. To wife Anne, extx., personalty; residue of estate to children at marriage or 21 yrs. of age. (Will: 2:13; 23 Sept 1674; 13 Oct 1674)

PEARSON, John, age 17 yrs. Servant of Ralph Shaw, 11 Jan 1675. (Ct.&Land: F#1.163)

PEARSON, Nathaniell, age 16 yrs. Servant of Dennis Husoula, 11 April 1676. (Ct.&Land: F#1.173)

PEELE. (See PEALE.)

PEESO, Cornape, age 13 yrs. Servant of William Marshall, 12 Jan 1668/9. (Ct.&Land: D#1.42)

PELLEFUL (PELLUFUL, PELLUFUR, PELLUFUS), Joseph and Mary his wife conveyed on 9 June 1710, to Thomas Sanders a parcel called *Wapping* on w. side of Portobacco Creek, cont. 100 acres. On 14 March 1720 Thomas Sanders (Gent.), conveyed to Thomas Osborn (planter) a tract called *York*, cont. 40 acres, previously belonging to afsd. Joseph and Mary Pellufur. On 18 Nov 1728 Joseph and his wife Mary conveyed to Thomas Sanders, tract called *Littleworth*, being part of a tract called *York*, 40 acres. (Land: C#2.188; H#2.427; L#2.446)

PEMBROOKE, Mary, age 20 yrs. Servant of Robert Rowland, 11 June 1678. (Ct.&Land: G#1.157)

PEMBROOKE, Jane wife of John Pembrook. Gift dated 16 Oct 1686, from William Watkins, a cow. (Ct.&Land: N#1.27)

PEMBROOKE, John. Items in the possession of Jane Pembrooke (relict). (Inv.: 9.313; 22 June 1687; ----)

PENN, William and Mary, at the head of Wicomico River. Their children: Marke, born 24 Nov 1692; Elizabeth, born 2 June 1695. (Ct.&Land: P#1.211; QRev.18, 26)

PENN, William, age 46. Deposition, 24 Sept 1719, regarding the tract *Baynes*. (Chas LandComm: M2.53)

PENN, William (Gent.) and Fantelenah his wife on 4 June 1720 conveyed parcels of land called *Russell Tract, Fortune & Penn Freehold*, and *Fortune*. (Ct.&Land: H#2.349)

PENN, John (planter). Married the relict of Arther Smith prior to 31 Jan 1721. (Ct.&Land: H#2.477)

PENN, John. Signed 25 March 1737. To his son John Penn Jr., gives Negro man named Toney. (Land: O#2.194)

PENN, William. To son William, ex., 290 acres dwelling plantation *Pensalvania*; 2/3 of personal estate. To dau. Elizabeth wife of Joseph Joy, 1 guinea. To wife Fantalenah, 1/3 of personal estate. (Will: 21.749; 9 Feb 1736; 14 March 1736) Next of kin: John Penn, Mark Penn. Ex.: William Penn. (Inv.: 22.271; 12 May 1737; 6 June 1737)

PENN, Mark. To wife Jane, extx., dwelling plantation, *Bergen's op Zoem*, 30 acres called *Gwinn's Hope*, 38 acres called *Penn's May Flower*. To dau. Jane, dwell. plan., also *Gwinn's Hope* and *Penn's May Flower*. Mentions dau. Ann; dau. Sarah. To sister Ann Chandler, 100 acres of *Chandler's Purchase*. To Thomas Bateman, personalty. (Will: 22.21; 6 Jan 1735; 4 Jan 1738) Next of kin: John Penn, William Penn. Extx.: Jane Penn. (Inv.: 24.97; 31 April 1739; 14 May 1739)

PENN, Fantalony (widow). Deed of gift signed 20 Feb 1744/5. To her son Philip Jinkins, Negro woman Bess, &c. (Land: Z#2.12)

PENNY, James. Mentions: Elisabeth Penny (relict). (Inv.: 19½A.73; 22 Aug 1699; ----) Admr.: Elisabeth Penny (relict), who is disabled by sickness. She is represented by her father in law Capt. Henry Hardy. (Acct: 20.194; ----; [c1701])

PENNEY, Anne. 22 Dec 1703, binds her son Samuel, age 2 yrs. July last, for 18 years and 6 months (at age 21) to John Blee, with permission of her master, James Lattemore. (Ct.&Land: C#2.82)

PERFIT, William. Admr.: John Gooch. (Inv.: 8.452; 3 Aug 1685; ----)

PERKINS, James, age 13 yrs. Presented by Joseph Harrisson, 8 March 1663/4. (Ct.&Land: B#1.258)

PERKINS, Robert, Portobacco. In his will he left to Jane, wife of Arch. Wahob, Patrick Forrest, son of testator's wife, and Richard Corner, personalty. Wife Anne, extx. (Will: 1.354; 30 Dec 1668; ----)

PERRIE, Samuel (Gent.), of Prince George's Co., son of Samuel Perrie, dec'd, of said county. 15 June 1738. To Alexander Hawkins, three tracts: *Daniels Mount*, 100 acres; *Johnsons Enlargement*, 100 acres; *Bartons Enlargement*, 50 acres. (Land: O#2.334).

PERRIE, Samuel (merchant of Prince George's Co.) and Sarah his wife. Indenture, 6 Aug 1720, to Philip Lee. (Ct.&Land: H#2.406).

PERRIE, Samuel, and his wife Margaret. 1 March 1742/3. To Charles Smoot, part of a tract called *Daniels Mount*, cont. 45 acres; and a part of *Johnson Retirement*, cont. 80 acres. (Land: X#2.6).

PERRIE, Samuel and Sarah his wife, granddau of William Barton. Indenture 11 Nov 1713, from William Barton; a parcel called *Daniel's Mount*, cont. 100 acres; *Barton's Hope*, cont. 100 acres; *Johnson's Retirement*, cont. 100 acres; *Johnson's Enlargement*, cont. 100 acres; *Hatfield*, cont. 100 acres; and *Barton Enlargement*, cont. 52 acres. (Ct.&Land: F#2.1).

PERRY (PERRIE), Samuel, Maj. Next of kin: "minors." Admr.: Mrs. Sarah Perrie. (Inv.: 15.296; 16 Dec 1729; 2 Jan 1729)

PERRY, Thomas (Gent.) late of St. Mary's Co. Indenture, 19 Dec 1709 to Cornelius White, Gent.; Thomas binds himself for seven yrs., after three yrs. of service a house to be provided for Thomas to marry Margaret Smith. (Ct.&Land: C#2.210)

PERY (PERRY), Thomas. To sons John, Thomas, William, Hugh and Samuel at 18 yrs., and to daus. Mary and Anne, personalty. Wife Mary, extx. (Will: 14.519; ----; ----) Appraisers: Henry Brett, John Barker. (Inv.: 1.87; 9 Jun 1718; ----)

PERRIE, Samuell. Next of kin: Levin Wailes, Ann Wailes. Admr.: Mary Perrie. (Inv.: 29.334; 25 April 1744; 15 Aug 1744)

PERSIVALL, Charles, age 12 yrs. Servant of Mrs. Coates, 10 June 1673. (Ct.&Land: E#1.132)

PETERS, Samuell. Admr.: Martha Peters (relict). (Acct: 26.334; ----; 7 April 1707) Admr.: Martha Peters by John Andrews. (Acct: 28.94; ----; 18 Nov 1707)

PETERS (PETTERS), Martha (Mrs.), of All Faith Parish. To James Knight, personalty. To son or godson (mention is made in both ways) John Haggatt, ex., residue of estate, including dwell. plant. during term of lease. (Will: 13.219; 10 Jan 1710; 30 Jan 1710) (Inv.: 32B.159; 3 Feb 1710; ----) Ex.: John Hagget. (Acct: 32C.168; ----; 26 Sept 1711)

PETERS, Martha. Ex.: John Haggett. (Acct: 36A.240; ----; 7 Aug 1714)

PETTIT, Thomas, and his wife Susanna on 27 July 1745 conveyed remainder of a tract called *St. Margarets*, cont. 48 acres. (Land: Z#2.56)

PEW, David. (Inv.: 16.1; 21 June 1698; ----)

PHEGG (PHOGG), Charles, age 14 yrs. Servant of Thomas Gerrard, 14 March 1681. (Ct.&Land: I#1.258)

PHILBERT, John (planter), grandson of Thomas Wharton on 15 Dec 1724 conveyed part of a tract called *Christian Millford*, cont. 50 acres. (Land: L#2.196)

PHILBERT, John, and his wife Eliza on 14 June 1727 conveyed a tract called *Archibalds Desert*, cont. 100 acres. (Land: L#2.363)

PHILIPS, Nicholas, age ca. 21 yrs. Swore in court 2 July 1661. (Ct.&Land: A#1.142)

PHYLLIPS, Hugh, age 21 yrs. Servant of Col. Gerrard Fowke, 8 Sept 1668. (Ct.&Land: D#1.4)

PHILLIPS, Edward, age 17 yrs. Servant of Thomas Dent, 11 Jan 1675. (Ct.&Land: F#1.163)

PHILLIPS, Thomas, age 17 yrs. Servant of James Bowling, 13 March 1676. (Ct.&Land: G#1.16)

PHILLIPS, John, age 16 yrs. Servant of John Fearson, 12 March 1677. (Ct.&Land: G#1.119)

219

PHILLIPS, Zephaniah and Catherine Scott, married 8 Jan 1744. Their son: Zephaniah, born 4 Dec 1745. (Trinity: 106)

PHILPOT, Charles, son of Edward Philpot, born 19 Feb 1667. (Ct.&Land: P#1.204; QRev.3)

PHILPOTT, Edward. (Inv.: 7A.63; 20 March 1679; ----)

PHILPOTT, Edward and Susanna, of head of Wicomico River. Their children: Edward, born 14 Jan 1687; Susanna, born 9 June 1690; John, born 13 Oct 1692. (Ct.&Land: C#1.252; P#1.210; QRev.13, 16, 18)

PHILPOTT (PHILLPOTT), Edward. To son Edward, tract of land in Charles Co., adj. 300 acres sold by James Walker to father Edward Philpott. To sons John, Edward and Charles, 60 acres, *Timber Neck*. To son Charles, remainder of land on n. side of Hospital Run. To daus. Eleanor and Mary, and to granddau. Susanna Musgrave (at age of 16 or marriage), personalty. To wife Eleanor, dwelling plantation, adjoining that of Capt. Jno. Fendall's. afsd. Exs.: Wife Eleanor and son John, jointly. (Will: 14.672; 19 Aug 1718; 28 Oct 1718) Next of kin: Gustavus Brown. (Inv.: 2.111; 31 Oct 1718; 9 June 1719)

PHILPOT, Charles and Elizabeth his wife conveyed on 7 Oct 1720, a parcel at the head of Wicomico River. (Ct.&Land: H#2.395)

PHILPOTT, Elinor, Mrs. Next of kin: Henry Hawkins, Thomas Hawkins. (Inv.: 8.214; 24 April 1723; ----)

PHILLPOT(T), Eleanor. To son Edward, personal estate, excepting legacies to following: Jane Morley, Marg. Phillpott, Mary Gattwick and Wm. Hungerford. Bro. John Phillpott, ex., to have care of son Edward till of age at 21. (Will: 18;343; 22 Jan 1724; 23 Feb 1724) Mentions: Edward Phillpot, Charles Phillpot, Peter Harrant. Executrix: (name not given). (Inv.: 10.369; 10 March 1734; 29 May 1725)

PHILLPOTS (PHILPOTT), Edward. To sons John and Edward, 100 acres called *Courses Pallace*; personalty at age of 16. To god-dau. Elizabeth Fairfax, personalty. To wife Margaret, extx., dwelling plantation. (Will: 18.428; 30 Jan 1724/5; 27 Jan 1725) Next of kin: Charles Philpott, John Philpott. (Inv.: 11.258; 25 Feb 1725; 16 March 1725)

PICHERD, Robert, age 17 yrs. Servant of John Lambert, 11 March 1678. (Ct.&Land: H#1.130)

PICKERING, Michael. Petitions that he hath since his arrival in the Province, being at that time the age of 18 and upwards, one Robert Henly of Charles Co. term of five years without an indenture; now demands his freedom. Court held 13 March 1665/6; jury finds him to be 21 yrs. old and orders his freedom. (Arch. of Md.: XLIX.565; Ct.&Land: B#1.525)

PIDGON (PIGION), John (planter) and his wife Joan received a ten year lease, dated 10 Nov 1724, on a parcel *Lordships Favour*, on w. side of Zachia Swamp, cont. 50 acres. (Land: L#2.198)

PIGOTT, Sarah, dau. of Bartholomew Pigott (physician), dec'd. Deed of gift from Richard Boughton, dated 20 April 1686. (Ct.&Land: M#1.32)

PIGOTT (PIGGOTT), Sarah. To Eliza: Lampton, Mary Birth, Daniel Celly, Darby Cain and Rose, his wife, personalty. To William Hunter, residue of estate in trust for the poor. Ex.: William Chandler. (Will: 3.5; 29 Dec 1703; 14 Feb 1703) Legatees: Derby Cane, Mary Birth, Elisabeth Lampton (infant under age), William Hunter (gentleman). Ex.: William Chandler. (Acct: 25.87; ----; 18 April 1705)

PILE, Joseph, son of Joseph Pile, dec'd. and Luke Gardiner of Prince George's Co. Indenture, 9 March 1713, to John Parnham and Elizabeth his wife, sister to said Joseph Pile. Parcel called *Horne*, cont. 100 acres; located on the w. side of Wicomico R. (Ct.&Land: F#2.12)

PILES, Joseph, age 30. Deposition on 12 xber 1719, regarding tract called *Salisbury*. (Chas LandComm: M2.75)

PILE(S), Joseph. To daus. Ann, Elisa: and Mary and their hrs., 300 acres out of upper end of *Sarum*. To two sons Joseph and Bennett and their hrs., 700 acres of *Sarum*, with 150 acres of *Baltimore's Bounty*. To nephew Joseph Power, 400 a. of *St. Barbaries* (St. Mary's Co.). Wife Eliza:, extx. Sons to be of age at 21, daus. at 16 or marriage. (Will: 18.312; 15 June 1724; 28 Sept 1724) Appraisers: Next of kin: Benedict Boreman, John Parnham. Executrix: (name not given) (Inv.: 10.265; 29 Dec 1724; 1 Jan 1724)

PINNER (PINNAR), William, youngest son of Richard Pinner, dec'd. Deed of gift dated 1 March 1669, from Andrew Watson (planter), Stafford Co., Virginia to Alexander White, parcel of land called *Watson's Addition*, cont. 75 acres; to be held by White for the use of Wm: Pinnar during his minority. (Ct.&Land: E#1.17½)

PINNER, Richard. Indenture, 14 Sept 1675, to his brother William Pinner; parcel cont. 300 acres. (Ct.&Land: F#1.136)

PINNER, Richard. Wife Mary, extx.. To daus. Anne and Eliza:, 300 acres equally at death of their mother. (Will: 4.147; 21 Feb 1684; 17 June 1685)

PINNER, William. To wife Rose, estate now in hands of her father in law Richard Clowder. To brother Richard and cous. Anne Pinner, personalty. Mother Anne Attkins, extx. (Will: 4:146; 10 Nov 1684; 17 June 1685)

PIPER, John, age ca. 30 yrs. in court 26 Oct 1658. Age ca. 34 yrs. in court 9 July 1662. (Ct.&Land: A#1.25-26, 232)

PIPER, James, age 11 yrs. Servant of Richard Morris, 12 March 1672. (Ct.&Land: E#1.54)

PLATER, Francis. (Inv.: 29.330; 6 July 1709; ----) Admr.: Elisabeth Hamilton. (Acct: 30.304; ----; 9 Feb 1709)

221

PLAYER, John. Judged to be 15 yrs. old, presented by John Wright, 10 Jan 1664. (Ct.&Land: B#1.397)

POKE, Margarett, age 19 yrs. Servant of George Dent, Nov 1710. (Ct.&Land: D#2.5)

POLLY, Roger, accused of intermarrying a slave of Richard Boughton. 1671. (Arch. of Md.: LXV.19)

POORE, Peter, age 21 yrs. Servant of William Smith, 14 Nov 1682. (Ct.&Land: K#1.25)
POOR(E), Walter (planter). Admr.: Margaret Poore (widow). (Inv.: 1.616; 2 Sept 1702; 2 Sept 1702) Admr.: Margarett Poor (relict). (Acct: 3.29; ----; 20 June 1703) Admr.: Margrett Poore (relict). (Acct: 24.254; ----; 21 June 1703)

POPE, Francis. To eldest sons Thomas and Francis, exs., 400 acres called *Bryan's Clift*, and 350 acres called *Batten's Clift*. To two youngest sons Richard and John, 400 acres called *Roome*, at 21 yrs. of age. (Will: 1.470; 1 Oct 1671; 27 Jan 1671)
POPE, Thomas. Payments include William Hinsey guardian for Richard Smith's orphan, Thomas Harris guardian of John Pope (son of Francis Pope), Thomas Clipsham (administrator of Charles Grigory), John Borland (overseer upon Smith's plantation — Thomas Pope was Smith's guardian). Admr.: Mary Pope. (Acct: 5.203; ----; 11 July 1678)
POPE, John. To Joseph Cornell, 350 acres, *Batton's Clifts*. To kinswoman Eliza: Burford, 200 acres, *Brian's Clifts*. Mentions Thomas Burford, brother of sd. Eliza:. To Bereshebay and Mary Harris, 400 acres, *Rome*. To Mary Peter, Edward Baxter, Chris. Shadwell, personalty. Ex.: Jos. Carvill. (Will: 4.64; 5 Sept 1684; 18 Oct 1684) (Inv.: 8.290; 18 Oct 1684; ----) Legatees: Edward Boteler, Mary Pratt, Christopher Shottwell. Ex.: Joseph Cornell. (Acct: 9.131; ----; 10 Aug 1686)

PORTINGALL, Hugh. (Inv.: 32C.170; 24 Aug 1711; ----) Admr.: Margaret Youp, wife of Roger Youp. (Acct: 33A.41; ----; 12 Nov 1711)

POSEY, Anne (spinster), dau. of Francis Posey, to marry John Mould (carpenter), 12 April 1669. (Ct.&Land: H#1.248)
POSEY, John and Susanna of head of Wicomico River. Their children: Humphrey, born 1 Feb 1683; John, born 30 July 1685. (Ct.&Land: P#1.211; QRev.9, 11)
POSEY, Susanna, relict of John Posey. Indenture 4 July 1689, from George Thompson of St. Mary's Co.; parcel called *Johnson's Choise*, cont. 250 acres in *Zachia Manor*. (Ct.&Land: P#1.199)

POSEY, John. Petition regarding two tracts left by will of John Posey to his wife Susanna during her widowhood, then to his two sons; Susanna now the wife of Thomas Austin. Court held 2 March 1690. (Ct.&Land: Q#1.22)

POSEY, John. Dated 13 Jan 1690, regarding administration of estate of John Posey by widow Susanna Posey, now Susanna Austin; distribution to Susanna Philpott, wife of Edward Philpott, Elizabeth Posey, Mary Posey, Jane Posey, Humphrey Posey and John Posey, children of the deceased. (Ct.&Land: Q#1.25-26)

POSEY, Benjamin and Mary. Their children: Susanna, born 1 June 1691; Mary, born 10 Sept 1693. (Ct.&Land: P#1.212; QRev.17, 22)

POSEY, John and Lydia his wife, on 28 April 1711, conveyed all rights in *Southvielle*, cont. 20 acres and on 9 Nov 1736 part of a tract called *Ordington Hall*, and on 26 May 1740 a tract called *Horn Fair*, lying in Nanjemy, cont. 150 acres and a tract called *Poseys Chance* in Nanjemy Parish, cont. 100 acres. (Ct.&Land: C#2.253; Land: O#2.173, 343, 345.)

POSEY, Mary (widow). Deed of gift, 17 Feb 1717, to her sons Benjamin Posey, Francis Posey, Belayne Posey. (Ct.&Land: H#2.126)

POSEY, Humphry. William Wilson, James Allen. (Inv.: 1.64; [c1717/8]; ----)

POSEY, Humphrey. Deed of gift, 16 Aug 1717, to his son Benjamin Posey. (Ct.&Land: H#2.126)

POSEY (POSSEY), John. In his will he left to mother, Mary Posey, extx., tract of land, *Shrimp's Neck*, and dwelling plantation. At her decease to pass to brother Francis. To bro. Benjamin, 100 acres, *Burlains Hill*, which is the plantation now called *Holt's Divising*. To bro. Francis, *St. John's* and personalty. To bro. Bolaine, *Noddall's Brand*. To sister Mary, personalty. (Will: 14.270; 21 March 1716; 28 April 1717) (Inv.: 37B.86; 20 June 1716; ----) Payments to: Mary Posey Jr. (sister of deceased). Extx.: Mary Posey. (Acct: 39C.95; ----; 17 Feb 1717)

POSEY, John, age 34. Deposition, 5 Nov 1719, regarding part of tract called *Christian Temple Manor*. (Chas LandComm: M2.66)

POSEY, John, age 37. Deposition, 31 May 1721, regarding tract called *Christian Temple Manor*. (Chas LandComm: M2.122)

POSEY, Mary. In her will she left to bros. Francis, ex., Benjamin and Belaine, godson John Coe, Beane Griggs, god-daus. Elizabeth Coale and Mary Penn, mother Mary Miller, Mary Caretts, two sisters (unnamed), Jemina Coale, Susannah Phillpott and Elizabeth Musgrave, personalty (some of which described as in Virginia at Richard Rollins's). (Will: 18.342; 5 Feb 1725; 23 Feb 1724/5) Next of kin: Benjamin Possey, Bolean Possey. (Inv.: 10.336; ----; [c1724/5])

POSEY, Francis (carpenter) and Anne his wife. Deed dated 24 March 1729/30. To James Lattimar (Lattimore), part of the tract called *Gores Addition*. (Land: M#2.227)

POSEY, Belane (carpenter), late of Charles Co., but now of Prince William Co., Virginia, and his wife Mary, one of the daus. of John Wilkenson, dec'd. Deed dated 19 Feb 1733/4, to Samuel Hanson Sr. Said John

Wilkinson had by two warrants laid out; one tract called *Wilkinson's Throne*, cont. 556 acres; sd. Wilkinson died intestate and left issue, two daus., afsd. Mary and Eleanor Wilkinson. (Land: O#2.24) See also Land: O#2.9, 26, 27.)

POSEY, Richard. Next of kin: John Posey, John Posey Jr. Admr.: Ann Posey. (Inv.: 18.481; ----; 7 Aug 1734)

POSEY, Benjamin, of Prince William Co., Virginia (planter), son of Humphrey Posey, late of Charles Co., and Benjamin's wife Ann, on 13 Aug 1735 conveyed a tract called *Willford*, lying at Nanjemy, cont. 100 acres. (Land: O#2.117)

POSTON, John Sr. (planter). 12 Nov 1740. To Philip Key (Gent.) of St. Mary's Co., in partial payment of debt owed by John Poston Sr. and his son John Poston Jr., the tract where John Poston Sr. lives, being 1/2 of tract called *Goodwill*, cont. 50 acres. (Land: O#2.490)

POSTON (POSTAN), John. Next of kin: Frances Postan, Thom Postan. Ex.: William Postan (surviving executor). (Inv.: 29.177; ----; 12 June 1744)

POSTEN, John and his wife Priscilla. Deed to Priscilla Briscoe. On 12 March 1745 Priscilla Posten released her dower. (Land: Z#2.18)

POSTON, Jeremiah, son of William and Priscilla Poston, born 26 Aug 1745. (Trinity: 120—rev.)

POTTER, William, age ca. 28 yrs. Swore in court 14 Nov 1665. (Ct.&Land: B#1.493)

POTTER, George, son of Robert Potter. Gift dated 19 July 1690, from Charles Barrow; cattle. (Ct.&Land: P#1.202)

POTTER, John. Admr.: Simon Smith. (Inv.: 17.480; ----; 28 Sept 1733)

POTTS, John. Servant of Capt. Bowling, age judged to be 24 yrs. old, 8 June 1686. (Ct.&Land: M#1.220)

POTTS, Robert. (Inv.: 10.86; 23 Feb 1687; ----) Extx.: Jone Lindsey, (relict), wife of Thomas Lindsey. (Acct: 10.160; ----; 1 Oct 1688)

POUNCY, George. Deed of gifts 6 April 1687, to children of his wife, Mary Pouncy, to be received immediately after her death, to: Mathew Boswell, John Boswell, Mary Boswell, Martha Boswell, Michell Boswell, William Boswell. (Ct.&Land: N#1.137, 206)

POUNSEY, Mary. Gift dated 12 Feb 1690/1, to her children: Michael Boswell, William Boswell and Martha Boswell; cattle. (Ct.&Land: P#1.203)

POWCHER, Thomas, age 20 yrs. Servant of John Court, 9 Feb 1685/6. (Ct.&Land: M#1.89)

POWELL (POWLL), Robert, age 16 yrs. Servant of Mr. Adams, 8 March 1669/70. (Ct.&Land: D#1.127)

POWELL, Edward and his wife Elizabeth, servants of John Davis in 1677. (Arch. of Md.: LXIX.90)

POWELL, David. Mentions: A note from Mr. Henry Rocher to Mr. John Busey (dead) to deceased. (Inv.: 4.558; 28 Nov 1677; ----) Ex.: Thomas Alcocke. (Acct: 6.651; ----; 18 Feb 1679)

POWELL, James. One of the appraisers was John Powell. (Inv.: 10.250; 1689; ----)

POWELL, Robert, son of Robert and ——— of Pickawaxen, born 17 Nov and bapt. 10 Jan 1692. (Ct.&Land: P#1.211; QRev.18)

PRATHER, Thomas (Gent.), of Prince George's Co., and his wife Elizabeth, on 4 April 1744 conveyed Lot #58 in Charles Town. (Land: X#2.102)

PRICE, John, age ca. 20 yrs. Swore in court 4 March 1661. (Ct.&Land: A#1.191)

PRICE, William and Hanna Price, his wife, relict of Hugh Lee, dec'd. William Hollingsworth demands warrant against the afsd. William and Hanna. Court documented 8 Nov 1664. (Ct.&Land: B#1.396)

PRICE, Edward of Charles County, married by June 1673, the relict of John Thompkinson. (Arch of Md: 60.495)

PRICE, Edward. His will he left to Eliza: Williams, personalty. Wife Jane, extx. received 500 acres, *Locust Thicket*. (Will: 2.68; 26 Jan 1676; 15 March 1679; Inv.: 7A.58; 5 Feb 1679; ---)

PRICE, John (of Charles). (Inv.: 7C.192; 10 June 1682; ----) Payments include George Bright for nursing deceased's son (unnamed). Admr.: Richard Garforth. (Acct: 8.85; ----; 1 Aug 1683)

PRICE (PRISE), Mary, dau. of Robert and Anne Prise of Portobacco, born 12 Nov 1692. (Ct.&Land: P#1.211; QRev.18)

PRISE, Jane, widow. Indenture, 12 Feb 1695, to Henry Hawkins, Gent., and Elizabeth his wife, to care for her throughout her lifetime, parcel called *Locust Thickett*, on branch of Piscataway, 500 acres, patented by Edward Prise (planter), on 26 Jan 1676, and left by his will to his wife Jane Prise; mentions children, Ruth Hawkins and Henry Holland Hawkins. (Ct.&Land: Q#1.80)

PRICE, Thomas. (Inv.: 24.101; 10 Sept 1703; ----) Admr.: Elisabeth Price. (Acct: 25.147; ----; 1 March 1704)

PRICE, Robert and his wife Juliana, To Samuel Peele of London Town in Anne Arundel Co. (merchant). Lease for 2000 years, 20 June 1712 of several tracts in Charles Co.: *St. Ignatius*, 100 acres; *Haggesters Addition*, 50 acres; *Spring Plain*, 50 acres; and *St. Patrick Hill*, 300 acres. (Land: O#2.168)

PRICE, Robert (planter). In his will he left to dau. Eliza: and dau. Mary, by 2nd and last marriage, all land. Wife Julianah, extx. Daus. to remain with their mother during minority or until marriage. To dau. Mary Shaw,

personalty. (Will: 14.64; 8 Dec 1714; 22 June 1715) (Inv.: 38B.50; 1715; ---
-) Extx.: Juliana Price. (Acct: 38A.133; ----; 11 May 1717)
PRICE, Thomas. Next of kin: none. (Inv.: 37B.84; 5 Feb 1716; 24 April 1717)
Ex.: Charles Jones. (Acct: 37B.83; ----; 24 April 1717)
PRICE, Juliana (widow). Indenture, 23 Dec 1717, to her dau. Eliza: Lucket, wife of Thomas Hussey Lucket, Gent. By will of Robert Price (dec'd.) [See Robert's will: Liber 14, folio 64 proved 22 June 1715], tract *St. Patricks Hill* on w. side of main branch of Potobacco Ck., 200 acres. (Ct.&Land: H#2.140)
PRICE, Juliana (widow). Indenture dated 13 May 1718, to Thomas Hussey Lucket; for love of her dau. [Elizabeth who is married to Lucket], regarding *St. Ignatius, Haggister's Addition*, and *St. Patrick's Hill*. (Ct.&Land: H#2.163) Also Deed of Gift: dated same to her youngest dau. Mary Price; a Negro girl. (Ct.&Land: H#2.167)
PRICE, Juliana (widow). Enters into a bond, 19 May 1718, regarding a gift of 12 year Negro boy, for love of her youngest dau. Mary who is shortly to be married to Andrew Simpson. (Ct.&Land: H#2.173). Also an indenture from Juliana Price dated 28 April 1718, to Robert Hanson; tract of land on the w. side of the main fresh of Portobacco Creek called *St. Patrick's Hill*; part of the tract lying between *Lampton* and *St. Patrick's Hill* lately resurveyed for Juliana Price, cont. 136 acres. (Ct.&Land: H#2.173-4)
PRICE, Edward, age 55. Deposition, 12 xber 1719, regarding tract called *Salisbury*. (Chas LandComm: M2.75)
PRICE, John, age 36. Deposition, 12 xber 1719, regarding tract called *Salisbury*. (Chas LandComm: M2.77)
PRICE, Thomas. Next of kin: Mary Wright, Sarah Meeks. Admr.: Richard Price. (Inv.: 17.344; 18 May 1732; 13 Aug 1733)

PRINCE, Abigall, age 23 yrs. Servant of Thomas Dent, 11 Jan 1669/70. (Ct.&Land: D#1.117)

PROBERT (PROBARTT), John. (Inv.: 8.493; 26 April 1686; ----) Admr.: Maj. John Wheeler. (Inv.: 9.418; 25 July 1687; ----. Acct: 9.418; ----; 13 Sept 1687)

PROCTER (PROCTOR), Eliza. To son Charles Proctor, goods and chattels, signed 4 June 1727. (Land: L#2.367)
PROCTOR, Elizabeth. To son Charles, ex., entire estate. (Will: 23.445; 3 Feb 1740; 15 March 1743)

PRODDY (PRODY), Nicholas (nunc.). To mother, two brothers and two sisters (all unnamed) in England; Thomas Dickenson, Thomas Deaverel, Dr. John Wine, Edward Mines, personalty. To Peter Dent, *Barnaby*, 1/2 land at Piscataway. John Addison, ex. (Will: 5.201; 2 Feb 1676; 2 April 1676) (Inv.: 6.239; 13 Aug 1679; ----)

PRODDY, Thomas and his wife Jane. Thomas, late of *Barnabye*, now of *Gisbrough*, County of York, Kingdom of England, bro. and heir of Nicholas Proddy, late of Nanjemy, (dec'd). To Thomas Hobb of St. George's in St. Mary's Co., dated 13 Aug 1688; two tracts, *Barnabye* of 545 acres and *Batchelor's Horne*, 280 acres. (Ct.&Land: R#1.32)

PROSER, Anne, age 25 yrs. Servant of Robert Price, Nov 1710. (Ct.&Land: D#2.7)

PROWSE, Robertt. (Inv.: 1.324; 22 Jan 1674; ----) Mentions: amount due the executor in Virginia. Admr.: Benjamin Rozer. (Acct: 4.288; ----; 4 Oct 1677)

PRYOR, William (planter) and his wife Marie, dau. of Nicholas and Elizabeth Emerson, dec'd. Quit claim dated 8 Nov 1685, to Henry Hawkins and Elizabeth his wife, relict of Francis Wine; parcel *Glovers Point* on Nanjemy Creek, formerly sold by Eliza: Emerson to Francis Wine 16 June 1671. (Ct.&Land: M#1.212)

PURNIE, John. Servant of Mary Chandler, age judged to be 18 yrs. (Ct.&Land: M#1.67)

PYE, Edward, St. Mary's Co., and his wife Ann, admx. of Benjamin Rozer of Charles Co. who died intestate. 1682. (*Arch. of Md.*: LXX.276)

PYE, Edward, Col. (Inv.: 15.44; 8 Jan 1696; ----) (Inv.: 15.44; 6 Sept 1696; ----) Mentions: Notley Rozier. (Inv.: 15.131; 15 March 1696; 10 June 1697) (Inv.: 15.240; 28 Sept 1697; ----) Admr.: Notley Rosier (gentleman). (Acct: 18.128; ----; [c1698]) Payments to: Notley Rosier his share of his father's (unnamed) estate. Admr.: Notley Rosier. (Acct: 19.163; ----; 17 July 1699)

PYE, Edward, Esq. (Inv.: 18.195; 28 June 1698; ----)

PYE, Charles of the Mynde, County of Hereford, and his bro., Walter Pye of same, are bound to James Gunter of City of Hereford (Gent.) for £500, in exchange for the estate of late Sr. Walter Pye. Bond recorded 24 Feb 1723. (Land: L#2.116)

PYE, Walter (Gent.), and his wife Margret. Deed dated 9 March 1736/7; to Ralph Falkner of Prince William Co., Virginia, tract in Portobacco Parish called *Beeches Neck*, 480 acres, patent granted to Walter Pye 17 Sept 1715; and on 22 March 1738/9 to James Scot (Gent.), Lot #94 in Charles Town. (Land: O#2.191, 394)

RACHFORD (See ROCHFORD).

RAINES, John and Elizabeth of Mattawoman. Their children: Elizabeth, born 26 June 1684; Henry, born 3 Sept 1686; Lucy, born 7 Dec 1688. (Ct.&Land: P#1.209; QRev.10, 12, 14)

RAINES, Lucy and Elizabeth, daus. of John Raines. Cattle mark recorded 4 July 1689. (Ct.&Land: P#1.200)

RAYNES, John. Admr.: Henry Tanner. (Acct: 31.111; ----; 1 April 1710)

RALE (See REALY, REALEY).

RAMSEY, John. Next of kin: Jonathon Willson, John Willson. Admr.: Anne Ramsey. (Inv.: 23.516; 30 Nov 1738; 7 Feb 1738)

RAMSEY, Ann, extx. of John Ramsey. Signed 12 March 1741/2. The following persons of Charles Co. and Calvert Co. acknowledge being satisfied with a child's part from any demands from sd. Ann Ramsey: John Dainty, Neffelt Leach, Abraham Wilson, James Thomas, James Nutwell, James Leach, Richard Estep, Susannah Ramsey. (Land: Z#2.37)

RANDALL, Richard. To John Pinke of Boston, New England, Antony Bridges and Thomas Cooper, personalty. To Protestant Church, 200 acres called *The Addition*. To father Richard Randall, and Ann Randall, residue of estate. Exs.: Stephen Montague and Jos. Harrison. (Will: 1.290; 3 Aug 1667; ----)

RANDALL, Richard, died 7 Sept 1667. (Ct.&Land: C#1.253; P#1.204; QRev.3)

RANFORD, William, age 13 yrs. Servant of John Clarke, 10 June 1673. (Ct.&Land: E#1.132)

RASPIN, Samuell. Mentions: estate of Henry Pratt (admr. of Samuell Raspin), estate of John Dudick (admr. of Samuell Raspin). (Inv.: 7A.197; 13 Aug 1680; ----) (Inv.: 8.75; 29 March 1681; ----) Admr.: Thomas Marshall. (Acct: 8.245; ----; 13 March 1684)

RATCLIFE (RATELIFE), Richard, son of John and Bat(h)sheba Ratelife of Wicomico, born 16 Dec 1692. (Ct.&Land: P#1.211; QRev.19)

RATLIFFE, Richard. Next of kin: Thomas Nickolls, Benony Nickouls. Admr./Ex.: Ann Ratliffe. (Inv.: 16.608; 23 Aug 1732; 23 Sept 1732)

RATLIFF, Mullenex (Mullinex, Mullence) (planter). Mentions dau. Uilindor; sons Joseph and John, to be of age at 16 yrs.; sons Charles and Josuway. Residue of estate, after wife's thirds are deducted, to be divided between three youngest children, Joseph, John and dau. Mary. Ex.: Son Joseph. (Will: 21.62; 18 March 1722/3; 15 May 1734) Next of kin: Joshua Ratlif, John Ratlif. Ex.: Joseph Ratcliff. (Inv.: 18.497; 24 May 1734; 13 Aug 1734)

RATLIFF (RATLIEFF), Joshua. To eldest son John, dwelling plantation. Mentions son Joseph; son James; son Joshua. To son Joseph, personalty had of Charles Mountoe. To dau. Mary, personalty. Residue of estate to be divided bet. wife Mary and children. Exs.: Wife and son John. (Will: 21.842; 19 July 1737; 4 Jan 1737) Creditors: Daniell Chambers, John

Hobson. Next of kin: Joseph Ratlieff, John Ratlieff. Extx.: Mary Ratlieff. (Inv.: 23.26; 9 Feb 1737; 15 Feb 1737)

RATLIFF, Joseph, signs agreement with John Ratliff to warrant that he will abide by the division made to a tract called *St. Edwards*, given to him and John by their father, Mulinex Ratliff. Recorded 30 Nov 1742. (Land: O#2.589)

RAWLINGS, Mary, sister of Daniel Rawlings of Patuxent, died 24th of 8th month 1699; Ann, wife of Daniel Rawlings, died 18th of 4th month 1713. (Clifts Monthly Meeting, Quaker Records of So. MD, p. 56)

RAWLINGS, Daniel, too old to represent Patuxent Meeting. 24th of 2nd month, 1722. (Quaker Records of So. MD, p. 76)

RAWFIELD, John, age 15 yrs. Servant of Anne Lynes, Nov 1710. (Ct.&Land: D#2.8)

RAWSON, Susan. Judged to be 17 yrs. old, presented by Daniell Johnson, 14 March 1664. (Ct.&Land: B#1.436)

RAY, Edward, age 14 yrs. Servant of James Bowling, 13 March 1676. (Ct.&Land: G#1.16)

RAYNES. (See RAINES.)

REA, John, age 5 yrs. (bound to age 21). Servant of Robert Rowland, 8 March 1669/70. (Ct.&Land: D#1.127)

REA, James and his wife Mary. Late of Charles Co., but now of Stafford Co., Virginia, on 11 May 1722 conveyed pt. of *St. Barbaries Manor*. (Land: L#2.19)

READ. (See REED.)

REAGON, John. Next of kin: James Ross, Peter Fernandie. Admr./Ex.: Elisabeth Reagon. (Inv.: 13.476; 11 Dec 1728; 26 Feb 1728)

REALY (REALEY, RALE), Michael (Mical). (Inv.: 27.2; 13 May 1707; ----) Admr.: Barbury Realey. (Acct: 28.100; ----; 14 Feb 1707) Admr.: Barbery Spearing, wife of John Spearing. (Acct: 29.396; ----; 31 May 1709)

REALY (PEALEY), Philip. Admr.: Elisabeth Realey. (Acct: 35A.381; ----; 26 April 1714) Distribution to: wife (unnamed). Admr.: Elisabeth Holiwood (relict), now wife of James Holiwood. (Acct: 37A.18; ----; 30 Jan 1715)

REAS, John. Admr.: Stephen Yoakley. (Acct: 36B.178; ----; 23 July 1715) Mentions Capt. John Reas, mariner of the City of London. Admr.: Capt. Stephen Yoakley. (Acct: 38A.72; ----; 30 April 1717)

REDFERNE, Mary, dau. of James and Faith Redferne of Portobacco, born 16 Dec 1694. (Ct.&Land: QRev.25)

REED, Thomas, age 18 yrs. Presented by Robert Hendley for William Hinshaw, 10 Jan 1664. (Ct.&Land: B#1.397)

REED, John. Next of kin: Margaret Reed, Edward Ganne. (Inv.: 1.414; 22 Feb 1717; ----)

READ, Richard, son of Capt. Richard Read, late of Prince George's Co., transfers part of the tract called *The Mare and Colt*, 106 acres, dated 25 Feb 1734/5. (Land: O#2.83).

REED, Thomas. In his will he mentions wife Elizabeth and child., Sarah Cooksey, Susanna Duley, Mary Cooksey and Elizabeth Duley (eld. dau. and wife of James Duley). (Will: 24.384; 18 Dec 1741; 2 April 1746)

REEDING, Isabell, age 19 yrs. Maid servant of Thomas Hussey, 10 Nov 1674. (Ct.&Land: F#1.13)

REEDING, Isable, had a bastard child. Servant of Thomas Hussy, 9 Nov 1680. (Ct.&Land: L#1.37)

REEDER, John, son of Benjamin Reeder. 5 Oct 1741. See Williams, William. (Land: O#2.528).

REEVES, William (planter) and Anne his wife on 18 Feb 1692 conveyed half part of tract of 200 acres called *Harguesse's Hope*. (Ct.&Land: S#1.109)

REAVES, Samuel. Next of kin: William Reeves, Edward Reeves. Admr.: Thomas Reeves. (Inv.: 29.172; 19 March 1743; 2 ---- 1744)

REGON, James (bricklayer) and Joan, of Nanjemy. Their children: Mary, born 28 Aug 1683; John, born 24 March 1685; Matthew, born 24 April 1687; William, born 31 Jan 1690; Charles, born 20 May 1692; Margarett, born 12 Feb 1694. (Ct.&Land: QRev.9, 11, 13, 16, 20, 23)

REGON, James. Admr.: Joan Regon, wife of John Wood. (Acct: 16.247; ----; 1 April 1698)

REILY, Phillip. (Inv.: 34.195; 26 April 1713; ----)

RENISSON, John. Judged to be 19 yrs. old, presented by Daniell Johnson for William Robisson, 10 Jan 1664. (Ct.&Land: B#1.398)

RENNICKE, Anne, age 16 yrs. Servant of Mrs. Elinor Beane, 10 Nov 1674. (Ct.&Land: F#1.13)

RENNICK, Anne. Presented in March court—had a bastard child, guilty and given 20 lashes, 14 June 1681. (Ct.&Land: I#1.124)

RENOLD (REINOLD), James. Admr.: Capt. Joseph Douglas. (Inv.: 18.148; 1 Feb 1733; 10 June 1734)

REUSE (See ROUSE.)

RICHARDSON, Joseph, age 21 yrs. Servant of John Clark, 12 Jan 1674. (Ct.&Land: F#1.41)

RICHARDSON, Bernard, age 17 yrs. Servant of Col. John Duglas, 13 March 1676. (Ct.&Land: G#1.16)

RICHARDSON, Nicholas. (Inv.: 4.407; 10 Oct 1677; ----) (Acct: 4.408; ----; 11 Oct 1677) Admr.: William Rozwell (gentleman).

RICHARDSON, Thomas, age 13 yrs. Servant of Henry Adams, 1680. (Ct.&Land H.242)

RICHISON, Joseph, son of William Richison. Cattle mark recorded 25 March 1706. (Ct.&Land: Z#1.209)

RICHARDSON, William. (Inv.: 34.52; 22 July 1713; ----)

RICHARDSON, John, son of John Richardson, county of York, age 25. Indenture, 3 March 1714, to John Larkin of the county of Lancaster, mariner, service for five years from arrival in Virginia. (Ct.&Land: H#2.10)

RIGG, Mary, dau. of Thomas Rigg. Cattle mark registered 14 June 1686. (Ct.&Land: M#1.100)

RIGGE, Thomas. (Inv.: 10.208; 5 Sept 1688; ----) Admr.: John Gardner. (Acct: 10.228; ----; 5 April 1689)

RIGG, John. (Inv.: 33A.40; 15 Sept 1711; 26 Sept 1711) Mentions: poor widow (unnamed). Admr.: Susanna Rigg. (Acct: 33A.216; ----; [c.1712])

RIGG, Thomas, son of Susanah Lom... [ink blot] (widow). Cattle mark recorded 23 May 1729. (Land: M#2.161)

RIGG (RIGGE), Peter (planter), and his wife Violetta. 21 June 1744. To Richard Tubman (Gent.) of Prince George's Co., his right to the tract called *Nonsuch*, on s. side of Mattawoman, cont. 87 acres. (Land: X#2.151)

RIGHT. (See WRIGHT.)

RILEY (RELEY), Thomas. Lease dated 23 July 1733, from Peter Attwood, to Thomas Reley of 140 acres, lying in St. Thomas' Mannor, during the lives of Thomas Reley, Mary his wife, and William Carriel, her son. (Land: M#2.351)

RING, Ralph, age 22 yrs. Servant of Samuel Cressey, 10 March 1670/1. (Ct.&Land: E#1.35)

ROBARTS. (See ROBERTS.)

ROBERTS (ROBARTS), Edward. To Thomas Allanson, ex., entire estate, for his children, Charles and Eliza:, including property in Eng., belonging to testator by death of uncle, John Reade, son of grandfather, George Reade. (Will: 5.321; 15 Jan 1676; 22 Nov 1677) (Inv.: 4.556; 29 Nov 1677; ----) Admr./Ex.: Thomas Alleson (also Thomas Allanson). (Acct: 6.649; ----; 17 Feb 1679)

ROBERTS, Anne, age ---. Servant of James Neale, 1680. (Ct.&Land: H#1.308)

ROBERTS, Anne, had bastard child, servant of James Neale, 1680. In later court proceedings, found guilty and given 21 lashes on bare back, 10 Jan 1681. (Ct.&Land: I#1.231)

ROBERTS, Richard, age 22 yrs. Servant of William Boareman, 13 June 1682. (Ct.&Land: I#1.293)

ROBERTSON, Marie, age 17 yrs. (to serve for six yrs.). Servant of John Coates, 10 March 1667/8. (Ct.&Land: C#1.255)

ROBERTSON, Jane. Indicted for having a bastard child, living at John Marloes, 13 March 1710. (Ct.&Land: D#2.136)

ROBERTSON, Francis. (Inv.: 39A.45; 21 April 1718; ----)

ROBERSON (ROBERTSON), Robert. To William Middleton, ex., dwelling plantation. To wife Joan, personal estate. One of the witnesses was Eleanor Middleton (at date of probate des. as Eleanor Taylor of Virginia). (Will: 21.259; 7 July 1733; 2 Oct 1734)

ROBERSON (ROBISON), William. Next of kin: Mary Taylor, Jane Newton. Admr.: Mary Robison. (Inv.: 28.159; ----; 27 July 1743)

ROBEY. (See ROBY.)

ROBINS, Robert, charges his wife Elisabeth with adultery, claiming her child was not begotten by him, 4 June 1658. (Ct.&Land: A#1.4)

ROBINS, Robert and Elisabeth Weekes charged with having a bastard child, 1 Oct 1662. (Ct.&Land: A#1.243)

ROBINS, Henry, age 17 yrs. Servant of Benjamin Rozer, 11 April 1676. (Ct.&Land: F#1.173)

ROBINS, Robert. Deed of gift 8 March 1680/1, to his son John Robins. (Ct.&Land: I#1.123)

ROBINS, William, son of Henry Robins. Cattle mark recorded, 10 Nov 1691. (Ct.&Land: R#1.333)

ROBBINS, Henry of Mattawoman. Cattle marks for his children: Thomas, James and Margarett, recorded on 15 Nov 1704. (Ct.&Land: Z#1.160, 161)

ROBINS, Richard. To dau. Margaret, *Sensey* at marriage. To dau. Elizabeth, dwelling plantation, *Homefare*. To bro. John and godson Benjamin, son of John Banester, personalty. To John Banester, 100 acres adjoining *Sensey* afsd. One of the witnesses was Jno. Robins. (Will: 3.647; 4 Dec 1704; 2 Sept 1705) (Inv.: 3.683; 24 June 1705; ----) Extx.: Lydia Posey (relict), now wife of John Posey. (Acct: 26.45; ----; 30 May 1706)

ROBINS, John. To Diana Harrison, Lawrence Banester, Frances Banester, Francis Lyn, Timothy Banester and Jno. Posey, personalty. Benjamin Banester, residuary legatee, and his father, John, ex. (Will: 12.325; 25 Nov 1708; 15 Dec 1708) Admr.: Morris Fitsgerald. (Inv.: 29.244; 15 Dec 1708; ---;) Ex.: John Banister. (Acct: 30.313; ----; 10 Dec 1709) (Acct: 29.67; ----; 21 Jan 1708)

ROBINS, Thomas, of Prince George's Co., son of Henry Robins on 8 Nov 1715, conveyed a parcel called *The Mudhole*, cont. 173 acres. (Ct.&Land: H#2.3)

ROBISSON, William (carpenter) of Portobacco, and his wife Susan. Deed dated 17 Feb 1658, to tract of land. (Ct.&Land: C#2.157)

ROBINSON, William, age ca. 29 yrs. Swore in court 4 Sept 1660. (Ct.&Land: A#1.100)

ROBINSON, William and his wife Susanna. Mentioned in court records betw. June and Sept 1660. (Ct.&Land: A#1.97, 105)

ROBINSON, John married Elizabeth Browne, 21 March 1666. (Ct.&Land: C#1.253; P#1.204; QRev.2)

ROBINSON, John and his wife Elizabeth. Indenture 11 June 1667; a parcel called *Troope's Rendezvous*, lying on e. side of Avon R., cont. 350 acres. (Ct.&Land: C#1.192)

ROBINSON, Ann, age 23 yrs. Servant of John Clark, 12 Jan 1674. (Ct.&Land: F#1.41)

ROBINSON, Susanna, dau. of Richard Robinson. Cattle mark recorded June 1678. (Ct.&Land: G#1.165)

ROBINSON, Richard and Joyce, of head of Wicomico River. Their children: Susanna, born 20 Oct 1677; Mary, born 17 Dec 1679. (Ct.&Land: P#1.208; QRev.5, 6)

ROBINSON, Samuell, age 21 yrs. Servant of Capt. Humphrey Warren, 11 June 1678. (Ct.&Land: G#1.157)

ROBINSON, Thomas, of Nanjamy. To wife Ann, dower rights. To dau. Ann Price, all land. To Richard Price and his wife, residue of estate. Ex., sd. Richard Price. (Will: 4:211; 19 Nov 1685; 6 Aug 1686)

ROBISON, John. Appraisers: John Banester, William Mire. (Inv.: 29.61; 10 Nov 1708; ----)

ROBINSON, Peter. John Browne, ex. and sole legatee of estate. (Will: 13.641; 8 Sept 1712; 16 Jan 1713) (Inv.: 35A.53; 22 Jan 1713; ----) Ex.: John Browne. (Acct: 36A.25; ----; 27 Dec 1714)

ROBINSON, William. To Anna Maria Parnham and Eliza. Parnham, residue of estate, both here and in England. Ex.: John Parnham. (Will: 20.336; 4 Dec 1731; 18 Dec 1731) Ex.: John Parnham. (Inv.: 17.350; 18 Dec 1731; 18 Sept 1733)

ROBY, John Sr. Next of kin: William Roby, Richard Roby. Admr.: Sarah Roby. (Inv.: 11.346; 23 April 1726; 24 May 1726)

ROBY, Michael Hinds, son of Sarah Roby (widow). Cattle mark recorded 11 Oct 1726. (Land: L#2.317).

ROBY, Benjamin. Next of kin: Thomas Robey, Richard Robey. Admr.: Mary Robey. (Inv.: 29.345; 3 May 1744; 10 July 1744)

ROBY, Peter, son of John Roby. Cattle mark and heifer given to him by Samuel Luckett, 15 Feb 1707. (Ct.&Land: C#2.157)

ROBY, Sarah. Relict of John Roby Sr., dec'd., is discharged from all legacies that may be due from her to us on the estate of John Roby. Signed 29 Aug 1726—John Roby, Edward Darnell, Thomas Roby, John Wornell, William Roby, Richard Roby, Michael Hinds Roby, John Henly, Joseph Gardiner, George Gibbens, Ralph Roby, Daniel Howard. Deed of gift, 30 Nov 1734, to her son Peter Roby. 22 Dec 1738, from her children, John Roby Sr., Richard Roby, Elizabeth Henley, John Warnall, Ralph Roby, Thomas Roby, Samuel Roby, William Roby, George Gibbens, Michael Winds, part of the goods and chattels left to them by the death of their bro., Peter Roby. (Land: L#2.313; O#2.76, 466)

ROBY, Peter. Next of kin: John Roby Sr., Benjamin Roby. Admr.: Michael Hinds Roby. (Inv.: 23.25; 30 Jan 1737; 15 Feb 1737)

ROBEY, Sarah. Deed of gift signed 18 Aug 1739. To William Robey, son of Benjamin Robey (planter), furniture. To Victoria Robey, dau. of Benjamin Robey, pot and pot hooks. (Land: O#2.410)

ROCH, William, son of Charles Roch. Cattle mark recorded 28 Nov 1718, for mare given him by his godmother Mary Shaw. (Ct.&Land: H#2.213)

ROCHFORD, Michaell. Left his brother John Cole, ex., 100 acres of the tract called *Phames (Thames?) Street*, and 100 acres of *Tower Dock*. (Will: 3.739; 11 Feb 1705; 28 Feb 1705/6)

ROCHFORD (RACHFORD), Michaell. Extx.: Margret Cole, wife of William Cole. (Acct: 7A.144; ----; 20 July 1680) (Inv.: 25.346; 18 March 1705; 26 March 1706) Ex.: John Cole. (Acct: 28.261; ----; 15 July 1708)

ROCK, Charles. (Inv.: 3.332; 11 May 1720; ----)

ROCK, John. Next of kin: Henry Rock, Charles Rock. Admr.: James Rock. (Inv.: 16,561; 20 May 1732; 31 July 1732)

ROCKWOOD (See ROOKWOOD).

ROELANTS (ROOLANTS), Dinah, dau. of Roger and Margery Roolants of Wicomico, born 2 May 1677. (Ct.&Land: P#1.210; QRev.5)

ROWLANTS, Robert. Admr.: Margery Warren (relict), wife of Humphry Warren (married immediately after deceased's death). (Acct: 7A.166; ----; 27 July 1680)

ROGERS, Mary, age 20 yrs. Servant of Philip Lines, 14 March 1681. (Ct.&Land: I#1.258)

ROGERS, John (gentleman). To wife Eliza:, extx., dwell. plantation. Mentions son Richard [minor]; son John [minor], testator's interest in right of his mother, deceased, to part of estate of Charity Courts, in hands of his uncle, John Courts and interest in tract in Pr. Geo. Co., called *Clean Drinking*; to son Roadham, land testator had with his mother. To Revd. Wm: Maconchie, for the church, personalty. To Alex: Contee, John Courts, Robert and Sam: Hanson, neighbor Mary Theobalds and to Johanna Price, personalty. Mentions three children and unborn child. Shd. she marry, Alex: Contee to have care of Rich: and John. (Will: 14.521; 4 Nov 1717; 13 Jan 1717) Next of kin: Robert Hanson, A. Contee. (Inv.: 1.279; 22 May 1718; 18 Sept 1718)

ROGERS, William, city of Annapolis, and his wife Mary. On 26 Oct 1723 conveyed part of a tract called *Strife*, cont. 135 acres; on 4 April 1724, lot #20, on e. side of the main fresh or head of Portobacco Ck. On 28 Oct 1724, three tracts at Chinqomuxon [Chicomuxen] Ck.: one called *Morecrofts Friendship*, cont. 200 acres; another called *The Gift*, cont. 300 acres; and one called *Speakes Inclosure*, cont. 283 acres. (Land: L#2.156, 204, 398)

ROGERS, Richard, of St. Mary's Co., son of John Rogers, dec'd., on 30 April 1730 conveyed two lots in Chandler Town. (Land: M#2.206)

ROGERS, John. Next of kin: Rod. Rogers. Admr.: Charles Courts. (Inv.: 22.342; 19 July 1734; 18 July 1737)

ROGERS, Richard, of Stafford Co., Virginia, and his wife Mary, on 16 May 1743 conveyed 200 acres. John Rogers, of Charles Co., by his will, gave a tract on Portobacco Creek cont. 200 acres to his son Rhodam Rogers and in case of his death, to his son Richard, and in case of his death then to his son John Rogers. Said John Rogers is dead and afsd. Rhodam Rogers is long absent and not heard from. (Land: X#2.14)

ROOKERD (ROOKED), Edward (planter) and Mary his wife conveyed on 8 June 1680, a parcel of land lying northward of Goose Bay, cont. 150 acres; also parcel called —— *Addition*, cont. 50 acres. (Ct.&Land: H#1.302)

ROOKEWOOD (ROOKWOOD), Edward, son of Edward and Mary Rookewood of Pickawaxen, born 25 Dec 1692. (Ct.&Land: P#1.211; QRev.19)

ROOKWOOD, Edward. In his will he mentions dau. Mary Sanders and children of his wife Mary (unnamed); and son Thomas. (Will: 14.519; 13 Feb 1717; ----)

ROOKWOOD (ROCKWOOD), Thomas. To dau. Mary, *Allensons Folly*, 1/3 thereof excepted during life of her mother; *Preston* adj.; and personalty at age of 16 yrs. To dau. Anne, *St. Davids, Found Hills, Hard Frost*. To wife Heneretta, extx. 1/3 interest in *Allenson's Folly*. To god-dau. Winniford Speake, personalty formerly belonging to Charles Talfer. (Will: 18.442; 21 Nov 1725; 1 Feb 1725) Mentions: Sarah Nelson,

Richard Wade, Elisabeth Parandier, Stephen Brown. Extx.: Henrietta Rockwood. (Inv.: 11.344; 21 May 1726; 24 May 1726)

ROSE, John, age 15 yrs. Servant of Mr. Adams, 8 March 1669/70. (Ct.&Land: D#1.127)

ROSEE, James. Admr.: Edmund Devene. (Inv.: 23.25; 4 April 1737; 27 Jan 1737)

ROZER, Benjamin and Mary, of Portobacco. Their children: Notley, born 1 July 1673; Mary, born 6 April 1675. (Ct.&Land: E#1.140; P#1.205, 206; QRev.4, 5)

ROSIER (ROZIER, ROZER), Benjamin, Col. (gentleman). Mentions: partnership with Marke Lampton. (Inv.: 7C.98; 25 May 1681; ----) Distribution to: Madam Ann Rosier, Notley Rosier (son). Admr.: Notley Rosier (administrator of Col. Edward Pye (administrator of deceased)). (Acct: 19.164; ----; 17 July 1699)

ROZER, Notley. Orphan son of Col. Benjamin Rozer, 14 June 1692. (Ct.&Land: Q#1.54)

ROZER, Anne, relict of Benjamin Rozer. Court dated 9 Aug 1692 refers to her marriage to Edward Pye. (Ct.&Land: Q#1.57)

ROZER, Notley and Jane his wife. Acknowledge indenture, 10 May 1703, to James Semms. Indenture, 1 March 1703, to Col. Henry Darnall; land called *Rozer's Refuge* of 1000 acres on Portobacco Creek in Zachia Manor. (Ct.&Land: Z#1.61, 141)

ROZER, Notley. Deed, 20 Nov 1711, to William Hunter, land which by the death of Benjamin Rozer became the right of his eldest son Notley Rozer. Parcel called *Splittfield*, cont. 30 acres. Also part of a parcel called *Piercefield* on the e. side of Portobacco Creek, cont. 20 acres; also parcel called *Hazard*, above Portobacco Creek, cont. 100 acres. (Ct.&Land: C#2.265)

ROUGHT, Anne, dau. of William and Sarah Rought. Gift dated 19 July 1690; bay mare. (Ct.&Land: P#1.202)

ROUZE, John, servant to John Cage, died 25 Jan 1666. (Ct.&Land: C#1.252; P#1.204; QRev.2)

ROUZE, Anne, age 19 yrs. Servant of William Smith, 11 March 1678. (Ct.&Land: H#1.130)

ROUSE, William (planter). To son John, part of land on n. side of road. To son-in-law John Gallwith, personalty. Wife Ann extx. (Will: 18.445; 28 Nov 1725; 24 Feb 1725) Next of kin: John Rouse, John Gallaway. Extx.: Ann Williams, wife of Thomas Williams. (Inv.: 11.348; 24 May 1726; 9 June 1726)

REUSE (ROUSE), John (planter). Lease, 7 July 1739, to John Reuse, of part of *His Lordships Manor* of Calverton, 210 acres called the *Mountains*, for the natural lives of sd. John Reuse, Bethia Reuse and Tabitha Reuse, his two daus. (Land: O#2.432).

ROWLAND, Ribert. Servants mentioned: William Harbot, John Wray (boy). (Inv.: 6.665; 12 May 1679; ----)

ROWLANTS. (See ROELANTS.)

ROWLES, Elizabeth, dau. of Eleanor Lees. Ordered to be delivered to her mother by James Smallwood, who paid the security. (Ct.&Land: M#1.221)

ROZER, ROZIER (See ROSIER).

RUE, Elizabeth. Bounds her dau. Temperance Rue (to the full age of 16, she being nine yrs. old 14th Oct next), to James Finley, 8 March 1691. (Ct.&Land: R#1.372)

RUMNEY, Edward, of Anne Arundel Co., and his wife Elizabeth. Deed dated 3 Nov 1736. To Edward Brawner of Charles Co., parcel called *Hazard*, cont. 83 acres. (Land: O#2.178)

RUSSELL, Christopher, age ca. 45 yrs. Swore in court 26 Jan 1658. (Ct.&Land: A#1.35)

RUSSELL, John. (Inv.: 26.87; 25 Sept 1706; ----) Admr./Ex.: Richard Coe. (Acct: 27.138; ----; 1 Sept 1707)

RUSSELL, Brutus, bound for England, married the widow and admx. of Richard Southerland. Court held ca. 1711; Brutus made over his estate belonging to his predecessor's children by his widow to Thomas Taney (Gent.). (Ct.&Land: D#2.142)

RUSSELL, Mary. Binds her son, 20 May 1714, Michael Richard Sotherland, to John Rogers, to age 21. (Ct.&Land: F#2.72)

RUSSELL, Luke, of St. Mary's Co., and his wife Mary. Deed dated 25 Nov 1725, to Hudson Wathen, 50 acres, part of a tract called *Westwood Mannor*, now divided between the two granddaus. of said Gilbert Cropper, whereof the said Luke Russell, by marrying Mary, the widow of William Watkins, became seized with a right of inheritance. (Land: L#2.244)

RUSSELL, Thomas Truman and his wife Susanna. Deed dated 18 Aug 1735. To Samuel Perrie of Prince George's Co. On 15 Feb 1727/8 Henry Darnal leased Samuel King a tract in *his Lordship's Manor* of Calverton called *My Clear Land*, 41 acres, during the lifetime of sd. Samuel King and Elizabeth King and Mary King. Samuel King assigned his right to Thomas Truman Russell, with agreement of his wife Ann King. (Land: O#2.129)

RUSSELL (RUSSEL), Luke (planter) and his wife Mary, of St. Mary's Co., on 11 March 1728 conveyed, 100 acres, part of tract called *Westwood Mannor*. (Land: M#2.151)

RUSSELL, James of Prince George's Co. (merchant), and his wife Ann on 30 Sept 1741 conveyed a tract called *Thompsons Hope*, 193 acres, and on 12

Sept 1745, 2/3 of lot #15 in Benedict Leonard Town on Patuxent River. (Land: O#2.543; Z#2.76)

RUSTON, Margaret. Servant of Col. Edward Pye, she had a bastard child, 12 Jan 1691. (Ct.&Land: R#1.337)

SACKIMORE, Edward. Servant of Henry Hawkins, age judged to be 14 yrs., 12 Jan 1685. (Ct.&Land: M#1.67)

SACOAT(E) (See SAPCOATE).

SAFFRON, James. (Inv.: 2.58; 13 Aug 1718; 13 Aug 1718)

SAINT CLARE, Robert. Next of kin: Peter Wood. Admrs.: Priscilla Saint Clare, George Saint Clare. (Inv.: 11.504; 22 March 1725; 9 Sept 1726)

ST. CLARE, George. Creditors: Francis Parnham, James Nevison. Next of kin: Thomas St. Clare, John Slye. Admr.: Dorothy St. Clare. (Inv.: 29.339; ----; 18 July 1744)

SALSBY (See SOLSBY).

SALT, Mary, age 20 yrs. Servant of Thomas Speeke, St. Mary's Co., 11 March 1678. (Ct.&Land: H#1.129)

SALYERD, Charles. Mentions wife. Admr./Ex.: Clement Barkstone. (Acct: 32A.44; ----; 28 Aug 1710)

SAMPLE, Charles and his wife Frances, one of the three daus. of William Sanders and his wife Alice, the surviving heiress of John Falkner, late of Charles Co., dec'd., conveyed to John King a tract called *Chairmans Purchase*, cont. 200 acres. Sd. John Falkner and his wife Alice, by deed dated 17 Dec 1689 leased the 200 acres to Philip Lynes for 99 yrs. which lease was sold by his legal representatives Anne Story and John Marten to afsd. John King. (Land: M#2.183, 349; O#2.166)

SANDERS (SANDER, SAUNDERS)

SANDERS, Mathew, judged to be 15 yrs. old, 8 July 1662. (Ct.&Land: A#1.220)

SANDERS (Sand.ᵉˢ), William, age 17 yrs. Servant of John Hanson, 10 March 1684/5. (Ct.&Land: L#1.93)

SANDERS, Edward, Gent., (admr. to Henry Brayne, dec'd.), and Jane, wife of Edward Sanders. Indenture to Giles Blizard. Obligation of Henry Brayne, dated 2 July 1674, to John Cane for use of his dau. Susanna Cane, assigns on the day of marriage of Susanna 20,000 lbs. of tobacco; marriage was 21 Aug 1684 between Giles Blizard and Susanna Cane.

Edward and Jane Sanders convey parcel on 8 April 1683 called *Bowplain* on e. side of Anacostia R. on St. John's Creek, cont. 1000 acres. (Ct.&Land: S#1.285)

SAUNDERS, Edward and Jane of west side of Portobacco Creek. Their children: Edward, born 6 Nov 1685; Thomas, born 30 March 1688; Charles, born 18 July 1690; Mary, born 19 April 1692. (Ct.&Land: QRev.11, 14, 15, 18)

SAUNDERS, John, son of Matthew Saunders. Cattle mark recorded 12 Feb 1690. (Ct.&Land: P#1.203)

SAUNDERS, Mary, dau. of John and Sarah Saunders of Portobacco, born 19 April 1692. (Ct.&Land: P#1.212)

SAUNDERS, Mary, dau. of John Saunders. Cattle mark recorded 16 Dec 1692. (Ct.&Land: S#1.47)

SAUNDERS, Mary, dau. of John and Sarah Saunders. Cattle mark recorded 25 Aug 1694. (Ct.&Land: S#1.334)

SAUNDERS (SANDERS), Edward. To son John, all lands in Virginia except 400 acres. To son Thomas, afsd. 400 acres in Virginia; he dying without issue to pass in turn to son Charles and dau. Jane, son Edward already having his share of real estate. To William Hunter, priest, grandchildren Mary, Thomas and Sarah Saunders, personalty. Wife Jane, extx. and residuary legatee of estate. (Will: 6.248; ----; 29 March 1699) His date of death is cited as 14 November 1698. Admr./Ex.: Jane Sanders (widow). (Inv.: 19½A.12; 17 April 1699; ----) Legatees: William Hunter. Extx.: Mrs. Jane Saunders (also Joane Saunders). (Acct: 11B.46; ----; 27 Sept 1700)

SANDER(S) (SAUNDERS), Jane (widow). Mentions Jane Keene and William Hunter. Mentions sons Edward, Thomas, Charles and dau. Jane. Ex.: Wm. Chandler who is to have charge of children during minority. By note attached to aforegoing will Susanna Blizzard is given 100 acres on which testatrix lived. (Will: 11.181; 15 Aug 1700; 3 Feb 1701/2) Relict and executrix of Edward Saunders. (Inv.: 21.56; ----; 9 Oct 1701) (Inv.: 23.174; ----; 5 April 1702) Legatees: legacy by Edward Sanders whose widow the said Jane was to the children (unnamed) of John Sanders, Thomas Sanders and Charles Sanders. Ex.: William Chandler. (Acct: 29.249; ----; [c1709])

SANDERS, James. Legatees: William Hunter, Samuell Peckle. Ex.: Margarett Hollinsworth. (Accts. from Wills: 5.360; ----; 1 Oct 1703)

SANDERS, James. Legatees: William Hunter, Samuell Peckle. Ex.: William Chandler. (Acct: 5.360; ----; 1 Oct 1703)

SANDERS, Edward (planter). Conveyed on 25 March 1708, to John Sanders (his brother) a parcel formerly belonging to John Ocaine and now in possession of Edward Sanders, grandson of John Ocaine; land called *Caines Purchase*; on w. side of Portobacco Creek, cont. 350 acres. Edward Sanders and Jane his wife, late dec'd, father and mother to afsd. Edward Sanders conveyor of this indenture to his brother John Sanders. (Ct.&Land: C#2.99)

SANDER, John and Sarah his wife and Thomas Sympson and Mary his wife had a right to land assigned from William Matthews to Maj. William Dent; recorded at request of George Dent, 4 Oct 1709. (Ct.&Land: (C#2.143)

SANDERS, Jane. Next of kin: John Sanders, Thomas Sanders, Charles Sanders. (Inv.: 32B.191; 26 March 1711; ----)

SANDERS, Matthew. Deed of gift 6 Aug 1713, to his son William Sanders; part of a tract called *Prichard*, lying on s. side of St. Thomas Creek. (Ct.&Land: F#2.18)

SANDERS, Mathew Sr. Gift of moiety of tract, *Sanders Pleasure*, on s. side of Mattawoman Creek; to his dau. Frances Saunders, now Frances Robinson, 13 Aug 1717; Martha Saunders give power of attorney to John Sanders of Mattawoman to ack. moiety of tract. (Ct.&Land: H#2.76)

SANDERS, Robert. (Inv.: 39A.33; 15 April 1718; ----)

SANDERS, John, age 48, pomfret. Deposition, 12 Aug 1719, re *Glovers Point*. (Chas LandComm: M2.48)

SANDERS, Robert. To Ann Coulson, widow, two sets of bills of exchange for £14 sterling. Mentions bro. Mathew, father Mathew, Henry Ward, sister Margaret Ward, bro. John (Sanders). Mentions Capt. Samuell Bowman's cabin boy, Anthony Smith, Wm., son of Mary Johns (an orphan bound to Wm. Sanders), when of age, Mary, dau. of Geo. Ares, 20s. when at age of 16 yrs., Elizabeth and Chas. Camill, they to live with Francis Robinson and Wm. Sanders during minority. Exs.: Francis Robinson and Wm. Sanders, jointly. (Will: 14.445; 22 Jan 1717; 4 Feb 1717)

SANDERS, William, age 71. Deposition, 4 Nov 1719, regarding part of tract called *Christian Temple Manor*, on the s. side of Mattawoman (petition of John Sanders). (Chas LandComm: M2.66)

SAUNDERS, Mathew, age 71. Deposition, 5 Nov 1719, regarding part of tract called *Christian Temple Manor*, on the s. side of Mattawoman (petition of John Sanders). (Chas LandComm: M2.67)

SANDERS, Mathew. Next of kin: John Sanders, William Sanders. (Inv.: 5.150; 2 April 1720; ----)

SANDERS, Mathew Sr. To grandson Robt. Roberson, 100 acres, dwelling plantation, *Prickard*. Mentions two sons, John and William; eldest son Mathew; dau. Margt. Ward. Wife Elinor extx. (Will: 15.313; 19 Dec 1719; 20 Feb 1719/20)

SANDERS, Edward. To bros. Charles and Thomas, land adj. Ck., and personal estate. (Will: 16.213; 17 Sept 1720; 4 Oct 1720) Next of kin: John Sanders (son). (Inv.: 4.327; 6 Oct 1720; ----)

SANDERS, Thomas (planter). Brothers: Charles and Edward Sanders. Indenture dated 13 June 1721, to bro. Charles; (Edw:, by his will 17 Sept 1720, gave his land to his afsd. bros.); Thos. conveys his part to Charles; land located on the w. side of Portobacco Creek. (Ct.&Land: H#2.433)

SANDERS, John, Mattawoman. To eldest son Mathew, 100 acres in *Christian Temple Mannor*; 100 acres of *Sympson's Supply*, *Woodstock Bower*, n. side Collier's Branch. To son John, 450 acres called

Whittland. To dau. Sarah, part of *William's Purchase.* To dau. Mary [minor], half of last-named tract. To dau. Martha [minor], part of *Woodstock Bower.* Wife Eliza., extx. To Nimrod Duncan, an orphan boy, his freedom. Overseers: Wm. Sanders and Henry Ward. (Will: 17.168; 29 Aug 1720; 30 April 1722)

SANDERS, Matthew. Next of kin: Elisabeth Parnander, Mary Sanders. Admr.: William Nellson. (Inv.: 11.412; 14 April 1726; 2 July 1726)

SANDERS, Thomas, son of John Sanders, dec'd. conveyed on 27 April 1730 lot #72 in Chandler Town, at head of Portobacco Creek. (Land: M#2.205)

SANDERS, John. Mentions wife Mary, dau. Mary Power, grandson John Power, daus. Mary Power, Jane Doyne. To son John, 100 acres of *Cane's Purchase* at Port-tobacco. To son Edward, pt. of last named tract. To dau. Ann, personalty. To son William, residue of land at *Port-tobacco*. To eldest son Thomas, ex., residue of estate (except land in Virginia sold by father Edward Sanders to Nicholas Russell). Codicil: 6th July 1729. Testator states that estate of Ethelbert Doyne, dec'd, with three small children being in his hands, is to be distributed as follows: Grandson Ethelbert Doyne, to care of Clement Gardiner until of age to receive his estate, as designated; two granddaus. Mary and Jane Doyne, with personalty, to care of Thomas Thompson, Port-tobacco. (Will: 19.892; 22 Oct 1724; 15 April 1730) Next of kin: John Sanders, Edward Sanders. Ex.: Thomas Sanders. (Inv.: 15.634; 1 Aug 1730; 17 Aug 1730)

SANDERS, William (planter). To dau. Frances (wife of Charles Sample), 1/2 of *Hazard*; sd. land not to be sold or mortgaged. To dau. Elizabeth (wife of Benjamin Stennett), residue of *Hazard*, same conditions. To dau. Ann, land where mother Eleanor Sanders now lives. To dau. Rachel, after her mother's decease, dwell. plan.; she dying without issue, to pass to dau. Anne after decease of her mother in law Catherine. Wife Katherine, extx., to keep dau. Anne until of age or marriage. (Will: 20.239; 25 Aug 1731; 14 Oct 1731) Next of kin: Matthew Sanders, William Robertson. Extx.: Catherine Bell, wife of Moses Bell. (Inv.: 16.323; 12 Nov 1731; 4 Dec 1731)

SANDERS, John. To son Ignatius, lands and dwell. plant. at Port-tobacco as left to testator by will of his father. To wife Valinda, ex., residue of estate to be divided bet. three children, viz, Ignatious, Prudence and Richard; sons to be of age at 18, dau. at 16 yrs. or day of marriage. Test: Sarah Combs (Coombes), Thomas Sanders, William Sanders. (Will: 20.339; 18 Nov 1731; 7 Feb 1731)

SANDERS, John. Next of kin: Thomas Sanders Jr., Edward Sanders. Extx.: Virlinda Sanders. (Inv.: 16.448; 11 May 1732; 6 June 1732)

SANDERS, Thomas. Next of kin: Edward Saunders, Joseph Camsanders. Admr.: Virlinda Sanders. (Inv.: 20.484; 7 May 1735; 17 June 1735)

SANDERS (SAUNDERS), Eleanor (widow). Mentions son Matthew; dau. Margaret Ward; Elizabeth and Anne Ward and Jane Newton; grandson John; grandson, William Robertson. Exs.: William Robertson and dau.

Margaret. (Will: 21.751; 14 June 1732; 16 March 1736) Next of kin: John Ward, Mary Taylor. Ex.: William Robison (Robertson). (Inv.: 22.518; 18 July 1737; 4 Oct 1737)

SANDERS, Charles. Next of kin: Thomas Sanders, John Sanders. Admr.: Prudence Sanders. (Inv.: 13.117; March 27 1727; 22 May 1728) Admr.: Prudence Green. (Inv.: 17.488; 8 Oct 1731; 8 Nov 1733)

SANDERS, Joseph. Next of kin: William Cooper, Mary Sanders. Admr.: Robert Doyne, Jane (surname not given). (Inv.: 22.343; ----; 20 July 1737)

SANDERS, Mary. To sons Benedict, John Baptist and Francis Boarman, exs., personal estate. To daus. Mary Sly, Elizabeth Hamozly and Clare Shirbin, personalty. (Will: 22.119; 12 March 1739; 17 Dec 1739) Next of kin: Leonard Borman, Richard Borman. Exs.: Benedict Leonard Boarman, John Bablist [sic] Boarman, Francis Ignatius Boarman. (Inv.: 25.416; 21 Dec 1739; 1 April 1741)

SANDERS, Edward. Next of kin: John Sanders, Ann Howard. Ex.: William Sanders. (Inv.: 25.336; ----; 15 Sept 1740)

SANDERS, John, son of John Sanders of Mattawoman, Charles Co., dec'd., conveyed on 9 May 1741, 195 acres called *Williams Purchase*, being part of a tract called *Christian Temple Manor*, being the land purchased of John Smoot and his wife Posthuma by John Sanders, father of sd. John Sanders. (Land: O#2.386)

SANDERS, Thomas (planter). To priest, Mr. Mullineux, personalty. To wife Eleanor, personalty and life interest in *Cow Branch* where Robert Thompson now lives. At her death to pass to youngest son Thomas. To eld. son John, 400 acres called *St. Mathews*. To daus. Mary and Sarah, personalty. Mary to live with her aunt —— Howard. Ex.: Bro. William. (Will: --.---; 25 June 1740; 23 May 1741) Next of kin: John Sanders, Sarah Sanders. Admr./Ex.: William Sanders. (Inv.: 26.371; 23 July 1741; 2 Oct 1741)

SANDERS, John. (Inv.: 27.47; ----; [c1742])

SANDERS, John Jr. (planter), and his wife Eleanor. 1 Dec 1743. To Jeremiah Mudd, lease of 100 acres lying near the Irish Race. (Land: X#2.55)

SANDERS, Edward (planter), on 14 March 1743/4, conveyed land to his brother Thomas Sanders. Thomas Sanders, Charles Co., dec'd., father to afsd. Edward and Thomas Sanders, by deed dated 9 June 1710, purchased of Joseph Pallufeis and his wife Mary, a tract called *Napping* on w. side of Portobacco Creek, 40 acres; and another called *Littleworth*, being part of a tract called *York*. He died intestate and the land became the property of afsd. Edward the eldest son. (Land: X#2.120)

SANFORD, William. Gave nails, &c. for the use and in behalf of his father in law, Capt. William Batten [Battin], dated 2 Oct 1662. (Ct.&Land: B#1.177)

SAPCOATE (SAPERCOTE), Elizabeth, dau. of Abram and Rachell Sapcoate "of ye River side," born 12 Nov 1677. (Ct.&Land: P#1.208; QRev.5)

SAPCOAT(E) (SACOAT), Abraham (nunc.). To dau. in law Rachel, wife of Morris Fittsgerroll, entire estate. (Will: 7.181; 23 Sept 1695; 4 Oct 1695) (Acct: 14.72; ----; 12 Oct 1696) (Acct: 3.404; ----; 12 Oct 1696) Ex.: Morrice Fitzgerrell in right of his wife Rachell Fitzgerrell. (Acct: 3.404; ----; 12 Oct 1696)

SARRAT, Samuel (planter), of Prince George's Co. and his wife Ann. 11 March 1744/5 convey a tract called *Bride Watter*, cont. 70 acres. (Land: Z#2.59)

SAUNDERS (See SANDERS.)

SCARRY, Elias. (Inv.: 38A.16; 12 March 1716; ----)

SCARRYOTT, Richard, age 12 yrs. Servant of Archibald Wahob, 9 Jan 1671/2. (Ct.&Land: E#1.52)

SCHALES, George, age ca. 25 yrs. Swore in court 7 May 1661. (Ct.&Land: A#1.130)

SCOTT, Eribecca. Servant, judged to be 14 yrs. old, presented by James Lindsey, 12 July 1664. (Ct.&Land: B#1.314)

SCOTT, Edward (planter) and Mary his wife. Conveyed on 28 Nov 1690, a parcel called *Thomas his Chance* on Piscataway Creek, cont. 200 acres. (Ct.&Land: R#1.131)

SCOTT, James, age 22 yrs. Servant of Anthony Neale, Nov 1710. (Ct.&Land: D#2.8)

SCOTT, John Jr., age 34. Deposition on 12 xber 1719, regarding tract called *Salisbury*. (Chas LandComm: M2.75)

SCOTT, John Sr., age 60 odd years. Deposition on 12 xber 1719, regarding tract called *Salisbury*; refers to a tract called *Ferry* formerly belonging to John Piles grandfather of Joseph Piles. (Chas LandComm: M2.75)

SCOTT, John Sr. Next of kin: John Scott Jr., William Scott. Executrix: (name not given). (Inv.: 10.347; ----; 19 April 1725)

SCOT, John. Mentions: Joseph Simpson, Christian Lemaster, Christian Scott, William Scott. Admr./Ex.: Elisabeth Scott. (Inv.: 25.417; 25 Sept 1740; 9 April 1741)

SCOTT, James. Admr.: Walter Scott. (Inv.: 27.288; 7 Jan 1742; 10 Jan 1742)

SCOTT, Charles, cooper. In his will he left to children William, John Preston and Henry, 5s. To younger son Charles and dau. Susanna, residue of estate. Ex.: Wife Grace. (Will: 23.179; 22 Aug 1742; 27 Aug 1743)

SCROGGIN, George and Susanna, of Pickaaxon. Their children: Elizabeth, born 14 May 1686; John, born 27 Dec 1687; Mary, born 16 March 1688;

George, born 13 Nov 1692; Susanna, born 5 Feb 1694. (Ct.&Land: P.211; QRev.12, 13, 14, 18, 24)

SCROGGIN, George. Admr./Ex.: John Lofton. (Inv.: 1.677; 18 Sept ----; 19 Sept 1700) Items committed to John Loftus. (Inv.: 20.31; 18 Sept 1700; 19 Sept 1700) Admr.: John Loften. (Acct: 23.73; ----; 30 Sept 1702)

SCROGGIN (SCROGGEN), John. Mentioned wife Jane, extx.; oldest son Joseph; son John; son James; dau. Sarah Oakley; dau. Mary. Note: Heir at law lived on Eastern Shore at time of probate of above will. (Will: 23.143; -- --- 1742/3; 24 June 1743) Next of kin: Sarah Olklys, George Scroggen. Admr./Ex.: Jane Scroggen. (Inv.: 28.236; ----; 16 Sept 1743) (Inv.: 29.351; ----; 27 July 1744)

SEAWELL, Rebeckah, age 20 yrs. Servant of Thomas King, 13 March 1676. (Ct.&Land: G#1.16)

SEER, Thomas, age 13 yrs. Servant of Col. Gerrard Fowke, 10 March 1667/8. (Ct.&Land: C#1.256)

SEES [LEES?], Thomas, age 22 yrs. Servant of John Court Jr., 9 March 1685/6. (Ct.&Land: M#1.90)

SELBY, Parker. (Inv.: 25.296; 2 April 1706; ----)

SELBY, William Magruder, of Calvert Co., and his wife Martha, dau. of Major Josiah Willson, late of Prince George's Co. on 3 July 1735 conveyed a tract in St. Mary's Co. called *Indian Giant Sepulchre*, cont. 203 acres. (Land: O#2.107)

SIMMES, Francis. Servant of William Barton, age judged to be 17 yrs., 12 Jan 1685. (Ct.&Land: M#1.88)

SYMMES, John. Servant judged to be 9 yrs., presented by George Plater, Gent., 9 June 1691. (Ct.&Land: R#1.189)

SEMMES (SIMES, SIMS, SIMMES), Fortune. She left to son John Semmes, 319 acres, part of *St. George's*, bought by her late husband, Marmaduke Semmes; to son Marmaduke Semmes, 319 acres; to son Anthony Semmes, 200 acres. To son Thomas Medford; Thomas, son of sd. Thomas; and Marmaduke, son of Anthony Semmes, personalty. (Will: 11.200; 1 May 1699; 10 Dec 1701) (Inv.: 21.270; 22 Jan 1701; ----) Exs.: John Simms, Marmaduke Simms. (Acct: 23.100; ----; 19 Sept 1702)

SIMMS, James (planter) and Mary his wife conveyed on 26 Feb 1707 part of *Rozer's Refuge*, cont. 19 acres. (Ct.&Land: C#2.91)

SEMMS (SIMMES, SIMS), Anthony. To sons Anthony and Marmaduke, 200 acres, *Sems Settlement*, Marmaduke to have dwelling plantation. To children Elictions, Fidellimus, Mary and Bathia, 400 acres, *Semms Forest* in Cecil Co. To dau. Jane, personalty. Wife Dusebella, extx. Mentions bro. James Semmes and Barnaby Anctill. (Will: 12.326; 15 Aug 1708; 12

Jan 1708) (Inv.: 29.56; 17 Jan 1708; --) Extx.: Dusabella Sims. (Acct: 31.285; ----; 25 April 1710)

SEMMS (SIMS), Marmaduke of Newport. Mentions eldest dau. Ruth; son Francis and dau. Eleanor and child unborn; James Haddock; wife Elizabeth, extx. (Will: 14.518; 11 May 1717; 29 July 1717)

SEMMS, James, age 50. Deposition, 21 May 1720, regarding a tract called *Mattinglys Hope*. (Chas LandComm: M2.87)

SEMMES, James (planter) and his wife Mary on 26 May 1725 conveyed parcel of land, part of two tracts lying nr. the head of Portobacco Creek, one called *Roundhills*; the other called *Chandlers Invention*. (Land: L#2.218)

SEMMS (SIMMS, SIMES, SIMMES), John. To son Thomas, 110 acres dwelling plantation. To son Cleburne (Cleaburn), 110 acres of *St. George's*. To daus. Ann and Rebecka, 125 acres of *St. George's*. To cousin Marmaduke, 100 acres of *Sime's Settlement*. To cousin Anthony, 100 acres of *Simes Settlement*. To cousin Elizabeth, part of *St. George's*. To cousin Elinor, 100 acres. To cousin Ruth, 100 acres. Son Cleburne to be ex. with son Thomas. One of the witnesses, Benj. Higdon, dec'd at date of probate. (Will: 18.368; 15 April 1723; 12 Jan 1724) Next of kin: Marmaduke Simms, Anna Duke. Executrix: Cleborn Semmes. (Inv.: 11.418; 1 Feb 1724; 6 July 1726)

SEMMES, James. Title to William Chandler, title in *Burnt Quarter* at Portobacco. To son Marmaduke, *Chandler's Invention* to path leading from Andrew Simpton's quarter to John Ashman's. To wife Mary, dwell. plan. and residue of *Chandler's Invention* at her decease to sons Joseph Milburn Semmes and Ignatius. To four daus., Mary, Ann, Juliana and Susannah, personalty. To son James, personalty. Exs.: Wife and son Marmaduke. Codicil: 7 Aug 1727. To son James, money in Liverpool which Garard Slye is empowered to recover, not to exceed £70. (Will: 19.366; 5 Aug 1727; 12 March 1727/8) Next of kin: Anthony Semmes, Aleatius Semmes. Exs.: Mary Semmes, Marmaduke Semmes. (Inv.: 13.263; 18 June 1728; 13 Aug 1728)

SEMMES, Marmaduke, and his wife Henrietta on 20 March 1731 conveyed lot #38 in Charles Town at Portobacco to his bro. of Joseph Milburn Semmes and on 16 Jan 1734/5 they conveyed all lands left to him by the will of his father, James Semmes, a tract called *Chandlers Invention*, and the other called *Round Hill*. (Land: M#2.302 O#2.80)

SEMMES, Francis. Deed of gift signed 14 Aug 1733. To his dau. Catherine Semmes, a cow. (Land: O#2.2)

SEEMS, Francis and Lucretia Chapman, married 14 Jan 1733. Their children: Elizabeth, born 24 Oct 1734; Jane, born 28 June 1736; Joseph, born 3 March 1738/9; Marmaduke, born 23 May 1741; Chloe, born 2 Oct 1743; Ignatious, born 5 Sept 1745; (Trinity: 108--rev.)

SEMMES, Fidellimus, and his wife Elizabeth conveyed on 10 Nov 1736 a tract called *Eatons Delight*, 200 acres. (Land: O#2.171)

SIMMS (SEMMES), Cleborn (Cleyborn), and his wife Mary on 11 Nov 1736 conveyed part of a tract called *St. Georges*, 110 acres. (Land: O#2.179, 381)
SIMMS, Anthony (planter), of St. Mary's Co., Deed dated 9 Dec 1736. To Marmaduke Simms, a tract left him by his father, Antho: Simms, being part of the tract *St. Georges*, 100 acres. (Land: O#2.189)
SEMMES, Juliana (nunc.). To bro. Ignatius, personalty. Test: Mary Speake, widow, mother of testatrix. (Will: 21.731; 16 Dec----; 2 Feb 1736)
SIMMS (SIMMES), Marmaduke, and his wife Mary. Deed dated 11 Nov 1736. To Francis Simmes, a part of the tract *St. Georges*, 103 acres, 40 perches. (Land: O#2.174. Also see Land O#2.175 {land sold to Cleborne Simms}, and Land O#2.176, 177)
SEEMS (SIMMES, SIMES), Marmaduke. To son Anthony, plantation where Thomas Higdon lives. To son Marmaduke, *New Design*. To son James, dwelling plantation. To three sons afsd., 50 acres called *Seemses Chance*, Zacciah Swamp. To cousin Ann Cooksey, 59 acres of *St. George's*. To dau. Jane, personalty. To wife Mary, extx., dwelling plantation. (Will: 22.22; ----; 17 Jan 1738) Next of kin: Anthony Simmes. Extx.: Mary Semmes. (Inv.: 24.96; ----; 5 May 1739)
SEMMES, Ignatius. Next of kin: Marmaduke Semmes, Julianah Simson. Admr.: Joseph Milburn Sr. (Inv.: 25.497; 27 April 1741; 28 April 1741)
SEMMES, Marmaduke, elder bro. of Ignatius Semmes (dec'd.); 9 Nov 1741. To Joseph Milburn Semmes, bro. also of Marmaduke Semmes, 300 acres, which land was purchased of William Chandler, dec'd. by James Semmes, father of sd. Marmaduke and Joseph Milburn Semmes; also a tract called *Chandles Invention*, taken up by the sd. James Semmes by an assignment from sd. William Chandler. These lands were by the will of sd. James Semmes, devised to sd. Joseph Milburn Semmes and his bro. Ignatius, now also dec'd. Heneretta, wife of Marmaduke Semmes, released her dower. (Land: O#2.535)
SEMMES, Joseph Milburn, and his wife Rachel conveyd on 9 Nov 1743 tract called *Miricks Chance*, cont. 115 acres. (Land: X#2.69)
SEMMES (SIMMES), Mary (widow). On 10 June 1729 conveyed to her son Joseph Milburn Semmes, her right to part of a tract called *Round Hills*, lying at Portobacco Creek, part of a devise left to said Jos: Milburn Semmes by the will of his father, James Semmes, cont. 50 acres. (Land: M#2.175)

SENEY, Daniell, age 14-15 yrs. Servant of Henry Moore, 11 June 1667. (Ct.&Land: C#1.164)

SENNETT, Gerrard and his wife Ann. Deed of gift dated 11 Jan 1672, to John Lumbrozion (Lumbroso), a black cow. (Ct.&Land: E#1.73)

SENNETT, Elizabeth, dau. of Gerrard Sennett, dec'd. Age 6 yrs., last day of Aug, bound to William Newman and his wife, 13 March 1710. (Ct.&Land: D#2.141)

SERJEANT (SERGENT), William. (Inv.: 39C.129; 3 March 1717; ----) Admr.: Thomas Price. (Acct: 39A.32; ----; 21 April 1718)

SETTELF (See SUTCLIFF).

SHACKERLEY, Edward, son of John and Francis Shackerley of head of Wicomico River, born 3 Aug 1694. (Ct.&Land: QRev.23)

SHACKALET (SHALALET, SHAKULETT, SHAKALETT), Michael (planter) and wife Elizabeth who was the dau. of Mary Campbell. Said Mary Campbell was dau. of Elizabeth Dermon, sister of Robert Downes, the purchaser of land called *Cowspring*. Said Robert Downes was the son of Robert Downes. Deed dated 11 Aug 1724. To Joseph Harrison, son of Richard Harrison, tract at Nanjemy, *Cowspring* (or *Coolespring*), cont. 400 acres. (Land: L#2.152, 162)

SHACKERLY, John and Mary his wife conveyed on 16 Nov 1716 part of a tract, 300 acres at the head of Nanjemy Creek, nr. Nanjemy Road, cont. 50 acres. (Ct.&Land: H#2.50)

SHACKLET, Michael. To dau. Tabitha, entire estate. Bro. in law and sister, Thomas Taylor and Tabitha, his wife, to have charge of her and her estate until of age at 16. (Will: 19.369; 14 March 1727; 6 April 1728) Next of kin: Hen: Taylor, Mary Lambeth. Admr.: Edward Shacklet. (Inv.: 13.265; --- -; 13 Aug 1728)

SHACKERLIT (SHAKERLETT), Benjamin, and his wife Sarah conveyed on 10 April 1734, tract called *Ingothorp*, lying on e. side of main fresh of Pointen Creek, cont. 100 acres. (Land: O#2.47)

SHACKER, Sarah, dau. of John Shacker. Cattle mark recorded 26 April 1694. (Ct.&Land: S#1.278)

SHADWELL, Christopher. (Inv.: 34.51; Aug 1713; ----)

SHAW, John, age 17 yrs. Servant of Railph Smith, 13 June 1682. (Ct.&Land: I#1.293)

SHAW, John. Cattle mark, 15 Oct 1709, for heifer given by John Hartick to his godchild, John Shaw, son of above John Shaw. (Ct.&Land: C#2.148)

SHAW, Ralph Sr. Agreement, 19 March 1710/11, with Edward Marlow Sr. of Prince George's Co., giving Marlow all stock, grain. Marlow to give Shaw and wife Ann a room for their lifetime. (Ct.&Land: C#2.223)

SHAW, Ralph and Anne his wife. Indenture, 12 Nov 1711, to Ralph Shaw Jr.; a parcel on the e. side of Portobacco Creek now in posesion of Ralph Jr., called *Mobile*, cont. 90 acres. (Ct.&Land: C#2.268)

SHAW, Ralph and his wife Mary conveyed on 2 May 1718 a tract called *New Exchange* on the e. side of Portobacco Fresh, cont. 30 acres and on 7 Apr 1719 part of a tract *New Exchange* on the e. side of Portobacco main fresh, cont. 64 acres. [NOTE: Mary dau. of Juliana Price, widow]. (Ct.&Land: H#2.168, 225)

SHAW, John. (Inv.: 8.302; 17 Aug 1723; ---)

SHAW, John Sr. To son John, ex., entire personal estate. To daus. Mary, wife of James Rock, Sarah, wife of William Gug, Elizabeth, wife of James Freeman, Dorothy, wife of William Asphen, and Monacak, wife of John Bateman and to granddau. Elizabeth, wife of William Wakefield, 1s. each. (Will: 22.120; 23 Nov 1739; 24 Dec 1739) Next of kin: James Rock, James Freeman. Ex.: John Shaw. (Inv.: 24.473; 4 Jan 1739; 10 March 1739)

SHEARMAN, John. To bro. William Moncaster and Eliza:, dau. of James Moncaster, personalty. To dau. Eliza: Shearman, at 16 yrs. of age, dwelling plantation. Richd: Waye to have use of land. To wife Susan (or Susannah), residue of estate. (Will: 12.270; 18 April 1708, 5 July 1708) (Inv.: 28.297; 30 Aug 1708; ----)

SHAREMAN, John. Extx.: Susannah Cooper (relict), now wife of John Cooper. (Acct: 31.287; ----; 27 May 1710)

SHELTON, Thomas, of Charles Co., age 28. 1661. (Arch. of Md.: XLI.497)

SHELTON, Mary, age 17 yrs. Servant of John Piles, 14 March 1681. (Ct.&Land: I#1.258)

SHENSTONE, George (planter) and Mary his wife. In reference to sale of tract called *Pinner*, cont. 200 acres dated 10 Nov 1674. (Ct.&Land: F#1.14, 42)

SHEPHERD, Demaris. Petitions for letters of admin. of estate of her late husband, Charles Shepherd, 8 March 1691. (Ct.&Land: Q#1.53)

SHINER, Daniell. Judged bo be 15 yrs. old, presented by John Duglas on behalf of Robert Hundley, 27 March 1662. (Ct.&Land: B#1.101)

SHINGLETON, John (goldsmith). To John Smith Prather, ex., entire estate. Note: John Smith Prather and Matthew Williamson make over their rights of administration to John West. (Will: 23.238; 23 Feb 1742/3; 7 Oct 1743)

SHORT, George, age 17-18 yrs. Servant of Clement Theobalds, 10 Jan 1670. (Ct.&Land: E#1.1)

SHORT, George (planter). Mentions wife Anne, son Daniel; dau. Eliza: Dent; son George. To son Daniel, 60 acres, *Smith's Purchase*. Tract

Simpson's Supply to grandson George Short. (Will: 15.315; 17 Oct 1718; 4 March 1719) (Inv.: 3.334; 13 April 1720; ----)

SHORT, Daniel (planter) and his wife Katherine, John Williams (late of Charles Co., now St. Mary's), and James Williams and his wife Elizabeth (or Easter?) conveyed on 6 April 1730 part of a tract called *St. Thomas*, cont. 70 acres. (Land: M#2.223)

SHORT, Daniel. Next of kin: Thomas Williams, William Williams. Admr.: Catherine Short. (Inv.: 19.93; 14 Aug 1734; 2 Oct 1734)

SHUTTLEWORTH, Lydia and Edward, children of Thomas Shuttleworth. Deed of gift 9 Sept 1682, from William Nevill; parcel called *Homefaire*(?) in Nanjemy Creek. (Ct.&Land: K#1.273)

SIGELOY, Samuell, age 16 yrs. Servant of John Mun, 9 Nov 1680. (Ct.&Land: I#1.33)

SIMMES, SIMES, SIMS (See SEEMS, SEMMES).

SIMMONS, Mary, age 14 yrs. Maid servant, presented by James Boulin, 17 Dec 1662. (Ct.&Land: B#1.38)

SYMMONS, Elinor, wife of George Symmons. Ordered by court, 14 June 1681, to take care of Elizabeth Brafitt. (Ct.&Land: I#1.124)

SIMPSON, Paul (mariner), age 60. 28 June 1650. Said that March last he was with Lt. William Lewis at Appamattocks in the county of Northumberland, Virginia and heard John Hallowes wife say to Lt. Lewis, that she suspected he had inveigled and invented to carry away William Greenestead and Thomas Meredith who she said were servants that had run away from their Mrs. service. About a fortnight later he saw them at Lt. Lewis's house at Portobacco. (Arch. of Md.: X.20, 73)

SIMPSON, Alexander. To goddau. Margaret Wahob, dau. of Archibald Wahob, 120 acres (unnamed). To Eliza: Wahob, dau. of sd. Archibald, 120 acres. In event of death of both Margaret and Eliza: during minority, land to pass to Jane Wahob, their mother. To Jacob Leah, bro. of sd. Jane Wahob, 300 acres. *Simpson's Delight*. To Thomas Borker, personalty. Extx.: Jane Wahob. (Will: 1.379; 30 Dec 1669; 12 April 1670)

SIMPSON, Samuell, age 15 yrs. Servant of John Goodge, 2nd Tues in Aug 1673. (Ct.&Land: E#1.135)

SIMPSON (SIMSON), William. To son Thomas, 100 acres, *Liverpool*, on which he now lives. Wife Eliza:, extx. 150 acres, &c. (Will: 11.95; 18 Jan 1700; 18 March 1700) (Inv.: 21.1; 8 May 1701; ----) Legatees: Thomas Simpson. Extx.: Elisabeth Jones (relict), wife of John Jones. (Acct: 23.65; ----; 19 Dec 1702)

SIMPSON, Elizabeth, age ca. 22 yrs. Servant of Robert Sanders, 13 March 1710. (Ct.&Land: D#2.67)

SYMPSON, Thomas (planter) and Mary his wife conveyed on 14 March 1710/11 a parcel formerly taken up by Thomas Matthews called *Saint Matthew's*, formerly conveyed from Leonard Brooke and Anne his wife to Francis Green, father of Leonard Green; by defect in the will of sd. Thomas Matthews the parcel became the property of Thomas Simpson and Mary his wife; cont. 100 acres. (Ct.&Land: C#2.236)

SIMPSON (SYMPSON), John. (Inv.: 30.15; 26 July 1709; ----) Admr.: Elisabeth Mahaune, wife of Robert Mahaune. (Acct: 32C.127; ----; 6 April 1711)

SYMPSON, Thomas (planter) conveyed on 9 June 1713 part of a tract granted to Thomas Sympson, father of said Thomas Sympson, called *St. Thomas*. Also *Sinkin*, in Charles Co., formerly of St. Mary's Co., cont. 200 acres. (Ct.&Land: D#2.67)

SIMPSON, Thomas, Sr., age 58. Deposition on 12 xber 1719, regarding tract called *Salisbury*. (Chas LandComm: M2.75)

SYMPSON, Thomas Sr. and Thomas Sympson Jr., and his wife Sarah on 17 Feb 1719 conveyed tract called *Huckleberry Swamp*, nr. the Potomac River, cont. 100 acres. (Ct.&Land: H#2.319)

SIMPSON, Thomas, age 57. Deposition in 1720 regarding tract called *Westwood Mannor*. (Chas LandComm: M2.95)

SYMPSON, Thomas, Sr. age 58. Deposition in 1721 regarding tract called *Wadestone's Enlargement* in Durham Parish. (Chas LandComm: M2.129)

SYMPSON, Thomas Sr., and Thomas Sympson Jr. and his wife Sarah on 7 Aug 1727 conveyed 168 acres, being part of a tract formerly taken up by Thomas Sympson Sr., dec'd., it being resurveyed by Thomas Sympson Jr., called *Saint Thomas'*. (Land: L#2.385, 387)

SYMPSON, Thomas Sr. and Thomas Sympson Jr. and his wife Sarah on 7 Aug 1727 conveyed to William Sympson (carpenter), 112 acres, part of a tract formerly taken up by Thomas Sympson Sr., dec'd., it being resurveyed by Thomas Sympson Jr., called *St. Thomas'*. (Land: L#2.252, 253, 383)

SYMPSON, Thomas Jr. and his wife Sarah, and Thomas Sympson Sr. (planters), conveyed on 31 Dec 1730, to Igna: Sympson (carpenter), being part of a tract formerly taken up by Thomas Sympson Sr., dec'd., it being resurveyed by Thos: Sympson Jr., called *St. Thomases*, cont. 60 acres. (Land: M#2.252, 253)

SYMPSON, Thomas (planter), and his wife Sarah, on 13 Aug 1738 part of a tract called *Huckleberry Swamp*, 12 acres. (Land: O#2.346)

SYMPSON, Andrew (planter). Deed of gift dated 30 April 1739. To his dau, Clear (Clare) Sympson, a Negro boy called Nacy alias Ignatius, about 12 years old. (Land: O#2.398)

SIMPSON (SYMPSON), Andrew. To sons Thomas, and Joseph Green Simpson, personalty. To dau. Ann Clark, personalty. To grandson, Jno. Semmes, son of Cleburn Semmes, 5 shillings. To daus. Mary, and Clare,

personalty. To wife Juliana, personalty and residue of estate, sole extx.
(Will: 23.659-660; 2 Nov 1744; 3 Dec 1744) Next of kin: Joseph Green
Sympson, Thomas Sympson. Extx.: Juliana Sympson. (Inv.: 30.290; 14
Dec 1744; 3 March 1744)

SIMSON (See SIMPSON).

SINGLETON, Richard, age 13 yrs. Servant of Richard Beck, 10 June 1674.
(Ct.&Land: E#1.171)

SYNNETT, Garrett of Charles County, married 21 Nov 1666, Alice Hunt.
(Arch of Md: 60.116).

SENNETT, Garrett (planter), and his wife Anne. Indenture 9 March 1676;
parcel called *St. Peter's*, lying on w. side of a fresh run of Portobacco
Creek, cont. 50 acres. (Ct.&Land: G#1.20)

SINNETT (SYNNET), Garret married Alice Hunt 21 Nov 1666. Margaret,
dau. of Garrett Sinnett, born 24 Oct 1667. (Ct.&Land: C#1.253; P#1.204;
QRev.2, 3)

SINNETT, Alice, had a bastard child, servant of Philip Lines, 8 Nov 1681.
Court ruling quilty, given 20 lashes, 29 Nov 1681. (Ct.&Land: I#1.174, 180)

SINNETT, Garrett (planter) and Ann his wife on 4 April 1705 conveyed a
parcel *Friendship*, 50 acres. (Ct.&Land: Z#1.178)

SINNET, Robert. Lease, 13 Aug 1740, of land in *St. Thomas Manor*, 230
acres, for the term of the lives of sd. Robert Sinnet, his wife Hannah, and
his dau. Benedicta. (Land: O#2.464)

SKIDMORE, Nicholas and his wife Anne. Indenture 7 Nov 1681, to John
Posey; 50 acre parcel at head of Wicomico R. called *Southbury*; also
Aldgate, cont. 41 acres. (Ct.&Land: I#1.181)

SKIDMORE, Nicholas and his wife Ann. Indenture 8 Sept 1685, to Robert
Hagar of St. Mary's Co.; parcel called *Skidmore Rest*, cont. 80 acres.
(Ct.&Land: L#1.183)

SKIDMORE, Nicholas (tailor) and Anne his wife on 12 Aug 1690 conveyed a
parcel called *Hill Port*. (Ct.&Land: R#1.31)

SKIDMORE, Nicholas. (Inv.: 13A.261; 21 Jan 1694; ----)

SKIDMORE, Nicholas. Admr.: John Beale who married Ellinor relict and
executrix of Hugh Tears (carpenter) (administrator of deceased). (Acct:
32B.8; ----; 23 Jan 1710)

SKINNER, Thomas, age 15 yrs. Servant of Robert Hunly, 11 June 1667.
(Ct.&Land: C#1.164)

SKINNER, Thomas, son of Thomas Skinner. Cattle mark recorded 25 Feb
1722. (Land: L#2.78)

SKINNER, Thomas. Mentions wife Constance; son Thomas (160 acres of
Milerne); son William (160 acres of *Doncaster* and *Aspinnall's
Chance*); son James (160 a.) at 18 yrs. Exs.: Wife and son Thomas.

(Will: 19.318; 8 Oct 1727; 19 Feb 1727) Next of kin: William Skinner, "minors." Ex.: Thomas Skinner. (Inv.: 13.113; 4 May 1727; 20 May 1728)
SKINNER, Constance, Signed 30 June 1740. To her son Richard Masten, he gives a Negro man called Lowhill, age 26, and Negro boy called Ned about 2 years old. (Land: O#2.458)

SLATER, John, age 16 yrs. Servant of Thomas King, 13 March 1676. (Ct.&Land: G#1.16)

SLAYDE, Anne, relict and admr. of George Goer who died intestate, now wife of George Slayde, 8 Sept 1691. (Ct.&Land: Q#1.41)

SLY, Robert, age ca. 34 yrs. Swore in open court 25 Sep 1661. (Ct.&Land: A#1.157)
SLY, Robert. (Inv.: 18.24; 18 Oct 1698; --) Ex.: William Jones. (Acct: 19.178; ----; [c1699])
SLYE, Robert, son of John and Eleanor Slye, born 15 Nov 1745. (Trinity: 114B—rev.)

SMALDRIGE, Elisabeth. Presented for having a bastard child, 14 Nov 1665. (Ct.&Land: B#1.492)

SMALLPAGE, Robert. To son in law Joshua Graves and to Sarah Graves, personalty. Wife, extx. and residuary legatee of estate, including *Nassemore*. (Will: 6.75; 11 Feb 1697; 2 April 1698) (Inv.: 18.66; 5 July 1698; ----)
SMALLPADGE (SMALLPAGE), Ellinor. To dau. Mary Griffen, 1s. To sons John and James Boyce, residue of estate, including land *Mallemore*, the latter to pass to granddau. Mary Griffin should sd. sons die without issue. (Will: 12.269; 31 Oct 1702; 5 July 1708) (Inv.: 29.1; 11 July 1708; 22 Nov 1708)

SMALLWEELL, James. Appraisers: William Tannehill, Gawen Hamiltowne. Admr./Ex.: Elisabeth Smallweell (relict). (Inv.: 13B.68; 15 Nov 1695; 27 Feb 1695)

SMALLWOOD, James and Esther. Their children: John, born in Jan 1666.; James, born in Oct 1668; Mary, born in Jan 1670; Matthew, born in April 1673. (Ct.&Land: E#1.163; P#1.205; QRev.2, 3, 4)
SMALLWOOD, James. Deed of gift 16 March 1685/6, to his dau. Mary Maddocks, a cow and mare. (Ct.&Land: M#1.27)
SMALLWOOD, James and his wife Hester, complaint against Thomas Fowlkes, 9 Aug 1692. (Ct.&Land: R#1.456)
SMALLWOOD, John. Mentions wife Lettes; dau. Esther; brother ——— Prayer; sister Mary Maddocks; brothers James, Matthew, Thomas, and William Smallwood, and William's wife (unnamed), brother Benjamin Smallwood; sister Sarah; brother ——— Ladstone, brother ——— Bayne;

bro. in law Cornelius Maddocks; and Hannah More. (Will: 7.18; 20 March 1693; 6 Aug 1694)

SMALLWOOD, John. To Mordecai Moore, of Anne Arundel Co., ex., entire estate. (Will: 7.189; 6 Nov 1695; 3 Jan 1695)

SMALLWOOD, William (Capt.). To wife Eleanor, estate which was hers at marriage. To children Jane, John and Ann, all estate which was testator's at marriage afsd. To son John afsd., two tracts in Charles Co., one 100 acres at head of Portobacco Ck. and the other on Mattawoman, at present in possession of brother Pryar Smallwood; also lot and house in Portobacco. Exs.: Wife Eleanor and brother James Smallwood. (Will: 12.27; 17 Feb 1705, 12 June 1706) (Inv.: 26.106; [c1706]; ----) Extx.: Ellinor Philpott, wife of Edward Philpott. (Acct: 28.129; ----; 23 June 1708) (Inv.: 29.376; 26 Nov 1708; ----) Payments to: James Wilson, cause of estate of George Tubman by Randolph Garland, Elinor Tubman before her marriage to deceased, [and] Thomas Bordley. Extx.: Elinor Philpot (relict), now wife of Edward Philpot. (Acct: 29.383; ----; 3 Aug 1709)

SMALLWOOD, James, Col. Bill of exchange, 26 July 1706, on behalf of his son James Smallwood Jr., to John Godwin, London merchant. (Ct.&Land: C#2.135)

SMALLWOOD, Bayne (Baine) of Port Tobacco. To brother James (Smallwood), ex. and rest of brothers and sisters, all estate which came by father. To sd. father, personalty. To wife Charity, all estate which came through her father, Col. Jno. Courts. (Will: Part 2—12.208; 28 June 17--; 2 Dec 1709) Ex.: James Smallwood. (Inv.: 31.145; [c1709]; ----)

SMALLWOOD, James (Gent.) and his wife Mary. Deed of gift, 13 Jan 1709, to John and Anne Frazer, natural dau. of Mary; also to Mary Frazer, natural dau. of John and Anne Frazer, and granddau. of said Mary Smallwood. Parcel of land in Prince George's called *Bean Plaine*, cont. 100 acres on the Potomac R. (Ct.&Land: C#2.154)

SMALLWOOD, Samuel (carpenter) of Baltimore County and Martha his wife conveyed on 17 April 1712 parcel called *Strife*, cont. 135 acres. (Ct.&Land: D#2.18)

SMALLWOOD, James Sr. (Col.). To wife Mary, extx., 2/3 of personal estate on plantation *Bew Plains*, in Prince George's Co. To child., viz., James, Thomas, Prier and Leadstone Smallwood, Mary Tayler and Sarah More, residue of estate on sd. plantation. Test: Jno. Done, Jno. Doddson. (Will: 14.31; 16 Sept 1712; 12 Jan 1714)

SMALLWOOD, James, Col. (Inv.: 36C.255; 24 April 1715; ----) Extx.: Mary Harbert, wife of Alexander Harbert. (Acct: 37B.135; ----; 24 Sept 1717)

SMALLWOOD, James Sr. Mentioned wife's children Elenor, John, William, Mathew and James (at 18 yrs.); dau. Lydia (at 16 or marriage). To wife Mary, extx., personalty, including an English woman Mary Daginat. (Will: 18.209; 13 Nov 1723; 12 Dec 1723)

SMALLWOOD, Ledstone, age 36. Deposition re *Lynes Delight*, 22 Dec 1718. (Chas LandComm: M2.41)

253

SMALLWOOD, Pryer (Gent.) and his wife Elizabeth conveyed on 9 Aug 1720, to Daniel Bryon of Stafford Co., Virginia, parcel called *St. Bridgett* on w. side of Portobacco Creek, cont. 250 acres. (Ct.&Land: H#2.377)

SMALLWOOD, Pryor, age 40. Deposition, 31 May 1721, regarding tract called *Christian Temple Manor*. (Chas LandComm: M2.122)

SMALLWOOD, James. Indenture, 14 Nov 1721, to his bro. Ledstone Smallwood (both are sons of James Smallwood, dec'd.), regarding two tracts of their father; one tract called *Welcome*, cont. 200 acres; also *May Day* of 300 acres. (Ct.&Land: H#2.471)

SMALLWOOD, James. Next of kin: John Smallwood, William Smallwood. Executrix: (name not given). (Inv.: 9.337; 21 Feb 1723; 10 March 1723)

SMALLWOOD, Mary, extx. and widow of James Smallwood. Deed dated 12 Aug 1725. From William Hoskins, parcel called *Friendship*, on the s. side of Mattawoman Fresh, 333 acres. (Land: L#2.231)

SMALLWOOD, Mary and John, exs. of the will of James Smallwood. Bind themselves to Charles Byrne and his wife Margery; whereas a parcel of land formerly belonging to Hugh Thomas, father of said Margery, of 200 acres, part of tract called *Friendship*, originally granted unto Bennett Hoskins, lying on Mattawoman Swamp, was by reciprocal consent of sd. Mary Smallwood and John Smallwood and Charles Byrne and Margery his wife on 29 Nov last [1725], divided. Recorded 25 May 1727. (Land: L#2.354)

SMALLWOOD, Mary (alias Mary Boydon) and James Griffin, her son, conveyed on 22 Feb 1731; a tract called *Ashbrook's Rest*, cont. 150 acres. (Land: M#2.280)

SMALLWOOD, William and his wife Mary, and James Smallwood, conveyed on 4 Aug 1733 a small parcel of two acres called *Pinee*. (Land: M#2.354)

SMALLWOOD, John. To wife Mary and dau. Ann, personalty, including servant David McCrackin. To son William, dwelling plantation. (Will: 21.299; 21 Dec 1734; 19 Feb 1734)

SMALLWOOD, Prior (Pryor). To son William, 200-acre dwelling plantation called *Christian Temple Manner*, bought by father James Smallwood from Thomas Witcherly and wife. To son Bayne, ex., residue of real estate; sd. son to allow his sisters Ann and Elizabeth to work so much of tract called *Bayne* or *New Design* as will employ their negroes while sd. sisters remain unmarried. To dau. Hester, personalty. (Will: 21.1; 23 Feb 1732/3; 29 March 1734) Next of kin: Ledstone Smallwood, Mathew Stone Sr. Ex.: Bayne Smallwood. (Inv.: 18.473; ----; 7 Aug 1734)

SMALLWOOD, Thomas Sr. To son James, the part of *Poor Call*, Piney Branch. To son Thomas, 200 acres called *Moores Rest*. To son Pryor, part of *Poor Call*, *Batchelor's Delight*, 250 acres. adjoining *Smallwood Plain*. To daus. Elizabeth Cawood, Sarah Roby, Esther Harrison, personalty. To dau. Charity Davy, use of certain personalty, then to her daus. Ann and Eleanor Davy. To Humphrey Berry, 300 acres called *Smallwood's Plains*; at his decease to be divided between Humphry and Thomas Berry, his sons by testator's dau. Mary. Wife Alice, extx. (Will: 21.336; 14 April 1734; 9 April 1735) Next of kin: Thomas Smallwood, Esther Harrison. Extx.: Alice Smallwood (deceased by 17 Sept 1735), wife of Thomas Middleton. (Inv.: 21.85; 28 May 1735; 17 Sept 1735. See Robert Middleton (ca. 1651-ca. 1707) . . . by John Goodwin Hernadon, Lancaster, Penna.: privately published, 1955, p. 17, Smallwood-Middleton).

SMALLWOOD, John. Next of kin: William Smallwood, Ladstone Smallwood. Admr.: Mary Smallwood. (Inv.: 20.379; 8 May 1735[?]; 22 May 1734) Admr.: Mary Smallwood. (Inv.: 21.91; ----; 14 Oct 1735)

SMALLWOOD, Ledstone and his wife Elizabeth. Deed dated 10 June 1736. To his son William Smallwood, 100 acres, part of tract called *May Day*. (Land: O#2.154)

SMALLWOOD, Bayne (Bay:) (planter), and his wife Priscilla on 21 Aug 1739 conveyed part of tract called the *Expectation*, by last survey called *Winters' Possession*, cont. 225 acres. (Land: O#2.412. See also Land O#2.363.)

SMALLWOOD, Mary (widow). 27 March 1742. To John Smallwood, William Smallwood, Matthew Smallwood and James Smallwood Jr., planters, part of tract called *Friendship*, lying on s. side of Mattawoman fresh, 333 acres; also 100 acres, being part of 200 acres of *Friendship* formerly belonging to Hugh Thomas bounded according to the division made between sd. Mary Smallwood, John Smallwood, Charles Byrn and Margery his wife, dated 5 Jan 1725/6. (Land: O#2.439)

SMALLWOOD, Ledstone (Leadstone), and his wife Elizabeth, and William Smallwood and his wife Lidia on 12 June 1740 conveyed Lot #55 in Charles Town in Port Tobacco Parish. To Capt. Samuel Hanson, son of Robert Hanson, deed dated 11 Dec 1741, a tract called the *Goar*, 23 acres. To Francis Goodrick, deed dated 14 March 1744/5, part of tract called *Addition to May Day*, cont. 120 acres. (Land: O#2.457. See also Land O #2.545 and Land Z #2.25.)

SMALLWOOD, Pryor. Mentions: John Cawood, Humphry Beary Jr. Next of kin: Matt. Smallwood, Samuel Beary. Admr./Exs.: Walter Bayne and his wife Winifred Bayne. (Inv.: 26.441; 9 Jan 1741; 17 Feb 1741)

SMITH, Richard, age ca. 23 yrs. Swore in court 2 July 1661. (Ct.&Land: A#1.142)

SMITH, Richard. Mentions wife Mathew, unborn child (land on n. side Potete's Ck.), William, son of Edward Williams. (Will: 1.165; 25 Nov 1662; 2 Jan 1662)

SMITH, William, age ca. 17 yrs. Swore in court 8 July 1662. (Ct.&Land: A#1.220)

SMYTH, John married Margaret Barker, 14 Feb 1666/7. (Ct.&Land: C#1.252; P#1.204; QRev.2)

SMITH, Robert, age 15 yrs. Servant of John Munn, 10 June 1674. (Ct.&Land: E#1.171)

255

SMITH, James, age 12 yrs. Servant of Thomas Mudd, 8 Jan 1677. (Ct.&Land: G#1.85)

SMITH, Elizabeth, age 12 yrs. Servant of Thomas Clarke, 12 March 1677. (Ct.&Land: G#1.119)

SMITH, Ralph and Sarah his wife, relict of Col. John Duglas. Indenture, 3 April 1680, to Thomas Harris (planter); exchange of land. (Ct.&Land: H#1.291)

SMITH, Richard and Anne, of Pickawaxon. Their children: Richard, born 11 July 1688; Elizabeth, born 12 Sept 1690; Arthur, born 23 April 1692; James, born 23 Aug 1694. (Ct.&Land: QRev.14, 17, 20, 25)

SMITH, James, age 21 yrs. Servant of Samuell Luckett, 9 Feb 1685/6. (Ct.&Land: M#1.89)

SMITH, Richard (planter) and Anne his wife on 10 May 1688 conveyed part of a parcel of 80 acres lying nr. Picawaxon Creek, cont. 40 acres. (Ct.&Land: P#1.67)

SMITH, Alexander (planter). Deed of gift dated 11 March 1689, plantation at head of Wicomico River. Mentions: dau. Sarah Smith; dau. Mary Turner, wife of Edward Turner; dau. Elizabeth Rivett, wife of Jonas Rivett; dau. in law Grace Colliar, wife of Giles Colliar; grandsons Arthur Turner and Alexander Smith Turner, sons of Edward and Mary Turner—at age of 21. To Mary Turner, 500 acres at Piscataway and part of tract *Batchelor's Harbor*, cont. 400 acres. Administration of estate by Sarah, dau. of William Smith, now wife of Henry Hawkins Jr. (Ct.&Land: Q#1.2)

SMITH, John. Gift dated 19 July 1690, to his dau. in law, Elizabeth Symons; cow and calf. (Ct.&Land: P#1.202)

SMITH, Anthony who married Martha Baker, dau. of Thomas. Regarding estate of Thomas Baker, 2 March 1690; receiving part of *Baker's Rest* on Baker's Creek called *Baker's Addition*, along with Andrew Baker, Thomas Baker and John Baker, 9 June 1691. Indenture 25 Sept 1691, to William Dent, 6,500 lbs. tobacco; parcel laid out of Thomas Baker, dec'd, due Martha, dau. of Thomas Baker, known as *Lott Number Three*. [It appears Anthony Smith left his wife destitute and the court ordered William Dent to pay Joyse Garrett, wife of Charles Garrett, part of the afsd. tobacco for the maintenance of Martha Smith.]. (Ct.&Land: Q#1.23, 28; R.279)

SMITH, Daniell (carpenter) of St. Mary's Co., and Elizabeth, his wife. Indenture 31 Dec 1690, to Henry Goodridge; tract called *Lyons Hole*, cont. 100 acres. (Ct.&Land: R#1.144)

SMITH, William, son of William and Joan Smith of Wicomico, born 15 Sept 1691. (Ct.&Land: QRev.17)

SMITH, Thomas, son of Henry and Margery Smith of Portobacco, born 3 March 1692. (Ct.&Land: QRev.20)

SMITH, Arthur, son of Richard Smith. Cattle mark recorded 14 Nov 1693. (Ct.&Land: S#1.169)

SMITH, Elizabeth, dau. of Richard Smith. Cattle mark recorded 14 Nov 1693. (Ct.&Land: S#1.169)

SMITH, William. Wife Eliza:, extx. To William, son of Adam Smith, Berkshire, Eng., 1200 acres, *Southampton* at Pomonkey. Mentions Adam, the eldest brother of sd. William, and his sister (unnamed). (Will: 7.74; 22 Jan 1694; 13 March 1694) Extx.: Elisabeth Smith (relict). (Inv.: 13A.278; 25 April 1695; ----) Payments include Richard Harrison and Richard Wade (administrators of John Wright), William Bishop (administrator of John Smith), Capt. Phillip Hoskins on account of Thomas Love son of William Love. Extx.: Elisabeth Smith. (Acct: 15.58; ----; 13 Oct 1696)

SMITH, William, son of William. Cattle mark recorded betw. June-Aug 1694. (Ct.&Land: S#1.313)

SMITH, Thomas, son of Henry Smith. Cattle mark recorded betw. June-Aug 1694. (Ct.&Land: S#1.313)

SMITH, Richard. To Sarah Douglas, to dau. Eliza: and unborn child, personalty. To sons Richard and Arthur, all real estate equally. To wife Ann, estate during minority of children. Exs.: Wife and son Richd: afsd. (Will: 7.11; 14 June 1694; 18 July 1694) One of the appraisers is Ralph Smith. (Inv.: 10.417; 24 Aug 1694; ----) Distribution to: widow (unnamed), four children (unnamed). Extx.: (unnamed relict), wife of Joseph Wilson. (Acct: 10.418; ----; [c1694/5])

SMITH, Jane, dau. of William and Joan Smith of Wicomico, born 10 Sept 1694. (Ct.&Land: QRev.23)

SMITH, Henry, son of Henry and Margery Smith of Portobacco, born 5 Nov 1694. (Ct.&Land: QRev.24)

SMITH, John (planter) of Calvert Co., and Elizabeth his wife conveyed on 11 Nov 1694 a parcel called *Smith's Chance* on s. side of Mattawoman Run, located in *Manor of Zachia*, cont. 144 acres. (Ct.&Land: S#1.404)

SMITH, John. (Inv.: 13B.64; 1 Sept 1695; ----) Admr.: William Bishop. (Acct: 14.69; ----; 30 July 1696)

SMITH, Ralph. Wife Sarah, extx. and sole legatee. (Will: 6.217; 26 Dec 1698; 10 Feb 1698/9) Appraisers: Cleborne Lomax, Walter Storey. Extx.: Sarah Smith (relict). (Inv.: 18.154; 10 March 1698; ----) Mentions: no orphans. Admr.: Sarah Smith (widow). (Acct: 19½B.89; ----; 24 Feb 1699)

SMITH, Elizabeth (widow). To Mary, wife of John Martin Smith; Cleborne Lomax and Blanche, his wife; Eliza:, wife of Jno. Hawkins; Robbin, son of Ann Osborne; and to Revd. George Tubman, personalty. Cleborne Lomax and John Martin Smith, exs. and residuary legatees of personalty, they also to have charge of plantation until the heir (unnamed) comes to take possession of it. (Will: 6.84; 11 March 1697; 26 March 1698) Above Elizabeth Smith was wife of William Smith (dead) and Archibald Waughob (dead). (Inv.: 19½B.93; 19 March 1699; ----)

SMITH, William. (Inv.: 16.3; 27 June 1698; ----) (Inv.: 19½B.91; 6 March 1699; ----)

SMITH, Daniell. Mentions: widow (unnamed, very poor), four children (unnamed). (Inv.: 20.217; 7 Feb 1700; 8 Aug 1701)

257

SMITH, John and his wife Anne conveyed on 20 Oct 1702 100 acre of a 1500 acre called *Jordans*. (Ct.&Land: Land Z.92)

SMITH, John. To sister Mary Stevenson, cousins Elizabeth and John Williams and to Joan Branch, William Hunter, Wm. Kelleck, Robert Brookes and Benjamin Hall, personalty. To kinsman Gilles Hill, dwell. plantation, *Simson's Supply*. To kinswoman Susanna Hill, 40 acres, *Smith's Addition* and 50 acres, *The Addition*. Ex.: Richard Edelen, empowered to sell *The Hope* at Patuxent. Cousins John Gilles and Susanna Hill afsd. to receive proceeds of residue of estate. (Will: 3.741; 13 Nov 1705, 10 Dec 1705) (Inv.: 27.1; 26 March 1707; ----) Legatees: John Williams, Mary Stevenson, Elisabeth Cooksey, Mary Short, wife of George Short, William Hunter (priest), Capt. Benjamin Hall. Ex.: Richard Edelin. (Acct: 29.64; ----; 5 Feb 1708)

SMITH, James. (Inv.: 26.140; 7 Jan 1706; ----) Admr.: John Miller for Sarah (no surname given). (Acct: 28.98; ----; 11 March 1707)

SMITH, Richard. Extx. Hanna Wilson (relict). (Acct: 27.227; ----; 1707)

SMITH, John. Admr.: William Willson. (Acct: 30.305; ----; 4 Feb 1709)

SMITH, Henry. Admr.: Madam Mary Contee (widow). (Acct: 31.41; ----; 9 April [c1710])

SMITH, Margarett, age 19 yrs. Servant of Edward Millstead, Nov 1710. (Ct.&Land: D#2.8)

SMITH, John Jr., son of John Smith; married Ann Hagon, dau. of Thomas Hagon. Memorandum (12 April 1713), between John Smith and Thomas Hagon. John Smith gives his son tract of 300 acres called *St. Katherine*. (Ct.&Land: D#2.70)

SMITH, John and Anne his wife conveyed on 9 June 1713 part of 1500 acres called *Fordam*, on w. side of Zachia Swamp, cont. 100 acres. (Ct.&Land: D#2.48)

SMITH, John and his wife Ann conveyed on 10 March 1713 parcel called *Jordan* on w. side of Zachia Swamp, cont. 35 acres. (Ct.&Land: F#2.3)

SMITH, Arther. (Inv.: 36A.175; [c1714]; ---)

SMITH, John. Deed of gift to his son in law John Moore of Prince George's Co. (planter), 20 Xber 1715; tract of land bounded by Geo. Ascomb and Zachia Swamp, cont. 200 acres. (Ct.&Land: F#2.81)

SMITH, Jno: To son Jno., dwelling plantation, 300 acres, and personalty after decease of testator's wife. To son Martha (son of son Jno.), personalty. To dau. Priscilla (wife of Jno. More), 200 acres. To dau. Elizabeth, 300 acres. To dau. Sarah, 300 acres. To wife Ann, dwelling plantation; at her decease to son Jno:. After her decease to child. afsd. Exs.: Sons Jno. Smith and Jno. More, jointly. (Will: 14.195; 13 April 1716; 16 Nov 1716) Next of kin: Thomas Hagan, James Hagan. (Inv.: 38A.17; 30 Jan 1716; ----)

SMITH, William. To eldest son William, £30. To son Elias, 100 acres adj. land of Rich: Estey's. To wife Priscilla, extx., dwelling plantation. (Will: 14.509; 7 Feb 1717; 12 March 1717) Next of kin: Elisabeth Barnaby, Elias Smith. (Inv.: 2.234; 3 June 1719; 15 July 1719)

SMITH, Samuel. To friend Mary, dau. of Bowling Speak, £4. Exs.: Richard Odeton and John Stapleton. (Will: 14.426; 18 Oct ----; 12 Nov 1717)

SMITH, William. (Inv.: 1.75, 10 June 1718; ----)

SMITH, Adam (Gent.) of Reading, county of Berks, Great Britain, elder brother ? of William Smith, who was the nephew and divisee of William Smith, late of Charles Co., Md., dec'd. Indenture, 28 June 1718, to James Stoddart of Prince George's Co.; parcel called *South Hampton* formerly in Charles Co., now in Prince George's Co., of 1000 acres, and 200 acres adjoining at the riverside nr. Maryland Point; also rest of the estate. (Ct.&Land: H#2.194)

SMITH, John. (Inv.: 3.314; [c1719/20]; ----)

SMITH, William, son of William Smith. Cattle mark recorded 28 Feb 1723. (Land: L#2.119)

SMITH, John son of Thomas Smith. Cattle mark recorded 8 May 1724. (Land: L#2.139)

SMITH, Richard. Mentions: George Dent. Administrator: (name not given). (Inv.: 11.22; ----; 17 Aug 1725)

SMITH, Thomas. Next of kin: Elias Smith (brother), Charles Somersett Smith. Admr.: Jane Smith. (Inv.: 18.278; 7 June 1734; 17 Jan 1734)

SMITH, Simon (nunc.). To son Simon and dau. Sarah, entire estate. Mentions son John and son in law Richard Wilson (who married dau. ———). Test: John Stokes (aged about 23). (Will: 20.40; ----; 30 June 1730) Next of kin: Richard Wilson, Sarah Smith. Admr.: Simon Smith. (Inv.: 15.641; 5 Sept 1730; 9 Sept 1730) Admr.: Simon Smith. (Inv.: 18.307; 20 Oct 1730; 17 July 1734)

SMITH, James. Next of kin: Richard Smith, W. Cage. Admr.: Elisabeth Smith. (Inv.: 19.61; 23 July 1734; 31 Aug 1734)

SMITH, Charles Somerset. Signed 14 Nov 1738. To his dau. Mary Smith, a mulatto child called James. (Land: O#2.374)

SMITH, Charles Somerset(t), Capt. To wife, extx., 1/3 personal estate. To son Richard, land on Southwest side of St. Nicholas's Ck. To son Charles Somerset Smith, land on n. side of sd. creek, where dwell. plant. stands. To Francis Wilkinson, he having married dau. Elizabeth, the moyety of *Wiltshire Plains*. To children, viz.: Richard, Charles Somerset, Ann, Dikanda, Mary and Jane, residue of personal estate. Overseer, bro. Walter. (Will: 22.23; 17 Nov 1738; 20 Feb 1738/9) Next of kin: Francis Wilkinson, William Wilkinson. Extx.: Margarett Smith. (Inv.: 24.183; 1 June 1739; 13 June 1739)

SMOOT, William (planter). Has 400 acres of land due him for transporting Elisabeth Ann and Aels Smoote, his daus., Elisabeth Wood, his wife's dau. — before 1651; parcel lying on w. side of Wicokomeco River, at head of branch called Smoote's Branch in the Manor of West St. Mary's. (Ct.&Land: B#1.99-100)

SMOOTE, William, age ca. 63 yrs. Swore in court 25 Sept 1661. (Ct.&Land: A#1.158)

SMOOT, Thomas. Acknowledged note to his father, William Smoote, where Thomas was to deliver up the child William Hungarford and his estate to his father during his life, 14 Nov 1665. (Ct.&Land: B#1.492)

SMOOTE, Elizabeth, dau. of Richard Smoote, born 15 Dec 1666. (Ct.&Land: C#1.252; P#1.204; QRev.2)

SMOOTE, Grace, wife of William Smoote, died 14 Jan 1666. (Ct.&Land: P#1.204; QRev.2. Ct.&Land C.252 has a date of 1665.)

SMOOTE, Richard. To eld. son Richard, home plantation at 21 yrs. of age. To 2nd son Edward, 100 acres, *Smoote's Purchase* at 21 yrs. of age. To five child., viz., Richard, Edward, Eliza:, William, and Ellinor, residue of estate, equally. Overseers: Brothers William Barton and Robt. Rowland. (Will: 5.157; 23 April 1676; 31 Oct 1676)

SMOOTE, William, age now 9 yrs. this instant June, son of Richard Smoote. To serve William Hatton until age 21, 8 June 1680. (Ct.&Land: H#1.299)

SMOOTE, William (planter). Indenture 17 May 1683, to Thomas Smoote, his brother; parcel formerly granted John Goldsmith of St. Mary's Co., lately dec'd, lying on w. side of Wicomico R., cont. 150 acres. (Ct.&Land: K#1.180)

SMOOTE, William (planter) and Anne his wife conveyed on 5 Aug 1684, part of a tract called *Wicomico Fields*, 105 acres. on west side of Wicomico River, and on 7 Aug 1686, part of tract called *The Hills* formerly occupied by Richard Smoot, dec'd., cont. 50 acres; and a parcel called *Wicomico Fields*, cont. 100 acres. Witnessed by Edward Smoot, Richard Smoot, Thomas Smoot, and Thomas Warren. (Ct.&Land: M#1.222; N#1.213)

SMOOTE, Edward and Lydia, of Wicomico. Their children: John, born 22 Nov 1686; Edward, born 20 June 1693. (Ct.&Land: QRev.12, 21)

SMOOTE, Thomas. To sons Thomas and Charles jointly, *Cabin*, 150 acres, *Gwinn's Choice*, 32 acres, *Bargain*, 21 acres - all on w. side Wiccomoco R. Mentions sons William and John Nathan; daus. Elizabeth, Rachell, Ann and Mary; eldest son Barton to be joint ex. together with bro. in law Lt. Col. William Barton. Should Col. Barton die during minority of sd. son Barton, Thomas Taney, Richard Harrison, Robert Yates and Wm. Herbert to assist in administration of estate. (Will: 3.486; 6 Jan 1704; 30 Jan 1704/5) (Inv.: 3.715; 13 April 1705; ----) Mentions: widow (unnamed, dead). Ex.: Barton Smoot. (Acct: 26.125; ----; 22 Nov 1706)

SMOOT, Edward. (Inv.: 27.84; ----; 16 Aug 1707)

SMOOT, Barton (planter) and Sarah his wife. Indenture 11 March 1712, to Henry Hawkins Jr., son of Sarah for love and affection; parcel called *Smith's Venture*; also tract formerly in possession of Richard Morris adjoining *Smith's Venture*, cont. 200 acres. (Ct.&Land: D#2.41)

SMOOT, Thomas. Next of kin: Barton Hungerford, Barton Smoot. (Inv.: 3.199; 20 Nov 1719; ----)

SMOOT, John and Postuma his wife conveyed on 7 Aug 1721, part of *Christian Temple Manor*, land bequeathed Postuma Smoot by the will of her father. (Ct.&Land: H#2.466)

SMOOT, William (planter). To son Thomas, personalty; to be under the charge of Mark Penn, ex., until 21 yrs. of age. To son William, personalty; to be under the charge of John Wilder until 21 yrs. of age. (Will: 19.12; 9 Nov 1726; 18 Nov 1726) Creditor: Thomas Smoot. Next of kin: Barton Smoot, Thomas Smoot. Ex.: Mark Penn. (Inv.: 11.824; 3 March 1726; 15 March 15 1726)

SMOOT, Thomas and his wife Abigail. Deed dated 13 Nov 1728; to Charles Smoot, tracts called, *Smoots Branch*, cont. 150 acres, and *Smoots Chance*, cont. 160 acres. (Land: L#2.462)

SMOOT(E), John. Next of kin: Lidia Smoot, James Smoot. Admr./Ex.: John Groves "(his wife, who is joined with him in the administration is not capable of riding at this time)." (Inv.: 13.352; 4 Dec 1728; 15 Dec 1728) Mentions: John Courts, George Dent. James Smith, Lydia Smoote, Alexander Hannay, Mark Penn. (Inv.: 14.37; ----; [c1729])

SMOOT, Barton and his wife Ann conveyed on 8 May 1731, tract called *Lomax's Addition*, cont. 30 acres. (Land: M#2.248)

SMOOT, Thomas and Abigal. Their children: Mary, born 17 May 1739; Arthur, born 16 Aug 1742. (Trinity: 107)

SMOOT, Barton. To wife Anne, divided plantation, and 200 acres of land at Port Tobacco, *Skipten*, 100 acres near Charles Baker's *Fishpond*. To son Barton, 200 acres *Brant's (?) Cliffs*; also *Mt. Clipsham*, cont. 68 acres; also 100 acres Marsh land; at his death to testator's grandson Henry Smoot, then to Geo: Smoot. To son Isaac, 88 acres called *Smoot's Delight*; 50 acres called *Smoot's Swamp*; 55 acres called *Smoot's Swamp Addition*; and 68 acres called *Lomax Addition*. To son William, 100 acres called *Barton's Hope*; 25 acres, part of *Daniel's Mount*; 100 acres called *Monday's Disappointment*. To son Thomas, ——. Residue of estate to be divided among my four sons and dau.: Thomas, Barton, Isaac, William, dau. Elizabeth Guyther. (Will: 23.662-664; 22 Sept 1744; 16 Jan 1744) Next of kin: Thomas Smoot, Charles Smoot. Exs.: Ann Smoot, Thomas Smoot. (Inv.: 31.31; 24 Jan 1744; 15 April 1745)

SMOOT, Thomas and his wife Elinor, and Ann Smoot (widow). To Revd. Henry Ogle (Gent.), Rector of Portobacco Parish, on 15 June 1745, lease of a tract called *Skipton*, cont. 200 acres. (Land: Z#2.48)

SMOOTH, Richard. Admr.: Mary Davis. (Acct: 6.504; ----; 24 Oct 1679)

SMOOTH, Edward. Admr.: Garrard Ocaine. (Acct: 28.128; ----; 19 June 1708)

SMOOTH, Thomas. Ex.: Barton Smooth. (Acct: 29.235; ----; 25 April 1709)

SNELL, Margaret, age 20 yrs. Servant of Ann Fowkes, 12 March 1672. (Ct.&Land: E#1.54)

SNETON, John, age 19 yrs. Servant presented by James Mackey, 8 March 1663/4. (Ct.&Land: B#1.259)

SNOSELL, Christopher, age 20 yrs. Man servant presented by Richard Stone, 8 March 1663/4. (Ct.&Land: B#1.257)

SNOWDEN, William, age 10 yrs. Servant of Jno: Vaudry, St. Mary's Co., 11 March 1678. (Ct.&Land: H#1.129)

SOLSBY (SALSBY), Nicholas. (Inv.: 1.58; 27 May 1674; ----) Admr.: John Allen. (Inv.: 1.138; 4 Dec 1674; ----) Admr.: John Allen. (Acct: 1.153; ----; 4 Dec 1674)

SOMMER, Jonathan. Judged to be 12 yrs. old, presented by Capt. Josias Fendall, 17 Dec 1662. (Ct.&Land: B#1.38)

SOTHERLAND, David, son of David and Elizabeth Sotherland, age ca. 19 years. On 15 Sept 1738 he said he was harrowing corn and his bro. Alexander Sotherland, then about 10 years of age, was leading the horses, which horse raised up and fell upon the sd. Alexander, and he saw the side of his head and face bloody and discovered that a piece of his right ear was gone. (Land: O#2.376)

SOTHORON, Richard. Admr.: Mrs. Mary Sothoron (widow). (Inv.: 26.18; 6 June 1706; ----) Admr.: Mary Russell, wife of Brutus Russell. (Acct: 28.124; ----; 20 May 1708)

SOTHORON, John. To son John Johnson (Southorn), that land, bought from Edward Barber by John Johnson, father of wife, also 135 acres, *Long Monkshire*. To son Samuell, two tracts in St. Mary's Co., plantation with mill. To son Richard, *Southerns Desire*. To son Charles, *Southorn's Hills*. To dau. Ann, lease of parts of Chaptico Manor in St. Mary's Co., and jointly with dau. Mary, 175 acres, *Southorn's Delight*. To wife Mary, extx., dwelling plantation part of *Two Friends*; at her decease to pass to young. son Benjamin. (Will: 13.402; 18 March 1711; 1 May 1712) Next of kin: Elisabeth Price, William Wells. (Inv.: 33B.140; 1 May 1712; -----)

SOTHORN, Benjamin. To Bro. Samuel Sothorn, *Two Friends*, cont. 125 acres, then to his [brother's] son, Leaven Sothorn. To bro. Samuel's sons, Richard Sothorn, and John Johnson Sothorn, personalty. Mentions sister Mary Clerk; dau. Elizabeth Sothorn; bro. Richard Sothorn; his son John Sothorn. Ex. not mentioned. Wit.: includes Elizabeth Clerk, Leonard Clark. (Will: 24.383; 21 Jan 1745; 4 April 1745)

SPAKE (See SPEAKE).

SPALDING (SPAULDING), John. To wife Priscilla, dwell. plantation *Collier Tone Manner*. Mentions youngest son Charles; son John, 100 acres of *Batchelors Rest*, in Clement's Bay Forest; sons William and Bassell at age 18. Mentions tracts *Five Brothers*, and *St. Giles*, St. Mary's Co., *Greens Inheritance*, nr. Port Tobba.; tract on Beavour Dam Mannour, St. Mary's Co. Mentions dau. Mary. Exs.: Wife and son John. One of the witnesses was Wm. Spalding. (Will: 19.23; 18 Jan 1724/5; 14 Sept 1726) [This will replaces 18.524.] Next of kin: Edward Spalding, Peter Spalding. Exs.: Priscilla Spalding, John Spalding. (Inv.: 11.704; 4 Nov 1726; 5 Jan 1726) (Inv.: 13.265; ----; 11 Dec 1727)

SPEAKS, John and Winifred his wife. Indenture 11 Aug 1685, from John Wheeler, father of said Winifred; parcel called *Plimoth* on a fresh of the Piscattaway River, cont. 350 acres. (Ct.&Land: L#1.178)

SPEAKE, James, son of John Speake. From Charles Shepherd, a heifer, signed 6 Jan 1691. (Ct.&Land: R#1.333)

SPEAKE, Richard, son of John Speake. Cattle mark recorded 8 Oct 1713. (Ct.&Land: D#2.61)

SPEAK, John, age 54. Deposition on 21 Xber 1719, regarding the tract *Christian Temple Mannour*. (Chas LandComm: M2.68)

SPEAKE, John and Winnifred his wife. Indenture, 28 Nov 1720, to their son Richard Speake; part of a parcel called *Reserve* in the woods at Chingamuxon, cont. 210 acres. Indenture, 28 Nov 1720, to their son Thomas Speake; part of a parcell called *Reserve*, cont. 143 acres. (Ct.&Land: H#2.400, 402)

SPEAKE, Richard, son of John Speak Jr. Mark recorded 8 April 1724, of cows and calves given him by his grandfather, Richard Wade. (Land: L#2.128)

SPEAKE, John Jr. and Elizabeth his wife. Deed dated 27 Jan 1722, to Richard Speake, part of two tracts: *Mackeys Park* and *Allinsons Supply*, 100 acres. Conveyed on 11 June 1729 part of a tract called *Mackeys Park* and on 28 May 1731, part of a tract called *Mackeys Park*, and part of a tract called *Allinsons Supply*; both bounded by Richard Speak's land. Deed dated 8 June 1731 to John Speake (innholder), father of afsd. John Speake Jr., tracts called *Allinsons Supply*, 200 acres, and *Mackey's Park*, 200 acres, to sd. John Speake Sr. and the heirs of Winifred (his late wife), and if her (Winifred) hrs. die before adults, then to hrs. of her father, John Wheeler. (Land: L#2.71; M#2.173, 255, 256)

SPEAK, John Sr. (innholder) of Chandler Town and Winifred his wife conveyed on 9 March 1725, two lots in Chandler Town. (Land: L#2.261)

SPEAKE, Richard, to his father John Speake. Deed recorded 10 Sept 1729; part of tract called *Reserve*, cont. 110 acres. (Land: M#2.172)

SPEAKE, Richard and his wife Theodocia conveyed on 8 Sept 1729 part of tract called *Reserve*, cont. 103 acres; and on 25 March 1734, a tract called *Maiden Fair*, cont. 450 acres. (Land: M#2.171; O#2.33)

SPEAKE, John (innholder) and his wife Mary conveyed on 20 April 1730 part of tract called *the Reserve*, cont. 383 acres. (Land: M#2.207)

SPEAKE, John, son of Thomas Speake. Cattle mark recorded Jan 13, 1731/2. (Land: M#2.274)

SPEAKE (SPAKE), John (innholder). To wife Mary, extx., lot and house in Charles Town; at her decease to grandson John, son of Thomas Speake; refers to his wife's former husband James Semmes. To sons John, Richard and Thomas and dau. Jane, wife of Edward Maddocke, residue of estate. (Will: 20.337; 4 Dec 1731; 1 Jan 1731) Next of kin: Thomas Speake, Edward Maddock. Exs.: John Speake, Richard Speake. (Inv.: 16.445; ----; 20 May 1732) (Inv.: 17.351; ----; [c1733])

SPEAKE, John, and his wife Elizabeth of Prince George's Co. 26 Dec 1734. To Daniel Bryan, a 10-year lease, 26 Dec 1734, of 240 acres called *Allison's Supply*. (Land: O#2.101. See also Land O#2.215.)

SPEAK(E), Bowling (planter), and his wife Mary, on 13 March 1743/4 conveyed part of the tract called *the Mistake*, cont. 250 acres. (Land: X#2.93)

SPEAKE, Mary, widow of John Speake. 12 June 1745. Leased a lot in Charles Town on 12 June 1745. (Land: Z#2.42)

SPERING, John (of Chester Co., Pennsylvania) and his wife Barbara, conveyed on 4 Feb 1718, part of tract on the n. side of the Piscataway River called *St. John's*, cont. 800 acres. (Ct.&Land: H#2.234)

SPICER, Haniball and his wife Elisabeth. Court held 26 October 1658, case of defamation. Court ordered six lashes, but Elisabeth alleging shie is with child, her whipping delayed until after delivery. (Ct.&Land: A#1.25-26)

SPURLING, Jeremiah. Servant of Henry Hawkins, age judged to be 18 yrs., 12 Jan 1685. (Ct.&Land: M#1.67)

ST. CLARE (See SAINT CLARE).

STAFFORD, Richard and his wife Rachael, conveyed on 15 Nov 1727, part of a tract called *Dukes Delight*, cont. 56 acres. Deed of gift signed 14 Nov 1732, to their son and daughter in law, Freeman Hagitt and his wife Alice, part of a tract called *Dukes Delight*, cont. 40 acres. Deed dated 9 June 1741, to John Hawkins Jr. (Gent.) of Prince George's Co., part of tract called *Dukes Delight*, cont. 164 acres. (Land: L#2.401; M#2.308; O#2.386B)

STAFFORD, William (planter), of Prince George's Co., and his wife Sarah, conveyed on 7 March 1744/5 a tract called *Safford Rest*, cont. 20 acres. (Land: Z#2.51)

STANDBURY, John. (Inv.: 34.46; 27 June 1713; ----)

STANDFORTH, Richard. Next of kin: Richard Anderson, John Anderson. Admr./Ex.: Jonathon Davis Jr. (Inv.: 26.215; 7 June 1740; 5 Sept 1741)

STANDIDGE (STANDISH), Alexander. Next of kin: none. (Inv.: 36B.293; 7 June 1715; ----) Admr.: Elisabeth Hawret, wife of Peter Hawret. (Acct: 37C.136; ----; 15 Aug 1716)

STANDLY, Thomas, age 14 yrs. Servant presented by Humphery Warren for John Piles, 8 March 1663/4. (Ct.&Land: B#1.258)

STANFIELD, Robert. Admr.: William Thimbley. (Inv.: 10.108; 22 June 1724; 25 Aug 1724)

STEARMAN, Richard, married the relict widow of Edmond Brent. Court held 17 Dec 1662. (Ct.&Land: B#1.43)

STEEDE, Thomas, age 13 yrs. in November next (bound to age 21). Servant of Richard Waye, 1678. (Ct.&Land: H#1.47)

STEPHENS, Mary, age 19 yrs. Servant of John Lambert, 10 March 1673. (Ct.&Land: E#1.152)

STEPHENS, Mary, age 19 yrs. Servant of Thomas Stonestreet, 13 June 1682. (Ct.&Land: I#1.293)

STEPHENS, Charles. Items in possession of Mary Sarjent (relict), now wife of William Sarjent. Appraisers: Richard Land, John Wheeler. (Inv.: 10.251; 17 Feb 1692; ----)

STEVENS, Kezia. Next of kin: none. (Inv.: 38A.165; 24 March 1717; ----)

STEPHENS, Richard, age 40. Deposition, 30 Aug 1720, regarding tract *Farthings Discovery*. (Chas LandComm: M2.99)

STEVENS, Esther (spinster). Indenture made 16 Dec 1740. Binds her son, James Stevens, now age one year, to John MacDonald (planter). (Land: O#2.364)

STEVENS, Henry (planter), and his wife Blanch conveyed on 15 March 1738/9, a tract called *Stevens Hope*, cont. 100 acres. (Land: O#2.390)

STEPHENSON, Issabella, of Whitehaven, County of Cumberland in Great Britain (spinster), dau. of William Stephenson, dec'd., in Virginia or Maryland (merchant), appointed William Dent of Nangemy in Maryland as her attorney. Signed 12 April 1743. (Land: X#2.53)

STUART, Elinor. Admr.: John Combes. (Acct: 11B.56; ----; 5 June 1700)

STEWARD (STUART), Daniell. (Inv.: 26.187; 12 March 1706; ----) Admr.: Ellinor Stuart. (Acct: 28.118; ----; 20 April 1708)

STEWARD, George, age 16 yrs. Servant of Walker Winter, Nov 1710. (Ct.&Land: D#2.8)

STUART (STEWARD), John. Admr.: Timothy Dunaway. (Inv.: 36A.243; [c1714]; ----) (Acct: 36B.331; ----; 7 June 1715) (Inv.: 39C.96; 22 Oct [c1717]; ----)

STUART, John, son of Daniel Stuart. Cattle mark recorded 2 March 1723. (Land: L#2.119)

STEWARD, Eleanor. Mentions dau. Katherine Mosgrove, granddau. Eleanor and granddau. Katherine Mosgrove; son John Parandier and granddau. Eleanor Criger; son James Parandier, ex. (Will: 20.207; 12 Oct 1725; 9 June 1731)

STEWARD, Daniel Sr. (planter). 3 Jan 1737/8. To his son William Steward, 84 acres, part of tract called *The Three Brothers*. (Land: O#2.311)

STUERT (STWERT), Daniel and his wife Mary on 4 Feb 1744/5 conveyed part of tract called *The Three Brothers*, cont. 83 acres. (Land: Z#2.19)

STIDMAN, Edward, age 14 yrs. Servant of Capt. Ignatius Causine, 12 June 1676. (Ct.&Land: G#1.37)

STIGELEER, Jane. Dau. of James Stigeleer and Mary his wife of Portobacco Parrish; born 4 June 1702. (Ct.&Land: Q#1.26, 123)

STIGELER, Jane, dau. of James Stigeler and Mary his wife of head of Wicomico. Cattle mark, 9 June 1707. (Ct.&Land: Z#1.272)

STICKLER (STIGELEARE), Mary. Next of kin: William Jackson. (Inv.: 35A.366; 1 April 1714; ----) Admr.: Stephen Mankin. (Acct: 36B.341; ----; 31 March 1715)

STINIT, Benjamin (house carpenter), and his wife Elizabeth, one of the three daus. of William Sanders and his wife Alice, the surviving heir of John Falkner, later of Charles Co. Deed dated 14 March 1733. To John King, the tract called *Cheerman's Purchase*. Said John Falkner and his wife Alice by their deed of 1689 leased 200 acres to Philip Lines, late of Charles Co., for 99 years. (Land: M#2.330)

STINNETT (STENNETT), Benjamin, and his wife Elizabeth, of Virginia, leased on 21 June 1737, 1/2 of a tract called *Hazard* on the head of Daniels Branch for 11 years. (Land: O#2.220)

STODDERT, James Jr., of Prince George's Co., Gent., and Elizabeth his wife, conveyed on 19 May 1720, a parcel called *Ruden* on the w. side of the Patuxent River, cont. 270 acres. (Ct.&Land: H#2.367)

STONE, William, Capt. To wife Verlinda, estate at St. Mary's. To eld. dau. Eliza Stone, 900 acres at Bustard's Island, Patuxent R., and 600 acres at *Nangemy*; that which testator formerly gave her in trust by his brother Sprigg Stone. To son Richard, 500 acres of *Nangemy Manor*, and cattle in consideration of that given him by his uncle, Richard Stone.

To son John, 500 acres of *Nangemy*. To son Mathew, 500 acres of *Nangemy*. To daus. Mary and Katharine, personalty. Eldest son Thomas, exs. Overseers and guardians of minor child: Gov. Josias Fendall, bro. in law Francis Doughty, and bro. Matthew Stone. (Will: 1.89; 3 Dec 1659; 21 Dec 1660)

STONE, Richard, age ca. 18 yrs. Swore in court 6 June 1660. (Ct.&Land: A#1.94)

STONE (Stoane), Elisabeth. Judged to be 14 yrs. old, presented by William Heard, 27 March 1662. (Ct.&Land: B#1.101)

STONE, Verlinda, Mrs. Appoints her son Richard Stone as attorney, 3 Feb 1663/4. (Ct.&Land: B#1.247)

STONE, Thomas and his wife Mary. Acknowledge 350 acres to be the right of Richard Smith. 9 Sept 1663. (Arch. of Md.: XLIX.58)

STONE, Thomas. Mentions his bro. John Stone and another bro. Richard Stone, 12 July 1664. (Ct.&Land: B#1.328-329)

STONE, Richard, brother of Mathew Stone. Gives to his brother his interests in land on the south side of the Sassafras River. 20 Dec 1664. (Arch. of Md.: XLIX.335)

STONE, Thomas and his wife Mary, of Poynton, in Chas. Co. Let to John Stone that plantation called Nangemie in Chas. Co. late in the occupation of Richard Stone. 28 May 1667. (Arch. of Md.: LXV.133)

STONE, Mathias, age 14 yrs. Servant of Archebald Walkup (Wahob), 10 March 1673. (Ct.&Land: E#1.152)

STONE, Mathew. Mentions John, son of Francis Fernly; Eliza: Cornahill. Exs.: Wm. Marshall Sr., Jonathan Marler. (Will: 1.523; 24 Dec 1672; 2 April 1673)

STONE, Verlinda. To Benony Thomas, 400 acres called *St. Verlindas*. To dau. —— Doyen, personalty. To son John, ex., residue of estate, at 21 yrs. of age. (Will: 2.364; 3 March 1674/5; 13 July 1675)

STONE, Matthew. Wife Margery, extx., sole legatee of estate. (Will: 5.97; 11 May 1676; 5 Oct 1676) Extx.: Marjery Maddock (relict), wife of Edward Maddock. (Acct: 7C.250; ----; 26 July 1682) (Ct.&Land: I#1.125) (Inv.: 2.258; 14 Aug 1676; ----)

STONE, Thomas. To wife Mary, extx., estate in trust for children:, son Richard, plantation now leased by Symon Stevens, and part of *Pointon Manor* at 18 yrs. of age; son William, residue of lands at 18 yrs. of age. Test: Jno. Stone, Eliza Stone. (Will: 5.94; 24 April 1676; 5 Oct 1676)

STONE, John. To sons Thomas and Walter, dwelling plantation, 500 acres, part of *Poynton Manor*, and 80 acres, *St. John's*. To sons Matthew and John, *Mangawoman*, cont. 500 acres. To daus. Ellinor and Eliza:, 400 acres, *Durum*. Exs.: Wife Ellinor together with son Thomas; son to administer upon his own estate and that of his two bros., Matthew and John, and wife to administer upon her estate and her children's. (Will: 6.153; 17 Sept 1697; 10 Aug 1698) (Inv.: 17.6; [c1697/8]; ----) (Inv.: 17.11; 16 Dec 1697; ----) Mentions: seven children (unnamed). Admr.: Dorothy Stone (widow). (Acct: 18.88; ----; 21 March 1698)

STONE, John. Mentions brother Matthew, Ann Bayne and Ann Fowlkes. Brother Thomas, ex. (Will: 11.361; 27 Jan 1702; 1 June 1703)

STONE, John, son of John Stone (cooper), in "ye manor." Cattle mark recorded 9 Sept 1707. (Ct.&Land: Z#1.260)

STONE, William, age 52. Deposition, 12 Aug 1719, regarding *Glovers Point*. (Chas LandComm: M2.48)

STONE, William, age 50. Deposition, 2 Nov 1719, regarding tract near Nanjemy called *Moulds Adventure*. (Chas LandComm: M2.63)

STONE, Thomas (Capt.), age 44. Deposition in 1721 (petition of William Stone Sr.) regarding tract called *Paynton Manor*. (Chas LandComm: M2.137)

STONE, William Sr., one of the petitioners, age 55. Deposition in 1721 regarding tract called *Paynton Manor*. (Chas LandComm: M2.138)

STONE, William (Gent.) and his wife Theodosia. Deed dated 25 Nov 1723. To Joseph Harrison son of Richard Harrison, for 20 shillings and for sd. Joseph Harrison's marrying his dau. Virlinda, tract called *Virlinda's*, formerly held and occupied by Benoni Thomas who died without issue and the land became the right of said William Stone by the will of Virlinda Stone, dec'd. (patentee of sd. land), 300 acres. (Land: L#2.108)

STONE, Matthew (Gent.) and his wife Rachel conveyed on 23 May 1726 part of a tract, on w. side of main fresh of Nanjemy Creek, cont. 100 acres. (Land: L#2.283)

STONE, Thomas [Sr.] of Nanjemy Parrish. Mentions children David and Mary, grandson Gerrard Fowke, wife Katherine, extx. (Will: 19.254; 25 May 1727; 7 Nov 1727) Next of kin: Mathew Stone, William Stone. Extx.: Mrs. Catherine Stone. (Inv.: 13.311; 23 Nov ----; [c1727/8])

STONE, William. Next of kin: William Stone, Thomas Stone. Admr.: Eleanor Stone. (Inv.: 13.9; 4 Dec 1727; 4 March 1727/8)

STONE, William. To eldest son Thomas, plant. beginning at mouth of Could Spring Branch and plantation adj. land of cousin David Stone and Gerd. Fowke. To dau. Mary, plant. where she and her husband Thomas Matthews now live, adj. lands of cousin Matthew Stone and Robert Doyne; and 1/2 of *O'Neales Dezearts*. To youngest son Richard, residue of dwell. plan. *Poynton Manner*. To dau. Verlinda Harrison, 100 acres *Dover's Clifts*, tract bou. of Martin Campbell and Mary, his wife; 39 acres adj. to *Dover Clifts*. To dau. Theodosia, other half of *O'Neales Dezearts* and part of *Market Overton* at Pomankka. To dau. Pretious (Precious) Jones, 300 acres called *Millner*, and 113 acres called *Langham's Rest*, Prince George's Co. To youngest dau. Bethia Barnes, 143 acres, *Stone's Rest*, and 1/2 of *Market Overton*. Mentions wife Theodosia. [Proviso regarding son Thomas and plantation where his bro. William lived and Daniel McDaniell now lives.] Exs.: Wife and sons Thomas and Richard. (Will: 20.221; 17 April 1730; 12 Aug 1731) Next of kin: John Manning, Matthew Stone. Exs.: Mrs. Theodosia Stone, Thomas Stone, Richard Stone. (Inv.: 16.321; 22 Sept 1731; 10 Nov 1731)

STONE, Richard. Signed 23 Sept 1734. Leased for 15 yrs., part of a tract called *Pointon Manor*. Refers to his bro. Thomas Stone. (Land: O#2.76)

STONE, Mathew (Gent.). 30 Jan 1737/8. To his son John Stone, part of a tract called *Pointon Manor*, 100 acres. (Land: O#2.313)

STONE, Thomas (Gent.), and his wife Margery, on 12 Nov 1740 leased 1 acre, lying on w. side of Stones Run. (Land: O#2.483)

STONE, Mathew Sr. (planter) and his wife Rachael. 8 Jan 1741/2. To Barton Stone, part of *Pointon Manor*, 75 acres. (Land: O#2.428. Also see Land O#2.429.)

STONEHOUSE, Thomas, age 13 yrs. Servant of Richard Pinner, 8 June 1675. (Ct.&Land: F#1.101)

STONESTREET, Thomas Sr. (planter) of Prince George's Co. Indenture, 11 June 1706, to Thomas Stonestreet Jr., of Prince George's Co., younger son of Thomas Sr., part of *Birth Denn*, 150 acres. (Ct.&Land: C#2.7)

STONESTREET, Thomas. To son Edward, ex., dwell. plant. and land 100 acres, *Morrises Helpe*, 50 acres of which is in a lease from Joseph Pile Sr. Said land to pass to grandson Buttler, son of Thomas Stonestreet, To grandson Thomas Mastin, personalty. (Will: 12.77; 14 Oct 1706; 13 Nov 1706) (Inv.: 26.189; 11 Jan 1706; ----) Ex.: Edward Stonestreet. (Acct: 27.139; ----; 1 Oct 1707) Legatees: Robert Hager, Thomas Stonestreet, Sarah Tedman. Ex.: Edward Stonestreet. (Acct: 28.95; ----; 18 Dec 1707)

STONESTREET, Thomas and Christian. Child.: Butler, born 26 Aug 1703; Edward, born 23 Dec 1705; Thomas, born 7 June 1708; and Anne, born 23 March 1710. (King George's Parish: p. 248)

STONESTREET, Thomas. Legatees: Sarah Sedman, Thomas Stonestreet. Ex.: Thomas Stonestreet. (Acct: 32B.258; ----; 25 June 1711)

STONESTREET, Thomas and Christian his wife. Authorize William Hickford Leman to handle conveyance of a parcel called *Birch Denn* of 150 acres, 9 March 1713/14. (Ct.&Land: D#2.84)

STONESTREET, Thomason, dau. of Thomas and Mary Stonestreet, born 2 June 1741. (Trinity: 109)

STORY, Anne, widow and extx. of Walter Story, one of the exrs. of Anne Lynes, sole extx. of Philip Lynes. John Marten, exr. of Michael Marten, who was joint exr. with afsd. Walter Story, of will of sd. Anne Lynes. Deed dated 14 June 1727; to John King (shipwright). John Falkner, late of Charles Co., and his wife Alice, by their deed of 17 Dec 1689, leased to afsd. Philip Lynes for 99 years, 200(?) acres called *Charomans Purchase*. They now sell the remaining time of lease. (Land: L#2.360)

STORY, Walter and Mary his wife. Indenture, 5 June 1719, to John Magrah; parcel called *Preston*, cont. 60 acres; also *The Wilderness*, cont. 50 acres. (Ct.&Land: H#2.268).

STORY, Walter who married the relict of Thomas Dixon. Plantation of said Dixon viewed by panel, 14 May 1720. (Ct.&Land: B#2.347).

STORY, Walter. Mentions grandson Walter Hanson; wife Ann; daus. Sarah Douglas, Elizabeth, Charity and Jane. Exs.: Wife Ann and Robert Yates. (Will: 18.498; 2 March 1725/6; 4 April 1726) Next of kin: Sarah Douglas, Elisabeth Story. Extx.: Mrs. Ann Story. (Inv.: 12.29; 10 April 1727; 3 June 1727)

STOREY, Ann. Next of kin: Robert Martin. Admr./Ex.: John Dixon. (Inv.: 16.302; 26 June 1731; 22 Oct 1731)

STORY, Elizabeth, dau. of Col. Walter Story conveyed on 16 Oct 1739, part of tract called *Stump Dall* and 1/4 of tract called *Brandts Discovery*, both tracts in William and Mary Parish. (Land: O#2.417)

STRATTON, Luci. Court held 24 Nov 1658, identifies Arthur Turner as father of her child; she could not prove her charge, court orders thirty lashes. (Ct.&Land: A#1.32)

STRATTON, Philise. Judged to be 19 yrs. old, presented by Henry Warren, 14 March 1664. (Ct.&Land: B#1.436)

STRINGER, George, age 15 yrs. Servant of Henry Hawkins, 8 Jan 1677. (Ct.&Land: G#1.85)

STROMAT, John Baptist. Next of kin: John Stromat, Con. Hibeart. Admr.: Elisabeth Stromat. (Inv.: 19.63; 3 Aug 1734; 18 Sept 1734)

STROMATT, John and William Williams, passed bonds to warrant their abiding by the determination of arbiter, Richard Harrison, relating to John Stromatt's right of his wife Ann, relict of William Williams, father of afsd. William Williams, of two tracts called *Frankum* and *Williams' Addition*. Signed by Richard Harrison 26 Jan 1744/5. (Land: Z#2.30)

STUART/STUERT/STWERT (See STEWARD.)

SUDBERIE, Gregorie, age 16 yrs. Servant of Robert Hunley, 9 June 1668. (Ct.&Land: C#1.268)

SUMMERS, William. (Inv.: 1.68; 17 May 1716; ----)

SUTCLIF(F) (SETTELF), John. To Jane Wright, personalty. To wife Anne, extx. (Will: 23.297; 7 April 1739; 24 Nov 1743) Extx.: Ann Sutclif. (Inv.: 29.169; ----; 31 May 1744)

SWAINE, George, age 14 yrs. Servant of Capt. Josias Fendall, 1676. Presented by his bro., Samuel Fendall. (Ct.&Land: F#1.193)

SWANN, Thomas Sr. of Prince George's Co., age about 49 years. Depositions recorded 21 Feb 1723; states his father, Edward Swann, about 30 years previously, showed him the first bounded tree of tract called *Eaglton*. Samuel Swann, aged about 47 years, stated his bro., Thomas Swann Sr., showed him the bounded tree. Witnesses present at the bounded tree this date, 21 Feb 1723 include Joseph Ward and Benjamin Ward, sons of Wm. Ward Sr.; James Swann, son of Thos. Swann Sr. and Mary Lewis dau. of Thos. Lewis. (Land: L#2.115-116)

SWANN, Thomas and his wife Abigal conveyed on 17 July 1732 a tract called *Egleton*, cont. 12 acres. (Land: M#2.298)

SWANN, Samuel. To son Edward, 80 acres called *Egleton*. To sons Samuel and Mercer; dau. Sarah Dyer, personalty. Mentions son Burch; daus. Susanna ———, Elizabeth Wheeler and Barbara Muggleston. Exs.: Wife Anne and son Edward. (Will: 23.136; 17 April 1743; 1 June 1743) Next of kin: Burch Swann, Edward Swann. Extx.: Ann Swann. (Inv.: 28.161; -- --- 1743; 17 Aug 1743)

SWANN, Thomas. Next of kin: James Swann Jr., John King. Admr.: Abigail Swann. (Inv.: 28.162; 24 Aug 1743; 27 Aug 1743)

SWATEWELL, John. Ex.: Dr. Mordecay Moore of Anne Arundel County. (Acct: 19.168; ----; 10 July 1699)

SWEEN, Sarah, age 20 yrs. Servant of Francis Goodwick, 12 March 1677. (Ct.&Land: G#1.119)

SWINBURNE (SWINEBURNE), Nicholas. (Inv.: 8.440; 25 Aug 1685; ----) Admr./Ex.: Edward Rookewood. (Acct: 9.28; ----; 10 July 1686)

SYMPSON (See SIMPSON).

SYZOR, Phillip. Admr./Ex.: Mrs. Elinor Bayne. (Inv.: 10.262; 1691; ----)

TAFT, Thomas. (Inv.: 14.17; 14 May 1696; 10 July 1696)

TAILOR. (See TAYLOR.)

TALFORD, Charles. Next of kin: John Payne Jr., Edmund Bury Payne. Admr.: Elisabeth Talford. (Inv.: 11.920; 20 April 1727; 20 May 1727)

TALLOR. (See TAYLOR.)

TANNER, Henry, age 70 odd years. Deposition, 20 Aug 1719, regarding *Saint Davids*. (Chas LandComm: M2.50)

TANNER, Henry (cooper) and Anne his wife conveyed on 22 Dec 1719, a part of a tract called *St. Thomas*. On 14 Feb 1719 Henry and Anne conveyed another parcel of the tract *St. Thomas*, cont. 228 acres. (Ct.&Land: H#2.304, 418)

TANNER, Henry, age 82. Deposition in 1721 regarding tract called *Paynton Manor*. (Chas LandComm: M2.137)

TANNER, Henry. Mentions wife Ann, son Joseph, son John, son Henry and daus. Ann and Elizabeth. Exs.: William Williams and Joseph Chambers. (Will: 20.206; ----; 8 June 1731) Next of kin: Joseph Tanner, Ann Webb. Extx.: Ann Tanner. (Inv.:16.409; 19 July 1731; 11 March 1731) Creditors include Joseph Tanner. Next of kin: Ann Webb, James Tanner. Admr.: Elleanor Tanner. (Inv.: 21.171; 15 July 1735; 5 Nov 1735)

TANNER, Henry (planter), son of Henry Tanner, dec'd. 12 June 1734. To Thomas Hudson, tract called *Tanners Discovery*, 87 acres; and by deed dated 13 July 1738 to Thomas Hudson, parcel of land bounded by the south line of St. Barbary's Manor, 48 acres; and any tracts that his father, died possessed of. (Land O#2.50B, 340)

TANSHALL, Margarett, dau. of Edward Tanshall. Cattle mark recorded 1678. (Ct.&Land: H#1.185)

TANSHALL, Edward. Cattle mark recorded, 13 Sept 1681 for his sons: John and Thomas. (Ct.&Land: I#1.173)

TARLINE, Richard, age ca. 23 yrs. Deposition in court 23 Oct 1660; mentions his master Hennery Lilly. (Ct.&Land: A#1.108)

TARLINE, Richard, age ca. 25 yrs. and his wife (unnamed). Swore in court 24 Sept 1661. (Ct.&Land: A#1.153)

TARLIN, Mary, age ca. 24 yrs. Swore in court 11 Feb 1662. (Ct.&Land: B#1.89-90)

TARVIN, Richard. To wife Elizabeth, extx., dwelling plantation *Matiawoman*. To son George, 100 acres called *Laurel Branch*. To sons Richard and John, 300 acres called *St. Micholass* at Port Tobacco. To son William, 150 acres called *Laurel Branch*. To son Thomas, plant. at death of his mother. To daus. Elizabeth, Ann and Rebecca, personalty. (Will: 23.45; 8 Dec 1742; 27 Dec 1742)

TARVIN, Richard. Mentions eldest bro. George; sis. Martha Noble; godson Richard; bro. John; mother Elizabeth, extx. (Will: 23.448; 14 Jan 1743/4; 26 March 1744) Next of kin: George Dent, G. Tarvin. Extx.: Elisabeth Tarvin. (Inv.: 29.342; ----; 14 Aug 1744)

TATE, George. Admr.: John Glasshon. (Inv.: 11.426; 11 April 1726; 16 July 1726)

TATTERSHALL (TOTTERSHALL), Charles. Next of kin: William Carter, Philip Tottershall. (Inv.: 32A.66; 10 Feb 1709; ----) Admr.: Thomas Tattershall. (Acct: 32B.8; ----; 8 Dec 1710)

TATTERSALL, Philip. Next of kin: John Thomas, Thomas Thomas. (Inv.: 33A.121; 31 Dec 1711; ----) Admrix.: Terasha Tattersall. (Acct: 34.217; ----; 13 May 1713)

TATTERSHELL, William. Deed recorded 5 June 1730 from Simon Reader to Joseph Chambers; tract being part of a tract given to William Tattershell, and left by sd. Tattershell to his bro. James Tant, bounded by the land laid out for Wm: Tattershell, at the mouth of Coles Creek, cont. 200 acres. (Land: M#2.217)

TAYLOR, Jheromie, age 21 yrs. Presented by John Lumbroso, 8 March 1663/4. (Ct.&Land: B#1.259)

TAYLOR, Elizabeth, age 19-20 yrs. Servant of Alexander Smyth, 11 June 1667. (Ct.&Land: C#1.164)

TAYLOR, Morgan. Admr.: Thomas Notley. (Inv.: 1.57; 30 May 1674; ----) Admr.: Thomas Notley. (Acct: 1.62; ----; 6 Sept 1674)

TAYLOR, Richard, age 16 yrs. Servant of John Posie, 11 Jan 1675. (Ct.&Land: F#1.163)

TAYLOR, George, age 14 yrs. Servant of William Porfit, 11 April 1676. (Ct.&Land: F#1.173)

TAYLOR, Thomas, age 13 yrs. Servant of George Godfrey, 12 June 1676. (Ct.&Land: G#1.37)

TAYLOR, Edmond. To unborn child of Eliza: Bossell, personalty. To Henry Norton, 1/3 of personal estate. Charles Cullis, ex. of estate. (Will: 5.160; 26 Nov 1676; 22 Feb 1676/7) Ex.: Charles Cullis. (Acct: 4.403; ----; 11 Oct 1677)

TAYLOR, Samuell of Prince George's Co., and Verlinda his wife, one of the daus. of Robert Doyne (Gent.), conveyed on 9 Jan 1702, two tracts: 550 acres patented 9 June 1676 called *Rotterdam*, and tract called *The Indian Towne*, 600 acres, conveyed 11 March 1685 by William Whittington (Gent.), of Accomack, Virginia, now of Somerset Co. Robert Doyne died intestate and his children were Wharton, William, Sarah, Virlinda, Ellinor and Mary; estate descended to Wharton as eldest son. William inherited this land at the death of Wharton; William died intestate and Virlinda who married Samuel Taylor inherited 1/4 of the land. (Ct.&Land: Z#1.8)

TAYLOR (TAYLER), Thomas and Anne, of Pickawaxon. Their children: John, son, born 8 Jan 1692; Thomas, born 3 March 1694. (Ct.&Land: P#1.211; QRev.19, 24)

TAILOR, William. Admr.: Magdalene Tailor. (Acct: 16.245; ----; 20 Nov 1697)

TAYLOR (TALLOR), Thomas (planter). Admr.: Ann Taylor. (Inv.: 17.110; 15 Oct 1698; ----) (Acct: 19½A.97; ----; 3 Feb 1699) Admr./Ex.: widow (unnamed), wife of John Gwin. (Acct: 19½B.113; ----; 25 April 1700)

TAYLOR, Thomas (tailor) and Barbara his wife conveyed to John Speake Jr. on 17 April 1719, two tracts on Chingamuxon Creek called *Allinsons Supply* and *Machies Park*, cont. 135 acres; and on 15 May 1722, tract called *Allinsons Supply* on s. side of Chinquamuxon Creek, 200 acres, and tract called *Mackey Park*, 200 acres. (Ct.&Land: H#2.243; Land: L#2.17)

TAYLOR, Robert, age 53. Deposition, 6 Dec 1720, regarding tract called *Friendship*. (Chas LandComm: M2.107)

TAYLOR, Thomas. Next of kin: Tubman Mankin. Admr.: Sarah Taylor. (Inv.: 11.20; 20 Aug 1725; 8 Sept 1725)

TAYLOR, Henry. One of the witnesses to the will of Henry Tanner was Henry Taylor (Tayler) who died before probate in 1731. (Will: 20.206; --—; 8 June 1731)

TAYLER (TAYLOR), William (planter). To Henry Acton Jr., ex., entire estate. (Will: 20.842; 2 Nov 1733; 22 Nov 1733) Next of kin: John Taylor Sr. Ex.: Henry Acton. (Inv.: 18.308; 11 Dec 1733; 17 July 1734)

TAYLOR, John. Mentions wife Eliza:, extx., son James, minors. (Will: 21.9; 20 Feb 1733; 2 April 1734) Next of kin: John Pigeon, John Roy. Extx.: Elisabeth Taylor. (Inv.: 18.306; 15 July 1734; 15 July 1734)

TAYLOR, James. Admr.: Hannah Ewing, wife of Samuel Ewing. (Inv.: 18.281; 26 June 1734; ----)

TAYLOR, William Smallwood (planter) and his wife Mary. 9 May 1741. To John Sanders, son of John Sanders, dec'd. In consideration of a parcel (which is part of a tract called *Christian Temple Manor* at Mattawoman) that was purchased by deed of John Smoot and Posthuma his wife by the afsd. John Sanders, dec'd.; and by the will of sd. John Sanders devised to his afsd. son John Sanders who by deed dated today conveyed the same to sd. William Smallwood Taylor; Taylor sells a tract called *Williams Purchase*, 195 acres, originally granted to William Seargent and by him sold to afsd. John Sanders, dec'd., who by his will devised it to his dau., the aforementioned Mary. (Land: O#2.507)

TAYLOR, Ann. Next of kin: Edward Maddox, Phile: Clements. Admr.: William Smallwood Taylor. (Inv.: 30.148; 18 Nov 1744; 17 Dec 1744)

TEARES, Elizabeth, dau. of Hugh Teares. Cattle mark, 25 Aug 1694. (Ct.&Land: S#1.334)

TEARES, Hugh of Nanjemy. Mentions wife Ellinor, extx.; dau Eliza:; Ann Bayne Jr., and Ebsworth Bayne; Henry and Ruth Hawkins; Ellinor and Eliza: Stone; Charles and Edward Philpot Jr. Certain personalty which belonged to dec'd wife is bequeathed to dau. Eliza: afsd. Proviso for glebe land to be given to the churches at Newport and Portobacco in King and Queens' Parish. (Will: 11.189; 23 Jan 1699; 20 Feb 1699) (Inv.: 21.262; 23 Feb 1699; ----)

TENNIS [TENNISON], Justinian. He left to daus. Barbara, Mary, Catherine, Eliza:, Sarah, and Dracie, son John, and grandchild John Mansfield at 21 yrs. of age, personalty. Wife (unnamed), extx. His estate to pass to dau. Christian at wife's decease. (Will: 6.251; 23 Jan 1699; 8 July 1699)

TENNISON (TENESON), Justinian. His eldest brother, John Teneson, was born in Holland and his mother was big with child with him when they went to England to Yarmouth where Justinian was born. Deposition of John Vadry, 13 Aug 1720, recalling statement of Justinian Teneson, made about 40 yrs. ago. (Ct.&Land: H#2.366, 415) John Noe, age ca. 21 yrs., on 14 June 1720, said that he heard Justinian Tennison say he was born in Weymouth, England. (Ct.&Land: H#2.415)

TENESON, Samuel, St. Mary's Co., and his wife Elizabeth, conveyed on 2 May 1726 part of tract called *Westwood Mannor*, 100 acres. Also, one tract of land nr. Mattawoman Creek called *Lumber Street*, cont. 100 acres. (Land: L#2.287)

TENNISON, Sarah. Her sons Jesse Tennison and Ignatius Tennison, of Prince George's Co., conveyed on 24 July 1745, part of tract called *Strife*, 135 acres, Sarah Tennison to remain on part of the land. Releases of dower by Rachel Tennison, wife of Jesse Tennison, and Elizabeth Tennison, wife of Ignatius Tennison. (Land: Z#2.67)

THATRYER (THATCGER?) Mary, age 19 yrs. Servant of John Clarke, 11 March 1678. (Ct.&Land: H#1.130)

THEOBALDS, Clement. Deed of gift dated 8 July 1662 to his dau. Elisabeth, a heifer. (Ct.&Land: A#1.236)

THEOBALD, Clement. (Inv.: 4.507; 9 June ----; 4 July 1676) Distribution to: James Wheeler who married the widow of Thomas Corker. Administratrix.: Thomas Corker is the administrator of Clement Theobald and Elisabeth Wheeler is the executrix of Thomas Corker. (Acct: 4.509; ----; 26 Oct 1677)

THEOBALDS, Clement. Mentions: William Thomas. Admr.: Penelope Morris. (Acct: 8.275; 20 July 1682; ----) "killed by the strock of a horse." Admr.: Richard Morris. (Acct: 8.85; ----; 1 Aug 1683)

THEOBALDS, John, son of John and Mary Theobald(s) of Portobacco, born [blank] Sept 1692. (Ct.&Land: QRev.20)

THEOBALDS, John (planter). To eld. son William [minor] dwelling plantation, two tracts, viz., 50 acres, *Betty's Delight* and 100 acres, *Planter's Delight* and a mare branded H. S. To son John, 100 acres, *Greens* on w. side main branch of Portobacco Creek, about two miles from head of sd. Creek, and mare formerly belonging to Penelope Theobald. To dau. Mary and to dau. Charity, at 16 yrs. or marriage, personalty. Wife Mary, extx. (Will: 13.540; 18 Oct 1712; 24 July 1713) (Inv.: 35A.55; [c1713]; --) Extx.: Mary Theobald. (Acct: 36A.241; ----; 22 July 1714)

THEOBALDS, John. Creditors include Charity Theobalds. Next of kin: William Theobalds, John Muschett. Admr./Ex.: Eliza: Theobalds. (Inv.: 27.216; ----; 16 Nov 1742)

THEOBALD, Elizabeth (widow). Recorded 26 Dec 1743. To her children: Elizabeth Theobalds, Negro girl named Juda, age 2 years, at age 16; Samuel Theobalds, Negro girl named Lucy, age 5 years, at age 21; and Jane Theobalds, a Negro girl named Monica, age 3 years, at age 16. (Land: X#2.51)

THOMAS, Hugh (Hewgh), age ca. 24 yrs. Swore in court 1 Oct 1662. (Ct.&Land: A#1.247)

THOMAS, Anne, age 22 yrs. Servant of John Buttler, 11 Jan 1675. (Ct.&Land: F#1.163)

THOMAS, John. To John Wall, ex. in Stafford County, entire estate. (Will: 2.101; 17 April 1680; 11 Aug 1680)

THOMAS, Edward, age 12 yrs. Servant of Capt. Ignatius Causene, 11 Aug 1685. (Ct.&Land: L#1.161)

THOMAS, William and his wife Susanna conveyed on 8 Feb 1673 a tract called *Thomas His Chance*, cont. 200 acres. (Ct.&Land: E#1.160)

THOMAS, Susanna, relict of William Thomas. Requests probate of his will, 10 Nov 1691. (Ct.&Land: Q#1.44)

THOMAS, William. Will proved 10 Nov 1691. To son John Thomas, 100 acres of *Mannis Cledre*. To my three children, George, Guyott and Elizabeth, remainder of parcel. To wife Susanna, half of the 100 acres "I now live on" and other half to son William Thomas. To dau. Mary, a colt. (Ct.&Land: Q#1.44)

THOMAS, Anne (widow). Petitions court for freedom of her dau., Elizabeth Thomas; Thomas Mitchell (master) and his wife Mary, 8 March 1691. (Ct.&Land: R#1.372)

THOMAS, Ann, dau. of George Thomas. Cattle mark recorded, 16 March 1713. (Ct.&Land: D#2.82)

THOMAS, James. To wife Teratia, extx., entire estate. At her decease estate, including 300 acres, *Ware*, formerly in Calvert Co. and now in Chas. Co., on w. side Patuxent R., to pass to their children, viz., John and Thomas and Anna Mary, equally. (Will: 11.196; 7 June 1701; 10 Dec 1701) (Inv.: 21.372; 26 April 1702; ----) Admrix.: Tracey Thomas. (Acct: 21.381; ----; 17 June 1702)

THOMAS, John. Appraisers: Thomas Stone, Edward Williams. Next of kin: Thomas Stone, William Watkins. (Inv.: 35A.245; 19 Jan 1713; ----)

THOMAS, William (planter). Presented for unlawfully cohabiting with Anne Coleson, wife of Robert Coleson, Aug 1711. (Ct.&Land: D#2.190)

THOMAS, John. Payments mention Benoni Thomas. Admr.: Marjery ———, relict of Francis Lynn. (Acct: 36B.95; ----; 5 March 1714)

THOMAS, Benony. To wife Katharine, extx., estate, including tract of land in Stafford Co., Virginia, at hd. of Poluck Ck., *Acquinkekas Hill* at Pomokey, Prince George's Co., and land, at head of Bordick's Ck. (Will: 13.678; 10 Oct 1711; 25 Feb 1713)

THOMAS, Benoni, Capt. Next of kin: Thomas Stone, Matthew Stone. (Inv.: 36A.62; 29 June 1714; ----)

THOMAS, Richard. Next of kin: Thomas Stone, William Watkins. (Inv.: 35A.244; 15 March 1713; ----) Admr.: Marjery Lynn (administratrix of Francis Lynn (administrator of deceased)). (Acct: 36B.99; ----; 5 March 1714)

THOMAS, William, age 50. Deposition, 20 Aug 1719, regarding tract called *Saint Davids*. (Chas LandComm: M2.50)

THOMAS, William, age 50. Deposition, 29 Sep 1719, regarding the tract *Martins Freehold*. (Chas LandComm: M2.52)

THOMAS, Susannah, age 59. Deposition, 29 Sep 1719, based on the information of John Courts, grandfather of the petitioner (John Courts), regarding tract *Martins Freehold*. (Chas LandComm: M2.58)

THOMAS, George, age 45. Deposition, 29 Sep 1719, regarding the tract *Martins Freehold*. (Chas LandComm: M2.58)

THOMAS, William, age 50. Deposition in 1721 regarding tract called *Wadestones Enlargement* in Durham Parish. [In a second deposition re same tract in 1721 his age is give as 52.] (Chas LandComm: M2.131)

THOMAS, Susannah. Mentions son George, dau. Elizabeth Adams, son William. Ex.: Son Thomas (sic). T. P. shows son William to have been appointed. (Will: 18.335; 20 Feb 1723/4; 31 Aug 1724)

THOMAS, William. Cattle mark recorded for his son Geo. Salisbury Thomas, on 24 June 1725. (Land: L#2.227)

THOMAS, William. Next of kin: Mary Pirrie, George Thomas. Admr.: Jane Thomas. (Inv.: 15.300; 19 Nov 1729; 5 Dec 1729)

THOMAS, Thomas. He left to eld. son James part of *Ware*. To son Thomas, *Thomas's Fancy*. Wife Elizabeth, extx., residue of *Ware*. Mentions son William and four daus.: Elizabeth, Sophia, Teresa, Sophonia and unborn child. Codicil: 18th May 1734, refers to three sons and five daus. (Will: 21.216; 6 March 1733; 22 Oct 1734) Next of kin: James Thomas, Thomas Thomas. Extx.: Elisabeth Thomas. (Inv.: 20.317; 19 Nov 1734; 19 Feb 1734)

THOMAS, George. To eldest son James, 200 acres of *Godfrey's Chace* [sic], where he now lives. To son George, 120 acres of *Saint George*. To dau. Brooks, 200 acres *Thomas' Port*. To dau. Susannah Farr, pt. of tract where she now lives. To dau. Elizabeth Tompkins, personalty. To grandson Benjamin Compton, 86 acres where his mother lived. To son William, 94 acres *Bowen's Dispute*. To son Benjamin, ex., residue of estate, sd. son to care of Capt. Benjamin Douglas, and son George, until he arrives at age of 21. (Will: 22.20; 21 Nov 1738; 22 Dec 1738) Mentions: James Thomas, William Thomas. Admr.: George Thomas. (Inv.: 24.42; 13 Jan 1738; 6 April 1739)

THOMAS, Joseph. Next of kin: Mathew Cooffer, Henry Cooffer. Admr.: Henry (surname not given) and his wife Keziah. (Inv.: 25.396; ----; 21 Feb 1740)

THOMAS, James (planter), and his wife Sarah, and Benjamin Thomas. Deed dated 19 Dec 1744; to James Gow (cordwainer), their right to a parcel called *Godfreys Chase*. (Land: Z#2.31)

THOMAS, James (planter) and his wife Sophania. Deed dated 25 Nov 1745. To William Thomas, part of tract called *Ware*. (Land: Z#2.79)

THOMPKINS. (See TOMPKINS.)

THOMPKINSON, John (carpenter). Deed of gift 2 Oct 1672, to his wife Jane, all his estate. (Ct.&Land: E#1.101)

THOMPSON (TOMSON), Henry, age 17 yrs. Servant boy presented by Walter Beane, 8 March 1663/4. (Ct.&Land: B#1.258)
THOMPSON, James, age 12 yrs. Servant of Hugh Ellis, 12 Jan 1674. (Ct.&Land: F#1.41)
THOMPSON, John, age 15 yrs. Servant of Robert Greene, 11 June 1678. (Ct.&Land: G#1.157)
THOMPSON, Henry, age 16 yrs. Servant of Thomas Clipsham, 11 March 1678. (Ct.&Land: H#1.130)
THOMPSON, William. (Inv.: 6.682; 23 Nov 1679; ----) Admr.: John Faning (gentleman). (Acct: 7A.149; ----; 21 July 1680)
THOMPSON, William, son of William and Mary Thompson of St. Mary's Co., (she being dau. of William Britton of sd. county), married Victoria Matthews, dau. of Thomas and Jane Matthew(e)s of Charles Co., 11 April 1681. (Ct.&Land: QRev.8)
THOMPSON, Robert Jr. Deed of gift, 9 March 1680/1, to Anne Thompson, his mother in law; a heifer. (Ct.&Land: I#1.122)
THOMPSON, John. Servant of Henry Hawkins, age judged to be 17 yrs., 12 Jan 1685. (Ct.&Land: M#1.67)
THOMPSON, Robert. To two child., viz.; John and Mary, entire estate equally at majority. Ex.: Capt. Humphery Warren. (Will: 6.46; 26 Aug 1688; 26 Dec 1688)
THOMPSON, Robert. (Inv.: 10.196; 28 Jan 1688; ----)
THOMPSON, William and Victoria, of head of Wicomico River. Their children: Thomas, born 12 Sept 1682; William, born 5 March 1684; Victoria, born 30 May 1687; Jane, born 13 Nov 1689; Cuthbert, born 12 Sept 1692; Mary, born 12 Feb 1694. (Ct.&Land: QRev.9, 10, 12, 15, 20, 25)
THOMPSON, Grace. Servant of John Stone, had bastard child, dated 14 Jan 1691. (Ct.&Land: R#1.372)
THOMPSON, Mary, dau. of John and Mary Thompson of Portobacco, born 8 Jan 1694. (Ct.&Land: QRev.25)
THOMPSON, Robert Jr. Admr.: Mary Smallwood, wife of Maj. James Smallwood. (Inv.: 13A.308; 8 Jan 1694; ----. Acct: 13A.310; ----; 15 May 1695) Payments to: William Thompson and others. Admrs.: Maj. James Smallwood and his wife Mary Smallwood. (Acct: 13B.25; ----; [c1696]) Admr.: Mary Smallwood, wife of James Smallwood. (Acct: 10.396; ---- 4 Oct 1695)

THOMPSON, Issabella. List of debts: mentions Henry Thompson (husband of deceased). (Inv.: 19½A.13; 11 Nov 1699; ----)

THOMPSON, Anne, dau. of Thomas Thompson. Cattle mark, recorded 25 March 1706, for heifer given her by her grandfather, William Thompson. (Ct.&Land: Z#1.233)

THOMPSON, William (planter). (Acct: 30.19; ----; 19 Aug 1709)

THOMPSON, John and Mary his wife conveyed on 11 Aug 1713 to John Clemons Jr. and William Clemons a tract called *Greens Forrest*, cont. 183 acres. (Ct.&Land: D#2.53)

THOMPSON, William (Gent.) of St. Mary's Co. and Eleanor his wife. Dated 24 Nov 1722; to Cuthbert Thompson (Gent.), son of afsd. William Thompson, tract called *Little Worth*, cont. 189 acres. (Land: L#2.56)

THOMPSON, William (Gent.) of St. Mary's Co., and Eleanor his wife, conveyed to his children, Jane Brent and William Matthews Thompson, tract called *Thompsons Chance*, 230 acres, jointly while Jane remains a widow, and then to said William Matthews Thompson. (Land: L#2.129)

THOMPSON, Cuthbert. Next of kin: Thomas Thompson, William Thompson. Admr.: Elisabeth Thompson. (Inv.: 11.420; 17 Dec 1724; 11 July 1726)

THOMPSON, William Mathews. (nunc.) Mentions wife and minor child. (Will: 19.370; 24 March 1727/8; 25 March 1728) Next of kin: Will Thompson, Thomas Thompson. Admr.: Mrs. Katherine Thompson. (Inv.: 13.474; 18 Dec 1728; 4 Feb 1728)

THOMPSON, William. To his grandson, William Thompson Jr., part of the tract called *Simpsons Supply*, cont. 200 acres. Signed 22 April 1731. (Land: M#2.247)

THOMPSON, James and his wife Jane. Signed 14 July 1733. To Richard Standforth (sawyer), for a Negro man called Cezar and 40 shillings, a tract called *Thompsons Hope*, cont. 191 acres. (Land: O#2.5)

THOMPSON, William Sr. Signed 13 Oct 1733. To his son Thomas Thompson, tract called *Thompsons Delight*, cont. 120 acres. (Land: O#2.22)

THOMSON (THOMPSON), John. Mentions sons Thomas and William, ex. and land at Piscattaway, where they now live; son John and dwelling plantation, where he now lives. To dau. Winefred, part of dwelling plantation; at her decease to grandson Joseph, son of son William. To daus. Ann, Magdalen and Susannah, personalty. (Will: 22.66; 2 March 1733; 8 May 1739) Next of kin: John Thompson, Winfr: Thompson. Exs.: Thomas Thompson, William Thompson. (Inv.: 24.186; 14 May 1739; 18 July 1739)

THOMPSON, James. Mentions wife Jane, extx., to whom he leaves 1/3 part of *Thompson's Hope*, lying on s. side of the North Branch; after her decease to John McPherson, remaining part to John McPherson. To Richard McPherson, the part of afsd. tract lying on n. side of sd. branch. (Will: 21.188; 30 March 1733; 14 Aug 1734)

THOMPSON, William of St. Mary's Co. Deed of gift signed 17 May 1735. To his granddau., Ann Thompson, dau. of his son, Thomas Thompson, a mulatto slave named Martha, when Ann is age 16 or day of marriage. (Land: O#2.101)

THORNE, Absalom and his wife Elizabeth conveyed on 10 March 1720, 50 acres, tract formerly conveyed to Elizabeth Noble by William White. (Land: M#2.225)

THORN(E), Absalom. To wife Elizabeth, extx., entire estate. (Will: 21.343; 9 Jan 1733/4; 7 May 1735) Extx.: Elisabeth Thorn. (Inv.: 21.87; ----; 22 Sept 1735)

THORN, William Sr. Mentions dau. Elizabeth and son William; eldest son John; "rest of children." Ex.: Son in law Isaac Shamwell. (Will: 21.816; 22 Nov 1737; 15 Dec 1737) Next of kin: John Thorn, James Thorn. Ex.: Isaac Shamwell. (Inv.: 23.61; 28 Feb 1737; 14 March 1737)

TIBBITT, John, age 17 yrs. Servant of James Bowling, 10 June 1673. (Ct.&Land: E#1.132)

TIBLEE, Thomas, age 20 yrs. Servant of Nathaniel Barton, 9 June 1668. (Ct.&Land: C#1.268)

TIDROR, James. Servant, judged to be 15 yrs. old, presented by John Bouls, 27 March 1662. (Ct.&Land: B#1.101)

TILL, Edward. Heirs and legatees are sons Edward and John; John and Thomas Craxon; Thomas Chapman Jr.; wife Sarah, extx. (Will: 7.371; 6 May ----; 11 June 1698)

TILL, Sarah. (Inv.: 18.65; [c1698]; ----) Relict of Edward Till. Admr.: Thomas Craxon. (Acct: 18.72; ----; 5 Nov 1699) Executrix of Edward Till. Admr.: Thomas Craxon. (Inv.: 19.41; 19 June 1699; ----)

TILL, William. Admr.: John Groves. (Inv.: 27.390; 7 Jan 1742; 2 April 1743)

TILLOTSON, James, age 70. Deposition, 4 Nov 1719, regarding part of tract called *Christian Temple Manor*. (Chas LandComm: M2.65, 66)

TILLSEY, Mabella, age 18 yrs. Servant of Thomas Harrison, 13 March 1676. (Ct.&Land: G#1.16)

TILLYARD, Richard of All Faith's Parish. To Susannah Willson, personal estate. To sister Mary Russell, extx., residue of estate, including 125 acres, on Bush River. (Will: Part 2—12.212; 15 Dec 1709; 17 Feb 1709) (Inv.: 31.412; 20 Feb 1710; ----) Extx.: Mary Russell, wife of Brutus Russell. (Acct: 32B.116; ----; 10 Feb 1710)

TIMMS, Joseph (planter). 23 Dec 1743. A lease, 23 Dec 1743, to Joseph Timms of 117 acres in St. Thomas Manor for the term of the lives of sd. Joseph Timms Sr., Joseph his son, and William Amos. (Land: X#2.86)

TYMOTHIE, Will, age 15 yrs. Servant of John Bowles, 11 June 1667.
(Ct.&Land: C#1.164)

TYMOTHY, Mabella, dau. of William and Mabella Tymothy of Pickawaxon, born 12 Oct 1693. (Ct.&Land: QRev.22)

TIMOTHY, William. Items in the possession of Samuell Compton of St. Mary's County. (Acct: 11B.27; 21 May 1700; ----) Payments to: Grace Timothy (widow of deceased), William Herbert and his wife Sarah (executrix. of Ralph Smith) and others. Admr.: Samuell Compton. (Acct: 20.264; ----; 14 May 1701) Admr.: Samuell Compton (deceased on folio 123) by Thomas Dixon. (Acct: 25.123; ----; 12 April 1705)

TIPTON, Edward, age 18 yrs. Servant of Humphrey Warren Jr., 11 Aug 1668. (Ct.&Land: D#1.2)

TISKERELL (TINKERELL), Thomas (tailor) and his wife Anne conveyed on 10 Aug 1680 a parcel of 200 acres of tract called *Partnership*. (Ct.&Land: H#1.331)

TICKERELL, Jane, wife of Thomas Tickerell (dec'd). Her son John Tickerell be bound over for apprentice servant to William Hatch, 13 June 1683. (Ct.&Land: K#1.179)

TOD, Thomas, age 13 yrs. Servant of William Love, 10 Jan 1670. (Ct.&Land: E#1.1)

THOMPKINS, Giles. Son Giles (minor), ex. and sole legatee of estate. Mentions Mary Christian, dau. of testator's sister. (Will: 4.152; 16 Nov 1682; 27 April 1685) (Inv.: 8.381; 26 May 1685; ----) Admr.: Thomas Stone. (Acct: 10.190; ----; [c1688])

TOMKINS, Joan, age 20 yrs. Servant of Rando: Hanson, 8 March 1686. (Ct.&Land: N#1.151)

THOMPKINS, Giles, son of Giles and Sarah Thompkins of Pickawaxen, born 23 Nov 1692. (Ct.&Land: P#1.211; This conflicts with birth date of Giles, son of Giles and Sarah Thompkins of Pickawaxon, born 20 Nov 1692 found in Ct.&Land: QRev.19)

TOMPKINS (TOMKINS), Giles. (Inv.: 25.405; 13 April 1706; ----) Admr.: Sarah Tomkine (also Sarah Tompkins). (Acct: 26.191; ----; 24 March 1706)

THOMPKINS, John. (Inv.: 1.12; 28 May 1718; 29 May 1718)

TOMKINS, Sarah (widow). Dated 29 June 1719, orders that her eldest son Newman Tomkins, 5 years of age, be free at age 18 and have management for his estate. Recorded 28 June 1720 at request of George Newman (planter). That Charles Denny shall in no way hinder Newman Tomkins from obtaining his estate and freedom at 18. (Ct.&Land: H#2.363)

THOMPKINS, Giles. (Inv.: 6.18; 26 June 1721; ----)

THOMPKINS (TOMPKINS), Newman, on 10 Aug 1737 conveyed part of a tract called *Thompkins Purchase*. Newman Thompkins's mother is now

the wife of John Woodman. Elizabeth Tompkins, wife of Newman
Tompkins, acknowledges her right of dower. (Land: O#2.223, 309)

TOMKINS (TOMPKINS, THOMPKINS), Newman (planter), and his wife
Elizabeth on 31 March 1740 convey part of tract called *Tomkins
Purchase*, 46 acres, not to leave possession until the death of Sarah
Woodman, wife of John Woodman. (Land: O#2.441)

TOMSON. (See THOMPSON.)

TOPPING, John. (Inv.: 39B.70; 8 June 1717; ----)

TOTTERSHALL, TOTTERSALL (See TATTERSHALL).

TOWELL, David. Thomas Allcox and Edward Ruckwood, exs. and sole
legatees of estate. (Will: 5.319; 10 July 1677; 22 Nov 1677)

TRENCH, Ann, age 21 yrs. Servant of Mr. Rozer, 2nd Tues in Nov 1670.
(Ct.&Land: D#1.169)

TREW, Ann, age ca. 26 yrs. Deposition made and "put her mark to," dated
29 June 1663. (Ct.&Land: B#1.163)

TREW, Richard, age ca. 58 yrs. Deposition made and "put his mark to," dated
29 June 1663. (Ct.&Land: B#1.162)

TRINKENS, TOMPKINS (See THOMPKINS).

TROOPE, Robert, Capt., age ca. 28 yrs. Deposition made by same and sworn
2 Nov 1663; mentions "the King of Nangemy." (Ct.&Land: B#1.200)

TROOPE, Robert, Capt. To Eliza:, wife of Joseph Harrison; Mary Harrison,
dau. of said Joseph; Mary, wife of James Lindsey; Eliza: Lindsey, dau. of
said James, personalty. To Richard Harrison, son of sd. Joseph, 150 acres
French Lewis, 100 acres *Troupe's Supply*, and 150 acres adjoining
Henry Sylly's. To James Lindsey and James Macoy, 150 acres on
Anacostine River. To goddau. Eliza: Theobald, residue of estate. In event
of death of said Eliza: before majority, estate to be divided among John
Browne, Thomas Elleson, Mary Lindsey, dau. of James Lindsey, and exs.
Ignatius Cursine and Stephen Montague. (Will: 1.260; 20 July 1666; 1 Aug
1666)

TROUTON, John. (Inv.: 19½A.92; 1 Jan 1689; ----)

TROVER, Patrick. Next of kin (relation to the orphan): Richard Byrch.
Admr./Ex.: Mary Trover. (Inv.: 31.141; 5 June 1710; ----) Admr.: Mary
Farrell, wife of Patrick Farrell. (Acct: 32C.167; ----; 14 July 1711)

TRUE, Richard (boatwright) and his wife Anne. Indenture 11 March 1672; parcel called *Nonesuch*, lying at the head of Lambert's Valley, cont. 100 acres. (Ct.&Land: E#1.103½)

TRUEMAN, Edward and his wife Elizabeth, only dau. and heiress of Thomas Hutcheson (Hutchinson), late of St. Mary's Co. (merchant), dec'd. Deed dated 27 Sept 1728. Capt. Charles Beale, eldest son of Ninian Beale, confirms that the land, called *Edenburgh (Edinburgh)*, 380 acres, was sold by his father to sd. Thomas Hutcheson who by his will of 3 Jan 1697 bequeathed said land to his only dau., Elizabeth Hutcheson. Acknowledged Mary Beale, wife of Charles Beale. (Land: L#2.440, 442)

TRUMAN (TRUEMAN), Thomas Greenfield. Next of kin: Henry Truman, James Truman. Admr.: Mrs. Sarah Truman. (Inv.: 18.488; 9 May 1734; 10 Aug 1734)

TUBB, Thomas, age 21 yrs. Servant of Zach: Wade, 2nd Tues in April 1668. (Ct.&Land: D#1.63)

TUBMAN, George, Revd. Admr.: Elinor Tubman. (Acct: 3.410; ----; 18 May 1704)

TUBMAN, Elinor (widow). Deed of gift, 4 June 1705, to her son, Richard Tubman, at age 18 and dau. Elizabeth Tubman at age 16 or marriage. Recorded at request of Elinor Phillpott, wife of Edward Phillpott. (Ct.&Land: (C#2.129)

TUBMAN, George. Mentions: Col. James Smallwood whose son William Smallwood married Ellinor Phillpott (the widow and wife of Edward Phillpott), admrix. of the deceased. (Inv.: 29.374; 26 Nov 1708; --) Admr.: relict (unnamed) (admrix. of William Smallwood), wife of Edward Philpot. (Acct: 31.75; ----; 12 April 1710)

TURLING, Rebeckah, dau. of Isable Onell. Cattle mark recorded 16 Feb 1693. (Ct.&Land: S#1.239)

TURLOW, Orlock, aged 15 yrs. Servant of Col. William Diggs, 13 March 1682. (Ct.&Land: I#1.124)

TURNER (TURNOR), Arthur. Made over to his two sons, Arthur and James Turner, 600 acres of land (500 bought of Francis Posey and 100 bought of Walter Gest), dated 31 Aug 1659. (Ct.&Land: A#1.104)

TURNER, Arthur. Enters mark of hogs and cattle, for his son Edward Turner, 2 July 1661. (Ct.&Land: A#1.145)

TURNER, Arthur and his wife Margarite acknowledge the right of 100 acres in Charles Co. to Capt. James Neale. 30 Oct 1665. (Arch. of Md.: XLIX.528; LVII.8)

TURNER, Edward, orphan of Arthur Turner, Charles Co., dec'd. His cattle mark recorded by James Bowling on 17 July 1668. (Arch. of Md.: LVII.345)

283

TURNER, Richard, Charles Co., killed on 24 Oct 1668, with a gun by Thomas Corker of Charles Co., Portobacco Ck. (Arch. of Md.: LVII.353)

TURNER, William, age 22 yrs. Servant of Humph: Warren, 11 June 1669/70. (Ct.&Land: D#1.117)

TURNER, Alexander Smith, son of Edward Turner. Cattle mark, 9 June 1691. (Ct.&Land: R#1.234)

TURNER, Edward and Elinor. Their children: John, born 11 Feb 1729, died 5 Sept 1743; Lydia, born 13 Dec 1731; Samuel, born 7 Oct 1733; Edward, born 24 Aug 1735; died 2 Sept 1743; Randal, born 20 Sept 1739; Joshua, born 14 July 1741; Mary, born 9 May 1743; Charles, born 21 April 1745; Joseph, born 1 March 1746/7; Elizabeth, born 7 Nov 1748. (Trinity: 108, 108—rev.)

TURNER, Edward and his wife Elinor. To George Dement, a lease dated 7 Jane 1730/1 to tract called *Watson's Choice*, 137 acres; also a tract called *Hingstone*, 47 acres. (Land: M#2.262)

TURNER, Edward, binds himself to Samuel Amery, bond recorded 24 May 1731. Said Edward Turner has married Elinor Wilson, one of the daus. of John Wilson, dec'd., whereby the right to 1/2 of said Willson's estate did devolve, part of the tract *Watsons Choice*, 237 acres; and a tract called *Hingistone*, 47 acres. (Land: M#2.251)

TURNER, Samuel and Virlinda. Their children: Zephaniah, born 19 Sept 1737; Hezekiah, born 23 July 1739; Dorcas, born 21 Nov 1741; Deborah, born 25 Jan 1743/4. (Trinity: 106)

TURTON, John and Catherine. Their children: Mary Ann, born 26 April 1745; John, born 9 July 1747. (Trinity: 110—rev.)

TURVEY, Thomas, son of Edward Turvey (planter). Cattle marks recorded, 3 Aug 1721. (Ct.&Land: H#2.452)

TURVY, Edward. To sons Thomas, William and John, entire estate; sd. sons to be of age at 18. Ex.: John Wilder. (Will: 19.14; 30 Aug 1726; 16 Sept 1726) Next of kin: William Orde. Ex.: John Wilder. (Inv.: 11.822; 27 Jan 1726; 26 Feb 1726)

TUSON, Zara, age 16 yrs. Maid servant presented by Robert Hudley, 8 March 1663/4. (Ct.&Land: B#1.257)

TWAMBROOKS, John Ingham (tailor) and his wife Margrett on 8 March 1728 conveyed part of tract called *Lemley*, 100 acres. (Land: L#2.463)

TWIFER, Ann. Judged to be 17 yrs. old, presented by William Marshall, 22 April 1662. (Ct.&Land: A#1.201)

TYBALLS, John, son of Clement Tyballs, dec'd. John enters complaint that James Wheeler his guardian has taken cattle mark for himself. Court dated 14 March 1681, orders mark be ousted and John's added. (Ct.&Land: I#1.259)

TYER, James. Extx.: Mrs. Rebecah Tyer. (Inv. 9.300; 19 April 1687; ----)
TYER, James (planter), and Margarett his wife. Indenture, 5 Aug 1704, to Robert Yates, (gent.), two tracts: one parcel called *Heard's Mountaine*, cont. 150 acres, land which on 2 Jan 1681 John Ward and Susannah his wife conveyed to James Tyer; 26 July 1686 by his will James Tyer conveyed 150 acres to his sons James Tyer and John Tyer; James survived his brother and became sole owner. James and Margarett Tyer also conveyed tract *Arabia* on west side of main swamp, being 50 acres and a parcel on the s. side of the main swamp of Pile's Fresh; cont. 700 acres called *Oneales Desart*. (Ct.&Land: Z#1.134; C#2.50)
TYRE, James and his wife Margrit Tyre, dau. of Joseph Cornall, dec'd., conveyed land on 8 Jan 1706. (Ct.&Land: H#2.287)
TYER, Bowles. (Inv.: 3.690; 1 Nov 1705; --) Admr.: Jane Jones, wife of Charles Jones. (Acct: 28.102; ----; 26 March 1708) Admr.: Jane Jones (relict), now wife of Charles Jones. (Inv.: 29.60; 28 June 1708; 14 Jan 1708) (Acct: 29:252; ----; 7 June 1709) Admr. (de bonis non): Charles Jones. (Acct: 35A.71; ----; 13 Feb 1713)
TYER, James. To wife Margarett, extx., and daus. Rebecca and Ann, entire estate. (Will: 13.400; 29 Dec 1711; 20 May 1712) Creditors and Next of kin: Robert Yates, Charles Jones. (Inv.: 33B.44; 16 June 1712; ----) Extx.: Margaret Connor, wife of John Connor. (Acct: 34.31; ----; 22 Aug 1713)
TYER, James. Extx.: Margaret Wallow, wife of James Wallow. (Acct: 38B.26; ----; 8 Oct 1716)
TYER, Rebeccah and Ann Tyer. Assets listed, 22 March 1717, by James Waters, their guardian. (Ct.&Land: H#2.149)
TYARS (TYER), Rebecca, eldest dau. of James Tyars (Tyer) Jr., dec'd., with William Cole who is married to Anne (not of age), dau. of said James Tyars. Deed dated 12 Feb 1729; to William Lloyde (Loyde), tract called *Bonners Retirement*, cont. 200 acres [Rebecca and Anne being sisters]. (Land: M#2.188)

UPPENBIRDGE, John, age 13 yrs. Servant of John Breade, 8 June 1680. (Ct.&Land: H#1.299)

VADREY. (See VAUDRY.)

VAINE, Henrie, age 14 yrs. Servant of George Newman, 7 April 1668. (Ct.&Land: C#1.263)

VANDREYS, John and Elizabeth his wife. Acknowledge their right to *St. Nicholas*, 8 Aug 1671. (Ct.&Land: E#1.52½)
VAUDRY, John. Deed dated 29 Jan 1722, to his son William Ward (planter), and his wife Anne, 1/2 of all his lands. (Land: L#2.79)

VADREY (VAUDRY), John. To son in law William Ward, ex., 200 acres. To eldest son John, sons George and Philemon and dau. Susannah, 1s. each. To two daus. Ann Ward and Elizabeth Ward, widow, residue of estate. (Will: 18.173; 16 Aug 1723; 8 Sept 1723) Next of kin: Elisabeth Ward, George Ward. (Inv.: 9.284; 10 Oct 1723; 18 Jan 1723)

VAUDREY, John, of St. Mary's Co., one of the sons of John Vaudrey, late of Charles Co. on 2 Dec 1731 conveyed all the estate due him by reason of his father. (Land: M#2.273)

VASSALL, Thomas, son of Lewis and Elizabeth Vassall, born 8 Sept 1680. (Ct.&Land: P#1.206; QRev.7)

VAUHOP. (See Waghob, Waghop.)

VAUX, Joseph, age 19 yrs. Servant of Phillip Lynes, 8 June 1686. (Ct.&Land: M#1.221)

VENEABLE (VENABLE, VHENSON), George. Next of kin: John Galwith, George Walls. Admr.: Margaret Venable. (Inv.: 19.94; 5 Aug 1734; 2 Oct 1734)

VENNOUR (VENOUR, VENNOR), Joseph, of Portobacco Parish (apothecary). Towards repairing parish church, and boy Marke Pensuch, personalty. To aunt Abigall Harrington, extx., of England, residue of estate. Hickford Leman to have charge of estate in Maryland. Test: Robert Power, Joseph Leman, James Connill, Hickford Leman. (Will: 12.188; 9 Sept 1707; 10 Oct 1707) (Inv.: 28.51; 23 Oct 1707; ----) (Inv.: 32B.188; ----; 16 July 1711) (Inv.: 32B.189; 16 July 1711; ----) Legatees: Vestry of Port Tobacco Parish, Hickford Leman, John Frasier (minister), Mark Penn paid to his brother William Penn. Mentions: Capt. Hide. Extx.: Dame Abigail Harrington by Hickford Leman (trustee). (Acct: 32C.158; ----; 16 July 1711)

VENOUR, Robert. (Inv.: 39C.80; 7 Dec 1717; ----)

VEREN (VEIRING, VERING), Nathaniell. Admr.: James Tyrce. (Inv.: 9.99; 10 Oct 1685; 13 Dec 1685) Admr.: Mrs. Rebeckah Tyer (executrix of James Tyer (executor of deceased)). (Acct: 9.443; ----; 28 Oct 1687) Admr.: Rebecca Yates (relict of James Tyre (administrator of deceased)), now wife of Robert Yates. (Acct: 10.164; ----; 5 Oct 1688)

VERNON, Robert. Admr.: Dorothy Vernon. (Acct: 39C.108; ----; 7 Dec 1717)

VERRITT, John, age 17 yrs. Servant of John Hatch, 11 April 1676. (Ct.&Land: F#1.173)

VILELE, VILLET (See WILLET).

VILLET, Peter. Deed of gift signed 4 June 1734. To his dau., Mary Greer, Negro boy and after her death, to her son Thomas Greer. (Land: O#2.45)

VINCENT, John and his now wife Susannah. Bind themselves to Christopher Kirkeley, joiner, 24 May 1706, for 20,000 lbs. of tobacco, giving quit claim on the estate of Christopher Kirkeley. (Ct.&Land: Z#1.261)

VINSON, John and his wife Elizabeth. Lease dated 10 Oct 1725, being of pt. of land he bought from John Moor(e). (Land: L#2.250)

VINSON (VINCENT), John. Next of kin: William Cole, James Carrick. Admr.: Sine Vincent. (Inv.: 12.521; 6 Dec 1727; 8 Feb 1727)

VINCENT (VINSON, VENSON), Sina (Siner), widow. In her will she left to sons John and Nathan; Will son of James Kerrick and Mary his wife; Rebeckah, dau. of Will Cole and Ann his wife; Sina dau. of Thomas Raley and Mary his wife; John Macfarding and Sarah Smith — personalty. Son John, about 19 yrs., to have liberty to choose for himself; son Nathan, about 13 yrs., to be bound to George Scrogin to learn shoemaker's trade, or to Mark Pen to learn the smith's trade; dau. Elizabeth Cole, being the county charge, to be taken care of by Thomas Raley and Mary his wife. Residue of estate to be divided between sons John and Nathan and Thomas Raley, ex. (Will: 21.66; 5 May 1734; 17 May 1734) Next of kin: William Venson, Benjamin Venson. Ex.: Thomas Reyley. (Inv.: 18.309; 27 May 1734; 17 July 1734)

VINSON (VINCENT), William (planter), and his wife Sarah, conveyed on 30 Nov 1738, a tract called *Burnhams Beginning*, near Pickawaxon, 85 acres. They conveyed on 24 March 1740 part of tract called *Long Acre*, 20 acres. (Land: O#2.377, 444)

VINTON, Solomon (carpenter). 12 June 1745. To John Marten Sr., lease of two lots in Charles Town, #60 and #64. Vinton gives Marten the power to receive all debts due to Vinton in his own right to the estate of William Ansel, dec'd., with whose widow, Ann Ansel, now wife of sd. Solomon, admx. of sd. William Ansel. (Land: Z#2.77)

W[torn]d, Margrett, age 20 yrs. Servant of Mr. Rozer, 2nd Tues in Nov 1670. (Ct.&Land: D#1.169)

WAALWORT, Isaac, age 22 yrs. Servant of William Marshall, 11 June 1667. (Ct.&Land: C#1.164)

WADE, John (Dr.). He left to his son Edward, all property given to him and his wife Mary by Edward Attkins of Chilvercoton in Warwickshire by will or by deed of gift. To his dau. Mary Wade, personalty which is to be paid at the death of Nicholas Houkins and Elizabeth his wife, the bond of which money is in the hands of John Wade of Chilvercoton. To son John Wade, son of Anne Smith, who formerly lived with testator in Maryland, personalty, in event of death of dau. Mary during minority. Mentions child. of brother William Wade in Cecil, Warwickshire. Residue of estate to Anne Smith and child. afsd. of testator. Wm. Wright, Zacharias Wade, John Harwood and Jas. Johnson to have property until coming of Anne Smith. Admr.: Zacharias Wade. (Will: 1.101; ----; 4 Sept 1658)

WADE, Zacharie. His children: Marie (Mary), born 21 April 1661, died 21 July following; Sarah, born 7 July 1662, died 17 Aug following; a child born 22 Sept 1666, died before baptized; Edward, born 2 Nov 1670, died 22 Aug 1672; William, died 3 Nov 1673. (Ct.&Land: A#1.139, 240; C#1.222; D#1.168; E#1.170, 172; P#1.204, 205; QRev.1, 4. NOTE: A#1.240 gives date of birth of Mary as 20 April 1661. E#1.170 gives date of death of William as 3 Dec 1673.)

WADE, Zacharie. Court held 2 July 1661; mentions his father in law, Capt. Bankes. (Ct.&Land: A#1.140)

WADE, Zachary of Chas. Co. and his wife Mary, have acknowledged 400 acres in Talbot Co. called *Wades Point*, to be the right of William Leeds of Talbot Co. 12 Oct 1665. (Arch. of Md.: XLIX.515)

WADE, Zachary (Zac, Zachariah). In his will he left to eldest son Richard, 550 acres, *Limme* and *Limmis Enlargement*; 400 acres, *Wadeson* and *Wadeson's Enlargement*, and 1/2 of 1,060 acres, *Locust Thicket*, being land bought by testator and brother, Randolph Hinson, from Thomas Brookes; also land at hd. of Piscataway Ck. To son Robert, 600 acres, part of *Market Overton*; 500 acres, *Forest Green*, 350 acres, *Stony Harbor*, on Piscataway Ck.; and 200 acres, *Friendship*. To dau. Theodosia, land on eastern branch of Piscataway, taken up by testator and brother, Luke Gardner; also remainder of *Market Overton* afsd. To Mary Hinson, personalty. Mentions brother in law Randolph Hinson's sons (unnamed) and William Hatton's son (unnamed). Exs.: Brother Ran. Hinson, Wm. Hatton. (Will: 9.16; 5 March 1677; 25 May 1677) (Acct: 8.389; ----; 5 March 1684) Payments include Teodotia Dyet (dau. of deceased). Ex.: Randolph Hinson. (Inv.: 5.197; 30 May 1678; 20 June 1678)

WADE, Richard, age 56. Deposition in 1721 regarding tract called *Wadestones Enlargement* in Durham Parish. (Chas LandComm: M2.127)

WADE, Zachariah, son of Richard Wade. Cattle mark recorded 25 March 1725. (Land: L#2.253)

WADE, Mary. Next of kin: John King, Zachary Wade. (Inv.: 13.110; 6 March 1727; 15 May 1728)

WADE (WADD), Richard. In his will he left to eldest son Zachariah, tracts: *Lynn* (*Lim*); *Lynn's Inlargement*; *Douglas Adventure* and *Douglas' Addition*; and personalty after his mother's decease. To son Robert, *Wade's Adventor*, Prince George's Co. To daus. Mary Manning and

Ginnitt Godfrey, personalty after decease of their mother in law. To daus. Elizabeth Speeak and Theodoshea Speeak (after their mother's decease), personalty. Exs.: Sons Zachariah and Robert. Mary Wade, widow, renounced above will on 10 Oct 1727. (Will: 19.232; 7 Aug 1727; 18 Sept 1727) Next of kin: Theadoshia Stone, Thomas Stone. Exs.: Zachariah Wade, Richard Wade. (Inv.: 13.317; ----; 18 Oct 1727)

WADE, Zachariah (planter). In his will he left to eldest son Richard, *Douglas' Adventure* and *Douglas' Addition* on the little dam. To two youngest sons, Zachariah and John Courts Wade, *Lim*, and *Lim's Enlargement*. To son Zachariah, land on n. side of Wade's marsh. To son John Courts Wade, lands on s. side of sd. marsh. Sons Richard and Zachariah to care of wife, to have two yrs. schooling, and be for themselves at 18. (Will: 21.748; 30 Nov 1736; 3 March 1736) Next of kin: Theodosia Speak, Francis Meek. (Inv.: 24.96; ----; 8 May 1739) Admr.: Charity Adams, wife of Samuel Adams. (Inv.: 22.366; ----; 21 Sept 1737).

WADE, Robert (planter), of Prince George's Co., and his wife Elizabeth conveyed on 6 July 1744 to Daniel Jenifer of St. Thomas Jenifer (scrivener), part of tract called *St. Edmonds* lying on e. side of main fresh run, 100 acres, which was devised by John Hamilton to his dau. Elizabeth Hamilton and wife of sd. Robert Wade. (Land: X#2.128)

WAEDMAN, Rice. Servant judged to be 21 yrs. old, presented by Archibell Whahob, 14 March 1664. (Ct.&Land: B#1.436)

WAGER, Joseph. Admr.: Mary Harper. (Acct: 35A.241; ----; 19 Feb 1713)

WANGHOB, Archibald. Deed of gift 7 July 1675, to his dau. Margaret Lemaire, a mare. (Ct.&Land: F#1.155)

WAGHOPE, Archibald. Deed of gift 1 Feb 1676, to John Lemaire (physician), husband of Margarett Lemaire, dau. of Archibald; tract called *Waghope Purchase* on w. side of Portobacco Creek, cont. 300 acres. (Ct.&Land: G#1.21)

WAHOB (WAGHOB), Archibald of Portobacco. Wife Elizabeth, extx. Mentions possible unborn child; dau. Margaret, wife of John Lemare; dau. Eliza:, wife of Philip Hoskins; granddaus. Benedicta and Jane, daus. of Philip and Eliza: Hoskins. (Will: 4.23; 1 Dec 1683; 10 March 1684) Extx.: Elisabeth Wahob (relict). (Inv.: 8.189; 26 April 1684; ----)

VAUHOP, Archibald. Payments to: Capt. Phillip Hoskins by order of Thomas Lowe, son of William Lowe. Ex.: Cleborne Lomax (surviving executor of Elisabeth Smith (executrix deceased)). (Acct: 19.158; ----; 24 July 1699)

WAKEFIELD, Abel (planter) and his wife Elizabeth on 8 March 1702 conveyed a parcel of land which on 29 July 1673 Jonathan Markes willed *Manchester* to Thomas Wakefield, father of Abel Wakefield. On 13 April

1694 Thomas Wakefield and Ann his wife conveyed same to Abell
Wakefield. (Ct.&Land: Z#1.13)

WAKEFIELD, Thomas, son of Abell Wakefield. Cattle mark, betw. June-Aug
1694. (Ct.&Land: S#1.313)

WAKEFIELD (WALKEFEILD), Thomas. In his will he left to wife Ann,
extx., dwelling plantation, 100 acres, *Wakefield's Beginning*, and 80
acres, *Ratchdale*. To Thomas, eldest son of Abell Wakefield, sd. estate
at death of wife. To son Abell, 180 acres, *Manchester*. (Will: 6.335; 2
Nov 1697; 19 Feb 1699) (Acct: 20.194; ----; [c1701]) Extx.: Ann Shaw, wife
of Ralph Shaw. (Inv.: 19½B.134; 2 April 1700; ---)

WAKEFIELD, Thomas. Next of kin: Abell Wakefield Jr., John Wakefield.
Admr.: Sarah Wakefield. (Inv.: 11.622; 1726; 7 Nov 1726)

WAKEFIELD, Sarah. Next of kin: Mary Bateman, Thomas Bateman.
Admr.: William Jenkins. (Inv.: 15.82; 1 Feb 1728; 5 Sept 1729)

WAKEFIELD, Abel Sr. In his will he left to wife Elizabeth estate, at her
decease to be divided among children. (Will: 20.676; 26 Feb 1731; 17 Aug
1732) Next of kin: Abel Wakefield, John Wakefield. Admr.: Elisabeth
Wakefield. (Inv.: 16.621; 5 Sept 1732; 28 Oct 1732) Next of kin: John
Wakefield, William Jenkenson. Admr.: John Groves. (Inv.: 18.282; 11
April 1734; 29 June 1734)

WAKEFIELD, Elisabeth. Next of kin: John Wakefield, William Incius.
Admr.: Abel Wakefield. (Inv.: 17.126; 19 Feb 1732; 5 May 1733)

WAKELIN, Richard and his wife Mary conveyed on 13 March 1682 parcel
called *Green Chase* at Nanjemy, cont. 200 acres. (Ct.&Land: K#1.130)

WAKELIN, Catherine, wife of Richard Wakelin Jr., on 9 June 1691 binds her
son Richard Wakelin, age 4 yrs. on 18 Aug next, to serve John Godshall,
to age 21 yrs., 9 June 1691. (Ct.&Land: R#1.189)

WAKELIN, Richard. Mentions wife Mary; dau. Mary; son John; Geo.
Wakelin and Violata Harrison. (Will: 13.248; 28 Dec 1708; 7 May 1711)

WAKELIN, John. (Inv.: 31.145; [c1709]; ---) Admr.: Elinor Wakelin. (Acct:
31.344; ----; 20 July 1710)

WALDEN, William Next of kin: John Jackson, Richard Warden. Admr.:
Margaret Loyde, wife of William Loyde. (Inv.: 21.167; ----; 5 Nov 1735)

WALES, George, age 58. Deposition, 30 Aug 1720, regarding tract
Farthings Discovery. (Chas LandComm: M2.99)

WALKER, William (planter) of Westmoreland Co., Virginia and Mary his wife
on 14 March 1709 conveyed 300 acre parcel of land. (Ct.&Land: C#2.170)

WALKER, James, age ca. 40 yrs. Swore in court 24 Sept 1661. (Ct.&Land:
A#1.155)

WALKER, James. To wife Alice, ex., lands in Chas. Co., including *Docker's Delight*. Mentions John Newby, Henry Randall. To Cous. James Docker, provided he come into the province within 10 yrs. and have issue, residue of lands. Proviso for Protestant Church. (Will: 2.47; 31 Oct 1673; 10 March 1674)

WALKER, John. (Inv.: 1.394; 10 June 1675; ----)

WALKER, Alise, relict of James Walker on 13 Sept 1675 conveyed tract called *Docker's Delight*, cont. 150 acres. (Ct.&Land: F#1.151)

WALKER, Alice, relict and extx. of James Walker acknowledges a bill of sale of 18 Jan 1674/5, from James Walker to John Worland for a parcel called *Dockers Delight*. (Ct.&Land: P#1.199)

WALKER, George, age 17 yrs. Servant of Patrick Maggotee, Nov 1710. (Ct.&Land: D#2.5)

WALKER, Charles, age 55. Deposition, 1 March 1720, regarding tract called *Canterbury* (petition of Joseph Gates). (Chas LandComm: M2.116)

WALLIS, Michael (nunc.). In his will he left to William Wilson, estate in trust during minority of son John. (Will: 11.308; ----; 30 May 1702) (Inv.: 1.623; 20 June 1702; ----) (Acct: 23.66; ----; 18 Nov 1702) Ex.: William Willson.

WALLS, George. In his will he left to wife Alice, entire personal estate, she to have charge of children during minority and to bring them up Protestants. To son William, 50 acres *Hanover* in St. Mary's Co. To son George, 50 acres *Hanover* in St. Mary's Co. To sons Larrance and Joseph at 18 yrs., and to daus. Ann and Monokey, personalty. (Will: 22.90; 13 May 1738; 31 July 1739) Next of kin: William Walls, George Walls. Admr.: Alice Walls. (Inv.: 25.62; 19 Dec 1739; 11 June 1740)

WALLS, George Jr. Deed of gift from Richard Lemaster, 13 June 1716 for love and favour of his friend George Walls Sr. (Ct.&Land: H#2.14)

WALSON, William (planter), his wife Jane and his dau. Elizabeth. Indenture 10 Dec 1690, from William Huchison (gent.), a tract called *Vineyard*, cont. 70 acres. (Ct.&Land: R#1.376)

WALTERS, Robert. Admr.: John Breton. (Acct: 38A.124; ----; 11 May 1717)

WALTERS, John, son in law of John Barron. Recorded cattle mark, 24 Feb 1718. (Ct.&Land: H#2.214)

WALTHEN (See WATHEN).

WALTOM, John, age ca. 40 yrs. Swore in court 28 July 1663. (Ct.&Land: B#1.136)

WALTOM, Ralph. Judged to be 14 yrs. old, presented by Peeter Car, 14 March 1664. (Ct.&Land: B#1.436)

WANGHOB. (See WAGHOB.)

WAPLE, Thomas. Next of kin: Osm. Waple, brother. (Inv.: 36B.125; 27 Jan 1714; --) (Inv.: 36B.127; 8 March 1714; ----)

WAPLE, James (planter). (Inv.: 38A.113; 8 March 1716; ----) Admr.: John Bradford of Prince George's county. (PG County Acct: 38A.114; ----; 1 May 1717) Admr.: Maj. John Bradford. (Acct: 38A.116; ----; 31 July 1717)

WAPLE, Osmond, gent. In his will he left to cousin Sarah Waple, 200 acres, *Neck Pastime*, for the use of her son John. To Ann Gooman, 100 acres and 2 tobacco houses, *Healy's Plantation*. To Robt. Hanson, £20. To Col. Philip Hoskine, residue of estate, for the use of children by his late wife Ann. To wife Elizabeth, 1/3 of estate. Exs.: Phil. Hoskine and Robt. Hanson, jointly. (Will: 14.423; 10 Dec 1717; 28 Dec 1717) (Inv.: 1.67; 20 March 1717; ----)

WAPLES, Thomas. Admr.: Phillip Hemsley. (Inv.: 2.231; [c1719]; ----)

WAPPLE, James. Next of kin: Stephen Mankin, Joshua Wapple. Admr.: Margaret Wapple. (Inv.: 17.346; ----; 25 Aug 1733)

WAPLE, George (planter), and his wife Elsabeth (Elce). Deed dated 9 Nov 1736. To William Cooper Sr., a tract called *Waples Chance*, 80 acres of the 100 acre tract. (Land: O#2.183)

WARD, John. Indenture made 20 Aug 1652 between Arthur Turner and John Ward to bind Ward to age 20. On 3 Nov 1663 John Nevill swore that he knew John Ward since he came into the county which was 17 years earlier; he was then about 4 or 5 years old. (Ct.&Land: B#1.193)

WARD, Anne. Servant maid judged to be 16 yrs. of age, presented by John Nevill, 10 May 1663. (Ct.&Land: B#1.124)

WARD, John and Damaris. Their children: Anne, born 5 Feb 1663; Mary, born 5 July 1665; Anne, born 10 April 1667. (Ct.&Land: C#1.253; P#1.204; QRev.1, 2)

WARD, John, son of John Ward, born 16 March 1671. (Ct.&Land: E#1.163 (has date of 15 March 1674); P#1.205; QRev.4)

WARD, Henry, age 15 yrs. Servant of Richard Smoote, 8 June 1675. (Ct.&Land: F#1.101)

WARD, Richard, age 12 yrs. Servant of Humphrey Warren, 11 April 1676. (Ct.&Land: F#1.173)

WARD, John. Admr.: Arthur Turner. (Inv.: 7B.6; 10 Oct 1680; 1681. Acct: 7B.148; ----; 6 Oct 1681)

WARD, Mary, wife of William Ward. She state her life was in danger by John Bracher and Eliza: Vassall, 13 June 1682. (Ct.&Land: I#1.303)

WARD, William. In his will he left to Richard, Mary, and Halalugha Fowke, personalty. Wife Mary, extx. (Will: 4.155; 26 March 1685; 21 May 1685) (Inv.: 8.390; 27 May 1685; ----)

WARD, John Sr. To wife Dameris, 112 acres, *Angerstone*, during widowhood. To son John, 300 acres, consisting of *Charlestown* and *Ward's Delight*. To son Thomas at 19 yrs. of age, 250 acres, *Old Plantation*, at hd. of Nanjemy; 100 acres, *Ingorthorpe*, and 50 acres adjoining William Stone's. To 3rd son James at 19 yrs. of age, 112 acres, *The Mountain*. To 4th and youngest son Henry, and to youngest dau. Catherine at 19 yrs. of age, 550 acres lying between Pamunkey and Nating, equally. Mentions sisters of afsd. children, viz., Mary, Eliza:, Prudence,. To daus. Audray Ward and Mary Wells, personalty. Exs.: Wife Dameris and son John. (Will: 4.252; 4 Sept 1686; 10 June 1687)

WARD, Henry, youngest son of John Ward (dec'd.). On 17 Aug 1690, Charles Shepherd gave young Ward, a slave. Mentions Catherine Ward, youngest dau. of aforesd. John Ward. (Ct.&Land: R#1.332)

WARD, James, son of John Ward (dec'd.) and Deamaris, his wife, alias Damaris Sarjeant, the natural mother of James Ward. Indenture 17 July 1694, in which James bounds himself to Robert Edmondson. (Ct.&Land: S#1.430)

WARD, John. (Inv.: 17.3; 15 May 1698; ----) Admr.: John Ward. (Acct: 19.39; ----; 28 April 1699)

WARD, John, age 50. Deposition, 2 Nov 1719, regarding tract near Nanjemy called *Moulds Adventure*. (Chas LandComm: M2.63)

WARD, John son of Henry Ward (planter). Cattle mark recorded 14 June 1722. (Land: L#2.89)

WARD, Benjamin. Next of kin: William Ward Sr. (Inv.: 8.139; 16 May 1723; ----)

WARD, William Sr. (planter) and his wife Anne of St. Mary's Co. on 31 March 1729 conveyed part of a tract called *Wilton*, cont. 30 acres. (Land: M#2.152)

WARD, Thomas of Durham Parish. To dau. Catherine Lemaster, grandson Thomas Lemaster and daus. Christian Pickum, Mary Goldring, Sary and Ann, personalty. To son Thomas, ex., 250 acres dwell. plan. (Will: 20.45; 2 May 1730; 7 Aug 1730) Next of kin: John Ward, Henry Ward. Ex.: Thomas Ward. (Inv.: 16.99; ----; 29 Dec 1730)

WARD, William (planter), son of James Ward on 19 April 1732 sold to Moses Bell, cows, calves, a gun, tract called *Mountain*, cont. 112 acres. (Land: M#2.291)

WARD, Joseph and his wife Margaret on 17 June 1732 conveyed part of a tract called *Marshland*, cont. 40 acres. (Land: M#2.305)

WARD, John, planter. In his will he left to son Acallis, 76 acres, *Ward's Addition* adjoining to *Charlestown*. Mentions son in law Simon Smith; wife Agnes, extx. (Will: 20.895; 5 --- 1733; 16 Jan 1733) Next of kin: Augustine Ward, Akellis Ware. Extx.: Agnes Ward. (Inv.: 18.34; 28 March 1734; 1 May 1734)

WARD, William, of St. Mary's Co., and his wife Ann. Deed dated 10 Sept 1735, to his dau., Susanna Pettit, wife of Thomas Pettit, part of tract called *St. Margaretts* in St. Mary's Co. and Charles Co., 90 acres (giving her the part in Charles Co.). Deed dated 31 Oct 1740, To Notley Ward, their grandson, 1/2 of tract called *Wilton*, on n. side of main fresh that falls into Budds Creek, 300 acres. (Land: O#2.141, 485)

WARDER, Mary of Portobacco. Deed of gift dated 9 Jan 1712/3, to her son William Warder. (Ct.&Land: D#2.36)

WARNER, Christopher, age 20 yrs. Servant of Robert Downes, 2nd Tues in April 1669. (Ct.&Land: D#1.62)

WARNER, Thomas and his wife Elizabeth. Indenture 16 May 1688, land *Witten*, cont. 150 acres. Mentions father of Thomas, named Thomas Warner (dec'd. 2 Aug 1669). (Ct.&Land: P#1.30)

WARING, Marsham (of Prince George's County), Next of kin: Sarah Haddock, Will. Murdock. (Inv.: 17.13; [c1732]; ----)

WARRING, Basil of Prince George's Co., and his wife Martha. Deed dated 28 June 1732. To Robert Mahony (planter), 300 acres, part of tract called *Hadlow*, devised to sd. Basil by the will of William Barton. (Land: M#2.300)

WARING, Basil (Gent.) of Prince George's Co. (son of Marsham Waring) and his wife Mary on 1 Jan 1744/5 conveyed two tracts one called *Indian Field*, 300 acres and the other being part of *Boarmans Manor*, 96 acres. (Land: Z#2.6)

WARREN, Humphrey and Margery, of Wicomico. Their children: Notley, born 16 Dec 1675; Benjamin, born 23 Jan 1682; Charles, born 10 Nov 1684; John, born 18 June 1687; Humphrey, born 15 Nov 1691. (Ct.&Land: P#1.210; QRev.5, 8, 13, 17)

WARREN, Humphrey Sr. (Inv.: 1.33; 27 March 1674; ----)

WARREN, Thomas (planter) and his wife Mary. Indenture 13 June 1688, from William Barton (Gent.) for his natural love for his dau. aftsd. Mary Warren; parcel called ------, cont. 140 acres. Mentions Thomas Smoot and his wife Elizabeth in case of default. (Ct.&Land: P#1.6)

WARREN, Elinor, dau. of Thomas and Mary Warren of Wicomico, born 7 March 1690. (Ct.&Land: QRev.16) A cattle mark was recorded for Elinor on 26 April 1694. (Ct.&Land: S#1.278)

WARREN, Humphrey, and Abraham, sons of Humphrey Warren. Recorded cattle mark, 26 April 1694. (Ct.&Land: S#1.279)

WARREN, Humphrey (Humphery, Humphry), Col. To wife Margery, *Hatton's Point*, 500 acres. To son Notley, sd. land at death of wife afsd. In event of testator's brother (unnamed) coming into the Province, wife Margery is forced to renounce 250 acres, she is to have 190 acres, part of *The Hills*. To son Benjamin, 190 acres, part of *The Hills*, on w. side

Wicocomico R., and 280 acres, *Warren's Discovery*. To son Charles, 50 acres, residue of *The Hills*, and 100 acres, *Smoote's Purchase*, and 100 acres, part of *Wicomico's Fields*. To son John, 400 acres on w. side of Wicocomico R. To unborn child, two tracts, 170 acres, *The Town House*. To son Notley, personalty in lieu of that bequeathed him by Hon. Thomas Notley. By note dated Jan 21st, 1694, testator bequeaths to son Humphery two tracts of land bequeathed in his will to supposed unborn child, and appoints son Notley joint ex. with wife Margery afsd. (Will: 7.65; 14 Aug 1689; 25 Feb 1694) (Inv.: 10.371; 18 July 1695; 29 July 1695) Mentions: four children (unnamed) plus the accountant. Admr./Ex.: Notly Warren (son). (Acct: 14.74; ---; 7 Oct 1696)

WARREN, Notley. (Inv.: 19½B.157; 13 April 1700; ----) Mentions: Capt. Hardy. (Inv.: 21.79; 13 April 1700; ----)

WARREN, Humphry, Col. Admr.: Benjamin Warren (son). (Inv. from Wills: 3.706; 15 May 1705; ----)

WARREN, John (Gent.). Quit claim 19 Nov 1708, to Samuel Hanson and his wife (Elizabeth), extx. of Benjamin Warren, being brother of John Warren; 190 acres part of a tract called *The Hills*, containing a total of 240 acres. (Ct.&Land: C#2.123)

WARREN (WOREN), Benjamin. (Inv.: 26.341; 18 June 1706; 14 Feb 1706) Extx.: Elisabeth Hanson, wife of Samuell Hanson. (Acct: 27.132; ---- 2 Oct 1707) Extx.: Elisabeth Hanson (relict), now wife of Samuel Hanson. (Acct: 32A.37; ----; 6 Oct 1710)

WARREN, Notley. Admr.: Walter Bayne (admr. of John Bayne (admr. of deceased)). (Acct: 33B.24; ----; 1 Aug 1712)

WARREN, Thomas. To wife, Jane, extx., 50 acres, dwelling plantation, part of 300 acres, *Frailty*. Mentions son Thomas; unborn child; son Barton; daus. Eliza: and Sarah; (Will: 13.152; 6 Jan 1708; 23 Nov 1710) Next of kin: John Harris, John Duley. (Inv.: 32B.192; 10 Jan 1710; ----) Extx.: Jane Warren. (Acct: 33A.42; ----; 12 Nov 1711) Extx.: Jane (surname not given). (Acct: 35A.184; ----; 10 April 1714)

WARREN, John. In his will he left to dau. Mary, *Rich Thicketts*, with tract 50 acres, adjacent, also *The Hills*, *Warren's Discovery*. To dau. Anne, tract, *The Tanyard*, *Smoot's Purchase*, now in tenure of Edward Lloyd. To wife Judith, extx., dwelling plantation and land *Hatton's Point*. (Will: 13.627; 12 Aug 1713; 13 Feb 1713)

WARREN, Judith, widow of John Warren conveyed on 21 Jan 1715 parcel of land on the Wicomico R., 500 acres; bequeathed by John Warren to his widow Judith. (Ct.&Land: F#2.84)

WARREN, John. (Inv.: 3.200; 22 Feb 1719; -) (Inv.: 3.201; 16 March 1719; ---)

WARREN, Humphry (Gent.) of Hattons Point. Indenture, 1 Nov 17--, to Josias Fendall (Gent.) for love of Ellen his wife and to Thomas his youngest son for their maintenance. A tract of land on the w. side of

Wicomico called *Frailty*. Recorded 12 June 1721 at request of Barton Warren. (Ct.&Land: H#2.431)

WATERS, Joseph. (Inv.: 29.332; 23 March 1708; ----) Admr.: John Dyson. (Acct: 30.306; ----; 10 Feb 1709)

WATERS, Anne, widow. Binds her son, 12 July 1715, John Waters, now age 11 years on 3 June, to serve John Manning to age 21. (Ct.&Land: F#2.88)

WATERS, James (tailor) and his wife Margaret convey on 19 Oct 1717 three parcels: *Hopewell*, *Batton's Clifts*, and *Dover*. On 9 June 1719, they sold another part of tract called *Hopewell*; cont. 200 acres; also land adjoining land of Richard Watson cont. 350 acres; and a tract called *Dover* on Hampton Creek and the Potomac River, cont. 200 acres. (Ct.&Land: H#2.104, 255)

WATERS, Joseph and Mary. Their children: Ann, born 27 Aug 1735; Joseph and Mary Waters, twins, born 10 March 1737/8; Sarah, born 10 Sept 1740; John, born 8 March 1742/3; Thomas, born 11 Aug 1745; Elizabeth, born 11 Jan 1747/8. (Trinity: 111)

WATERS, James and Susanna. Their children: James, born 8 Dec 1737; Ann, born 1 Nov 1741; William, born 15 Aug 1745. (Trinity: 108)

WATERS, James. In his will he left to wife Elizabeth, 1/3 dwelling plantation *Dover*. Mentioned son William; dau. Catherine; Peter Garret Sr., a tailor of St. Marys Co., and his son Peter; "any heirs named Waters living in Co. Sloughah in the west of Ireland"; Mary Price and widow Smith; If any of his family break away from the Catholic Church, their share of estate to be divided bet. other members. (Will: 22.295; 3 Oct 1740; 21 Feb 1740) Next of kin: William Waters, Kathrine Waters. Admr./Ex.: Elisabeth Waters. (Inv.: 26.143; 18 March 1740; 16 June 1740) Next of kin: John Waters, Lidia Waters. Admr.: James Waters Jr. (Inv.: 27.303; ----; 18 Feb 1742)

WATERWORTH, Catherine, age 14 yrs. Servant of John Munn, 8 Aug 1682. (Ct.&Land: I#1.317)

WATERWORTH, John, age 12 yrs. Servant of John Bayne, 8 Aug 1682. (Ct.&Land: I#1.317)

WATHEN (WALTHEN), John. To wife Ann, extx., dwelling plantation, to pass to son John at her decease. To son Ignatius, 200 acres, *Warren's Adventure*. To son James, houses, lotts, &c., at Newport. To sons Hudson, Henry, daus. Judea, Jane and Ann, personalty. (Will: 3.453; 28 Feb 1704/5; 10 July 1705) Admr.: John Wathen. (Acct: 26.182; ----; 25 Feb 1704) (Inv.: 3.698; 14 Sept 1705; ----) (Acct: 26.39; ----; 14 Sept 1706) (Acct: 28.127; ----; 4 June 1708)

WATHEN, Ignatius. Cattle mark, 20 Oct 1707; mentions brother John Wathen. (Ct.&Land: Z#1.276)

WATHEN, John, age 38. Deposition in 1720 regarding tract called *Westwood Mannor*. (Chas LandComm: M2.95)

WATHAN, Hudson and his wife Mary conveyed on 25 Nov 1725 a tract called *Pan*, taken up by Gilbert Cropper, cont. 50 aces. (Land: L#2.241)

WATHEN, Hudson. Cattle mark recorded for his sons, John and Basel Wathen dated 8 Nov 1734. (Land: O#2.63)

WATHEN, Henry. Next of kin: John Wathen, Hudson Wathen. Admr.: Elisabeth Wathen. (Inv.: 23.170; 20 April 1738; 5 June 1738)

WATHEN, Martin, son of Hudson and Sarah Wathen, born 2 Feb 1739. (Trinity: 110)

WATHEN, Bennet, son of Hudson and Sarah Wathen, born 30 Nov 174-. (Trinity: 110)

WATHEN, Elinor, dau. of Hudson and Sarah Wathen, -- Nov 1744. (Trinity: 110)

WATHEN, John. Ann Wathen, wife; Child.: John, Joseph, Bennett, Clement, Barton, Mary, and Susanna. Son John Wathen, and bro. Hudson Wathen, exs. (Will: 24.299; 16 Dec 1745; 13 Jan 1745)

WATKINS, William (tailor) and Mary his wife conveyed on 2 Dec 1723, 50 acres, part of 100 acres bought by Gilbert Cropper of Thos. Gerrad and part of *Westwood Manor*, and now divided between two granddaus. of said Gilbert Cropper. (Land: L#2.131) Admr.: Luke Russell. (Inv.: 11.169; ----; 4 Dec 1725)

WATRIDGE, Anne, had a bastard child. Servant of William Hatch, 1680.

WATSON, Andrew, age ca. 30 yrs. Swore in court 12 May 1659. (Ct.&Land: A#1.56)

WATSON, Richard (nunc.), Pickiawaxen. In his will he left his estate to John Wader, his wife Margery and William, son of afsd. John and Margery Wader. (Will: 1:566; 13 Nov 1673; 6 Dec 1673)

WATSON, John (joiner). From Yorkshire, left from London, age 28 yrs., bound to William Haneland, merchant of London for four years from the time of his arrival in Maryland; signed 9 May 1683. (Ct.&Land: N#1.308)

WATSON, Charles. Mentions: widow (unnamed, dead). Admr.: John Kelley. (Acct: 19.27; ----; 17 March 1698)

WATSON, James. Admr.: Robert Sanders. (Acct: 39C.109; ----; [c1717])

WATSON, Mathew (Matthew), Admr.: William Dent. (Inv.: 27.302; 13 Oct 1742; 18 Feb 1742)

WATTERMAN, Thomas. Admr.: John Suttle. (Inv.: 3.238; 4 Nov 1719; 2 Feb 1719)

WATTS, John, mariner. Codicil to will in hands of Capt. John Hyde, late mcht. in London, dec'd, and now in hands of Samuel Hyde, his ex.; whereby bro. Richard Watts and bro. in law John Carr are appointed exs. Said will confirmed except as hereafter specified, viz.: To wife, 100 acres of *Panton Mannor*, in Nanjamoy; also personalty on plantation now occupied by son in law William Brents. To son in law William Brent, personality. John Parnham Sr., and Walter Pyes, exs. of estate in Maryland. (Will: 21.788; 12 Sept 1735; 7 Sept 1737) Admr.: Dr. Andrew Scott. (Inv.: 23.354; 16 Nov 1737; 9 Aug 1738)

WAYE, Jane wife of Richard Waye, on 7 Sept 1685, gave to Ruth Martin, dau. of John Martin, a heifer. (Ct.&Land: N#1.217)

WAYE, Joan, wife of Richard Waye on 14 Jan 1689, gave to her god-dau. Ruth Martin, dau. of John Martin and his wife Mary, cattle. (Ct.&Land: P#1.190)

WAYE(E) (WHEY), Richard. To son in law Daniel Procter, personality, provided he stay with wife during his minority. To Mary, dau. of William Mungister, personality. Wife Mary, extx. (Will: 13.406; 11 Feb 1711; 8 May 1712) Legatees: Daniell Proctor. Extx.: Mary Barker, wife of John Barker. (Acct: 34.184; ----; 23 Jan 1712) Next of kin: none. (Inv.: 33B.101; 29 July 1712; 4 Sept 1712)

WEAVER, John. (Nunc. will) To Mrs. Mary Weaver (spinster), Bristol, England, entire estate. Ex.: Dr. John Pilsworth of Bristol. (Will: 12.153; 6 Aug 1707; 28 Aug 1707)

WEBB, John and Mary his wife. Lease dated 3 Dec 1722, from George Brett (planter), a tract called *Find One*, now in the possession of said Brett, cont. 150 aces. (Land: L#2.80)

WEBSTER, Nicholaus, age 17 yrs. Servant presented by Humphery Warren for John Piles, 8 March 1663/4. (Ct.&Land: B#1.258)

WELLS, William. Next of kin: Furten Ward (daughter), Mary Ward (daughter). (Inv.: 34.194; 29 Dec 1712; ----)

WELLS, William. Admr.: Mary Wells. (Acct: 34.31; ----; 7 Aug 1713)

WELLS, Mary, widow of William Wells. Deed of gift, 27 March 1719, to granddau. Catherine Wells, cattle at age 16. (Ct.&Land: H#2.230)

WENMAN, Mary. In her will she left to Thomas Plouket, Winifrede Fardenand, and Margaret Hammons, personality. To Mary Wolfe at age, residue of estate. Ex.: Jno. Godson. (Will: 4.211; 11 Feb 1685/6; 25 Aug 1686)

WENNAM, William (planter) of Charles Co., age 24 yrs. 1661. (Arch. of Md.: XLI.563)

WENNAM, William. Accused in court held 2 July 1661, of fathering a child of Anne Marden. (Ct.&Land: A#1.142)

WENTWORTH (WINTWORTH), Thomas. Indenture 5 Aug 1664; to Daniell Methenia (Mathenia), parcel of land called *Wentworth Wood House*, on n. side of Pascatoway R. and s. side of Matawoman Ck. (St. Thomas Ck.),

300 acres. (Ct.&Land: B#1.509-512) [NOTE: Daniell Methenia was Thomas Wentworth's son in law.]

WEST, John (joiner), and Walter West his son. Indenture on 8 June 1741. Walter West binds himself an apprentice to Philip Wood (tailor) for seven years. (Land: O#2.527)

WEST, John (joyner), Admrs.: George Godfrey, John Clerke Jr. (Inv.: 31.126; 1 April 1745; 23 June 1745)

WESTMAN, Arthur. Creditors: Robert Whythill, George Riddell. Admr.: Janet Freeman, wife of James Freeman. (Inv.: 28.157; 19 April 1743; 26 July 1743)

WETHERINGTON, Richard. Next of kin: Richard Witherenton. Admr./Ex.: Vincent Askin. (Inv.: 27.46; 22 Sept 1740; 10 June 1742)

WHARTON, Thomas and wife Margaret. Testified in court 6 June 1660. (Ct.&Land: A#1.93)

WHARTON, Elizabeth (spinster). Deed dated 23 May 1722. To her sister's eldest son, John Philbert, 1/2 of tract *Christian Wellford* in Nanjemy Parish nr. Burdits Ck. The whole tract was bought by Thomas Wharton, father to sd. Eliza: Wharton, from Francis Thornton by deed of 10 June 1673. (Land: L#2.35)

WHARTON, Jesse. Admr.: Elisabeth Diggs (relict), wife of William Diggs. (Inv.: 7B.141; 15 Aug 1676; ----. Acct: 7B.144; ----; 24 Aug 1681)

WHARTON, Elizabeth, dau. of Thomas Wharton. Cattle mark recorded, 1680. (Ct.&Land: H#1.292)

WHARTON, Margaret, wife of Thomas Wharton. Cattle mark recorded, 1680. (Ct.&Land: H#1.292)

WHARTON, Elizabeth, wife of Jesse Wharton, patentee of grant of 10 March 1673, tract called *Barbadoes*, 1000 acres; she later became the widow of Col. William Digges, father of sd. John Digges who on 4 Oct 1697 conveyed same to her son Edward Digges, who by his will devised same to John Digges who now conveys same to Francis Goodrick, cont. 702 acres. Conveyance dated 27 Sept 1728; also relinquishing her right of dower is Eleanor, the wife of John Digges. (Land: L#2.460)

WHARTON, Thomas. Admr.: Seymour Moor. (Acct: 31.278; ----; 21 April 1710)

WHARTON, Elizabeth, dau. of Thomas Wharton, dec'd. Court held 13 March 1710, ordered to live with Martha Barker to age 16 yrs. or marriage. (Ct.&Land: D#2.64)

WHARTON, Henry of St. Mary's Co. and his wife Jane. Deed dated 12 Nov 1722. To John Briscoe, part of a tract *Baltemores Gift*, on the e. side of Wicomico R. nr. the mouth of Birds Ck., 108 acres, and a parcel of 60 acres. (Land: L#2.63)

WHARTON, Jesse. Whose land descended to his eldest son, who died an infant, and whose land then descended to his bro., Henry Wharton who mortgaged the land on 6 Dec 1704 to John Hyde. Tract of land commonly called *Rices Mannor*, alias *Lewis' Neck*. (Land: M#2.162; also see 209-215)

WHEATLE (WHEATLEY), John. In his will he left to wife Luckey, extx., entire estate. (Will: 23.511; 20 April 1744; 12 June 1744)

WHEELER, John and Mary. Their children: John, born in 1654; James, born "nine dayes before Christmas in 1656; Mary, born 22 March 1658; Thomas, born 18 March 1660; Winifrid (son), born in March 1663; Ignatius, born in May 1665. (Ct.&Land: C#1.253; P#1.205; QRev.1, 2)

WHEELER, John Jr., age about 22 yrs., 10 Jan 1675. (Ct.&Land: H#1.145)

WHEELER, David, age 18 yrs. Servant of Thomas Mitchell, 10 Jan 1681. (Ct.&Land: I#1.224)

WHEELER, John, age ca. 25 yrs. Swore in court 26 Oct 1658. (Ct.&Land: A#1.25) 1694).

WHEELER, John and his wife Mary. Ordered in court 23 Oct 1660, to make good the sale of 350 acres of land. (Ct.&Land: A#1.108)

WHEELER, Robert and Mary his wife conveyed on 8 June 1677 a parcel of land from the estate of Henry Fletcher, dec'd., by letter of administration. (Ct.&Land: G#1.39)

WHEELER, Robert and his wife Mary. Indenture 8 March 1681, to Cuthbert Musgrove; parcel called *Shrewsberry* in Chingamuxon Creek, cont. 150 acres. (Ct.&Land: I#1.259)

WHEELER (WHEELAR), James (planter). Appraisers: John Godshall, John Clarke. (Inv.: 8.388; 11 Feb 1684; ----) Extx.: Katharine Jones, wife of Moses Jones. (Acct: 9.188; ----; 16 Aug 1686) (Inv.: 10.1; 24 March 1687; ----) Mentions: Maj. John Wheelar & Moses Jones at difference on behalf of orphans (James and Anne). Extx.: Katharine Jones (relict), deceased wife of Moses Jones. (Acct: 10.364; ----; [c1693])

WHEELER, John (Gent.). Indenture 10 Nov 1685, to his dau. Wennifred and her husband John Speake, a parcel called *Plymouth* near fresh of Piscattaway, cont. 350 acres. (Ct.&Land: M#1.32)

WHEELER, Thomas. Cattle marks recorded 15 Dec 1686; by Thomas, father of Richard, Thomas, and Benjamin Wheeler. (Ct.&Land: N#1.9)

WHEELER, John (Gent.) and Mary his wife conveyed on 8 Jan 1688 a parcel called *Exiler*, on s. side of main fresh of Piscataway Creek, cont. 316 acres. (Ct.&Land: P#1.92)

WHEELER, Luke, son of Ignatius Wheeler. Cattle mark recorded, 10 Jan 1692. (Ct.&Land: R#1.548)

WHEELER, Anne, dau. and Thomas and Ignatius, sons, of Thomas Wheeler. Cattle mark recorded 21 Feb 1693. (Ct.&Land: S#1.240)

WHEELER, Luke, son of Ignatius and Francis Wheeler of Portobacco, born 8 Feb 1693, died 8 Jan 1694. (Ct.&Land: QRev.22, 24)

WHEELER, John. In his will he left to son Thomas, 200 acres (unnamed) on which he now lives, and 230 acres, *Wheeler's Rest*. To wife Mary, extx., 600 acres, *Planter's Delight*. To son Ignatius, sd. *Planter's Delight* at death of wife. To son Francis, 187 acres, *Mayor's Choice*, and 96 acres, *Middleton's Lot*. To grandson, John Wheeler, son of dec'd. son James, 200 acres, part of 500-acre, *Wheeler's Purchase*. To grandson James, son of sd. dec'd son James, 200 acres, part of *Wheeler's Purchase*. To granddau. Ann Wheeler, dau. of sd. dec'd son James, 100 acres, residue of *Wheeler's Purchase*. To granddau. Ann, 165 acres, *Wheeler's Delight*. Mentions grandson Richard, son of son Thomas. (Will: 7.70; 11 Nov 1693; 9 Jan. 1694)

WHEELER, Ignatius. In his will he left to wife Frances, extx., life interest in 600 acres, *Planter's Delight*. To son Luke, *Planter's Delight* afsd. at death of his mother, and *Rich Neck*, being in possession of testator through his marriage. To unborn child, 208 acres, *No Design* at Pormunky. Mentions James Fendall and William Hatton. In event of death of wife during minority of child or children, bro. in law Luke Gardner to hold estate in trust. (Will: 6.296; 14 March 1698; 3 Aug 1698)

WHEELER, Thomas (planter). Indenture, 19 April 1710, to Richard Wheeler, son of Thomas; a tract of land called *Wheeler's Rest* and part of a tract called *Wheeler's Addition*, cont. 110 acres. (Ct.&Land: C#2.204)

WHEELER, Thomas, age 58. Deposition on 22 Dec 1719, regarding the tract *Christian Temple Mannour*. (Chas LandComm: M2.69)

WHEELER, Thomas, age 60. Deposition, 31 May 1721, regarding tract called *Christian Temple Manor*. (Chas LandComm: M2.122)

WHEELER, John of Baltimore Co., son of Thomas Wheeler, of Charles Co. Deed dated 24 Oct 1724. Thomas Wheeler to his son John; two tracts, *Wheelers Delight* and *Wheelers Rest*, cont. 120 acres. (Land: L#2.171; O#2.511)

WHEELER, Thomas. Deed dated 9 Nov 1724; to his son, Richard Wheeler, part of a tract called *Wheelers Addition*, nr. Mattawoman, cont. 17 acres, and on 12 April 1726 to his son Richard Wheeler, a part of tract called *Wheelers Addition*, cont. 17 acres. (Land: L#2.247, 269)

WHEELER, Richard. In his will he left to Kindrick Bane, dwelling plantation and 17 acres until son Richard comes to age of 18. To son Thomas, 20 acres, and the mill on sd. land; Kindrick Bane to have 500 lbs. tob. yearly until Thomas arrives at age of 18. Thomas Mitchell to be paid 500 lbs. tob. yearly for education of sons Richard and Thomas. To dau. Elizabeth Bravner, dau. Martha, dau. Mary Madox, dau. Ann Ellder, personalty. To sons Richard and Thomas and dau. Annastasia Kean, 1/2 of personal estate, other 1/2 to Kindrick Bane and her child. Should Ebsworth Bane come to molest or take any part or parcel thereof, Patrick Connelly is empowered to secure the afsd. estate to sd. Kindrick and her children. Ex.: Thomas Mitchell. Test: William Nelson, Charity Smallwood, Ignatius

Mitchell. (Will: 21.57; 1 April 1734; 1 May 1734) (Inv.: 18.509; ----; 21 Aug 1734) Next of kin: Thomas Wheeler, Elisabeth Browne. Ex.: Thomas Mitchell.

WHEELER, Thomas. Signed 29 July 1734. All he owns to his grandsons, Ignatius Mitchell and Thomas Mitchell Jr., sons of Thomas Mitchell (planter). (Land: O#2.48).

WHEELER, Thomas. Next of kin: Ann Mitchell, Elisabeth Green. Admr.: John Wheeler. (Inv.: 22.72; 10 Sept 1736; 6 Oct 1736)

WHEY. (See WAYE.)

WHICHALEY, Jane, wife of Thomas Whichaley of Pickawaxon Parish, died 7 Nov 1693. (Ct.&Land: QRev.21)

WHICHALEY, Thomas married Elizabeth Ford (wife of Edward Ford, decd:), dau. of Thomas Allanson of Chingamuxon, dec'd., 25 April 1694. (Ct.&Land: QRev.23)

WHICHALEY, Thomas and his wife Elizabeth, relict and extx. of Edward Ford. Indenture, 13 Nov 1695, to Thomas Austin. Edward Ford had sold a parcel called *Wellford* at Nanjemy of 100 acres to Thomas Austin. Indenture, 14 Jan 1703, to Susanna Mason of St. Mary's Co.; 13 April 1659 a patent was granted to Thomas Allanson (Gent.); tract called *Christian Temple Manor* on the s. side of Piscataway River. Charles Allanson inherited this land from his father, Thomas, 14 Feb 1689, conveyed same to Edward Ford who by his will dated 6 Jan 1693 devises 200 acres on St. Thomas Creek to his wife Elizabeth. (Ct.&Land: Q#1.72; Z.76)

WICHERLY, Elizabeth, dau of Thomas Allison, former owner of *Christian Temple Manour*, age 46. Deposition, 5 Nov 1719, regarding part of tract called *Christian Temple Manor*, on the s. side of Mattawoman (petition of John Sanders). (Chas LandComm: M2.66)

WHICHERLY, Elizabeth, age 46. Deposition, 31 May 1721, regarding tract called *Christian Temple Manor*. (Chas LandComm: M2.122)

WHILDEN, John, age 24 yrs. Servant of Edward Swanne, 11 June 1667. (Ct.&Land: C#1.164)

WHITE, William, age ca. 36 yrs. Deposition to court 10 March 1658. (Ct.&Land: A#1.43)

WHITE, Cornelius. (Baltimore Inv.: 35A.237; 25 May 1714; ----) Payments to: Jonathon Tipton of Baltimore County, Dr. Philip Briscoe for maintenance of Eleanor Charlesworth. Admrs.: John Parry, Luke Barber, Andrew Norton. (Acct: 35A.237; ----; 5 June 1714) Admrs.: John Parry, Luke Barber, Andrew Norton. (Acct: 36C.47; ----; 31 Aug 1715) Received from: Richard Lewellin on account of Mrs. Mason. Exs.: John Parry, Luke Barber, Andrew Norton. (Acct: 37C.141; ----; 19 Jan 1716)

WHITE, William and his wife Mary of Stafford Co., Virginia. Indenture to Elizabeth Noble (spinster), 28 March 1719. Part of a tract called *Green Chance*, cont. 100 acres that Rich: Wakelin left his dau. Mary Wakelin. (Ct.&Land: H#2.227, 228)

WHITE, John. Admr.: William Campbell. (Inv.: 22.344; ----; 13 Aug 1737)

WHITEHEAD, John, age 18 yrs. Servant of Humphrey Warren, 8 Jan 1677. (Ct.&Land: G#1.85)

WHITEHORNE, John, age 16 yrs. Servant of Thomas Mudd, 14 March 1681. (Ct.&Land: I#1.258)

WHITOM, William. (Inv.: 17.31; [c1698]; ----)

WHITT, Samuel, age 11-12 yrs. Servant of Benjamin Rozer, 14 Nov. 1676. (Ct.&Land: F#1.222)

WHITTER. (See WITHER).

WHITTER, Thomas (Acct: 26.185; ----; 18 Feb 1706). Admr.: William Whitter.

WHITTYMORE, Christopher and Anne, of Portobacco. Their children: Anne, born 5 Sept 1694; Richard, born 2 Sept 1690. (Ct.&Land: QRev.16, 25)

WHITTYMORE, Anne, dau. of Christopher Whittymore. Cattle mark recorded 24 April 1693. (Ct.&Land: S#1.112)

WHORTON, John. Judged to be 17 yrs. old, presented by Thomas Mathews, 14 March 1664. (Ct.&Land: B#1.446)

WICHERLY. (See WHICHERLY.)

WIETTAM (WITTAM), William. Uncle Richard Jenkins, ex. and sole legatee of estate. (Will: 6.156; 13 May 1698; 24 June 1698)

WIGGS, David, age 13 yrs. Servant of Robert Downes, 2nd Tues in April 1669. (Ct.&Land: D#1.62)

WILDER, Robert, age 16-17 yrs. Servant of John Bowles, 8 Aug 1671. (Ct.&Land: E#1.43)

WILDER, John and EverElday of Wicomico. Their children: Edward, born 27 Nov 1689, bapt. 1 Dec 1689; John, born 30 Sept 1692, bapt. 2 Oct 1692. (Ct.&Land: P#1.201, 210; QRev.15, 18)

WILDER, Francis. In his will he left to children Mary, John, Ann and Assence, personal estate. Brother in law Wm. Browne and sister Mary, his wife, to care for testator's children Mary and Assence, and Robert

Yates to care for John and Ann during minority. (Will: 3.648; 10 April 1705; 7 Aug 1705) (Inv.: 25.18; 21 Aug 1705; ----) Admr.: William Browne. (Acct: 26.183; ----; 18 March 1706)

WILES (WILD, WEALES), Elisabeth, age ca. 22 yrs. 29 June 1663. (Ct.&Land: B#1.163, 164, 166)

WILFRAY, Lusi, age 18 yrs. Servant of Bennett Marshegay, 8 June 1675. (Ct.&Land: F#1.101)

WILKINSON, William. In his will he mentions Elizabeth Budden, dau. of Margaret Budden, "my last wife," two grandchild.: William Dent, eld. son of Thomas and Rebecca Dent, and William Hatton, eld. son of William and Elizabeth Hatton; son in law Thomas Dent and Rebecca his wife; son in law William Hatton and Elizabeth his wife. (Will: 1.190; 29 May 1663; 21 Sept 1663)

WILKINSON, Lancelot, age 18 yrs. Servant of Humphry Warren, 9 Jan 1671/2. (Ct.&Land: E#1.52)

WILKINSON, John, age 18 yrs. Servant of John Taylor, 10 June 1674. (Ct.&Land: E#1.171)

WILKINSON, Richard. List of debts: including William Wilkinson of St. Mary's Co. (Inv.: 3.117; 22 Feb 1676; ----)

WILKINSON, Mary, dau. of Lancelot and Mary Wilkinson of Mattawoman, born 15 Oct 1687. (Ct.&Land: QRev.13)

WILKINSON, Mary, dau. of Lancelott and Mary. Cattle mark, 14 Nov 1693. (Ct.&Land: S#1.169)

WILKINSON, Thomas. Cattle marks for his children: Minor, Thomas Jr., and William. Recorded 9 Aug 1706. (Ct.&Land: C#2.12).

WILKINSON, John. Admr./Ex.: John Williams (his wife being dead). (Inv.: 11.171; 4 Oct 1725; 5 Feb ----)

WILKINSON, William, merchant. In his will he left to dau. Sophia Wilkinson (alias Sophia Hicks); 86 acres adjoining; both in Prince George's Co.; and 1/2 revenue from mill. To grandson William, 1/2 revenue from mill, and debts due testator in London. To grandson Francis and granddau. Susanna, personalty. To dau. Sophia and three grandchild., afsd., 600 acres *The Enclosure*, Patuxent. Mentions widow Craycroft, Prince George's Co. Thomas Grant, Prince George's Co., joint ex. with dau. Sophia. (Will: 19.16; 4 Nov 1725; 29 Aug 1726) Next of kin: Will. Wilkinson, Francis Wilkinson. Admrs.: Col. Thomas Truman Greenfield, Richard Smith. (Inv.: 11.815; 30 Jan 1726; 15 March 1726)

WILKINSON, Francis. Elizabeth Morris took oath that Francis Wilkinson said on his death bed that his son Francis shd. inherit only his personalty. (Will: 22.296; ----; 4 March 1740) Next of kin: William Wilkinson, Ann Greenfield. Admr.: Ellis Parran, wife of Young Parran. (Inv.: 27.213; 27 April 1741; 10 Nov 1742)

WILLARD, John. Lease dated 22 April 1728, from Barton Smoot of that plantation being a tract called *Smoots Fish Pond*, 100 acres, for lifetime of said John and Anne his wife and James his son. (Land: L#2.412)

WILLARD, James, son of John. Cattle mark recorded 25 March 1728/9. (Land: L#2.467)

WILLBEE, Michael, age 12 yrs. Servant of George Godfrey, 11 March 1678. (Ct.&Land: H#1.129)

WILLET (VILLET, VILELE), Peter. In his will he left to wife Cecelia, daus. Elizabeth Hulks, Mary Greer and Rachel, son Peter, and daus. Mary Ann and Rebeckah personalty. To wife Cecilia, extx., plantation in Calverton Manor during her lifetime. Residue of personalty to be divided among four youngest children, viz.: Rachel, Peter, Mary Ann and Rebeckah, who are to be in care of wife until they come of age. (Will: 22.65; 31 Dec 1737; 23 April 1739) Next of kin: John Moran, Elisabeth Hulks, William Cantar. Extx.: Cecilia Villet. (Inv.: 24.313; ----; 24 Sept 1739)

WILLIAM, Edward, age ca. 33 on 26 Jan 1658. (Ct.&Land: A#1.36)

WILLIAM, Anne, sues Richard Smith for maintenance of her child, 6 June 1660 (Ct.&Land: A#1.93)

WILLIAM, Edward, age ca. 34 on 19 Nov 1661. (Ct.&Land: A#1.169)

WILLIAMS, John, died Feb 1661; entered by Joseph Harrison. (Ct.&Land: A#1.217)

WILLIAMS, Peter, age 13 yrs. Servant of Thom: Hussy, 12 Jan 1668/9. (Ct.&Land: D#1.42)

WILLIAMS, Jenkins, age 21 yrs. Servant of Benjamin Rozer, 12 Jan 1674. (Ct.&Land: F#1.41)

WILLIAMS, Jane, age 14 yrs. Servant of Philip Lines, 13 March 1676. (Ct.&Land: G#1.16)

WILLIAMS, John, age 21 yrs. Servant of Thomas Gerrard, 13 March 1676. (Ct.&Land: G#1.16)

WILLIAMS, Katherine, age 17-18 yrs. Servant of Josias Fendall, 1676. (Ct.&Land: F#1.193)

WILLIAMS, Edward, age 20 yrs. Servant of Henry Hawkins, 11 March 1678. (Ct.&Land: H#1.129)

WILLIAMS, William, age 22 yrs. Servant of Capt. Ignatius Causin, 11 March 1678. (Ct.&Land: H#1.130)

WILLIAMS, Benjamin, age now about 3 yrs., son of Abice [Maris]. To serve Haman Norton until age 21, 10 Aug 1680. (Ct.&Land: H#1.330)

WILLIAMS, John, age 10 yrs. Servant of John Allward, 14 March 1681. (Ct.&Land: I#1.258)

WILLIAMS, Rise. (Inv.: 10.252; 27 April 1685; ----)

WILLIAMS, William, son of John and Sarah Williams "of ye river side," born 2 Oct 1685. (Ct.&Land: P#1.208; QRev.11)

WILLIAM, John, son of John and Sarah Williams "of ye River side," born 2 Aug 1688. (Ct.&Land: P#1.208; QRev.14)

WILLIAMS, William, son of John Williams. Cattle mark, 12 Sept 1692. (Ct.&Land: S#1.65)

WILLIAMS, William, age 53. Deposition 24 April 1693, for conveyance of land from Thomas Mudd to John Saunders in right of his wife Sarah, dau. of Maj. William Boarman. In 1673 deponent was a tenant to Major, then Capt. Wm. Boarman on his tract where Thomas Mudd now dwells; deponent heard Boarman say that 400 acres of the 800 acres in the patent went to his dau. Sarah in marriage to Joseph Piles; the match was broken by disagreement of parents of Mr. Piles; then a match was proposed with Thomas, the eldest son of Dr. Thomas Matthews of Portobacco, and Sarah; when deponent returned from 5-6 months in England, Sarah and Thomas were living on land where Thomas Mudd now lives. Deponent asked how Capt. Boarman "would do by ye son George to whom you have promised this land now given your daughter." He replied other provisions had been made for George. (Ct.&Land: S#1.110)

WILLIAMS, John (planter), on 10 April 1709, by his will, devised to his wife Sarah, 100 acres, and after her death to his son, John Williams. The son died without attaining full age leaving Ann, his sister, who married James Connell. By this deed dated 26 May 1740, James Connell (planter) of St. Mary's Co. and Anne his wife, sell to John Dunbar the tract of 100 acres. Recorded at the request of Elizabeth Hanson, 12 Nov 1745. John Hanson (sometime deputy clerk) stated that after the death of his father, Samuel Hanson, late clerk of Charles Co., John Dunbar lodged with him a deed from James Connell and Ann his wife, to be recorded after the alienation money was paid. Deed was lost for some time. (Land: Z#2.74)

WILLIAMS, Edward. (Inv.: 6.19; 7 July 1721; ----)

WILLIAMS, James. In his will he left to all his children (unnamed), 158 acres and at wife's decease. Exs.: Wife Elizabeth and sons John and Thomas. (Will: 18.170; 27 July 1723; 7 Sept 1723) Next of kin: John Lemaster, John Scott. (Inv.: 9.340; 15 Jan 1723; 26 March 1724)

WILLIAMS, Elizabeth, and Thomas Williams, twin children of Thomas and Ann Williams, born 21 Aug 1745. (Trinity: 110)

WILLIAMS, John (planter). To wife Sarah, 100 acres, to pass at her decease to son John. To eldest son William, residue, 150 acres. Wife extx. Mentions daus. Eliza: Mackay and Mary and Ann Williams (when 14 yrs. of age); god-son John Smoot (at majority). (Will: Part 2—12.58; 10 April 1709; 18 April 1709) (Inv.: 30.2; 27 April 1709; ----) Ex.: William Williams, Sarah Osborn (wife of Thomas Osborn). (Acct: 31.282; ----; 27 May 1710)

WILLIAMS, John. Next of kin: none. (Inv.: 35A.361; 8 March 1713; ----)

WILLIAMS, John. Admr.: Boswell Smith. (Acct: 36B.96; ----; 11 Feb 1714)

WILLIAMS, Thomas. Legatees: Elisabeth the wife of Thomas Short, John Williams (son). Extx.: Ann Mackey, wife of James Mackey. (Acct: 35A.380; ----; 24 May 1714)

WILLIAMS, William, age 33. Deposition, 29 Sep 1719, regarding the tract *Martins Freehold*. (Chas LandComm: M2.59)

WILLIAMS, John, Thomas Williams, James Williams, Daniel Short and his wife Catherine, Justinian Williams, William Williams, Gilbertus Simpson and his wife Elizabeth—heirs of James Williams. Deed dated 6 April 1730; being part of tract called *St. Thomas'*, lying on the w. side Piles Fresh, cont. 150 acres. From Thomas Sympson Jr., and his wife Sarah. (Land: M#2.222)

WILLIAMS, William. In his will he left to son Thomas, 72 acres *Williamses Chance*. To son William, 250 acres *Frankum*, 28 acres adj. thereto called *Williames Addition*. To children, viz: William, Thomas, Lewcresea and Mary, and Elizabeth Annis, personalty. Sons to be free at age of 19. Wife Ann extx. Test: Thomas Wright, John Wright, Jonathan Williams. (Will: 21.548; 19 Nov 1735; 5 May 1736) Next of kin: William Williams, Elisabeth Annis. Extx.: Ann Williams. (Inv.: 21.405; ----; 16 June 1736)

WILLIAMS, William (planter), and his wife Sarah, on 14 March 1738/9 conveyed tract that William Williams purchassed of Barton Hungerford, 100 acres. (Land: O#2.389)

WILLIAMS, William, and his wife Anne, heir of James Tant, dec'd., and John Reeder, son of Benjamin Reeder, dec'd. Said Anne Williams is heir to James Tant, late of St. Mary's Co., bro. in law to Laurence Totershall, dec'd. To Francis Ware (planter) of Portobacco, a tract called *Totershall's Gift*, 400 acres. 5 Oct 1741. (Land: O#2.528)

WILLIAMS, Mary, wife of David Williams, and her sister Priscilla Mirick, both of Charles Co. From George Brett of Charles Co., but now of Prince William Co., Virginia, 14 Nov 1744. Tract called *Chosen*, in Durham Parish, 80 acres. George Brett binds himself, 14 Nov 1744, to David Williams and Mary his wife, and Priscilla Mirick in case his wife Constant does not release her right of dower. (Land: Z#2.11)

WILLIAMS, Justinian, son of James and Esther Williams, born 29 Jan 1745/6. (Trinity: 109—rev.)

WILLIAMSON, William. In his will he left to Capt. Henry Aspinall, 1/2 of estate. To Mary Aspinall, wife of sd. Henry, and to their unborn child, residue of estate. (Will: 5.159; 19 Nov 1676; 20 Feb 1676/7)

WILLMAN, Henry, age 12 yrs. Servant of William Smith, 11 June 1678. (Ct.&Land: G#1.157)

WILSON, Robert, age ca. 30, 26 Jan 1658 (Ct.&Land: A#1.38)

WILSON, Gils. Judged to be 22-23 years old, presented by Alexander Smith, 14 March 1664. (Ct.&Land: B#1.436)

WILSON, Lawrence, age 20 yrs. Servant of Capt. William Boreman, 9 Jan 1671/2. (Ct.&Land: E#1.52)

WILSON, Joseph (Inv.: 24.251; 27 July 1703; ----) Hannah Wilson. (Acct: 27.233; ----; -- Aug 1707)

WILSON, Margarett, dau. of Joseph Willson. Cattle mark, 5 Feb 1703/4. (Ct.&Land: Z#1.67)

WILLSON (WILSON), Alexander. In his will he left to William, Ignatius, James and Mary Sympson (Simpson), entire estate. Ex.: Rich'd Edling. Among witnesses was Thos. Sympson. (Will: 14.109; 8 Feb 1715/16; 3 April 1716) (Inv.: 37A.52; 29 March 1716; ----) Ex.: Richard Edelen. (Acct: 39B.71; ----; 22 March 1716)

WILLSON, Richard, age 45. Deposition on 12 Jan 1719, regarding the tract *Lees Purchase*. (Chas LandComm: M2.56)

WILSON, Hannah. Next of kin: Richard Smith, James Smith. (Inv.: 2.118; 8 April 1719; ----)

WILLSON, John. Next of kin: Joseph Allen, Mary Allen. (Inv.: 5.151; 1 May 1721; --) (Inv.: 6.18; 22 July 1721; ---)

WILLSON, William. Admr.: Edward Grey. (Inv.: 17.250; 14 May 1733; 6 Aug 1733)

WILSON, James, and his wife Sophia, of Prince George's Co., conveyed on 7 March 1739/40, a tract on the w. side of Patuxent River called *Enclosure*. (Land: O#2.437)

WILLSON, John, and his wife Lydia conveyed on 6 Dec 1742 to Jonathan Willson (planter), parcel called *Black Oak Thicket*, 250 acres. (Land: O#2.590)

WINDSOR, Thomas (planter), and his wife Sarah, conveyed on 13 June 1744, a tract called *Windsor Castle*, on n. side of branch falls in Zachia Swamp, 100 acres. (Land: X#2.134)

WINE, Francis. Age ca. 30 years, 13 June 1665 (Ct.&Land: B#1.448)

WINE, Henry, now of Pitchley, Northampton-shire. Dated 5 Oct 1688, exchanges a parcel of land left him by his father, Francis Wine, in Wicomico called *Burton*, 90 acres with his mother Elizabeth Hawkins. (Ct.&Land: P#1.178)

WYNE, Elizabeth, widow of Burton plantation, relict of Francis Wyne, dec'd. Deed of gift, 4 June 1682, to her children, Henry Wyne, Elizabeth Wyne and Jno. Wyne, not yet 21 years old. (Ct.&Land: I#1.309)

WYNE, Francis. In his will he left to son Henry of London, 1/2 of properties, viz.; *Ireland, Angell,* and *Pinwell Closes*, in Northamptonshire, England. To dau. Eliza:, residue of above mentioned properties. To son John, sd. properties in event of death of sd. Henry or Eliza: without issue; also 300 acres *Simpson's Delight*; 200 acres *Wassell*; 100 acres *London*; 100 acres *Blockstitch*; 100 acres *Glowers' Point*; 200 acres *Pithly*; 90 acres *Burton*; 37 acres *Scidmore's Adventures*; and 37 acres *Susquehanna*; all in Chas. Co. Wife Eliza:, extx. and residuary legatee of estate. Extx.: Elisabeth Hawkins, wife of Henry Hawkins. (Will: 2.173; 14 Nov 1681; 6 March 1682; Inv.: 7C.239; 19 April 1682; ----; Acct: 8.56; ---; 26 June 1683)

WYNE, Elizabeth (widow of *Burton* plantation), relict of Francis Wyne. Deed of gift, 4 June 1682, to her children: Henry, Elizabeth, and John Wyne (not yet 21), gift of cattle, goods, &c. (Ct.&Land: I#1.309)

WINE, Robert, son of John, of Blowmoris in county of Anglicey Comp., age 17 yrs. To serve William Whaley of Liverpoole, merchant, 7 years after his arrival in Virginia or other colony, 10 May 1717. (Ct.&Land: H#2.167)

WINE, Sarah, of the Parish of Hemel Hempstead, County of Hertford of England, widow and relict of Francis Wine, late of Hemel Hempstead, afsd., husbandman, dec'd. (who was the grandson of Francis Wine, late of Charles Co., Gent., dec'd.), and also the mother and guardian of Henry Wine (the eldest son of my late husband Wine), an infant age 10 yrs., has appointed her son's attorney to recover from Henry Hawkins, and others all rents, money or other compensation as are due her said son Henry. Sd. Henry Hawkins (son of Henry Hawkins) occupying certain lands (which descended to her late husband), lying in Portobacco, called *Sympsons Delight*, 300 acres; and three parcels of land, one called *Wassell*, 200 acres, the other called *London*, 100 acres, and other called *Blocksitch*, 100 acres; and parcel at Nanjemy, called *Glovers Point*, 200 acres; and parcel nr. Piscataway, called *Pitchley*, 200 acres. Also three parcels at the head of Wicocomoco R.: *Burton*, 90 acres; *Skidmores Adventure*, 37 acres; and *Susquehana*, 37 acres. Signed 7 Aug 1732. (Land: M#2.338-339) Thomas Wright (yeoman), of the Parish of Redbourn nr. Burrough of St. Albans, County of Hertford, England; says he has several yrs. known Francis Wine who was married in Hemel Hempstead Church on 1 Oct 1721, to Sarah Elkins, then a single woman, and which said Francis Wine died ab. 20 Nov 1730. Francis always lived with his wife; he being only son of Henry Wine, late of Pikesley in the County of Northampton; he heard that sd. Henry Wine had a bro. named Francis who died before the age of 14. Said Francis Wine, the grandson who died in 1730 left issue, Henry his eldest son now living and aged ab. 10 yrs., and three other sons, Francis, aged ab. 8, William aged ab. 5, and John aged 3 yrs. Signed 8 Aug 1732. Affirmed by Edward Wright of St. Albans. (Land: M#2.340)

WINSER (WINSOR), Garvis. Mentions son William, son Joseph, dau. Elizabeth, dau. Ann, son Thomas and son John. Wife Elizabeth, extx. He directs that he be buried beside first wife on dwell. plan. Test: Richard Chidley (dec'd at date of probate), Edward (Eadman) Grainman, Giancet Crecian (mentions Jennat Club, lately called Jennet Bryan). (Will: 20.165; ---- 1727; 10 March 1730)

WINSOR, Jarvis. Bequeathed to his son and dau., William and Elizabeth Winsor, a tract called *Smiths Chance*, cont. 144 acres. The land was divided by agreement betw. William Winsor and Edward Walker, who married sd. Elizabeth. Signed 13 Nov 1733. (Land: O#2.19)

WINTER, Ignatius and his sister Ann Winter. Indenture dated [early 1732/3]. Tract called *Addition to the Orphants Loss*, originally to be divided betw. afsd.; Ann to have the upper part where the widow Carpenter now lives, bounded by a tract of land called *Good Luck*, land called *Ingerstone*, the northeast Branch of Nanjemie Creek. (Land: M#2.316)

WINTER, Walter. Next of kin: Edward Millstead, Thomas Millstead. Admrs.: Catherine Winter, William Winter, John Winter. (Inv.: 17.710; ----; 3 April 1734)

WINTER, Katherine, widow, of Walter Winters. Signed 3 Sept 1734. To her two children, Ignatius and Ann Winter, two Negro women, Sarah Toge and Rose. Mentions other three children (unnamed). Admx. with her sons, John and William Winter, quit claims to her son's part of the estate of Walter Winter. (Land: O#2.50E, 63)

WINTER, John, son of Walter Winter, and Elizabeth Bruce, married 6 Dec 1736, by Rev. John Donaldson. (Trinity: 110—rev.)

WINTER, Judith Townley, dau. of John and Elizabeth Winter, born 4 Nov 1743. (Trinity: 110—rev.)

WISE, Richard. Next of kin: Two children, unnamed and under age. (Inv.: 36C.251; 19 July 1715; ----)

WITTER, Thomas and Mary. Their children: Thomas, born 9 Feb 1672; Buckley (Bulkeley), born 26 July 1675; William, born 26 Sept 1678; George, born 9 Oct 1683. (Ct.&Land: P#1.207, 210; QRev.4, 5, 6, 9)

WITTER, Thomas, planter, and his wife Mary. Indenture, 7 Sept 1675, to Francis Wine, cooper (Ct.&Land: F#1.140)

WITTER, William, son of Thomas Witter. Chooses his father in law [stepfather] John Duglas (cooper), as his guardian, 2 Jan 1693. (Ct.&Land: S#1.212)

WITTER, George, son of Thomas Witter, dec'd. Apprenticed for four years to John Martin (boatwright) and Demaris his wife; with consent of John Duglas (cooper), his father in law [step-father], 2 Jan 1693. (Ct.&Land: S#1.211)

WITTER, Margaret, former wife of Walter Poore, dec'd., now wife of Walter Witter (a cooper). Deed of gift, 100 acres, 21 July 1703, to son Robert Poore at age 18; mentions daus. Margaret the younger and Mary Poore. (Ct.&Land: Z#1.103)

WITHER (WHITTER), William, planter, Port Tobacco Parish. In his will he left to wife Ann, extx., entire estate. (Will: 21.730; 5 Dec 1736; 24 Jan 1736) Next of kin: George Whitter, James Latimre. Extx.: Ann Whitter. (Inv.: 22.517; 9 June 1737; 12 Oct 1737)

WOOFE, Robert, age 17 yrs. Servant of Robert Rowlants, 11 June 1678. (Ct.&Land: G#1.157)

310

WOLPH, Mary, dau. of Joseph Wolph. Cattle mark recorded June 1678.
(Ct.&Land: G#1.164)
WOLPH, Mary, dau. of Joseph Wolph. Cattle mark recorded, 8 Aug 1682.
(Ct.&Land: I#1.316)
WOLF, Joseph. (Inv.: 8.444; 20 Nov 1685; ----)

WOLLIS, Anne. Maid servant judged to be 18 years old, presented by John Courts, 27 March 1662 (Ct.&Land: B#1.101)

WOMMAN, Mary. (Inv.: 9.178; 23 Oct 1686; ----)

WOOD, Mary, dau. of John Wood. Cattle mark recorded, 1676. It being the previous cattle mark of Robert Troope. (Ct.&Land: H#1.227)
WOOD, John, son of John Wood. Cattle mark recorded, 13 Feb 1684.
(Ct.&Land: L#1.92)
WOOD, John Sr. To wife Margaret, extx., 50 acres, between Goose and Nanjemy Cks., on n. side Rotterdam. Son John, daus. Mary Williams and Eliza: Killingsworth have received their portions. To children Elijah, Jane, Ann, Sarah and Hannah Wood, residue of land in Stafford Co., Virginia. Codicil 10 Dec 1715 — Dau. Margaret, born after making of will, to share with children named in sd. land in Virginia, and son Elijah live with his mother until he is 21 yrs. of age. (Will: 14.106; 5 Jan 1709; 6 April 1716)
WOOD, John Jr. Next of kin: John Wood. (Inv.: 34.236; 19 Aug 1713; ----)
WOOD, John Jr. Admr.: Elisabeth Wood. (Acct: 36A.244; ----; 12 Oct 1714)
WOOD, John. Next of kin: Edward Williams, Jeane Wood. (Inv.: 36C.259; 9 April 1716; ----)
WOOD, John. Extx.: Margaret Wood. (Acct: 37C.140; ----; 20 Dec 1716)
WOOD, Abraham, of St. Mary's Co. (tailor), and his wife Ann, conveyed on 21 April 1736 part of a tract of land in St. Mary's Co. called *Woods Pleasure*, 70 acres. (Land: O#2.150. See also Land O#2.160)
WOOD, Peter, and his wife Susanna, on 9 Dec 1736 conveyed part of a tract called *Lyons Den*, on w. side of Zachia Swamp, 140 acres, and an adjoining tract of 38 acres called *Woods Addition*. (Land: O#2.181)
WOOD, John. Next of kin: Matthew Reagon, Anne Ross. Admr.: Elisabeth Carroll, wife of James Carroll. (Inv.: 24.476; ----; 16 April 1740)
WOOD, Elisabeth. To godson Ralph Gardner, Elizabeth Coble and Mary Owen, entire estate. Note: Mary Roby, sister of Eliz: Wood agrees to probate of above will. (Will: 22.377; 1 April 1741; 6 June 1741) Next of kin: Robert Senit, James Mankin, Jean Mankin. Admr./Ex.: Benjamin Robey. (Inv.: 26.213; 23 June 1741; 1 Sept 1741)
WOOD, Isaac (planter), of St. Mary's Co., and his wife Mary, on 9 Nov 1743 conveyed part of a tract called *Woods Pleasure*, lying on e. side of Piles Fresh, 77 acres. (Land: X#2.57)

WOODARD. (See WOODWARD.)

WOODMAN, John and his wife Sarah, one of the daus. of George Newman, dec'd. Partition of moiety, of the lands lately in the possession of George Newman; also partitions for Eleanor Noe, James Williams and Eliza: his wife, and for Mary Newman — each 75 acres; agreement witnessed by John Hamill (Hammill) and his wife Sarah; signed 6 March 1729/30. To John Harris Jr., parcel cont. 75 acres; deed recorded 3 May 1733. (Land: M#2.235, 334, 336)

WOODKEEPE, Richard, age 12 yrs. Servant of Cornelius Mackaries, 9 Sept 1673. (Ct.&Land: E#1.137)

WOODARD (WOODERD), John. (Inv.: 6.18; 30 Jan 1678; ---) Admr.: John Butcher. (Acct: 7A.230; ----; 21 Sept 1680)

WOODGARD, Richard, son of Henry Woodgard. Gift dated ca. 1685/6, from Richard Pinnar, a heifer. (Ct.&Land: M#1.10)

WOODYARD, John (carpenter) and Jane his wife. Indenture, 18 Feb 1712/3, to Henry Brett; parcel called *Southrick Beginning*, cont. 20 acres. (Ct.&Land: D#2.40)

WOODYARD, John and Jean his wife, dau. of Gerrard Browne, dec'd. and John Newton, son of Richard Newton, dec'd. Indenture, 26 Feb 1716, to John Sanders. A parcel on s. side of St. Thomas Creek, part of *Christian Temple Manor*. (Ct.&Land: H#2.73)

WOODWARD, John and Jane his wife and John Newton, conveyed on 7 March 1717, a tract called *Simpsons Supply* on the e. side of Piscataway River and s. side of Mattawoman Creek, cont. 100 acres. (Ct.&Land: H#2.145)

WOODYARD, John, age 44. Deposition, 5 Nov 1719, regarding part of tract called *Christian Temple Manor*, on the s. side of Mattawoman; he visited site with John Sanders and his father Matthew Sanders and John Newton. (Chas LandComm: M2.123)

WOODWARD, John, age 43. Deposition on 22 Xber 1719, regarding the tract *Christian Temple Mannour*. (Chas LandComm: M2.68)

WOODYARD, John, age 44. Deposition, 9 Aug 1721; refers to conversation about seven years ago of Martha Cornish and John Cornish. (Chas LandComm: M2.123)

WOODYARD, John, son of Richard Woodyard. Cattle mark recorded 24 Oct 1726. (Land: L#2.318)

WOODWARD, John (Gent.), of St. Mary's Co., and his wife Mary. 17 Nov 1738. To Edward Sanders (Saunders), a tract called *Anns Delight*, being on s. side of Zachia Swamp. (Land: O#2.379)

WOODARD (WOODWARD), John. In his will he left to son Henry, plan. on which he now dwells. To wife's eldest son, land. To children Elizabeth, Mary, James, personalty. Wife, extx. (Will: 23.141; 5 April 1743; 23 June 1743) Mentions: John Cunningham, Richard Woodward, Henry Woodward. Admr./Ex.: Jane Woodward. (Inv.: 28.235; ----; 10 Sept 1743)

WOOLCOCK, Christian, dau. of Christopher and Mary Woolcock of
Portobacco, born 10 Dec 1694. (Ct.&Land: QRev.24)

WOOLF, Joseph, age 13 yrs. Boy servant, presented by Robert Perkins, 8
March 1663/4. (Ct.&Land: B#1.258)

WORLAND, John, son of John Worland, born 2 Jan 1685. (Ct.&Land: M#1.10)
WORLAND, John, of William and Mary Parish. In his will he left to son
John at majority, entire estate, including 86 acres, *New Allsford* in
Pickawaxen, and 150 acres *Docker's Delight*. In event of his death
unmarried or without issue, *Allsford* afsd. to pass to Protestant minister
of William and Mary Parish, and *Docker's Delight* to pass to Thomas
Whichaley. Ex.: Thos. Whichaley afsd., who is appointed quardian of son
John during minority. (Will: 11.203; 6 Sept 1701; 11 Nov 1701) (Inv.:
21.374; 29 Dec 1701; ----)
WORLAND, John (planter) and his wife Mary conveyed on 12 Oct 1709 tract
called *Dockers Delight*, cont. 60 acres. (Ct.&Land: C#2.144)
WORLAND, John, and Stacey his wife conveyed on 12 June 1711 part of a
360 acre tract called *Docker's Delight*, cont. 50 acres. (Ct.&Land:
C#2.251)

WORRALL, Robert. (Inv.: 8.125; 12 Feb 1683; ----) Admr.: Margrett
Cornell, wife of Joseph Cornell. (Acct: 9.76; ----; 13 Aug 1686)

WORTHINGTON, Joseph, age 15 yrs. Servant of Edward Rookard, 11 Aug
1685. (Ct.&Land: L#1.161)

WOTTON, James, of Ogburn St. George in the County of Wilts in Great
Britain (clerke) and Frances, his wife (lately called Frances Townley, one
of the sisters of Mary Rogers dec'd., formerly called Mary Contee of
Charles Co., widow). To John Fendall, William Marshall, dec'd., by virtue
of a patent of 20 March 1650, for 500 acres called *Mash Land* [*Marshalls
Land*]. Walter Bayne became seized in fee to 450 acres and died
possessed, which land descended to John Bayne, son of Walter Bayne who
died and the land descended to Walter Bayne, his son who conveyed the
land to Mary Contee called Mary Rogers and when she died the land
descended to the hrs. of Judith Bruce, dec'd, lately called Judith Townley,
one of the sisters of the afsd. Mary. Deed dated 13 Dec 1731. (Land:
M#2.294, 345)
WOTTON (WOOTTON), James, of Ogburn, St. George in the county of
Wilts, England (clerk) and Frances, his wife, (lately called Frances
Townley, one of the sisters of Mary Rogers, dec'd., formerly called Mary
Contee of Charles Co., widow). To John Fendall, tract called *Marshalls
Land*, on w. side of Wicomoco River. Another sister Judith Bruce, late of
Chas. Co., dec'd., lately called Judith Townley. 13 Dec 1731. (Land: O#2.6B)

WRIGHT, George, age 18-19 yrs. Servant of Benjamin Rozer, 1676.
(Ct.&Land: F#1.194)
WRIGHT, Elinor, dau. of George and Anne Wright, born 7 Oct 1683.
(Ct.&Land: P#1.207; QRev.9)
WRIGHT, William. Admr.: Robert Thompson Sr. (Acct: 8.448; ----; 3 Dec 1684)
RIGHT, Robert. (Inv.: 10.77; 25 March 1688; ----)
WRIGHT (WRITE), John. Admr.: Richard Harrison, Richard Wade. (Inv.: 13A.276; 4 May 1695; ----) Payments include Dr. Hugh Mockella for care of Ann Wright. Mentions: four orphans (unnamed). Admrs.: Richard Harrison, Richard Wade. (Acct: 13B.8; ----; 16 May 1696) Admrs.: Richard Harrison, Richard Wade. (Acct: 19½A.100; ----; 16 Dec 1699)
WRIGHT, Thomas and Mary his wife conveyed on 4 March 1714 a parcel called *St. Thomases*, cont. 300 acres. (Ct.&Land: F#2.29)
WRIGHT, Thomas (planter), and his wife Mary conveyed on 13 July 1738 a parcel of land of 48 acres and on 31 July 1738, 48 acres. (Land: O#2.342, 343)
WRIGHT, Daniel. Lease, 30 Dec 1743, to 100 acres in St. Thomas' Manor, for the term of 3 lives of Daniel Wright, his wife (unnamed) and his dau. Susanna Wright. (Land: X#2.126)

WYOTT, John, age 16 yrs. Servant of Mrs. Beane, 10 June 1673. (Ct.&Land: E#1.132)

WYNE. (See WINE.)

YAPPE, Roger. Servant of Henry Hawkins, age judged to be 21 yrs., 12 Jan 1685. (Ct.&Land: M#1.67)

YATES, Robert. In right of his wife Rebecca, of goods and chattels of Nathaniell Vering (dec'd.), 12 June 1688. (Ct.&Land: N#1.329)
YATES, Robert. Married Rebeckah, relict of James Tyer, dec'd., who was exr. of Lawrence Hoskins, dec'd., dated 5 Oct 1688. (Ct.&Land: Q#1.42)
YATES, Robert, son of Robert and Rebeckah Yates of Pickawaxen, born 10 April 1690. (Ct.&Land: P#1.211; QRev.16)
YATES, Charles, son of Robert and Rebeckah Yates of Pickawaxon, born 29 April 1692. (Ct.&Land: P#1.211; QRev.18)
YATES, Robert Jr., eldest son of Robert Yates. Deed of gift, 9 Jan 1703, from James Tyler. (Ct.&Land: Z#1.67)
YATES, Robert, age 30, son of Robert Yates, dec'd. Deposition in 1710 (petition of John Maddox) regarding a tract on the w. side of Wicomico River, originally patented for John Courts, 200 acres. (Chas LandComm: M2.83)
YATES, Charles, son of Robert Yates. Deposition in 1710 (petition of John Maddox) regarding a tract on the w. side of Wicomico River, originally patented for John Courts, 200 acres. (Chas LandComm: M2.83)

YATES, Robert Sr. In his will he left to eldest son Robert, ex., 250 acres, on Wiccomico R., bought of Benony Foning and Hannah, his wife. To son Charles, 180 acres, tract called *Manchester*, and 150 acres, *Herds Mountains*, also 50 acres, *Arabia*. To wife Lydia, 160 acres, *Wollring Field* and personalty belonging to Mr. Hatton's estate. (Will: 13.638; 19 Nov 1713; 26 Dec 1713)

YATES, Robert (gentleman). Next of kin: --din Yates, Charles Yates. (Inv.: 35A.230; 16 Feb 1713; ----. Another Inv.: 36B.36; 28 Dec 1714; ----)

YATES, Robert. A second inventory was cited. Payments to: mother (unnamed) and brother (unnamed) of executor, Thomas Britaght. Legatees: Charles Yates, Mrs. Lydia Yates. Ex.: Robert Yates. (Acct: 36B.30; ----; 3 March 1714) Ex.: Robert Yates. (Acct: 37C.134; ----; 5 March 1716)

YATES, Lydia, Mrs. Next of kin: John Maddox, William Hawton. (Inv.: 39A.42; 18 April 1718; --)

YATES, Ledia. (Inv.: 2.233; 1719; ----)

YATES, Charles and his wife Jane (Jean) conveyed on 7 March 1729 two tracts, *Heards Mountain*, 150 acres, and *Arabia*, 50 acres. (Land: L#2.464)

YATES, Robert (Maj.). Next of kin: Charles Yates, Eliza Gwinn. Admr./Ex.: Ann Yates. (Inv.: 28.239; 27 July 1743; 3 Oct 1743) (Inv.: 28.498; ----; 10 April 1744)

YATES, Robert, and his wife Sarah, acquired on 1 March 1743/4 from Charles Bruce (son of John Bruce), three tracts, one being near Wicomico River, which was conveyed by Walter Bayne and his wife Martha, to Mary Contee, a tract called *Himslays Marsh* on the w. side of Wicomico River, 70 acres; also a tract called *Hemesley Meadows* bounded by Wicomico Marsh, 130 acres. In consideration Robert Yates and his wife Sarah, relict and extx. of John Bruce, relinquish dower right to two tracts, *Hatton's Point* and *Chesnut Point*, late the estate of said John Bruce. (Land: X#2.83, 106)

YOAKLEY, Stephen, Capt. Admr.: Martha Yoakley. (Inv.: 18.33; 29 Jan 1733; 1 May 1734)

YOAKLEY, Martha, Mrs., widow. In her will she mentions dau. Rachel Semmes; son Aaron Prather; grandson Aaron, minor son of Aaron; grandson Baruch Williams; Charity Theobald; children Eleanor Williams, Thomas Prather, John Smith Prather, and Philip Prather. To sons, Thomas, Philip, and John Smith Prather, tract called *Sprigs Request* at Collington, in accordance to their father's will. Exs.: Thomas and John Smith Prather, and Thomas Williams. (Will: 22.524; 19 June 1742; 13 Nov 1742) Next of kin: Baruck Williams, Josiah Prather. Exs.: Thomas Prather, John Smith Prather, Thomas Williams. (Inv.: 27.385; 3 Dec 1742; 1 April 1742)

315

YOPP, Charles. In his will he left to father Roger Yopp, personalty. Legacies left in his hands by his grandfather, Jno. Alward, to be delivered to Sarah and Jane Yopp and Dorothy Brown. Wife, extx. (Will: 15.105; 5 Jan 1717; 21 April 1719) Next of kin: Roger Yopp, Jane Yopp. (Inv.: 2.235; 22 April 1719; ----)

YOPP, Roger. Next of kin: Sarah Yopp, Susannah Mathews. (Inv. 3.190; [c1719]; ----)

YOUNG, Arthur and Ann of Patuxent. Their children: Frances, born 3rd day of 10th month, 1683, about 2 in the morning; Anna, born 22nd of 9th month, 1685; Peter, born 12th of 11th month 1687/8; Mary, born 2nd of 5th month 1689; Arthur, born 3rd of 1st month 1690/1; Constant, born 20th of 5th month 1693; Ann, born 23rd of 9th month 1695; Elizabeth, born 2nd of 11th month 1697/8; Sarah and Elizabeth, born 2nd of 11th month 1698/9. (Clifts Monthly Meeting, Quaker Records of So. MD, p. 54-55)

YOUNGE, Charles, age 10 yrs. Servant of Samuel Fendall, 2nd Tues in Aug 1673. (Ct.&Land: E#1.135)

YOUNGE, Lawrance and Sarah Younge of the head of Baker's Ck. Their child: John, born 4 Dec 1673; Thomas, born 18 May 1678. (Ct.&Land: P#1.206; QRev.5, 6)

YOUNGE, Lawrence (planter) of St. Mary's Co. Deed of gift 5 Sept 1677, to his wife Sarah Younge. (Ct.&Land: G#1.55)

YOUNG, Jane, age 20 yrs. Servant of Elinor Bayne, 11 March 1678. (Ct.&Land: H#1.130)

YOUNGE, Thomas, son of Lawrance and Sarah Younge, of the head of Baker's Creek, born 18 May 1678. (Ct.&Land: P#1.206)

YOUNG, Elizabeth. In her will she left to Robert Yates, Mr. Boules and James Tyre, and goddau. Ellinor Boreman, daughter of Maj. Wm. Boreman, William Hunter, and Mr. Hall, personalty. Richard Hobbart, residuary legatee. Ex.: Wm. Boarman Jr. By codicil (7.145) dated 19 Oct 1695, testatrix bequeaths 60 acres, *Bullen*, in Chas. Co. to grandson Boules, son of James Tyre. (Will: 7.142; 7 Oct 1695; 21 Jan 1695/6) Ex.: William Boarman Jr. (Acct: 14.149; ----; 19 May 1697) Legatees: Robert Yates, Mr. Hunter & Mr. Hall, Richard Hubbard, James Tiers, Bowles Tyers. Ex.: William Boreman. (Acct: 19.113 (Dupe: 19.156); ----; -- June 1699)

YOUNG, John. In his will he left to Gilbert, youngest son of Jno. Sympson, personalty. John Crane, ex. (Will: 3.234; 29 Nov 1704; 7 Dec 1704) Ex.: John Crane. (Acct: 25.129; ----; 23 April 1705)

[torn], Rurthe, age 14 yrs. Servant of John Stone, 2nd Tues in Nov 1670. (Ct.&Land: D#1.169)

INDEX

-A-

A Trifle, 177
Abberdeen, 1
ABBOTT, Edward, 1, 29
  Susanna, 137
  Thomas, 1
Aberdeene, 182
ABERNATHY, James, 90, 191
  John, 90
  Thomas, 90, 91, 191
  William, 90
ABINGTON, John, 150
  Mary, 150
ABURNATHY, Ann, 204
ACHILLES, Peter, 80
Acquinkekas Hill, 275
ACTON, Anne, 1
  Eleanor, 182
  Henry, 1, 182, 273
  John, 1
ADAIR, Alexander, 1, 66
  Christian, 1
ADAMES, Henry, 56, 169, 209, 215
ADAMS, Benjamin, 2, 175
  Charity, 132, 288
  Charles, 1, 2
  Elizabeth, 1, 2, 201, 276
  Francis, 1, 57
  George, 1, 2
  Grace, 1
  Henry, 1, 107, 118, 154, 174, 181, 230
  Hester, 2
  James, 91
  John, 2, 201
  Joseph, 58
  Lodowick, 1
  Lodwick, 2
  Luke, 2
  Margaret, 1
  Marie, 1
  Mary, 1, 2
  Mr., 223, 235
  Richard, 2
  Samuel, 110, 288
  Sarah, 1
Adamses Delight, 1
ADDAMES, Henry, 42, 107, 138, 150
  Mr., 42
ADDAMS, Charles, 1
  Francis, 109
  George, 1
  Mary, 109
Addams Delight, 1, 2
ADDISON, Jane, 2
  John, 2, 81, 225
  Rebecca, 79
  William, 2
Addition, 35, 36, 140, 151, 187, 227, 257
Addition of St. Johns, 204
Addition to Belmont, 177
Addition to Cattles Grave, 195
Addition to Clair, 119
Addition to Hereford, 126
Addition to May Day, 254
Addition to the Adventure, 177
Addition to the Orphants Loss, 309
ADERTON, Anne, 173
  Jeremiah, 173
Adventure, 3, 154, 177
A'GAMBRA,
  Domindigue, 103
  Richard, 103
AGAMBRAH,
  Domindigo, 39
AGBOROUGH,
  Thomas, 2
AILER, Elizabeth, 2
  Mary, 2
ALAVERY, Faith, 62
Albergirn, 24
ALCOCK(E), Mary, 2
  Thomas, 2, 224
ALDEN, Mary, 2
Aldgate, 250
ALDIS, William, 2
ALEXANDER, Ann, 100
  Robert, 100, 101
ALLANSON, Charles, 230, 301
  Elizabeth, 230
  Thomas, 4, 230, 231, 301
ALLCOCK, Thomas, 2, 89
ALLCOCKS, Thomas, 83
ALLCOKE, Thomas, 83
ALLCOX, Thomas, 99, 281
ALLEN, Ann(e), 3
  Barbara, 3, 4
  Barbary, 1, 4
  Catherine, 4
  Elisabeth, 4
  Elizabeth, 3
  Ellinor, 3, 161
  Esther, 3
  George, 3

James, 3, 222
John, 3, 4, 20, 96, 115, 131, 161, 261
Joseph, 4, 56, 65, 92, 307
Katherine, 3, 4
Martha, 2, 39
Mary, 3, 307
Pentheceelia, 4
Philip, 3, 182
Robert, 3
Susanna, 3, 4
Thomas, 3, 4, 182
William, 2, 39
Allens Addition, 72, 75
Allens Grove, 75
ALLENSON, Charles, 4
Thomas, 4, 121
Allenson's Folly, 234
ALLESON, Thomas, 231
ALLIN, George, 3
James, 3, 4
Jane, 3
John, 3
Susan, 4
William, 3
ALLING, Barbary, 1
ALLINSON, Annabella, 4
Thomas, 4
Allinsons Supply, 262, 272, 273
ALLISON, Barbary, 42
Charles, 4
Elizabeth, 301
Thomas, 4, 301
Allisons Manor, 24
Allison's Supply, 263
Allissons Secret, 4
ALLITON, Susannah, 4
ALLONSON, Thomas, 4
ALLORD, John, 5

Allsford, 312
ALLWARD, Anne, 5
John, 5, 57, 304
Margarett, 5
Mary, 5
ALLWOOD, John, 5
Susannah, 5
William, 5
ALVEY, Leonard, 5
Margret, 5
ALWARD, John, 315
AMBROSS, Margaret, 5
Richard, 5
Amendment, 110
AMERY, Elinor, 5
John, 5
Lydia, 5
Mary, 5
Samuel, 5, 283
AMOS, William, 279
Amsterdam, 131
ANCHORAM, Mary, 5, 6, 9
Richard, 5, 6, 9
ANCTILL, Barnaby, 243
ANDERSON, Ann, 6
Anne, 6, 197
Archbald, 6
Bartholomew, 6
Edward, 6, 46, 72, 197
Elizabeth, 6
George, 6
James, 6
John, 6, 264
Katherine, 6
Mary, 6
Richard, 6, 264
Robert, 6
Sarah, 6
Andersons Chance, 6
ANDERTON, Ann, 6
Jeremiah, 6

ANDRASS, Benjamin, 7
Lawrence, 7
William, 7
ANDRES, Elizabeth, 7
Henry, 7
Lawrence, 7
Mary, 7
ANDREWS, John, 218
ANDROSIE, Lawrence, 46
ANGE, Elizabeth, 7
William, 7
Angell, 307
Angerstone, 292
Anglicey Comp., Blowmoris, 308
ANGLISH, John, 7
ANKREM, John, 7
Mary, 7
ANKRUM, Mary, 99
Richard, 99, 100
Anne Arundel County, 27, 28, 137, 162, 165, 224, 236, 252, 270
Annapolis, 136, 137, 234
London Town, 224
ANNES, Sarah, 7
Thomas, 7
ANNIS, Elisabeth, 306
Elizabeth, 7, 306
J., 7
Thomas, 7, 150
William, 7, 150
Anns Delight, 311
ANSEL(L), Ann, 8, 286
William, 7, 8, 108, 109, 286
ANSIL(L), Ann, 8
William, 8
APLEBY, Charles, 36
APPLEYARD, John, 8

Susanna, 8
AQUANTANCE,
  Robert, 11
Aquenseek, 203
Aquimsick?, 6
Arabia, 284, 314
ARCELIS, Elizabeth,
  99
Archibalds Desert, 212,
  218
ARCHIBALL, John, 8
ARNLEY, James, 8
ARROWSMITH,
  Gerrard, 8
ASCOMB, George, 257
ASH, Anne, 176, 188
  Thomas, 176, 188
Ashar, 32
ASHBROOKE, Anne, 8
  Edward, 8
  Elizabeth, 8
  James, 8, 59
  John, 8
  Lettise, 8
  Rose, 8
  Thomas, 8
Ashbrook's Rest, 253
ASHCOM, Judith, 37
ASHFORD, Michael, 8
  Michaell, 9
  Rachell, 8, 9
ASHFORTH, Mary, 9
  Michaell, 9
  Rachell, 9
ASHMAN, Allward
  Hardy, 9
  Allwood Hardy, 9
  Ann(a), 9
  Anne, 9
  Elizabeth, 9
  John, 5, 6, 9, 99, 123,
    126, 244
  Mary, 9

Richard, 9, 99, 100,
  123, 127
Standidge, 9
Standish, 9
Thomas, 49
Ashman Parche, 9
ASHTON, Burdit, 9
  James, 176
  Mary, 9
ASKIN, Beththyah
  Harrison, 9
  George, 9, 123
  Vincent, 298
ASKINS, Mark, 61
  Mary, 61
ASPEANWALL,
  Henry, 9
ASPENALL, Elisabeth,
  10
  Elizabeth, 9
  Henry, 9, 10, 144
Aspenalls Chance, 9
ASPHEN, Dorothy, 247
  William, 247
ASPINALL, Henry, 9,
  99, 171, 306
  Mary, 9, 99, 306
Aspinalls Chance, 189
Aspinals Chance, 173
Aspinnall's Chance,
  250
Assentons, 91
ASTEN, Thomas, 4
ASTERE, George, 10
ATCHISON, Ann, 10
  James, 10
  John, 10
  Joseph, 10
  Vincent, 16
  William, 10, 50
Atchison's Hazard, 10
Atchison's Strife, 10
Atchison's Woodyard,
  10

ATHEE, Ann, 10
  George, 10
Atheshoop, 88
ATHEY, George, 10
  John, 10
  Sarah, 10
ATTKINS, Anne, 220
  Edward, 286
  William, 10
ATTWOOD, Peter, 26,
  59, 153, 230
ATWICKS, Elisabeth,
  147
ATWOOD, Peter, 88
AUSHISH, William, 10
AUSIL, William, 109
AUSTIN, John, 10
  Mary, 10
  Susanna, 10, 222
  Thomas, 10, 89, 222,
    301
AYLET, Elizabeth, 94
  William, 94
AYLMER, Justianian,
  10
  Justinian, 34
AYRES, Ellinor, 10
  George, 10, 11
  John, 10
  Joseph, 10

-B-
BAARNS, Richard, 41
BABB, Elizabeth, 11
  Peter, 11
BABTISTA, John, 11
Bachelor's Hope, 156
BACKER, Barbara, 15
BAGGOTT, Alice, 11
  John, 11
  Mary, 120
  Samuel, 11
  Thomas, 11
BAILD, John, 41

BAILEY, Grace, 11
  Sarah, 119
BAILY, William, 11
BAITEMAN, Patrick, 18
BAKER, Andrew, 12, 255
  Charles, 3, 260
  Elizabeth, 12
  Hamlet, 12
  John, 24, 84, 116, 141, 200, 255
  Margaret, 12
  Martha, 12, 35, 255
  Mary, 12
  Stephen, 12
  Susannah, 24
  Thomas, 12, 22, 23, 84, 93, 94, 107, 120, 255
Baker's Addition, 5, 9, 64, 255
Bakers Enlargement, 179
Baker's Rest, 255, 179
BALEY, James, 83
BALL, John, 13
  Thomas, 13
  Winifred, 13
BALLIYS, Sharp, 72
BALSE, Oliver, 1
Baltemore Bounty, 64
Baltemores Gift, 213, 298
Baltimore County, 79
Baltimore County, 64, 82, 95, 107, 154, 187, 252, 300, 301
Baltimore Gift, 158
Baltimore's Bounty, 64, 220
Baltimore's G(u)ift, 82, 37, 132

Baltimores Kindness, 26
BALTROP, Ann, 13
  Francis, 13
BALY, John, 11
BANCKES, Mary, 13
  Richard, 13
  Samuel, 13
  Sarah, 13
BANE, Ebsworth, 300
  Kindrick, 300
BANESTER, Benjamin, 231, 232
  Frances, 232
  John, 231, 232
  Lawrence, 232
  Timothy, 232
BANISTER, Elizabeth, 13
  John, 13, 232
  Timothy, 13
BANKES, Capt., 287
BARACLOW, Tobie, 13
BARAN, Mary, 16
  Richard, 16
Barbadoes, 32, 82, 298
Barbadoes, Island of, 33, 69
  St. Michaels, 32
BARBER, Baptist, 209
  Cornelius, 209
  Edward, 261
  Luke, 103, 209, 301
  Mary, 13
  Richard, 9, 13
BAREFOOT, John, 13
Bargain, 259
BARGESS, Elizabeth, 43
  Samuel, 43
  Thomas, 43
Bargids?, 166
BARKER, Ann, 14
  Catrine, 14

  Dorothy, 14
  Elizabeth, 14, 35
  George, 14, 35
  Joan, 14
  John, 14, 28, 35, 77, 105, 215, 218, 297
  Katherine, 14
  Leonard, 14
  Margaret, 254
  Martha, 14, 28, 35, 298
  Mary, 76, 297
  Peter, 14
  Robert, 14
  Samuell, 123
  Sarah, 161
  William, 14, 28, 35
  ———, 14
Barker's Enlargement, 14
Barker's Rest, 14
BARKSTONE, Clement, 237
BARLOW, Joel, 14
Barn Hill, 70
BARNABY, Elisabeth, 257
Barnabye, 225, 226
Barnehill, 69
BARNES, Barbara, 15
  Benjamin, 15
  Bethia, 132, 267
  Christian, 14
  Edmond, 14
  Edward, 14
  Elizabeth, 14
  Francis, 14
  Godshall, 14
  Henry, 14, 15, 94, 151
  Jane, 14
  Joseph, 108
  Mary, 97
  Mat(t)hew, 14, 18, 118, 146

Sarah, 14, 118
Thomas, 14, 15
BARNHAM, Jane, 213
  John, 213
BARNS, Mathew, 156
  Matthew, 60
BARON, John, 15
  Martha, 15
  Mary, 15
  Richard, 15
BARRAN, Priscilla, 166
BARREN, Thomas, 15
BARRET, Joseph, 15
  Samuel, 15, 88
BARRETT, Elizabeth, 15
  James, 15
  John, 15
  William, 15
BARRON, Ann, 15
  John, 15, 290
  Martha, 15
  Mary, 166
  Peter, 15
  Thomas, 15, 158, 166
BARROTT, Robert, 31
BARROW, Charles, 15, 223
  John, 15
BARRY, John, 33
BARTLET, Elisabeth, 8
  Thomas, 8
BARTLETT, Elisabeth, 16
  Mary, 16
  Ralph, 16
  Thomas, 16
BARTON, Ann, 16
  David, 17
  Elizabeth, 16, 17
  George, 16, 89
  Grace, 16
  Margaret, 147
  Margret, 192

Martha, 16
Mary, 293
Nathan, 16, 17, 186
Nathaniel, 279
Rachell, 17
Robert, 16
Sarah, 119
Thomas, 17
William, 16, 17, 24, 66, 101, 106, 107, 119, 130, 136, 144, 147, 148, 160, 192, 206, 217, 243, 259, 293
Bartons Enlargement, 217
Barton's Hope, 217, 260
Bartons Wood Yard, 147, 148, 192
Bartoyne Hill, 61
BARTTON, Elizabeth, 17
  Nathan, 17
  Rachel, 17
  Ralph, 95
Bastable, 59, 75
Bastford Manor, 94
BASWELL, William, 123
BATCHELER, Francis, 17
Batchellors Forrest, 164
Batchelor's Agreement, 78
Batchelor's Delight, 148, 253
Batchelor's Harbor, 25
Batchelor's Hope, 55, 110, 153
Batchelor's Horne, 226
Batchelors Rest, 262

BATEMAN, Benjamin, 18
  Elizabeth, 18
  George, 18, 152
  John, 17, 18, 153, 247
  Lawrance, 18
  Mary, 17, 18, 152, 289
  Monacak, 247
  Murdoe, 18
  Thomas, 18, 217, 289
BATHERTON, John, 18
BATMAN, Thomas, 153
BATON, Murdo, 18
BATTEN, William, 29, 241
Batten's Clift(s), 47, 221
Battessey, 185
BATTIN, Margery, 18
  William, 18, 241
BATTLE, Anthony, 18
Batton's Clifts, 295
BAWLDING, Robert, 30
BAXTER, Edward, 221
BAYLEY, James, 11
  John, 183
Bayley's Rest, 183
BAYLIE, John, 11
  William, 11
BAYLY, James, 11
  John, 11
  Mary, 11
  Nicholas, 11
BAYNE, Ann, 18, 19, 267, 273
  Anne, 18, 19
  Burditt, 19
  Ebsworth, 18, 19, 171, 273
  Elinor, 270, 315
  Ellinor, 19

John, 18, 19, 80, 294, 295, 312
Kindrick, 19
Martha, 19, 314
Walter, 18, 19, 20, 97, 254, 294, 312, 314
Winifred, 254
———, 251
Baynes, 216, 253
Beach Neck, 24
BEACHFIELD, Elizabeth, 33
BEAD, Elizabeth, 19
John, 19
Mary, 19
Nicholas, 19
Sarah, 19
Susanna, 19
BEADE, John, 20
BEADON, Daniel, 20
BEAKE, Elizabeth, 93
BEALE, Charles, 282
Ellinor, 19, 250
Jeoffrey, 20
Johanah Catherine, 152
Johanna, 73
Johanna Catherine, 20
John, 20, 73, 152, 250
Jone, 20
Mary, 282
Ninian, 282
Richard, 20
BEALL, Elizabeth, 97
Ninian, 20
Ruth, 20
BEAMONT, John, 21
Thomas, 21
BEAN, Eleanor, 20
Walter, 20
Bean Plaine, 252
BEANE, Elenor, 21
Elinor, 229

Elizabeth, 21
Ellinor, 21
Mrs., 38, 313
Thomas, 21
Walter, 21, 57, 154, 182, 212, 277
Bean's Land, 174
BEARY, Humphry, 254
Samuel, 254
BEAUMONT, Anne, 21
BEAUMOUNT, Mary, 21
Richard, 21
BEAUMUNT, James, 21
BEAVAN, Charles, 158
BEAWAN, Basil, 73
BECK, Elisabeth, 21
Elizabeth, 21
Lewis, 21
Margarett, 21
Mary, 21, 205
Richard, 21, 45, 250
William, 104
Beckley, 186
BEE, Thomas, 21
Beeches Neck, 226
BEEMAN, William, 210
Beginning Lott, 12
BELAYNE, Elisabeth, 21
Elizabeth, 21
Jemima, 21
John, 21
Mary, 21
Nichola(u)s, 21
Belaynes Addition, 61
BELL, Bridgett, 20
Catherine, 20, 240
Charles, 20
Elizabeth, 20
Katherine, 20
Moses, 20, 240, 292
Ninian, 20

Richard, 20
William, 20
Bellconnell, 175
BELLINGHAM, Alice, 23
BELLOWS, George, 21
Belmont, 177
BENATHON, Christian, 22
BENCRAFT, Elenor, 41
BENJAR, Robert, 22
BENN, Fantolena, 58
BENNAM, Margaret, 22
BENNET, Isaac, 22
Susanna, 22
BENNETT, John, 22, 203
Mary, 22
BENNITT, John, 22
Mary, 22
BENSON, John, 22
Mary, 141
Robert, 22, 61, 138, 170
William, 6, 22
BENSTONE, Patrick, 22
BENT, Jeane, 35
Mary, 35
Robert, 35
William, 34
Bergen ap Zoen, 40, 197
Bergen-ap-Zome, 6, 124, 171
Bergen's op Zoem, 216
BERREY, Samuel, 22
Berry, 166
BERRY, Agnes, 64
Allice, 22
Edmond, 132
Elizabeth, 22, 64

Index

Esther, 22
Humphrey, 253
Humphry, 254
John, 22
Mary, 254
Thomas, 254
William, 22
Bettyes Delight, 152, 165, 274
BEVAN, Basil, 22, 23
　Blanford, 23
　Charles, 22, 23
　Henry, 23
　Martha, 23
　Mary, 22
　Richard, 23
Bevans Addition, 23
BEVENS, Mary, 198
Bew Plains, 252
BIAS, Elizabeth, 23
　Mary, 23
BIGGER, James, 140, 146
BIGGS, Ambros, 23
　Charity, 23
　Eliner, 23
　Elizabeth, 23
　John, 23
　Priscilla, 23
　Ruth, 23
　Sarah, 23
BILE, James, 23
BILLINGHAM, Mary, 23
BINNS, James, 23
BIRCH, John, 4
　Mary, 23
Birch Den, 148, 189
BIRD, John, 23
　Mary, 23, 102
Birds Head, 76
Birds Nest, 9, 100
BIRKHEAD, Jane, 49
Birmingham, 2

BIRTCH, Robert, 42
BIRTH, Mary, 220
　Robert, 42
Birth Denn, 268
BISHOP, Archibald, 23
　Elisabeth, 23
　Will, 23
　William, 23, 256
Black Oak Thicket(t), 154, 307
BLACKBEARD, Peeter, 23
BLACKFAN, Elizabeth, 24
　John, 24
　Mary, 24
　Richard, 24
BLADEN, Ann, 24
　Barbara, 24
　Thomas, 24
　William, 24, 99, 136, 174
BLAKWOOD, John, 24
BLANCH, John, 24
BLANCHET, Henry, 154
　John, 192
BLANCIT, Henry, 24
BLANFORD, Charles, 73
BLANSET(T), Henry, 212
BLANSHAT, Henry, 24
BLANSHET, John, 24
BLEE, John, 24, 170, 217
　Margaret, 24
Blew Plane, 25, 45
Blithwood, 86
BLIZAR, Giles, 45
BLIZ(Z)ARD, Anne, 25
　Giles, 25, 122, 140, 201, 237
　Susanna(h), 25, 238

Blocks(t)itch, 307, 308
Blowplaines, 45
Blueberry, 1
BLYZARD, Ann, 25
　Gyles, 25
　Mary, 25
　Susanna, 25
BOARD, Jane, 25
BOAREMAN, Capt., 46
　William, 16, 98, 231
BOARMAN, Baptist, 25
　Benedict, 25, 26, 27, 241
　Benedict Leonard 241
　Benjamin, 25, 26
　Clare, 25, 39
　Elizabeth, 26, 27
　Francis, 27, 241
　Francis
　　Ignatius, 25, 26, 27, 116, 241
　George, 305
　Gerard, 27
　Ignatius, 27
　James, 26
　Jane, 202
　Jean, 26, 27
　John, 27
　John Bablist, 241
　John Baptist(a), 25, 26, 27, 241
　Joseph, 26
　Maj., 25, 141
　Mary, 25, 26, 27, 205
　Sarah, 305
　Thomas James, 26, 27
　William, 25, 26, 27, 39, 75, 101, 116, 141, 162, 165, 198, 202, 305, 315
Boarmans Manor, 293
Boarmans Reserve, 39, 198

Boarmans Rest, 25, 31, 122
Boatsail, 79
BOBO, Gabriell, 28
Boden, 63
BODKIN, Anasta, 27
  Andrew, 27
  Anne, 27
  Augustine, 27
  Dominick, 27
  Edward, 27
  Ellinor, 27
  James, 27
  Jane, 27
  Patrick, 27
BOICE, Elinor, 165
BOLAYN, John, 21
BOLLETT, Elisabeth, 41
BOLTON, James, 27
  Mary, 27, 130
  Nathaniel, 130
BONARD, Henry, 77, 121
Bonds Purchase, 62
BONE, Isabell, 27
BONNER, Elizabeth, 27
  Henry, 27, 116, 164
Bonner's Retirement, 27, 62, 284
BOOK, Richard, 96
BOOKER, Ann, 28, 35
  Elizabeth, 28
  John, 15, 28
  Martha, 28
  Mary Ann, 28
  Sarah, 28
BOOTH, Jane, 143
  John, 28
  Mary, 28
BORBANCKS, Joyce, 115

BORDLEY, Thomas, 80, 252
BOREMAN, Ann, 118
  Benedict, 220
  Capt., 186
  Ellinor, 315
  Maj., 198
  Mary, 25, 186
  Sarah, 25
  William, 25, 118, 141, 198, 306, 315
Boreman's Reserve, 198
BORKER, Thomas, 248
BORLAND, John, 221
BORMAN, Leonard, 241
  Richard, 241
BOSELL, John, 29
BOSSELL, Elizabeth, 272
BOSWEL, John, 28
  Marie, 28
  Martha, 28
  Mathew, 28
  Michael, 28
  William, 28
Boswell, 63
BOSWELL, George, 29
  John, 28, 29, 138, 147, 223
  Marmaducke, 29
  Martha, 223
  Mary, 29, 175, 223
  Mary Ann, 138
  Mathew, 29, 223
  Michael, 223
  Michell, 223
  Thomas, 29
  William, 29, 223
BOTELER, Edward, 221
  Henry, 80
  Katherine, 80

BOUGHTON, Catherine, 42
  Elizabeth, 42
  Francis, 42
  Parthenia, 42
  Richard, 13, 29, 42, 115, 220, 221
  Samuell, 29
  Sarah, 42
  Verlinda, 29, 42
  Virlinda, 29
Boughton's Disappointment, 101
BOULD, Jane, 29
  John, 29
BOULES, James, 30
  John, 29
  Margery, 29
  Mr., 315
BOULIN, James, 248
Boulins Plaine, 42
BOULLIN, Mary, 30
BOULS, John, 279
  Margaret, 29
BOURN, Elizabeth, 30
  James, 30
BOURNE, Daniel, 30, 182
  Jesse Jacob, 30
  Mary, 30
BOUTCHER, Francis, 30
BOWDER, Roger, 30
BOWEN, Catharine, 62
Bowen's Dispute, 276
BOWIE, John Pidgon, 187
BOWING, William, 30
BOWLD, Elizabeth, 29
  Jane, 29
  John, 29
  Mary Anne, 29
BOWLEING, John, 31
BOWLES, Edward, 29

Index

Isabel, 29
John, 18, 29, 30, 138, 142, 280, 302
Margery, 18
Sarah, 29
William, 29
Bowles Land, 86
Bowles Purchase, 13
Bowles' Purchase, 30
BOWLIN, James, 21, 23
John, 30
Mary, 30
Bowling, 172
BOWLING, Capt., 223
James, 27, 30, 218, 228, 279, 282
John, 30, 31, 70
Mary, 30, 31
Thomas, 30, 31
William, 30, 31
Bowling Plains, 30
Bowlings Reserve, 58
Bowlston(e), 13, 30
BOWMAN, John, 31
Samuell, 239
BOWPLAIN, 238
BOY, Jennett, 160
John, 160
BOYCE, Eleanor, 31
Elinor, 31
Elizabeth, 31
Helenor, 31
James, 31, 251
John, 31, 251
William, 31
BOYD, John Pigeon, 184
BOYDE, James, 31
Katherine, 31
BOYDEN, Elinor, 31
Elizabeth, 31, 195
John, 31
Mary, 31

Roger, 31
William, 31, 195, 215
BOYDON, Mary, 253
BOYE, Abraham, 32
Bowman, 32
Elizabeth, 32
Jane, 32
John, 32
Pigeon, 32
Thomas, 32
BOYER, John, 195
BOYNE, Elizabeth, 32
John, 32
Mary, 32
BOZWELL, John, 29
BRACHER, Jane, 32
John, 32, 291
BRADFORD, John, 291
BRADSHAW, George, 98
John, 32
Thomas, 32
BRAFITT, Elizabeth, 248
Brambry, 169
BRANCH, Joan, 257
BRAND, Charles, 32
BRANDT, Ann, 33
Anne, 33, 189
Catherine, 33
Charles, 32, 33, 145
Elisabeth, 33
Elizabeth, 32, 33, 145
Jacob, 32, 33, 145
Katharine, 33
Marcus, 32, 33
Margaret, 32
Mary, 32, 33
Randolph, 32, 33, 95, 98
Sarah, 33
Brandts Discovery, 269
Branford Enlarged, 182

BRANNER, Edward, 33
Henry, 33, 96
BRANSON, Abraham, 213
Michael, 33
Rebecca, 33
BRANSONER, Henry, 191
Brant's Cliffs, 260
Brathwood, 18
BRAVNER, Elizabeth, 300
BRAWNER, Edward, 33, 34, 236
Elisabeth, 34
Henry, 33, 34
John, 33
Mary, 33
Thomas, 33
William, 33, 34
BRAYFIELD, Elisabeth, 34
John, 34
Margaret, 34
Mary, 34
BRAYNE, Henry, 237
Jane, 34
BRAYSALE, Agnes, 34
BREAD(E), Jane, 34, 149, 186
John, 34, 149, 284
BREDD, John, 141
BREDING, Mathew, 212
BREEDEN, Elizabeth, 34
Gerrard, 34
BREEDING, John, 34
Mary, 34
Mat(t)hew, 24, 34, 88
Susannah, 24
Thomas, 182
William, 34
Breels Beginning, 76

BRENDT, Charles, 32
  Randolph, 32
BRENT, Ann, 38, 41
  Anne, 41
  Edmond, 264
  Elizabeth, 35
  Francis, 35
  George, 34, 35, 52, 115
  Henry, 34, 38, 53, 115
  Jane, 34, 35, 53, 278
  Katharine, 41
  Margaret, 34
  Martha, 34, 115
  Mary, 35, 52, 115
  Nicholas, 34, 35
  Randle, 41
  Robert, 34, 35
  Susanna, 35
  William, 34, 35, 53, 296
  ———, 264
BRENTS, William, 296
BREST, George, 28
  Richard, 28
BRETON, John, 290
BRETT, Anne, 36
  Constant, 306
  Contant, 36
  Elisabeth, 35
  Elizabeth, 35
  George, 28, 35, 36, 42, 66, 190, 297, 306
  Henry, 28, 35, 36, 218, 311
  John, 36
  Richard, 35, 36
  Sarah, 35, 36
  Susanna(h), 36, 66
  William, 28, 35, 161
BRETTON, Thomas, 108
Bretts Addition, 35
Brett's Discovery, 36
Brian's Clifts, 221
Bride Watter, 242
Bridge Town, 48, 49, 158
BRIDGES, Antony, 227
  Steaphen, 36
BRIDGETS, Elizabeth, 35
Brierwood, 198
BRIGHT, Edward, 36
  George, 224
  Thomas, 36
BRIGHTWELL, Elisabeth, 62
  John, 62
BRIMBLECUM, John, 37
BRIMINS, Christopher, 197
BRISCOE, Ann, 37
  Anne, 37
  Edward, 37, 38
  Elanore, 38
  Eleanor, 37
  Eliner, 37
  Elizabeth, 37, 38
  George, 37
  Hesekiah, 37
  Hezekiah, 37
  Hezikiah, 38
  James, 37, 38, 145
  John, 37, 38, 93, 127
  Leonard, 37, 38
  Lydda, 37
  Martharn, 37
  Mary, 37, 38
  Philip, 37, 38, 113, 127, 145, 301
  Priscilla, 37, 223
  Rebecca, 38
  Robert, 37, 38
  Samuel, 37, 38
  Samuel Williamson, 37, 38
  Susanna(h), 37, 38
  Williamson, 37, 38
BRISON, John, 38
  Mary, 38
BRITAGHT, Thomas, 314
Britain, 134, 151
  Balle Easton, 214
  Berks County, 258
  Burbige Green, 209
  Buxton in Darbyshire, 209
  Cheshire, 209
  Cumberland County, 264
  Fairfield Stope Parish, 209
  Ogburn St. George, 312
  Reading, 258
  Somersetshire, 214
  Whitehaven, 264
  Wilts County, 312
BRITT, Eliza, 35
  George, 28, 35, 205
  Henry, 28, 35
  Richard, 28, 35, 36
  William, 28, 35
BRITTAIN, Ann, 98
  Thomas, 98
BRITTON, Mary, 277
  William, 277
Britts Adventure, 36, 131
BROGDEN, Eliza, 38
  William, 38
BROMLEY, Michael, 38
  Mile, 38
BRONAUGH, John, 185
BROOK, Judith, 38
  Mary, 38
  Richard, 27
  Sarah, 38

Index

BROOKE, Anne, 249
  Baker, 38
  Clare, 39
  Dorothy, 201, 202
  James, 201, 202
  John, 28, 38, 43
  Leonard, 115, 141, 249
  Mary, 199
  Mathew, 38
  Mr., 143
  Rebecca, 145
  Richard, 27
  Roger, 201, 202
  Thomas, 38
BROOKES, Ann, 141, 199
  Henry, 38
  Jane, 43
  John, 43
  Nathaniel, 38
  Robert, 141, 257
  Thomas, 287
  William, 38
BROOKS, Ann, 25
  Elizabeth, 38
  Jane, 38
  John, 38
  Margaret, 39
  Mary, 38
  Matthew, 38
  Sarah, 38
  William, 39
BROONELY, Thomas, 39
Brother Wood, 171
Brotherood, 56, 63
Brotherwood, 19
Brothwood, 19, 136
BROWN, Ann, 40
  Anne, 137
  Dorothy, 5, 315
  Dr., 91
  Frances, 40, 100
  Francis, 40, 91, 170
  Gukstavus, 101
  Gustavus, 40, 100, 219
  James, 40
  Jane, 39
  John, 39, 40, 72, 152, 197
  Martha, 39
  Mary, 39, 40, 91
  Penelope, 40, 197
  Philip, 68
  Ruth, 170
  Sarah, 40, 91
  Stephen, 40, 177, 235
  Verlinda, 40
  Virlinda, 40
  William, 40
BROWNE, Ales, 39
  Alice, 40
  Ann, 40, 137
  Assence, 302
  Elisabeth, 39, 301
  Elizabeth, 39, 40, 232
  Gerrard, 39, 311
  Henry, 40
  James, 39
  Jean, 311
  Joane, 39
  John, 27, 39, 40, 232, 281
  Mary, 39, 129, 302
  Mary Anne, 40
  Mereon, 27
  Philip, 39
  Thomas, 39, 40
  William, 39, 40, 129, 302, 303
BRUCE, Charles, 41, 137, 314
  Elizabeth, 137, 309
  Francis, 137
  John, 40, 314
  John, 314
  Judith, 137, 312
  Sarah, 40, 314
  Tounley, 40
  Townley, 41, 137
BRUMLEY,
  Elizabeth, 41
BRUXBANKE,
  Abraham, 41
BRYAN, Daniel, 41, 195, 263
  Frances, 41
  Jennat, 308
  William, 41
Bryan's Clift, 221
BRYFIELD, John, 41
BRYON, Daniel, 253
Buck Range, 64
BUCKLOW, Benjamin, 41
BUCKNAN, Thomas, 26
BUDDEN, Elizabeth, 303
  Margaret, 303
BULL, Thomas, 41
  William, 41
Bullen, 315
BULLET(T), Benjamin, 41, 188
  Elizabeth, 32, 41
  John, 188
  Joseph, 32, 41, 188
BULLIT, Benjamin, 41
  Elizabeth, 41
  Joseph, 41
Bullit's Folly, 41
BULLOT, Joseph, 48
BULLOTT, Benjamin, 41
  Elizabeth, 41
  Joseph, 41
BUMPUS, Thomas, 41
BUNCRAFT, Thomas, 41

Buplaine, 25
BURCH, Barbary, 42
　Benjamin, 42
　Edward, 6, 42
　Elisabeth, 42
　Ellinor, 42
　John, 42, 56
　Jonathan, 42
　Jonathon, 42
　Justenian, 42
　Justinian, 42
　Oliver, 42
　Susana(h), 42, 76
　Thomas, 42, 136
BURDETT, Sarah, 100
　Thomas, 100
BURDIT, Thomas, 29, 42, 85
　Verlinda, 29, 42
Burdit's Nest, 42
Burdit's Rest, 9, 42
BURDITT, Parthenia, 42, 52
Burditts Rest, 100
BURFORD, Ann, 43
　Anne, 11, 42, 52
　Benjamin, 42
　Elizabeth, 42, 68, 221
　Frances, 68
　Thomas, 11, 42, 68, 221
BURGES, Elisabeth, 54
　John, 130
BURGESS, Anne, 43
　Benjamin, 43
　Eleanor, 43
　Elizabeth, 71
　John, 43, 71, 128
　Mary, 21
　Samuel, 43, 71
　Thomas, 71
BURKHAINE, John, 43
Burlains Hill, 222
Burloyns Hill, 74

BURN, James, 11
BURNAM, Alice, 43
　John, 43
　Samuel, 43
　William, 43
Burnhams Beginning, 286
BURNS, G., 142
　Matthew, 44, 142
Burnt Quarter, 244
BUROS, Paull, 43
BURROUGHS, Mary, 43
　Thomas, 43
BURRUS, Thomas, 43
Burton, 307, 308
BUSEY, John, 224
BUSHY, John, 99
BUTCHER, Francis, 123
　John, 43, 311
　Mary, 43
BUTLER, Elizabeth, 43
　John, 43
　Lydia, 43
　William, 43
Butney, 32
BUTTERIS, John, 212
BUTTERY, Francis, 43
　John, 43
BUTTLER, Ann, 14
　John, 275
BUTTRUNE, William, 44
BUTTS, Christian, 112
　John, 121
　Mary, 44
　Richard, 44
Byfield Close, 53
BYRCH, Richard, 281
BYRN, Charles, 254
　Elizabeth, 44
　James, 44
　Margery, 254

BYRNE, Charles, 44, 253
　Margery, 44, 253

-C-
CABLE, John, 44, 78, 82
　Mary, 78
CADE, Elizabeth, 42
CADEL, Anna, 44
　John, 44
CADELL, John, 44
　Robert, 44
CADLE, Abigail, 44
　Anna, 44
　Edward, 44
　Elizabeth, 44
　John, 44
　Mary, 44
　Robert, 44
CADY, Ellenor, 44
　Robert, 44
CAGE, Anna, 44
　John, 44, 45, 74, 103, 118, 212, 235
　Margaret, 45
　Susanna(h), 44
　W., 210, 258
　William, 40, 44, 45, 169
CAGER, Mr., 16
CAHOW, James, 127
CAIN, Darby, 220
　John, 152
　Judeth, 210
　Rose, 220
CAINE, Elizabeth, 45
　John, 34, 45
　Thomas, 45
Caines Purchase, 238
CALLIHON, Ann, 45
　Patrick, 45, 202
CALRY, William, 128
CALVERT, Ann, 45

Charles, 45
Elisabeth, 85
Elizabeth, 45, 88
William, 45
Calvert County, 43, 44, 70, 185, 227, 243, 256, 275
Calverton Manor, 140
Calverts Hope, 26, 27, 122, 213
CALVIN, Elisabeth, 46
John, 46
CAMBELL, Dunkin, 180
CAMPBELL, Archibald, 173
John, 46
Martin, 46, 67, 80, 267
Mary, 46, 67, 246, 267
William, 302
CAMSANDERS, Joseph, 240
CANE, Derby, 220
John, 25, 45, 237
Susanna, 25, 45, 237
Susannah, 45
CANEDAY, Darby, 168
Cane's Purchase, 25, 240
CANLAND, John, 46
CANTAR, William, 304
Canterbury, 33, 105, 148, 149, 290
CANTWELL, Thomas, 46
Capell, 147, 192
CAPSHAW, Francis, 46
James, 43
John, 46
CAR, Peeter, 27, 291
Peter, 39
CARETTS, Mary, 222
CAREW, Henry, 38

CAREY, Cornelius, 46
Hugh, 46
Philip, 46
Susan, 46
CARICO, Abel, 48
Elisabeth, 48
Mary Ann, 48
CARLETON, Arden, 47
Bostock, 47, 185
Catherine, 47, 185
Dudley, 47
Edward, 47, 185
John, 47
Josiah, 47
Margaret, 47
Mary, 47, 185
Matthew, 47
Theodore, 47
Theodosia, 47
Thomas, 47, 185
CARLILE, Charles, 47
CARNAGGEY, James, 47
Carnavan, 198
CARNELL, Joseph, 47
Margaret, 47
Thomas, 39
CARNER, Richard, 47
CARNEY, Thomas, 47
CARPENTER, Christopher, 48
Henry, 47
Sarah, 158
widow, 309
Carpenter's Square, 130, 131
CARR, Arthur, 48
Grace, 177
John, 296
Peter, 32, 48, 107, 117, 157, 168, 196
Rebocah, 48
CARRE, Richard, 48
CARRICK, James, 286

CARRICO, Abel, 48
Elizabeth, 48
CARRICOE, Catherine, 48
James, 48
Sarah, 48
CARRIEL, William, 230
CARRINGTON, Timothy, 128
CARROLL, Elisabeth, 310
James, 310
Jane, 48
John, 48
Carrot Bed, 178
CARTEE, Charles, 22
CARTER, Elizabeth, 49
Jane, 49
Sophia, 49
Timothy, 48
William, 48, 49, 271
CARTIE, Demund Mack, 49
CARVER, Richard, 87
CARVILE, Susanna, 10
Thomas, 10
CARVILL, Joseph, 221
CARVILLE, Robert, 27
CARY, Adam, 46
Philip, 46
CASELTON, John, 68
Mary, 68
Robert, 68
CASEY, Charles, 96
Thomas, 96
CASH, Mary, 49
Rebeckah, 49
William, 49
CASHE, James, 49
Mary, 49
CASSICK, Benjamin, 49
John, 49

CASSOCK, Benjamin,
    49
  John, 49
  Sarah, 49
Cassocks Lopp, 189
CATHEW, Christopher,
    49
CATLET, Daniell, 172
  Elisabeth, 172
CATTLE, Elizabeth, 42
  James, 42
CAUS, Thomas, 210
CAUSEEN, John, 50
  Mary, 50
CAUSEENE, Ignatius,
    1
CAUSENE, Ignatius,
    275
CAUSIN, Ignatius, 15,
    50, 207, 304
  Jane, 50
  John, 50
  William, 50
CAUSINE, Ignatius,
    11, 13, 49, 50, 265
  Jane, 50
  John, 50
  Nicholas, 49
  Nicolas, 49
  William, 50
Causin's Manor, 50
CAUSONE, William, 50
CAUSOON, John, 50
  William, 50
CAVE, Mary, 50
  Thomas, 50
CAVENOUGH, Mary,
    50
  William, 50
CAWOOD, Elizabeth,
    253
  John, 50, 254
  Mary, 50, 59
  Stephen, 50, 61

Thomas, 10, 50
William, 10, 50, 59
CAWSINE, Ignatius, 49
  Jane, 49
  Nicholas, 49
  Nicolas, 49
CAYNE, James, 45
CAYTON, Charles, 51
CECIL, Isaac, 23
  Joshua, 23
Cecil County, 149, 243
CEECUBES, William,
    94
CELLY, Daniel, 220
CERICK, Patrick, 51
CERRECK, John, 51
Chairmans Purchase,
    237
CHAMBER, Ann, 132
  Thomas, 132
CHAMBERS,
  Christopher, 51
  Daniel, 51
  Daniell, 227
  Elizabeth, 51
  Joseph, 51, 271, 272
CHAMPE, Stephen, 51
Chance, 70
CHANDLER, Ann(e),
    51, 52, 53, 100, 217
  Col., 2
  Jane, 52
  Job, 51, 52, 53, 100
  Jobe, 51, 52
  John, 53, 74
  Mary, 52, 53, 79, 89,
    199, 226
  Nancie, 52
  Richard, 51, 52, 67,
    84, 100, 103, 196
  Stephen, 53, 145
  William, 18, 34, 35,
    51, 52, 53, 67, 79,
    100, 115, 121, 143,

153, 155, 168, 169,
    192, 203, 205, 220,
    238, 244, 245
Chandler Hill, 202
Chandler Hills, 53
Chandler Town, 180
Chandler's Addition,
    53
Chandler's Hope, 53
Chandler's Invention,
    244
Chandler's Purchase,
    53, 217
Chandles Invention,
    245
CHAPLIN, Thomas, 53
CHAPMAN, Barbara,
    53
  Barbary, 54, 137
  Edward, 46, 54
  Elisabeth, 54, 71
  Elizabeth, 54, 156
  George, 53
  Jane, 54
  John, 54, 113, 151,
    156, 180
  Lucretia, 244
  Margaret, 54
  Mary, 54, 71
  Richard, 53, 54, 71,
    113, 137, 156
  Thomas, 22, 53, 54,
    71, 213, 279
  William, 54, 137, 156
Chaptico Manor, 37
CHARLESON, Charles,
    54
  Dorothy, 54
Charlestown, 292
CHARLESWORTH,
  Eleanor, 301
  Ellinor, 55
  Robert, 10, 55

Index

CHARLEWORTH,
  Elinor, 10
  Robert, 10
Charly, 31
CHARMAN, Elizabeth,
  199
  John, 199
Charomans Purchase,
  268
CHASE, J., 55
  Richard, 55
  Thomas, 55
CHATTAM, Joseph, 55
Cheerman's Purchase,
  265
CHERIBUB, Elizabeth,
  55
  John, 55
  Mary, 55
  William, 55
CHERMAN, Elisabeth,
  55
  John, 197
CHERRYBUB,
  Elizabeth, 55
  John, 55
  Mary, 55
  Walter, 55
  William, 55
CHESELDYNE,
  Kenelme, 86
Cheshire(s), 52, 177
Chesnut Point, 41, 314
CHESSON, Barbary,
  55
  John, 55
  Mary, 55
CHEW, Edith, 55
CHIDLEY, Richard,
  308
CHILDMAN, Joane, 55
CHING, Elinor, 55
  John, 55
  Mary, 55

CHISELDYNE,
  Kenelm, 56
  Mary, 56
CHISMUND, Mary,
  174
CHITTAM, Isaac, 55
  Phillis, 55
  Rebeckah, 55
CHOLMLY, Francis, 73
CHOMLEY, Francis, 56
Chosan, 36
Chosen, 35, 36, 161,
  306
CHRISMOND, Joseph,
  56, 108
CHRISTIAN, Mary,
  280
Christian Milford, 66,
  131, 218
Christian Temple
  Manor, 4, 66, 69, 99,
  110, 176, 185, 195,
  205, 222, 239, 241,
  253, 259, 262, 273,
  279, 300, 301, 311
Christian Wellford, 298
CHUMBLY, Barbara,
  73
  Frances, 73
CHUN, Andrew, 56
CHUNN, Andrew, 56
  Aquila, 56
  Benjamin, 56
  Cassandra, 56
  Chloe, 56
  Dorothy, 56
  Elizabeth, 56
  John, 56
  Joseph, 56
  Judith, 56
  Lydia, 56
  Mary, 56
  Mary Ann, 56
  Mersilva, 56

  Muriel, 56
  Peregrine, 56
  Rachel, 56
  Rebeckah, 56
  Richard, 56
  Samuel, 56
  Susanna, 56
CHURCH, Ann, 8
CHURCHYARD,
  Elizabeth, 56
  Harman, 56
Clahammond, 44
Clair, 119
Clare, 120
CLARK, Ann, 249
  Benjamin, 180
  Carter, 58
  John, 57, 230, 232
  Juliana, 58, 172
  Leonard, 261
  Luke, 58
  Mary, 58
  Robert, 57
  Thomas, 58
  William, 180
CLARKE, Abigail, 57
  Ambros, 57
  Andrew, 57
  Ann(e), 57
  Beteres, 57
  Conyers, 59
  Esther, 57
  Fantalona, 57
  George, 57
  Gilbert, 57, 59, 182,
    202
  James, 57
  Jane, 57
  John, 57, 59, 102, 162,
    184, 227, 274, 299
  Julian, 198
  Mary, 57
  Nicholaus, 57
  Robert, 57, 62

Samuel, 57
Sarah, 57
Susanna(h), 31, 57
Thomas, 57, 140, 198, 209, 255
Clarke's Inheritance, 57
Clarke's Purchase, 127
CLARKSON, Elisabeth, 119
Elizabeth, 120
CLARY, Morris, 58
CLASH, John, 58
Mary, 58
Nicholas, 58
Clean Drinking, 234
CLEARKE (CLARKE), Robert, 211
CLEMENCE, Nicholaus, 58
CLEMENS, John, 58
CLEMENT, Elizabeth, 58
John, 58
CLEMENTS, Agnes, 58
Ann, 58
Barbary, 58
Benjamin, 58
Edward, 58
Elinor, 175
Elizabeth, 58, 59, 204
Francis, 58, 204
George, 58, 204
Jacob, 58, 59
Jean, 58
John, 58, 59
Lydia, 58
Mary Ann, 58
Phile:, 273
Rosamond, 58
Rosomond, 175
Samuel, 58, 59
William, 58
CLEMONS, John, 278

William, 278
CLERKE(E), Cosimer, 57
Elizabeth, 261
John, 298
Mary, 261
CLIMPSON, Ignatius, 59
CLINKSCALES, Adam, 59
Mary, 59
Clipsham, 68
CLIPSHAM, Susannah, 44, 45, 59, 68
Thomas, 44, 59, 68, 90, 105, 116, 221, 277
CLOUDER, Elizabeth, 75
Richard, 59, 75
Temperance, 59, 75, 98
Clovers Point, 239
CLOWDER, Richard, 220
CLOWTER, Elizabeth, 59
Richard, 59
Temperance, 59
CLUB, Jennat, 308
CLUBB, Anna, 59
Anne, 59
Elizabeth, 59
John, 59
Matthew, 59
Philip, 59
CLYPSHAM, Thomas, 30
COALE, Elizabeth, 222
Jemina, 222
Coate Back, 65
COATES, Bartholomew, 146
Charity, 64

Charles, 64
John, 64, 231
Mrs., 218
Thomas, 59
William, 64
Coate's Retirement, 152
COATS, Hewgh, 59
John, 59
COBB, Samuel, 59
COBLE, Elizabeth, 310
COCKIN, Anne, 38
COCKLEY, Jesse, 167
William, 167
COCKRIN, Ann, 60
John, 60
Cocksetts, 187
COCKSEY, Elizabeth, 65
CODDINGTON, Elizabeth, 60
CODWELL, William, 60, 196
COE, John, 222
Richard, 60, 236
William, 92
COF(F)ER, Elizabeth, 58, 60
Francis, 60
Gerrard, 60
Henry, 60
John, 44, 60
Mary, 60
Mat(t)hew, 60
Richard, 60
Sarah, 60
Thomas, 60
Violata, 60
William, 60
Coffer's Chance, 60
Coffers Chance, 188
COGGHILL, Anne, 61
Lidia, 61
Mary, 61
Smallwood, 61

COGHILL, Christian, 60
  James, 60
  William, 60
COGILL, David, 187
  Peter, 187
COGWELL, Anne, 61
  Christian, 61
  James, 61
  William, 61
COHOW, Martha, 127
Colchester, 102
Cold Spring, 67
Cold Spring Manor, 85, 86
Coldspring, 46
Cole, 205, 214
COLE, Ann, 62, 203, 204, 286
  Anne, 284
  Benjamin, 61
  Edward, 61, 62, 203, 204
  Elizabeth, 61, 62, 286
  Giles, 61
  Jeffery, 61
  Jeffrey, 61
  Jemima, 62
  Jeoffre, 61
  John, 61, 62, 233
  Linas, 61
  Margret, 233
  Mary, 61, 62
  Philip, 61, 117
  Rebeckah, 286
  Sina, 61
  Will, 286
  William, 61, 62, 233, 284, 286
COLEMAN, Catharine, 62
  Catharine Samways, 62
  Elizabeth, 62
  Martha, 62
  Richard, 62
  Thomas, 62
  Ursilla, 62
COLESON, Anne, 275
  Robert, 275
COLL, John, 72
COLLIAR, Giles, 255
  Grace, 255
COLLIER, Barbara, 62
  William, 62, 67
Collier Tone Manner, 262
COLLINGS, Anthony, 104
COLLINGWOOD, Robert, 62
COLLINS, Alice, 62
  Frances, 33
COLLSON, Ann, 62
  Eleanor, 62
  George, 62
  Robert, 62
COLLYER, William, 4
COLSON, Robert, 197
COLTON, Ann, 63
COLVIN, Charles, 12
COMBES, John, 264
  Philip, 44
  Richard, 66
Comber Chance, 87
COMBS, Richard, 115
  Sarah, 240
Come By Chance, 133
COMPTON, Anne, 63
  Barton, 63
  Benjamin, 276
  Elinor, 127
  Elisabeth, 63
  Elizabeth, 63
  John, 63, 86, 119, 127, 136
  Mary, 63
  Mat(t)hew, 63, 145
  Rache(a)l, 63, 145
  Samuell, 63, 280
  Susanna(h), 37, 63
  William, 63
COMTON, Susanna, 38
CONER, John, 64
CONNALLY, Patrick, 78
CONNELEY, Patrick, 53
CONNELL, Angellica, 210
  Ann, 305
  Dennis, 30, 63, 210
  Elizabeth, 210
  James, 305
  Mary, 44, 63, 210
  William, 44, 63, 210
CONNELLY, Anna Statia, 63
  Annastasia, 63
  Patrick, 63, 300
CONNER, Ellenor, 44
CONNERY, Elizabeth, 64
  Thomas, 64
CONNETT, Mary, 79
  William, 79
CONNILL, Elizabeth, 62
  James, 285
CONNOR, John, 284
  Margaret, 284
CONSTABLE, Jane, 163
  John, 64
  Marmaduke, 163
CONTEE, A., 234
  Alex, 64
  Alexander, 12, 64, 169, 234
  Charity, 64, 70
  Grace, 64
  Jane, 64

John, 12, 64, 65, 70
Mary, 64, 174, 257, 312, 314
Peter, 64
Content, 25, 116
Conveniency, 3, 131
COOCHE, John, 98
COODE, Sarah, 65
 William, 56
 William Gerard, 65
COODY, William, 65
COOFFER, Henry, 276
 Mathew, 276
COOK(E), Eleanor, 65
 Henry, 65
 John, 65
 Samuel, 65
 Sarah, 65
 Thomas, 65
COOKSEY, Ann, 245
 Christian, 65
 Elisabeth, 65, 257
 Elizabeth, 65
 Jestinian, 65
 John, 65, 166
 Justinian, 65
 Mary, 65, 229
 Phillip, 65
 Priscilla, 65
 Samuel, 65, 106
 Sarah, 65, 229
 Susanna, 65
 William, 65
COOMBES, Sarah, 240
COOMES, Elizabeth, 65, 66
 Philip, 65
 Thomas, 66
 William, 94
COOPER, Anne, 66
 Elisabeth, 66
 Jesse, 11
 John, 66, 67, 150, 159, 247

Jon:, 199
Joseph, 66
Mary, 66
Mary Anne, 67
Nicholas, 46, 52, 66, 67, 87, 114, 161
Penelope, 66
Philip, 66
Prudence, 66, 161
Richard, 66
Robert, 66
Roger, 66
Sarah, 66
Susannah, 247
Thomas, 66, 227
Walter, 66
William, 66, 67, 159, 241, 291
COPE, Ann, 209
COPPER, Elisabeth, 7
 William, 7
CORAM, Jurat, 79
CORKER, Elizabeth, 67
 Thomas, 67, 68, 274, 283
Corkers Hogg Hole, 174
CORNAHILL, Elizabeth, 266
CORNALL, Joseph, 67, 284
 Margaret, 67
 Margrit, 284
CORNELL, Joseph, 185, 221, 312
 Margrett, 312
CORNER, Ellenor, 44
 Richard, 217
CORNISH, Edward, 67, 89
 Elizabeth, 67
 Jane, 67
 John, 67, 311
 Margarett, 67

Martha, 67, 311
Richard, 67
CORNOR, Anne, 68
 Job, 68
CORNUTE, Hendrick, 68
CORNWALL, Francis, 68
CORNWELL, Joseph, 68
Correck Measure, 120
CORRICKE, James, 68
 Jone, 68
 Patrick, 68
CORSPHER, Henry, 172
COSSLETON, Mary, 68
 Robert, 68
COSTEKIN, Daniel, 68
COSTER, John, 14
COSTLETON, Mary, 68
 Robert, 68
COTTERELL, Elizabeth, 68
 James, 68
COTTINGTON, Edward, 69
COTTON, William, 69
COTTRELL, Ann(e), 69
 Elizabeth, 68
 James, 68, 69, 84, 153
 Jane, 69
 Thomas, 69
COTTWELL, James, 68
COULSON, Ann, 239
 Anne, 69
 Robert, 69
COUPPER, Mary Ann, 67
 William, 67

Courses Pallace, 219
COURT, Cleat:, 69
  Elisabeth, 69
  Elizabeth, 69
  John, 36, 69, 223, 243
COURTE, Elizabeth, 69
  John, 69, 102
COURTES, John, 137, 212
COURTS, Ann(e), 69, 70
  Charity, 19, 44, 69, 70, 137, 234, 252
  Charles, 70
  Elizabeth, 69
  Henl(e)y, 70
  Henry, 70
  Hery, 70
  Hugh, 69
  John, 19, 41, 64, 69, 70, 113, 132, 137, 152, 201, 234, 252, 260, 276, 310, 313
  Margaret, 70
  Margarett, 69
  William, 70
Courts Choice, 157
Courts' Discovery, 70
Courts Marsh, 70, 132
COVART, Robert, 93
COVENT, Robert, 104
Coventry, 26, 27, 140
COVERT, Christian, 70, 110
  Robert, 70, 110
Cow Branch, 241
Cow Land, 186
Cow (or Cool Spring), 131
Cow Spring(s), 46, 67, 80, 87
COWARD, Robert, 3
  Stephen, 61

Cowland, 17
COWPER, Isaac, 67
  Thomas, 24
COWSEEN, John, 187
Cowsking, 66
Cowspring, 246
COX, Anne, 71
  Charles, 60
  James, 70, 71
  John, 24, 111
  Margarett, 70
  Mary, 60
  Richard, 69
  Sarah, 24, 71
  Thomasine, 70, 71
  William, 60
CRABB, Elizabeth, 71
  Jane, 71
  Margt:, 71
  Ralph, 71
  Thomas, 71, 192
Crabbtree, 78
CRAEN, John, 71
CRAIN, Dorothy, 71
CRAKSON, Thomas, 71
CRANE, Dorathy, 71
  Elizabeth, 71
  John, 71
  John, 315
Crane's Low Grounds, 71
CRAXON, Ann, 71
  Anne, 200
  John, 82, 279
  Thomas, 200, 279
CRAXSON, Ann, 71
  John, 54, 71, 199
  Thomas, 71
CRAYCROFT, Charles, 72
  Clement, 214
  Elisabeth, 213
  Ignatius, 72
  Jane, 72

  John, 72
  Mr., 143
  Susanna, 72
  widow, 303
CRAYSTONE, Thomas, 200
CRE(A)DWELL, George, 72, 100
CRECIAN, Giancet, 308
CRENEY, Samuell, 128
CRESSEY, Mary, 72
  Samuel, 72, 92, 230
  Susanna, 72
CRESSY, Samuel, 72
  Susanna, 72
CRIGER, Eleanor, 265
CRISMAN, Joseph, 56
Cristen Tempellman, 39
CROCKER, William, 160
CROOKSHANKS, Christopher, 72
CROPPER, Gilbert, 236, 296
  Phillip, 72
CROSON, Mary, 72, 157
  Thomas, 72, 157
CROUCH, Anne, 72
  Ralph, 121
Croutches Gift, 70
CROWN, Mary, 98
CRUMMEY, Oliver, 72
  Thomas, 72
CRUMMY, John, 72
CRUMP, Adam, 36
CRUMPTON, Francis, 73
  Johanna, 73
CRY, Patrick, 73
Cuckholds Delight, 16
CULLES, Charles, 73

CULLINS, Peter, 73
CULLIS, Barbara, 73
  Charles, 272
  James, 73
  Mary, 73
CULVER, Ann, 73
  Cathrine, 73
  Mary, 73
  William, 73
CUMBER, Catherine, 73
CUMBERBITCH, Rebecca, 209
CUMPTON, Christopher, 63
  William, 63
CUNNINGHAM, George, 73
  John, 126, 311
  Mary, 126
CUNNINGHAME, John, 73, 126
  Mary, 73, 126
CURRICK, Hugh, 73
  James, 73
  Joan, 73
  Mary, 73
  Patrick, 73
CURRY, Andrew, 73
CURSINE, Ignatius, 281
CURTIS, John, 73
Cusine's Manor, 50
CUSSEEN, John, 50
CUTTANCE, Josias, 21, 74
CUTTLER, Margaret, 73

-D-
DAGG, John, 48, 74
  Sarah, 74
DAGINAT, Mary, 252
DAINE, Charles, 74
DAINTY, John, 227
DAMER, Thomas, 74
DAMES, John, 74
DANEL, John, 54
Danfrit, 205
DANIELL, Francis, 62
  William, 62
Daniel's Mount, 217, 260
Daniel's Quarter, 131
DANIVAN, Cornelius, 29
  Jane, 29
DANSEY, John, 74
DANSY, Jane, 74
DARNAL, Henry, 236
DARNALL, Anne, 82
  Edward, 74
  Henry, 82, 235
  John, 74
  Rushell, 74
  Thomas, 74
DARNELL, Edward, 74, 233
  Elizabeth, 74
  Sarah, 74
  Thomas, 74
DAUGLAIS, Gilford, 86
DAUGLAS, Mary, 86
DAVERILL, Thomas, 74
DAVID, Ann, 74
  Priscilla, 74
  Thomas, 74
  William, 74
DAVIES, Alise, 75
  Allen, 75
  Deborah, 75
  Edward, 75, 166
  Griffith, 75
  James, 74, 75, 103
  Jon:, 75
  Jonathan, 75
  Martha, 75
  Mary, 76
  Mary Price, 75
  Thomas, 76
DAVIS, Allen, 213
  Ann(e), 76
  Barton, 76
  Benjamin, 76
  Briscoe, 38
  Charity, 76
  Cornelious, 76
  David, 76
  Edward, 75, 76, 78
  Elisabeth, 76
  Elizabeth, 75, 76
  George, 38
  Griffin, 205
  Griffith, 75
  Henry, 75, 76
  Isiah, 33
  James, 76
  John, 75, 76, 158, 224
  Jonathon, 213, 264
  Joseph, 76
  Luke, 76
  Margaret, 75
  Mary, 39, 62, 75, 76, 260
  Onor, 75
  Peter, 76
  Priscilla, 75, 76
  Rachell, 75
  Randolph, 76
  Richard, 30, 76, 180, 181
  Salome, 76
  Sarah, 213
  Susanna, 4
  Thomas, 8, 75, 76, 110
  Walter, 39
  William, 75, 76
Davis' Hazard, 75
DAVISE, Edward, 78
Davises Addition, 76

Davises Hazard, 75, 76
DAVY, Ann, 253
　Charity, 253
　Eleanor, 253
DAWGLASS, John, 145
DAWSON, Elizabeth, 76
　John, 76
　Mary, 50, 76, 77
　Nicholas, 76, 77
de CREYGER, John, 77
DEAKONS, Thomas, 77
DEALE, James, 77
　Thomas, 77
DEAN, Sarah, 77, 207
　William, 115
DEANE, Charles, 77
　Edward, 77
DEATON, Mary, 203
DEAVEREL, Thomas, 225
DEAVERSON, Humphrey, 189
Debt, 53
DECRAGOE,
　Elizabeth, 77
　William, 77
　———, 77
DECREGOE,
　Elizabeth, 77
　Joane, 61
　William, 77
DECREVEIR, John, 77
DELAHAI, Susan, 78
DELAHAY, George, 78
　Jane, 77
　John, 77
　Susanna, 78
Delahayes Chance, 131
DELAHEY, John, 167
Delahey's Chance, 130
DELAP, James, 90
DELL, Henry, 78

Margret, 78
DELOZEAR, Daniel, 78
　Thomas, 78
DELOZ(I)ER, Daniel, 78, 99
　George, 78
　John, 78
　Mary, 78
　William, 78
DEMENT, Anne, 78
　Benajah, 78
　Elizabeth, 78
　George, 78, 283
　Jesse, 78
　John, 78
　Margaret, 78
　Mary, 78
　Susanna, 78
　William, 78
DEMPSIE, John, 79
　Mary, 79
DEMSEY, Allicen, 78
　John, 78
DENE, George, 127
DENEGO, Joanah, 20
　William, 20
DENEGOE, Anna, 79
　John, 79
DENNIS, Justinian, 46
DENNY, Charles, 280
DENT, Ann(e), 79, 80, 81, 127, 166
　Benjamin, 81
　Capt., 130
　Catherine, 81
　Elizabeth, 52, 79, 80, 206, 247
　Esther, 81
　George, 79, 80, 81, 84, 117, 127, 136, 138, 144, 145, 221, 239, 258, 260, 271
　Gerrard, 79
　Hatch, 81

Hilip, 80
John, 2, 81, 130, 158
Lydia, 81
Mary, 81
Michael, 81
Mr., 80, 130
Peter, 79, 80, 225
Philip, 79
Rebecca, 303
Rebecka, 145
Rebeckah, 127
Rhoda, 81
Thomas, 74, 79, 80, 81, 136, 166, 213, 218, 225, 303
William, 12, 79, 80, 81, 99, 115, 145, 161, 174, 178, 206, 239, 255, 264, 296, 303
Dents Inheritance, 81
Denyal, 72
DERMON, Elizabeth, 246
DERMONT, Elizabeth, 46
　John, 46
Desert, 29
DEVENE, Edmund, 81, 235
DEVERELL, Anne, 81
　Elizabeth, 81
　Thomas, 81
DEVERILLE, Ann, 189
　Thomas, 189
DEVINCK, Cornelius John, 81
Devray, 42
DEWLICK, Nicholas, 141
DIAMONDS, George, 81
　Mary, 81

DICKASON, Charles, 82
　Jeremiah, 82
　Thomas, 82
DICKENSON,
　Jeremiah, 123
　Thomas, 225
DICKESON, Jeromy, 205
　Thomas, 82
DICKINSON, Anne, 82
　Jeremiah, 43, 81
　Mr., 208
　Roger, 199, 200
　Thomas, 81, 82
DICKISON, Jeremiah, 212
　Mary, 82
　Thomas, 82
DICKSEY, John, 82
DICKSON, Elizabeth, 83
　Mary, 154
DIFFERT, Douglas, 127
DIGGES, Ann, 82
　Anne, 83
　Charles, 82
　Dudley, 82
　Edward, 82, 298
　Eleanor, 298
　Elinor, 82
　Elizabeth, 53, 82
　Jane, 82
　John, 82, 298
　Mary, 82
　Nicholas, 82
　William, 82, 83, 298
Digges Addition, 82, 124
Digges Baltimore Gift, 124
Digges Baltimore's Gift's Addition 82
Digges' Purchase, 82
DIGGS, Charles, 82, 203
　Dudley George, 82
　Edward, 82, 205, 298
　Elisabeth, 82, 298
　Elizabeth, 82
　John, 213, 298
　John Nedd, 82
　Monica, 205
　William, 82, 102, 203, 282, 298
Digg's Addition, 214
DIKE, Elizabeth, 83
　Marie, 2
　Mary, 2, 83
　Mathew, 2, 83
　Matthew, 83
DILLAHAY, Elizabeth, 83
　Thomas, 83
DINES, Mary, 83
　Thomas, 83
DIRKHEAD, Jane, 49
Discovery, 75, 124, 149
DISON, Ann, 89
　Thomas, 89
Dison's Chance, 89
DIVELL, James, 83
Dividing Run, 127
DIXON, Ann, 83
　Anne, 63
　Hannah, 21
　John, 21, 83, 269
　Mary, 83
　Sarah, 83, 118
　Thomas, 63, 83, 118, 269, 280
　——, 269
Doags Neck, 9, 121
DOBSON, Samuell, 83
DOCKER, James, 290
Docker's Delight, 95, 290, 312
DOD, Anne, 83, 84
　Jane, 68, 83
　John, 84
　Mary, 84
　Richard, 68, 83, 84, 93, 96
DODD, Jane, 42
　Richard, 42, 84
DODDSON, John, 252
DODE, Marie, 84
　Richard, 84
DODS, Thomas, 84
DODSON, Frances, 84
　John, 84
　Leaticia, 84
　Lettica, 147
　Lettisha, 84
　Walter, 84, 138, 147
Dodsons Courage, 84
Doeg's Neck, 24
Dog's Point, 99
DOLTON, Richard, 84
DONAHAU, Fincene, 84
DONALDSON, Daniel, 85
　John, 309
DONASTLE, J., 91
Doncaster, 173, 189, 250
DONCASTLE, John, 91
DONE, John, 252
DONOHAU, Cornelius, 85
DOOLEY, Elizabeth, 85
　James, 85
　John, 85
　Thomas Read, 85
Dorchester County, 42
Dorey Lane, 49
DORROSELL, Joseph, 85
Dorsett County, 155
DORSEY, Thomas, 4

DORUMPLE, Elinor, 179
John, 179
DOSETT, Edward, 85
DOUGHLASS, John, 86
Mary, 86
Robert, 86
DOUGHTIE, Enock, 85
Francis, 85
DOUGHTY, Ane, 85
Anne, 85
Burdit, 85
Enoch, 85
Enock, 85
Francis, 85, 266
Robert, 85
DOUGLAS, Benjamin, 33, 127, 276
Charles, 86
Col., 128
Elizabeth, 51, 105
Gilford, 86
John, 85, 190, 197
Joseph, 33, 86, 127, 174, 177, 230
Josh:, 124, 127
Mary, 86, 127, 174
Penelope, 174
Robert, 86
Sarah, 85, 177, 256, 269
Thomas, 51, 105, 127, 215
Douglas' Addition, 287, 288
Douglas Adventure, 287, 288
DOUGLASE,
Joseph, 163
Penelope, 163
DOUGLASS, Benjamin, 86, 126, 174
Charles, 48

Eleanor, 126
Elizabeth, 48, 86, 126, 174
John, 48, 57, 86, 127
Joseph, 48, 86, 123, 127, 138
Robert, 48
Sarah, 48, 86
Thomas, 86, 105
William, 86
Douglass' Clame, 86
DOUGLASSE,
Benjamin, 107
Joseph, 107
DOUGLIS, Charles, 86
DOUL, George, 127
DOVE, Phillip, 86
Dover, 64, 178, 295
Dover, Christopher, 86
Dover's Clifts, 267
DOWEN, Dennis, 79
John, 79
DOWGLASS, Elenor, 145
John, 145
DOWIN, John, 87
Sarah, 87
DOWING, Dennis
Nicod:, 87
Ellis, 87
DOWN, Ellisa, 79
DOWNES, Elizabeth, 87
Robert, 46, 87, 246, 293, 302
Robertt, 87
DOWNING, Denis, 87
John, 87
DOWTY, Francis, 210
DOYEN, ———, 266
DOYNE, Dennis, 87, 88
Elinor, 40, 77
Ellinor, 87, 272
Ethelbert, 87, 240

Ethelbirth, 88
Ignatius, 88, 186, 187
Jane, 88, 169, 240
Jesse, 87, 88
Joseph, 88
Joshua, 87, 88
Joshuah, 180
Mary, 40, 77, 87, 240, 272
Robert, 40, 77, 87, 88, 175, 241, 267, 272
Sarah, 40, 77, 87, 272
Verlinda, 40, 272
Virlinda, 40, 77, 87, 272
Wharton, 40, 77, 87, 272
William, 40, 77, 87, 88, 272
DOYNES, Dennis, 87
Ethelbert, 87

Jesse, 87
Jonathon, 187
William, 87
DRAPER, John, 127
Railph, 88
DRAYDEN, Isabella, 88
DRINKING, Nimrod, 88
DROYDEN, George, 88
DRYDEN, George, 10
Idabella, 10
Isabella, 62
Duck Marsh, 86, 144
Duckes Delight, 120
DUDICK, John, 227
DUELY, John, 88
DUFFEY, Anne, 88
Cassandra, 88
Elizabeth, 88
Leonard, 88
Martha, 88, 188
Patrick, 88

DUGLAS, Benjamin, 86
  Catherine, 86
  Elizabeth, 85
  John, 31, 85, 86, 136,
    189, 230, 247, 255,
    309
  Mary, 86
  Robert, 86
  Sarah, 85, 255
DUGLASS, Benjamin,
    86
  John, 86
  Joseph, 86
DUKE, Anna, 244
Dukes Delight, 263
DULEY, Elizabeth, 229
  James, 229
  John, 294
  Susanna, 229
DUNAWAY, Timothy,
    265
DUNBAR, John, 305
DUNCAN, Nimrod, 240
DUNCASTLE, John,
    134
DUNCKLY, Bassill, 33
  Rebekah, 33
DUNINGTON, Ann, 28
  Francis, 28
  Rebecca, 28
DUNINTON, Margrett,
    28
DUNN, Isaac, 88
  Mary, 46
  Susanna, 46, 88
DUNNAK, Danniell, 89
DUNNAWAY,
  Francis, 89
  Mary, 89
  Richard, 89
DUNNINGTON,
    Elizabeth, 35
  Francis, 35, 89, 187
  Margaret, 89
  Margarett, 35
  Margret, 28
  Rebekah, 35
DUPHEX, Rebecca,
    153
DUPLEX, Ann, 209
  Rebecca, 209
DUPPE, Thomas, 89
Durham, 20, 152
Durum, 266
DUTTON, Edith, 146
  Elizabeth, 19, 89
  Garratt, 89
  Gerard, 89
  Judeth, 210
  Judith, 89
  Mathew, 89, 210
  Matthew, 89
  Notley, 89, 146
  Nottley, 89
  Thomas, 89
  ———, 146
DYAMEND, George, 81
  Mary, 81
DYET, Teodotia, 287
DYSON, Abigall, 89, 90
  Ann, 89
  Bennet, 89
  James, 89, 90
  John, 295
  John, 89
  John Baptist, 89
  Maddox, 89
  Mary, 89
  Sarah, 89, 90
  Thomas, 5, 89, 200

-E-

EADY, Elizabeth, 90
Eaglton, 270
EARL, William, 90
EARLE, Mary, 128
EARLES, William, 90
EASON, John, 90
East Marling, 56
EATEN, Samuel, 97
EATIE, Elizabeth, 90
  Nathanell, 90
EATON, Nathaniel, 42
  Samuel, 42
  Thomas, 90
  Verlinda, 29, 42
Eaton's Delight, 44,
    169, 244
EATY, Arthur, 45
  Nathaniel, 45
EBDEN, Katharine,
    182
EBERNATHY, Ann, 84
EBERNETHY, Anne,
    91
EBORSELL, William,
    147
EBURNATHY, Ann(e),
    90, 92, 204
  James, 90, 91
  John, 90
  Thomas, 90, 91
  William, 90
EBURNETHY, Ann,
    91, 125
  John, 90, 91, 125
EDELEN, Ann, 91
  Catharine, 91
  Christopher, 91
  Edward, 91
  Richard, 43, 57, 72,
    91, 101, 114, 167,
    203, 257, 307
  Sarah, 91, 119, 120
  Thomas, 91
EDELIN, Richard, 91,
    257
  Sarah, 91
*Edenburgh
    (Edinburgh)*, 282
EDGAR, Elizabeth, 91
  Joanna, 91

John, 91
Richard, 91
Sarah, 91
William, 91
EDGE, Thomas, 91
EDLEN, Mary, 153
Richard, 91
EDLING, Richard, 307
EDMONDSON, Robert, 292
EDWARDS, John, 92
Katherine, 92
EDZARD, Esdras Theodore, 92
Effton Hills, 64
Egglestone, 37
EGGLIN, Margaret, 204
Egleton, 270
EGLIN, Richard, 92
EILBECK, William, 114
ELDER, John, 92
ELERY, Elizabeth, 92
James, 92
John, 24
Mark, 24
ELGIN, Elisabeth, 1
ELIOT, Jone, 92
Elizabeth's Delight, 82
ELKINS, Sarah, 308
ELLDER, Ann, 300
ELLESON, Thomas, 281
ELLIOTT, Joan, 92
Joane, 92
William, 92
ELLIS, Hugh, 92, 277
James, 27
John, 92
ELLISON, John, 92
ELLITT, Ann, 92
William, 92
ELLIXSON, Haines, 93

ELLSON, Anne, 93
Nicholas, 93
EMANSON,
Elizabeth, 93
Mary, 93, 194
Nicholas, 93, 194
Phebe, 93
EMERSON, Anthoni, 93
Elizabeth, 226
Marie, 226
Nicholas, 93, 226
William, 93
EMMETT, Abraham, 93
Hannah, 93
John, 93
EMMS, Thomas, 115
EMPSON, Eleanor, 196
Elenor, 93
Elinor, 93
Mary, 93
William, 93, 196
Enclosure, 303, 307
England, 11, 19, 52, 58, 64, 80, 118, 164, 173, 182, 197, 200, 213, 225, 230, 232, 236, 274, 285, 305
Gisbrough, 226
Barnstable, 64
Beedale, 135
Berkshire, 256
Blackheath, 47
Bristol, 144, 297
Camberwell, 185
Carshelton, 47
Catticke, 135
Cecil, Warwickshire, 287
Chichester, 121
Chilvercoton, 286, 287
Clapham, 185

Cumberland County, 150
Dartmouth, 215
Dearham, 150
Goodman's Fields, 146
Hemel Hempstead Parish, 7, 308
Hereford County, 226
Hertford County, 7, 308
Kent County, 47
Lancaster County, 230
Lessester County, [Leicestor], 127
Lewisham, Parish of, 47
Liverpool, 46
Liverpoole, 308
London, 10, 18, 23, 25, 45, 85, 99, 130, 144, 174, 185, 192, 200, 201, 202, 228, 252, 296, 303, 307
Loughborow, 127
Manchester, 181
Middlesex, 146
Middlesex County, 24, 47, 185
Mynde, 226
Never Newington, 185
Newington, 47
Northampton County, 7, 308
Northamptonshire 307
Ogburn, St. George, 312
Pikesley, 308
Pitchley, 307
Redbourn Parish, 308
Seamore, 135
St. Albans, 308

St. Gile's Parish, 202
St. Mary White
  Chapel, 146
Surrey County, 47,
  185
Sussex County, 121
Tunstall, 135
Warwickshire, 17,
  286, 287
Westminster, 17
Weymouth, 208, 274
Whitehaven, 150
Wilts County, 312
Yarmouth, 274
York County, 135, 226
Yorkshire, 296
ENGLAND, John, 182
ENIBURSON,
  Christopher, 93
  Derick, 93
ENNIS, David, 150
ENSEY, Catherine, 94
  Elisabeth, 94
  Ennis, 94
  John, 94
  Margaret, 94
  Mary, 94
  William, 94
  Win(n)ifred, 94
  Winifrit, 94
ESKRIDGE, George,
  94
  Robert, 94
  Samuel, 94
  William, 94
Essex, 118
Esston Hills, 80
ESTEP, John, 210
  Richard, 227
ESTEY, Richard, 257
ETIE, Elizabeth, 95
  Mary, 95
  Nathan, 95
  Nathaniell, 95

ETTYE, Arthur, 90
  Elizabeth, 90
  Rachell, 90
ETY, Elisabeth, 90
  Nathaniell, 90
EURE, Christopher, 94
EVANS, Ann, 94
  Anne, 116
  Charles, 116
  Edward, 94, 117, 165
  Elizabeth, 94
  Henry, 94
  Jane, 120, 131
  Joanne, 94
  John, 94
  Mary, 94
  Roger, 94
  Rowland, 94
  Sarah, 94
  Stephen, 94
Evans Reserve, 44
EVERAD, Francis, 95
EWING, Hannah, 273
  Samuel, 273
Exiler, 299
Expectation, 32, 254
EYRES, George, 55
EYTON, Richard, 144

-F-

FAARNANDEZ, Pedro,
  96
Fair Fountain, 133,
  134
FAIRFAX, Anne, 95
  Catarn, 95
  Elizabeth, 95, 219
  John, 95, 209
  Mary, 95
  William, 95
FAIRSON, Samuell, 40
FALKNER, Alice, 237,
  265, 268
  John, 237, 265, 268

Peter, 204
Ralph, 226
FANING, Benonie, 95
  Benony, 95
  Elizabeth, 95
  Jane, 95
  John, 66, 95, 277
  Mary, 95
Faning's Venture, 95
FANNING, Alice, 95
  Benjamin, 45
  Benoni, 90, 95
  Benony, 95
  Elizabeth, 95
  Hanna, 95
  Hannah, 95
  James, 95
  John, 39, 95
  Mary, 95
Fanning's Adventure,
  90
FAR, Peter, 112
FARDENAND,
  Winifrede, 297
FARDINANDO, Peter,
  73, 96
FARFAX, Catorn, 95
  Mary, 95
FARLOE, Patrick, 96
  William, 95
FARLOWE, Ambros,
  95
  William, 95
FARLUM, Patrick, 96
FARLUN, Patrick, 96
FARMER, Rice, 96
FARNANDIS,
  Elizabeth, 96
  Peter, 33, 96
FARR, Mary, 55
  Susannah, 276
FARRAND, John, 96
  Mary, 96
  Thomas, 96, 185

Index

FARRELL, Mary, 281
  Patrick, 281
  Richard, 33
FARRING, Elizabeth, 148
FARROW, James, 96
FARROWS, James, 96
FARSEN, Atwix, 207
  Walker, 207
FARSON, Samuel, 77
FARTHING, Anne, 96
  William Maria, 96
Farthings Discovery, 6, 96, 213, 264, 289
Farthings Penny Worth, 96, 104
FEARSON, Grace, 98
  John, 98, 215, 218
  Percival, 209
  Perry, 98
  Samuel, 64, 98
FEATHERSTON, Mr., 87
FECTRER, Thomas, 98
FEILD, Edward, 210
  Eleanor, 210
FEIRSON, Samuel, 40
FENCOKE, Ane, 96
FENDAL, Benjamin, 97
  Elisabeth, 97
  Elizabeth, 97
  John, 97
  Mary, 97
FENDALL, Benjamin, 97, 136
  Brigett, 111
  Elizabeth, 24, 96, 97
  Ellen, 97, 294
  James, 300
  Jane, 98
  John, 19, 24, 96, 97, 111, 131, 159, 183, 219, 312

  Josias, 96, 98, 146, 160, 170, 261, 266, 269, 294, 304
  Mary, 24, 96, 97
  Samuel, 181, 269, 315
  Samuell, 157
  Thomas, 294
Fendalls Delight, 40, 77
FENER, Francis, 210
FENNELL, Joseph, 97
  Mary, 97
FENNER, Thomas, 97
FERNANDEZ, Pedro, 96
FERNANDIE, Peter, 228
FERNANDOS, Peter, 96
  Winefrett, 96
FERNANDRIS, Peter, 96
FERNE, 114, 213
FERNES, 30, 210
FERNLY, Ann, 98
  Francis, 266
  John, 266
FERRALL, Fran:, 98
  John, 98
  Mathew, 98
Ferry, 242
FERSON, Alwicks, 67
  Elisabeth, 98
  Elizabeth, 98
  Jane, 98
  Percy, 98
  Perseful, 98
  Samuel, 98
  Sarah, 98
  Sophia, 98
FIELD, Charles, 98
  Enoch, 98
Field Close, 71
FILBURT, John, 189

FILLPOT, Edward, 34
Find One, 297
FINLEY, James, 98, 139, 236
FIRE, Ralph, 98
FISH, Elinor, 98
FISHER, Elisabeth, 98
Fishpond, 260
FITSGERALD, Morris, 232
FITTSGERROLL, Morris, 242
  Rachel, 242
FITZGARRALD, Morris, 99
FITZGERALD, Morrice, 99
FITZGERRALD, Edward, 98
  Elizabeth, 99
  Morris, 99
FITZGERRELL, Morrice, 242
  Rachell, 242
Five Brothers, 262
FLANNIN, Benjamin, 45
FLETCHER, Henry, 99, 299
FLIN, Bryan, 133
  Mary, 133
FLINN, Edward, 43
FLOWER, Elizabeth, 74
  Jane, 74
  Richard, 74
FLYE, Elizabeth, 23
FOGG, David, 159
  Susanna, 159
FONING, Benony, 314
  Hannah, 314
FOOKE, Gerard, 66
FOOKES, Garret, 19
FORBIS, William, 99

FORD, Charles, 99
  Edward, 4, 66, 99, 301
  Elizabeth, 4, 99, 301
  Posthuma, 99
  Temperance, 99
Fordam, 257
FORDE, Christopher, 99
  Edward, 117
FORDINANDOE,
  Agatha, 96
  Elinor, 96
  Peter, 96
Forest Green, 287
FORREST,
  Patrick, 217
FORSTER, Ann, 99
  Dorothy, 99, 193
  William, 99, 193
Fortune, 44, 216
Fortune & Penn Freehold, 216
FOSTER, Anne, 5, 9
  Leonard, 99
  Michael, 27, 181
  Mr., 202
  Ralph, 10
FOUCKE, Richard, 111
FOUKE, Gerrard, 52
  Richard, 29, 100
FOUKES, Roger, 100
FOULKE, Anne, 100
  Richard, 100
Found Hills, 234
Fountain Head, 34
FOWKE, Ann, 80, 100, 200
  Anne, 52, 79, 100
  Chandler, 100, 101
  Elizabeth, 79, 100
  Frances, 100
  Gerard, 52, 79, 80, 100, 101

  Gerrard, 100, 218, 243, 267
  Halalugha, 292
  Hallilujah, 100
  Jane, 101
  Katherine, 100
  Mary, 52, 79, 292
  Maryland, 100
  Richard, 100, 170, 292
  Roger, 9, 100, 101
  Sarah, 100, 101
  William Chandler, 101
FOWKES, Ann, 260
FOWLER, William, 101
FOWLKES, Ann, 267
  Thomas, 251
FOWTRELL, George, 101
FOX, Edward, 101
  Henry, 121
Fox(es) Race, 6
Foxhall, 20
FOXLEY, Elisabeth, 136
FOXTON, Richard, 22
Frailty, 294, 295
France, 49
FRANCIS, John, 101
FRANCISSON,
  Francis, 101
FRANCKLIN, Henry, 101
  Jane, 101
  Mary, 101
FRANCKUM, Francis, 101
  Henry, 101, 102
FRANCUM, Amey, 101
  Elizabeth, 101
  Henry, 101
FRANK, Henry, 45
FRANKAM, Henry, 101
FRANKBURN, Henry, 102

FRANKLIN, Henry, 45
  John, 101
FRANKUM, 269, 306
FRASIER, John, 285
FRAWNER, Edward, 102
  Mathew, 147
FRAWNES, Ellinor, 102
FRAZER, Anne, 102, 252
  John, 102, 252
  Mary, 102, 252
FRAZIER, Owen, 102
FREEMAN, Anne, 102
  Elizabeth, 247
  James, 102, 197, 247, 298
  Janet, 298
  Nathaniel, 102
FREETE, Teague, 102
FREMAN, Nathaniell, 102
FRENCH, Hugh, 22
French Lewis, 281
French Lewiss, 114
Freshes, 44
Friendship, 29, 60, 79, 91, 126, 143, 250, 253, 254, 287
FRISSELL, Hannah, 102
  Thomas, 102
Frogs Nest, 1
FRONER, Mathew, 11
FROST, William, 57, 193
FRY, Elizabeth, 148
  Joseph, 148
FRYE, Constance, 102
  John, 102
FURNIS, Francis, 102
  Mary, 102
FURTH, Joseph, 102

-G-

GABRIELL,
  Bartholome, 102
GAILE, Edward, 103
  Ruth, 103
GAILY, Thomas, 103
Gaily's Discovery, 103
GALAHAW, Katherine, 175
GALBREATH,
  George, 103
GALEY, Lorance, 102
Galeys Discovery, 48
GALLAWAY, John, 235
Galleys Discovery, 74
GALLWITH, John, 235
GALWITH, Elizabeth, 103
  Ignatius, 103
  James, 103
  John, 103, 285
  Jonas, 103
  Mary, 103
  Sarah, 103
  Tamer, 103
GAMBILL,
  William, 103
GAMBRA, Domingo, 103
  Elizabeth, 103
  Richard, 103, 182
GAMBRAL, Elizabeth, 25
GANDI, William, 103
GANDIE, William, 118
GANNE, Edward, 229
GANT, Magery, 103
  Thomas, 103, 105
GARDINER, Ann, 104, 105, 110
  Ben, 104
  Benjamin, 43, 104, 105
  Bullet, 104

Clement, 240
Constant, 105
Douglas Gifford, 104
Edward, 104
Eleanor, 43, 104
Elizabeth, 105
Howard, 108
Hugh, 104, 107
Ignatius, 104
John, 103, 105
Joseph, 104, 105
Luke, 104, 110, 220
Martha, 104
Mary, 26, 76, 107
William, 103
GARDNER, Ann, 104
  Annastasia, 104
  Benjamin, 104
  Biningman, 104
  Bullat, 104
  Edward, 104
  Eliner, 104
  Elizabeth, 103, 104, 163
  Francis, 104
  John, 163, 230
  Joseph, 104
  Luke, 103, 163, 174, 287, 300
  Mary, 104
  Michael, 104
  Ralph, 104, 310
  Samuel, 104
GARFORTH, Richard, 105, 224
GARLAND, Ann, 105
  Mary, 105
  Randolph, 105, 252
GARNER, Benjamin, 105
  Elizabeth, 38
  John, 60, 104, 105
  Joseph, 104
  Michael, 104

Samuell, 104
Zephaniah, 60
GARRARD, Jane, 107
  John, 107
  Mary, 56
  Thomas, 56, 107
GARRET, James, 105
  John, 105
  Peter, 295
GARRETT, Amos, 174
  Ann, 105
  Charles, 105, 215, 255
  Joyce, 105
  Joyse, 255
GARTHERELL,
  Bartholme, 105
GARVER, Charity, 13
GARY, Jephari, 105
GASKOYNE, Samuel, 105
GATELEY, Edward, 105
GATES, Elizabeth, 106
  James, 203
  John, 92, 105, 106, 119, 200
  Joseph, 105, 106, 214, 290
  Mary, 106
  Peter, 106
  Robert, 105, 106
GATTWICK, Mary, 219
GAVAN, Thomas, 27
GAVIN, Mr., 202
  Thomas, 103
GAZEY, Jonathon, 106
  Martha, 106
GEDDAS, George, 199
GEDDES, George, 106
GEE, Henry, 106
  John, 106
GEER, James, 106
GENTS, Elisabeth, 106
GEORGE, Jane, 102

John, 111
Georges Rest, 26, 165, 177, 201
GERMAN, George, 106
GERRAD, Thomas, 296
GERRARD, Daniell, 106
  Thomas, 68, 150, 154, 178, 182, 193, 201, 218, 304
GES, Ane, 107
  Lewis, 107
  Mary, 107
  Walter, 107
GEST, Walter, 282
GEY, Anne, 107
GHOUGH, Jane, 107
GIBBENS, George, 233
  Thomas, 107
GIBBS, Elizabeth, 111
  John, 107
GIBSON, Elizabeth, 107
  John, 107
  Thomas, 31, 69, 93, 107, 118, 195
  William, 107
Gibson Close, 108
GIBSON?, Dorothy, 107
Gibson's Neck, 108
GIFFARD, Douglas, 127
GIFFERD, Douglas, 127
GIFFORD, Douglas, 107
  Henry, 104, 107
  Ursula, 167
GIFFORDE, Douglass, 108
  Roseaman, 108
Gift, 234
GILBARD, James, 108

GILBERT, Jane, 108
GILE, William, 10
Gill(s) Land, 203, 205
GILLCHRIST, Samuel, 108
GILLES, John, 257
Gilliod, 205
GILPEN, Charity, 108
  Edward, 108
  Henry, 108
  Isaac, 108
  Jane, 108
  Mary Ann, 108
  Thomas, 108
  William, 108
GILPIN, Benjamin, 108
  Charety, 108
  Charity, 108
  Edward, 108
  Eleanor, 108
  Elizabeth, 108
  Henry, 108
  Isaac, 108
  Jane, 108
  Mary, 108
  Mary Ann, 108
  Sylvanus, 108
  Thomas, 108
  William, 108
GINNEY, John, 108
Gi(n)sbrough, 79
GIURBERT, Josua, 26
GLASCOCK, James, 108
GLASE, Benjamin, 109
  Sarah, 109
GLASHEN, Elinor, 109
GLASS, John, 26, 109, 113
GLASSCOCK, James, 7, 8
GLASSHON, John, 271
GLAWSHEN, James, 109

GLAZE, Benjamin, 109
  Elizabeth, 109
  John, 109
  Joseph, 109
  Margaret, 109
  Mary, 109
  Samuel, 109
  Sarah, 109
  Thomas, 109
GLOOVER, George, 109
GLOSSE, George, 109
  John, 109
GLOSSINGTON, Hannah, 102
GLOVER, John, 37
  Mary, 109, 211
  William, 211
Glovers Point, 3, 93, 143, 226, 267, 308
Glowers' Point, 307
GOADY, William, 109
GOALLY, Mary, 210
Goar, 254
Goate's Lodge, 154
Goat's Lodge, 133
Goats Lodge, 134
GODAH, William, 92
GODEY, William, 39
GODFREY, Ann, 110
  Anne, 109
  Archibald, 110
  Francis, 110
  George, 1, 109, 110, 162, 194, 215, 272, 298, 304
  Ginnitt, 288
  Janet, 110
  Jannet, 104, 110
  Jennet(t), 110
  Mary, 109, 110, 215
  Stephen, 110
  Thomas, 109

Index 347

William, 11, 104, 109, 110
Godfrey's Chase, 276
GODFRY, George, 109
  Mary, 28, 109
GODRING, Mary, 292
GODSHALL, John, 57, 111, 289, 299
  Mary, 111
  Sarah, 14
GODSON, John, 297
GODWIN, John, 252
GODY, Margaret, 39
  Matthew, 109, 112
  Samuel, 109
  William, 39, 109, 112
GOER, Ami, 111
  Ann(e), 111, 251
  George, 111, 251
  Mary, 111
  Sarah, 111
GOLDSMITH, John, 259
GOLETIE, Thomas, 156
GOLEY, Ann, 54
  Elisabeth, 111, 192
  Susanna, 54
  Thomas, 54, 111
GOOCH, John, 107, 111, 217
GOOD, Lewis, 111
  Lucie, 111
Good Fortune, 174
Good Intent, 120
Good Luck, 5, 309
Good Will, 76
GOODALE, Elizabeth, 111
  Isabella, 111
GOODERICK, Francis, 140
GOODGE, John, 248
GOODHALL, John, 57

GOODRICH, Francis, 112, 141
  Stran, 147
GOODRICK, Ann, 112
  Aron, 112
  Benjamin, 112
  Elizabeth, 112
  Francis, 112, 254, 298
  George, 112, 167
  Henry, 116
  Mary, 112
  Robert, 112
  Susanna, 39
  Theodosia, 112
  Ursule, 112, 167
  William, 112
GOODRICKE, Francis, 92
GOODRIDGE, Henry, 255
GOODWICK, Francis, 270
Goodwill, 214, 223
GOODY, Henry, 112
GOOLD, John, 112
  Margerie, 112
GOOMAN, Ann, 291
GOOMES, John, 147
Goose Creek, 35, 100
GOOSEY, Jonathan, 112
  Martha, 106, 112
GOOSH, John, 41
GOR, George, 111
GORDIAN, Daniel, 113
  Mary, 113
GORE, George, 111
Gores Addition, 222
GORLEY, Dianah, 113
  John, 113
GORLY, Barbary, 54, 137
  John, 54, 137
  Thomas, 156

GOSH, Richard, 112
GOSLIN, Robert, 113
GOSTING, Robert, 113
GOTFARD, Douglass, 138
GOUGH, William, 208
GOULE, James, 113
GOURDON, Daniel, 113
  Mary, 113
GOUR(E)LEY,
  Barbary, 113
  Elizabeth, 113
  John, 113
  Thomas, 113
GOURLY, Elizabeth, 161
  John, 161
GOW, James, 98, 276
GOYLE, John, 113
  Thomas, 113
GRADINER, Joseph, 233
GRAHAM, Anne, 113
  James, 113
GRAINMAN, Eadman, 308
  Edward, 308
GRANDSWORTH,
  Mary, 113
GRANT, Robert, 113
  Thomas, 303
GRAVES, Dorothey, 113
  Dorothy, 113, 114
  George, 61
  Josha, 251
  Joshua, 113
  Mary, 113
  Samuel, 113
  Sarah, 113, 251
  Thomas, 113
GRAY, Alexander, 90
  Ann, 114

Edward, 114
Francis, 114
James, 114
John, 114, 205
Joseph, 114, 155
Mary, 28, 35, 114, 169, 205
Ruth, 114
GREAVES, Ann, 114
John, 114
GREEN, Charity, 119, 120
Cudburth, 116
Elisabeth, 301
Elizabeth, 115
Francis, 115, 116, 249
Giles, 116
Jane, 115
John, 115, 116
Joseph, 115
Joshua, 115
Leonard, 115, 116, 249
Lewis, 81
Luke, 2, 114
Margaret, 115
Mary, 115, 116
Mildred, 116
Prudence, 116, 241
Richard, 115
Robert, 25, 115, 116
Thomas, 115, 116
William, 46
Winifrid, 115
Green Banck, 117
Green Branch, 191
Green Chance, 302
Green Chase, 289
Green Land, 125
Green Spring, 53, 169
Greenbank, 53
GREENE, Anne, 116
Claire, 115
Elizabeth, 115

Francis, 1, 115, 116
Giles, 115
James, 115
Leonard, 1, 115, 116
Luke, 129
Margaret, 115, 116
Mary, 115, 116
Robert, 1, 115, 116, 163, 197, 277
Thomas, 115, 116
Verlinda, 115
William, 115
Winefred, 116
Winnifrid, 116
GREENESTEAD, William, 248
GREENFIELD, Ann, 303
Dorothy, 209
Joane, 174
Thomas, 116, 174
Thomas Randolph, 2
Thomas Trueman, 10
Thomas Truman, 303
GREENHALGE, Edward, 130
GREENHILL, John, 52
GREENING, Jabez, 116
Susannah, 116
Greens, 274
Greens Forrest, 278
Green's Inheritance, 5, 115, 116, 126, 262
Green's Rest, 116
Greenwigh, 32
GREER, Mary, 286, 304
Thomas, 286
GREGORY, Charles, 116
Christopher, 9, 80
GREMER, Willeford, 27
GREW, John, 192

GREY, Edward, 114, 307
Elizabeth, 114
Francis, 114
James, 114
Johannah, 114
John, 114
Richard, 114
Samuel, 110
Thomas, 114
William, 114
GREYDEN, Margarett, 116
GREYSON, Jane, 135
William, 135
GRIFFEN, Mary, 251
GRIFFERD, Douglass, 138
GRIFFETH, William, 116
GRIFFIN, James, 253
John, 116
Mary, 251
Robert, 116
William, 116
GRIGES, John, 116
GRIGGS, Bayne, 18
Beane, 222
GRIGORY, Charles, 221
GRINAN, Virlinda, 51
GRODTWELL, George, 100
GROSSER, Mary, 117
GROVES, Alice, 117
Elizabeth, 117
George, 117
Jane, 117
John, 117, 260, 279, 289
Mary, 117
Matthew, 117
Possume, 117
William, 117

Index

GRUB, John, 117
  Mary, 117
GRUBB, John, 72
Grubb Street, 10
Grubs Venture, 19
GRYANT, Daniel, 123
GRYER, John, 118
GUESSE, Richard, 118
GUG, Sarah, 247
  William, 247
GUIBERT, Ann, 118
  Elizabeth, 118
  Joshua, 118
  Thomas, 118
GUIFORD, Henry, 118
GUNBY, Constant, 112
  ——, 112
GUNNER, Moyses, 118
GUNTER, James, 226
GUTRIDGE, James, 112
GUY, Charles, 118
  Elizabeth, 118
GUYTHER, Elizabeth, 260
GUYUN, John, 117
GWIN, John, 113, 118, 272
  Richard, 118
Gwines Hope, 197
GWINN, Ann, 119
  Anna, 118
  Benjamin, 119
  Eliza, 314
  James, 11
  John, 83, 117, 118, 119
  Joseph, 11, 118, 119
  Joshu:, 119
  Mary, 119
  Ralph, 108, 118
Gwinn's Choice, 259
Gwinn's Hope, 124, 216, 217

Gwins Hope, 171
GWITHER, Mary, 119
  Nicholas, 119
GWYNN, Anne, 118
  Christopher, 118
  Susanna, 118

-H-
Hab Nab at a Venture, 184
Habnabala Venture, 10
HADDOCK, James, 17, 65, 244
  Sarah, 119, 293
Hadlow, 119, 176, 293
HADLOWE, Idy, 139
HAGALL, Elisabeth, 119
HAGAN, Basil, 119
  Benjamin, 119
  Henry, 119
  Ignatius, 119
  James, 119, 120, 257
  Joseph, 119
  Mary, 119
  Rebecca, 119
  Sarah, 119
  Thomas, 119, 120, 257
  William, 119
HAGAR, Elizabeth, 120
  Mary, 120
  Robert, 120, 250
  William, 120
HAGER, Robert, 268
HAGERTEE, Mary, 113
  Robert, 113
HAGERTY, Honner, 75
  John, 75
HAGGAT, Anne, 100
  Humphery, 100
HAGGATE, Humpherie, 120
HAGGATT, John, 218

Haggesters Addition, 224
HAGGETT, Alice, 120
  Ann(e), 120
  Freeman, 120
  Humphrey, 100, 120
  John, 120, 218
  Mary, 120
Haggister's Addition, 225
HAGGIT, John, 120
HAGGON, Sarah, 199
HAGITT, Alice, 263
  Freeman, 263
HAGNER, John, 120
HAGOE, Ann, 120
  Charity, 120
  Elizabeth, 120
  Ignatius, 120
  James, 120
  Mary, 120
  Sarah, 120
  Thomas, 120
  William, 120
HAGON, Ann, 257
  Thomas, 257
HAGUE, Elisabeth, 120
HAIL, Thomas, 120, 163
HAINES, Bennard, 181
HAISLIP, Henry, 71, 111, 132
  Richard, 132
  Robert, 132
  Susanna, 71
  Susannah, 111
HAISTINGS, Henry, 71
HAKSON, James, 121
HALERD, William, 121
HALEY, John, 121
Hall, 165
HALL, Alice, 122

Benjamin, 30, 122, 141, 165, 257
Charles, 121
Dorothy, 122
Francis, 26, 122
Ignatius, 122
Isaack, 121
John, 38, 121, 122, 141
Margrett, 121
Mary, 30, 57, 121, 122
Mr., 315
Rebecca, 121
Richard, 57, 121
Sarah, 5, 41, 122
Thomas, 5, 122
Thomas Lant, 122
Walter, 24, 121
William, 121, 161
HALL?, Katherine, 122
HALLOWES, John, 248
Hall's Lott, 151
Hall's Place, 151, 198
HALY, Clement, 171
Elisabeth, 121
Elizabeth, 171
Mary, 171
HAMARSLEY,
Frances, 122
Francis, 122
HAMBLETON,
Elizabeth, 122, 130
John, 122, 123, 130
HAMBLIN, James, 122
HAMBYE, Francis, 122
HAMERLY, Mary, 33
HAMERSLEY, Francis, 17, 33
HAMERSLY, Frances, 122
Francis, 122
Margrett, 32
Mary, 122

HAMILL, John, 122, 311
Sarah, 53, 122
Hamills Discovery, 122
HAMILTON,
Alexander, 123
Elisabeth, 123, 130, 220
Elizabeth, 123, 288
James, 123
Jane, 143
John, 42, 52, 118, 123, 288
Mary, 123
Patrick, 123
Samuel, 123
Thomas, 123
William, 123
HAMITOWNE, Gawen, 251
HAMLETON, John, 122
HAMMERSLEY,
Francis, 32
Margaret, 32
Hammersmith, 32
HAMMILL, John, 311
Sarah, 311
HAMMILTON,
Elizabeth, 130
John, 130
Joseph, 130
HAMMON, John, 123
HAMMOND(S),
Benjamin, 176
John, 123, 140
HAMMONS, Margaret, 297
HAMOZLY, Elizabeth, 241
HANBY, Alise, 123
Francis, 123
HANCE, Benjamin, 185, 196

HANCOCK, George, 123
HANDLY, Mr., 128
HANDY, Henry, 123
HANELAND, William, 296
HANNA, Alexander, 123
Mary, 123
HANNAY, Alexander, 260
Hanover, 290
HANSON, Ann, 124
Anne, 102, 123
Benedicta, 123
Benjamin, 124, 125
Charity, 124, 126
Chloe, 126
Dorothy, 124
Elisabeth, 90, 126, 172, 173, 294
Elizabeth, 97, 123, 124, 125, 126, 149, 178, 294, 305
Helloise, 126
Heloise, 126
Jane, 124, 126
Joan, 126
John, 52, 65, 90, 123, 124, 125, 126, 149, 172, 173, 191, 196, 237, 305
Mary, 97, 123, 124, 125
Randolph, 280
Robert, 34, 60, 90, 97, 123, 124, 125, 126, 143, 144, 166, 207, 214, 225, 234, 254, 291
S., 97, 125
Samuel(l), 20, 65, 70, 97, 123, 124, 125, 126, 134, 177, 178,

222, 234, 254, 294, 305
  Sarah, 123, 124
  Thomas, 102
  Violetta, 125, 126, 144
  Walter, 123, 125, 126, 178, 269
  William, 124, 125, 126
Hanson Green, 125
Hanstone?, 12
Haphazard, 80, 130
HARBEN, Joanna, 4
HARBERT, Alexander, 252
  Ann, 127
  Mary, 252
  Sarah, 127
  William, 40, 47, 55, 127, 162
Harbert's Chance, 127
HARBOT, William, 236
Hard Frost, 234
Hard Shift, 26
Hardfrost, 2
HARDING, Robert, 58
Hardshift, 75, 103, 190
HARDY, Ann(e), 9, 127
  Capt., 294
  Elinor, 127
  Elizabeth, 127
  George, 127
  Henry, 9, 22, 100, 127, 174, 217
  Ignatius, 127
  John, 127
  Rebecah, 127
  William, 127
HARDYE, Henry, 100
Hardy's Purchase, 127
HARE, James, 127
HARGAY, William, 127
HARGESS, Abraham, 128
  Francis, 128

  Thomas, 128
  William, 128
Hargess Hope, 128
HARGIS, Abraham, 201
  Anne, 127
  Roger, 127
  William, 66, 127
HARGISS, Ann, 114
  William, 114
Hargisses Hope, 114
HARGIST, Ann, 127
Hargrass' Hope, 1
HARGUESS, William, 107
HARGUESSE, Ann, 128
  William, 128
Harguessee's Hope, 229
HARIS, George, 128
HARISON, Jos., 227
HARKLEY, Ann, 128
  Elizabeth, 128
  Jane, 128
  Mary, 128
  Richard, 128
  Robert, 128
HARPER, Daniel, 128
  Daniell, 199
  Mary, 35, 128, 199, 288
  Peter, 128
HARRANT, Peter, 219
HARRARD, William, 128
HARRINGTON,
  Abigail, 285
  Abigall, 285
  John, 128
HARRIS, Ales, 128
  Barton, 129
  Bereshebay, 221
  Bethseba, 129
  Bethsheba, 137

  Elisabeth, 129, 167
  Jane, 128
  John, 88, 119, 129, 154, 167, 170, 294, 311
  Katharine, 129
  Mary, 129, 137, 221
  Nathan, 129
  Nathaniell, 129
  Richard, 128, 129
  Samuel, 128
  Susanna, 129
  Thomas, 105, 128, 129, 137, 207, 221, 255
HARRISE, George, 128
HARRISON, 132
  Alice, 131
  Anne, 130
  Benjamin, 129, 130
  Benoni, 132, 197
  Catherine, 129
  Cathrine, 131
  Diana, 232
  Elizabeth, 81, 129, 130, 131, 132, 281
  Ester, 132
  Esther, 131, 132, 253, 254
  Francis, 11, 98, 129, 130, 131, 132
  Hester, 131
  Hezekiah, 131
  Jane, 130
  John, 12, 130, 131
  Jone, 78
  Jos., 66
  Jos:, 131
  Joseph, 2, 3, 11, 13, 62, 80, 129, 130, 131, 132, 141, 192, 246, 267, 281, 304, 80
  Joseph Hanson, 94

Katharine, 129
Martha, 12, 130
Mary, 2, 129, 131, 132, 281
Oliver, 130
Priscilla, 131
Richard, 3, 11, 47, 66, 77, 80, 94, 119, 120, 122, 129, 130, 131, 132, 149, 211, 246, 256, 259, 267, 269, 281, 313
Robert, 130
Susanna, 130
Tabathia, 131
Tabitha, 130, 132
Thomas, 82, 120, 130, 131, 132, 197, 279
Verlinda, 131, 267
Violata, 289
Violatta, 131
Virlanda, 132
Virlinda, 131, 132, 267
William, 131
Harrison's Adventure, 130
Harrison's Gift, 79
Harrisons Land, 114
Harrisons Venture, 61, 77, 131
HARRISS, Elizabeth, 129
  John, 129
  Mary, 129
  Nathan, 129
  Thomas, 129
HARRISSON, Elizabeth, 130
  Jane, 130
  Joseph, 114, 130, 193, 217
  Richard, 130, 193
  Tabitha, 130
Harrisson's Gift, 12

HARROLD, Catherine, 148
HARROW, John, 147
  Peter, 147
HARSTON, William, 132
HARTICK, John, 246
HARWOOD, John, 287
HASLINGS, Thomas, 132
HASLIP, Henry, 51, 132
  Richard, 132
  Robert, 132
HASTEAD, Elizabeth, 83
  Michaell, 83
HATCH, John, 63, 132, 215, 285, 88
  Mary, 132
  Mr., 16
  Sarah, 132, 135
  Thomas, 132, 133
  William, 15, 41, 108, 132, 135, 159, 280, 296
Hatfield, 217
HATHERTON, John, 133
Haton, 174
Hattens Point, 117
HATTON, Benoni, 133
  Elisabeth, 133
  Elizabeth, 303
  George, 133
  Lidia, 133
  Lydia, 133
  Mr., 314
  William, 128, 133, 259, 287, 300, 303
Hattons Improvement, 133
Hatton's Point, 293, 294, 314

HAUGE, Elisabeth, 123
  John, 123
HAULE, Henry, 27
HAUSE, John, 46
HAW, John, 36, 133
  Mary, 37, 133, 171
HAWES, Thomas, 147
HAWKING, Henry, 133
  Mary, 135
  Sarah, 133
  William, 135
HAWKINS, Alexander, 133, 134, 217
  Alexander Smith, 133
  Catharine, 33
  Elisabeth, 61, 133, 182, 307
  Elizabeth, 61, 133, 134, 191, 224, 226, 256, 307
  Ellinor, 133
  Henery, 149
  Henry, 38, 57, 60, 61, 133, 134, 160, 172, 179, 182, 195, 206, 207, 208, 209, 219, 224, 226, 237, 255, 259, 263, 269, 273, 277, 304, 307, 308, 313
  Henry Holland, 133, 134, 224
  Joan, 134
  John, 61, 133, 134, 256, 263
  Mary, 133, 172
  Ruth, 133, 224, 273
  Sarah, 133, 134, 255
  Thomas, 61, 133, 134, 219
  Tubman, 133
  William, 134
Hawkin's Addition, 133

Hawkin's Barrens, 133
Hawkin's Lot, 133
Hawkin's Purchase, 133, 134
HAWLING, Mary, 135
William, 135
HAWLTON, William, 135
HAWRET, Elisabeth, 264
Peter, 264
HAWSSE, John, 139
HAWTON, Benja:, 135
Benoni, 135
Benony, 135
Hannah, 135
John, 135
Joseph, 135
Lydia, 135
Marg(a)ret, 135
Thomas, 135
William, 51, 132, 135, 314
Hawton's Improvement, 135
HAXBY, Isabell, 135
HAYES, John, 180
Margaret, 67, 136
Mary, 166
Peter, 136
Samuel, 136
Thomas, 166
HAYFIELD, Richard, 136
HAYLES, Mary, 120
HAYS, James, 136
Patrick, 136
Thomas, 165
HAYSE, Peter, 136
HAYWARD, John, 136
HAYWOOD, Mary, 136
Hazard, 235, 236, 240, 265
HEADLOW, Edith, 139

HEAGAN, John, 119
Healy's Plantation, 291
HEARBEN, Allen, 136
Elisha, 136
Elizabeth, 136
HEARBIN, John, 4
HEARD, Bridgett, 136
Bridgit, 136
Brigit, 136
William, 64, 136, 163, 212, 266
Heards Mountain, 314
Heard's Mountaine, 284
HEATH, James, 48, 208
Hedlow, 17
HEETH, George, 106
HEIGHFEILD, Richard, 136
HELGAR, Anne, 136
Thomas, 136
HELMES, John, 136
Hemesley Meadows, 314
Hemirad, 208
HEMLSEY, Mary, 97
Philemon, 97
HEMSLEY, Ann, 137
Mary, 64, 70, 137
Phil:, 70
Philemon, 64, 70, 137
Phillip, 291
William, 137
HEMSLY, Mary, 136, 137
Phelemon, 137
Philemon, 136
HENDLEY, Robert, 57, 179, 229
HENLEY, Elizabeth, 233
Henry, 128

Robert, 10, 20, 23, 84, 150, 182, 211
HENLY, Charity, 137
John, 233
Robert, 30, 137, 155, 219
HENSEY, William, 137
HENSLEY, Edward, 138
Mary, 137, 174
Philemon, 137, 174
HENSLY, William, 121
HENSON, Barbara, 140
Barbarah, 138
Randolph, 138
William, 138
Her Excellency's Gift, 52, 124
HERALD, William, 180
HERBERD, Elizabeth, 138
John, 138
William, 138
HERBERT, Catherine, 138
Elizabeth, 138
John, 138
Mary, 47, 138
Sarah, 138, 280
William, 47, 55, 67, 68, 138, 259, 280
Herds Mountains, 314
Hereford, 126
HERGESSON, Susannah, 114
HERMAN, Mary, 68
Robert, 138
HERNADON, John Goodwin, 254
HERRANT, John, 138
Peter, 138
HERRICKSON, Hans, 138

Judith, 138
HERRINGTON,
  Thomas, 138
HESELDEN, Elizabeth,
  138
HETTON, William, 209
HEUTON, Allen, 138
  George, 138
  Mary, 138
HEWLITT, Mary, 35
HEWS, Even, 147
HEWTON, Allen, 84,
  138
  Frances, 84
  George, 138
  Mary, 138
HEY, Charles, 139
HEYDON, Francis, 139
  Thomasine, 139
HIBEART, Con:, 269
HICKS, Sophia, 303
HICKSON, Edward,
  139
  Henry, 139
  James, 98, 139
  Mary, 139
Hicory Thicket, 23
HIDE, Ann, 161
  Capt., 285
HIGDEN, Benedict
  Leonard, 139
  Benjamin, 139
  Ignatious, 139
  Jane, 139
  Martha, 139
  Susanna, 139
  William, 139
HIGDON, Benjamin,
  139, 244
  Charles, 139
  John, 139
  Thomas, 245
HIGDONS, Thomas,
  139

William, 139
HIGGINS, Elizabeth,
  156
  John, 156
  Margaret, 156
  Mary, 156
  Richard, 156
HIGONS, John, 139
HIGTON, Bathia, 139
  Benjamin, 139
  Charles, 139
  John, 139
  Mary, 139
  Menesenca, 139
  Millasaint, 213
  Thomas, 139, 213
  William, 139
HILL, Ann(e), 140
  Clement, 27, 140
  Edith, 21
  Eleanor, 146
  Gil(l)es, 140, 257
  John, 140
  Margaret, 140
  Mary, 139, 140
  Mathew, 21, 146
  Matthew, 23, 139
  Onsley, 139, 140
  Philip, 140
  Richard, 140
  Robert, 140
  Susanna, 257
  Thomas, 139, 140
  Vall:, 139
  Walt, 139
Hill Freehold, 186
Hill Port, 250
Hills, 125, 127, 178,
  259, 293, 294
Hills, Edee, 139
  Edith, 139
  Idy, 139
  Susanna Marea, 139
  William, 139

Hills and Dales, 103
Himslays Marsh, 314
HINCH, Mathew, 140
HINCKS, Dorothy, 140
HINDE, William, 140
HINDLE, Joshua, 140
Hingistone, 283
HINSEY, William, 66,
  139, 221
HINSHAW, William,
  229
HINSLEY, Thomas,
  140
HINSON, Barbara, 140
  Blanch, 140
  Mary, 287
  Randolph, 140, 287
HIPKIS, Peter, 140
*His Lordship's
  Favour*, 20, 91, 190,
  191
*His Lordship's
  Manor*, 37, 56, 75,
  214, 235, 236
*His Lordships Manor
  of Calvert*, 103
Hispaniola, 189
Hitchin, 37, 75
HITCHINSON, John,
  140
HITON, Millsant, 30
HOBART, Richard,
  141, 179
HOBB, Isable, 141
  Thomas, 141, 226
HOBBART, Richard,
  315
HOBERT, Richard, 202
HOBSON, Eliza, 141
  Elizabeth, 141
  J., 141
  John, 141, 228
  Phoebe, 141
  Thomas, 141

HOCTON, Adam, 141
  Joseph, 141
HODGINS, Charles, 141
HODGLY, John, 141
HODGSON, Elinor, 142
  Elisabeth, 13, 142
  Elizabeth, 141, 142
  Johana, 141
  Johannah, 141, 142, 196
  Philip, 141
  Richard, 13, 141
  William, 141
HOE, Frances, 174
  Rice, 174
  Tabitha, 132
HOGAN, Katharine, 107
HOGDIN, Johnathan, 141
HOGGIN, Henry, 142
Hoggs Island, 131
Hoggs Quarter, 8
HOGIN, John, 141
HOLE, Thomas, 86
HOLIWOOD,
  Elisabeth, 228
  James, 228
Holland, 77, 274
HOLLAND,
  Mary, 103
  Richard, 103
HOLLINGSWORTH,
  William, 224
HOLLINSWORTH,
  Margarett, 238
HOLLYDAY, Leonard, 157
HOLMES, Grace, 142
HOLT, Ann, 36
  James, 142
  Jane, 142
  John, 142
  Margaret, 24
  Margarett, 142
  Mary, 142
  Milicent, 142
  Robert, 36, 142
  William, 142
HOLTON, Joseph, 142
Holt's Divising, 222
Holy Spring, 130, 131
HOMAN, Dorothy, 142
  Herbert, 142
Homefaire, 248
Homefare, 231
Homely, 62
HONNKER, Elisabeth, 142
Hope, 257
HOPE,
  Elizabeth, 50
  George, 142
Hopefull Blessing, 185
Hopewell, 10, 47, 50, 59, 184, 295
HOPEWELL,
  John, 142
HOPKINS, Phillip, 188
  William, 29
HOPPER, Dave, 17
  Rachel, 17
HORDUILT, Rachel, 49
Horn Fair, 222
Horne, 220
HORTON, Alice, 40
HOSKINE, Philip, 291
HOSKINGS, Thomas, 142
HOSKINS, Ann(e), 143, 144, 174, 198, 205
  Ballard, 143
  Baylard, 144
  Baylord, 143, 144
  Benedicta, 288
  Benedista, 143
  Benjamin, 144
  Bennet, 143, 144, 204
  Bennett, 143, 144, 253
  Eleanor, 144
  Elizabeth, 126, 143, 211, 288
  Jane, 143, 288
  Jeremi:, 142
  Lauran:, 142
  Lawrence, 143, 313
  Margarett, 143
  Martha, 143, 144
  Mary, 73, 126, 143, 205, 211
  Mary Ann, 143
  Mary Anne, 144
  Oswald, 143, 144
  Oswell, 143
  Phil:, 143
  Philip, 23, 121, 126, 143, 144, 156, 174, 288
  Phillip, 143, 198, 256, 288
  Violetta, 126
  Will, 211
  William, 29, 126, 143, 144, 253
Hoskins' Lot, 143
HOSKYNS, Elizabeth, 143
  Philip, 143
HOTTON, William, 133
HOUGHTON, James, 144
HOUKINS, Elizabeth, 287
  Nicholas, 287
HOULT, Ann, 36
  Robert, 36
  Susannah, 36
HOWARD, Ann, 146, 241

Anne, 145
Daniel, 233
Edmond, 80, 145
Edmund, 119, 144, 145
Edward, 145
Elenor, 145
Elisabeth, 33, 145
Elizabeth, 127, 144, 145
George, 144, 145
Jane, 145
John, 59, 144, 145, 150
Margaret(t), 144
Mary, 179
Mary Ann, 146
Philise, 144
Rachel, 145
Rebecca, 145
Sarah, 38, 145, 146
Susannah, 145
Thomas, 33, 144, 145, 179
William, 38, 144, 145
William Stevens, 144, 145
———, 241
HOWELL, Thomas, 75, 146
HOWES, Thomas, 146
HOWISON, Ann, 146
John, 11, 138, 146
Howland, 89, 194, 205, 210
HOWLING, Mary, 146
William, 146
HOWSON, John, 146
HOYLE, Samuell, 146
HUBART, Richard, 141
HUBBARD, Eleanor, 146
Ellinor, 19
Mr., 202

Nathaniel, 146
Richard, 27, 315
HUBBERTON, Mary, 146
HUCHISON, William, 290
Huckleberry Swamp, 186, 249
HUDLEY, Robert, 283
HUDSON, Elener, 15
Elizabeth, 15, 146
Joanna, 15
Johanna, 146
Richard, 14
Robert, 146
Thomas, 146, 176, 271
William, 146
Hudsons Disappointment, 176
Hudsons Sinnagouge, 146
HUGH, Even, 147
HUGHS, Dorothy, 147
Even, 138
HUGHTON, Allen, 147
HULKS, Elisabeth, 304
Elizabeth, 304
Hull, 50
HULSE, James, 147
Menshall, 147
Meverell, 147
Meverill, 116
HULSEY, Elizabeth, 147
HUMBLE, Barbary, 147
HUNDBY, Henry, 147
HUNDLEY, Robert, 141, 247
HUNDLY, Robert, 31, 147
HUNGARFORD, William, 259
HUNGER, William, 115

HUNGERFORD, Ann, 16, 147
Barten, 119
Barton, 76, 119, 147, 148, 191, 192, 259, 306
Charles, 147
Elizabeth, 119, 147, 148
John, 147
Margaret(t), 147
Margret, 192
Mary, 17, 147
Thomas, 147, 192
William, 16, 147, 192, 219
Hungerford's Choice, 147
Hungerford's Choyce, 147
HUNLEY, Robert, 269
HUNLY, Robert, 250
HUNT, Alice, 250
Ann(a), 76, 148
Dorothy, 148
John, 78, 148
Joseph, 148
Mary, 148
Philip, 148
Thomas, 148
HUNTER, Alexander, 36
Mr., 315
Richard, 148
William, 32, 38, 46, 141, 148, 203, 235, 238, 257, 315, 220
HUNTINGTON, Elias, 148
Hunt's Venture, 148
HURRIE, Ann, 148
George, 148
Mary, 73
Thomas, 73

HURST, Samuell, 148
HUS, Robert, 148
HUSBAND, Alice, 149
  James, 149
  William, 149
Huscullens Addition, 201
Husinlows Addition, 177
Huskilow's Addition, 201
HUSOULA, Dennis, 216
HUSSEY, Elizabeth, 124, 149
  Jane, 149
  Joan, 149
  Johanna(h), 8, 149
  Thomas, 8, 84, 85, 124, 148, 149, 150, 155, 158, 170, 229
Huss(e)yes Lott, 125, 134
Hussey's Discovery, 172
HUSSY, Elisabeth, 149
  Elizabeth, 125
  Johannah, 149
  Thomas, 109, 125, 149, 304
Hussyes Addition, 125, 134
Hussyes Lodge, 125, 134
Hussyes Reserve, 125, 134
HUTCHESON, Elizabeth, 282
  Thomas, 282
  William, 150
HUTCHINS, Elianor, 149
HUTCHINSON, Ann, 150

John, 40, 150
Sarah, 149
Thomas, 150
William, 40, 149
HUTCHISON, Ann, 150
  Mary, 150
  Thomas, 150
  William, 150
HUTCHYSON, Ann, 150
  Elizabeth, 150
  Thomas, 150
HUTTON, Charles, 150
  John, 150
HYDE, Henry, 19
  John, 296, 299
  Joseph, 93
  Margaret, 93
  Mary, 142
  Samuel, 296
  Thomas, 142

-I-
IBBETSON, Francis, 150
  John Thomas, 150
  Teresa, 150
IDE, Margere, 150
INCIUS, William, 289
Inclosure, 72
Indian Cabbin, 19
Indian Cabin, 18,
Indian Field(s), 122, 151, 293
Indian Giant Sepulchre, 243
Indian Princess, 130
Indian Quarter, 129
Indian Town(e), 40, 77, 87, 272
Ingerstone, 124, 149, 309
Ingorthorpe, 292

Ingothorp, 246
INNIS, Thomas, 150
Ireland, 307
Ireland, Armagh County, 90, 91
  Ballihaden, 90
  Drummanon, 90
  Grange Oneland, 90
  Kilmore, Parish of, 91
  Sloughah County, 295
IRELAND, Elisabeth, 150
IVERY, Catherine, 150

-J-
JACKSON, Elizabeth, 150
  James, 150
  Jane, 151
  John, 289
  Mary, 150
  Thomas, 71, 150, 159
  William, 151, 265
Jamaica, 133, 134
JAMES, Edward, 82
  William, 151
JAMESON, Ann, 151
  Barbara, 151
  Benjamin, 151
  Elisabeth, 151
  Elizabeth, 151
  Frances, 151
  Henneretta, 151
  Henry, 151
  Henry Joshua, 151
  John, 151
  Joseph, 151
  Martha, 151
  Mary, 88, 151
  Richard, 151
  Thomas, 88, 151, 164, 186, 198
JAMIESON, John, 151
  William, 151

JARBO, John, 152
  Mary, 152
JARBOE, John, 152
  Mary, 152
JARRETT, Charles, 215
Jarvis, 151, 172
Jarviss, 198
JAXSON, William, 151
Jeamind, 162
JEFFERS, Marie, 152
JEFFERSON, James, 152
  Michael, 152
JEFFS, John, 152
JENCKINS, Abednego, 153
  Jane, 84
JENIFER, Ann, 152
  Daniel, 46, 152, 166, 199, 288
  Elizabeth, 152
  Mary, 152
  Saint Thomas, 152
  St. Thomas, 152, 288
JENKENSON, William, 289
JENKINGS, Richard, 152
JENKINS, Abenigo, 153
  Ann(e), 152, 153
  Daniell, 152
  Edward, 153
  Elizabeth, 152, 153
  Enock, 152
  George, 153
  Henerilla, 153
  Henrietta, 153
  John, 153
  Margaret, 153
  Mary, 152, 153
  Philip, 153
  Richard, 153, 302
  Susannah, 153
  Thomas, 68, 136, 152, 153
  William, 152, 153, 170, 289
  Zantalina, 153
JENKINSON, Ignatius, 154
  Mary, 58, 154
  Philip, 154
  William, 154, 170
JERRATT, Capt., 65
JESSOP, Joseph, 61
JINKINS, Philip, 217
JOANES, Jane, 155
  Mary, 154
  Morgan, 155
  Philip, 156
JOHNES, Elizabeth, 159
JOHNS, Abraham, 154
  Hannah, 154
  Mary, 239
  Richard, 12, 196
  William, 239
JOHNSON, Ann, 169
  Annastasia, 154
  Daniel, 154
  Daniell, 14, 69, 154, 158, 162, 228, 229
  Donnell, 158
  Elisabeth, 154
  Elizabeth, 163
  George, 154
  James, 214, 287
  Jemima, 154
  John, 154, 261
  Mary, 36, 154, 261
  Richard, 154
  Thomas, 154
  William, 36, 154, 213
Johnson Retirement, 217
Johnson's Addition, 184
Johnson's Choice, 147, 172, 221
Johnsons Enlargement, 217
JOHNSTONE, Archibald, 62
JONES, Ann(e), 155, 156
  Barbara, 156
  Catherine, 155
  Charles, 46, 119, 136, 156, 157, 225, 284
  Edward, 155
  Elinor, 156
  Elisabeth, 156, 248
  Elizabeth, 15, 155, 156, 159
  Evan, 22, 54
  James, 208
  Jane, 155, 156, 284
  Joanna, 154
  John, 155, 156, 248
  Katharine, 299
  Katherin, 155
  Katherine, 155
  Lewis, 156, 161, 204
  Margaret, 156
  Margarett, 155
  Mary, 155, 156
  Moses, 16, 155, 156, 299
  Owen, 2, 15, 109, 154, 155
  Philip, 155, 156, 159
  Pretious (Precious), 267
  Rice, 49
  Richard, 128, 130, 155, 156, 196
  Robert, 155
  Thomas, 156
  William, 251

Index

JONSON, Mary, 78
Jordan(s), 91, 190, 195, 257
JORDAN, John, 33
  Margaret, 157
Joseph Bullit's Folly, 41
Josephs Lott, 88
JOY, Elisabeth, 89
  Elizabeth, 216
  Joseph, 216
JUBB, James, 157
JUDD, Susannah, 92
JUSTIS, Henry, 169
  Mary, 169

-K-
KARNES, Henry, 157
  Mary, 157
  Robert, 157
  William, 157
KARR, Robert, 157
KEAN, Annastasia, 300
KEE, Henry, 158
  Sarah, 158
KEECH, Courts, 157, 200
  Elisabeth, 157
  Elizabeth, 69, 134, 157
  James, 69, 134, 157
  John, 134, 157
  Martha, 134
  Ruth, 134
KEELBY, John, 157
KEEN, James, 20, 157
  Nicholas, 157
  Susanna, 20
KEENE, Anne, 157
  Frances, 157
  James, 157
  Jane, 238
  Jeane, 157
  John, 157

Mary, 157
Nicholas, 157
KEETE, Martha, 72
  Mary, 72, 157
  William, 72, 157
Keeths Purchase, 72
Keets Purchase, 71
KEETT, Elizabeth, 157
  William, 157
KELLECK, William, 257
KELLEY, John, 296
KELLY, John, 3
  Mary, 66
  Thomas, 66
KENDALL, Francis, 157
KENDAY, James, 158
KENEDY, Elizabeth, 158
  John, 158
KENNADY, John, 158
KENNER, Hawson, 94
  Margret, 94
KENT, Robert, 158
Kent County, 13
KERKLEY, William, 160
KERRICK, James, 286
  Mary, 51, 286
  Will, 286
KERSEY, Margaret, 158
  Thomas, 158
  William, 158
KEY, Henry, 49, 158
  Philip, 106, 158, 223
  Sarah, 158
  Susannah, 158
  William, 158
KEY, Jobe, 15
  William, 15
KEYBERT, Constant, 158

Thomas, 158
KEYTH, Elizabeth, 158
  George, 158
KIDWELL, Anne, 158
  Anne, 158
  Benjamin, 158
  Elizabeth, 158
  Haggit, 158
  James, 158
  John, 158
  Thomas, 158
  Tracy, 158
  William, 158
KILBORNE, Elizabeth, 158
  Francis, 158
  Margaret, 158
KILINGSWORTH, John, 159
KILLCART, John, 159
KILLINGSWORTH, Elizabeth, 310
  John, 117
KING, Alice, 265
  Ann, 66, 159, 236
  Benjamin, 159
  Catherine, 159
  Charity, 123, 132
  Elisabeth, 159
  Elizabeth, 159, 236
  Joanna, 159
  Johannah, 141
  John, 15, 35, 41, 123, 159, 237, 265, 268, 270, 287
  Margarett, 116
  Mary, 107, 159, 236
  Richard, 159
  Robert, 107, 108, 159, 211
  Samuel, 159, 236
  Thomas, 59, 88, 159, 199, 207, 243, 251
  William, 40, 88, 159

KINGE, Thomas, 159
KINGERSLEY,
    Elizabeth, 159
    George, 159
    Mary, 159
KINGLAND, William, 159, 160
KINGSBURY, George, 160
KINGSTONE, Thomas, 160
KINIKIN, James, 160
KINNEY, William, 159
KIRBY, John, 160
    Paul, 160
KIRKELEY,
    Christopher, 286
KIRKL(E)Y, Catherine, 160
    Christopher, 160
    Elizabeth, 160
    Susanna(h), 160
KIRTEN, Zachary, 160
KITTES, Elizabeth, 21
Kitts Choice, 209
KNIGHT, Anne, 160
    Edward, 74, 160
    Elinor, 74
    Hannah, 160
    James, 160, 218
    Jane, 74
    Jennett, 160
    John, 74, 160, 161
    Mary, 160
    Rebecca, 74
    Sarah, 161
KNIPE, Ann, 199
KNOWLAND, Mary, 63
    Stephen, 63
KNOX, James, 195
KUE, John, 161

-L-

LADSTONE, ——, 251
LAMASTER, Abraham, 165
    John, 165, 166
Lamastres Delight, 166
LAMBER, Ami, 161
LAMBERT, Amy, 117
    Elinor, 161
    Elizabeth, 161
    Ellen, 3, 161, 206
    Ellenor, 68
    Ellinor, 3, 161
    John, 3, 38, 68, 155, 161, 206, 219, 264
    Mary, 161
    Samuel, 161
    Samuell, 161
    Sarah, 161
    William, 161
LAMBETH, James, 161
    John, 161, 162, 169
    Mary, 246
    Sarah, 162
    William, 161
LAMBETTY, John, 131
Lampton, 125, 162, 225
LAMPTON, Ann(e), 162
    Elisabeth, 220
    Elizabeth, 162, 220
    Esther, 162
    Isabell(a), 162
    Isable, 162
    Issabella, 162
    Jane, 162
    John, 162
    Lisabella, 162
    Mark, 35, 162
    Marke, 162, 235
    Mary, 162
    Sarah, 162
    Victoria, 162
    Victory, 162
    William, 162
LANCASTER,
    Elizabeth, 204, 205
    Jane, 146
    John, 13, 144, 170, 185, 203, 204, 205
    Joseph, 146
    Raphael, 205
LAND, Anne, 162
    Elinor, 162
    Elizabeth, 162, 163
    John, 162, 163
    Mary, 163
    Penelope, 162, 163
    Philip, 162
    Richard, 162, 264
    Susanna, 162, 163
    Thomas, 162
    William, 162
LANDEN, Robert, 163
Land's Lane, 131
LANE, Anne, 163
    Elizabeth, 163
    Florence, 171
    William, 163
Lane's Land, 130
LANG, Francis, 153
    John, 153
    Robert, 153
    William, 153
LANGHAM, George, 67
Langham's Rest, 267
Langley, 201
LANGWORTH,
    Agatha, 111, 132, 163, 181
    Elizabeth, 163
    James, 163
    John, 163
    Mary, 163
    William, 163
LANNUM, John, 163
LANS, William, 162
Lanterman, 25

Index 361

Lanternam, 13, 26
LARKIN, John, 230
LASTELY, Alexander, 163
LATEMERE, James, 95
LATIMAR, James, 104
  Mary, 104
LATIMER, James, 32, 122
LATIMRE, James, 309
LATTEL, Ann, 163
  John, 163
LATTEMORE, James, 32, 217
  Mary, 32
LATTIMAR, James, 222
LATTIMER, James, 163
LATTIMORE, Hannah, 69
  James, 32, 222
  Mary, 32
LATTMER, Mary, 33
Laurel Branch, 271
LAURENCE, Thomas, 164
Lauturnan, 119
LAW, Rose, 24
LAWN, Edward, 172
Lawrel(ls) Branch, 80, 79, 91
LAWRENCE, Benjamin, 164
LAWREY, David, 172
LAWSON, Elisabeth, 164
  Elizabeth, 164
  John, 164, 166
  Rachel, 164
  Thomas, 103, 164
  William, 103, 164
LE MARE, John, 61
LEACH, James, 227

Neffelt, 227
LEAH, Jacob, 248
LEAKE, Richard, 31
LEAMER, Margret, 164
LEAPTROT, Mary, 13
LECKONBY, Thomas, 26
LEE, Ann, 165
  Arthur, 164, 165
  Bridget, 164
  Elizabeth, 164
  Frances, 165
  Francis, 164, 165
  Hanna(h), 164, 224
  Henry, 164, 165
  Hugh, 164, 224
  James, 142, 164
  Jane, 164
  John, 164
  Lettice, 164
  Marg(a)ret, 164
  Phil(l)ip, 137, 164, 165, 217
  Richard, 165
  Robert, 164, 165
  Roger, 164
  Sarah, 164
  Thomas, 164, 165
  Winifier, 164
  Winifred, 164
Lee Langly, 164
LEECH, James, 165
LEEDS, Robert, 165
  William, 287
LEEK, George, 165
LEES, Eleanor, 236
Lees Freehold, 165
Lees Purchase, 307
LEES?, Thomas, 243
LEETE, Elinor, 165
  George, 165
  John, 165
LEGATE, Briget, 111

LEGATT, John, 106, 176
LEGET, Bridgett, 168
  John, 168
LEMAIRE, John, 21, 288
  Margaret(t), 288
Lemaister's Delight, 152
LEMAISTRE,
  Abraham, 166
  John, 166
  Sarah, 166
LEMAN, Hickford, 285
  Joseph, 285
  William Hickford, 268
LEMARE, John, 61, 288
  Margaret, 288
Lemarr's Purchase, 189
LEMASTER, Abraham, 137, 165, 166
  Anne, 166
  Catherine, 292
  Christian, 65, 166, 242
  Isaac, 166
  John, 65, 166, 305
  Justinian, 166
  Martha, 165
  Mary, 166
  Priscilla, 166
  Richard, 165, 290
  Sarah, 166
  Thomas, 292
  William Cooksey, 166
LEMASTRE, Abraham, 166
  John, 165, 166
  Richard, 165, 166
Leml(e)y, 89, 283
LENDSEY, Anne, 168
  Edmond, 168

Ellenor, 168
LENOIR, John, 166
  Mary, 166
LENTON, Joseph, 17, 166
  Ursula, 120
LEONARD, Sarah, 37
LESLEY, Alexander, 163
LETTON, Joseph, 70
LEVERETT, John, 167
LEVERTON, Ephram, 25
LEVETT, John, 172
LEVRITT, Jane, 167
  John, 167
LEWELLIN, Jane, 211
  John, 56, 94, 211
  Margtt:, 211
  Richard, 211, 301
LEWEN, Joseph, 167
LEWGAR, John, 167, 186
  Martha, 167
  Thomas, 191
LEWGER, Elizabeth, 167
  John, 167
  Martha, 167
  Thomas, 167
LEWIN, John, 167
  Joseph, 40
LEWIS, Ann, 148
  David, 167
  Elisabeth, 43
  Elizabeth, 134, 148
  George Rogers Williams, 168
  Gilbert, 167
  Henrietta Lewis Williams, 167
  Henry, 167
  Isable, 167
  James, 167
  Jane, 167
  Katharine, 25
  Mary, 148, 167, 168, 270
  Rebecca, 167
  Richard, 25
  Samuel, 129
  Thomas, 25, 148, 167, 168, 270
  Ursula, 167
  Ursule, 112, 167
  William, 112, 167, 212, 248
  ———, 134
Lewis' Neck, 299
LIEUGER, Thomas, 103
LIGET, Bridgett, 168
  John, 168
LIGN, Michaell, 169
LILLEY, Thomas, 168
LILLY, Elizabeth, 168
  Hennery, 271
  Thomas, 168
Lim(m)e, 287, 288
Limmis Enlargement, 287
Lim's Enlargement, 288
LINDAR, Mary, 169
LINDESAY, Elizabeth, 77
  James, 77
  Mary, 77
Lindsey, 126
LINDSEY, Edmond, 39, 52, 53, 55, 146, 154, 168
  Edmund, 151, 168
  Elinor, 168
  Elizabeth, 168, 281
  Henry, 168
  James, 168, 242, 281
  Jane, 155
  Jone, 223
  Mary, 168, 281
  Thomas, 155, 223
LINE, Francis, 175
LINEGAR, John, 169
LINES, James, 174
  Philip, 4, 49, 63, 88, 108, 112, 140, 141, 142, 147, 181, 185, 201, 215, 234, 250, 265, 304
Lines' Gore, 156
LING(E), Francis, 169, 215
  Mary, 121, 169, 215
  Michaell, 169
  William, 121, 169, 215
LINGGAN, Katherine, 80
Linner Sheet, 171
LINOE, John, 169
Linsey, 3, 96, 168
LINSEY, Cornelius, 168
  James, 168
  Marie, 168
Lisbon, 34, 63, 154
Little Wood, 126
Little Worth, 97, 126, 278
Littleworth, 216, 241
LIUGE, Michael, 169
Liverpool, 248
LLEWELLIN, Jane, 169
  Margaret, 169
  Richard, 169
LLOYD, Edward, 294
  Henrietta Marea (Maria), 202
  Henrietta Mary, 202
  James, 202
  Martha, 169
  Maurice, 169

Index

Richard, 169
LLOYDE, William, 284
LOCK, William, 168
Locust Thicket(t), 18, 224, 287
LOE, Rice, 174
LOFLING, John, 169
LOFTAS, Margrett, 170
LOFTEN, Frances, 170
  John, 170, 243
  Onah (Oriah), 170
  Priscilla, 170
  Robert, 170
LOFTING, Frances, 170
  John, 170
LOFTON, John, 170, 243
  Robert, 170
LOFTUS, John, 243
LOMAX, Blanch, 170
  Blanche, 256
  Catherine, 170
  Cleborn, 170, 171, 197
  Cleborne, 24, 83, 170, 256, 288
  Cliborne, 170
  John, 170
  Margaret, 170
  Margery, 197, 215
  Marjery, 171
  Ra(i)lph, 94, 170
  Susanah, 49
  Susanna, 170
  Susannah, 171
  Thomas, 24, 39, 170, 171
Lomax's Addition, 260
Lomley, 200, 208
LOMMES, Mary, 139
LOM—, Susannah, 230
London, 307, 308

LONE, Elizabeth, 163
  John, 163
  William, 163
LONG, Elenor, 171
  Jemima, 171, 212
  John, 171
  Robert, 171
Long Monkshire, 261
Longnor, 1
Lonist Thickett, 138
LOOFE, William, 171
Lordships Favour, 219
Lordships Manors of Panquiah, 204
Lott Number Three, 255
LOVE, Charles, 171
  Elinor, 171
  Elizabeth, 171
  Florence, 171
  John, 171
  Kindrick, 171
  Lucy, 171
  Mary, 129, 171
  Pintheselia, 171
  Samuel, 160, 171
  Susanna, 56, 171
  Thomas, 171, 256
  William, 171, 256, 280
LOVEDAY, William, 171
Loves Enjoyment, 37
Love's Injoyment, 37
LOVETT, John, 172
  Margaret, 172
  Mary, 47
Loving Brothers, 106
LOVLY, William, 58
LOWE, Edward, 172
  John, 172
  Mary, 172
  Thomas, 288
  William, 288
Lower Poole, 94, 157

LOWRY, David, 172
LOXTON, Robert, 170
LOYD, Edward, 169, 210
  Elizabeth, 169
  Morris, 169
  Richard, 169
  Roydrick, 169
LOYDE, Eliza, 169
  Margaret, 289
  Richard, 169
  William, 284, 289
LUCAS, Anne, 172
  Jane, 109
  Thomas, 172
LUCE, Thomas, 167
LUCK, Clark, 172
  Thomas, 172
LUCKET, Anne, 173
  Elisabeth, 170
  Elizabeth, 225
  Ignatius, 125, 173
  Jane, 125, 173
  John, 125
  Samuel, 172, 173
  Samuell, 90, 170
  Thomas, 173
  Thomas Hussey, 149, 173, 225
  William, 125
Luckets Addition, 173
LUCKETT, Ann, 172, 173
  Charity, 173
  Eleanor, 173
  Elizabeth, 125, 149, 172, 173
  Hassey, 46
  Ignatious, 173
  Ignatius, 123, 125, 172, 173
  Jane, 125, 173
  John, 173

Samuel, 125, 172, 173, 233
Samuell, 123, 172, 255
Sarah, 173
Thomas, 172, 173
Thomas H., 173
Thomas Huss(e)y, 125, 172, 173
William, 173
Luckett's Level, 173
LUCUS, Jane, 8
LUDWELL, James, 72, 157
Martha, 72, 157
LUES, Thomas, 167
LUGAR, John, 167
Thomas, 167
LUKES, Ann, 108
James, 108
Lumber Street, 56, 274
LUMBROSO, Jacob, 173
John, 128, 173, 245, 272
LUMBROZION, John, 245
LUMBROZO, Elizabeth, 174
John, 174
Ribna, 174
Lumbrozo's Discovery, 174
Lumley (Lombey), 42
Lumley Round, 42
LUTIE, Elizabeth, 174
Nathaniel, 174
LUTWIDE, James, 11
LUTWIDGE, James, 105
LYBSCOME, Dorothy, 174
LYLE, John, 174
LYN, Francis, 232

LYNDSEY, James, 168, 200
Jane, 155, 156
Thomas, 155, 156
LYNES, Ann, 174
Anne, 174, 228, 268
James, 174
Philip, 80, 156, 174, 237, 268
Phillip, 32, 155, 161, 285
Lynes Delight, 52, 112, 252
LYNG, Francis, 169
LYNGE, Francis, 169
Michael, 169
LYNN, Elizabeth, 175
Francis, 175, 275, 276
Margery, 175, 275
Marjery, 276
Mary, 22
Michael, 22
Michaell, 169
Richard, 175
Lynn (Lim), 287
Lynn's Inlargement, 287
Lynsei (Lindsey), 153
LYNTON, Ursuly, 167
LYON, John, 175
Mary, 175
Lyons Den, 26, 184, 310
Lyons Denn, 40, 76
Lyons Hole, 255

-M-
MACARTIE, Denis, 175
MACATEE, Patrick, 175
MACAY, John, 175
MCBRIDE, John Duncan, 188
Mary, 188

MACCABE (MCCABE), Barbara, 176
MACCAN, Timothy, 188
MACK CORMACK, Margarett, 92
MCCLAINE, Laughlane, 187
MCCLANE, Elisabeth, 187
MCCORMICK, Margarett, 92
MCCOY, Hugh, 188
MCCRACKIN, David, 253
MCDANIEL, Elizabeth, 187
John, 187
MACDANIEL(L), Alexander, 176
Charles, 176
MCDANIELL, Daniel, 267
Daniell, 103, 123
MACDANIELL, Elizabeth, 176
MACDONALD, Alexander, 176
Ann, 40
Daniel, 40
John, 264
MCDONALD, Daniel, 187
Owen, 185
MACDONALL, Daniel, 176
Hen:, 106
MACDONELL, Daniel, 176
MACFARDING, John, 286
MCFERSON, Daniel, 189
Elizabeth, 189

MCGRIG(G)ER, Anne, 188
  Duncan, 188
  Elizabeth, 188
  Frances, 188
  John, 188
  Katherine, 188
MCHAN, Ann, 188
  Daniel, 188
  Timothy, 188
MACHETEE, Edmond, 175
  Elinor, 175
  Frances, 175
  James, 175
  Katherine, 175
  Mary, 175
  Patrick, 175
  Rosamond, 175
  Rosomond, 175
Machies Park, 272
MACHON, Anne, 176
  Elizabeth, 176
MCHON, Elizabeth, 188
MACHON, Jane, 176
MCHON, Martha, 88
  Prisalla, 188
  Priscilla, 188
MACHON, Robert, 176
MCHON, Robert, 188
  Virlinda, 188
MACHON, William, 176
MCHON, William, 188
MACKALEY, Margaret, 94
MACKARIES,
  Cornelius, 311
MACKATEE, Patrick, 40
MACKAY, Elizabeth, 305

MACKDONLAD,
  Daniel, 187
MACKENCE, Lomax, 176
MACKENEARD,
  Elinor, 175
MACKENHINE, John, 175
MACKENY, Elinor, 92
MACKEY, Anguis, 177
  Ann, 305
  Elizabeth, 7
  James, 7, 175, 177, 261, 305
MCKEY, James, 176
Mackey Park, 273
Mackeys Park, 262
MACKHORN, Anne, 188
  Elizabeth, 188
  Jane, 188
  Martha, 188
  Robert, 188
  William, 188
MACKHORNE, Robert, 119
MACKINTOSH, James, 187
MACKLANAN,
  Margret, 177
MACKLOGHLIN,
  Kenelme, 168
MACKMILLION,
  Arthur, 48
  George, 48, 177
  Grace, 177
  Peter, 41, 48, 177, 188
MACKY, Elizabeth, 176
  James, 176
MCMILLION,
  Elizabeth, 188
  Peter, 188

MACONCHIE,
  Alexander, 177
  Anne, 177
  John, 177
  Mary, 124, 177
  William, 124, 177, 234
Maconchie's Dale, 177
MACONOKIE, William, 152
MACOUCHIE, Ann, 177
MACOY, Hugh, 188
  James, 281
  John, 177
  Mary Ann, 188
  William, 188
MCPHERSON,
  Alexander, 189
  Alexander
  Wilkinson, 188
  Daniel, 188, 189
MACPHERSON,
  Eleanor, 177
MCPHERSON, Elinor, 188
  Elizabeth, 189
  John, 188, 278
  Kerenhappuck, 188
  Mary, 189
  Richard, 278
  Richard Bassill, 189
  Thomas, 188
MACPHERSON,
  William, 177
MCPHERSON,
  William, 108, 188
MACQUEEN
  (MCQUEEN),
  George, 177
  Katherine, 189
  William, 169
MADDOCK, Annah, 101
  Anne, 101

Cornelius, 178
Edward, 89, 101, 177, 178, 266
James, 178
Margery, 177, 178
Marjery, 266
Mary, 178
Notly, 178
William, 178
MADDOCKE, Edward, 263
Jane, 263
MADDOCKS,
Cornelius, 252
Elizabeth, 178
John, 70, 178
Mary, 251
MADDOKE, James, 178
Mary, 178
MADDOX, Ann, 178
Dr., 81
Edward, 273
James, 178
John, 133, 135, 178, 313, 314
Mary, 178
Notley, 167, 178, 184
Sarah, 135, 178
Walter, 178
William, 178
MADOX, Mary, 300
MAGGATEE, William, 94
MAGGOTEE, Patrick, 290
MAGGOTTEE, Edmund, 58, 204
MAGITEE, James, 175
Patrick, 175
Rose, 175
MAGITTEE, James, 175
Patrick, 175

Rose, 175
MAGLOCKERY, William, 178
MAGLOUGHLIN, Elizabeth, 176
Keneline, 176
MAGRAH, John, 268
MAGRAUGH, John, 198
Mary, 198
MAGREGER, Dunking, 179
MAGRIGGER, Frances, 188
MAGRUDER,
Alexander, 150
Ann, 150
MAHAUNE, Elisabeth, 249
Robert, 249
MAHAWNEY, Tymothy, 179
MAHONEY, Dennis, 179
Elizabeth, 179
MAHONY, Dennis, 179
Elizabeth, 179
Robert, 293
Timothy, 179
Maiden Fair, 103, 262
Maiden's Pleasure, 59
Maidens Point, 86
Maidston, 158
MAINSTER, John, 180
Thomas, 180
Maismire, 195
Maismore, 195
MAKEY, Elizabeth, 176
James, 7, 143, 176
MALCOM, W., 179
MALDEN, James, 179
Mallemore, 251
MALLOW, John, 5
MALOW, Margaret, 5

MANAREL, John, 91
Mary, 91
Manchester, 63, 180, 288, 289, 314
Mangawoman, 266
MANING, Edmond, 180
John, 180
MANITHURB, Thomas, 179
Mankester's Craft, 199
MANKIN, Elizabeth, 179, 180
Hope, 179
Jame, 180
James, 142, 179, 310
Jane, 5
Jean, 310
John, 51, 179, 180
Joseph, 180
Josiah, 179, 180
Josias, 147, 179, 180
Margaret(t), 51, 179, 180
Mary, 51, 179
Stephen, 46, 51, 109, 121, 177, 179, 180, 265, 291
Tub(b)man, 5, 179, 180, 273
William, 180
Mankins Adventure, 180
MANNERLEY, Margaret, 180
MANNING, John, 47, 142, 180, 267, 295
Joseph, 24, 54, 66, 128, 169, 180
Mary, 180, 287
Richard, 180
Sarah, 142
Mannings Discovery, 180

Index 367

Mannis Cledre, 275
MANNISTER, John, 180
  Thomas, 180
MANNOTH, Lidia, 107
Manor of Chaptico, 55
Manor of West St. Mary's, 55
Manor of Zachia, 256
MANSELL, Benjamin, 180
  Mathew, 30
  Thomas, 203
  William, 180
MANSFIELD, John, 273
Manson Folly, 2
MANTE, John, 181
MANWAREN, Walter, 181
MANWARING, Anne, 181
  George, 181
MANZEY, Margarett, 32
MARBERRY, Francis, 115
  Mary, 115
MARCHEGAY, Bennett, 181
MARDEN, Anne, 297
  John, 181
MARHALL, Richard, 181
MARIS, Abice, 196, 304
  Alice, 196
  Anise, 196
  Elizabeth, 196
  Sarah, 196
  Thomas, 49, 52, 196
MARKEAT, Anthonie, 181
MARKEN, John, 181

MARKES, Jonathan, 288
Market Overton, 267, 287
MARKINFIELD, George, 47
MARKWICH, Catherine, 47, 185
MARLER, John, 5, 181, 182
  Jonathan, 181, 266
  Margaret, 5, 182
  Mary, 181
  Samuel, 181
MARLES, Elizabeth, 132
MARLOE, Edward, 182
  John, 5, 181
  Susannah, 5
  William, 181, 182
MARLOES, John, 231
MARLOR, Mary, 164
MARLOW, Anne, 182
  Anthony, 181
  Bartholomew, 182
  Bur, 181
  Edward, 182, 246
  Elizabeth, 181
  Ellinor, 182
  James, 182
  John, 182
  Joseph, 182
  Mary, 182
  Richard, 182
  Susanna, 181
  William, 182
MARROME, James, 182
Marrowbone, 53
MARSH, Gilbert, 182
  John, 182
  Margaret, 182
  Thomas, 182
  William, 182

Marsh Land, 37
MARSHALL, Barbara, 183
  Barbary, 183
  Elisabeth, 183
  Elizabeth, 97, 182, 183
  Hugh, 182
  Joshua, 182
  Josua, 183
  Mary, 183
  Mr., 128
  Rebecca, 97
  Rebeckah, 183
  Richard, 97, 183
  Thomas, 97, 183, 227
  William, 19, 34, 39, 51, 57, 94, 97, 182, 183, 216, 266, 283, 286, 312
Marshalls Land, 312
MARSHEGAY, Bennett, 303
Marshland, 292
MARSTIN, Constance, 183
MARSTON, Constance, 183
  Elizabeth, 183
  Henry, 183
  Mary, 183
  Richard, 183
  Robert, 183
MARTEN, Elizabeth, 184, 185
  Henry, 184
  John, 22, 184, 185, 191, 237, 268, 286
  Michael, 175, 268
  Sarah, 191
Marten's Supply, 184
MARTIN, Ann(e), 175, 183, 184
  Catherine, 183

Damaris, 184
Demaris, 184, 309
Elizabeth, 183, 184
Henry, 184
James, 183, 184
Jillian, 184
Joan, 184
Joane, 92
John, 121, 128, 134, 183, 184, 297, 309
Margaret, 184
Mary, 121, 169, 183, 184, 297
Michael, 134, 175
Michaell, 43, 133, 184
Nicholas, 175
Penelope, 184
Robert, 269
Ruth, 297
Sarah, 184
Thomas, 92
William, 183, 184
MARTING, Ann, 184
William, 184
Martin's Freehold, 5, 69, 70, 276, 306
MARWICH, Catherine, 185
MARWICK, Catherine, 47, 185
Maryland, 11, 13, 23, 77, 84, 90, 146, 150, 155, 264, 296, 297
Mary's Delight, 29
Mash Land [Marshalls Land], 312
MASON, Ann, 185
Elizabeth, 185
George, 30, 185, 197
John, 185
Mary, 185, 195
Mathew, 185
Mrs., 301
Philip, 185

Samuel, 195
Samuell, 185
Susanna, 301
William, 185
Massemore, 208
MASSEY, Margaret, 185
Mr., 202
Thomas, 27, 141, 185
MASSON, Francis, 185
MASTEN, Richard, 251
MASTERS, Mary, 185
William, 185
MASTIN, Charles, 186
Francis, 186
Robert, 83
Susanna, 186
Thomas, 268
MASTON, John, 186
Mary, 186
Richard, 183, 186
Robert, 186
MATHENA, Daniel, 186
Daniell, 186
Elizabeth, 186
Mary, 186
Sarah, 186
MATHENIA, Daniell, 297
MATHEWES, Thomas, 86
MATHEWS, Esther, 180
Ignatius, 186
Jane, 1
John, 180, 186
Joseph, 186
Lucas, 186, 187
Luke, 151, 186
Martha, 187
Mary, 187
Susannah, 187, 315

Thomas, 28, 131, 180, 186, 187, 302
William, 186, 187
Mathew's Purchase, 186
Mathias Obyrans Old Plantation, 208
Matiawoman, 271
Mattawoman, 113
MATTHEWS, Ann, 187
Anne, 34
Hester, 54
Ignatius, 34, 187
Jane, 34, 186, 187, 277
Jesse, 187
Jonathan, 79
Joseph, 187
Lucas, 187
Luke, 151, 187
Martha, 151
Mary, 186, 187, 267
Sarah, 198, 305
Susana, 187
Susannah, 187
Thomas, 1, 34, 54, 181, 186, 198, 249, 267, 277, 305
Victoria, 34, 277
William, 34, 50, 186, 187, 239
Matthews' Hope, 186
Matthew's Purchase, 187
Mattinglys Hope, 124, 244
MATTOX, David, 178
Thomas, 178
MAUD, John, 187
Susanna, 187
Susannah, 24
Mauniss (Mannes) Eleture, 2
MAURISE, Ales, 196

Richard, 196
May Day, 253, 254
MAYBANCK,
  Elizabeth, 187
MAYCOCKE,
  Seabright, 98
Mayor's Choice, 300
MAYROOK, Mary, 187
  Seabright, 187
Mayrooks Rest, 187
Maysemow, 31
Maze, 103
Ma———, 195
Meadows, 18
MECARTEE, Dennis, 189
MEDCAPH, Robert, 189
Meddows, 19
MEDLEY, Anne, 189
  George, 189
MEDLY, John, 157
MEDREY, George, 146
MEE, Elizabeth, 189
  Hugh, 72, 189
MEEK, Francis, 36, 132, 146, 176, 189, 288
  Mary, 132, 189
MEEKE, Francis, 132, 159, 189
  Mary, 189
MEEKES, John, 55, 100
MEEKS, Francis, 176
  Sarah, 225
MELLAR, John, 111
  Sarah, 111
MELLOR, John, 189
  Mary, 189
  Nathaniel, 189
MELTON, James, 189
Mendment, 110
MERCER, ———, 185

MERCHANT,
  Thomasine, 189
Merchant Tailor's Hall, 39
Merchant Taylor's Hall, 133, 157
MEREDITH, Thomas, 248
MERICK, Elizabeth, 190
  John, 190
  William, 190
Mericks Chance, 190
MERRICK, William, 189
MERTIN, Ann, 175
  Rebechak, 175
METHENIA, Daniell, 297, 298
MEWMAN, Mary, 166
MICANEY, Andrew, 190
MICHELL, Joan, 193
  Marke, 193
  Thomas, 45, 193
MICHLE, ———, 35
MICKELL, Thomas, 161
Middle Green, 66
MIDDLETON, Alice, 254
  Ann, 190
  Eleanor, 191, 231
  Elizabeth, 134, 190
  James, 91, 190
  Mary, 190
  Robert, 190, 254
  Samuel, 191
  Smith, 190
  Susannah, 190
  Thomas, 190, 254
  William, 91, 134, 180, 190, 191, 231

Middletons Kindness, 58
Middleton's Lot, 300
MIDDLETOWN, Mary, 190
  Robert, 11, 190
MIDGELEY, Richard, 57, 146
MIDGELY, Elizabeth, 103, 191
  Richard, 191
MIDLETON, Elisabeth, 157
  William, 157
MILBURN, Joseph, 245
Milerne, 173, 250
Milersie, 9
MILES, Anne, 151
  Edward, 153
  Elisabeth, 84
  Elizabeth, 191
  Henry, 191
  Mary, 191
  Nathaniel, 191
Miles End, 78, 81
Milford, 3
MILL, Isabella, 191
MILLBORNE, Rachell, 191
MILLER, Andrew, 191
  Dinah, 191
  Francis, 191
  Grace, 191
  Isaac, 192
  Jacob, 147, 168, 191, 192
  John, 49, 117, 191, 192, 257
  Margaret, 17, 192
  Margarett, 204
  Margett, 147
  Margret, 147, 191
  Mary, 192, 222

Peter, 191
Sarah, 49, 191, 192
Sophia, 191
Millner, 267
MILLNER, Anne, 192
Isaac, 192
Thomas, 192
MILLOR, John, 192
Mary, 192
MILLS, John, 136
MILLSTEAD,
Catherine, 14
Edward, 192, 257, 309
John, 192
Sarah, 192
Thomas, 110, 309
William, 192
MILLSTEADE,
Edward, 192
Susanna, 192
William, 192
MILLSTED, Edward, 192
John, 192
Mary, 192
William, 192
Millum, 110
MILSHAW, John, 192
MILSTEAD, Edward, 192
Elizabeth, 192
Joseph, 111, 192
Thomas, 20, 192
William, 192
MILSTEED, Edward, 192
William, 192
MINES, Edward, 225
MING, Edward, 193
Mary, 193
Minges Chance, 131, 193
MINGOE, Charles, 193
Elizabeth, 193

Joseph, 193
Lewis, 193
Thomas, 193
MINGS, Edward, 121, 193
Jane, 193
Mary, 193
MINOAKE, Michaell, 99
MINOCK, Dorothy, 193
Michaell, 193
Michall, 193
MINORK, Michael, 15
MIRE, William, 232
MIRES, Christopher, 200
MIREX, Jacob, 193
William, 193
MIRICK, Priscilla, 306
Miricks Chance, 245
Miry Branch, 153
Mistake, 263
MITCHEL, Peter, 84
William, 187
Mitchel Platt, 45
MITCHELL, Agnes, 193
Ann, 193, 301
Anthony, 193
Collin, 193
Esther, 193
Ignatius, 301
Janet, 193
John, 193
Mary, 193, 275
Peter, 193
Thomas, 1, 41, 45, 62, 159, 162, 193, 209, 275, 299, 300, 301
Mitchell Platt, 45
Mobile, 246
MOCKELLA, Hugh, 313
Mole's Venture, 95

MOLLER, Jane, 194
John, 194
MONCASTER,
Elizabeth, 247
James, 80, 121
Mary, 80
William, 247
MONCESTER, James, 199
Mary, 199
Prudence, 199
William, 199
Monday's Disappointment, 260
MONKESTER,
Elizabeth, 199
William, 14
Monmoth, 207
MONROE, George, 19
MONROW, William, 108
MONTAGUE, Mr., 139
Stephen, 194, 227, 281
Montagues Addition, 9
MONTEAL, Richard, 194
MONTGOMERY,
Peter, 118
MONTREW, William, 194
MOOD, Henry, 198
MOODY, Ann, 194
Jane, 194
William, 194
MOOKATEE, William, 94
MOONEY, Thomas, 87
MOOR, Henry, 195
Sarah, 195
Seymour, 298
MOORE, Ann, 8
Elisabeth, 194
Elizabeth, 194, 195

Index 371

Henry, 15, 36, 194, 195, 245
Hugh, 195
John, 194, 195, 257, 286
Lilias, 195
Mordecai, 252
Mordecay, 270
Priscilla, 195
Sarah, 36, 195
Thomas, 194, 195
Mooredith, 206
Moore's Branch, 133, 194
Moore's Ditch, 8, 9, 173
Moores Fishing Place, 15, 67, 87
Moore's Folly, 133, 194
Moore's Gore, 124, 149
Moores Lodge, 124, 149
Moore's Rest, 194, 253
MORAN, Andrew, 195
  Elisabeth, 195
  Elizabeth, 195
  Gabriel, 195
  John, 195, 304
  Peter, 195
  William, 195
MORDOCK, James, 192
MORE, Christopher, 195
  Hannah, 252
  Hugh, 195
  John, 190, 257
  Priscilla, 257
  Sarah, 252
Morecrofts Friendship, 234
MORELAND, Jacob, 78
  John, 78
  Mary, 78
  Patrick, 78
  Philip, 78

William, 78
More's Branch, 133
Mores Ditch, 125
More's Hope, 5
MORETON, Ann, 195
  Margaret, 195
  William, 195
MORGAN, Anne, 33
  Frances, 196
  Jane, 3
  Mary, 33
MORIS, John, 196
MORLEY, Jane, 219
MORPHEY, Daniel, 200
  Rachel, 200
  William, 200
MORREING, John, 87
MORRELL,
  Christopher, 196
MORRICE, Randall, 58
  Richard, 196
MORRIS, Ales, 196
  Annas, 196
  Anne, 196, 197
  Christopher, 196
  Dinah, 197
  Eleanor, 196
  Elinor, 93
  Elisabeth, 196
  Elizabeth, 196, 303
  Ellis, 196
  John, 15, 93, 196
  Margery, 197
  Mary, 196
  Penelope, 196, 197, 274
  Randolph, 92, 196
  Richard, 45, 160, 171, 196, 197, 220, 259, 274
  Sophia, 195
  Stephen, 196, 197

Thomas, 102, 195, 196, 197
Morris His Hope, 55, 197
Morris His Mount, 65
Morrises Discovery, 67, 99
Morrises Helpe, 268
Morrises Mount, 56
MORRISS, Randolph, 56
  Sophia, 197
  Thomas, 197
Morris's Venture, 37
MORWOOD, William, 209
MOSGROVE, Eleanor, 265
  Katherine, 265
MOSS, Edward, 197
  William, 197
MOSSE, John, 32
  Margrett, 32
MOULD, Barbara, 197
  Frances, 197
  John, 197, 221
MOULDIN, John, 197
Moulds Adventure, 180, 292
Moulds Venture, 117
MOULTON, Margarett, 197
Mounds Adventure, 267
MOUNKE, Elisabeth, 197
Mount Clipsham, 59
Mount Paradise, 150
Mount Pleasant, 104, 149
Mountagues Addition, 173
Mountagues Mountains, 173
Mountain, 20, 292

Mountains, 235
MOUNTO, Charles, 197
MOUNTOE, Charles, 227
MOW, Peter, 197
MOWLAND, Patrick, 198
Mt. Clipsham, 260
Muckhaddam, 44
MUDD, Ann, 198
 Barbara, 198
 Benedick, 199
 Bennett, 198
 Casander, 198
 Casandra, 199
 Elisabeth, 198
 Elizabeth, 198
 Ellen, 199
 Ellinder, 198
 George, 198, 199
 Heneretter, 198
 Henry, 198
 James, 185, 199
 Jane, 198
 Jeremiah, 199, 241
 John, 198, 199
 Julian, 198
 Mary, 185
 Monaca, 198
 Sarah, 198, 199
 Thomas, 198, 199, 205, 255, 302, 305
 William, 199
Muddle's Branch, 18
Mudd's Rest, 198
Mudhole, 232
MUGGLESTON,
 Barbara, 199, 270
 Thomas, 199
MULLET, Winifrede, 199
MULLINEUX, Mr., 241
——, 205

MUN, John, 155, 248
MUNCASTER,
 Catherine, 159
 James, 94, 146, 199
 Mary, 159, 199
 William, 199
MUNCESTER, Ann, 11
 Jean, 11
MUNES, John, 199
MUNGISTER, Mary, 297
 William, 297
MUNKASTER, James, 199
MUNKESTER,
 Elizabeth, 199
 James, 199
 William, 199
MUNKISTER,
 Elizabeth, 199
 James, 128
 William, 128
 ——, 199
MUNN, John, 2, 3, 155, 199, 254, 295
MUNROE, Elisabeth, 194
 William, 108, 154, 194
MURDOCK, William, 293
MURFREY, Dennie, 200
Muriells Choice, 56
MURPHEY, Dennis, 200
 Edmond, 200
 Elisabeth, 71
 Elizabeth, 71, 200
 James, 71
 Mary, 71
 Monachy, 71
 Monica, 71
MURPHY, Ann, 54, 200

 Daniel, 200
 Daniell, 200
 Edward, 54, 200
 James, 200
 John, 200
 Mary, 200
 Rachell, 200
 William, 200
 Zephaniah, 200
MURRAINE, Nicholas, 200
MURREY, John, 32
MUSCHET, John, 201
MUSCHETT, John, 141, 274
MUSGRAVE,
 Benjamin, 58
 Charles, 212
 Elizabeth, 222
 Mary, 58
 Susanna, 219
MUSGROVE,
 Cuthbert, 200, 299
 Dorothy, 54, 200
 William, 200
MUSSHELL, John, 210
 Penelope, 210
My Clear Land, 236
MYERS, Christopher, 200
 Mary, 200

-N-
Nailas Range, 2
NAILL, James, 201
NAILOR, Elizabeth, 201
 George, 201
 James, 201
 Priscilla, 201
Nailor's Range, 201
NALLEY, Dennis, 177, 201
 John, 201

Mary, 201
William, 201
NALLY, Denis, 201
Elianor, 201
John, 201
Joseph, 201
Mary, 201
William, 201
Nangemy, 265, 266
Nangemy Manor, 265
Nanjemy Indian Town, 77
NAPER, Edward, 182
Naping, 68
Napping, 241
NASH, Samuell, 201
Nassemore, 251
NEAL, Ann, 202
Anthony, 202
Benjamin, 203
Bennet, 58, 204
Edward, 58, 204
Elisabeth, 202
Elizabeth, 203
Henry, 128, 202, 203
James, 202, 203
Martha, 58, 204
Mary, 202, 203
Raphael, 26, 203
William, 203
NEALE, Ann, 61, 202, 204, 205
Anna, 201
Anne, 150, 202, 204
Anthony, 82, 141, 150, 201, 202, 203, 204, 242
Ash, 203
Barton, 204
Benjamin, 91, 202, 203, 204
Bennett, 203
Catherine, 204
Charles, 53, 203, 204

Daniel, 204
Edward, 6, 53, 144, 202, 203, 204
Elisabeth, 202, 204
Elizabeth, 17, 82, 91, 118, 201, 202, 203, 204
Garrett, 205
H., 205
Henrie, 201
Henrietta, 205
Henrietta Maria, 202
Henry, 53, 128, 185, 202, 203, 204, 205
Jacob, 204
James, 14, 45, 61, 62, 77, 91, 93, 96, 102, 109, 111, 118, 172, 196, 201, 202, 203, 204, 205, 207, 231, 282
Jane, 26, 202, 204
John, 17, 91, 203, 204
Joseph, 202
Madam, 201
Margaret, 202, 203, 204
Martha, 6, 204
Mary, 34, 53, 202, 203, 204, 205
Mary Ann, 204
Mildred, 203, 204
Monica, 205
Oswald, 34
Raphael, 18, 98, 107, 144, 201, 203, 204, 205
Raphaell, 202, 203
Raphel, 207
Richard, 205
Robert, 201
Roswell, 203
Sarah, 205
Trinso, 205

William, 53, 128, 144, 203, 204, 205
Zachariah, 204
Neals's Chance (or Choice), 204
Neale's Gift, 203
NEALL, James, 39
Raphaell, 203
Neck Pastime, 291
NEEVES, Mary, 205
NEISBUT, Edmond, 205
NELLIS, Hannah, 30
NELLSON, Alice, 205
Barbary, 205
Eleanor, 205
John, 205
Margrett, 205
Mary, 205
Richard, 205
William, 205, 240
NELSON, Alice, 205
Ann, 205
Barbary, 205
Elinor, 205
John, 205
Margret, 205
Mary, 205
Richard, 205
Sarah, 234
William, 205, 300
NENAN, Dennis, 205
NEVETT, John, 205
Richard, 205
Nevett's Desire, 18
NEVILL, Ellen, 206
Joane, 206
Johanna, 149, 206
John, 69, 149, 161, 206, 291
William, 149, 206, 248
Nevill's Desert, 19
Nevil's Desire, 4, 5
NEVISON, James, 237

NEVIT, John, 4
New Allsford, 312
New Bradford, 6
New Design, 245, 253
New England, Boston, 227
New Exchange, 247
New Street, 132
NEWBY, John, 290
NEWEN, Owen, 58, 79, 206
NEWITT, John, 206
  Melesaint, 206
Newitts Desire, 206
NEWMAN, Ann, 206
  Charles, 206
  Elisabeth, 48, 98, 207
  Elizabeth, 206, 207
  George, 12, 30, 48, 73, 107, 159, 203, 206, 207, 280, 284, 311
  Grace, 206
  Hannah, 206
  John, 48, 77, 170, 207
  Loften, 207
  Lydia, 48
  Mary, 48, 166, 206, 207, 311
  Parsiler, 170
  Priscilla, 207
  Prissilla, 207
  Richard, 65
  Sarah, 206, 311
  William, 48, 206, 207, 246
  ———, 48
Newport, 124, 149
NEWTON, Jane, 207, 231, 240
  John, 38, 135, 157, 164, 207, 311
  Richard, 155, 207, 311
  Sarah, 94
  Willoughby, 94

New York, 86, 144
NICHOLAS, John, 207
NICHOLLS,
  Bathsheba, 207, 208
  Bersheba, 129
  Elizabeth, 208
  John, 207, 208
  Jonathan, 208
  Solomon, 31
NICHOLS, Anne, 207
  Elizabeth, 137
  John, 207
  Jonathan, 207
  Rachell, 207
  Solomon, 207
  William, 207
NICHOLSON, Esther, 208
  Hester, 208
  John, 208
  Margarett, 208
  Nicholas, 208
  William, 208
NICKOLLS, Thomas, 227
NICKOULS, Benony, 227
NICOLL, James, 162
NICOLLS, Christobell, 207
NIVISON, James, 56
No Design, 300
NOBELL, Elizabeth, 35
NOBLE, Elizabeth, 28, 35, 279, 302
  Joseph, 208
  Martha, 208, 271
  Mary, 36
  Susanna, 35
Noddall's Brand, 222
NODDOR, Nathaniel, 108
NOE, Abell, 208
  Eleanor, 208, 311

  Helena, 66
  Henrietta, 208
  John, 208, 274
  Peter, 208
  Samuel, 66
  Sarah, 208
NOELAND, Mary, 208
  Stephen, 208
Noe's Desart, 165
Noes Desart, 166
NOLAND, Daniel, 208
  James, 208
  Stephen, 208
NOLININ, Patrick, 208
Nonesuch, 44, 282
Nonsuch, 184, 230
NORMAN, John, 208
  Thomas, 209
NORMANSELL,
  Thomas, 209
NORRICE, Robert, 45
NORRIS, Henry, 209
  Mary, 153
North Carolina, 25
Northwick, 107
NORTON, Amy, 209
  Andrew, 209, 301
  Cornelius, 209
  Haman, 304
  Henry, 272
  Mary, 209
Norwick, 190
NOTELY, Thomas, 182
NOTLEY, Thomas, 149, 272, 294
Nowlan[d], 30
NUMAN, Mary, 206
  William, 206
Nutshall, 178
NUTWELL, James, 227

-O-
OAKES, Francis, 209

Index   375

OAKLEY, Giles, 209
  John, 209
  Sarah, 243
  Thomas, 61
  thomas, 151
OARD, Ann, 211
  Peter, 211
  William, 135
OBRIAN, Mathias, 210, 174
OBRYAN, Eleanor, 44
  Elinor, 210
  Elizabeth, 210
  Ellinor, 210
  Magdalen, 210
  Mary, 210
  Mathias, 210
  William, 210
OCAIN, Martha, 210
OCAINE, Darby, 210
  Garrard, 260
  Garrat, 210
  Gerrard, 210
  John, 238
O'CAINE, Judith, 135
OCANE, Garrard, 169
  Gerrard, 210
Ocbridge, 95
OCCAINE, Judith, 210
ODEN, Elisabeth, 50, 210
  Elizabeth, 45
  Francis, 45, 210
ODETON, Richard, 258
OGDEN, Andrew, 210
  Elisabeth, 210
  Mary, 210
  Thomas, 210
OGILVY, John, 210
OGLE, Henry, 260
OKEANE, John, 18, 68
OKELEY, John, 209
OKEY, Mary, 82

Old Branford Enlarged, 4
Old Plantation, 292
Old Woman's Branch, 115
OLKLYS, Sarah, 243
OLLAND, John, 12
OLLARD, John, 210
OLLOVER, Ann, 99
ONEAL, Daniel, 210
  Hew, 85
  Joy, 210
O'Neal's Desert, 30
ONEALE, Arthur, 211
  Heugh, 85
  Hugh, 210, 211
  Joye, 85
  Wenifret, 211
Oneales Desart, 284
Oneales Desert, 187
O'Neales Dezearts, 267
ONEALL, Hugh, 85
ONELL, Idable, 282
ORD, Anne, 211
  James, 211
  Mary, 211
  Peter, 211
  Thomas, 211
ORDE, William, 283
Ordington Hall, 222
ORELL, Isabell, 211
  Jane, 211
  Thomas, 211
ORRELL, Jane, 211
  Thomas, 211
  ———, 169
ORSON, Bearer, 211
OSBORN, Sarah, 305
  Thomas, 216, 305
OSBORNE, Ann, 256
  Elisabeth, 211
  Elizabeth, 62
  Robbin, 256
  Thomas, 62, 109, 211

OSBOURNE, Joseph, 211
OSBURN, Joseph, 211
  Thomas, 211
OULSON, John, 211
OVERSEE, Elizabeth, 211
  Simon, 102, 211
  Symon, 52
OVERSEES, Symon, 52
OVERZEE, Symon, 51
OWEN, Elisabeth, 42
  Mary, 211, 310
  Sarah, 211
  Thomas, 104
  William, 211
Owens Purchase, 184

-P-

PACEY, Thomas, 212
PAGAN, Peter, 192
PAGE, Margerie, 212
  Robert, 136
PAGETT, Mary, 212
PAGGET, Benjamin, 212
  Mary, 212
  William, 212
Paggets Purches, 212
PAIN, John, 161, 215
  Mary, 215
PAINE, John, 32, 215
PALINTEAR, Elisabeth, 212
PALLUFEIS, Joseph, 241
  Mary, 241
PALMER, Samuel, 129, 192
  Samuell, 212
Pan, 296
Panton Mannor, 296
Paquaseat, 183

Paquescoe, 97
PARANDEOR, James, 212
John, 212
PARANDIER,
Elisabeth, 235
James, 46, 265
John, 265
PARKER, Abraham, 213
Ann, 212
Anne, 135, 213
Elisabeth, 213
Eliza, 213
Elizabeth, 17
Farner, 213
Francis, 36, 142
Galwith, 213
Jo:, 212
Joane, 212
John, 17, 164, 212, 213
Jonas, 212, 213
Laurence, 135
Samuel, 212
Sarah, 38, 213
Thomas, 213
William, 212
PARKES, Robert, 213
PARNANDER,
Elisabeth, 240
PARNHAM, Ann, 213
Anna Maria, 213, 232
Elizabeth, 213, 220, 232
Francis, 56, 214, 237
Francis Xavier, 213
Fras: Xaverius, 213
Jane, 213
John, 11, 27, 31, 82, 91, 98, 106, 213, 220, 232, 297
Richard, 48
Sophania, 48

PARRAN, Elizabeth, 214
Ellis, 303
Young, 196, 214, 303
PARRANDER,
Elizabeth, 51
PARRANDIER,
Elisabeth, 212
Parrandyer Lott, 212
PARRY, Dorothy, 124, 214
Hannah, 214
John, 124, 209, 214, 301
Joseph, 214
Thomas, 124, 214
Walter, 214
PARSONS, David, 214
William, 214
Partner's Content, 70, 104, 110
Partner's Purchase, 5, 19, 145
Partnership, 5, 56, 87, 139, 280
PASE, Margaret, 5
PASTAN, Charity, 214
Edward, 214
Francis, 214
Jeremiah, 214
John, 214
Mary, 214
Rebecca, 214
Susanna, 214
Thomas, 214
William, 214
PATRICK, Thomas, 215
PATRIGE, Mary, 215
PATTISON, John, 215
PAUDING,
William, 215
PAYN, Eleanor, 215
Jacob, 58

John, 215
Mary, 215
PAYNE, Edmund Bury, 270
Godfry, 132
John, 215, 270
Marie, 215
Mary, 215
Thomas, 215
Payn's Addition, 215
Payns First Addition, 215
Payns Second Addition, 215
Paynton Manor, 87, 267, 271
PEACH, William, 108
PEACOCK, Margret, 187
PEACOCKE, William, 215
PEALE, Henry, 215
PEALEY, Philip, 228
PEARCE, Anne, 215
Joseph, 215
PEARSON, John, 216
Nathaniell, 216
Peccattoway, 183
PECKLE, Samuell, 238
PECOCK, Ann, 123
PEELE, James, 215
Samuel, 224
Peer (Peir), 83
PEESO, Cornape, 216
PEIRCY, Thomas, 215
PELLEFUL, Joseph, 216
Mary, 216
PELLUFUR, Joseph, 216
Mary, 216
PEMBROOK, Jane, 216
John, 216

PEMBROOKE, Jane, 216
  John, 32, 216
  Mary, 216
PEN, Mark, 286
PENN, Ann, 217
  Anne, 24
  Elizabeth, 146, 216
  Fantalenah, 216
  Fantalony, 217
  Fantelenah, 216
  Jane, 69, 153, 216, 217
  John, 38, 216, 217
  Mark, 69, 153, 216, 260, 285
  Marke, 216
  Mary, 53, 216, 222
  Sarah, 217
  William, 28, 53, 89, 146, 154, 169, 216, 217, 285
PENNEY, Anne, 217
  Samuel, 217
PENNINGTON, Francis, 27
Penn's May Flower, 216, 217
Pennsylvania, 174
  Chester Co., 263
  Lancaster, 254
PENNY,
  Elisabeth, 217
  James, 99, 217
Penrick (Penray), 42
Pensalvania, 216
PENSUCH, Marke, 285
PERCEI, Thomas, 127
PERFECT, William, 13, 162, 194
PERFIT, William, 217
PERKINS, Anne, 217
  James, 217

Robert, 217, 312
PERRIE, Margaret, 217
  Mary, 218
  Samuel, 217, 218, 236
  Sarah, 217
PERRY, Anne, 218
  Hugh, 141, 218
  John, 218
  Margaritt, 17, 18
  Mary, 218
  Samuel, 217, 218
  Thomas, 79, 217, 218
  William, 8, 218
PERSIVALL, Charles, 218
PERSON, Francis, 113
PERY, Thomas, 218
PETER, Mary, 221
PETERS, Martha, 120, 160, 218
  Samuell, 218
PETTERS, Matha, 14
PETTIT, Susanna, 218, 293
  Thomas, 218, 293
PEW, David, 218
Phames (Thames?) Street, 233
PHEGG, Charles, 218
PHILBERT, Archibald, 176
  Eliza, 218
  John, 218, 298
PHILIPS, Nicholas, 218
PHILLBUNT, John, 109
PHILLIPS, Anne, 42
  Catherine, 219
  Edward, 218
  James, 42
  John, 218
  Thomas, 218
  Zephaniah, 219
Phillips Town, 63

PHILLIS, John, 136
PHILLPOT, Charles, 219
  Edward, 219
  Eleanor, 219
  John, 58, 95
PHILLPOTS, Edward, 219
  John, 219
  Margaret, 219
PHILLPOTT, Edward, 41, 282
  Elinor, 282
  Ellinor, 282
  John, 92, 219
  Margaret, 219
  Margrett, 41
  Susannah, 222
PHILPOT, Ann(e), 69
  Brigit, 117
  Charles, 219, 273
  Edward, 219, 252, 273, 282
  Elinor, 252
  Elizabeth, 219
  John, 34, 69, 95
PHILPOTT, Charles, 17, 219
  Edward, 219, 222, 252
  Eleanor, 219
  Elinor, 219
  Elizabeth, 17
  Ellinor, 252
  John, 219
  Mary, 219
  Susanna, 219, 222
PHYLLIPS, Hugh, 218
PICHERD, Robert, 219
PICKERING, Michael, 219
PICKUM, Christian, 292
PIDGON, Joan, 219
  John, 219

Piercefield, 235
Pierce's Encouragement, 82
PIGEON, John, 273
PIGOTT, Bartholomew, 29, 220
  Sarah, 29, 220
PILE, Ann, 220
  Bennett, 220
  Elisabeth, 220
  Elizabeth, 122, 220
  John, 26
  Joseph, 122, 220, 268
  Mary, 220
PILES, John, 247, 264, 297
  John, 242
  Joseph, 220, 242, 305
PILSWORTH, John, 297
PINDOWELL, Elisabeth, 179
Pinee, 253
PINKE, John, 227
PINNAR, Richard, 311
  William, 220
Pinner, 1, 247
PINNER, Anne, 220
  Elizabeth, 220
  Mary, 220
  Mr., 53
  Richard, 220, 268
  Rose, 220
  William, 220
Pinner Enlargement, 1
Pinwell Closes, 307
PIPER, James, 220
  John, 220
  Thomas, 141
PIRRIE, Mary, 276
Piscattaway, 97
Pitchley, 308
Pithly, 307
PLANT, James, 120

Planter's Delight, 274, 300
PLATER, Ann, 68
  Francis, 220
  George, 38, 43, 68, 178, 208, 243
PLAYER, John, 221
Plimoth, 262
PLOUKET, Thomas, 297
PLUNKETT, Christopher, 141
  William, 109
Plymouth, 299
Pointon Manor, 268
POKE, Margarett, 221
POLEY, Humphrey, 4
POLK, Francis, 167
POLLARD, Richard, 103
POLLETT, Francis, 107
POLLY, Roger, 221
POLTON, Thomas, 15, 88, 89
Pomfrett, 112
POOR, Margarett, 221
  Walter, 221
Poor Call, 253
POORE, Margaret, 221, 309
  Margrett, 221
  Mary, 146, 309
  Peter, 221
  Robert, 309
  Walter, 221, 309
POPE, Francis, 118, 221
  John, 221
  Mary, 221
  Mr., 128
  Richard, 221
  Thomas, 221
Poppleton, 89, 146

PORFIT, William, 47, 272
PORFRAY, Elisabeth, 16
  Peter, 16
Pork Hall, 2
Port-Tabacco, 240
PORTINGALL, Hugh, 221
POSEY, Ann, 58, 223
  Anne, 221
  Belaine, 222
  Belane, 222
  Belayne, 222
  Benjamin, 4, 18, 49, 192, 222, 223
  Bolaine, 222
  Elizabeth, 222
  Frances, 171
  Francis, 58, 192, 221, 222, 282
  Humphrey, 13, 221, 222, 223
  Humphry, 222
  Jane, 222
  John, 221, 222, 223, 231, 232, 250
  Lydia, 222, 231
  Mary, 94, 222
  Richard, 223
  Susanna, 221, 222
Poseys Chance, 222
POSIE, John, 272
POSSEY, Benjamin, 222
  Bolean, 222
  John, 222
POSTAN, Frances, 223
  John, 223
  Thom, 223
  William, 223
POSTEN, John, 223
  Priscilla, 223

POSTON, Jeremiah, 223
  John, 223
  Priscilla, 223
  William, 223
POSY, Belaine, 62
  Benjamin, 62
POTTER, George, 223
  John, 223
  Robert, 223
  William, 223
POTTS, Jane, 130, 155, 156
  John, 223
  Jone, 223
  Robert, 12, 130, 156, 223
POULSON, Elizabeth, 135
  John, 135
POUNCY, George, 223
  Mary, 223
POUNSEY, Mary, 223
Poverty, 214
POWCHER, Thomas, 223
POWELL, David, 224
  Edward, 224
  Elizabeth, 224
  James, 224
  John, 224
  Robert, 137, 223, 224
  Sarah, 213
  ———, 224
POWER, John, 240
  Joseph, 220
  Mary, 146, 240
  Robert, 285
Poynton Manor, 52, 100, 168, 177, 266, 267
PRATHER, Aaron, 314
  Elizabeth, 224
  John Smith, 247, 314
  Josiah, 314
  Thomas, 224, 314
PRATT, Henry, 227
  Mary, 221
PRAYER, ———, 251
Preston, 2, 151, 234, 268
Prevention, 65
PRICE, Ann, 232
  Anne, 224
  Charles, 224
  Diana, 131
  Edward, 18, 22, 46, 133, 224, 225
  Elisabeth, 224, 261
  Elizabeth, 46
  Hanna, 224
  Hannah, 164, 181
  Jane, 224
  Johanna, 234
  John, 224, 225
  Juliana, 46, 224, 225, 247
  Julianah, 224
  Mary, 224, 225, 295
  Richard, 36, 225, 232
  Robert, 224, 225, 226
  Ruld, 13
  Thomas, 28, 137, 224, 225, 246
  William, 164, 224
Prichard (Prickard), 239
PRINCE, Abigall, 225
Prince George's County, 2, 6, 19, 22, 23, 27, 33, 40, 64, 70, 72, 75, 76, 77, 78, 82, 83, 87, 97, 102, 103, 104, 106, 110, 114, 119, 122, 129, 133, 134, 140, 148, 149, 150, 154, 158, 164, 172, 174, 183, 185, 187, 189, 190, 195, 201, 210, 217, 220, 224, 229, 232, 234, 236, 242, 243, 246, 252, 257, 258, 263, 265, 267, 268, 269, 272, 274, 275, 287, 288, 291, 293, 303, 307
Prior Cleve, 185
PRISE, Anne, 224
  Edward, 224
  Jane, 224
  Mary, 224
  Robert, 224
PROBARTT, John, 225
PROBERT, John, 225
PROCKTER, Betty, 26
PROCTER, Charles, 225
  Daniel, 297
  Elizabeth, 225
PROCTOR, Charles, 225
  Elizabeth, 225
PRODDAY, Nicholas, 75
PRODDY, Jane, 226
  Nicholas, 81, 141, 225, 226
  Thomas, 226
Promise, 9, 49
PROMROY, Ann, 157
PROODY, Nicholas, 81
PROSER, Anne, 226
PROUCE, Mr., 22
Providence, 130
PROWSE, Robertt, 226
PRYOR, Marie, 226
  William, 226
PULTON, Thomas, 51
PURNIE, John, 226
Putney, 81
PYE, Alice, 53

Ann, 199, 226
Anne, 235
Charles, 226
Edward, 199, 226, 235, 237
Jane, 53
Margret, 226
Walter, 226
PYES, Walter, 297
Pyes Chance, 108
Pyes Hardshift (Pyeshard Shift), 153

-Q-
QUEEN, Marsham, 151
Mary, 151
Ralph, 112
Queen Anne's County, 136
Queen Mary, 151
Quick Dispatch, 158
QUIGLEY, Charles, 27
John, 111

-R-
RAAY, Elisabeth, 23
James, 23
RACHFORD, Michaell, 233
RADFIELD, John, 174
RAINES, Elizabeth, 226, 227
Henry, 226
John, 180, 226, 227
Lucy, 226, 227
RALE, Mical, 228
Michael, 228
Raley, 215
RALEY, Mary, 286
Sina, 286
Thomas, 286
RALLEY, John, 49
RAMSEY, Ann, 227

Anne, 227
John, 157, 227
Susannah, 227
RANDALL, Ann, 227
Henry, 290
Richard, 66, 227
RANFORD, William, 227
Rangle, 119
RANKIN, Ann, 188
John, 188
Mary, 187
Robert, 188
RASPIN, Samuell, 227
Ratchdale, 289
RATCLIFE, Richard, 227
RATCLIFF, Joshua, 110
RATELIFE, Bathsheba, 227
John, 227
Richard, 227
RATFIF, Mary, 199
RATLIEFF, John, 228
Joseph, 228
Joshua, 227
Mary, 228
RATLIFF, Charles, 227
James, 227
John, 227, 228
Joseph, 227, 228
Joshua, 176, 227
Josuway, 227
Mary, 227
Mulinex, 228
Mullenex, 227
Uilindor, 227
RATLIFFE, Ann, 227
Richard, 227
RATTCLIF, Mary, 207
Richard, 207
Rause, 88
Raven's Denn, 110

RAWFIELD, John, 228
RAWLINGS, Ann, 228
Daniel, 228
Mary, 228
RAWSON, Susan, 228
RAY, Edward, 228
RAYNES, John, 227
REA, James, 228
John, 228
Mary, 228
READ, Richard, 229
READE, George, 231
John, 231
READER, Simon, 272
REAGIN, Elizabeth, 54
REAGON, Elisabeth, 228
John, 228
Matthew, 310
REALEY, Barbury, 228
Elisabeth, 228
Michael, 228
Thomas, 51
REALY, Michael, 228
Philip, 228
REAS, John, 228
REAVES, Samuel, 229
Ubgatt, 50
Redd Clift, 192
Redding, 62
REDFERNE, Faith, 229
James, 229
Mary, 229
REDISH, John, 141, 185
REDMAN, Sarah, 43
REED, Elizabeth, 229
John, 229
Margaret, 229
Mary, 229
Sarah, 229
Susanna, 229
Thomas, 229

REEDER, Benjamin, 229, 306
John, 229, 306
REEDING, Isabell, 229
Isable, 229
REEVES, Anne, 229
Edward, 229
Jane, 50
Thomas, 50, 229
Ubgate, 50
Ubgatt, 50
William, 229
REGON, Charles, 229
James, 229
Joan, 229
John, 229
Margarett, 229
Mary, 229
Matthew, 229
William, 229
REILY, Phillip, 229
REINOLD, James, 230
RELEY, Mary, 230
Thomas, 230
Remainder, 76, 110, 114
Renewment, 110
RENISSON, John, 229
RENNICK, Anne, 229
RENNICKE, Anne, 229
RENOLD, James, 230
RENOLDS, Edward, 190
Elizabeth, 190
Reserve, 262, 263
REUSE, Bethia, 235
John, 235
Tabitha, 235
REYLEY, John, 81
Thomas, 286
REYNOLDS, Elizabeth, 190
Rices Mannor, 299
RICH, Richard, 85

Rich Delight, 156
Rich Hill(s), 70, 130, 137, 170
Rich Neck, 300
Rich Thicketts, 294
Richard's Delight, 193
Richard's Pleasure, 131
RICHARDSON, Bernard, 230
Edward, 22, 165, 174
John, 230
Joseph, 230
Nicholas, 230
Thomas, 230
William, 230
RICHISON, Joseph, 230
William, 230
RIDDELL, George, 298
RIDER, Mary, 159
RIGG, Elizabeth, 68
John, 146, 230
Mary, 230
Peter, 230
Susanna, 230
Thomas, 68, 230
Violetta, 230
RIGGE, Penelope, 67
Peter, 230
Thomas, 67, 230
Violetta, 230
RIGGS, Thomas, 208
RIGHT, Robert, 313
RILAY, Ann, 157
RILEY, Thomas, 230
RING, Ralph, 230
River Spring, 24
RIVERS, Christopher, 34
River's Spring, 34
RIVETT, Elizabeth, 255
Jonas, 255

ROASE, John, 36
ROBARTS, Edward, 230
ROBBINS, Henry, 231
James, 231
Margarett, 231
Richard, 171
Robert, 29
Thomas, 231
ROBERSON, Joan, 231
Mary, 83
Robert, 231, 239
ROBERTS, Anne, 231
Edward, 230
Richard, 231
ROBERTSON, Francis, 231
Jane, 231
Marie, 231
William, 240, 241
ROBEY, Benjamin, 233, 310
John, 22
Mary, 233
Penelope, 50
Richard, 233
Sarah, 233
Thomas, 233
Victoria, 233
William, 233
ROBINS, Ann, 148
Elisabeth, 231
Elizabeth, 231
Henry, 231, 232
John, 231, 232
Lydia, 231
Margaret, 231
Richard, 231
Robert, 62, 155, 231
Thomas, 205, 232
William, 148, 231
ROBINSON, Ann, 232
Elizabeth, 232
Frances, 239

Francis, 239
George, 72
Hester, 50
John, 232
Joyce, 232
Mary, 232
Peter, 232
Richard, 115, 232
Samuell, 232
Susanna, 72, 232
Thomas, 192, 232
William, 72, 213, 232
ROBISON, John, 232
Mary, 231
Robert, 231
William, 241
ROBISSON, Susan, 232
William, 162, 229, 232
ROBY, Benjamin, 233
John, 232, 233
Mary, 310
Michael Hinds, 233
Penelope, 50
Peter, 233
Ralph, 50, 233
Richard, 232, 233
Samuel, 233
Sarah, 232, 233, 253
Thomas, 233
William, 232, 233
ROCH, Charles, 233
William, 233
ROCHER, Henry, 224
ROCHFORD, Michaell, 233
ROCK, Charles, 233
Henry, 233
James, 233, 247
John, 233
Mary, 247
ROCKWOOD, Edward, 83
Henrietta, 235

RODGERS, Richard, 169
ROELANTS, Dinah, 233
Margery, 233
Robert, 233
ROGER, Benjamin, 67
Richard, 211
ROGERS, Anne, 70
Elizabeth, 52, 124
John, 70, 90, 234, 236
Mary, 137, 234, 312
Rhodam, 234
Richard, 234
Roadham, 234
Rod:, 234
Rodham, 152
William, 137, 234
Rogers Refuge, 65
Rolen Plaine, 102
ROLLINS, Richard, 222
Rome, 207, 221
ROOKARD, Edward, 312
ROOKED, Edward, 234
Mary, 234
ROOKERD, Edward, 234
Mary, 234
ROOKEWOOD, Edward, 155, 234, 270
Mary, 234
ROOKWOOD, Anne, 234
Edward, 10, 234
Elisabeth, 10
Heneretta, 234
Mary, 234
Thomas, 234
ROOLANTS, Dinah, 233
Margery, 233
Roger, 233

Roome, 221
ROSAN, Sarah, 154
ROSE, John, 235
Roseberry, 80, 174
ROSEE, James, 235
ROSEWELL, Elizabeth, 202
William, 202
ROSIER, Ann, 235
Benjamin, 235
Notley, 226, 235
ROSS, Anne, 310
James, 51, 228
Rotterdam, 40, 77, 87, 272
ROUGHT, Anne, 235
Sarah, 235
William, 235
Round Hill, 244, 245
Round Hills, 245
Roundhill, 244
ROUSE, Ann, 235
John, 235
William, 235
ROUZE, Anne, 235
John, 235
ROWLAND, Margery, 44
Ribert, 236
Robert, 138, 211, 216, 228, 259
ROWLANTS, Margery, 233
Robert, 233, 309
ROWLES, Elizabeth, 236
ROWLING, John, 70
ROY, John, 273
ROZAR, Sarah, 154
Rozenbury, 64
ROZER, Ann, 53
Anne, 235
Benjamin, 53, 101, 107, 115, 139, 141,

148, 154, 174, 181, 215, 226, 231, 235, 302, 304, 313
Jane, 82, 235
Katrine, 53
Madam, 196
Mary, 235
Mr., 139, 140, 142, 281, 286
Notley, 235
ROZERS, ——, 53
Rozer's Refuge, 64, 235, 243
Rozers Refuge, 126
ROZIER, Notley, 226
ROZWELL, William, 230
RUCKWOOD, Edward, 281
Ruden, 265
RUE, Elizabeth, 236
Temperance, 236
RUMNEY, Edward, 236
Elizabeth, 236
RUSSEL, Luke, 236
Mary, 236
RUSSELL, Ann, 236
Brutus, 236, 261, 279
Capt., 163
Christopher, 236
James, 236
John, 71, 236
Luke, 236, 296
Mary, 236, 261, 279
Nicholas, 240
Susanna, 38, 236
T. T., 38
Thomas Truman, 236
Russell Tract, 216
RUSTON, Margaret, 237
RUTHERFORD, James, 86

RYAN, Thomas, 91

-S-
SACKIMORE, Edward, 237
Safford Rest, 263
SAFFRON, James, 237
St. Barbaries, 220
St. Barbaries Manor, 167, 228
St. Barbary's, 79
St. Barbary's Manor, 167
Saint Bennetts, 155
St. Bernard, 88
St. Bridgett, 253
St. Bridgetts, 111
St. Catherine's, 198
ST. CLARE, Dorothy, 237
George, 237
Thomas, 237
SAINT CLARE, George, 237
Priscilla, 237
Robert, 237
St. Davidge, 2
Saint Davids, 3, 101, 270, 276
St. Davids, 234
St. Edmond's, 9, 99, 152, 193, 288
St. Edmonds Bury, 81
St. Edmunds, 6, 126
St. Edward, 193
St. Edwards, 228
Saint George, 276
St. George's, 23, 26, 48, 65, 120, 243, 244, 245
St. George's Rest, 25
St. Giles, 262
St. Ignatius, 224, 225
St. James, 25, 120, 201

St. John's, 131, 140, 143, 144, 163, 222, 263, 266
Saint John's, 7, 97
St. Johns, 96, 176
St. John's Addition, 144
St. John's Freehold, 211
St. Katherine, 257
St. Margarets, 218
St. Margaretts, 293
St. Marthis, 208
St. Mary's County, 4, 5, 10, 16, 18, 21, 26, 27, 30, 31, 33, 35, 37, 38, 39, 45, 50, 56, 58, 61, 62, 63, 65, 72, 75, 79, 81, 82, 87, 88, 89, 93, 94, 95, 96, 98, 106, 113, 114, 116, 118, 120, 127, 129, 130, 131, 136, 139, 140, 148, 152, 153, 157, 158, 164, 165, 169, 172, 174, 179, 181, 185, 189, 197, 198, 202, 204, 206, 217, 220, 221, 223, 226, 234, 236, 237, 243, 245, 248, 249, 250, 255, 258, 261, 262, 265, 274, 277, 278, 280, 282, 285, 290, 292, 293, 295, 298, 301, 303, 305, 306, 310, 311, 315
St. George's, 226
St. George's Hundred, 79
St. Mary's Manor, 58
St. Mathew's, 45
St. Mathews, 241

Saint Matthew's, 249
St. *Matthews*, 203
St. *Michals*, 60
St. *Nicholass*, 271
St. *Nicholas*, 284
St. *Nicholls*, 206
St. *Patrick Hill*, 224
St. *Patricks Hill*, 125, 225
St. *Peter's*, 250
St. *Stephen Coleman*, 44
Saint Thomas, 212
Saint Thomas', 249
St. *Thomas'*, 30, 87, 91, 153, 248, 270
St. *Thomas Manor*, 250
St. *Thomases*, 313
St. *Verlindas*, 266
Saint Vincents, 201
St. *Vincents*, 201
Salisbury, 55, 91, 159, 220, 225, 242
Salsbury, 213
SALSBY, Nicholas, 261
SALT, Mary, 237
SALYERD, Charles, 237
SAMPLE, Charles, 237, 240
Frances, 237, 240
SANDER, John, 239
Sarah, 239
SANDERS, Alice, 237, 265
Ann(e), 240
Charles, 238, 239, 241
Edward, 44, 237, 238, 239, 240, 241, 311
Eleanor, 240, 241
Elinor, 239
Elizabeth, 240, 265
Frances, 237, 239, 240
Ignatious, 240

Ignatius, 240
James, 238
Jane, 237, 238, 239
John, 25, 66, 88, 92, 104, 198, 207, 238, 239, 240, 241, 273, 301, 311
Joseph, 241
Katherine, 240
Margaret, 239
Martha, 104, 240
Mary, 25, 92, 234, 240, 241, 273
Mat(t)hew, 237, 239, 240, 311
Prudence, 66, 240, 241
Rachel, 240
Richard, 240
Robert, 46, 239, 248, 296
Sarah, 92, 198, 240, 241
Thomas, 153, 216, 238, 239, 240, 241
Valinda, 240
Virlinda, 240
William, 146, 237, 239, 240, 241, 265
Sanders Pleasure, 239
Sandy Gravel, 119
SANFORD, William, 18, 241
SAPCOAT, Abraham, 242
SAPCOATE, Abram, 242
Elizabeth, 242
Rachell, 242
SARGENT, William, 169
SARJEANT, Damaris, 292
SARJENT, Mary, 264

William, 264
SARRAT, Ann, 242
Samuel, 242
Sarum, 220
Saturday Work, 27, 64, 144, 190
SAUNDERS, Charles, 238
Edward, 238, 240, 311
Eleanor, 240
Frances, 239
Jane, 238
Joane, 238
John, 238, 305
Margaret, 240
Martha, 239
Mary, 238
Mathew, 239
Matthew, 238, 240
Prudence, 146
Sarah, 198, 238, 305
Thomas, 238
SAVAGE, Joshua, 185
Mary, 185
SCALLON, Ann, 78
Peter, 78
SCARRY, Elias, 242
SCARRYOTT, Richard, 242
SCHALES, George, 242
Scidmore's Adventures, 307
SCOT, James, 226
John, 242
Scotland, Glasgow, 151
SCOTT, Andrew, 297
Catherine, 219
Charles, 242
Christian, 242
Edward, 242
Elisabeth, 242
Eribecca, 242
Grace, 242
Henry, 242

James, 242
John, 80, 129, 242, 305
John Preston, 242
Margaret, 204
Mary, 242
Susanna, 242
Walter, 242
William, 242
Scotts Folly, 95
SCROGGEN, George, 243
Jane, 243
SCROGGIN, Elizabeth, 242
George, 163, 242, 243
James, 243
jane, 243
John, 163, 242, 243
Joseph, 243
Mary, 242, 243
Sarah, 243
Susanna, 242, 243
SCROGIN, George, 286
John, 210
SEARGENT, William, 273
SEARSON, Alice, 179
Francis, 179
SEAWELL, Rebeckah, 243
Second Addition, 186
SEDMAN, Sarah, 268
SEEMES, Ignatius, 245
Joseph Milburn, 245
Marmaduke, 245
SEEMS, Anthony, 245
Chloe, 244
Elizabeth, 244
Francis, 244
Ignatious, 244
James, 245
Jane, 244, 245
Joseph, 244

Lucretia, 244
Marmaduke, 244, 245
Mary, 245
Seemses Chance, 245
SEER, Thomas, 243
SEES, Thomas, 243
SELBY, Martha, 243
Parker, 243
William Magruder, 243
SELLWOOD, Mary, 200
SEMMES, Aleatius, 244
Ann, 244
Anthony, 243, 244
Catherine, 244
Cleborn, 244, 245
Cleburn, 249
Douzabella, 25
Elizabeth, 244
Fidellimus, 244
Fortune, 243
Francis, 244
Heneretta, 245
Henrietta, 244
Ignatius, 244, 245
James, 122, 243, 244, 245, 263
John, 243, 249
Joseph Milburn, 244, 245
Juliana, 244, 245
Marmaduke, 6, 243, 244, 245
Mary, 112, 244, 245, 263
Milburn, 190
Rachel, 245, 314
Susannah, 244
Thomas Medford, 243
SEMMS, Ann, 15, 244
Anthony, 243, 244
Bathia, 243

Cleburne, 244
Dusebella, 243
Eleanor, 244
Elictions, 243
Elinor, 244
Elizabeth, 244
Fidellimus, 243
Francis, 244
James, 235, 244
Jane, 243
John, 139, 244
Marmaduke, 243, 244
Mary, 243
Rebecka, 244
Ruth, 244
Thomas, 244
Semms Forest, 243
Sems Settlement, 243
SEMSON, Joseph, 208
Sarey, 208
SENEY, Daniell, 245
SENIT, Robert, 310
SENNET, Garrat, 114
Robert, 73, 146
SENNETT, Ann, 245
Anne, 250
Elizabeth, 246
Garrett, 250
Gerrard, 245, 246
SENNIT, Robert, 38
Sensey, 231
SERGENT, William, 246
SERJEANT, William, 246
SETTELF, John, 269
SEWALL, Nicholas, 53
SEYMOUR, Jane, 174
John, 175
Thomas, 174
SHACKALET, Elizabeth, 246
Michael, 246
SHACKER, John, 246

Sarah, 246
SHACKERLEY,
　Edward, 246
　Francis, 246
　John, 246
SHACKERLIT,
　Benjamin, 246
　Sarah, 246
SHACKERLY, John,
　246
　Mary, 246
SHACKLET, Edward,
　246
　Michael, 246
　Tabitha, 246
SHADWELL,
　Christopher, 221,
　246
SHAKALIT, Benjamin,
　192
SHAKULETT, Michael,
　246
SHAMWELL, Isaac,
　279
SHAREMAN, John, 20,
　247
　Susanna, 20
　Susannah, 247
SHAW, Ann, 215, 246,
　289
　Anne, 246
　Dorothy, 247
　Elizabeth, 21, 247
　John, 21, 40, 246, 247
　Mary, 224, 233, 247
　Monacak, 247
　Ralph, 22, 108, 118,
　　216, 246, 247, 289
　Sarah, 40, 247
SHAW, John, 107
SHEARMAN,
　Elizabeth, 247
　John, 87, 247
　Susan, 247

Susannah, 247
SHELTON, Mary, 247
　Thomas, 247
SHENSTON, George,
　81
SHENSTONE, George,
　247
　Mary, 247
SHEPHERD, Charles,
　247, 262, 292
　Demaris, 247
SHILER, Jane, 147
SHINER, Daniell, 247
SHINGLETON, John,
　247
SHIRBIN, Clare, 241
SHORT, Anne, 247
　Catheine, 248
　Catherine, 306
　Daniel, 247, 248, 306
　Elisabeth, 305
　Elizabeth, 247
　George, 65, 247, 248,
　　257
　Katherine, 248
　Mary, 65, 257
　Thomas, 305
SHOTTWELL,
　Christopher, 221
Shrewsberry, 299
Shrimp's Neck, 222
SHUTTLESWORTH,
　Thomas, 129
SHUTTLEWORTH,
　Edward, 248
　Lydia, 248
　Thomas, 248
SIGELOY, Samuell,
　248
SIMES, Fortune, 243
Sime's Settlement, 244
Simkin and Crowback,
　166

SIMMES, Anthony,
　243, 245
　Francis, 243, 245
　Marmaduke, 245
SIMMONS, Mary, 248
SIMMS, Ann, 15
　Anthony, 245
　Cleborn, 245
　Cleborne, 245
　John, 243
　Marmaduke, 23, 48,
　　243, 244, 245
　Mary, 48, 245
SIMPSON, Alex, 17
　Alexander, 2, 10, 248
　Andrew, 225, 249
　Ann, 249
　Clare, 249
　Elisabeth, 248
　Elizabeth, 248, 306
　Gilbertus, 306
　Ignatius, 198, 307
　James, 307
　John, 249
　Joseph, 242
　Joseph Green, 249
　Juliana, 250
　Julianah, 112
　Mary, 198, 249, 307
　Paul, 248
　Samuel, 204
　Samuell, 248
　Sarah, 153
　Thomas, 198, 213,
　　248, 249
　William, 248, 307
Simpson's Delight,
　248, 307
Simpsons Reply, 67
Simpsons Supply, 20,
　140, 161, 187, 248,
　278, 311
SIMPTON, Andrew,
　244

SIMS, Anthony, 243
  Dusabella, 244
  Fortune, 243
  James, 6
  John, 65
  Marmaduke, 65
  Mary, 6, 139
SIMSON, Elizabeth, 198
  Julianah, 245
Simson's Supply, 257
SINGLETON, John, 147
  Richard, 250
SINKILTON, George, 138
Sinkin, 249
SINNET, Benedicta, 250
  Hannah, 250
  Robert, 250
SINNETT, Alice, 250
  Ann, 250
  Garratt, 53
  Garret, 250
  Garrett, 148, 250
  Margaret, 250
SISSON, William, 11
SKEENES, Ann, 32
  Susanna, 32
SKIDMORE, Anne, 250
  Nicholas, 250
Skidmore Rest, 120, 250
Skidmores Adventure, 308
SKINNER, Ann, 145
  Anne, 1
  Constance, 117, 250, 251
  Constant, 186
  James, 250
  Thomas, 81, 117, 145, 250

William, 1, 250, 251
Skipten, 260
Skipton, 22, 68, 260
SLATER, John, 251
SLAYDE, Anne, 251
  George, 251
SLY, Mary, 241
  Robert, 251
SLYE, Eleanor, 251
  Garard, 244
  John, 237, 251
  Robert, 52, 251
SMALDRIGE, Elisabeth, 251
Small Hope, 173
Small Hopes, 197
Smallhopes, 195
SMALLPADGE, Ellinor, 251
SMALLPAGE, Elinor, 67
  Robert, 67, 148, 251
SMALLWEELL, Elisabeth, 251
  James, 251
SMALLWOOD, Alice, 254
  Ann, 105, 252, 253
  Baine, 252
  Bayne, 18, 252, 253, 254
  Charity, 105, 252, 253, 300
  Eleanor, 252
  Elenor, 252
  Elisabeth, 188
  Elizabeth, 105, 253, 254
  Ellinor, 252, 282
  Esther, 251, 253
  Henrietta, 105
  Hester, 251, 253
  James, 36, 48, 52, 60, 98, 102, 236, 251,

252, 253, 254, 277, 282
  Jane, 252
  John, 116, 251, 252, 253, 254
  Ladstone, 254
  Leadstone, 252
  Ledstone, 252, 253, 254
  Lettes, 251
  Lidia, 254
  Lodstone, 105
  Lydia, 252
  Martha, 252
  Mary, 31, 60, 61, 102, 105, 251, 252, 253, 254, 277
  Mathew, 31, 61, 252
  Matthew, 251, 254
  Prier, 252
  Prior, 253
  Priscilla, 254
  Pry:, 19
  Pryar, 252
  Pryer, 188, 253
  Pryor, 110, 253, 254
  Samuel, 165, 252
  Sarah, 251, 253
  Thomas, 251, 252, 253, 254
  William, 105, 251, 252, 253, 254, 282
Smallwood's Plains, 253, 254
SMITH, Adam, 256, 258
  Alexander, 8, 46, 60, 73, 101, 130, 255, 306
  Ann, 119, 120, 256, 257, 258
  Anne, 255, 257, 287
  Anthony, 239, 255
  Arther, 216, 257

Arthur, 255, 256
Boswell, 305
Catherine, 76
Charles Somerset, 12, 71, 258
Daniell, 255, 256
Dikanda, 258
Elias, 257, 258
Elisabeth, 256, 258, 288
Elizabeth, 190, 255, 256, 257, 258
Hanna, 257
Henry, 255, 256, 257
James, 169, 255, 257, 258, 260, 307
Jane, 48, 71, 256, 258
Joan, 255, 256
John, 2, 48, 67, 141, 179, 190, 195, 255, 256, 257, 258
John Martin, 256
Margaret, 218
Margarett, 257, 258
Margery, 255, 256
Martha, 255, 257
Mary, 255, 256, 258
Mathew, 254
Priscilla, 195, 257
Rachell, 99
Railph, 246
Ralph, 48, 160, 162, 255, 256, 280
Richard, 137, 154, 169, 221, 254, 255, 256, 257, 258, 266, 303, 304, 307
Robert, 254
Samuel, 258
Sarah, 48, 255, 256, 257, 258, 286
Simon, 223, 258, 292
Somersett, 12

Thomas, 4, 160, 189, 255, 256, 258
Walter, 258
Widow, 295
William, 15, 57, 76, 99, 131, 178, 221, 235, 254, 255, 256, 257, 258, 306
———, 258
Smith's Addition, 140, 257
Smith's Be Served, 179
Smith's Chance, 256, 308
Smith's Purchase, 247
Smith's Venture, 259
SMOOT, Abigail, 260
Aels, 258
Ann, 17, 260
Anne, 33
Barton, 17, 22, 145, 259, 260, 304
Charles, 217, 260
Edward, 210, 259
Eleanor, 210
Elinor, 260
Elisabeth Ann, 258
Elizabeth, 260, 293
George, 260
Henry, 38, 145, 260
Isaac, 260
James, 161, 260
John, 79, 210, 241, 259, 273, 305
John Nathan, 22
Leonard, 187
Lidia, 260
Oriah, 170
Posthuma, 241, 273
Postuma, 259
Richard, 135, 181, 191, 259
Sarah, 259

Thomas, 17, 22, 133, 259, 260, 293
William, 17, 22, 172, 258, 260
SMOOTE, Ann(e), 259
Barton, 259
Charles, 259
Edward, 48, 259
Elizabeth, 259
Ellinor, 259
Grace, 259
John, 259, 260
John Nathan, 259
Leonard, 187
Lydia, 259, 260
Mary, 259
Rachell, 259
Richard, 39, 259, 291
Thomas, 259
William, 39, 258, 259
Smootes Chance, 172
Smoote's Purchase, 259, 294
SMOOTH, Barton, 260
Edward, 260
Richard, 260
Thomas, 260
Smoots Branch, 260
Smoots Chance, 260
Smoot's Choice, 147, 172
Smoot's Delight, 260
Smoots Fish Pond, 304
Smoot's Swamp, 260
Smoot's Swamp Addition, 260
SMYTH, Alexander, 89, 272
John, 254
Margaret, 254
SNELL, Margaret, 260
SNETON, John, 261
SNIVENS, Eliza, 24
Phillip, 24

Index

SNOSELL,
  Christopher, 261
SNOWDEN, William, 261
SNOWMAN, Grace, 98
SOLSBY, Nicholas, 261
Somerset County, 77, 272
SOMMER, Jonathan, 261
SOTHERLAND,
  Alexander, 261
  David, 261
  Elizabeth, 261
  Michael Richard, 236
SOTHORN, Benjamin, 261
  Elizabeth, 261
  John, 261
  John Johnson, 261
  Leaven, 261
  Richard, 261
  Samuel, 261
SOTHORON, Ann, 261
  Benjamin, 183, 261
  Charles, 261
  John, 183, 261
  John Johnson, 261
  Mary, 261
  Richard, 261
  Samuell, 261
South Hampton, 258
Southampton, 256
Southbury, 250
SOUTHERLAND,
  Richard, 236
Southerns Desire, 261
SOUTHORN, John
  Johnson, 261
Southorn's Delight, 261
Southorn's Hills, 261
Southrich, 35
Southrick Beginning, 311

Southvielle, 222
SPAKE, John, 263
SPALDING, Bassell, 262
  Charles, 262
  Edward, 262
  John, 116, 262
  Mary, 262
  Peter, 262
  Priscilla, 262
  William, 262
SPARKS, Thomas, 185
SPAULDING, Ann, 153
  John, 262
SPEAK, Bowling, 258
  John, 262
  Mary, 258
  Richard, 262
  Theodosia, 288
  Winifred, 262
SPEAKE, Bowling, 30, 263
  Elizabeth, 262, 263
  James, 262
  Jane, 263
  John, 23, 177, 262, 263, 272, 299
  Mary, 245, 263
  Richard, 262, 263
  Theodocia, 262
  Thomas, 262, 263
  Wennifred, 299
  Winifred, 262
  Winniford, 234
  Winnifred, 262
Speakes Inclosure, 19, 234
SPEAKS, John, 262
  Winifred, 262
SPEARING, Barbery, 228
  John, 228
SPEEAK, Elizabeth, 288

  Theodoshea, 288
SPEEKE, Thomas, 8, 121, 237
SPERING, Barbara, 263
  John, 263
SPICER, Elisabeth, 263
  Haniball, 263
SPIKMAN, Barbary, 197
SPINKE, Jane, 130
  Thomas, 130
Splittfield, 235
SPRATT, Helen, 199
Sprigs Request, 314
Spring Plain, 125, 224
Spring Run, 151
SPURLING, Jeremiah, 263
Square Adventure, 123, 173
STACY, Charity, 47
STAFFORD, Rachael, 263
  Richard, 263
  Sarah, 263
  William, 263
Stainland, 201
STANDBURY, John, 187, 263
STANDFORTH,
  Richard, 6, 264
STANDIDGE,
  Alexander, 264
STANDISH, Alexander, 264
  Thomas, 132
STANDIST, Alexander, 111
STANDLY, Thomas, 264
STANERD, William, 115

STANFIELD, Robert, 264
STAPLEFORD, Charles, 112
———, 112
STAPLETON, John, 258
STEARMAN, Richard, 264
———, 264
STEEDE, Thomas, 264
STENNETT, Benjamin, 240, 265
Elizabeth, 240, 265
STEPHENS, Charles, 264
Henry, 212
John, 212
Mary, 264
Richard, 264
STEPHENSON, Issabella, 264
William, 264
Stepney, 28
STEVENS, Blanch, 264
Esther, 264
Henry, 264
James, 264
Kezia, 264
Symon, 266
Stevens His Hope, 190
Stevens Hope, 264
STEVENSON, John, 192
Mary, 257
STEWARD, Daniel, 265
Daniell, 264
Eleanor, 265
George, 264
John, 265
William, 265
STICKLER, Mary, 265
STIDMAN, Edward, 265

STIGELARE, Mary, 78
STIGELEARE, Mary, 265
STIGELEER, James, 265
Jane, 265
Mary, 265
STIGELER, James, 265
Jane, 265
Mary, 265
STINIT, Benjamin, 265
Elizabeth, 265
STINNETT, Benjamin, 265
Elizabeth, 265
STOANE, Elisabeth, 266
STOCK, Mary, 6
STODDART, James, 258
STODDERT, Elizabeth, 265
James, 265
STOKES, Geane, 157
John, 258
STONE, Barton, 268
Bethia, 267
Catherine, 267
David, 267
Dorothy, 266
Eleanor, 267
Elisabeth, 266
Eliza, 265, 266
Elizabeth, 19, 45, 266, 273
Ellinor, 19, 266, 273
Hugh, 14, 157
Jean, 58
John, 2, 77, 155, 208, 266, 267, 268, 277, 315
Katharine, 266
Katherine, 267

Margery, 177, 266, 268
Mary, 157, 266, 267
Mathew, 17, 83, 117, 178, 253, 266, 267, 268
Mathias, 266
Matthew, 117, 153, 159, 177, 266, 267, 275
Pretious (Precious), 267
Rachael, 268
Rachel(l), 17, 267
Richard, 14, 24, 180, 205, 261, 265, 266, 267, 268
Sprigg, 265
Theadoshia, 288
Theodosia, 267
Thomas, 77, 83, 132, 143, 177, 180, 215, 266, 267, 268, 275, 276, 280, 288
Verlinda, 265, 266, 267
Virlinda, 267
Walter, 266
William, 24, 45, 52, 92, 131, 177, 178, 191, 265, 266, 267, 292
Stone Hill, 133
STONEHILL, Mathew, 57
STONEHOUSE, Thomas, 268
Stone's Rest, 267
STONESTREET, Anne, 268
Butler, 268
Buttler, 268
Christian, 268
Edward, 268

Mary, 96, 268
Thomas, 264, 268
Thomason, 268
Stony Harbor, 287
Stor Plantation, 187
Store Plantation, 9
STOREY, Ann, 269
  Walter, 163, 256
STORRY, Walter, 163
STORY, Ann, 269
  Anne, 237, 268
  Charity, 21, 269
  Elisabeth, 269
  Elizabeth, 125, 269
  Jane, 269
  Mary, 83, 174, 268
  Sarah, 174, 269
  Walter, 22, 43, 70, 83,
    136, 174, 175, 197,
    268, 269
  ———, 269
STRAMATE, John, 210
STRATTON, Luci, 269
  Mary, 83
  Philise, 269
Strife, 122, 165, 185,
  234, 252, 274
STRINGER, George,
  269
STROMAT, Elisabeth,
  269
  John, 269
  John Baptist, 269
STROMATT, Ann, 269
  John, 269
STUART, Daniel, 123,
  265
  Daniell, 264
  Elinor, 264
  Ellinor, 264
  John, 265
STUERT, Daniel, 265
  Mary, 265
Stump Dall, 269

SUDBERIE, Gregorie,
  269
SUDFIF, John, 199
SUITE, Richard, 92
SUPLE, Anthony, 67
SURLING, Robert, 130
Susquehana, 308
Susquehanna, 307
SUTCLIF, Anne, 269
  John, 269
SUTTLE, Ann, 156
  Elizabeth, 156
  John, 156, 296
SWAINE, George, 269
SWAN, Ann, 42
  Edward, 150
  Elizabeth, 69
  James, 69
  Judith, 69
  Katherine, 42
  Mary, 69
  Thomas, 69
Swan Hill, 89
SWANN, Abiga(i)l, 270
  Abigall, 89
  Anne, 270
  Barbara, 270
  Burch, 270
  Edward, 37, 206, 269,
    270
  Elizabeth, 270
  James, 270
  Mercer, 270
  Samuel, 37, 38, 270
  Sarah, 270
  Susanna, 270
  Thomas, 269, 270
Swann Hill, 5
SWANNE, Edward,
  301
SWATEWELL, John,
  270
SWEEN, Sarah, 270

SWIFT, Theophilus,
  126, 177
SWINBURNE,
  Elizabeth, 197
  Nicholas, 270
SYLLY, Henry, 281
SYMMES, John, 243
SYMMONS, Elinor, 248
  George, 248
SYMONS, Elizabeth,
  255
SYMPSON, Alexander,
  181
  Andrew, 115
  Clare (Clear), 249
  George, 215
  Gilbert, 315
  Ignatius, 249, 307
  James, 307
  John, 249, 315
  Joseph Green, 250
  Juliana, 250
  Mary, 239, 249, 307
  Sarah, 249, 306
  Thomas, 148, 239,
    249, 250, 306, 307
  William, 307
Sympsons Delight, 308
Sympson's Supply, 239
SYNET, Garrett, 55
SYNNET, Garrett, 250
SYNNETT, Alice, 250
  Garrett, 250
SYZOR, Phillip, 270

-T-

Tabitha's Lot, 131
TAFT, Thomas, 270
TAILOR, Magdalene,
  272
  William, 272
Talbot County, 287
TALFER, Charles, 234

TALFORD, Charles, 270
  Elisabeth, 270
TALLOR, Thomas, 272
TANEY, Mary, 205
  Ralph, 205
  Thomas, 236, 259
TANNEHILL, William, 251
TANNER, Ann, 163, 271
  Anne, 270
  Elizabeth, 271
  Elleanor, 271
  Henry, 227, 270, 271, 273
  James, 271
  John, 271
  Joseph, 271
  Thomas, 214
Tanners Discovery, 271
TANSHALL, Edward, 271
  John, 271
  Margarett, 271
  Thomas, 271
TANT, James, 272, 306
TANTE, Mrs., 162
Tanyard, 294
TARAIN, Ellen, 199
TARLIN, Mary, 271
TARLINE, Richard, 271
TARVIN, Ann, 271
  Elisabeth, 271
  Elizabeth, 166, 271
  G., 271
  George, 271
  John, 271
  Rebecca, 271
  Richard, 166, 271
  Thomas, 271
  William, 271
TARVIRE, G., 192

TASKER, Benjamin, 176
TATE, George, 271
Tatshall, 9
Tatter Shalls Gift, 189
TATTERSALL, Philip, 272
  Terasha, 272
TATTERSHALL, Charles, 271
  Thomas, 271
TATTERSHELL, William, 272
TAWNEY, Mary, 203, 204
TAYER, James, 48
TAYLER, Anne, 272
  Edmund, 103
  Henry, 273
  Mary, 252
  Thomas, 272
  William, 210, 273
TAYLOR, Ann, 272, 273
  Anne, 272
  Barbara, 272
  Edmond, 272
  Edmund, 165
  Eleanor, 231
  Elisabeth, 273
  Elizabeth, 27, 272, 273
  George, 272
  Hen:, 246
  Henry, 61, 273
  James, 273
  Jheromie, 272
  John, 27, 32, 272, 273, 303
  Mary, 104, 231, 241, 273
  Morgan, 272
  Richard, 272
  Robert, 273

  Samuel, 87
  Samuell, 272
  Sarah, 273
  Tabitha, 246
  Thomas, 7, 27, 98, 160, 189, 246, 272, 273
  Verlinda, 272
  Virlinda, 87, 272
  William, 165, 273
  William Smallwood, 104, 273
TEARES, Elizabeth, 273
  Ellinor, 273
  Hugh, 273
TEARS, Eleanor, 190
  Elizabeth, 190
  Ellinor, 250
  Hugh, 190, 250
TEDMAN, Sarah, 268
Temple Manor, 24
TENESON, Elizabeth, 274
  John, 274
  Justinain, 274
  Samuel, 274
  Sarah, 166
TENNIS, Barbara, 273
  Catherine, 273
  Christian, 273
  Dracie, 273
  Elizabeth, 273
  John, 273
  Justinian, 273
  Mary, 273
  Sarah, 273
TENNISON, Elizabeth, 274
  Ignatius, 274
  Jesse, 274
  Justinain, 274
  Justinian, 208, 273
  Samuel, 171

Index 393

Sarah, 274
TENNISSON, Mary, 38
THATRYER, Mary, 274
THEOBALD, Charity, 314
 Clement, 67, 274
 Elizabeth, 275, 281
 John, 67, 112, 163, 274
 Mary, 274
 Penelope, 274
THEOBALDS, Charity, 274
 Clement, 51, 247, 274
 Elisabeth, 152, 274
 Elizabeth, 274, 275
 Jane, 275
 John, 152, 174, 274
 Mary, 163, 174, 234, 274
 Samuel, 275
 William, 97, 204, 274
THEOBALLS,
 Clement, 53
THEOBOLD, William, 141
THIMBLEY, William, 264
THIRST, Elizabeth, 76
THOMAS, Ann, 50, 275
 Anna Mary, 275
 Anne, 275
 Benjamin, 276
 Benoni, 267, 275
 Benony, 80, 266, 275
 Brooks, 276
 Edward, 275
 Elisabeth, 276
 Elizabeth, 49, 60, 275, 276
 George, 2, 63, 275, 276
 George Salisbury, 276
 Guyott, 275

 Hugh, 60, 253, 254, 275
 James, 227, 275, 276, 277
 Jane, 276
 John, 51, 150, 172, 175, 272, 275
 Joseph, 60, 156, 276
 Katharine, 275
 Katherine, 29
 Margaret, 156
 Margery, 253
 Mary, 50, 88, 275
 Richard, 276
 Sarah, 276
 Sophania, 277
 Sophia, 276
 Sophonia, 276
 Susanna, 15, 88, 275
 Susannah, 276
 Teratia, 275
 Teresa, 276
 Thomas, 49, 272, 275, 276
 Tracey, 275
 William, 83, 88, 274, 275, 276, 277
Thomas and James Adventure, 113
Thomas' Choice, 40
Thomas' Disappointment, 176
Thomas His Chance, 275, 242
Thomas His Purchase, 132
Thomas' Port, 276
Thomas Town, 32
Thomas's Addition, 130
Thomas's Fancy, 276
THOMKINSON, Jane, 167
 John, 192

Thomkinson's Long Lookt For, 79
THOMPKINS, Giles, 280
 John, 74, 280
 Newman, 280
 Sarah, 280
Thompkins Purchase, 280
THOMPKINSON,
 Jane, 277
 John, 224, 277
Thompkinson's Longlook For, 51
THOMPSON, Ann, 58, 205, 278, 279
 Anne, 277, 278
 Blanch, 140
 Christopher, 170
 Cuthbert, 277, 278
 Eleanor, 278
 Elisabeth, 278
 George, 61, 105, 151, 221
 Grace, 277
 Henry, 179, 277, 278
 Issabella, 278
 James, 57, 278
 James, 277
 Jane, 277, 278
 John, 36, 115, 277, 278
 Joseph, 278
 Katherine, 278
 Magdalen, 278
 Mary, 25, 115, 277, 278
 Robert, 25, 31, 57, 81, 128, 138, 142, 241, 277, 313
 Susannah, 278
 Thomas, 140, 187, 240, 277, 278
 Victoria, 50, 277

Will, 278
William, 8, 143, 277, 278
William Mathews, 278
William Matthews, 278
Winefred, 278
Thompsons Chance, 278
Thompsons Delight, 152, 278
Thompsons Hope, 236, 278
Thompsons Humour, 50
Thompsons Rest, 115
Thompson's Square, 172
Thompson's Town, 108
THOMSON, Henry, 150
THORN, Elisabeth, 279
Elizabeth, 279
James, 279
John, 279
William, 279
THORNE, Absalom, 211, 279
Elisabeth, 211
Elizabeth, 211, 279
THORNTON, Francis, 298
THOROLD, George, 53, 148
Three Brothers, 145, 265
THRONE, William, 92
TIBBITT, John, 279
TIBLEE, Thomas, 279
TICKERELL, Jane, 280
Thomas, 280
TIDROR, James, 279
TIERS, James, 315
TILL, Ann, 71

Edward, 71, 279
John, 279
Sarah, 279
William, 279
TILLESON, James, 67
TILLOTSON, James, 279
TILLS, Edward, 148
TILLSEY, Mabella, 279
TILLYARD, Richard, 279
Timber Neck, 219
TIMEUS, Saragh, 43
TIMMS, Joseph, 279
Sarah, 39
Timnah Sarah, 88
TIMOTHY, Grace, 280
William, 280
TINKERELL, Thomas, 280
TIPPETT, Mary, 162
Phillip, 162
TIPTON, Edward, 280
Jonathon, 301
TISKERELL, Anne, 280
Thomas, 280
Tiverton, 189
TOD, Thomas, 280
TOMKINE, Sarah, 280
TOMKINES, Giles, 38
TOMKINS, Elizabeth, 281
Joan, 280
Newman, 280, 281
Sarah, 280
Tomkins Purchase, 281
Tomkinsons Long Looked For, 80
Tomkisens, 51
TOMPKINS, Ann, 40
Elizabeth, 276, 281
Giles, 40, 280
Newman, 280, 281

Sarah, 280
TOMPSON, James, 57
TOMSON, Henry, 277
TOPPING, James, 65
John, 281
TOTERSHALL, Laurence, 306
Totershall's Gift, 306
TOTTERSHALL, Charles, 271
Philip, 271
TOWELL, David, 99, 281
Tower Dock, 233
Tower Hill, 30, 182
Town House, 294
TOWNE, Henry, 11
TOWNLEY, Frances, 174, 312
Judith, 174, 312
TREIE, Richard, 139
TREN, Henry, 46
TRENCH, Ann, 281
TREW, Ann, 281
Priscilla, 74
Richard, 74, 281
TRIMBLE, Elizabeth, 62
TROOPE, Robert, 281, 310
Troope's Rendezvous, 232
Troop's Rendesvous, 1, 109, 177
Troublesom, 184
Troupe's Supply, 281
TROUTON, John, 281
TROVER, Mary, 281
Patrick, 281
TRUE, Anne, 161, 282
Priscilla, 75
Richard, 75, 161, 282
TRUEMAN, Edward, 282

Elizabeth, 282
Thomas Greenfield, 282
TRUMAN, Henry, 145, 282
  James, 145, 282
  Sarah, 282
  Thomas Greenfield, 282
Trumans Place, 72
Tryal, 48, 85, 143
TUBB, Thomas, 282
TUBMAN, Elinor, 252, 282
  Elizabeth, 282
  Ellinor, 133
  George, 134, 141, 252, 256, 282
  Richard, 134, 230, 282
TURBERVILL, William, 181
Turles, 158
TURLING, John, 79
  Rebeckah, 282
TURLINGE, John, 79
TURLOW, Orlock, 282
TURNER, Alexander, 283
  Alexander Smith, 255
  Arthur, 7, 181, 202, 255, 269, 282, 291
  Charles, 283
  Deborah, 283
  Dorcas, 283
  Dorothy, 124
  Edward, 5, 44, 81, 171, 211, 255, 282, 283
  Elinor, 283
  Elizabeth, 283
  Emma, 163
  Hezekiah, 283
  James, 107, 282
  John, 283
  Joseph, 283
  Joshua, 283
  Lydia, 283
  Margarite, 282
  Mary, 163, 255, 283
  Randal, 283
  Richard, 283
  Samuel, 44, 81, 283
  Thomas, 26, 124, 163
  Virlinda, 283
  William, 283
  Zephaniah, 283
TURNOR, Arthur, 282
TURTON, Catherine, 283
  John, 283
TURVEY, Edward, 283
  Thomas, 283
TURVY, Edward, 283
  John, 283
  Thomas, 283
  William, 283
TUSON, Zara, 283
TUTHER, Thomas, 203
TWAMBROOKS, John Ingham, 283
  Margrett, 283
TWIFER, Ann, 283
Two Friends, 182, 183, 261
TYARS, James, 284
  Rebecca, 284
TYBALLS, Clement, 283
  John, 283
TYER, Ann, 284
  Bowles, 284
  James, 27, 30, 48, 62, 68, 143, 284, 285, 313
  Jane, 284
  John, 284
  Margarett, 284
  Rebecah, 284
  Rebecca, 143, 284
  Rebeckah, 143, 285, 313
TYERS, Bowles, 315
TYLER, Benjamin, 191
  Eleanor, 191
TYMOTHIE, Will, 280
TYMOTHY, Mabella, 280
  William, 280
TYNDALE, Athelstand, 144
  Hester, 144
TYRCE, James, 285
TYRE, Ann, 174
  Boules, 315
  James, 29, 48, 143, 156, 160, 174, 284, 285, 315
  Margrit, 284
  Rebecca, 62, 143, 285
TYRWHITT, Anne, 33
  Charles, 33
  Frances, 33
  Margarett, 33

-U-

UPPENBIRDGE, John, 284
Urlinda (Verlinda), 131
USHER, Dorothy, 71
  Edward, 71
  Jane, 71
  Jean, 58

-V-

VADREY, Ann, 285
  Elizabeth, 285
  George, 285
  John, 285
  Philemon, 285
  Susannah, 285
VADRY, John, 274
VAINE, Henrie, 284

Index

Valle, 156
VANDREYS, Elizabeth, 284
  John, 284
VANSWERRING, Mary, 203
VASSALL, Elizabeth, 285, 291
  Lewis, 285
  Thomas, 285
VAUDREY, John, 261, 285
VAUDRY, John, 113, 284, 285
VAUHOP, Archibald, 288
VAUX, Joseph, 285
VECEN, Nathaniel, 35
VEIRING, Nathaniell, 285
VEN(E)ABLE, George, 285
  Margaret, 285
VENNER, Joseph, 115
VENNOR, Joseph, 285
VEN(N)OUR, Joseph, 285
  Robert, 285
VENSON, Benjamin, 286
  Sina, 286
  William, 286
VEREN, Nathaniell, 285
VERING, Nathaniell, 285, 313
VERNON, Dorothy, 285
  Robert, 285
VERRITT, John, 285
VHENSON, George, 285
VILELE, Peter, 304
VILLET, Cecilia, 304
  Mary, 286
  Peter, 286, 304
VILLETT, Charles, 51
  Mary, 51
VINCENT, Anna, 79
  Elizabeth, 286
  John, 79, 160, 210, 286
  Nathan, 286
  Sarah, 286
  Sina, 286
  Sine(r), 286
  Susannah, 160, 286
  William, 286
Vineyard, 290
VINSON, Elizabeth, 286
  John, 160, 286
  Sarah, 286
  Sina, 286
  Susanna, 160
  William, 160, 286
VINTEN, John, 40
VINTON, Ann, 8, 286
  Solomon, 286
Virginia, 11, 52, 53, 91, 100, 111, 121, 130, 174, 226, 230, 231, 238, 240, 264, 265, 308
  Accomack, 272
  Accomack Co., 77
  Appamattocks, 248
  Cople Parish, 107
  Corretoman, 130
  Essex County, 182
  Hanover County, 84
  King George County 13, 162
  Machodock Creek, 204
  Manchester, 56
  Northumberland County, 248
  Prince William, 222
  Prince William County, 110, 190, 223, 226, 306
  Princess Ann County, 126
  Quanticott, 172
  Rapahannock County, 85
  Richmond County, 12
  South Farnham Parish, 182
  Stafford County, 13, 17, 30, 35, 36, 44, 48, 66, 74, 83, 110, 115, 122, 135, 147, 161, 176, 178, 182, 186, 192, 220, 228, 234, 253, 275, 302, 310
  Upper Machoteck, 203
  Westmoreland County, 49, 52, 56, 94, 104, 107, 110, 192, 289
Virlinda's, 267

-W-
WAALWORT, Isaac, 286
WADD, Richard, 287
WADE, Anne, 138
  Edward, 286, 287
  Elisabeth, 123, 132
  Elizabeth, 288
  John, 286, 287
  John Courts, 288
  Marie, 287
  Mary, 189, 286, 287, 288
  Mr., 120

Index 397

Richard, 48, 138, 156, 189, 235, 256, 262, 287, 288, 313
Robert, 287, 288
Sachariah, 288
Sarah, 287
Theodosia, 287
William, 287
Zacharia, 215, 282
Zachariah, 287, 288
Zacharias, 287
Zacharie, 287
Zachary, 16, 91, 155, 287
Zachery, 57, 193
WADER, John, 296
Margery, 296
William, 296
Wade's Adventor, 287
Wades Point, 287
Wadeson, 287
Wadeson's Enlargement, 287
Wadestone, 110
Wadestones Enlargement, 1, 3, 6, 110, 249, 276, 287
WAEDMAN, Rice, 288
WAGER, Joseph, 288
WAGHOB, Archibald, 288
WAGHOPE, Archibald, 288
Waghope Purchase, 288
WAHOB, Archebald, 141, 266
Archibald, 143, 191, 217, 242, 248, 288
Archiball, 30
Elisabeth, 288
Elizabeth, 143, 248, 288
Jane, 217, 248
Margaret, 248, 288

WAIKFIELD, Thomas, 181
WAILES, Ann, 218
Levin, 218
WAINWRIGHT, Elizabeth, 36
Richard, 36
William, 36
WAKEFEILD, Abell, 39
Elisabeth, 39
WAKEFIELD, Abel, 22, 38, 288, 289
Abell, 289
Ann, 289
Elisabeth, 289
Elizabeth, 38, 247, 288, 289
John, 22, 289
Sarah, 289
Thomas, 181, 288, 289
William, 247
Wakefield's Beginning, 289
WAKELIN, Catherine, 289
Elinor, 289
George, 289
John, 289
Mary, 289, 302
Richard, 289, 302
Walberton Manor, 64
WALDEN, William, 289
WALES, George, 289
WALKEFEILD, Thomas, 289
WALKER, Alice, 95, 290
Alise, 290
Charles, 290
Edward, 109, 308
George, 290
James, 23, 95, 219, 289, 290
Jane, 215

John, 290
Mary, 289
William, 289
WALKUP, Archebald, 141, 266
WALL, John, 275
WALLIS, Michael, 290
Wallnut Thicket, 212
WALLOW, James, 284
Margaret, 284
Rebeccah, 284
WALLS, Alice, 290
Ann, 290
George, 285, 290
Joseph, 290
Larrance, 290
Monokey, 290
William, 290
WALSON, Elizabeth, 290
Jane, 290
William, 290
WALTERS, James, 64
John, 290
Margrett, 64
Robert, 290
WALTHEN, John, 295
WALTOM, John, 290
Ralph, 291
WANGHOB, Archibald, 288
Wanister, 75
WANRIGHT, Richard, 36
Want Water, 156
WAPLE, Ann, 291
Elizabeth, 291
Elsabeth (Elce), 291
George, 105, 176, 291
James, 291
John, 105, 291
Osmond, 291
Sarah, 291
Thomas, 291

WAPLES, Thomas, 291
Waples Chance, 67, 291
Wapping, 216
WAPPLE, James, 172, 291
  Joshua, 291
  Margaret, 291
WARD, Acallis, 292
  Agnes, 292
  Ann, 285, 292, 293
  Anne, 240, 284, 291, 292
  Audray, 292
  Augustine, 292
  Benjamin, 45, 270, 292
  Catherine, 292
  Christian, 292
  Damaris, 291
  Dameris, 292
  Deamaris, 292
  Elisabeth, 285
  Elizabeth, 240, 285, 292
  Francis, 94
  Furten, 297
  George, 285
  Henry, 93, 239, 240, 291, 292
  James, 292
  John, 67, 74, 85, 96, 108, 192, 241, 284, 291, 292
  Joseph, 270, 292
  Margaret, 43, 239, 240, 241, 292
  Mary, 72, 100, 291, 292, 297
  Notley, 293
  Prudence, 292
  Richard, 291
  Sary, 292
  Susanna, 293
  Susannah, 284
  Thomas, 292
  William, 45, 72, 100, 270, 284, 285, 291, 292, 293
WARDE, Mary, 100
WARDEN, Richard, 289
WARDER, Mary, 293
  William, 56, 92, 293
Wardle, 25, 71
Ward's Addition, 180, 292
Ward's Delight, 292
Ward's Runn, 114
Ware, 275, 276, 277
WARE, Akellis, 292
  Elizabeth, 91
  Francis, 91, 142, 306
  Mary, 3
  Sarah, 91
  Susannah, 91
WARING, Barton, 92
  Basil, 119, 293
  Marsham, 293
  Mary, 293
WARNALL, John, 233
WARNER, Christopher, 293
  Elizabeth, 54, 293
  Thomas, 293
WARRAN, John, 178
  Marsham, 26
WARREN, Abraham, 293
  Anne, 294
  Barton, 17, 88, 294, 295
  Benjamin, 19, 28, 42, 45, 293, 294
  Charles, 42, 293, 294
  Elinor, 293
  Elisabeth, 294
  Elizabeth, 294
  Henry, 181, 202, 269
  Humphery, 163, 264, 277, 294, 297
  Humphrey, 15, 43, 85, 90, 111, 123, 138, 179, 232, 280, 283, 291, 293, 302
  Humphry, 75, 233, 294, 303
  Jane, 294
  John, 19, 45, 64, 150, 174, 293, 294
  Judith, 174, 294
  Margery, 233, 293, 294
  Mary, 293, 294
  Notley, 42, 293, 294
  Notly, 294
  Sarah, 294
  Thomas, 123, 259, 293, 294
Warren's Adventure, 295
Warren's Discovery, 294
WARRING, Basil, 293
  Martha, 293
WARTON, Elizabeth, 108
  John, 108
  Thomas, 108
Wassell, 307, 308
Waterbeech, 132
WATERS, Ann(e), 295
  Catherine, 295
  Elisabeth, 295
  Elizabeth, 64, 295
  James, 73, 178, 284, 295
  John, 295
  Joseph, 295
  Kathrine, 295
  Lidia, 295
  Margaret, 62, 295
  Mary, 295

Sarah, 295
Susanna, 295
Susannah, 72
Thomas, 295
William, 64, 72, 178, 295
WATERWORTH,
  Catherine, 295
  John, 295
WATHAN, Hudson, 296
  Mary, 199, 296
WATHEN, Ann, 295, 296
  Barton, 296
  Basel, 296
  Bennet(t), 296
  Clement, 296
  Elinor, 296
  Elisabeth, 296
  Henry, 295, 296
  Hudson, 41, 236, 295, 296
  Ignatius, 213, 295
  James, 295
  Jane, 295
  John, 295, 296
  Joseph, 296
  Judea, 295
  Martin, 296
  Mary, 296
  Sarah, 296
  Susanna, 296
WATHER, Basil, 34
WATHIN, Hudson, 34
WATKINS, Mary, 236, 296
  William, 216, 236, 275, 276, 296
WATRIDGE, Anne, 296
WATSON, Andrew, 220, 296
  Anne, 135
  Charles, 296

  Elizabeth, 135
  Isabell, 135
  James, 296
  Jane, 135
  John, 140, 296
  Margarett, 135
  Mary, 140
  Mathew, 296
  Richard, 93, 135, 136, 295, 296
Watson's Addition, 220
Watson's Choice, 283
Watsons Choice, 5
WATTERMAN,
  Thomas, 296
WATTERS, John, 15
WATTS, Daniel, 214
  Jane, 35
  John, 296
  Richard, 296
WATTSON, Andrew, 11
Wattson's Purchase, 11, 66
WAUGHOB,
  Archibald, 256
WAUHOB, Archibald, 126
  Elizabeth, 126
WAY, Mary, 297
  Richard, 297
WAYE, Jane, 297
  Joan, 297
  Richard, 199, 247, 264, 297
WEALES, Elisabeth, 303
WEATE, Margarett, 197
  Walter, 197
WEAVER, Adam, 63
  John, 297
  Mary, 297
WEBB, Ann, 271

  John, 36, 150, 297
  Mary, 297
WEBSTER, Nicholaus, 297
WEDDING, Anne, 59
  Elizabeth, 59
  John, 59
WEEKES, Elisabeth, 231
  Mr., 39
Welcome, 253
WELER, John, 159
Wellford, 301
WELLS, Catherine, 297
  Mary, 292, 297
  William, 191, 261, 297
WENMAN, Mary, 297
WENNAM, William, 297
WENTWORTH,
  Thomas, 297, 298
Wentworth Wood House, 297
Wentworths Woodhouse, 186
WEST, John, 247, 298
  Walter, 298
  William, 16
West Wood Manor, 37, 56, 190
West Wood Marsh, 37
WESTMAN, Arthur, 298
Westwood, 94
Westwood Lodge, 25, 56
Westwood Mannor, 36, 91, 107, 142, 148, 236, 249, 274, 295, 296
WETHERINGTON,
  Richard, 298
WHAHOB, Archibell, 288

WHALEY, William, 308
WHARTON, Elisabeth, 298
  Elizabeth, 82, 298
  Francis, 213
  Henry, 82, 213, 298, 299
  Jane, 213, 298
  Jesse, 298, 299
  Margaret, 298
  Mary, 35
  Thomas, 108, 218, 298
WHARTOWN, Elizabeth, 28
Wheatland, 194
WHEATLE, John, 299
WHEATLEY, John, 299
  Luckey, 299
  Mary, 127
WHEELAR, James, 299
  John, 299
WHEELER, Ann, 300
  Annastasia, 300
  Anne, 299
  Benjamin, 299
  David, 299
  Elizabeth, 270, 300
  Frances, 300
  Francis, 115, 116, 299, 300
  Ignatius, 299, 300
  James, 155, 274, 283, 299, 300
  John, 20, 46, 105, 114, 140, 181, 190, 206, 225, 262, 264, 299, 300, 301
  Katharine, 299
  Leonard, 97
  Luke, 299, 300
  Martha, 300
  Mary, 190, 299, 300
  Richard, 299, 300
  Robert, 99, 299
  Thomas, 299, 300, 301
  Wennifred, 299
  Winifred, 262
  Winifrid, 299
  Winnifrid, 116
  Winnifried, 115
Wheeler's Addition, 300
Wheelers Delight, 34, 154
Wheeler's Hope, 190
Wheeler's Palme, 79, 149
Wheelers Paltrie, 80
Wheeler's Purchase, 300
Wheeler's Rest, 34, 154, 300
WHEY, Richard, 297
WHICHALEY, Elizabeth, 301
  Jane, 301
  Thomas, 301, 312
WHICHELEY, Thomas, 99
WHICHERLY, Elizabeth, 301
WHILDEN, John, 301
WHITCHALY, Jane, 95
  Thomas, 95
WHITE, Alexander, 28, 220
  Cornelius, 55, 209, 217, 301
  Elliner Haththorne, 212
  John, 302
  Marie, 215
  Mary, 215, 302
  Peter, 91
  Richard, 212
  William, 279, 301, 302
Whitehaven, 79
WHITEHEAD, John, 302
WHITEHORNE, John, 302
WHITELY, Susanna, 38
WHITOM, William, 302
WHITT, Samuel, 302
WHITTER, Ann, 309
  George, 309
  Thomas, 302
  William, 309
WHITTINGTON, William, 77, 272
Whittland, 240
WHITTYMORE, Anne, 302
  Christopher, 302
  Richard, 302
WHORTON, John, 302
WHYTHILL, Robert, 151, 298
Wiccocomico Fields, 70
WICHERLY, Elizabeth, 301
  Thomas, 66
Wickham, 59, 190
Wicomico's Fields, 206, 259, 294
WIETTAM, William, 302
WIGGS, David, 302
WILD, Elisabeth, 303
WILDER, Ann, 302, 303
  Assence, 302
  Diana, 40
  Edward, 302
  EverElday, 302
  Francis, 302
  John, 40, 102, 156, 197, 260, 283, 302, 303
  Mary, 135, 302
  Robert, 302
Wilderness, 122, 268

WILES, Elisabeth, 128, 303
WILFRAY, Lusi, 303
WILKENSON, John, 222
  Mary, 222
WILKINSON, Eleanor, 177, 223
  Elinor, 188
  Elizabeth, 258
  Francis, 214, 258, 303
  John, 177, 223, 303
  Lancelot, 303
  Lancelott, 197, 303
  Margaret, 303
  Margarett, 197
  Mary, 223, 303
  Minor, 303
  Richard, 303
  Sophia, 303
  Susanna, 303
  Thomas, 303
  William, 258, 303
Wilkinson's Throne, 223
Wilkinsons Throne, 126, 177
WILLARD, Anne, 304
  James, 304
  John, 304
WILLBEE, Michael, 304
WILLET, Cecelia, 304
  Cecilia, 304
  Elizabeth, 304
  Mary, 50, 304
  Mary Ann, 304
  Peter, 304
  Rachel, 304
  Rebeckah, 304
Willford, 223
WILLIAM, Anne, 304
  Edward, 304
  Marshall, 58

William Inlarged, 76
WILLIAMS, Ann, 235, 269, 305, 306
  Anne, 306
  Baruch, 314
  Baruck, 314
  Benjamin, 304
  David, 306
  Edward, 254, 304, 305, 310
  Eleanor, 314
  Elizabeth, 224, 248, 257, 305, 306, 311
  Esther, 306
  Ignatius, 1
  James, 65, 248, 305, 306, 311
  Jane, 304
  Jenkins, 304
  John, 161, 168, 248, 257, 303, 304, 305, 306
  Jonathan, 306
  Justinian, 306
  Katherine, 304
  Lewcresea, 306
  Lewis, 158
  Mary, 119, 305, 306, 310
  Peter, 304
  Rice, 118
  Richard, 101
  Rise, 118, 304
  Sarah, 1, 168, 304, 305, 306
  Thomas, 154, 235, 248, 305, 306, 314
  William, 3, 51, 128, 154, 229, 248, 254, 269, 271, 304, 305, 306
Williams' Addition, 269, 306

William's Purchase, 240, 241
Williams Purchase, 104, 241, 273
Williamses Chance, 306
WILLIAMSON, Matthew, 247
  Ralph, 46
  William, 306
  ———, 37
Williams's Folly, 203
WILLMAN, Henry, 306
WILLS, William, 149
Willshins Plains, 71
WILLSON, Alexander, 154, 307
  John, 5, 227, 307
  Jonathan, 307
  Jonathon, 227
  Josiah, 243
  Lydia, 307
  Martha, 38, 243
  Mary, 5
  Richard, 137, 307
  Susannah, 279
  Thomas, 95
  William, 290, 307
WILSON, Abraham, 227
  Alexander, 307
  Elinor, 283
  Gils, 306
  Gyles, 130
  Hanna, 257
  Hannah, 70, 307
  James, 252, 307
  John, 165, 283
  Joseph, 202, 256, 307
  Joshua, 119
  Lawrence, 306
  Margarett, 307
  Martha, 130
  Richard, 258

Robert, 306
Sophia, 307
William, 222, 257, 290
——, 256, 258
Wilton, 292, 293
Wiltshire Plains, 258
WINDS, Michael, 233
WINDSOR, Elizabeth, 153
Sarah, 307
Thomas, 307
Windsor Castle, 307
WINE, Elizabeth, 134, 226
Francis, 7, 73, 134, 182, 226, 307, 308, 309
Henry, 7, 134, 307, 308
John, 7, 225, 308
Mary, 134
Robert, 308
Sarah, 308
William, 7, 308
WINEARD, Ann, 128
WINSER, Ann, 308
Elizabeth, 153, 308
Garvis, 308
John, 308
Joseph, 308
Thomas, 308
William, 308
WINSOR, Elizabeth, 308
Garvis, 308
Jarvis, 308
William, 308
WINTER, Ann, 309
Catherine, 309
Elizabeth, 309
Ignatius, 309
John, 309
Judith Townley, 309
Katherine, 309

Walker, 264
Walter, 110, 309
William, 309
WINTERS, John, 14
Williams, 195
Winters Employment, 110
Winter's Imployment, 192
Winters' Possession, 254
WINTWORTH, Thomas, 297
Wintworth's Woodhouse, 17
WISE, Mary, 28
Richard, 309
Thomas, 28
Wistwood Mannor, 36
WITCHELL, Thomas, 161
WITCHERLY, Thomas, 253
WITHER, Ann, 309
William, 309
WITHERENTON, Richard, 298
WITLY, Francis, 127
WITTAM, William, 302
Witten, 293
WITTER, Buckley, 309
George, 309
Margaret, 309
Mary, 309
Thomas, 309
William, 309
WOLF, Joseph, 310
WOLFE, Mary, 297
Wolfs Dam, 10
Wolleston Manor, 202
WOLLIS, Anne, 310
Wollring Field, 314
WOLPH, Joseph, 310
Mary, 310

WOMMAN, Mary, 310
WOMRIGHT, Richard, 36
WOOD, Abraham, 310
Ann, 37, 38, 310
Benjamin, 71
Elijah, 310
Elisabeth, 258, 310
Elizabeth, 310
Hannah, 310
Isaac, 310
Jacob, 176, 188
Jane, 176, 188, 310
Jeane, 310
Joan, 229
John, 25, 39, 43, 187, 208, 229, 310
Margaret, 310
Mary, 38, 310
Peter, 237, 310
Philip, 298
Samuell, 157
Sarah, 310
Susanna, 310
Wood Stock Bower, 104
WOODARD, Elizabeth, 311
Henry, 311
James, 311
John, 207, 311
Mary, 311
Woodberrys Harbour, 35
Woodberry's Hope, 130, 131, 149
Woodborrough, 201
Woodbridge, 7, 9
WOODERD, John, 311
WOODGARD, Henry, 311
Richard, 311
WOODKEEPE, Richard, 311

Index

WOODMAN, John, 281, 311
  Sarah, 281, 311
Wood's Addition, 26, 310
Wood's Folly, 83
Woods Pleasure, 310
WOODSON, Bennett, 188
Woodstock Bower, 239, 240
WOODWARD, Henry, 311
  Jane, 311
  John, 311
  Margrett, 184
  Mary, 311
  Richard, 311
WOODYARD, Jane, 311
  Jean, 311
  John, 110, 311
  Richard, 311
WOOFE, Robert, 309
WOOLCOCK,
  Christian, 312
  Christopher, 312
  Mary, 312
WOOLF, Joseph, 312
Woollestan Mannor, 204
Woolleston Mannour, 202, 203
WOOTEN, James, 174
WOOTTON, James, 312
WORD, Benjamin, 78
WOREN, Benjamin, 294
WORLAND, John, 45, 181, 290, 312
  Mary, 312
  Stacey, 312
World's End, 35

WORLY, Catherine, 27
  William, 28
WORNELL, John, 233
WORRALL, Robert, 312
WORRELL, Margaret, 5
  Sarah, 135
  William, 47
WORTHINGTON,
  Joseph, 312
WOTTON, Frances, 312
  James, 312
WRAY, John, 236
WRIGHT, Ann(e), 105, 313
  Daniel, 313
  Edward, 308
  Elinor, 313
  George, 313
  Jane, 269
  John, 28, 87, 103, 105, 150, 221, 256, 306, 313
  Mary, 225, 313
  Susanna, 313
  Thomas, 28, 306, 308, 313
  William, 287, 313
WRITE, John, 313
WYCK, Thomas, 121
WYNE, Elisabeth, 182
  Elizabeth, 307, 308
  Francis, 2, 182, 307, 308
  Henry, 307, 308
  John, 307, 308
WYOTT, John, 313
W[*torn*]D, Margrett, 286

-Y-

YAPPE, Roger, 313

YARDLEY, Sarah, 52
YATES, Ann, 119, 314
  Charles, 64, 88, 156, 313, 314
  Jane, 314
  Jonathan, 165
  Ledia, 314
  Lydia, 135, 314
  Rebecca, 48, 143, 285, 313
  Rebeckah, 143, 313
  Robert, 48, 64, 92, 97, 119, 135, 143, 156, 165, 174, 210, 259, 269, 284, 285, 303, 313, 314, 315
  Sarah, 314
  Susanna, 88
  —din, 314
YEATES, Rebocah, 48
  Robert, 48
YOAKLEY, Martha, 314
  Stephen, 228, 314
YOPP, Charles, 5, 315
  Jane, 5, 315
  Roger, 315
  Sarah, 5, 315
  Susanna, 88
York, 216, 241
Yorke, 68
Yorkshire, 10
YOUNG, Ann(a), 315
  Arthur, 315
  Constant, 315
  Elizabeth, 315
  Frances, 315
  Jane, 315
  John, 315
  Lawrence, 315
  Mary, 315
  Mr., 36
  Mrs., 121
  Peter, 315

Sarah, 315
YOUNGE, Charles, 315
John, 315
Lawrance, 315
Lawrence, 315
Sarah, 315
Thomas, 315
YOUP, Margaret, 221
Roger, 221

-Z-
Zachia Manor, 10, 67, 134, 221

———
———, Ann, 54
———, Antonio, 51
———, Basill, 145
———, Beck, 75
———, Ben, 118
———, Bess, 217
———, Bett, 137
———, Billie, 100
———, Boatswain, 125
———, Cassine, 31
———, Catherine, 125, 187
———, Cezar, 278
———, Charles, 75
———, Chloe, 54
———, Dick, 91, 203
———, Doll, 145
———, Dubba, 137
———, Edward, 122
———, Elizabeth, 54
———, Elley, 134
———, Frank, 91, 129, 203
———, George, 118
———, Henry, 276
———, Ignatius, 213
———, Isabella, 34
———, Jack, 86
———, James, 129, 258
———, Jane, 54, 241
———, Jeany, 137
———, Jenny, 50
———, Jesse, 213
———, John, 54, 145, 213
———, Jonathan, 213
———, Juda, 275
———, Judeth, 165
———, Judith, 91, 125, 203
———, Kate, 125
———, Keziah, 276
———, Little Bess, 213
———, Lowhill, 251
———, Lucretia, 54
———, Lucy, 118, 275
———, Maquamps (*alias* Bennett) 163
———, Margaret, 213
———, Marjery, 175
———, Martha, 279
———, Mary, 54
———, Moll, 165
———, Monica, 213, 275
———, Nacey, 137
———, Nacy (*alias* Ignatius), 249
———, Nanny, 54, 125
———, Natt, 91, 203
———, Ned, 251
———, Nell, 118
———, Pegg, 97, 213
———, Peter, 153, 195
———, Ralph, 122
———, Rose, 309
———, Sarah, 137, 257
———, Sarah Rose, 125
———, Sarah Toge, 309
———, Sophia, 54
———, Sue, 75
———, Susan, 46
———, Susanna, 52, 270
———, Terrie, 118
———, Theodosia, 132
———, Thomas, 207
———, Tomacoe, 191
———, Toney, 137, 216
———, William, 54
———, Zachariah, 54
——— *Addition*, 234
——— *Choice*, 175
——— [*torn*], Ruthe, 315

Other books by Marlene Strawser Bates and F. Edward Wright:

York County, Pennsylvania Church Records of the 18th Century: Volumes 1-3

Other books by Marlene Strawser Bates:

Abstracts of Carroll County Newspapers, 1831-1846
Marlene S. Bates and Martha Reamy

Memoirs of the Dead, and Tomb's Remembrancer
Marlene S. Bates and Martha Reamy

Other books by F. Edward Wright:

Abstracts of Bucks County, Pennsylvania Wills, 1685-1785

Abstracts of Cumberland County, Pennsylvania Wills, 1750-1785

Abstracts of Cumberland County, Pennsylvania Wills, 1785-1825

Abstracts of Philadelphia County, Pennsylvania Wills, 1682-1726

Abstracts of Philadelphia County, Pennsylvania Wills, 1726-1747

Abstracts of Philadelphia County, Pennsylvania Wills, 1748-1763

Abstracts of Philadelphia County, Pennsylvania Wills, 1763-1784

Abstracts of Philadelphia County, Pennsylvania Wills, 1777-1790

Abstracts of Philadelphia County, Pennsylvania Wills, 1790-1802

Abstracts of Philadelphia County, Pennsylvania Wills, 1802-1809

Abstracts of Philadelphia County, Pennsylvania Wills, 1810-1815

Abstracts of Philadelphia County, Pennsylvania Wills, 1815-1819

Abstracts of Philadelphia County, Pennsylvania Wills, 1820-1825

Abstracts of South Central Pennsylvania Newspapers, Volume 1, 1785-1790

Abstracts of South Central Pennsylvania Newspapers, Volume 3, 1796-1800

Abstracts of the Newspapers of Georgetown and the Federal City, 1789-99

Abstracts of York County, Pennsylvania Wills, 1749-1819

Bucks County, Pennsylvania Church Records of the 17th and 18th Centuries Volume 2: Quaker Records: Falls and Middletown Monthly Meetings
Anna Miller Watring and F. Edward Wright

Caroline County, Maryland Marriages, Births and Deaths, 1850-1880

Citizens of the Eastern Shore of Maryland, 1659-1750

Cumberland County, Pennsylvania Church Records of the 18th Century

Delaware Newspaper Abstracts, Volume 1: 1786-1795

Early Church Records of Alexandria City and Fairfax County, Virginia
F. Edward Wright and Wesley E. Pippenger

Early Church Records of New Castle County, Delaware, Volume 1, 1701-1800

Frederick County Militia in the War of 1812
Sallie A. Mallick and F. Edward Wright

Inhabitants of Baltimore County, 1692-1763

Land Records of Sussex County, Delaware, 1769-1782

Land Records of Sussex County, Delaware, 1782-1789
Elaine Hastings Mason, F. Edward Wright

Marriage Licenses of Washington, District of Columbia, 1811-1830
Marriages and Deaths from the Newspapers of Allegany and Washington Counties, Maryland, 1820-1830
Marriages and Deaths from The York Recorder, *1821-1830*
Marriages and Deaths in the Newspapers of Frederick and Montgomery Counties, Maryland, 1820-1830
Marriages and Deaths in the Newspapers of Lancaster County, Pennsylvania, 1821-1830
Marriages and Deaths in the Newspapers of Lancaster County, Pennsylvania, 1831-1840
Marriages and Deaths of Cumberland County, [Pennsylvania], 1821-1830
Maryland Calendar of Wills Volume 9: 1744-1749
Maryland Calendar of Wills Volume 10: 1748-1753
Maryland Calendar of Wills Volume 11: 1753-1760
Maryland Calendar of Wills Volume 12: 1759-1764
Maryland Calendar of Wills Volume 13: 1764-1767
Maryland Calendar of Wills Volume 14: 1767-1772
Maryland Calendar of Wills Volume 15: 1772-1774
Maryland Calendar of Wills Volume 16: 1774-1777
Maryland Eastern Shore Newspaper Abstracts, Volume 1: 1790-1805
Maryland Eastern Shore Newspaper Abstracts, Volume 2: 1806-1812
Maryland Eastern Shore Newspaper Abstracts, Volume 3: 1813-1818
Maryland Eastern Shore Newspaper Abstracts, Volume 4: 1819-1824
Maryland Eastern Shore Newspaper Abstracts, Volume 5: Northern Counties, 1825-1829
F. Edward Wright and Irma Harper
Maryland Eastern Shore Newspaper Abstracts, Volume 6: Southern Counties, 1825-1829
Maryland Eastern Shore Newspaper Abstracts, Volume 7: Northern Counties, 1830-1834
Irma Harper and F. Edward Wright
Maryland Eastern Shore Newspaper Abstracts, Volume 8: Southern Counties, 1830-1834
Maryland Militia in the Revolutionary War
S. Eugene Clements and F. Edward Wright
Newspaper Abstracts of Allegany and Washington Counties, 1811-1815
Newspaper Abstracts of Cecil and Harford Counties, [Maryland], 1822-1830
Newspaper Abstracts of Frederick County, [Maryland], 1811-1815
Newspaper Abstracts of Frederick County, [Maryland], 1816-1819
Sketches of Maryland Eastern Shoremen
Tax List of Chester County, Pennsylvania 1768
Tax List of York County, Pennsylvania 1779
Washington County Church Records of the 18th Century, 1768-1800
Western Maryland Newspaper Abstracts, Volume 1: 1786-1798
Western Maryland Newspaper Abstracts, Volume 2: 1799-1805
Western Maryland Newspaper Abstracts, Volume 3: 1806-1810
Wills of Chester County, Pennsylvania, 1766-1778

www.ingramcontent.com/pod-product-compliance
Lightning Source LLC
Chambersburg PA
CBHW071943220426
43662CB00009B/967